Selected World Wide Web Sites for GS: The Middle East

All of these Web sites are hot-linked through the *Global Studies* home page:
http://www.dushkin.com/globalstudies (just click on a book).

Some Web sites are continually changing their structure and content, so the information listed may not always be available.

GENERAL SITES

1. CNN Interactive—World Regions: Middle East—*http://www.cnn.com/WORLD/meast/index.html*—This 24-hour news channel often focuses on the Middle East and is updated every few hours.

2. ReliefWEB—*http://www.reliefweb.int.*—UN's Department of Humanitarian Affairs clearinghouse for international humanitarian emergencies. It has daily updates, including Reuters and Voice of America.

3. United Nations System—*http://www.unsystem.org/*—The official Web site for the United Nations system of organizations. Everything is listed alphabetically, and data on UNICC and the Food and Agriculture Organization are available.

4. UN Development Programme (UNDP)—*http://www.undp.org/*—Publications and current information on world poverty, Mission Statement, UN Development Fund for Women, and much more. Be sure to see the Poverty Clock.

5. UN Environmental Programme (UNEP)—*http://www.unchs.unon. org/*—Official site of UNEP with information on UN environmental programs, products, services, events, and a search engine.

6. U.S. Central Intelligence Agency Home Page—*http://www.odci. gov/cia*—This site includes publications of the CIA, such as the *World Fact Book, Fact Book on Intelligence, Handbook of International Economic Statistics,* CIA maps and publications, and more.

7. U.S. Department of State Home Page—*http://www.state.gov/ index.html/*—Organized by categories: Hot Topics (i.e., Country Reports on Human Rights Practices), International Policy, Business Services, and more.

8. World Health Organization (WHO)—*http://www.who.ch/*—Maintained by WHO's headquarters in Geneva, Switzerland, the site uses the Excite search engine to conduct keyword searches.

MIDDLE EAST SITES

9. Access to Arabia—**http://www.accessme.com/**—Extensive information about traveling and working in the Arab world is presented on this Web site.

10. Arabia.On.Line—**http://www.arab.com/**—Discussions of Arab news, business, and culture are available at this site.

11. Camera Media Report—**http://world.std.com/~camera/**—This site is run by the Committee for Accuracy in Middle East Reporting in America, and it is devoted to fair and accurate coverage of Israel and the Middle East.

12. Center for Middle Eastern Studies—**http://w3.arizona.edu/ ~cmesua/**—This site is maintained by the University of Arizona Center for Middle Eastern Studies. The Center's mission is to further understanding and knowledge of the Middle East through education.

13. Centre for Middle Eastern and Islamic Studies—**http:// www.dur. ac.uk/~dme0www/**—The University of Durham in England maintains this site. It offers links to the university's extensive library of Middle East information; the Sudan Archive is the largest collection of documentation outside of Sudan itself.

14. The Middle East Institute—**http://www2.ari.net/mei/mei. html**—The Middle East Institute is dedicated to educating Americans about the Middle East. The site offers links to publications, media resources, and other links of interest.

15. Middle East Internet Pages—**http://www.middle-east-pages. com/**—A large amount of information on specific countries in the Middle East can be obtained on this site. Their engine allows you to browse through virtually every aspect of Middle East culture, politics, and current information.

16. Middle East Policy Council—**http://www.mepc.org/**—The purpose of the Middle East Policy Council's Web site is to expand public discussion and understanding of issues affecting U.S. policy in the Middle East.

17. Middle East Security Report—**http://www.me-dialogue. demon. co.uk/**—A comprehensive weekly review of defense and security information concerning Arab League countries, Iran, Israel, and Turkey. It also has links to a large number of other Web sites.

18. Middle Eastern and Arab Resources—**http://www. ionet.net/~usarch/WTB-Site.shtml**—This omnibus site offers extensive information on all of the Middle Eastern countries.

ISRAEL SITES

19. The Abraham Fund—**http://www.coexistence.org/**—The goal of peaceful coexistence between Jews and Arabs is the theme of this site. Information to various projects and links to related sites is offered.

20. Zionist Archives—**http://www.wzo.org.il/cza/index2.html** —This site is the official historical archives of the World Zionist Organization, the Jewish Agency, the Jewish National Fund, Karen Hayesod, and the World Jewish Congress.

We highly recommend that you review our Web site for expanded information and our other product lines. We are continually updating and adding links to our Web site in order to offer you the most usable and useful information that will support and expand the value of your book. You can reach us at: http://www.dushkin.com/globalstudies.

Contents

Global Studies: The Middle East

Page 26

Page 76

Page 82

Page 111

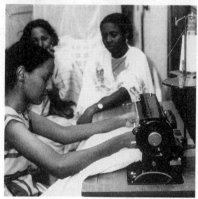

Page 128

Page 156

Introduction

THE GLOBAL AGE

As we approach the end of the twentieth century, it is clear that our future will be considerably more international in nature than we ever believed was possible. Each day, print and broadcast journalists as well as our own experiences make us aware that our world is becoming increasingly smaller and substantially more interdependent.

The energy crisis, world food shortages, and regional conflicts in the Middle East and other areas that threaten to involve us all make it clear that the distinctions between domestic and foreign problems are all too often artificial— that many seemingly domestic problems no longer stop at national boundaries. As Rene Dubos, the 1969 Pulitzer Prize recipient stated: "[I]t becomes obvious that each [of us] has two countries, [our] own and planet Earth." As global interdependence has become a reality, it has become vital for the citizens of this world to develop literacy in global matters.

THE GLOBAL STUDIES SERIES

It is the aim of this Global Studies series to help readers acquire a basic knowledge and understanding of the regions and countries in the world. Each volume provides a foundation of information—geographic, cultural, economic, political, historical, artistic, and religious—that allows readers to understand better the current and future problems within these countries and regions and to comprehend how events there might affect their own well-being. In short, these volumes attempt to provide the background information necessary to respond to the realities of our global age.

Author and Editor

Each of the volumes in the Global Studies series is crafted under the careful direction of an author/editor—an expert in the area under study. The author/editors teach and conduct research and have traveled extensively through the regions about which they are writing.

In this Middle East volume, the author/editor has written the regional essays and the country reports. In addition, he has been instrumental in the selection of the world press articles that relate to the region.

Contents and Features

The Global Studies volumes are organized to provide concise information and current world press articles on the regions and countries within those areas under study.

Regional Essays

For *Global Studies: The Middle East, Seventh Edition*, the author/editor has written narrative essays focusing on the religious, cultural, sociopolitical, and economic differences and similarities of the countries and peoples in the region. The purpose of the regional essays is to provide readers with an effective sense of the diversity of the area as well as an understanding of its common cultural and historical back-

(United Nations photo/Yutaka Nagata)

The global age is making all countries and all people more interdependent.

grounds. Preceding the regional essays is a two-page map showing the political boundaries of each of the countries within the region.

Country Reports

Concise reports are written for each of the countries within the region under study. These reports are the heart of each Global Studies volume. *Global Studies: The Middle East, Seventh Edition*, contains 20 country reports.

The country reports are comprised of six standard elements. Each report contains a small, semidetailed map visually positioning the country among its neighboring states; a "wild card" addressing an interesting facet of the country; a detailed summary of statistical information; an essay providing important historical, geographical, political, cultural, and economic information; a historical timeline offering a convenient visual survey of a few key historical events; and four graphic indicators, with summary statements about the country in terms of development, freedom, health/welfare, and achievements.

A Note on the Statistical Summaries

The statistical information provided for each country has been drawn from a wide range of sources. The most frequently referenced are listed on page 232. Every effort has been made to provide the most current and accurate information available. However, occasionally the information cited by these sources differs to some extent; and, all too often, the most current information available for some countries is somewhat dated. But aside from these difficulties, the statistical summary of each country is generally quite complete and reasonably current. Care should be taken, however, in using these statistics (or, for that matter, any published statistics) in making hard comparisons among countries. We have also included statistics on Canada and the United States, which follow on the next two pages.

World Press Articles

Within each Global Studies volume are reprinted a number of articles carefully selected by our editorial staff and the author/editor from a broad range of international periodicals and newspapers. The articles have been chosen for currency, interest, and their differing perspectives on the subject countries and regions. There are 16 articles in *Global Studies: The Middle East, Seventh Edition.*

The articles section is preceded by a *topic guide* as well as an *annotated table of contents.* The topic guide indicates the main theme(s) of each article, while the annotated table of contents offers a brief summary of each article. Thus, readers desiring to focus on articles dealing with a particular theme— say, religion—may refer to the topic guide to find those articles.

Spelling

In many instances, some articles use forms of spelling that are different from the U.S. style. Many publications reflect the European usage. In order to retain the flavor of the articles and to make the point that our system is not the only one, spellings have not been altered to conform with the U.S. system.

WWW Sites, Glossary, Bibliography, Index

An annotated list of selected World Wide Web sites can be found on page v in this edition of *Global Studies: Middle East.*

At the back of each Global Studies volume, readers will find a *glossary of terms and abbreviations,* which provides a quick reference to the specialized vocabulary of the area under study and to the standard abbreviations (OPEC, PLO, etc.) used throughout the volume.

Following the glossary is a *bibliography,* which is organized into general works, national histories, literature in translation, current events publications, and periodicals that provide regular coverage on the Middle East.

The *index* at the end of the volume is an accurate reference to the contents of the volume. Readers seeking specific information and citations should consult this standard index.

Currency and Usefulness

This seventh edition of *Global Studies: The Middle East,* like other Global Studies volumes, is intended to provide the most current and useful information available necessary to understand the events that are shaping the cultures of the region today.

We plan to issue this volume on a regular basis. The statistics will be updated, regional essays rewritten, country

reports revised, and articles replaced as new and current information becomes available. In order to accomplish this task we will turn to our author/editor, our advisory boards, and—hopefully—to you, the users of this volume. Your comments are more than welcome. If you have an idea that you think will make the volume more useful, an article or bit of information that will make it more current, or a general comment on its organization, content, or features that you would like to share with us, please send it in for serious consideration for the next edition.

(United Nations photo/John Isaac)

Understanding the problems and lifestyles of other countries will help make us literate in global matters.

Canada

GEOGRAPHY
Area in Square Kilometers (Miles):
9,976,140 (3,850,790) (slightly larger than the United States)
Capital (Population): Ottawa (920,000)
Climate: from temperate in south to subarctic and arctic in north

PEOPLE

Population
Total: 28,820,700
Annual Growth Rate: 1.06%
Rural/Urban Population Ratio: 23/77
Ethnic Makeup: 40% British Isles origin; 27% French origin; 20% other European; 1.5% indigenous Indian and Eskimo; 11.5% mixed
Major Languages: both English and French are official

Health
Life Expectancy at Birth: 76 years (male); 83 years (female)
Infant Mortality Rate (Ratio): 6/1,000
Average Caloric Intake: 127% of FAO minimum
Physicians Available (Ratio): 1/464

Religions
46% Roman Catholic; 16% United Church; 10% Anglican; 28% others

Education
Adult Literacy Rate: 97%

COMMUNICATION
Telephones: 18,000,000
Newspapers: 96 in English; 11 in French

TRANSPORTATION
Highways—Kilometers (Miles):
849,404 (530,028)
Railroads—Kilometers (Miles): 70,176 (48,764)
Usable Airfields: 1,138

GOVERNMENT
Type: confederation with parliamentary democracy
Independence Date: July 1, 1867
Head of State/Government: Queen Elizabeth II; Prime Minister Jean Chrétien
Political Parties: Progressive Conservative Party; Liberal Party; New Democratic Party; Reform Party; Bloc Québécois
Suffrage: universal at 18

MILITARY
Number of Armed Forces: 88,000
Military Expenditures (% of Central Government Expenditures): 1.6%
Current Hostilities: none

ECONOMY
Currency ($U.S. Equivalent): 1.41 Canadian dollars = $1
Per Capita Income/GDP: $24,400/$694 billion
Inflation Rate: 2.4%
Total Foreign Debt: $233 billion
Natural Resources: petroleum; natural gas; fish; minerals; cement; forestry products; fur
Agriculture: grains; livestock; dairy products; potatoes; hogs; poultry and eggs; tobacco
Industry: oil production and refining; natural-gas development; fish products; wood and paper products; chemicals; transportation equipment

FOREIGN TRADE
Exports: $185 billion
Imports: $166.7 billion

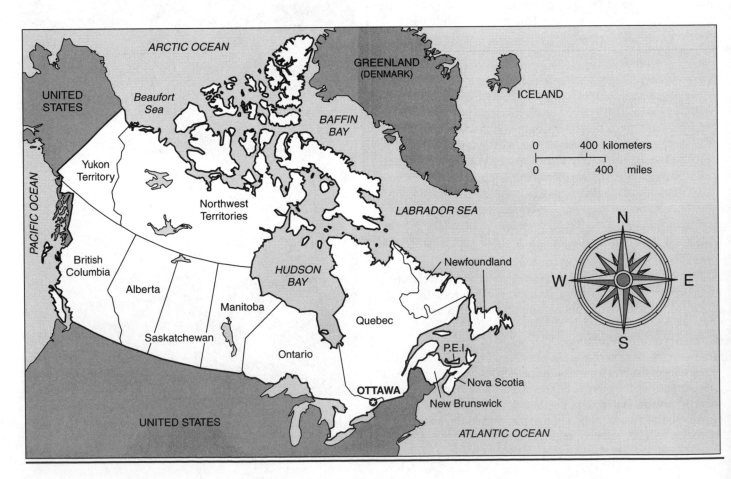

The United States

GEOGRAPHY
Area in Square Kilometers (Miles):
9,578,626 (3,618,770)
Capital (Population): Washington, D.C.
(606,900)
Climate: temperate

PEOPLE

Population
Total: 266,476,300
Annual Growth Rate: 0.91%
Rural/Urban Population Ratio: 25/75
Ethnic Makeup: 73% white; 12%
black; 10% Latino; 5% Asian, Pacific
Islander, American Indian, Eskimo,
and Aleut
Major Languages: predominantly
English; a sizable Spanish-speaking
minority; many others

Health
Life Expectancy at Birth: 73 years
(male); 79 years (female)
Infant Mortality Rate (Ratio): 6.7/1,000
Average Caloric Intake: 138% of FAO
minimum
Physicians Available (Ratio): 1/391

Religions
56% Protestant; 28% Roman Catholic;
4% Muslim; 2% Jewish; 10% others or
unaffiliated

Education
Adult Literacy Rate: 97.9% (official)
(estimates vary widely)

COMMUNICATION
Telephones: 182,558,000
Newspapers: 1,679 dailies;
approximately 63,000,000 circulation

TRANSPORTATION
Highways—Kilometers (Miles):
6,284,488 (3,895,733)
Railroads—Kilometers (Miles):
240,000 (149,760)
Usable Airfields: 13,387

GOVERNMENT
Type: federal republic
Independence Date: July 4, 1776
Head of State: President William
("Bill") Jefferson Clinton
Political Parties: Democratic Party;
Republican Party; others of minor
political significance
Suffrage: universal at 18

MILITARY
Number of Armed Forces: 1,807,177
*Military Expenditures (% of Central
Government Expenditures):* 3.8%
Current Hostilities: none

ECONOMY
Per Capita Income/GDP:
$27,500/$7.25 trillion
Inflation Rate: 2.5%
Natural Resources: metallic and
nonmetallic minerals; petroleum;
arable land
Agriculture: food grains; feed crops;
oil-bearing crops; livestock;
dairy products
Industry: diversified in both capital-
and consumer-goods industries

FOREIGN TRADE
Exports: $578 billion
Imports: $751 billion

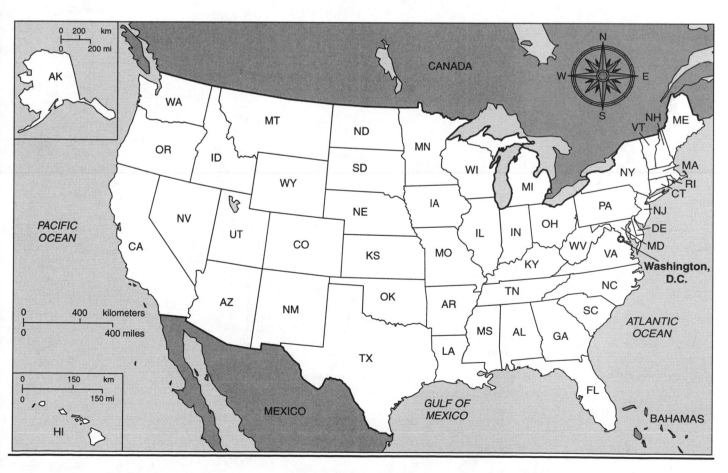

GLOBAL STUDIES

This map of the world highlights the Middle Eastern countries that are discussed in this volume. The following essays are written from a cultural perspective in order to give the readers a sense of what life is like in these countries. The essays are designed to present the most current and useful information available. Other books in the Global Studies series cover different global areas and examine the current state of affairs of the countries within those regions.

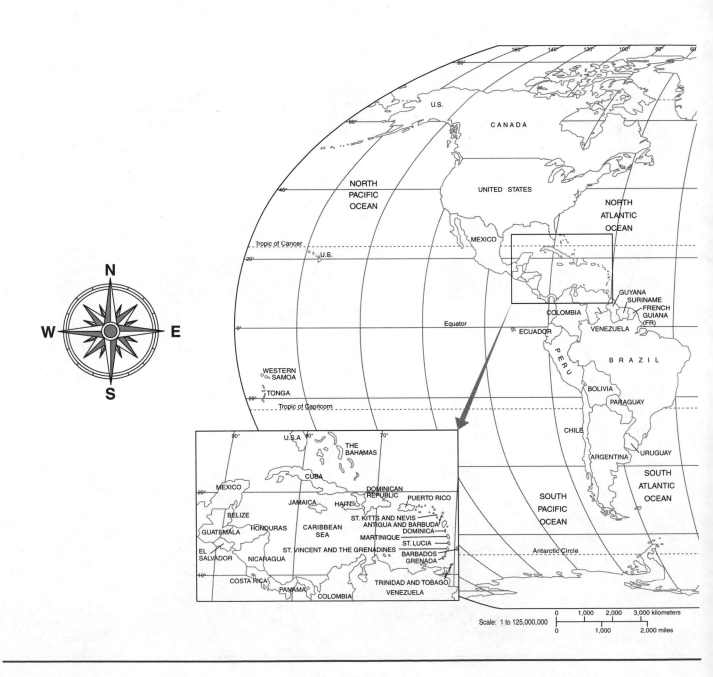

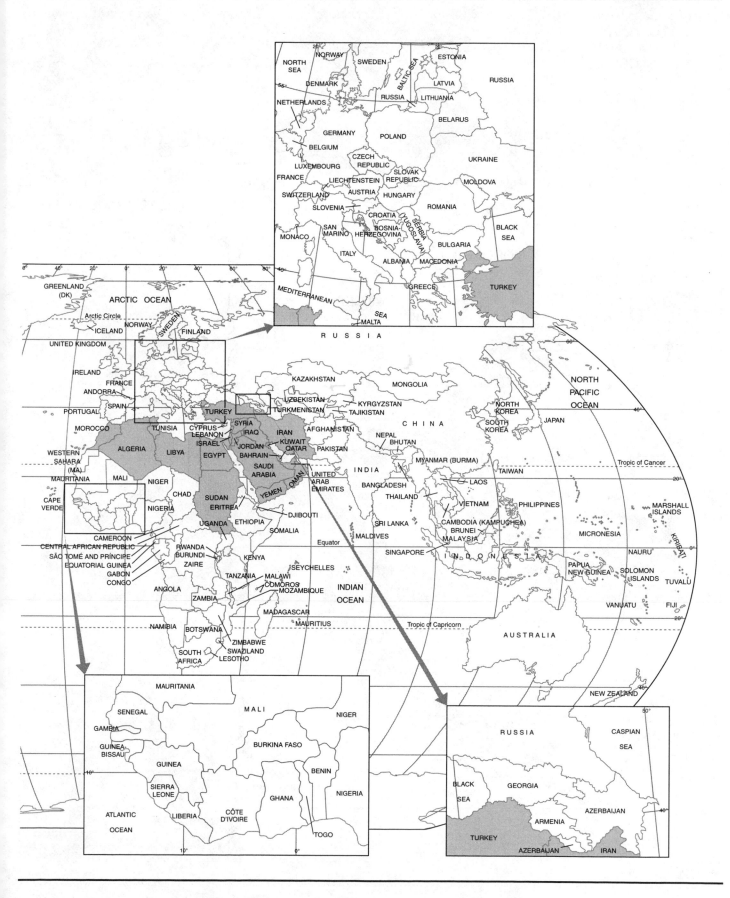

The Middle East

NORTH ATLANTIC OCEAN

FRANCE

ITALY

PORTUGAL

SPAIN

ALBANIA

GREECE

STRAIT OF GIBRALTAR

Algiers

Tunis

MALTA

MEDITERRANEAN SEA

TUNISIA

Rabat

Tripoli

MOROCCO

ALGERIA

LIBYA

WESTERN SAHARA

MAURITANIA

MALI

NIGER

CHAD

SENEGAL

GAMBIA

GUINEA-BISSAU

GUINEA

BURKINA FASO

BENIN

NIGERIA

SIERRA LEONE

CÔTE D'IVOIRE

GHANA

TOGO

CENTRAL AFRICAN REPUBLIC

SOUTH ATLANTIC OCEAN

LIBERIA

CAMEROON

| 0 | 500 | 1,000 | Kilometers |

| 0 | 500 | 1,000 Miles |

EQUATORIAL GUINEA

CONGO

GABON

● Capital cities

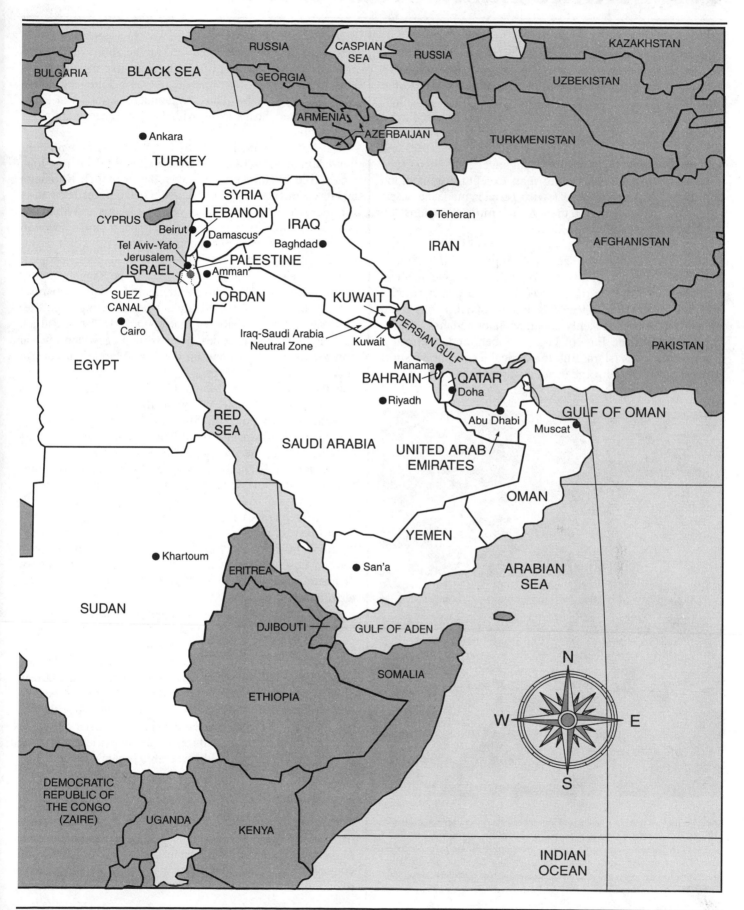

The Middle East: Cradle of Islam

ISLAM IN FERMENT

Until quite recently, the world of Islam, centered in the Middle East, was a remote grey area to most Americans. To many of those who passed through the area en route to the invasions of occupied Europe in World War II, it was a hot, dusty place, peopled by men dressed in what appeared to be bed sheets, who sat in fly-blown cafés at the outskirts of military bases drinking endless glasses of hot sweet tea and speaking an incomprehensible language. This stereotype changed little in the intervening years except for the addition of the State of Israel, whose Jewish peoples made the desert bloom and more than stood their ground militarily against the children of those men in "bed sheets."

Seen against the strong image of Israel, that country's Middle Eastern neighbors seemed unimportant. Most Americans knew little of their histories or of their struggles to attain dignity and stability in the new world of independent states. Many people had only a vague awareness of a religious group called Muslims (mistakenly called Mohammedans), who inhabited the Middle East in large numbers and practiced a religion known as Islam. But, in political terms, the Muslims seemed powerless, disorganized, always on the brink of con-

(UN photo)

The Middle East did not make a real impact on the American consciousness until 1979, when the followers of the Ayatollah Khomeini seized the U.S. Embassy in Teheran, Iran, and held its occupants hostage for more than a year. The extent to which fundamentalist Shia Muslims would follow Khomeini, pictured on the placard displayed above, was little recognized before this event.

flict. With the exception of Israel—often perceived as an extension of the United States—the predictability that Americans had come to expect of governments like their own was not to be found among the quarrelsome leaders of these Middle Eastern states. Thus the thunderous impact of Islam on the United States came with little advance warning or preparation.

The American public abruptly came face to face with militant Islam in 1979, when the U.S. Embassy in Teheran, Iran, was seized by supporters of Ayatollah Ruhollah Khomeini and its occupants were held hostage. Their enforced detention for more than a year made yellow ribbons a symbol of America's captivity to Islam and led to the political downfall of President Jimmy Carter but produced relatively little development in Americans' understanding of Islamic peoples. Later, misreading of their motivations by the Reagan administration led to the disastrous assignment of American marines to Lebanon as part of a multinational peacekeeping force after the 1982 Israeli invasion of that country. In 1983, a truck carrying what was later described as the largest non-nuclear bomb ever exploded blew up the U.S. Marine barracks in Beirut, killing 241 marines.

In the mid-1980s, the Islamic Jihad, a secret Lebanese Shia organization linked to Iran through Hizbullah (Party of God), Lebanon's most powerful Shia Muslim group, initiated a campaign of kidnappings of Americans and other foreigners in Beirut. Other shadowy organizations, such as Revolutionary Justice and Islamic Holy War for the Liberation of Palestine, followed suit. U.S. involvement in Lebanon after the Israeli invasion and revelations of the Reagan administration's secret arms deals with Iran shifted the kidnappers' focus to one of revenge for U.S. and Israeli actions against the "sacred Islamic soil" of Lebanon, whereas the original reason for the hostage taking had been to obtain the release of "Islamic brothers" held in Israeli and European jails for terrorist activities.

Altogether, more than a dozen Americans, plus Briton Terry Waite (the personal representative of the archbishop of Canterbury) and a number of British, French, German, and Italian citizens, were held hostage for periods of up to 7 years. The longest-held was Associated Press Middle East bureau chief Terry Anderson. Between 1986 and 1990, there were no hostage releases; but, in 1990–1991, protracted negotiations by then-United Nations secretary-general Javier Perez de Cuellar and his mediators, through intermediaries in Iran (the protective umbrella for Lebanese Shia organizations and essentially the only outside force capable of influencing the kidnappers), led finally to the resolution of the "hostage problem." One contributing factor in the complex negotiations was the release by Israel of Shia Lebanese prisoners held in south Lebanon. Another was the resolution of the Lebanese Civil War and establishment of de facto Syrian control over most of that country. However, Islamic Jihad's release of Anderson in December 1991 was accompanied by a statement re-emphasizing both the political and the Islamic aspects of the long-running hostage issue. It stated, in part: "The confrontation created by the kidnappings made the world listen to the voice of oppressed people and unmasked the ugly American and Israeli faces . . . but after finishing several stages we decided to free our last captive, thus folding this page in the hostage file before glorious Christmas."

These and other shocks since 1979 have brought the United States face to face with what appears to be a recent phenomenon of confrontation in the Middle East between Muslims and Westerners. To give the phenomenon a name, we call it "Islam in ferment."

What has caused this ferment? What does it consist of, and why is it directed so violently against the United States in particular? Is it a new phenomenon, or is it a natural progression for Islam, arising out of the circumstances in which Muslims find themselves in the late twentieth century? What are the elements that play a role in the Islamic ferment? We address these questions in this report.

THE CONCEPT OF JIHAD

Jihad is one of the most important elements in the Islamic ferment. It may be defined as "sacred struggle," "striving" (i.e., of the individual to carry out God's will), or, when exercised against the enemies of Islam, "holy war." The Afghan *mujahideen* (resistance fighters) who fought during the 1980s to expel Soviet forces from their homeland characterized their struggle as a jihad, as did Iranian Revolutionary Guards challenging U.S. forces in the Persian Gulf, to give just two of many examples.

But jihad can also be directed against apostates or weak believers *within* the House of Islam. In 1979, Muslims who seized the Great Mosque in Mecca, Saudi Arabia, argued that the Saudi government should be replaced, on these grounds: Islam does not allow secular kings or dynasties, and the Saudi government had deviated from "true" Islamic law and principles. And, during the trial of those arrested for the 1981 assassination of Egyptian president Anwar al-Sadat, their leader argued that there were three reasons for the justness of their act: 1) the incompatibility of Egypt's laws with Islamic law; 2) Sadat's peace with Israel; and 3) the sufferings of "good" Muslims under the regime.[1]

Another form of jihad-inspired violence within Islamic society has developed out of the religious divisions of Islam into Sunni and Shia groups. The Muslim Brotherhood, to give an example, is a Sunni Muslim organization, spread throughout the Islamic world, that seeks the replacement of all existing regimes by a universal Islamic state faithful to the ideals and practices of the original community of believers founded by Muhammad. As a result, it has at times been banned, proscribed, and ruthlessly repressed by those regimes. In Syria, the Brotherhood represents the principal opposition to the Alawi Shia minority government of President Hafez al-Assad. The Brotherhood's main power base was once the city

(Aramco Photo)

One of the Five Pillars of Islam, or five basic duties of Muslims, is to go on a pilgrimage to Mecca in Saudi Arabia once in their lifetime. There they circle seven times around the Black Box (the Ka'ba, pictured above), kiss the Black Stone, drink from the well of Zam Zam, and perform other sacred rites.

of Hama, home of a conservative Sunni population. Brotherhood members carried out a series of assassinations of Alawi officials from Hama and made two attempts on the life of the Syrian president. They called him an "enemy of Allah" and a Maronite (Lebanese Christian). In 1982, after the discovery of an Air Force plot to overthrow him that was linked to the Brotherhood, Assad ordered his troops into the city and all but obliterated it in the process of crushing his opposition.[2]

These militant events have not occurred in isolation. They are part of the struggle of Muslim peoples to come to terms with the modern world and to define an appropriate role for Islam in that world.

The difficulty for fundamentalist Muslims in defining such a role stems from the fact that their religion operates under very specific divine rules of conduct. These rules were laid down in the A.D. 600s by Muhammad the Messenger, who received them as revelations from God. The sum total of these revelations is the Koran, the Holy Book of Islam. Because Muslims believe that the Koran is the literal Word of God,

THE KORAN: THE HOLY BOOK OF ISLAM

Muslims believe that the Koran is the literal Word of God and that Muhammad was chosen to receive God's Word through the Angel Gabriel as a *rasul* (messenger). But the Koran does not cancel out the Bible and Torah, which preceded it. The Koran is viewed, rather, as providing a corrective set of revelations for these previous revelations from God, which Muslims believe have been distorted or not followed correctly. To carry out God's Word, as set down in the Koran, requires a constant effort to create the ideal Islamic society, one "that is imbued with Islamic ideals and reflects as perfectly as possible the presence of God in His creation."*

The Koran was revealed to Muhammad over the 22-year period of his ministry (A.D. 610–632). The revelations were of varying lengths and were originally meant to be committed to memory and recited on various occasions, in particular the daily prayers. Even today, correct Koranic practice requires memorization and recitation; during the fasting month of Ramadan, one section per day should be recited aloud.

In its original form, the Koran was either committed to memory by Muhammad's listeners or written down by one or more literate scribes, depending upon who was present at the revelation. The scribes used whatever materials were at hand: "paper, leather, parchment, stones, wooden tablets, the shoulder-blades of oxen or the breasts of men."** The first authoritative version was compiled in the time of the third caliph, Uthman, presumably on parchment. Since then, the Holy Book has been translated into many other languages as Islam spread to include non-Arab peoples.

All translations stem from Uthman's text. It was organized into 114 *suras* (chapters), with the longest at the beginning and the shortest at the end. (The actual order of the revelations was probably the reverse, since the longer ones came mostly during Muhammad's period in Medina, when he was trying to establish guidelines for the community.)***

Many of the revelations provide specific guides to conduct or social relationships:

When ye have performed the act of worship, remember Allah sitting, standing and reclining. . . . Worship at fixed times hath been enjoined on the believers. . . .
(*Sura IV,* 103)

Establish worship at the going down of the sun until the dark of night, and at dawn. Lo! The recital of the Koran at dawn is ever witnessed.
(*Sura XVII,* 78–79)

Make contracts with your slaves and spend of your own wealth that God has given you upon them. . . .
(*Sura XXIV,* 33)

If you fear that you will be dishonest in regard to these orphan girls, then you may marry from among them one, two, three or four. But if you fear you will not be able to do justice among them, marry only one.
(*Sura IV,* 3)

Much of the content of the Koran is related to the ethical and moral. It is an Arab Koran, given to Arabs "in clear Arabic tongue" (*Sura XLI,* 44) and characterized by a quality of style and language that is essentially untranslatable. Muslim children, regardless of where they live, learn it in Arabic, and only then may they read it in their own language, and then always accompanied by the original Arabic version. Recitals of selections from the Koran are a feature of births, marriages, funerals, festivals, and other special events and are extraordinarily effective, whether or not the listener understands Arabic.****

* Peter Awn, "Faith and Practice," in Marjorie Kelly, ed., *Islam: The Religious and Political Life of a World Community* (New York: Praeger, 1984), pp. 2–7.

** *The Qur'an, The First American Version,* Translation and Commentary by T.B. Irving (Brattleboro, VT: Amana Books, 1985), Introduction, XXVII.

*** On this topic, see Fazlur Rahman, *Major Themes of the Qur'an* (Chicago: Bibliotheca Islamica, 1980), *passim.*

**** "The old preacher sat with his waxen hands in his lap and uttered the first Surah, full of the soft warm coloring of a familiar understanding. . . . His listeners followed the notation of the verses with care and rapture, gradually seeking their way together . . . like a school of fish following a leader, out into the deep sea." Lawrence Durrell, *Mountolive* (London: Faber and Faber, 1958), p. 265.

they also believe that it is not subject to change but only to interpretation—and that to within a narrow range.

Conflict over interpretation of the term *jihad* has had a great deal to do with the ferment visible in Islam today. For example, members of Islamic Jihad believe that their interpretation of *jihad* as a holy war against the enemies of Islam is the correct one. The holy-war definition of *jihad* is the one most familiar to non-Muslims. Muslims have always believed that God intended them to struggle to establish Islam as a universal religion, although conversion of other monotheists (Jews and Christians) would not be required as long as these communities recognized the superiority of Islam. The military interpretation of *jihad* has led to the division of the world into the Dar al-Islam ("House of Islam") and the Dar al-Harb

("House of Dissidence"), the area yet to be brought into the House of Islam.[3]

Other Muslim groups, notably the Nakshbandi, a dervish order based in Bukhara (modern Uzbekistan) that dates back to the fourteenth century, reject the warlike view of *jihad.* Instead, they follow a policy of peace, tolerance, and cooperation with all faiths.

Another definition of *jihad,* the striving of the individual for justice, is perhaps the most controversial. Islam teaches that if rulers—whether elected or appointed over some Islamic territory—become unjust, their subjects should bear the injustices with fortitude; God will, in due course, reward their patience. Some Muslims interpret this injunction to mean that they should strive to help the leaders to see the error of their ways—by whatever action is necessary. Centuries ago, a secret society, the Hashishin ("Assassins"; so named because they reportedly were users of hashish), carried out many assassinations of prominent officials and rulers, claiming that God had inspired them to rid Islamic society of tyrants. Since Islam emphasizes the direct relationship of people to God—and therefore people's responsibility to do right in the eyes of God and to struggle to help other believers follow the same right path—it becomes most dangerous when individuals feel that they do not need to subject themselves to the collective will but, rather, to impose their own concept of justice on others.

In our own day, jihad is associated with the struggle of Shia Muslims for social, political, and economic rights within Islamic states. Inspired by the example of Iran, some seek to establish a true Islamic government in the House of Islam. But Iranian Muslims are not only militant, they are also strongly nationalistic. In this respect, they differ sharply in their approach to Islamic reform from the approaches of other militant Islamic groups, notably the Muslim Brotherhood. Its founder, Hassan al-Banna, stressed the gradualist approach, rejecting narrow or exclusivist philosophies and declaring that the Brotherhood stood ready to assist Muslim governments in the improvement of society through "basic Islamification of beliefs, moral codes and ruling institutions."[4]

No such strictures affect Iranians' view of jihad. An important element in their belief system derives from their special relationship with their religious leaders, particularly the late Ayatollah Khomeini. In his writings and sermons, Khomeini stressed the need for violent resistance to unjust authorities.

The best example of "internal" Islamic jihad in recent years developed during the annual *Hajj* ("Great Pilgrimage") to Mecca in August 1987. Iranian pilgrims, taking literally Khomeini's injunction that the Hajj is the ideal forum for demonstration of the "proper use of Islam in politics," staged a political rally after midday prayer services. Demonstrators carrying posters of Khomeini shouted, "Death to America! Death to the Soviet Union! Death to Israel!" Saudi police attempting to control them were attacked, and the demonstration swiftly grew into a riot. When it was over, more than 400 people had been killed, including 85 policemen, and 650 people had been injured. "To take revenge for the sacred bloodshed is to free the holy shrines from the wicked Wahhabi," an Iranian government official told a crowd in Teheran.[5]

ISLAMIC ORIGINS

The most negative view of Islam by Westerners is largely the result of the Crusades, highly colored by generations of Sunday-school textbooks. However, Islam developed among a particular people, the Arabs; was built on earlier foundations of Christianity and Judaism; and was primarily concerned with the transmission of the spiritual message of God to humankind as a corrective measure. It is an article of faith among Arab nationalists and Muslim Arab scholars that the Arabs were chosen as a people to receive God's revelations because they were cousins of the Jews through Abraham and therefore were included in the Judeo–Christian tradition. But they did not have scriptures of their own.

Islam was founded in the seventh century A.D. by Muhammad, a merchant in the small town of Mecca in southwestern Arabia. Muslims believe that Muhammad's religious teachings came from revelations that he received orally from God via the Angel Gabriel. After Muhammad's death, these revelations were put into book form in the *Koran* ("Recitation"), the Holy Book of Islam.

During Muhammad's lifetime, the various revelations he received were used to guide his followers along the "Way" of conduct (*Shari'a*, in Arabic) acceptable to God. The Arabs followed traditional religions in Muhammad's time, worshipping many gods. Muhammad taught belief in one God—Allah—and in the Word of God sent down to him as messenger. For this reason, Muhammad is considered the Prophet of Islam.

Muhammad's received revelations plus his own teachings issued to instruct his followers make up the formal religious system known as Islam. The word *Islam* is Arabic and has been translated variously as "submission," "surrender" (i.e., to God's will), and the fatalistic "acceptance." A better translation might be "receptiveness." Those who receive and accept the Word of God as transmitted to Muhammad and set down in the Koran are called Muslims.

Islam is essentially a simple faith. Five basic duties are required of the believer; they are often called the Five Pillars because they are the foundations of the House of Islam. They are:

1. The confession of faith: "I testify that there is no God but God, and Muhammad is the Messenger of God."

2. Prayer, required five times daily, facing in the direction of Mecca, the holy city.

3. Fasting during the daylight hours in the month of Ramadan, the month of Muhammad's first revelations.

4. Alms giving, a tax or gift of not less than 2½ percent of one's income, to the community for the help of the poor.

5. Pilgrimage, required at least once in one's lifetime, to the House of God in Mecca.

It is apparent from the above description that Islam has many points in common with Judaism and Christianity. All three are monotheistic religions, having a fundamental belief in one God. Muslims believe that Muhammad was the "seal of the Prophets," the last messenger and recipient of revelations. But they also believe that God revealed Himself to other inspired prophets, from Abraham, Moses, and other Old Testament (Hebrew Bible) figures down through history, including Jesus Christ. However, Muslims part company with Christians over the divinity of Jesus as the Son of God; the Resurrection; and the tripartite division into Father, Son, and Holy Ghost or Spirit.

THE ISLAMIC CALENDAR

The Islamic calendar is a lunar calendar. It has 354 days in all, divided into 7 months of 30 days, 4 months of 29 days, and 1 month of 28 days. The first year of the calendar, A.H. 1 (*Anno Hegira,* the year of Muhammad's "emigration" to Medina to escape persecution in Mecca), corresponds to A.D. 622.

In the Islamic calendar, the months rotate with the Moon, coming at different times from year to year. It takes an Islamic month 33 years to make the complete circuit of the seasons. The fasting month of Ramadan moves with the season and is most difficult for Muslims when it takes place in high summer.

Although Muhammad is in no way regarded as divine by Muslims, his life is considered a model for their own lives. His *hadith* ("teachings" or "sayings") that were used to supplement Koranic revelations (or to deal with specific situations when no revelation was forthcoming) have served as guides to Muslim conduct since the early days of Islam. The Koran and hadith together form the *Sunna* (translated literally as "Beaten Path"), which provides an Islamic code of conduct for the believers.

The importance of Muhammad's role in Islam cannot be overemphasized. Among Muslims, his name is used frequently in conversation or written communication, always followed by "Peace Be Unto Him" (PBUH). A death sentence (*fatwa*) imposed on the writer Salman Rushdie by Iran's revolutionary leader Ayatollah Khomeini resulted from an unflattering portrait of Muhammad in Rushdie's novel *The Satanic Verses* (1988); today, despite disclaimers by the post-Khomeini government, the sentence remains in effect. And an Israeli woman's depiction of Muhammad as a pig writing in the Koran, on a poster displayed in Hebron, roused a storm of protest throughout the Muslim world. She was arrested by Israeli police and given a 21-year jail sentence for "harming religious sensibilities."[6]

ISLAMIC DIVISIONS: SUNNIS AND SHIAS

The great majority (90 percent) of Muslims are called Sunnis, because they follow the Sunna, observe the Five Pillars, and practice the rituals of the faith. They also interpret as correct the history of Islam as it developed after Muhammad's death, under a line of successors termed *caliphs* ("agents" or "deputies") who held spiritual and political authority over the Islamic community. However, a minority, while accepting the precepts and rituals of the faith, reject this historical process as contrary to what Muhammad intended for the community of believers. These Muslims are called Shias (commonly, but incorrectly, Shiites). The split between Sunnis and Shias dates back to Muhammad's death in A.D. 632.

Muhammad left no instructions as to a successor. Since he had said that there would be no more revelations after him, a majority of his followers favored the election of a caliph who would hold the community together and carry on his work. But a minority felt that Muhammad had intended to name his closest male blood relative, Ali, as his successor. Supporters of Ali declared that the succession to Muhammad was a divine right inherited by his direct descendants. Hence they are known as Shias ("Partisans") of Ali.

The first three caliphs—Abu Bakr, Umar, and Uthman—were chosen by majority vote by the Mecca community. Under their leadership, Arab armies expanded Islam's territory far outside Arabia, changing what had been essentially a religious community into a political power through the conversion of non-Arab peoples to Islam and the imposition of rule by Islamic caliphs. These conquests compounded Sunni–Shia differences.

Ali was eventually elected as the fourth caliph; but, by this time, the divisions were so deep that his election was disputed. The Kharijites, an extremist group, who felt that Muhammad's original purpose in founding the Islamic community had been distorted, decided to assassinate Ali and his major rival, on the grounds that Ali had accepted arbitration in his dispute with this rival over the election. The Kharijites argued that the office of caliph could not be bartered away; it was a sacred trust transmitted from God to Muhammad. One of them murdered Ali outside a mosque in A.D. 661.

Ali's younger son and designated successor, Husayn, was ambushed and killed in A.D. 680 by the army of Yazid, the son of the fourth caliph's major rival, near the town of Karbala (in modern Iraq). This event led to the founding of a hereditary dynasty, the Umayyads. The Umayyad caliphs moved the Islamic capital from Mecca to Damascus. But the intrigues and rivalries of Muslim leaders continued to hamper political stability. A century and a half later, a rival group overthrew the Umayyads and established a third caliphate, the Abbasids. The caliphal capital was moved eastward, to Baghdad, where it endured for 500 years and developed the distinctive features of *Islamic* civilization, the successor in many respects of Greek and Roman civilizations and precursor of European civilization.

The Abbasid caliphs were Sunnis, and Shia resistance to them as presumed usurpers of the rightful heritage of Ali and his descendants resulted in much persecution. Shia rebellions were put down with bloody massacres by the ruling Sunnis. Forced to go underground, the Shia Muslims began to practice *taqiya* ("dissimulation" or "concealment"). Outwardly, they bowed to the authority of Sunni rulers; secretly, however, they continued to believe in the divine right of Ali's descendants to rule the Islamic world.

Most Shia Muslims recognize a line of 12 direct descendants of Muhammad, through Ali and Husayn, as their Imams, or spiritual leaders. When the 12th Imam died, a number of Shia religious leaders declared that he was not dead but hidden (alive, present in this world, but invisible) and would return at the end of time to pronounce the Day of Judgment. Until the Hidden Imam returned, the religious leaders would provide leadership and interpretation of God's will and make decisions on behalf of the Shia community. This doctrine gave the Shia religious leaders more authority over Shia Muslims than Sunni religious leaders have over Sunni Muslims. This helps to explain the tremendous power and prestige that Ayatollah Khomeini, leader of the revolution that established an Islamic republic in Iran, held among his people.

With one exception, Shia Muslims remained a minority in Islamic lands and did not acquire political power. The exception was Iran. In the early 1500s, Shaykh Safi, the leader of a religious brotherhood in northern Iran, preached a jihad against the Ottoman Turks, accusing them of unjust practices and discrimination against the non-Turkish subjects of their empire. His successor, as head of the brotherhood, claimed to be descended from Ali, which entitled him to act on behalf of the Hidden Imam. In order to obtain further sanction for his wars with the Ottomans, the successor reached an agreement with Shia religious leaders whereby they would recognize him as ruler of Iran in return for a commitment to establish Shia Islam as the majority there.

Since that time, Shia Islam has been the strongest bond unifying the Iranian people, regardless of ethnic, linguistic, or social differences. The relationship between the shahs of Iran and the clergy underwent many changes—from coexistence, to persecution, to a grudging acceptance. But it was not until the twentieth century, when Shah Mohammed Reza Pahlavi began to tamper with the bonds linking the Iranian people with their religious leaders through his programs of social modernization, particularly in the areas of emancipation and literacy, that the relationship became totally an adversarial one.

SHIA MUSLIMS AND MARTYRDOM

The murder of Husayn, far more than that of his father Ali, provided the Shia community with a martyr figure. This is due to the circumstances surrounding Husayn's death—the lingering image of Muhammad's grandson, with a small band of followers, surrounded in the waterless desert to be cut down by the vastly superior forces of Yazid, has exerted a powerful influence on Shias. As a result, Shias often identify themselves with Husayn, a heroic martyr fighting against hopeless odds. For example, an important factor in the success of Iran in repelling the invasion of Iraqi forces in the bitter 1980–1988 war was the Basijis, teenage volunteers led into battle by chanters in the firm belief that death at the hands of the Sunni Iraqi enemy was a holy action worthy of martyrdom.[7]

ISLAM AND EUROPE: CHANGING ROLES

The early centuries of Islam were marked by many brilliant achievements. An extensive network of trade routes linked the cities of the Islamic world. It was a high-fashion world in which the rich wore silks from Damascus ("damask"), slept on fine sheets from Mosul ("muslin"), sat on couches of morocco leather, and carried swords and daggers of Toledo steel. Islamic merchants developed many institutions and practices used in modern economic systems, such as banks, letters of credit, checks and receipts, accounting, and book-keeping. Islamic agriculture, based on sophisticated irrigation systems developed for the arid Middle East, introduced to the Western world the cultivation of citrus fruits, vegetables such as eggplant and radishes, coffee, cotton, and sugar. The very names of these products are derived from Arabic origins, all of them reaching Northern Europe via Spain, whence they were brought from the East and developed during the 700-year-long Muslim domination of the Iberian peninsula.

Islamic medical technology reached a level of excellence in diagnosis and treatment unequaled in Europe until the nineteenth century. Muslim mathematics gave Europeans Arabic numerals and the concept of zero. Muslim navigators made possible Columbus's voyages through their knowledge of seamanship and inventions such as the sextant and the compass. Their libraries were the most extensive in existence at that time.

The level of achievements of Islamic civilization from roughly A.D. 750–1200 was far superior to that of Europe. The first Europeans to come in direct contact with Islamic society were Crusader knights, who invaded the Middle East in order to recapture Jerusalem from its Muslim rulers. The Crusaders

'ASHURA

A special Shia Muslim festival not observed by Sunnis commemorates the 10 days of 'Ashura, the anniversary of the death of Husayn. Shia Muslims mark the occasion with a series of ritual dramas that may be compared to the Christian Passion Play, except that they may be performed at other times during the year. Particularly in Iran, the ritual, called *Ta'ziyeh,* is presented by strolling troupes of actors who travel from village to village to dramatize the story with songs, poetry, and sword dances. Ta'ziyeh also takes place in street parades in cities, featuring penitents who lash themselves with whips or slash their bodies with swords. Freya Stark, the great English travel writer, describes one such procession in her book *Baghdad Sketches:*

All is represented, every incident on the fateful day of Karbala, and the procession stops at intervals to act one espisode or another. One can hear it coming from far away by the thud of beaters beating their naked chests, a mighty sound like the beating of carpets, or see the blood pour down the backs of those who acquire merit with flails made of knotted chains with which they lacerate their shoulders; and finally the slain body comes, headless, carried under a bloodstained sheet through wailing crowds.

marveled at what they saw, even though they were the sworn enemies of Islam. This Christian occupation of the Holy Land, while short-lived (A.D. 1099–1187), contributed significantly to the mutual hostility that has marked Christian–Muslim relations throughout their coexistence. (A retired German diplomat who became a Muslim in 1980 expressed the difference between Christianity and Islam in cogent social terms: "The alternative to an increasingly amoral lifestyle in the West is Islam, but an Islam rigorously practiced and free from fanaticism, brutality, violence, violation of human rights and other practices erroneously associated in the Western mind with the religion.")[8]

The hostility between Muslims and Christians generated by the Crusades was intensified by the rise of the Ottoman Turks, one of the many newly converted Islamic peoples, to power in the Islamic world. By the 1400s, they had established a powerful Islamic military state. In 1453, the Ottomans captured Constantinople, capital of the East Roman (Byzantine) Empire, and soon controlled most of Eastern Europe.

During the centuries of Ottoman rule, many people from the Christian European provinces became converts to Islam. Islamic peoples from other parts of the empire also migrated there, drawn by opportunities for land or other inducements, and Ottoman soldiers were often given land grants in return for service to the state. Muslims in Eastern Europe remained there after countries such as Yugoslavia, Romania, Bulgaria, and Albania gained their independence from the sultan. Not until recently did their governments interfere substantially with the personal lives of their Muslim subjects. However, the wave of nationalism that swept over Eastern Europe in the late 1980s in the wake of Soviet efforts under Mikhail Gorbachev to revitalize the Communist system led at least one government—that of Bulgaria—to begin a forcible assimilation of its Muslim minority.

The Ottoman state not only ruled Eastern Europe for nearly 4 centuries but also dominated such emerging European nations as Russia, Austria, France, and England. These nations were struggling to limit the powers of absolute monarchs, develop effective military technology, and build systems of representative government. The Ottomans and the various Islamic peoples they governed did not think that any of these things were necessary. The Ottoman sultan was also the caliph of Islam. He was convinced that God had given him the right to rule and to know what was best for the people. Ottoman military success against Europe seemed to prove that God had given the Islamic world a stronger army, superior military technology, and a more effective way of life. The Ottomans were so sure of the superiority of Islam over anything that could be devised in the Christian West that they allowed Christian and Jewish communities under their control to practice their beliefs and rituals freely under their own leaders, in return for payment of a special tax and admission of their inferior military and political status in exchange for Ottoman protection.

Gradually, these roles were reversed. The first reversal came with the defeats of Ottoman armies by various European powers. The Ottoman sultans were forced to sign treaties with rulers they deemed inferior. Worse yet, they lost territories with each defeat. In the early nineteenth century, European powers seized control of Egypt; in Eastern Europe, meanwhile, the Greeks, Romanians, Serbs, and other subject peoples won their independence with European support. The defeat in Egypt was particularly shocking to Ottoman leaders, because Egypt had been part of the Islamic heartland for a thousand years.

An even greater shock came with the discovery by Muslims that the despised Europeans had developed a relatively advanced technology. Upper-class Muslim visitors to European lands in the late nineteenth century were astonished by this technology. Electric lights, railroads, broad boulevards sweeping through cities, telegraph lines, factories, and a long list of labor-saving inventions were all new to the Muslims. Most Islamic peoples were still living much as their ancestors had lived for centuries. When this apparent superiority in technology was added to European military dominance, it seemed to thoughtful Muslims that something had gone wrong.

The question was, What had gone wrong? How had it happened that the Islamic world had fallen behind Europe? Some Muslims believed that all one could do was to await the inevitable; God Himself had decided that it was time to bring the world to an end, and, therefore, the decline of Islam was a logical consequence. Other Muslims believed that the problem had developed because they had not been true to their religion or observed correctly the obligations of the faith. A third group of Muslims were convinced that Islam itself had to be "changed, modified, adapted or reformed to suit modern conditions . . . so as to overcome Western domination."[9]

The contrast between the second and third approaches to Islamic reform has been important in forming the Middle Eastern states of today. Two states, Saudi Arabia and, more recently, Iran, developed out of a movement to reestablish the Islamic community of Muhammad in its original form, basing their campaign on calls for strict adherence to the Koran and the Sunna. The other Middle Eastern states developed on an ad hoc basis through Western tutelage and gradual acceptance of Western methods and technology.

ISLAMIC FUNDAMENTALISM

The fundamentalism that appears to pervade the Islamic world today has its roots in earlier, nineteenth-century movements that sought to revitalize Islam through internal reform, thus enabling Islamic societies to resist foreign control. Some of these movements sought peaceful change; others were more militant. The most prominent of the militant groups was the Wahhabi movement, which laid the basis for the Saudi Arabian state—a pure Islamic state in form, law, and practice. Another was the Sanusiya, founded by a prominent scholar who sought to unite the nomadic and seminomadic peoples of Libya into a brotherhood. This movement was also based on strict interpretation and application of the Koran. A third movement, Mahdism, developed in Sudan; its purpose was not only to purify Sudanese Islam but also to drive out the British who had invaded Sudan from Egypt. The aims of these three movements were essentially parochial and territorial, either to expel foreigners from Islamic soil or to impose a "purification" on their tribal neighbors.

Twentieth-century reform movements such as the Muslim Brotherhood have concentrated their efforts on removal of secular Islamic governments, which, in their view, do not conform to the principles of the true faith and therefore are illegitimate. Islamic reform on the scale of the Christian Protestant Reformation has yet to be attempted, and the establishment of fixed national boundaries by Islamic governments bent on preserving their legitimacy makes it unlikely that a global Islamic state will emerge in the foreseeable future.

Fundamentalism is a somewhat incomplete term to apply to the twentieth-century Islamic movements, because it suggests to Westerners a religious view that is antimodernist, literal in interpretation, and with a strong emphasis on traditional ethics. Some fundamentalists would re-establish Islamic society peacefully through internal change, but others would revolutionize Islam in the manner of Marxist or other European revolutionary movements. Shia Muslim factions in Lebanon, such as the Hizbullah, view the revolutionary struggle as one aimed at expelling foreign influences first and achieving social justice second. This revolutionary movement, once centered around Khomeini in Iran, is committed to the rule of the religious leaders; while Libya's Muammar al-Qadhafi would eliminate the influence of the religious leaders entirely, substituting rule by "people's committees." The only common ground for these movements and groups is their fundamental opposition to the onslaught of materialistic Western culture. Their desire is to re-assert a distinct Islamic identity for the societies they claim to represent.

The great danger to Islam is that rather than being a true revival of the religion, these movements have disfigured its nature. Some of them would modernize Islam by grafting onto the religion negative and spiritually devastating ideas borrowed from the West. In the name of religious fervor, they close the door to the kind of open dialogue that could produce general agreement or understanding of what form Islam should take. A common concern among Muslims is how to achieve *Islamic modernization,* meaning a future wherein political and social development and economic progress appropriate for the realities of the twentieth century are firmly rooted in Islamic history and values.

The struggle between "modernizers" and "fundamentalists" for social control of Islamic peoples has become, in the final decade of the twentieth century, a contest for political control of governments. In most of the contemporary Islamic states, the struggle has involved efforts by opposition groups

(UN photo/John Isaac)

The mosque at Khan El Khalili, Egypt.

to overthrow their governments by violence. In Egypt and Jordan, the Muslim Brotherhood, focused in the past of violent opposition, has entered the political process as a more or less legitimate party and has disclaimed the use of violence to attain its goal of "Islamization" of the regime. This accommodation with the regime has enabled it to undertake a campaign of brutal repression of those Islamist groups outside the Brotherhood that were committed to antigovernment violence—a campaign that has largely succeeded.

Elsewhere in the Middle East, the Islamists have had varying success. The Islamic Salvation Front (FIS) in Algeria, for example, was declared illegal after winning elections in 1991 for the country's first multiparty National Assembly. But the annulment of the elections and the arrest of FIS leaders triggered a no-quarter war between the military regime and Islamists that has left Algerian society in shambles. In Turkey, the Islamic Welfare Party (Refah) won control of the government in the 1995 elections, bringing the country's first Islamic-oriented organization to power since the founding of the secular republic. After less than a year in office, however, its leader, Prime Minister Necmettin Erbakan, was forced to

MUSLIM HOUSING: FORM FOLLOWS FUNCTION

Muslim families in the Middle East live in many different kinds of houses. A common feature is the suitability of the traditional Islamic residence to the surrounding environment. Nomads in the desert live in woven goat-hair tents, easily dismantled when ready to break camp. In Syria and Turkey, one finds the cone-shaped beehive house, built of mud brick, which can be put up easily by unskilled labor and costs little in the way of materials. The high dome of the house collects the hot, dry air and releases it through narrow openings, while the dome shape sheds rainfall before the mud brick can absorb moisture and crumble. The construction provides natural air conditioning; interior temperatures remain in the 75°F–85°F range, while the outside temperatures may reach 140°F. The beehive house illustrates Frank Lloyd Wright's dictum that "form follows function."

Further illustrations of ingenious designs to suit the harsh climate are the cave houses in southern Tunisia. Caves have been hollowed out from a central shaft below the desert floor. (The movie *Star Wars* was filmed here.) Most residences on the Persian/Arab Gulf, where strong winds blow, have open-sided towers above the rooftops to catch any wind and funnel it into the rooms below. Many city residences are built with tiny windows and are joined together and covered by deep overhangs to provide shade for passersby.

In San'a, Yemen, houses are several stories high, are gaily decorated, and are painted with slatted overhangs for women to look out of without being seen. Some farmers in northern Tunisia utilize hay to construct their houses. These hay houses are sometimes elaborate and contain windows and wooden doors.

Mud brick, cut and sun-dried, has been a common building material in the Middle East for 8,000 years. Today, with the increased use of air conditioning and reinforced concrete, steel, and other prefabricated building materials, Middle Eastern cities have begun to take on the look of cities everywhere.

(UN photo/W. Graham)

This cave house in the Matmata Mountains suits the harsh climate of southern Tunisia.

Not only have most Middle Eastern cities lost their distinctive look, but widespread use of cement instead of the traditional and easily available building materials has had more dire consequences. To raise the cash to buy cement for housing in rural areas, someone must leave the village, thus disrupting family and community life.

---

resign by military leaders, who feared that Refah's policies would undermine secular Turkish values by imposing traditional Islamic principles and rules of behavior on society.

It should be noted that the long interaction between the West and the Islamic Middle East has resulted in the development of a large number of Western-oriented, if not Western-educated, leaders and professionals. Even the structure of the Middle East's Islamic regimes is modeled on Western institutions. Bernard Lewis reminds us that the Islamic Republic of Iran—the prototype for putative Islamic regimes—has an elected Assembly and a written Constitution, "for which there is no precedent in the Islamic past."[10] Both modernizers and fundamentalists view Islam as a divinely ordained alternative to communism and Western capitalism. Where they differ is that modernizers seek to superimpose Western principles and laws on Islamic society, while fundamentalists would establish *Islamic* law and Islamic social requirements (the *Shari'a*) as the controlling principle in Islamic states.

Muslims today, in the Middle East as elsewhere, are searching for an Islamic identity and way of life appropriate to the modern world of great ethnic, political, and religious diversity. The commonality of the faith, its overarching culture and social norms, is easily grasped and appeals to a great variety of peoples. But Islamic unity has thus far proven unworkable; Islams' cultural strength is also its political weakness. In practice, the process that outsiders call "Islamic fundamentalism" is actually a series of assaults on putative Islamic regimes by groups who feel either that they have been excluded from power or that the factors that legitimize the *Islamic* nature of these regimes have been ignored. But whatever the outcome, the Islamic revival has already proven its value in restoring a sense of dignity and purpose to Muslims, a sense that had long been lost to view.

ISLAMIC SOCIETY IN TRANSITION
I have come, I know not where,
but I have come.
And I have seen a road before me,
and have taken it.[11]

(UN photo/John Isaac)

A common concern among Muslims is how to achieve Islamic modernization, wherein social development considers the realities of the twentieth century. This dichotomy is illustrated by these Egyptian women in traditional dress waiting for a bus, a modern convenience.

Most Muslims inhabit a world still dominated by Islamic law, custom, spirituality, and belief, despite the waves of violence, puritanical reaction, revolution, ideological conflict, and power struggles among leaders that have threatened it. Islam is not only the bond that unites diverse peoples over a vast territory; it also brings equilibrium to counterbalance the visible disruptions that increasingly affect daily life.

One element of Islam that brings Muslims together in a ritual that transcends differences is the Hajj, the Great Pilgrimage to Mecca and Medina, the sacred shrines of the faith. It is the fifth of the Five Pillars and thus an obligation for believers. One may make a pilgrimage at any time, but the Great Hajj takes place only once a year, under the direct sponsorship of the Saudi Arabian government in its capacity as "Guardian of the Holy Places." Although it is intended to bring Muslims from all over the world in a spirit of harmony and reverence, the Hajj has become a vehicle for social and political protest in recent years.

Yet, for the *hajjis* ("pilgrims"), the Pilgrimage is still the ultimate religious experience. The Imam of the Muslim community of Toledo, Ohio, vividly described its impact: "You feel the weight of all the history. And everyone dresses identically in the *ihram* [the white seamless robe of the pilgrim] and sandals. You see the equality of all people before God: rich people, poor, women and men, kings and janitors, black and white, all in the same uniform, all together."[12]

In the Islamic lands of the Middle East, Islam provides a cultural uniformity that transcends ethnic, linguistic, and other differences among social groups. This Middle Eastern Islamic cultural order has many components, both real and intangible. The former include architecture, dress, arts and crafts, food, and living accommodations. In addition to these physical aspects of the culture, a wide range of social activities has evolved, built on religious foundations. The traditional social rituals of childbirth, marriage, adulthood, and death, and the festival celebrations, are duplicated with minor variations across the region. The intangible components of the system are harder to define, and they are perhaps more Middle Eastern than purely Islamic. Yet there is a common pattern of behavior. Most Middle Easterners practice bargaining in both business and personal relationships, emphasize the family as the responsible social unit above political parties and even nations, and follow a formal code of etiquette governing all aspects of behavior.

ARCHITECTURE: AN EXPRESSION OF RELIGIOUS FAITH

Islamic architecture is centered on the mosque, the house of worship. The first mosque was a simple structure of palm branches laid over a frame of tree trunks to provide shade from the desert sun for worshippers. As time passed, Muslim architects built more magnificent structures, dedicating their work to the glory of God, much as medieval Christian artisans did with the great cathedrals of Europe. The engineer-architect Sinan (1497–1588), who served as chief of the Imperial Architects under three sultans, designed and built 477 such structures, including mosques, royal tombs, public baths, and inns for travelers. His architectural genius is visible in many Turkish cities even today.

Along with mosques and other public buildings, which were usually decorated with elaborate designs in calligraphy and stonework, Islamic cities developed a distinct spatial order that made them functionally useful to their residents. Their outer limits were encircled by massive walls and gates, closed at night or in time of danger of invasion. An inner quarter, also fortified, marked the presence of government. Other quarters were reserved for the customary outdoor market (*suq*), with its tiny artisans' shops, produce stands, sacks of spice, and perfume sellers, tailors, and cloth and rug merchants. Nearby were residential areas and the religious quarter, with its mosque, Koranic school, libraries, and various social-service facilities. The modern American dichotomy of the central city divorced from its suburbs and industrial parks was until recently alien to the Islamic city; one was either an urbanite or a rural peasant or villager.

HOME AND FAMILY LIFE

Within the residential quarters of Islamic cities there existed, and in large measure still exists, a kinship arrangement very different from that of the typical American subdivision. The households of each quarter claim either a kinship relation or close personal ties to one another. Everyone knows everyone else, and most households are related. In one residential quarter of the town of Boujad, Morocco, the great majority of households claim descent from a common ancestor, the founder of the group from which they descended patrilineally. Other households regard themselves as being under the protection of that group.

(UN photo/J. Isaac)

Privacy is emphasized in the communities of the Middle East. The nondescript walls near this Moroccan child may very well surround beautiful courtyards decorated with fruit trees, flowers, and fountains.

The resulting cooperation establishes what anthropologists call the notion of closeness (*qaraba*), which defines the social organization of the quarter. Closeness is essential to the proper functioning of society. Christine Eickelman describes the *hayyan* (family cluster) in inner Oman as an essential support network for village women. The hayyan consists of those women (some of them relatives, others not related) whom each woman regards as her confidantes, and to whom she will confide matters that she may not reveal even to her own husband or immediate family. Visits among hayyan members are made on a daily basis, aside from the support provided in stressful situations such as birth, marriage, or death. Hayyan members also provide mutual protection and even share housework and child care.[13]

Within the Islamic family, the father has the final say on all matters, which gives him, in theory, absolute authority. However, the role of women in family life is crucial to its continuation. Women in Muslim families not only ensure successive generations but are also responsible for the discipline and informal education of the young. Mothers hold the family together through the transmission of cultural and religious traditions and values learned from *their* mothers. A tragic result of the turmoil in Lebanon and the Palestinian resistance movement in Israeli-occupied territories has been the breakup of the family, the loss of parental authority, and the substitution of war and violence for traditional family values among Lebanese and Palestinian youth.

Communities in the Middle East emphasize the private over the public life of residents. It is not possible for someone walking along a town or city residential street to know much about the economic or social circumstances of those who live there. Homes have blank, windowless walls facing the street; entry is usually achieved through a massive studded door set in the wall, a brass hand serving as a knocker. Inside, one may find, in a wealthier home, low-ceilinged rooms furnished with rich carpets, banquettes, and ottomans in lieu of chairs and sofas (though this is disappearing), and in the center an open courtyard with flowers, fruit trees, and a plashing fountain.

FAMILY CELEBRATIONS

Throughout the Middle East, the family is still the most important social unit, so much so that when rulers like King Hussein of Jordan and King Hassan II of Morocco describe their relationship with their subjects, they do so in terms of "my family" or "my children." Economic dislocations, the gap between illiterate parents and their educated children, and new social legislation have all affected the family. But the extended family is still where the individual places his or her trust, loyalty, and obedience.

Most celebrations and holidays in the Middle East are related to religion; although such holidays as No-Ruz (New Year) in Iran pre-date Islam and celebrate the onset of spring. Most modern Middle Eastern states observe a "national day" marking their independence from colonial rule. But the majority of festivals still spring essentially out of religious observances. Thus the most solemn festival in Judaism is collectively the "Days of Awe" or "High Holy Days," beginning each year with Rosh Hashanah (the Jewish New Year) and ending with Yom Kippur (the Day of Atonement). On that day, Jews are enjoined to pray, reflect on their lives, and avoid all customary activities; in Israel, even the buses do not run. Other festivals are more joyous, helping to bind families together in a closer relationship. Thus families join in building the thatched hut outdoors on Sukkot, celebrating the time when their ancestors wandered in the wilderness of Sinai. Similarly, Hanukkah, the "Festival of Lights," marks the victory of the Maccabees over the Syrian forces of the Emperor Antiochus more than 2,000 years ago. Purim, one of the most joyous holidays on the Jewish calendar, recalls the story of Esther, the Jewish queen of King Ahasuerus of Persia, who saved her people from death after the king had been persuaded by his chief minister, Haman, that they were disloyal and should be killed on a day chosen by the drawing of lots (*purim,* in Hebrew). Esther offered herself as a sacrifice, and, convinced by her honesty, King Ahasuerus changed his mind. This "day of deliverance" is celebrated with a multicourse feast, the giving of homemade sweets to relatives and friends, and triangular pastries called *oznei Haman* (Haman's ears). Similarly, the Hanukkah gelt themselves—gold-foil–covered chocolate "coins" hidden in households for children to find—symbolize the new coins minted long ago by Judas Maccabaeus to mark Jewish independence from religious and political persecution.

Muslim households observe a similar pattern. Ramadan, the ninth month of the Muslim year, is observed as a fasting month to mark Allah's first revelations to Muhammad. In principle, Muslim families go without food or nourishment of any kind from sunrise to sunset during the month. Increasingly, even in secular Muslim countries such as Turkey, the fast is being observed, as fundamentalism spreads across the Islamic world. The *iftar,* or "fast-breaking" evening meal that ends the day's observance, features special foods and spices, and there are daily Koranic readings until the 27th day. Then a cannon booms, and families joyfully celebrate Id al-Fitr, "The Breaking of the Fast."

A CUISINE SUITED TO THE ENVIRONMENT

Middle Eastern cooking largely transcends political, linguistic, religious, and other differences. It is a highly varied cuisine that makes much use of natural, unrefined foods. The pungent smells of lamb roasting over charcoal, stuffed eggplant and roasted sweet peppers, tiny cups of thick coffee and hot, sweet tea are common across national boundaries. The basics of Middle Eastern cooking originated in ancient Persia (modern Iran) and have been continually refined, with subtle differences developing from country to country.

Beef is relatively scarce in the region due to the aridity and lack of pasture, although this is changing with the introduction of Texas cattle and other breeds suited to the arid climate. There is abundant lamb and chicken, and people eat a great variety of seafood. Because of the lack of cattle, more olive oil is used in cooking than butter, and goat and sheep cheeses are more common than cheese made from cows' milk. Yogurt

is a staple dessert but is also used in soups and sauces. Potatoes are seldom used, but rice pilaf made with chicken broth, onions, and currants is popular. There is an almost limitless variety of herbs and spices.

Little milk is drunk. Fresh orange juice and guava juice are common, along with other fruit juices. Desserts are usually fruit, and sometimes cheese. Middle Easterners are also fond of rich, sweet pastries such as baklava and cakes, which are reserved for holidays and special occasions.

Coffee beans were first discovered growing wild in Ethiopia and were probably brought to Yemen by Ethiopian invaders. From there coffee spread throughout the Middle East as a popular beverage, the Port of Mocha becoming synonymous with export of the crop. Early Islamic religious authorities tried to ban its use because of its presumed narcotic properties, even driving coffee vendors from the precincts of the Great Mosque in Mecca, under the argument that coffee drinking interfered with the services. But in the end, public preference triumphed over religious zeal. The beverage was brought to Europe by the Ottoman Turks, probably during the siege of Vienna. Probably as a result, the heavily sweetened drink taken after dinner as a demitasse is often referred to as "Turkish coffee," although no coffee is grown in Turkey. In the Arab world, coffee is the universal symbol of hospitality, whether in a Bedouin tent, a princely palace, or a modest private residence. It is offered in demitasse cups, thick and strong and usually flavored with cardamom.[14]

Mint tea is also very popular in the Middle East, particularly in Morocco, where it is heavily laced with sugar and drunk from small glasses. The elaborate tea-making ceremony is an important part of a formal meal.

Each Middle Eastern country has its special dishes that serve as symbols of the cultural heritage of its people. In Israel and among Jewish communities elsewhere, for example, the *haroseth* ("clay," in Hebrew) has become an essential component of the Seder, the traditional formal Passover meal. Haroseth, small mashed balls of fruit and nuts in various combinations, are eaten during the Seder to remind Jewish families of the wanderings of their ancestors over the centuries of Jewish dispersion.

In similar fashion, *cous-cous,* a traditional North African dish of semolina wheat with vegetables, spices, and lamb or chicken added in a sort of stew, is usually the centerpiece of the Friday meal in Muslim homes marking the Islamic Sabbath. Although cous-cous has become a feature in restaurants not only in North Africa but throughout the Western world, it is best made and served at home. The cous-cous "ritual" calls for diners to spoon a mound from a platter into a small bowl, adding a ladleful of the hot sauce called *harissa* to blend the ingredients into a delicious mixture of tastes.

Middle Easterners are very conscious of their need to make use of every part of the things they grow. The date palm is a good illustration of this ecologically sound practice. The leaves of the date palm provide rope, baskets, mats and rugs, cleaning pads, and shelter for people and animals. People eat the dates; camels feed on the pits. The trunk of the palm is used for roof beams, rafters, and window frames.

As is true elsewhere in the world, in the Middle East, the traditional distinctive culinary arts and specialties are giving way to a homogenized "international" cuisine, just as shoes and plastic sandals now adorn many Middle Easterners' feet. Labor-saving devices such as microwave ovens and refrigerators simplify the task of meal preparation in Middle Eastern homes, and McDonald's and Kentucky Fried Chicken stores have introduced a fast-food wedge into Middle Eastern life. But a strong undercurrent of traditionalism pervades Islamic society in the region. This undercurrent has been strengthened by the relative success of Khomeini's revolution in Iran and the appeal of this revolution to Muslims as a force independent of both the United States and the former Soviet Union. Traditions die hard anyway; and the more isolated Muslims become—by their own choice—from Western thought, behavior, and practice, the more likely it is that all elements in their social system that reflect preferences and values, including those related to food, will remain appropriate to that system.

CHALLENGES TO THE MUSLIM FAMILY

The Muslim family in the Middle East today is subject to many of the same strains and stresses as those that affect families everywhere, but they have somewhat greater impact on Muslim families because of their suddenness. The Middle East did not have the lengthy period of conditioning and preparation that Europe and the United States had due to the Industrial Revolution. The story is told that, when some Turkish villagers saw their first automobile, early in the 1940s, they could not believe that it ran on its own power. Where is the donkey that will pull it? they wondered. Similarly, King Ibn Saud, a former ruler of Saudi Arabia, was faced with angry opposition by the religious leaders of the kingdom when he wished to install a radio network to link the far-flung cities and towns of his realm. He satisfied the religious leaders by having the Koran read over a radio hookup between Mecca and Riyadh, his capital, pointing out to them that if the machine could carry the Word of God, then God must have approved its use.

One of the challenges to family solidarity in the contemporary Middle East is "Western" secular education, which separates parents from their children who have been educated to acquire university degrees and enter the world of modern technology. Until recently, this education had to be obtained abroad. As a result, a generation of young Muslim men (and, increasingly, women) trained and educated in Western countries have returned to take up leadership positions in their own countries. Particularly in the 1970s and early 1980s, oil-producing Arab countries channeled oil revenues into education, setting up universities, medical centers, and technical

institutes of high quality, staffed initially by expatriates but, in the 1990s, largely by indigenous personnel.

A more difficult challenge to the Muslim family, and to the economy and society in general, has been posed by labor emigration. In the 1970s and early 1980s, several million Turks, Yemenis, Moroccans, Tunisians, Egyptians, and others emigrated either to Europe or to Arab oil-prospecting states on work contracts. Although their work was seldom of a highly skilled nature, the pay differential was enormous. Remittances from expatriate labor were important to the home economies, particularly of oil-less Islamic states. The 1980s recession and drop in world oil prices, followed by the 1991 Gulf War, brought significant efforts by the Gulf states to reduce their dependence on foreign workers. Many of these workers came from poor countries, not only from Pakistan, the Philippines, and other Asian countries but also from neighboring Middle Eastern countries such as Yemen. The resulting expulsion has not only affected the economies of these less fortunate countries but also required some difficult social adjustments, as long-absent fathers known primarily for their remittances are suddenly brought home, unemployed and sometimes penniless.

In terms of the traditional Muslim family, perhaps the thorniest issue today involves the position and rights of women. The Koran would seem to confirm a degree of subservience of women to men (e.g., *Suras II,* 32 and *IV,* 34). But other revelations stipulate only that women dress modestly and conduct themselves decently in public. It should be noted also that Muhammad was an Arab, a member of a tribal society governed by men and emphasizing traditional patriarchal values and beliefs. While Muhammad's message was universal in its intent, in terms of practical implementation, Islam took root in a patriarchal society and has always taken a patriarchal family structure to be the norm.

The emergence of Islamic states committed to nation building has put a new spin on women's rights and obligations in Islamic societies. Secular leaders such as Mustafa Kemal Ataturk in Turkey and Habib Bourguiba in Tunisia recognized early that women could make significant contributions to national development and that they needed to be trained, educated, and emancipated in order to do so. These leaders viewed the patriarchal "dead hand of Islam" as an obstacle to the enhancement of women's rights and status. Under their leadership, laws were passed to provide legal safeguards and rights for women, notably in the areas of voting rights, personal relations, education, and work opportunities. Other Islamic leaders continued the emancipation process. Thus Reza Shah, Iran's new ruler after World War I, literally "tore the veil" from women's faces by outlawing it, in his zeal to modernize his country.

Women's active participation in national life was facilitated by transplanted U.S. educational institutions such as the American University of Beirut, The American University of Cairo, Robert College in Istanbul, and Beirut College for

Women. These institutions not only educated a new generation of national leaders but also helped to relax patriarchal opposition to women's education and male–female student relationships. As a result, women began to enter the labor force as skilled professionals in law, medicine, teaching, the sciences, and the arts.

Unfortunately, the hard-won rights of Muslim women to pursue professional careers and enjoy a degree of equality with men in society have come increasingly under attack in Middle Eastern Islamic countries with the rise of reactionary fundamentalism. The reversal began with the 1979 Iranian Revolution. Iran's new clerical leaders re-imposed strict Islamic dress and behavior codes for both men and women, enforced by "morals squads" who patrolled city streets and neighborhoods, watching for infractions. Similar restrictions have been imposed by the National Islamic Front (NIF), which rules Sudan in tandem with a military regime but which exercises social and moral control over the population. Thus women are not only required to be completely covered in public; they are also prohibited from working outside the home after dark. Algerian women made significant gains in access to education and professional careers, codified in the 1984 Family Law. But the violence that engulfed the country after annulment by military leaders of the 1991 elections has particularly targeted professional journalists, radio and television personalities, and professors, many of whom are women. Some 400 women professionals were murdered in Algeria in 1994–1995 alone.

The most extreme case of fundamentalist control of any Islamic society involves Afghanistan, a fringe country in the Middle East but potentially of concern to its neighbors due to its location and its political instability. The former Soviet Union occupied the country in the 1980s but was unable to crush guerrilla resistance; eventually, it withdrew its troops. The various Afghan tribal and ethnic groups that had united to defeat the Soviet invader then resumed their traditional conflicts. But, in the early 1990s, the Taliban, a movement organized by religious students from Afghan villages, armed and backed by Pakistan, won control of two thirds of the country, including the capital, Kabul. Its stated purpose was to rid Afghanistan of "un-Islamic influences." These "influences," defined by the religious police (officially the Department for Promoting Virtue and Prohibiting Vice), were applied with particular severity to women, they were required to wear all-concealing robes (*burqas*) in public; prohibited from attending school (girls' schools were closed); and directed not to wear cosmetics or white socks, as these would promote "improper thoughts" among men. Most critical from a humanitarian standpoint was an edict barring women and children from nonemergency health care in hospitals and limiting emergency care to a single Kabul hospital—one in which electricity, lab and x-ray facilities, and surgical operat-

ing instruments are almost totally lacking. Other "edicts" of the Department for Promoting Virtue and Prohibiting Vice, which would seem to have no Koranic basis, have banned flying kites, playing cards or soccer, and keeping caged birds. While the Taliban brand of uncompromising Islamic fundamentalism is unlikely to be exported, given Iran's distrust of this Sunni movement and increasing opposition to it within Afghanistan, the "Afghan card" continues to play a major role in the fundamentalist movements elsewhere in the Middle East that have turned to violence in their campaign to overthrow secular regimes. Members of the Palestinian Hamas group, as well as al-Gamaa al-Islamiya in Egypt and the Armed Islamic Group in Algeria, for example, learned their craft as volunteers fighting the Soviet Army in Afghanistan.

NOTES

1. R. Hrair Dekmejian, *Islam in Revolution* (Syracuse, NY: Syracuse University Press, 1985), p. 99.

2. Emmanuel Sivan, *Radical Islam: Medieval Theology and Modern Politics* (New Haven, CT: Yale University Press, 1985). Reports the comment of an imprisoned Brotherhood member that underscores this violence: "These regimes are animated by vicious hatred of Islam; no dialogue with them is possible, for their sole answer is repression" (p. 41). Thomas L. Friedman, in *From Beirut to Jerusalem* (New York: Farrar Straus Giroux, 1989) devotes a chapter to "Hama Rules" to describe the uses of power by secular rulers in Islamic nation-states.

3. Peter Awn, "Faith and Practice," in Marjorie Kelly, ed., *Islam: The Religious and Political Life of a World Community* (New York: Praeger, 1984), p. 26.

4. Tareq Y. Ismael and Jacqueline S. Ismael, *Government and Politics in Islam* (New York: St. Martin's Press, 1985), pp. 64–67.

5. *Time* (August 17, 1987). The Koran, *Sura II,* verse 197, enjoins: "Anyone who undertakes the Pilgrimage should not engage in . . . any immorality or wrangling."

6. *The Los Angeles Times* (July 3, 1997). Muslims follow Jewish dietary laws in regarding pigs as unclean animals, and Muslim scholars called her action "a declaration of war against Islam."

7. V. S. Naipaul, "After the Revolution," *The New Yorker* (May 26, 1997), pp. 46–70. The Basijis were reminded of "the unequal battle of Karbala, where the Prophet's grandson and his followers were massacred by Iraqis—the Shia tragedy and passion, unendingly rehearsed" (p. 68).

8. Stephen King, in *The New York Times* (April 13, 1997).

9. Seyyed Hossein Nasr, "Islam in the West Today, an Overview," in C. K. Pullapilly, ed., *Islam in the Contemporary World* (Notre Dame, IN: Cross Roads Books, 1980), p. 7.

10. Bernard Lewis, "The Roots of Muslim Rage," in *The Atlantic Monthly* (September 1990), p. 60.

11. Eliya Abu Madi, quoted in Michael Asher, *In Search of the Forty Days' Road* (London: Longman, 1984), p. 132.

12. Rebekah Scott, in *The Toledo Blade* (June 8, 1997). American Muslim leader Malcolm X wrote of his Hajj experience in his autobiography: "I lay awake among sleeping Muslim brothers and I learned that pilgrims from every land—snored in the same language" (p. 344).

13. Christine Eickelman, *Women and Community in Oman* (New York: New York University Press, 1984) pp. 80–111.

14. Cardamom, an aromatic spice ground from pods of a tall, palm-like plant, came originally from India. Today, the bulk of the crop is grown at high altitudes in Guatemala and exported to the Arab countries, which do not grow any. See Larry Luxner, "The Cardamom Connection," *Aramco World,* Vol. 48, No. 2 (March–April 1997).

The Middle East: Theater of Conflict

As defined here, the Middle East, a region approximately equal in size to the continental United States and slightly larger in population, extends from the Atlantic coast of Morocco, in North Africa, to the mountains of Afghanistan, where the Indian subcontinent begins. The Middle East is thus intercontinental rather than continental, with the diversity of topography, climate, and physical and social environments characteristic of the two continents, Africa and Asia, that define its territory. Geography and location have dictated a significant role in world affairs for the Middle East throughout recorded history; humankind's earliest cities, governments, organized societies, and state conflicts were probably located there. In the twentieth century, this traditional role has been confirmed by the exploitation of mineral resources vital to the global economy and by the rivalries of nations that regard the Middle East as strategically important to their national interests.

The nations of the contemporary Middle East are very different, however, from their predecessors of 100 or 200 years ago. One important difference is political. When the United States became independent of England, there were three more or less "sovereign" Middle Eastern nation-states and empires: the Sherifian Sultanate of Morocco; the Ottoman Turkish Empire; and Iran, reunited by force under the new Qajar Dynasty, which would remain in power until it was succeeded by the Pahlavi Dynasty in the 1920s. These three states were still in place late in the nineteenth century, but European influence and control over their rulers had effectively robbed them of most of their independence. Since then—a process accelerated since World War II—the Middle Eastern map has been redrawn many times. The result of the redrawing process is the contemporary Middle East, 20 independent states with diverse political systems overlaying a pastiche of ethnic groups, languages, customs, and traditions.

The diversity of these states is compensated for, in part, by the cohesion provided by various unifying factors. One of these factors is geography. The predominance of deserts, with areas suitable for agriculture compressed into small spaces where water was available in dependable flow, produced the *oasis-village* type of social organization and agricultural life. Beyond the oases evolved a second type of social organization suited to desert life, a less settled lifestyle termed *nomadism*. Another type of village settlement evolved in plateau and mountain regions, wherever the topography afforded physical protection for the defense of the community. In Egypt, and to a lesser extent in the Tigris and Euphrates River Valleys, *villages* were established to take advantage of a dependable water supply for crop irrigation. Peoples living in the region mirrored these lifestyles, with the Middle Eastern city developing as an urban refinement of the same traditions.

The broad set of values, traditions, historical experiences, kinship structures, and so on, usually defined as "culture," is a second cohesive factor for the Middle East's peoples. Islam, for example, is either the official state religion or the leading

(UN photo)

Humankind's earliest governments, cities, and organized societies were probably located in what is known today as the Middle East. The ancient Roman town of Timgad, Algeria, pictured above, testifies to people's continued attempts over many centuries to live in the arid expanses of this part of the world.

religion in all but one (Israel) of the states. The Arabic language, due to its identification with Islam, is a bond even for those peoples who use another spoken and/or written language (such as Turkish, Hebrew, or Farsi); and, in any case, the social order of Islam is another unifying force.

A third unifying factor, while it is intangible and difficult to define, is a common historical experience. Without exception, the states of the Middle East are the products of twentieth-century international politics and the conflict of interests of outside powers. Clashing national interests and external involvement in regional affairs have set the tone for the internal and regional conflicts of Middle Eastern states. Thus, the intercommunal violence in modern Lebanon has its roots in foreign (French and British) support for various communal groups in the 1860s, setting the groups against one another under the guise of protecting them from the Ottoman government and its misrule. But Lebanon is only one example of a broad historical process. Throughout Middle Eastern history, invaders and counterinvaders have rolled across the region, advancing, conquering, and being conquered; below the surface of conflict, meanwhile, other peoples have crisscrossed the land in peace, building homes, establishing cities, forming the bedrock of settlement and social development.

THE LAND ISLAND

Until recently, the Middle East was compartmentalized. Its peoples had little awareness of one another and even less of the outside world. Months of arduous travel were needed for a directive from the caliph in Baghdad—the chief personage of the theocratic Islamic state—to reach his viceroy in far-off Morocco. Communications within the region were relatively poor; residents of one village often would know nothing of what was going on in other nearby villages—that is, if they were at peace and not feuding. Travel for caravans between cities was uncertain and often dangerous; the Tuareg of the Western Sahara Desert, a nomadic society, made a good living by charging tolls and providing mounted escorts for merchants crossing the desert.

Consequently, the combination of vast distances, poor communications, and geographical isolation brought about the early development of subregions within the larger Middle East. As early as the tenth century A.D., three such subregions had been defined: North Africa, the Arab lands traditionally known to Europeans as the Near East, and the highland plateaus of Turkey and Iran. In the twentieth century, these three areas were further separated from one another by foreign political control—the French in North Africa, the French and British jointly in the Arab lands, with Turkey and Iran nominally independent but subject to pressures from various outside powers. Alan Taylor's phrase "the Arab balance of power," referring to the "patterns of equilibrium, dislocation and readjustment that unfolded among the Arab states," applies equally well to the interaction of peoples and nations within the subregions.[1]

(UN photo/Kata Bader)

Life in the Sahara Desert is often perceived as nomadic, with the people living in tents and riding camels. To some extent this is still true, but there are many towns that offer a more settled way of life, such as this town in the Algerian Sahara.

Many years ago, naval historian Alfred Thayer Mahan defined the Middle East as a central part of the "land island" or heartland whose possession would enable some powerful nation to dominate the world. Mahan's definition stemmed from his view of naval power as an element in geopolitics; he saw the United States, as a growing naval power, and Russia, expanding across Asia, as the competitors for world domination in the twentieth century.

Mahan was not original in his geopolitical assessment. In the nineteenth century, Britain and Russia, the two superpowers of the period, were engaged in a "Great Game" of imperial expansion in Asia—the British *from* India, and the Russians moving southward from Moscow across the steppes *toward* India.[2] Each power worked assiduously to expand its territory or sphere of interest at the expense of the other. Their perceived national interests were thousands of miles from London and Moscow, in the mountains of Tibet, in the Caucasus, or along the Amu Darya (Oxus) River that separates modern-day Iran from Central Asia.

The Great Game was still being played in different locations, but under similar rules, by the United States and the Soviet Union during the 1980s; the Reagan administration's commitment to a strongly anti-Communist policy revived the Great Game in new locations. Thus U.S. president Ronald Reagan insisted in 1983–1984 that American marines were in Lebanon to defend vital U.S. interests. In 1987, the United States accepted a request from Kuwait to "reflag" Kuwaiti tankers in the Persian Gulf and provide them with naval protection, ostensibly to thwart Iran but also to forestall a Soviet move into the region. Reagan had warned Iran and Iraq earlier that any attempt to close the Strait of Hormuz to oil-tanker traffic would be regarded as a threat to the free world's access to Middle East oil and therefore to American national interests. Before its disintegration in 1991, the Soviet Union from time to time made equally strong pronouncements.[3]

SUBREGIONAL CONFLICTS

The periodic outbreak of local or subregional conflicts characteristic of Middle Eastern societies, which stem from their tribal or ethnic origins, has brought the region to the forefront of world affairs in recent years. Although such conflicts as the Lebanese Civil War, the Iran–Iraq War, the Gulf War, the Arab–Israeli conflict, Palestinian self-rule, and Morocco's absorption of the Western Sahara against the opposition of Saharan nationalists have from time to time drawn in outside powers, they have also developed an internal rhythm that resists negotiated solutions.

Although thus far these Middle Eastern conflicts have been confined to their areas of origin or mediated by outside powers to reduce tension levels, some U.S. policymakers continue to fear that they might spread and involve other nations in a wider war, possibly proving or at least demonstrating the effectiveness of the "domino theory" often invoked as a guide to modern international relations. The domino theory holds that tensions or unresolved disputes between two nations will widen as neighboring nations are drawn inevitably into the dispute, even without taking sides. The uninvolved nations will then become involved, as the particular dispute becomes buried in the rivalries of competing national interests. At some point, a specific incident ignites a general war, as nation after nation falls like a domino into the widening conflict. The classic example of the theory is World War I.

While the applicability of the domino theory to the Middle East has yet to be proven, regional conflict there thus far has not affected long-term global commerce or national survival, and international terrorist acts identified with Middle Eastern governments remain sporadic and uncoordinated. But there are very real limits to involvement or effective management, even by the superpowers. President Reagan recognized these limits implicitly by withdrawing American Marines from Lebanon; and, when Egypt's President Anwar al-Sadat ordered the withdrawal of all Soviet military advisers from his country some years ago, home they went.

A final point about these conflicts is that they are all direct results of European intervention in the Middle East. For much

IRANIANS AND ARABS

Iranians (or Persians) and Arabs are nearly all Muslims. But they have very different ethnic origins, linguistic and geographical backgrounds, and histories.

The Iranians were a loosely organized nomadic people from Central Asia who migrated into the Iranian plateau some 3,000 years ago and became sedentary farmers and herders. Very early, they displayed a talent for political organization and military prowess. Around 600 B.C., an Iranian prince, Cyrus, founded what is usually considered to be the world's first true empire. His successors, the Achaemenian Dynasty, expanded Iranian territory east to the Indus River and westward to the edge of Asia on the Mediterranean Sea. Despite a checkered history since then, Iranians have retained a lofty sense of their contributions to civilization beginning with this period. Except in Iraq and the Persian Gulf states, where there are significant Iranian communities, Iranians have largely remained in their country of origin.

The Arabs, in contrast, have gained their sense of unity and leadership primarily through Islam. The Arabs originated in the Arabian Peninsula and began to migrate to other parts of the Middle East after the rise of Islam. Today, the Arabs form the majority of the population in North Africa, the "Near Eastern" Arab states, and Sudan. They are also an important minority in Iran.

of its history, the Middle East was a region without defined borders, other than the intangible limits fixed for Muslims by their religion. Even the Ottoman Empire, the major power in the region for more than 5 centuries, did not mark off its territories into provinces with precise boundaries until well into the 1800s. But the European powers brought a different set of rules into the area. They laid down fixed borders sanctified by treaties, played ruler against ruler, divided and conquered. It was this European ascendancy, building on old animosities while creating new ones, that laid the groundwork for today's conflicts.

THE IRAN–IRAQ WAR:
BATTLE OF ISLAMIC BROTHERS

The Iran–Iraq War broke out in September 1980, when Iraqi forces invaded Iran and occupied large portions of Khuzestan Province. This measure was in retaliation for Iranian artillery attacks across the border and efforts by Iranian agents to subvert the Iraqi Shia Muslim population, along with propaganda broadcasts urging Iraqis to overthrow the Iraqi regime of Saddam Hussain. But, as is the case with most Middle Eastern conflicts, the causes of the war are complex.

One factor is the ancient animosity between Iranians and Arabs, which dates back to the seventh century A.D., when invading Arab armies overran the once powerful Sassanid Empire of Iran, defeating the Iranian Army at the famous Battle of Qadisiya in 637. The Iranians were converted to

Islam with relative ease, yet they looked down on the Arabs as uncivilized nomads who needed to be taught the arts of government and refined social behavior. The Arabs, in turn, despised the Iranians for what they considered their effeminateness—their love of gardens and flowers, their appreciation of wine and fine banquets. These attitudes have never entirely disappeared.[4] After the 1980 invasion, the controlled Iraqi press praised it as Saddam Hussain's Qadisiya, reminding readers of the earlier Arab success.

Iran and Iraq have been at swords' points over a number of issues in recent years. One is occupation of three small islands at the mouth of the Persian Gulf. The British had included these islands in their protectorate over eastern Arabia and transferred them to the United Arab Emirates after that country became independent. But Shah Mohammed Reza Pahlavi, then the leader of Iran, contested the transfer, on the grounds that historically they had belonged to Iran. In 1971, an Iranian commando force seized the islands. Although the islands had never belonged to Iraq, the Iraqis denounced the occupation as a violation of *Arab* sovereignty and mounted a campaign among the predominantly Arab population of Iran's Khuzestan Province, adjacent to the border, to encourage them to revolt against the central government.

Another issue was the shah's support for Kurdish guerrillas who had been fighting the Iraqi government for years to obtain autonomy for their mountain region. The shah also resented Iraq's grant of asylum to the Ayatollah Khomeini in 1963, because of the religious leader's continued anti-shah activities and propaganda broadcasts into Iran.

These disagreements intensified after the overthrow of the shah in 1979. Iraq accused the Khomeini regime of mistreatment of Khuzestan Arabs and of sending agents to incite its own Shia Muslim population to rebel. Iraqi governments have been dominated by the Sunni Muslim population since independence, although more than half of the population are Shia. The regime of Saddam Hussain, like its predecessors, is paranoid about opposition in general, but about Shia opposition in particular.[5]

The personal hatred between Saddam and Khomeini certainly contributed to the war. The two had been bitter enemies since 1978, when Saddam ordered Khomeini expelled from Iraq and accused him of working with Iraqi Shia Muslim leaders to undermine the regime. But differences in their views on the nature of authority and of social development also set the two leaders in opposition. For Saddam Hussain, the development of Islamic society to the fullest is best achieved by a secular Socialist party (e.g., the Ba'th); Islam is tangential. Khomeini, in the republic that he fashioned for Iran based on his Islamic political philosophy, argued for authority to be vested in religious leaders like himself, since they are qualified by wisdom, moral uprightness, and insight to know what is best for the Islamic community.

One issue often overlooked as a cause of the war is a territorial dispute, dating back many centuries, that has been aggravated by European intervention in the Middle East. The dispute concerns the Shatt al-Arab, the 127-mile waterway from the junction of the Tigris and Euphrates Rivers south to the Persian Gulf. The waterway was a bone of contention between the Ottoman and Iranian Empires for centuries, due to its importance as a trade outlet to the Gulf. It came entirely under Ottoman control in the nineteenth century. But, with the collapse of the Ottoman Empire in World War I, the new kingdom of Iraq, set up by Britain, came in conflict with a revitalized Iran over navigation and ownership rights. Iran demanded ownership of half the Shatt al-Arab under international law, which would mean to mid-channel at the deepest point. Iraq claimed the entire waterway across to the Iranian side. Conflict intensified as both countries built up their oil exports in the 1960s and 1970s. In 1969, the shah of Iran threatened to occupy Iran's side of the waterway with gunboats, and he began a program of military support to Kurdish (Sunni Muslim) rebels fighting the Iraqi government.

Iran was much wealthier and militarily stronger than Iraq at that time, and Iraq could do little about Iranian support for the Kurds. But the Iraqis did have the Shatt al-Arab as a bargaining chip, in that their rights were embodied in several treaties. In 1975, after lengthy negotiations, Houari Boumedienne, then the president of Algeria, interrupted an oil ministers' conference in Algiers to announce that "our fraternal countries Iran and Iraq have reached agreement on their differences."[6] Iraq agreed to recognize Iranian ownership of the Shatt from bank to mid-channel, and Iran agreed to stop supporting Kurdish rebels in Iraq.

The advantage to Iraq of bringing an end to the Kurdish rebellion was offset by the humiliation felt by Iraqi leaders because they had bartered away a part of the sacred Arab territory. Hussain considered the agreement a personal humiliation because he had been the chief negotiator. When he became president, he said that he had negotiated it under duress and that Iraq would one day be strong enough to revoke it.[7]

The fall of Shah Reza Pahlavi, followed by the internal upheaval in Iran let loose by the 1979 Revolution, seemed to Saddam Hussain to be an excellent opportunity to reverse Iraq's humiliation. In September 1980, he announced that the 1975 treaty was null and void, and he demanded Iran's recognition of Iraqi sovereignty over the entire Shatt al-Arab. He also called for the return of the three islands seized by the shah's forces in 1971 and the transfer of predominantly Arab areas of Khuzestan to Iraqi control. Although the two countries were roughly equal in military strength at the time, purges in Iranian Army leadership, low morale, and lack of spare parts for weapons due to the U.S. economic boycott convinced Saddam that a limited attack on Iran would almost certainly succeed.[8]

However, the quick and easy victory anticipated by the Iraqis did not materialize. Political expectations proved equally erroneous. Iraq had expected the Arabs of Khuzestan

(Gamma-Liaison/François Lochon)

These young Iranians, taken prisoner by Iraq, were typical of those fighting in the Iran–Iraq War. The Iranians' patriotic fervor produced thousands of volunteers, some barely in their teens.

to support the invasion, but they remained loyal to Iran's Khomeini regime. The Iraqi forces failed to capitalize on their early successes and were stopped by determined Iranian resistance. The war quickly turned into a stalemate.

In 1981–1982, the momentum shifted strongly in Iran's favor. The war became a patriotic undertaking as thousands of volunteers, some barely teenagers, headed for the front. An Iranian operation, appropriately code-named Undeniable Victory, routed three Iraqi divisions. Iran's blockade of Iraqi oil exports put a severe strain on the Iraqi economy. After the defeat, Saddam withdrew all Iraqi forces from Iranian territory and asked for a cease-fire. But Iran refused; Khomeini set the ouster of "the traitor Saddam" as a precondition for peace.

Iraqi forces fared better on their own soil and threw back a number of large-scale Iranian assaults, with huge casualties. Subsequent Soviet deliveries of missiles and new aircraft gave Iraq total air superiority. In early 1985, the Iraqis launched a campaign of "total war, total peace," combining air raids on Iranian ports and cities with an all-out effort to bring international pressure on Iran to reach a settlement.

In March 1985, Iranian forces launched another major offensive toward Basra from their forward bases in the Majnoon Islands, deep in the marshes, which they had captured by surprise in 1984. Although they were driven back with heavy losses, a year later, the Iranian forces captured the Fao (Faw) Peninsula southeast of Basra in another surprise attack and moved to within artillery range of Iraq's second city.

With the ground war stalemated, conflict shifted in 1986 and 1987 to the sky and sea lanes. Iraq's vast air superiority enabled the country to carry the war deep into Iranian terri-tory, with almost daily bombing raids on Iranian cities, industrial plants, and oil installations.

But the most dangerous aspect of the conflict stemmed from Iraqi efforts to interdict Iranian oil supplies in order to throttle its enemy's economy. The war had had a high-risk potential for broader regional conflict from the start, and in 1984, Iraqi missile attacks on tanker traffic in the Persian Gulf came close to involving other states in the region in active participation.

The internationalization of the war, which had been predicted by many analysts, became a reality in its seventh year, like a plague of locusts. The secret dealings with the United States (revealed in the 1987 Iran–Contra hearings) had immeasurably strengthened Iran's air power and defenses; Iraq lost one fifth of its aircraft in a series of battles in the marshes. Iranian arms dealers were successful in purchasing weaponry from many sources. One of their major suppliers was China, from which they purchased a number of Silkworm missiles, which were installed at secret launching sites along the coast facing the Strait of Hormuz and the Fao Peninsula. At the same time, Iranian Revolutionary Guards established bases in various small harbors from whence they could mount missile and grenade attacks in fast patrol boats against ships passing in the Gulf. The government warned that tankers bound for Kuwait and other Gulf ports would be attacked if Iraq continued its air raids.

The direct cause of the internationalization of the war, however, was an Iraqi air raid on the U.S. naval frigate *Stark* on May 17, 1987. Thirty-seven American sailors were killed in the raid. (Although more than 200 ships had been attacked by Iraq or Iran since 1984, the *Stark* was the first warship attacked, and it suffered the heaviest casualties.) Saddam apologized, calling the attack a "tragic mistake." The United States drastically increased its naval forces in the Gulf and, in the following month, accepted a request from Kuwait for tanker protection under the American flag, along with naval escorts. In June 1987, the first convoy of "reflagged" Kuwaiti tankers traversed the Gulf without incident, escorted by U.S. warships and overflying jets from the aircraft carrier *Constellation*.

Predictably, Iran's threat to make the Gulf "safe for every one or no one," following the U.S. buildup in the region, affected nearby countries as well as international shipping. Saboteurs blew up oil installations and factories in the United Arab Emirates, Bahrain, and Saudi Arabia. Revolutionary Guardsmen carried out their earlier threats with hit-and-run strafing and grenade attacks on passing tankers. But the most serious danger came from floating mines strewn at random in shipping lanes. After a number of tankers had been damaged, the United States and several European countries previously uninvolved in the conflict, notably Italy, began sending minesweepers to the area.

With the Gulf in a state of high tension, the United Nations (UN) Security Council mounted a major effort to end the war.

In July 1987, the Security Council unanimously approved *Resolution 598.* It called for an immediate cease-fire, the withdrawal of all forces to within recognized international boundaries, repatriation of all prisoners, and negotiations under UN auspices for a permanent peace settlement. Iraq accepted the resolution, but Iran temporized. Its then-president, Ali Khamenei, told the UN General Assembly: "The Security Council's stance in relation to the war imposed on us has not changed up to this moment."[9]

A year later, though, Iran accepted *Resolution 598,* in an abrupt about-face. A number of factors combined to bring about this change, but the principal one was probably Iraqi success on the battlefield. Iraqi forces recaptured the Fao Peninsula in early 1988; this success was followed by several other offensives that recovered all the territory in Iraq taken by Iranian forces. Iranian morale sagged after a series of unexpected Iraqi missile attacks on both military and civilian targets deep inside Iran. And the Iranian economy continued to weaken as the destruction of oil installations and factories by Iraqi aircraft took its toll.

Khomeini's death in June 1989 removed a major obstacle to peace negotiations. The Ayatollah had been persuaded with great difficulty to approve the cease-fire, and his uncompromising hatred of Saddam Hussain was not shared by many associates.

A real peace settlement would enable both regimes to turn their full attention to the enormous problems of reconstruction. Unfortunately, their diametrically opposed positions on war gains worked against dialogue. Iran insisted on the withdrawal of Iraqi troops from its territory as a first step, while Iraq demanded that prisoner exchanges and clearing of the Shatt al-Arab should precede withdrawal.

For the next 2 years, UN mediators shuttled between Baghdad and Teheran without effect. But Iraq's invasion of Kuwait in August 1990 brought about a drastic change in the relationship. Saddam, desperately searching for allies, abruptly agreed to the peace terms set by the UN and accepted by Iran in March. The terms specified a withdrawal of Iraqi troops from 1,560 square miles of occupied Iranian territory, prisoner exchanges, freedom of navigation in the Strait of Hormuz and the Gulf, and clearance of the Shatt al-Arab.

Iran stayed neutral during the Gulf War and even gave sanctuary to Iraqi pilots who flew their planes there to escape U.S./UN air attacks. But the agreed-upon prisoner exchange of some 30,000 Iraqis in Iran for 5,000 Iranians held in Iraq has yet to be completed. Iran unilaterally released 200 Iraqi POWs in October 1992, as a goodwill gesture.

THE GULF WAR AND ITS AFTERMATH

On August 2, 1990, the Iraqi Army, which had been mobilized along the border, invaded and occupied Kuwait, quickly overcoming light resistance as the ruling Kuwaiti emir and his family escaped into exile. The invasion climaxed a long dispute between the two Arab neighbors over oil-production

(AP Wide World Photos)

During Operation Desert Storm, the U.S./UN–led coalition mobilized a large number of air strikes that routed Iraqi forces. These F/A-18 fighters met with little resistance as they flew sorties over Iraqi defensive positions.

quotas, division of output from the oil fields of the jointly controlled Neutral Zone along the border, and repayment of Iraqi debts to Kuwait from the war with Iran. Saddam Hussain had criticized Kuwait for producing more than its quota as allotted by the Organization of Petroleum Exporting Countries (OPEC), thus driving down the price per barrel and costing Iraq $7 billion to $8 billion in lost revenues. The Iraqi leader also charged Kuwait with taking more than its share of the output of the Neutral Zone. The Iraqi charges found considerable support from other Arab states, most of which consider the Kuwaitis to be stingy and arrogant. However, an Arab League summit meeting of oil ministers failed to resolve the dispute. Kuwait agreed only to a month-long adherence to its OPEC quota and continued to press for repayment of Iraqi war debts.

What had been initially an inter-Arab conflict was globalized by the invasion. Although Iraq called its occupation a recovery of part of the Arab homeland, which had been "stolen" from the Arabs by the British and given its independence under false premises, the action was viewed as aggression by nearly all the countries in the world. The UN Security Council on August 6 approved *Resolution 660,* calling for an immediate withdrawal of Iraqi forces from Kuwait and restoration of the country's legitimate government. Pending withdrawal, a worldwide embargo would be imposed on Iraq, covering exports as well as imports and including medical and food supplies as well as military equipment. A similar resolution approved by the League of Arab States denounced Iraq's aggression against the "brotherly Arab state of Kuwait" and demanded immediate Iraqi withdrawal and restoration of Kuwaiti independence.

The invasion divided the Arab states, as several, notably Yemen and Sudan, agreed with Iraq's contention that Kuwait was historically part of Iraq and that Kuwaiti arrogance was partly responsible for the conflict. Others took the opposite view. Egyptian president Hosni Mubarak accused Saddam Hussain of breaking a solemn pledge not to invade Kuwait. Saudi Arabia, fearing that it might be Iraq's next victim, requested U.S. help under the bilateral defense treaty to protect its territory. Then–U.S. president George Bush and then–Soviet president Mikhail Gorbachev issued a joint pledge for action to expel Iraqi forces from Kuwait. A massive military buildup followed, largely made up of U.S. forces, but with contingents from a number of other countries, including several Arab states. Although led by U.S. military commanders, the collective force operated under the terms of UN *Resolution 660* and was responsible ultimately to the Security Council as a military coalition.

The UN embargo continued in effect for 6 months but failed to generate an Iraqi withdrawal from Kuwait, despite its severe impact on the civilian population. (The only concession made by Saddam Hussain during that period was the release of foreign technicians who had been working in Kuwait at the time of the invasion). As a result, the coalition forces launched the so-called Operation Desert Storm on January 16, 1991. With their total air superiority and superior military technology, they made short work of Iraq's army, as thousands of Iraqi soldiers fled or surrendered. On the express orders of George Bush, the campaign was halted on February 7, after Iraqi forces had been expelled from Kuwait. Yet Saddam remained in power, and uprisings of the Kurdish and Shia populations in Iraq were ruthlessly crushed by the reorganized Iraqi Army, which remained loyal to its leader. Although many felt that Saddam should be punished as well as driven from power, it was the consensus of U.S. policymakers that no alternative to the Iraqi leader existed and that a breakup of Iraq into competing factions would enable Iran to dominate the region and, perhaps, resume its anti-Western destabilizing activities.

Saddam Hussain's running battle with the United Nations kept world attention focused on Iraq in 1992–1993. Despite his country's sound defeat in the Gulf War, the Iraqi dictator had gained the support not only of some other Arab states but also of many developing-world leaders, for what appeared to them to have been an infringement on Iraq's sovereignty by the UN in its zeal to destroy Iraq's weapons of mass destruction. But for the UN and the United States, the main issue involved Iraq's noncompliance with UN resolutions. Thus *Resolution 687* directed the country to destroy all its long-range ballistic missiles and dismantle its chemical- and nuclear-weapons facilities, while *Resolution 715* would es-

tablish a permanent UN monitoring system, with surveillance cameras, for all missile test sites and installations as well as nuclear facilities. Iraq's compliance with these resolutions would end the embargo imposed after the invasion of Kuwait and would enable Iraq to sell $1.6 billion in oil to finance imports of badly needed medicines, medical supplies, and foodstuffs. Iraqi representatives argued that their country had complied with *Resolution 687* by demolishing under international supervision the al-Atheer nuclear complex outside Baghdad and by opening all missile sites to UN inspectors. But they said that *Resolution 715* was illegal under international law, since it infringed on national sovereignty.

Since then, Iraq and the United Nations (along with the United States) have been deadlocked over the issue of inspections in a potentially deadly cat-and-mouse game played with consummate skill by Saddam Hussain. In 1996, the Iraqi government accepted UN terms to allow it to sell $2 billion in oil every 6 months, in return for opening all missile-testing sites and biological- and chemical-weapons facilities to inspectors. The oil revenues would be used for purchases of critically needed food, medicines, and children's supplies. However, the UN Security Council was divided, with the United States insisting on Iraq's adherence to all its obligations specified in *Resolution 715,* while other Council members argued that the embargo was hurting the most vulnerable groups in the population without affecting the leadership.

The standoff hardened in late 1997, when Saddam Hussain ordered the American members of the inspection team to leave his country, saying that they were spies. The Clinton administration threatened to use force to compel their return and beefed up U.S. military strength in the Persian Gulf. However, mediation by Russia brought a compromise: Iraq agreed to "calm the waters" by accepting the return of the American inspectors.

A continued bone of contention was Iraq's refusal to open Saddam Hussain's numerous palaces and other nonmilitary buildings to UN arms inspection. The defection in 1995 of Saddam's son-in-law and chief of his bioweapons program had exposed some aspects of the program, which included production of anthrax and botulism spores at the Al-Hakam complex near Baghdad, and subsequently the complex was razed. But without full UN access to all sites of potential production and the ease with which biological and chemical weapons can be concealed, it remained almost impossible to assess the extent of Iraqi weaponry.

THE ARAB–ISRAELI CONFLICT

Until very recently, the Arab–Israeli conflict involved two peoples: those grouped into the modern Arab states, for the most part products of European colonialism, and the modern State of Israel. However, by the 1990s, this state-to-state conflict had been largely resolved. Israel's continued military superiority and the preoccupation of its Arab neighbors with internal problems has created a *modus vivendi* between these

ZIONISM

Zionism may be defined as the collective expression of the will of a dispersed people, the Jews, to recover their ancestral homeland. This idealized longing was given concrete form by European Jews in the nineteenth century. In 1882, a Jewish law student, Leon Pinsker, published *Auto-Emancipation,* a book that called on Jews, who were being pressed at the time between the twin dangers of anti-Semitism and assimilation into European society, to resist by establishing a Jewish homeland *somewhere.* Subsequently, a Viennese journalist, Theodor Herzl, published *Der Judenstaat (The Jewish State)* in 1896. Herzl argued that Jews could never hope to be fully accepted into the societies of nations where they lived; anti-Semitism was too deeply rooted. The only solution would be a homeland for immigrant Jews as a secular commonwealth of farmers, artisans, traders, and shopkeepers. In time, he said, it would become a model for all nations through its restoration of the ancient Jewish nation formed under a covenant with God.

Herzl's Zionist state would give equal rights and protection to people of other nationalities who came there. This secular view generated conflict with Orthodox Jews, who felt that only God could ordain a Jewish state and that, therefore, Zionism would have to observe the rules and practices of Judaism in establishing such a state.

long-term rivals. However, the core of the conflict, involving Palestinians and Israelis, continues to defy solution.

In essence, this conflict rests on ownership of land. The land in question is Palestine, ancient Judea and Samaria for Jews, claimed by modern Israel on historical, emotional, and symbolic grounds. The Jewish claim to possession is to fulfill God's original covenant with Abraham, patriarch of the ancient Jewish tribes. The modern Israelis are the returned Jews, immigrants from many lands, plus the small Jewish community that remained there during the centuries of dispersion. The modern Palestinians are the descendants of settlers who gravitated there under the occupation of Palestine by Roman, Byzantine, Crusader, and Ottoman Turkish rulers. Their attachment to the land has not had until very recently the sense of a sacred homeland, which it is for Jews.

In the twentieth century, the question of a Palestine homeland was given form and impetus by two national movements: Zionism and Arab nationalism. *Zionism,* the first to develop political activism in implementation of a national ideal, organized large-scale immigration of Jews into Palestine. These immigrants, few of them skilled in agriculture or the vocations needed to build a new nation in a strange land, nevertheless succeeded in changing the face of Palestine. In a relatively short time, a region of undeveloped sand dunes near the coast evolved into the bustling city of Tel Aviv, and previously unproductive marshland was transformed into profitable farms and kibbutz settlements.

Arab nationalism, slower to develop, grew out of the contacts of Arab subject peoples in the Ottoman Empire with Europeans, particularly missionary-educators sent by their various churches to work with the Christian Arab communities. It developed political overtones during World War I, when British agents such as T. E. Lawrence encouraged the Arabs to revolt against the Turks, their "Islamic brothers." In return, the Arabs were given to understand that Britain would support the establishment of an independent Arab state in the Arab lands of the empire. An Anglo–Arab army entered Jerusalem in triumph in 1917 and Damascus in 1918, where an independent Arab kingdom was proclaimed, headed by the Emir Faisal, the leader of the revolt.

The Arab population of Palestine took relatively little part in these events. But European rivalries and conflicting commitments for disposition of the provinces of the defeated Ottoman Empire soon involved them directly in conflict over Palestine. The most important document affecting the conflict was the Balfour Declaration, a statement of British support for a Jewish homeland in Palestine in the form of a letter from Foreign Secretary Arthur Balfour to Lord Rothschild, a prominent Jewish banker and leader of the Zionist Organization.

Although the Zionists interpreted the statement as permission to proceed with their plans for a Jewish National Home in Palestine, neither they nor the Arabs were fully satisfied with the World War I peace settlement, in terms of the disposition of territories. The results soon justified their pessimism. The Arab kingdom of Syria was dismantled by the French, who then established a mandate over Syria under the League of Nations. The British set up a mandate over Palestine, attempting to balance support for Jewish aspirations with a commitment to develop self-government for the Arab population, in accordance with the terms of the mandate as approved by the League of Nations. It seemed an impossible task; and, in 1948, the British gave up, handing the "Palestine problem" back to the United Nations, as the successor to the League of Nations. The UN had approved a partition plan for Palestine in November 1947; and, after the termination of the mandate, the Zionists proclaimed the establishment of the State of Israel.

Israel was established against the formal opposition of the neighboring Arab states. Since 1948, Israeli resolve has been tested with them in five wars. None of these wars led directly to a peace settlement, and with the exception of Egypt, Israel remains in a state of armistice and nonrecognition with these states.

Most state-to-state disputes are susceptible to arbitration and often outside mediation, particularly when they involve borders or territory. But Palestine is a special case. Its location astride communication links between the eastern and western sections of the Arab world made it essential to the building of a unified Arab nation, the goal of Arab leaders since World War I. Its importance to Muslims as the site of one of their

(Israeli Government Tourism Administration)

The Dome of the Rock in Jerusalem is the site of one of the holiest Muslim shrines. The Israeli control of Jerusalem is one of the reasons why the Palestinian Muslims turn to the Arab states for assistance in regaining control of the area.

holiest shrines, the Dome of the Rock in Jerusalem, is underscored by Jewish control—a control made possible by the "imperialist enemies of Islam," in the Arab Muslim view, and reinforced by the relatively lenient treatment given by an Israeli court to Jewish terrorists arrested for trying to blow up the shrines on the Dome and build a new temple on the site. Also, since they lack an outside patron, both the dispersed Palestinians and those remaining in Israel look to the Arab states as the natural champions of their cause.

Yet the Arab states have never been able to develop a coherent, unified policy toward Israel in support of the Palestinian cause. There are several reasons for this failure. One is the natural rivalry of Arab leaders—a competitiveness that has evolved from ancient origins, strong individualism, and family pride. Other reasons include the overall immaturity of the modern Arab political system and the difficulty of distinguishing between rhetoric and fact. The majority of Arab states today are still struggling to develop separate, viable political systems and to create legitimacy for their governments. But, because rhetoric urges them to subscribe to the ideal of a single Arab nation, they are torn between the ideal of this nation and the reality of separate nations. With the exception of Egypt, they lack the collective maturity that would enable them to negotiate on a firm basis with Israel. This lack of maturity has been amply demonstrated in the

past, as opportunities to make some sort of durable peace, even on somewhat unfavorable terms, were squandered regularly. The Arab states are thus probably more of a liability than an asset to the Palestinian cause.

Another reason for Arab disunity stems from the relationship of the Arab states with the Palestinians. During the British mandate, the Arab Higher Committee—the nexus of what became the Palestine national movement—aroused the anger of Arab leaders in neighboring countries by refusing to accept their authority over the committee's policies in return for financial support. After the 1948 Arab–Israeli War, the dispersal of Palestinians into Arab lands caused further friction; the Palestinians, often better educated than their reluctant hosts and possessed of greater political skills, seemed to threaten the authority of some Arab leaders and to dominate some Arab economies. Finally, the performance of the Arab states in the wars with Israel was a bitter disillusionment to the Palestinians. Constantine Zurayk of the American University of Beirut expressed their shame in his book *The Meaning of Disaster:*

> Seven Arab states declare war on Zionism, stop impotent before it and turn on their heels. . . . Declarations fall like bombs from the mouths of officials at meetings of the Arab League, but when action becomes necessary, the fire is still and quiet.[10]

Without the interference of Arab state rhetoric and instances of inept Arab military intervention, it is possible that the Palestinians might have come to terms with their Jewish neighbors long ago. As early as the 1930s, some Jews sought accommodation with Palestinian leaders. Chaim Weizmann, later the first president of Israel, wrote to an American friend: "Palestine is to be shared by two nations. . . . Palestine must be built without violating [by] one iota the legitimate rights of the Arabs."[11] Martin Buber, a distinguished Jewish philosopher and theologian, argued tirelessly for Jewish–Arab harmony. In 1947, on the eve of the UN partition resolution, he warned: "What is really needed by each of the two peoples . . . in Palestine is self-determination, autonomy . . . but this most certainly does not mean that each is in need of a state in which it will be the sovereign."[12]

More recently, Uri Avnery, a prominent Zionist and Knesset member, writing in the afterglow of Israel's triumph over the Arab states in the Six-Day War, said, "The government [should] offer the Palestine Arabs assistance in setting up a national republic of their own . . . [which] will become the natural bridge between Israel and the Arab world."[13]

The effort to distinguish between a rightful Jewish "homeland" and the occupied territories gained momentum in 1977 with the formation of Peace Now, a movement initiated by army officers who felt that the government of Menachem Begin should not miss the opportunity to negotiate peace with Egypt. Peace Now gradually became the engine of the Israeli peace movement, leading public opposition to invasion of Lebanon and establishment of Jewish settlements in the occupied territories. (With Labor's return to power in Israel in the 1992 election, Peace Now's policy of "exchanging land for peace and the ethical rights of Palestinians to national self-expression" became official government policy.)[14]

Continued Jewish settlement of the West Bank and East Bank remains a major obstacle to implementation of the

THE BALFOUR DECLARATION

The text of the Balfour Declaration is as follows: "I have much pleasure in conveying to you on behalf of His Majesty's Government the following declaration of sympathy with Jewish Zionist aspirations which has been submitted to and approved by the Cabinet:

"His Majesty's Government view with favor the establishment in Palestine of a National Home for the Jewish people and will use their best endeavors to facilitate the achievement of this project, it being clearly understood that nothing shall be done which may prejudice the civil and religious rights of existing non-Jewish communities in Palestine or the rights and political status enjoyed by Jews in any other country."

Palestinian–Israeli peace agreements. During its years in power, the Labor government kept settlement expansion at a moderate level, but the process was accelerated after Menachem Begin's Likud bloc took over the government in 1977. By 1985, Israel had acquired 51.6 percent of the West Bank through various methods, notably condemnation "for security needs." Numerous Jewish families, many of them new American migrants, established a defended ghetto in the midst of heavily populated Arab towns and villages.

The Rabin government continued this policy, although halting it briefly after the Bush administration warned that $2 billion in loan guarantees for new housing for Russian immigrants would be withheld if settlement expansion continued. But, by 1994, the settler population had increased nearly 10 percent.

The reluctance of U.S. policymakers to pressure Israel into compliance with international agreements governing occupied territories in general, or to observe Palestinian land rights, has increased the difficulty of finding an equitable resolution of the conflict. Since the establishment of Israel, nine U.S. presidents have struggled with the issue during their terms in office. Only two have had any substantial success— Eisenhower, by forcing Israel to withdraw from the Sinai Peninsula in 1956; and Jimmy Carter, by achieving peace with Egypt in 1977. The closest any American president has come in reconciling Israeli and Palestinian claims to the same homeland was Carter's 1977 statement defining a "Palestinian National Home" as precise as that defined for a "Jewish National Home" by the Balfour Declaration.

Domestic political pressures, the broad sympathy of Americans for Israel, and pragmatic support for the country as a dependable key ally in the volatile Middle East have been passed along from one U.S. administration to another, with little change. This innate preference has not been helped by the position taken on the issue by the Palestine Liberation Organization (PLO), the international exponent organization of the Palestinian cause. The PLO, at its founding in 1964, issued a charter calling for the destruction of Israel and the establishment of a sovereign Palestinian Arab state. The PLO until recently was also ambivalent about its acceptance of UN *Resolutions 242* and *338,* which call for Israeli withdrawal from the occupied West Bank and Gaza Strip as a prelude to peace negotiations.

During the 20-year Israeli occupation of the territories, the Palestinians there undertook few initiatives on their own to challenge the occupation. An entire generation grew up under Israeli control, living in squalid refugee camps or towns little changed since Ottoman times and deprived of even the elemental human rights supposedly guaranteed to an occupied population under international law. In December 1987, a series of minor clashes between Palestinian youths and Israeli security forces escalated into a full-scale revolt against the occupying power. This single event, called (in Arabic) the *intifada* (literally, "resurgence"), has changed the context of the Israeli–Palestinian conflict more decisively than any other in recent history.

The intifada caught not only the Israelis but also the PLO by surprise. Having lost their Beirut base due to the Israeli invasion of 1982, PLO leaders found themselves in an unusual situation, identified internationally with a conflict from which they were physically separated and could not control directly or even influence to any great degree. As more and more Palestinians in the territories were caught up in the rhythm of struggle, the routine of stone-throwings, waving of forbidden Palestinian flags, demonstrations, and cat-and-mouse games with Israeli troops, the PLO seemed increasingly irrelevant to the Palestinian cause.

Yet this organization, particularly its leader Yassir Arafat, had a talent for theater, for dramatic moves that not only kept the cause in the international spotlight but also provided hope for several million Palestinians that an apparently unwinnable conflict might someday be won. This talent was amply demonstrated in December 1988, the first anniversary of the intifada. Arafat concluded a meeting of the PLO National Council, the organization's executive body, in Tunis, Tunisia, with the historic statement that, in addition to formal acceptance of *Resolutions 242* and *338* as the basis for peace negotiations, the PLO would recognize Israel's right to exist. Arafat amplified the statement at a special UN General Assembly session in Geneva, Switzerland, formally accepting Israeli sovereignty over its own territory and renouncing the use of terrorism by the PLO.

The evidence of five wars and innumerable smaller conflicts suggests that the Arab–Israeli conflict will remain localized. Israel's invasion of Lebanon, like its predecessors, remained localized once the United States had intervened, and it proved only a temporary setback for the PLO, a displacement. The Arab states continue to be haunted by the Palestinians, an exiled, dispersed people who refuse to be assimilated into other populations or to give up their hard-won identity. Mohammed Shadid observes that "Palestine is the conscience of the Arab world and a pulsating vein of the Islamic world . . . perhaps the only issue where Arab nationalism and Islamic revivalism are joined."[15] In 1995, Libya's leader, Muammar al-Qadhafi, the Arab world's most fervent advocate of Arab unity since Gamal Abdel Nasser of Egypt, abruptly expelled 1,500 Palestinian workers long resident in his country. He did so, he said, to protest the Palestinian–Israeli peace agreements, which he called a sellout of Arab interests.

The Palestinians are equally present on the Israeli conscience. Israeli general Ariel Sharon's Lebanon War, ironically code-named "Operation Peace in Galilee," was intended to solve the Palestine problem by rough surgery—decapitation of the PLO head (that is, the leadership) on the assumption that the trunk and arms (that is, the West Bank Palestinians) would have no further reason for resisting incorporation into the Israeli state. The Lebanon War caused the

downfall of one Israeli government and the eclipse of Sharon himself, proving for the fifth time in Arab–Israeli history that military solutions do not work for essentially political problems. Sharon served as minister of housing in the last Likud government in 1990–1991. In that capacity, he oversaw the continued expropriation of Arab lands for new Jewish settlements in the West Bank. But, after the Rabin government took power, Sharon was largely discredited and left as a critic of government policy, writing letters to the editor of the *Jerusalem Post*.

The Arab states that surround Israel, although politically new, are heirs to a proud and ancient tradition, reaching back to the period when Islamic–Arab civilization was far superior to that of the Western world. This tradition and the self-proclaimed commitment to Arab brotherhood, however, have yet to bring them together in a united front toward Israel. A major obstacle to Arab unity is the variety of political systems that exist in the individual Arab states. These range from patriarchal absolute rule in Saudi Arabia by a ruling family to the multiparty system of Lebanon. Other Arab states reflect a variety of political systems—constitutional and patriarchal monarchies, authoritarian single-party governments, and regimes dependent on a single individual, to name a few examples. The only unification of Arab states that has stood the test of time is the merger of the Marxist People's Democratic Republic of Yemen (South Yemen) and the Yemen Arab Republic (North Yemen), and even this unification nearly collapsed due to civil war in 1994.

Aside from the immediate success of the Gulf War in its limited objectives, the one accomplishment of the Bush administration vis-à-vis the Middle East political situation was the launching of direct peace talks among Arab, Israeli, and Palestinian representatives to establish a "total Middle East peace." These talks, begun in Madrid, Spain, in 1991, were continued at various locations for nearly a dozen rounds, but without much progress toward a solution.

A major breakthrough, however, took place in September 1993, as negotiations conducted in secret by Palestinian and Israeli negotiators in Norway, a neutral country, resulted in a historic agreement. The agreement, although it fell far short of Palestinian objectives of an independent state, provided for Israeli recognition of Palestinian territorial rights and acceptance of a Palestinian "mini-state" in the Gaza Strip and an area around the West Bank city of Jericho, which would be its capital. It would be governed by an elected Council and would have limited self-rule for a 5-year transitional period, after which discussions would begin on its permanent status.

Somewhat unexpectedly—after many false starts, hopes raised and then blasted by extremist violence, delays on Israel's part to meet pact-imposed deadlines, and other difficulties—the two sides reached agreement in September 1995 on the next phase of Palestinian self-rule, confirmed with a handshake on the White House lawn. The new agreement would enlarge the area of Palestinian self-rule to include six towns. Israel began withdrawing its troops in stages over a 7-week period. As they withdrew, 12,000 Palestinian police gradually assumed the responsibility for internal security.

Israel also freed 1,200 Palestinian prisoners, to bring the total number released under the 1993 peace agreement to 7,000. Release of the remaining 2,800 would be determined during final talks on Palestinian autonomy.

Effective internalization of the long conflict enabled Israel to normalize its relations with several Arab states. A peace treaty was signed with Jordan in 1994; it provided for open borders, ambassadorial exchanges, water sharing, and the return to Jordan of territory seized in 1967. Morocco and Tunisia opened liaison offices in Tel Aviv also in 1994.

Unfortunately, the peace process began to unravel swiftly, after a series of suicide bombings and killings of Israelis by Hamas (the militant Islamic fundamentalist organization based in Gaza that opposes the Oslo agreement). Israel angrily sought retribution and demanded Palestinian cooperation in finding the perpetrators. The Israelis also re-imposed the border closures and other restrictions characteristic of their 30-year occupation of the West Bank, and they declared in 1997 that they would no longer be bound by the peace agreements.

WATER: A REGIONAL PROBLEM

Overshadowing territorial, ethnic, and religious conflicts and disputes over land ownership in the Middle East and North Africa is the issue of water sharing and control of water resources in this essentially arid part of the world. A 1996 World Bank report noted that in no other global region is water as important in development. With 5 percent of the world's population (280 million, but expected to double in 30 years at current birth rates), the Middle East has less than 1 percent of global annual renewable fresh water. Already by 1994, an earlier World Bank study had observed, "population and development have overwhelmed traditional water management practices, and problems of scarcity and pollution are as severe as anywhere in the world."

Water sharing and use have become politicized. For example, Turkey's construction of huge dams on the upper reaches of the Euphrates River—dams that are essential to the development of its Kurdish-populated, poverty-stricken southeastern region and would presumably solve the problem of Kurdish irredentism—has affected water-sharing downstream in Syria and Iraq. Both have rights as riparian states, but Turkish dam construction has at times sharply reduced their water supply.

A similar water-supply situation affects Jordan and Israel. The 1994 Israeli–Jordanian peace treaty guarantees Jordan 7.59 billion cubic feet annually from the Jordan and Yarmuk Rivers. But, to date, Jordan has received less than half this amount, adversely affecting its water supply. Israel also has been overdrawing its share of water from the coastal aquifer near Gaza by 10 percent annually, resulting in a high nitrate content in Gaza groundwater as well as saline intrusion and high chlorine levels in Lake Tiberias, the main Israeli water reservoir.

A similar disparity between allocation and actual use is involved in the Israeli relationship with the self-governing areas of the nascent Palestinian state. Israel draws 17.65 billion cubic feet of water from the West Bank aquifer for the Jewish settlers there. In contrast, the million Palestinians living in the West Bank are limited to 4,591 million cubic feet annually. The issue of equitable water distribution is one of the many unresolved issues in negotiations for a future Palestinian state that is often overlooked.

Aside from these political differences, it should be noted that, by 1997 overuse of water in the region had reached a critical stage. Across the region, per capita access to potable water had dropped from 123,599 cubic feet annually in 1960 to 44,142 cubic feet by 1996. In Gaza and Yemen, the hardest-hit places, access was down to 6,357 cubic feet in 1997. The only Middle Eastern country with a per capita renewable potable-water supply above the UN minimum of 105,942 cubic feet is Iraq, which has 186,634 cubic feet for each of its people. The overexploitation of groundwater, contamination of rivers and reservoirs from fertilizers and pesticides, waste dumping into the water supply, inefficiency in irrigation, and heavy subsidizing of water for crop production and industry all contribute to the Middle East's forthcoming water crisis.

The crisis has forced a number of governments to take politically unpopular but economically necessary steps. Algeria passed a law in 1996 prohibiting use of water at night. Also in 1996, the United Arab Emirates completed two new desalination plants, at enormous expense, in order to be able to meet the needs of its growing population; the rapid depletion of its underground water resources left it no alternative. Seven states in the region—Algeria, Bahrain, Iran, Iraq, Israel, Lebanon, and Libya—currently use 100 percent of available fresh water annually; and Libya, Jordan, Israel, Syria, Yemen, and the U.A.E. have less than 17,637 cubic feet of water per year per person.

Can the water crisis be headed off before it reaches major conflict levels? In 1997, the World Bank proposed a 20-year "action plan" to member states. The plan has several specific targets: a 40 percent reduction in water losses due to inefficiency, a 10 percent reduction in the use of water for irrigation, and a 50 percent increase in water for domestic and industrial use that could result from these savings. Achievement of these targets, the World Bank noted, would depend on the full support of states in the region. One encouraging response was the formation in June 1997 of the Middle East Desalination Research Center, based in Oman but funded jointly by the United States, Japan, Israel, and South Korea in addition to the Omani government. Its main purpose will be to develop ways to reduce the high cost of desalination. Given the limited amount of subsurface water available in the region, desalination offers almost the only avenue of hope for most of the Middle East's population.

THE WESTERN SAHARA: WHOSE DESERT?

It is a fearsome place, swept by sand-laden winds that sting through layers of clothing, scorched by 120°F temperatures, its flat, monotonous landscape broken occasionally by dried-up *wadis* (river beds). The Spanish called it Rio de Oro, "River of Gold," in a bitter jest, for it has neither. Rainfall averages 2 to 8 inches a year in a territory the size of Colorado. The population is largely nomadic. Before the twentieth century, this region, which we know today as the Western Sahara, was outside the control of any central authority. Other than a brief period of importance as the headquarters of the Almoravids, a dynasty that ruled most of North Africa for about a century, the Western Sahara was a backwater.

As a political entity, the Western Sahara resulted from European colonization in Africa in the late nineteenth century. Britain and France had a head start in establishing colonies. Spain was a latecomer. By the time the Spanish joined the race for colonies, little was left for them in Africa. Since they already controlled the Canary Islands, off the West African coast, it was natural for them to claim Rio de Oro, the nearest area on the coast.

In 1884, Spain announced a protectorate over Rio de Oro. The other European powers accepted the Spanish claim, under the principle that "occupation of a territory's coast entitled a colonial power to control over the interior."[16] But Spanish rights to the Saharan interior clashed with French claims to Mauritania and French efforts to control the independent Sultanate of Morocco to the north. After the establishment of a joint Franco–Spanish protectorate over Morocco in 1912, the boundaries of the Spanish colony were fixed, with Mauritania on the south and east and Morocco to the north. The nomads of the Western Sahara now found themselves living within fixed boundaries defined by outsiders.[17]

The Spanish moved very slowly into the interior. The entire Western Sahara was not "pacified" until 1934. Spain invested heavily in development of the important Western Sahara phosphate deposits but did little else to develop the colony. The Spanish population was essentially a garrison community, living apart from the Sahrawis, the indigenous Saharan population, in towns or military posts. A few Sahrawis went to Spain or other European countries, where they received a modern education; upon their return, they began to organize a Saharan nationalist movement. Other Sahrawis traveled to Egypt and returned with ideas of organizing a Saharan Arab independent state. But a real sense of either a Spanish Saharan or an independent Sahrawi identity was slow to emerge.[18]

Serious conflict over the Spanish Sahara developed in the 1960s. By that time, both Morocco and Mauritania had become independent. Algeria, the third African territory involved in the conflict, won its independence after a bloody

(UN photo/Y. Nagata)

The Western Sahara region is flat and very hot. At this time, it appears that this land eventually will be integrated with Morocco.

civil war. All three new states were highly nationalistic and were opposed to the continuation of colonial rule over any African people, but particularly Muslim peoples. They encouraged the Sahrawis to fight for liberation from Spain, giving arms and money to guerrilla groups and keeping their borders open.

However, the three states had different motives. Morocco claimed the Western Sahara on the basis of historical ties dating back to the Almoravids, plus the oath of allegiance sworn to Moroccan sultans by Saharan chiefs in the nineteenth and twentieth centuries. Kinship was also a factor; several important Saharan families have branches in Morocco, and both the mother and the first wife of the founder of Morocco's current ruling dynasty, Mulay Ismail, were from Sahrawi families.

The Mauritanian claim to the Spanish Sahara was based not on historical sovereignty but on kinship. Sahrawis have close ethnic ties with the Moors, the majority of the population of Mauritania. Also, Mauritania feared Moroccan expansion, since its territory had once been included in the Almoravid state. A Saharan buffer state between Mauritania and Morocco would serve as protection for the Mauritanians.

Algeria's interest in Spanish Sahara was largely a matter of support for a national liberation movement against a colonial power. The Algerians made no territorial claim to the colony. But Algerian foreign policy has rested on two pillars since independence: the right to self-determination of subject peoples and the principle of self-determination through referendum. Algeria consistently maintains that the Saharan people should have these rights.

In the 1960s, Spain came under pressure from the United Nations to give up its colonies. After much hesitation, the Spanish announced in August 1974 that a referendum would be held under UN supervision to decide the colony's future.

The Spanish action brought the conflict to a head. King Hassan declared that 1975 would mark the restoration of Moroccan sovereignty over the territory. The main opposition to this claim came from Polisario (an acronym for the Popular Front for the Liberation of Saguia al-Hara and Rio de Oro, the two divisions of the Spanish colony). This organization, formed by Saharan exiles based initially in Mauritania, issued a declaration of independence, and Polisario guerrillas began attacking Spanish garrisons, increasing the pressure on Spain to withdraw. In October 1975, Hassan announced that he would lead a massive, peaceful march of civilians, "armed" only with Korans, into the Spanish Sahara to recover sacred Moroccan territory. This "Green March" of half a million unarmed Moroccan volunteers into Spanish territory seemed an unusual, even risky, method of validating a territorial claim, but it worked. In 1976, Spain reached agreement with Morocco and Mauritania to partition the territory into two zones, one third going to Mauritania and two thirds to Morocco. The Moroccan Zone included the important phosphate deposits.

Polisario rejected the partition agreement. It announced formation of the Sahrawi Arab Democratic Republic (S.A.D.R.), "a free, independent, sovereign state ruled by an Arab democratic system of progressive unionist orientation and of Islamic religion."[19]

Polisario tactics of swift-striking attacks from hidden bases in the vast desert were highly effective in the early stages. Mauritania withdrew from the war in 1978, when a military coup overthrew its government. The new Mauritanian rulers signed a peace treaty in Algiers with Polisario representatives. Morocco, not to be outdone, promptly annexed the Mauritanian share of the territory and beefed up its military forces. A fortified "Sand Wall," which was built in stages from the former border with Rio de Oro down to the Moroccan–Mauritanian border and in 1987 extended about 350 miles to the Atlantic Ocean, provided the Moroccan Army with a strong defensive base from which to launch punitive raids against its elusive foe. The new segment also cut off the Polisario's access to the sea; Polisario raiders had begun to intercept and board fishing vessels in attempts to disrupt development of that important Moroccan resource and to bring pressure on foreign countries (such as Spain) that use the fishing grounds to push Morocco toward a settlement.

Although a large number of member states of the Organization of African Unity (OAU) subsequently recognized the Sahrawi Republic, Morocco blocked its admission to the OAU, on the grounds that it was part of Moroccan territory. However, the drain on Moroccan resources of indefinitely maintaining a 100,000-man army in the desert led King Hassan II to soften his obduracy, particularly in relation to Algeria. With both countries affected by severe economic problems and some political instability, a rapprochement became possible in the late 1980s. Diplomatic relations were restored in 1988; and in 1989, Morocco joined Algeria, Libya, Tunisia, and Mauritania in the Arab Maghrib Union (AMU). The AMU charter binds member states not to support resistance movements in one another's territory. As a result, Algeria withdrew its backing for S.A.D.R. and closed Polisario offices in Algiers.

Algeria's preoccupation with internal affairs and the withdrawal of Algerian and Libyan financial aid placed Polisario in a difficult position. Two of its founders, Omar Hadrami and Noureddine Belali, defected in 1989 and acknowledged Moroccan sovereignty over the territory. A 1990 amnesty offer by King Hassan for all Polisario members and Saharan exiles was accepted by nearly 1,000 persons; these included S.A.D.R.'s foreign minister, Brahim Hakim.

In 1991, Hassan agreed to a cease-fire and a UN–supervised referendum to allow the Sahrawis to decide their own future, the choice being between independence or incorporation into Morocco. The United Nations established a Mission for the Referendum on the Western Sahara (MINURSO), sending a small observer force to the region to supervise voter registration.

By this time, however, several hundred thousand Moroccan settlers had moved into the Western Sahara to take advantage of free land, housing, and other inducements offered by the government to help develop the new "frontier province" of Morocco. Their presence complicated the registration process, since Morocco insisted that they were Sahrawis and therefore entitled to take part in the referendum. Under these difficult circumstances, voter registration proceeded slowly. In May 1995, a demonstration by Sahrawis shouting "Independence Yes! Moroccan colonialism No!" stirred the United Nations to action. The Security Council passed *Resolution 995,* calling for a speedy implementation of the registration. The MINURSO observer force was increased to 240, plus 138 blue-helmeted police and soldiers, to implement the resolution.

Two later Security Council resolutions (*1042* and *1084*) extended the MINURSO mandate through May 1997. With the tenuous cease-fire still holding, peace talks between Moroccan and Polisario representatives began in June in Lisbon, Portugal. The talks were brokered by former U.S. secretary of state James Baker. His charge as special UN envoy was to bring to an end a 24-year conflict that had placed a heavy financial burden on Morocco and made 140,000 Sahrawis refugees in that part of the Western Sahara still controlled by Polisario. Whether Baker's high-profile involvement would bring about a solution acceptable to both parties or produce continued stalemate was unclear, although he was greeted as a "liberator" by the Sahrawis. A Polisario commander in Tindouf, the organization's main base in Algeria, told a reporter, "If Sahrawis are given an opportunity to choose we have no doubt they will choose independence in their own state. If they are not given a choice, we will continue our struggle to liberate our own country."[20]

NOTES

1. Alan R. Taylor, *The Arab Balance of Power* (Syracuse, NY: Syracuse University Press, 1982), Preface, XIII.

2. "Turkistan, Afghanistan, Transcaspia . . . they are the pieces on a chessboard upon which is played out a game for the domination of the World." Lord Curzon, viceroy of India, quoted in Shabbir Hussain *et al., Afghanistan Under Soviet Occupation* (Islamabad, Pakistan: World Affairs Publications, 1980), p. 54.

3. "The Soviet Action in Afghanistan was made necessary by the real threat of seeing the country transformed into an imperialist military platform on the Southern frontier of the U.S.S.R." Former Soviet leader Leonid Brezhnev, quoted in Hussain, *op. cit.,* p. 7.

4. Terence O'Donnell, *Garden of the Brave in War* (New York: Ticknor and Fields, 1980), p. 19, states that, in visits to remote Iranian villages, he was told by informants that the Arabs never washed, went around naked, and ate lizards.

5. Daniel Pipes, "A Border Adrift: Origins of the Conflict," in Shirin Tahir-Kheli and Shaheen Ayubi, eds., *The Iran-Iraq War: New Weapons, Old Conflicts* (New York: Praeger, 1983), pp. 10–13.

6. *Ibid.,* quoted on p. 20.

7. Stephen R. Grummon, *The Iran-Iraq War: Islam Embattled,* The Washington Papers/92, Vol. X (New York: Praeger, 1982), p. 10.

8. William O. Staudenmaier, "A Strategic Analysis," in Tahir-Kheli and Ayubi, *op. cit.,* pp. 29–33.

9. *The Christian Science Monitor* (September 23, 1987).

10. Quoted in Barry Rubin, *The Arab States and the Palestine Conflict* (Syracuse, NY: Syracuse University Press, 1981), p. 7.

11. Letter to James Marshall, January 17, 1930, in Camilo Dresner, ed., *The Letters and Papers of Chaim Weizmann*, Vol. 14 (New Brunswick, NJ: Rutgers University Press, 1979), pp. 208–211.

12. Martin Buber, *Land of Two Peoples,* ed. Paul Mendes-Flohr (New York: Oxford University Press, 1983), p. 199.

13. Uri Avnery, *Israel Without Zionists* (New York: Macmillan, 1968), pp. 187 and 189.

14. Yaron Ezrahi, *Rubber Bullets: Power and Conscience in Modern Israel* (New York: Farrar, Straus & Giroux, 1997), p. 220.

15. Mohammed Shadid, *The United States and the Palestinians* (New York: St. Martin's Press, 1981), p. 195.

16. John Damis, *Conflict in Northwest Africa: The Western Sahara Dispute* (Palo Alto, CA: Hoover Institution Press, 1983), p. 110.

17. "The borders zigzagged from Zag in the north to Zug in the south." David Lynne Price, *The Western Sahara,* The Washington Papers/63, Vol. VII (Beverly Hills, CA: Sage Publications, 1979), p. 11.

18. Damis, *op. cit.,* p. 13, notes that a tribal assembly (Jama'a) was formed in 1967 for the Sahrawis but that its 43 members were all tribal chiefs or their representatives; it had only advisory powers.

19. Quoted from *Le Monde,* in Damis, *op. cit.,* p. 75.

20. Scott Peterson, "Struggle in the Sahara," *The Christian Science Monitor* (July 15, 1997).

Algeria (Democratic and Popular Republic of Algeria)

GEOGRAPHY

Area in Square Kilometers (Miles):
2,381,740 (919,352) (about 3 times the
size of Texas)
Capital (Population): Algiers
(1,507,000)
Climate: mild winters and hot summers
on coastal plain; less rain and cold
winters on high plateau; considerable
temperature variation in desert,
February–May

PEOPLE

Population
Total: 29,539,400
Annual Growth Rate: 2.25%
Rural/Urban Population Ratio: 50/50
Ethnic Makeup: 99% Arab-Berber; less
than 1% European
Major Languages: Arabic; Berber
dialects; Ahaggar (Tuareg); French
widely spoken

Health
Life Expectancy at Birth: 67 years
(male); 69 years (female)
Infant Mortality Rate (Ratio): 50/1,000
Average Caloric Intake: 96% of FAO
minimum
Physicians Available (Ratio): 1/1,041

Religions
99% Sunni Muslim (Islam is the state
religion); 1% Shia Muslim, Christian,
and Jewish

Education
Adult Literacy Rate: 57%

COMMUNICATION
Telephones: 822,000
Newspapers: 6 dailies

The Casbah

The *Casbah* ("Fort" in Arabic), the walled inner city in the heart of Algiers
that served as the seat of government for the powerful Algerine corsair
state for 3 centuries, was neglected during the period of French colonial
rule and gradually became an urban slum. Far from the romantic image
portrayed in Hollywood films, the Casbah's narrow streets of rough
cobblestones and its crumbling tenements convey an atmosphere of
unspeakable gloom. Riots there in 1985 led the government to promise
to raze it and replace the ancient buildings with modern block housing.
However, the promise was not kept. Today, as occurred during the war
of independence of 1954-1962, the Casbah has become the main center
for armed Islamic groups seeking to overthrow the military government
and install one ruled under strict Islamic law.

TRANSPORTATION
Highways—Kilometers (Miles): 95,576
(59,639)
Railroads—Kilometers (Miles): 4,733
(2,953)
Usable Airfields: 139

GOVERNMENT
Type: republic, currently under military rule
Independence Date: July 5, 1962
Head of State/Government: President
Liamine Zeroual; Prime Minister
Ahmed Ouyahia
Political Parties: National Democratic Rally;
National Liberation Front; Movement for a
Peaceful Society; Front for Socialist Forces;
Rally for Cultural Democracy; Party for
Algerian Renewal; others
Suffrage: universal at 18

MILITARY
Number of Armed Forces: 125,500
*Military Expenditures (% of Central
Government Expenditures):* 2.7%
Current Hostilities: civil insurrection
led by breakaway guerrilla groups from
the Islamic Salvation Front

ECONOMY
Currency ($ U.S. Equivalent): 55.1
Algerian dinars = $1
Per Capita Income/GDP: $3,480/$97.1
billion
Inflation Rate: 15%
Total Foreign Debt: $26.4 billion
Natural Resources: crude oil; natural
gas; iron ore; phosphates; uranium;
lead; zinc; mercury
Agriculture: wheat; barley; oats; olives;
grapes; dates; citrus fruits; sheep; cattle
Industry: petroleum; light industries;
natural gas; petrochemicals; electrical;
automotive plants; food processing

FOREIGN TRADE
Exports: $14.27 billion
Imports: $11.24 billion

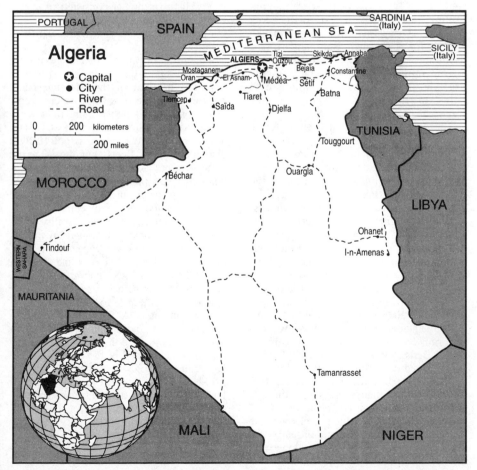

ALGERIA

The modern state of Algeria occupies the central part of North Africa, a geographically distinctive and separate region of Africa that includes Morocco and Tunisia. The name of the country comes from the Arabic word *al-Jaza'ir,* "the islands," because of the rocky islets along this part of the Mediterranean coast. The name of the capital, Algiers, has the same origin.

The official name of the state is the Democratic and Popular Republic of Algeria. It is the second-largest nation in Africa (after Sudan). The overall population density is low. However, the population is concentrated in the northern third of the country. The vast stretches of the Algerian Sahara are largely unpopulated. The country had an extremely high birth rate prior to 1988, but government-sponsored family-planning programs have significantly reduced the rate.

GEOGRAPHY

Algeria's geography is a formidable obstacle to broad economic and social development. About 80 percent of the land is uncultivable desert, and only 12 percent is arable without irrigation. Most of the population live in a narrow coastal plain and in a fertile, hilly inland region called the *Tell* (Arabic for "hillock"). The four Saharan provinces have only 3 percent of the population but comprise more than half the land area. The mineral resources that made possible Algeria's transformation in 2 decades from a land devastated by civil war to one of the developing world's success stories are all located in the Sahara.

Economic growth, however, has been uneven, generally affecting the rural and lower-class urban populations unfavorably. The large-scale exodus of rural families into the cities, with consequent neglect of agriculture, has resulted in a vast increase in urban slums. Economic disparities were a major cause of riots in 1988, which led to political reforms and the dismantling of the Socialist system responsible for Algerian development since independence.

Algeria is unique among newly independent Middle Eastern countries in that it gained its independence through a civil war. For more than 130 years (1830–1962), it was occupied by France and became a French department (similar to a U.S. state). With free movement from mainland France to Algeria and vice versa, the country was settled by large numbers of Europeans, who became the politically dominant group in the population although they were a minority. The modern Algerian nation is the product of the interaction of native Muslim Algerians with the European settlers, who also considered Algeria home.

Algeria's geography is a key to the country's past disunity. In addition to its vast Saharan territory, Algeria is broken up into discontinuous regions by a number of rugged mountain ranges. The Mediterranean coastline is narrow and is backed throughout its length by mountains, notably the imposing Kabyle range. The Algerian Atlas range, a continuation of the Moroccan Atlas, is a complex system of deep valleys, high plateaux, and peaks ranging up to 6,000 feet. In southeastern Algeria is the most impressive range in the country, the Aurès, a great mountain block.

The original inhabitants of the entire North African region were Berbers, a people of unknown origin grouped into various tribes. Morocco has the largest Berber population in the region—about 20 percent of the total in the Algerian case. The main Berber-speaking groups are found in Kabylia, the Aurès (Chaouia), and the Mzab, in the Algerian Sahara. The Tuareg, a nomadic people in southern Algeria, Mali, and Niger, are the only Berbers with a written script, called Tifinagh. They were formerly "lords of the desert," controlling trade routes on their swift racing camels and exacting tolls or serving as guides for caravans. But hard times, drought, and modernized transport have all but ruined their traditional nomadic lifestyle; the majority have migrated to cities to find work, usually at low wages.

The Arabs, who brought Islam to North Africa in the seventh century A.D., converted the Algerian Berbers after a fierce resistance. The Arabs brought their language as a unifying feature, and religion linked the Algerians with the larger Islamic world. Today, most follow Sunni Islam, but a significant compact minority, about 100,000, are Shia Muslims. They refer to themselves as Ibadis, from their observance of an ancient Shia rite, and live in five "holy cities" clustered in a remote Saharan valley where centuries ago they took refuge from Sunni rulers of northern Algeria. Their valley, the Mzab, has always maintained religious autonomy from Algerian central governments. The much larger Berber population of Kabylia has also resisted central authority, whether Islamic or French, throughout Algerian history. One of many pressures on the government today is that of an organized Kabyle movement, which seeks greater autonomy for the region and an emphasis on Berber language in schools, along with the revitalization of Kabyle culture.

HISTORY

The Corsair Regency

The foundations of the modern Algerian state were laid in the sixteenth century, with the establishment of the Regency of Algiers, an outlying province of the Ottoman Empire. Algiers in particular, due to its natural harbor, was developed for use by the Ottomans as a naval base for wars against European fleets in the Mediterranean. The Algerian coast was the farthest extent westward of Ottoman power. Consequently, Algiers and Oran, the two major ports, were exposed to constant threats of attack by Spanish and other European fleets. They could not easily be supported, or governed directly, by the Ottomans. The regency, from its beginnings, was a state geared for war.

The regency was established by two Greek-born Muslim sea captains, Aruj and Khayr al-Din (called Barbarossa by his European opponents because of his flaming red beard). The brothers obtained commissions from the Ottoman sultan for expeditions against the Spanish. They made their principal base at Algiers, then a small port, which Khayr al-Din expanded into a powerful fortress and naval base. His government consisted of a garrison of Ottoman soldiers sent by the sultan to keep order, along with a naval force called the corsairs.

Corsairing or piracy (the choice of term depended upon one's viewpoint) was a common practice in the Mediterranean, but the rise to power of the Algerine corsairs converted it into a more or less respectable profession.[1] The cities of Tetuan, Tunis, Salé (Morocco), and Tripoli (Libya) also had corsair fleets, but the Algerine corsairs were so effective against European shipping that, for 300 years (1500–1800), European rulers called them the "scourge of the Mediterranean." One factor in their success was their ability to attract outstanding sea captains from various European countries. Renegades from Italy, Greece, Holland, France, and Britain joined the Algerine fleet, converted to Islam, and took Muslim names as a symbol of their new status. Some rose to high rank.

Government in Algiers passed through several stages and eventually became a system of deys. The deys were elected by the Divan, a council of the captains of the Ottoman garrison. Deys were elected for life, but most of them never fulfilled their tenure due to constant intrigue, military coups, and assassinations. Yet the system provided considerable stability, security for the population, and wealth and prestige for the regency. These factors probably account for its durability; the line of deys governed uninterruptedly from the late 1600s to 1830.

Outside of Algiers and its hinterland, authority was delegated to local chiefs and religious leaders who were responsible for tax collection and remittances to the dey's treasury. The chiefs were kept in line with generous subsidies. It was a system well adapted to the fragmented society of Algeria and one that enabled a small military group to rule a large territory at relatively little cost.[2]

The French Conquest

In 1827, the dey of Algiers, enraged at the French government's refusal to pay an old debt incurred during Napoleon's wars, struck the French consul on the shoulder with a fly-whisk in the course of an interview. The king of France, Charles X, demanded an apology for the "insult" to his representative. None was forthcoming, so the French blockaded the port of Algiers in retaliation. But the dey continued to keep silent. In 1830, a French army landed on the coast west of the city, marched overland, and entered it with almost no resistance. The dey surrendered and went into exile.[3]

The French, who had been looking for an excuse to expand their interests in North Africa, now were not sure what to do with Algiers. The overthrow of the despotic Charles X in favor of a constitutional monarchy in France confused the situation even further. But the Algerians considered the French worse than the Turks, who were at least fellow Muslims. In the 1830s, they rallied behind their first national leader, Emir Abd al-Qadir.

Abd al-Qadir was the son of a prominent religious leader and, more important, was a descendant of the Prophet Muhammad. Abd al-Qadir had unusual qualities of leadership, military skill, and physical courage. From 1830 to 1847, he carried on guerrilla warfare against a French army of more than 100,000 men with such success that at one point the French signed a formal treaty recognizing him as head of an Algerian nation in the interior. Abd al-Qadir described his strategy in a prophetic letter to the king of France:

> France will march forward, and we shall retire. But France will find it necessary to retire, and we shall return. We shall weary and harry you, and our climate will do the rest.[4]

In order to defeat Abd al-Qadir, the French commander used "total war" tactics, burning villages, destroying crops, killing livestock, and levying fines on peoples who continued to support the emir.

These measures, called "pacification" by France, finally succeeded. In 1847, Abd al-Qadir surrendered to French authorities. He was imprisoned for several years, in violation of a solemn commitment, and was then released by Emperor Napoleon III. He spent the rest of his life in exile.

Although he did not succeed in his quest, Abd al-Qadir is venerated as the first Algerian nationalist, able by his leadership and Islamic prestige to unite warring groups in a struggle for independence from foreign control. Abd al-Qadir's green and white flag was raised again by the Algerian nationalists during the second war of independence (1954–1962), and it is the flag of the republic today.

Algérie Française

After the defeat of Abd al-Qadir, the French gradually brought all of present-day Algerian territory under their control. The Kabyles, Berbers living in the rugged mountain region east of Algiers, were the last to submit. The Kabyles had submitted in 1857, but they rebelled in 1871 after a series of decrees by the French government had made all Algerian Muslims subjects but not citizens, giving them a status inferior to French and other European settlers.

The Kabyle rebellion had terrible results, not only for the Kabyles but for all Algerian Muslims. More than 1 million acres of Muslim lands were confiscated by French authorities and sold to European settlers. A special code of laws was enacted to treat Algerian Muslims differently from Europeans, with severe fines and sentences for such "infractions" as insulting a European or wearing shoes in public. (It was assumed that a Muslim caught wearing shoes had stolen them.)

In 1871, Algeria legally became a French department. But in terms of exploitation of natives by settlers, it may as well have remained a colony. One author notes that "the desire to make a settlement colony out of an already populated area led to a policy of driving the indigenous people out of the best arable lands."[5] Land confiscation was only part of the exploitation of Algeria by the *colons* (French settlers). They developed a modern Algerian agriculture integrated into the French economy, providing France with much of its wine, citrus, olives, and vegetables. Colons owned 30 percent of the arable land and 90 percent of the best farmland. Special taxes were imposed on the Algerian Muslims; the colons were exempted from paying most taxes.

The political structure of Algeria was even more favorable to the European minority. The colons were well represented in the French National Assembly, and their representatives made sure that any reforms or laws intended to improve the living conditions or rights of the Algerian Muslim population would be blocked.

In fairness to the colons, it must be pointed out that many of them had come to Algeria as poor immigrants and worked hard to improve their lot and to develop the country. By 1930, the centenary of the French conquest, many colon families had lived in Algiers for two generations or more. Colons had drained malarial swamps south of Algiers and developed the Mitidja, the country's most fertile region. A fine road and rail system linked all parts of the country, and French public schools served all cities and towns. Algiers even had its own university, a branch of the Sorbonne. It is not surprising that to the colons, Algeria was their country, "Algérie Française." Throughout Algeria they rebaptized Algerian cities with names like Orléansville and Philippeville, with paved French streets, cafes, bakeries, and little squares with flower gardens and benches where old men in berets dozed in the hot sun.

Jules Cambon, governor general of Algeria in the 1890s, once described the country as having "only a dust of people left her." What he meant was that the ruthless treatment of the Algerians by the French during the pacification had deprived them of their natural leaders. A group of leaders developed slowly in Algeria, but it was made up largely of *evolués,* persons who had received French educations, spoke French better than Arabic, and accepted French citizenship as the price of status.[6]

Other Algerians, several hundred thousand of them, served in the French Army in the two world wars. Many of them became aware of the political rights that they were supposed to have but did not. Still others, religious leaders and teachers, were influenced by the Arab nationalist movement for independence from foreign control in Egypt and other parts of the Middle East.

Until the 1940s, the majority of the evolués and other Algerian leaders did not want independence. They wanted full assimilation with France and Muslim equality with the colons. Ferhat Abbas, a French-trained pharmacist who was the spokesperson for the evoluées, said in 1936 that he did not believe that there was such a thing as an Algerian nation separate from France.

Abbas and his associates changed their minds after World War II. In 1943, they had presented to the French government a manifesto demanding full political and legal equality for Muslims with the colons.

It was blocked by colon leaders, who feared that they would be drowned in a Muslim sea. On May 8, 1945, the date of the Allied victory over Germany, a parade of Muslims celebrating the event but also demanding equality led to violence in the city of Sétif. Several colons were killed, and in retaliation, army troops and groups of colon vigilantes swept through Muslim neighborhoods, burning houses and slaughtering thousands of Muslims. From then on, Muslim leaders believed that independence through armed struggle was the only choice left to them.

The War for Independence
November 1 is an important holiday in France. It is called *Toussaint* (All Saints' Day). On that day, French people remember and honor all the many saints in the pantheon of French Catholicism. It is a day devoted to reflection and staying at home.

In the years after the Sétif massacre, there had been scattered outbreaks of violence in Algeria, some of them created by the so-called Secret Organization (OS), which had developed an extensive network of cells in preparation for armed insurrection. In 1952, French police accidentally uncovered the network and jailed most of its leaders. One of them, a former French Army sergeant named Ahmed Ben Bella, subsequently escaped and went to Cairo, Egypt.

As the date of Toussaint 1954 neared, Algeria seemed calm. But appearances were deceptive. Earlier in the year, nine former members of the OS had laid plans in secret for armed revolution. They divided Algeria into six *wilayas* (departments), each with a military commander. They also planned a series of coordinated attacks for the early morning hours of November 1, when the French population would be asleep and the police preparing for a holiday. Bombs exploded at French Army barracks, police stations, storage warehouses, telephone offices, and government buildings. The revolutionaries circulated leaflets in the name of the National Liberation Front (FLN), warning the French that they had acted to liberate Algeria from the colonialist yoke and calling on Algerian Muslims to join in the struggle to rebuild Algeria as a free Islamic state.

There were very few casualties as a result of the Toussaint attacks; for some time, the French did not realize that they had a revolution on their hands. But, as violence continued, regular army troops were sent to Algeria to help the hard-pressed police and the colons. Eventually there were 400,000 French troops in Algeria, as opposed to about 6,000 guerril-las. But the French consistently refused to consider the situation in Algeria a war. They called it a "police action." Others called it the "war without a name."[7] Despite their great numerical superiority, they were unable to defeat the FLN.

Elsewhere the French tried various tactics. They divided the country into small sectors, with permanent garrisons for each sector. They organized mobile units to track down the guerrillas in caves and hideouts. About 2 million villagers were moved into barbed-wire "regroupment camps," with a complete dislocation of their way of life, in order to deny the guerrillas the support of the population.

The war was settled not by military action but by political negotiations. The French people and government, already worn down by the effects of World War II and their involvement in Indochina, grew sick of the slaughter, the plastic bombs exploding in public places (in France as well as Algeria), and the brutality of the army in dealing with guerrilla prisoners. A French newspaper editor expressed the general feeling: "Algeria is ruining the spring. This land of sun and earth has never been so near us. It invades our hearts and torments our minds."[8]

The colons and a number of senior French Army officers were the last to give up their dream of an Algeria that would be forever French. Together the colons and the army forced a change in the French government. General Charles de Gaulle, the French wartime resistance hero, returned to power after a dozen years in retirement. But de Gaulle, a realist, had no intention of keeping Algeria forever French. He began secret negotiations with FLN leaders for Algerian independence.

The colons and the army officers made one last effort. In 1961, several generals led an insurrection in Algiers against de Gaulle and demanded his removal from office. However, the majority of the army remained loyal. A cease-fire came into effect on March 19, 1962. But the Secret Army Organization (OAS), a group of army dissenters and colon vigilantes, then launched a new campaign of violence, terror, and indiscriminate murders of Muslims. Bombs exploded in Muslim hospitals and schools; victims were shot at random as they walked the streets. The OAS hoped that the FLN would break the cease-fire to protect its fellow Muslims and thus bring back the French Army. But the FLN held firm.

A RE-UNITED NATION
Algeria became independent on July 5, 1962. Few nations have started their existence under worse circumstances. Esti-mates of casualties vary, but, by the end of the war, hundreds of thousands of men, women, and children, Muslims, colons, and soldiers had been killed or wounded or had simply disappeared. A painful loss to the new nation was the departure of almost the entire European community. The colons panicked and crowded aboard ships to cross the Mediterranean and resettle in various European countries, but especially in France, a land that most knew only as visitors. Nearly all Algeria's managers, landowners, professional class, civil servants, and skilled workers left.

The new Algerian government was also affected by factional rivalries among its leaders. The French writer Alexis de Tocqueville once wrote, "In rebellion, as in a novel, the most difficult part to invent is the end." The FLN revolutionaries had to invent a new system, one that would bring dignity and hope to people dehumanized by 130 years of French occupation and 8 years of savage war.

The first leader to emerge from intra-party struggle to lead the nation was Ahmed Ben Bella, who had spent the war in exile in Egypt but had great prestige as the political brains behind the FLN. Ben Bella laid the groundwork for an Algerian political system centered on the FLN as a single legal political party, and in September 1963, he was elected president. Ben Bella introduced a system of autogestion (workers' self-management), by which tenant farmers took over the management of farms abandoned by their colon owners and restored them to production as cooperatives. Autogestion became the basis for Algerian socialism—the foundation of development for decades.

Ben Bella did little else for Algeria, and he alienated most of his former associates with his ambitions for personal power. In June 1965, he was overthrown in a military coup headed by the defense minister, Colonel Houari Boumedienne. Ben Bella was sentenced to house arrest for 15 years; he was pardoned and exiled in 1980. While in exile, he founded the Movement for a Democratic Algeria, in opposition to the regime. In 1990, he returned to Algeria and announced plans to lead a broad-based opposition party in the framework of the multiparty system.

Boumedienne declared that the coup was a "corrective revolution, intended to reestablish authentic socialism and put an end to internal divisions and personal rule."[9] The government was reorganized under a Council of the Revolution, all military men, headed by Boumedienne, who subsequently became president of the republic. After a long period of preparation and gradual assumption of power by the reclusive and taciturn Boumedienne, a National Charter (Constitution) was approved by voters in 1976. The Charter defined Algeria as a Socialist state with Islam as the state religion, basic citizens' rights guaranteed, and leadership by the FLN as the only legal political party. A National Popular Assembly (the first elected in 1977) was responsible for legislation.

In theory, the Algerian president had no more constitutional powers than the U.S. president. However, in practice, Boumedienne was the ruler of the state, being president, prime minister, and commander of the armed forces rolled into one. In November 1978, he became ill from a rare blood disease; he died in December. For a time, it appeared that factional rivalries would again split the FLN, especially as Boumedienne had named neither a vice president nor a prime minister, nor had he suggested a successor.

The Algeria of 1978 was a very different nation from that of 1962. The scars of war had mostly healed. The FLN closed ranks and named Colonel Chadli Bendjedid to succeed Boumedienne as president for a 5-year term. In 1984, Bendjedid was re-elected. But the process of ordered Socialist development was abruptly and forcibly interrupted in October 1988. A new generation of Algerians, who had come of age long after the war for independence, took to the streets, protesting high prices, lack of jobs, inept leadership, a bloated bureaucracy, and other grievances.

The riots accelerated the process of Algeria's "second revolution" toward political pluralism and dismantling of the single-party Socialist system. President Bendjedid initially declared a state of emergency; and, for the first time since independence, the army was called in to restore order. Some 500 persons were killed in the rioting, most of them jobless youths. But the president moved swiftly to mobilize the nation in the wake of the violence. Voters approved in national referendum changes in the governing system to allow political parties to form outside the FLN. Another constitutional change, also effective in 1989, made the cabinet and prime minister responsible to the National Assembly.

The president retained his popularity during the upheaval and was reelected for a third term, winning 81 percent of the votes. A number of new parties were formed in 1989 to contest future Assembly elections. They represented a variety of political and social positions. Thus, the People's Movement for Algerian Renewal advocated a "democratic Algeria, representative of moderate Islam," while the National Algerian Party, more fundamentalist in its views, had a platform of full enforcement of Islamic law and the creation of 2 million new jobs. The Socialist Forces Front (FFS), founded many years earlier by exiled FLN leader Hocine Ait Ahmed, resurfaced with a manifesto urging Algerians to support "the irreversible process of democracy."

For its part, the government sought to revitalize the FLN as a genuine mass party on the order of the Tunisian Destour while insisting that it would not duplicate its neighbor country's *democratie de façade* but embark on real political reforms. Recruitment of new members was extended to rural areas. Although press freedom was confirmed in the constitutional changes approved by the voters, control of the major newspapers and media was shifted from the government to the FLN, to provide greater exposure.

FOREIGN POLICY

During the first decade of independence, Algeria's foreign policy was strongly nationalistic and anti-Western. Having won their independence from one colonial power, the Algerians were vocally hostile to the United States and its allies, calling them enemies of popular liberation. Algeria supported revolutionary movements all over the world, providing funds, arms, and training. The Palestine Liberation Organization, rebels against Portuguese colonial rule in Mozambique, Muslim guerrillas fighting the Christian Ethiopian government in Eritrea—all benefited from active Algerian support.

In the mid-1970s, Algeria moderated its anti-Western stance in favor of nonalignment and good relations with both East and West. The government broke diplomatic relations with the United States in 1967, due to American support for Israel, and did not restore them for a decade. Relations improved thereafter to such a point that Algerian mediators were instrumental in resolving the 1979–1980 American–Iranian hostage crisis, since Iran regarded Algeria as a suitable mediator—Islamic yet nonaligned.

Until recently, Algeria's relations with Morocco were marked by suspicion, hostility, and periodic conflict. The two countries clashed briefly in 1963 over ownership of iron mines near Tindouf, on the border. Algeria also supported the Western Saharan nationalist movement fighting for independence for the former Spanish colony against Moroccan occupation. After Morocco annexed the territory, Algeria provided bases, sanctuary, funds, and weapons to the Polisario Front, the military wing of the movement. The Bendjedid government recognized the self-declared Sahrawi Arab Democratic Republic in 1980 and sponsored SADR membership in the Organization for African Unity.

However, summit meetings between Bendjedid and Morocco's King Hassan II led to improved relations. Algeria's concern with its own economic problems and internal political instability resulting from the move toward a multiparty system in the 1980s put the Western Saharan issue on the back burner. After Hassan accepted the principle of a UN–sponsored referendum for the territory, the Algerian government withdrew support from the Polisario and closed down its bases.

The success of Algerian mediators in resolving international disputes has been duplicated in recent years in conflicts involving its other neighbors. In 1987, they succeeded in influencing Libyan leader Muammar al-Qadhafi to provide compensation for Tunisian workers expelled from Libya; in 1989, they arranged a peace treaty between Libya and Chad. Subsequently, Algeria was instrumental in the formation of the Arab Maghrib Union, which links the country with Morocco, Tunisia, Libya, and Mauritania in a five-nation regional economic bloc.

THE ECONOMY

Algeria's oil and gas resources were developed by the French. Commercial production and exports began in 1958 and continued through the war for independence; they were not affected, since the Sahara was governed under a separate military administration. The oil fields were turned over to Algeria after independence but continued to be managed by French technicians until 1970, when the industry was nationalized.

Today, the hydrocarbons sector provides the bulk of government revenues and 90 percent of exports. Algeria ranks fifth in the world in natural gas and 14th in oil reserves. New oil strikes in 1996 and extension of an undersea pipeline to Spain in 1997 are expected to increase exports significantly while adding several billion barrels to reserves.

During President Boumedienne's period in office, all sectors of the Algerian economy were governed under the 1976 National Charter. This document set forth provisions for national development under a uniquely Algerian form of state socialism. However, persistent economic difficulties caused by a combination of lower oil prices and global oversupply led the Bendjedid government to scrap the Charter. Since then, Algeria has borrowed

(UN photo/Kata Bader)

The rapid growth in the population of Algeria, coupled with urban migration, has created a serious housing shortage, as this apartment building in Algiers testifies.

economic practice when it seemed to work—was totally abandoned.

By 1997, the Algerian economy was again on a sound footing. With structural reforms largely completed, increased privatization of state-owned enterprises (138 during the period 1991–1994), and a strong hydrocarbons sector largely unaffected by political violence, the country seemed an excellent prospect for greater foreign investment. However, the Algerian people themselves seemed to have realized little from their economic development. Unemployment was 25 percent in 1997, striking hardest at the large number of males under age 19, and some 87 out of the 138 privatized state enterprises were liquidated due to fiscal mismanagement.

THE FUNDAMENTALIST CHALLENGE

Despite the growing appeal of Islamic fundamentalism in numerous Arab countries in recent years, Algeria until very recently seemed an unlikely site for the rise of a strong fundamentalist movement. The country's long association with France, its lack of historic Islamic identity as a nation, and 3½ decades of single-party socialism militated against such a development. But the failure of successive Algerian governments to resolve severe economic problems, plus the lack of representative political institutions nurtured within the ruling FLN, have brought about the rise of fundamentalism as a political force during the 1990s. Fundamentalists took an active part in the 1988 riots; and, with the establishment of a multiparty system, they organized a political party, the Islamic Salvation Front (FIS). It soon claimed 3 million adherents among the then 25 million Algerians.

FIS candidates won 55 percent of urban mayoral and council seats in the 1989 local and municipal elections. The FLN conversely managed to hold on to power largely in the rural areas. Fears that FIS success might draw army intervention and spark another round of revolutionary violence led the government to postpone for 6 months the scheduled June 1991 elections for an enlarged 430-member National People's Assembly. An interim government, under the technocrat Prime Minister Sid Ahmed Ghozali, was formed to oversee the transition process.

In accordance with President Bendjedid's commitment to multiparty democracy, the first stage of Assembly elections took place on December 26, 1991, with FIS candidates winning 188 out of 231 contested seats. But, before the second stage could take place, the army stepped in. FIS leaders were arrested, and the elec-

heavily and regularly from international lenders to pay for continued industrial growth.

After a number of years of negative economic growth, the government initiated an austerity program in 1992. Luxury imports were prohibited and several new taxes introduced. The program was approved by the International Monetary Fund, Algeria's main source of external financing. In 1995, the IMF loaned $1.8 billion to cover government borrowing up to 60 percent under the approved austerity program to make the required structural adjustment. In August of that year, the Paris Club—the international consortium that manages most of Algeria's foreign indebtedness—rescheduled $7 billion of the country's foreign debts due in 1996–1997, including interest payments, to ease the strain on the economy.

With 42 percent of the labor force employed in agriculture, improvement in that sector is essential to economic development. For most of its 3½ decades of independence, Algeria has had to import 70 percent of its food; but, in 1992, cereals production increased significantly, to 3.5 million tons, reducing the need for imports. Domestic demand for potatoes, another important food crop, would be met by a seed potato plant completed at Guellal in 1993.

Structural reform has top priority. In 1988, 3,500 state farms were converted to collective farms, but with individual farmers holding title to lands. Low-income urban migrants were encouraged to return to farming, with financial incentives provided, and the autogestion system—introduced as a stopgap measure after independence and enshrined later in FLN

tions were postponed indefinitely. President Bendjedid resigned on January 17, 1992, well ahead of the expiration (in 1993) of his third 5-year term. He said that he did so as a sacrifice in the interest of restoring stability to the nation and preserving democracy. Mohammed Boudiaf, one of the nine historic chiefs of the Revolution, returned from years of exile in Morocco to become head of the Higher Council of State, set up by military leaders after the abortive elections and resignation of President Bendjedid. FIS headquarters was closed and the party declared illegal by a court in Algiers. Local councils and provincial assemblies formed by the FIS after the elections were dissolved and replaced by "executive delegations" appointed by the Higher Council.

Subsequently, Boudiaf named a 60-member Consultative Council to work with the various political factions to reach a consensus on reforms. However, the refusal of such leaders as former president Ben Bella and Socialist Forces Front (FFS) leader Hocine Ait Ahmed to participate limited its effectiveness. Boudiaf was also suspected of using it to build a personal power base. On June 29, 1992, he was assassinated, reportedly by a member of his own presidential guard.

With Boudiaf gone, Algeria's generals turned to their own ranks for new leadership. In 1994, General Liamine Zeroual, the real strongman of the regime, was named head of state by the Higher Council. Zeroual pledged that elections for president would be held in November 1995 as a first step toward the restoration of parliamentary government. He also released from prison two top FIS leaders, Abbasi Madani and Ali Belhaj, confining them to house arrest on the assumption that, in return for dialogue, they would call a halt to the spiraling violence.

However, the dialogue proved inconclusive, and Zeroual declared that the presidential elections would be held on schedule. Earlier, leaders of the FIS, FFS, FLN, and several smaller parties had met in Rome, Italy, under the sponsorship of Sant-Egidio, a Catholic service agency, and announced a "National Contract." It called for the restoration of FIS political rights in return for an end to violence, multiparty democracy, and exclusion of the military from government. The Alge-

rian "personality" was defined in the Contract as Islamic, Arab, and Berber.

Military leaders rejected the National Contract out of hand, due to the FIS's participation. However, the November 1995 presidential election was held as scheduled, albeit under massive army protection—soldiers were stationed within 65 feet of every polling place. Zeroual won handily, as expected, garnering 61 percent of the votes. But the fact that the election was held at all, despite a boycott call by several party leaders and threats of violence from the Armed Islamic Group (GIA), was impressive.[10]

THE KILLING FIELDS
Algeria's modern history has been well described as one of excesses. Thus "the colonial period was unusually harsh, the war for independence particularly costly . . . the insistence on one-party rule initially unwavering and the projects for industrialization overly ambitious," as specialists on the country have noted.[11] Extremes of violence are nothing new in Algerian life. But in addition to horrifying violence, the real tragedy of the conflict has been to pit "an inflexible regime and a fanatical opposition" against "innocent victims doomed by their secular lifestyle or their piety."[12]

Shortly after the 1995 election, Ahmed Ben Bella, Algeria's first president and the current leader of the opposition Movement for Democracy in Algeria (MDA), wrote a thoughtful analysis of the "dialogue at Rome" in which he had participated and that produced the National Contract. He noted: "A mad escalation of violence is the hallmark of everyday life. Nobody is safe: journalists, intellectuals, women, children and old people are all equally threatened. Yet the use of force, the recourse to violence, will not allow any of the protagonists to solve the problem to their advantage, and the solution must be a political one." The dialogue at Rome, he added, "was meant to lead to a consensus that would bring together everyone—including the regime in power—within the framework of the current Constitution, which stipulates political pluralism, democracy, respect for all human rights and freedoms."[13]

Unfortunately, neither the regime nor its opponents have been listening. As Ben

Bella noted, the GIA targeted not only military leaders but also writers, professors, journalists, prominent women, and eventually foreigners, in a savage campaign. Its victims included the head of the national theater and, ironically, the head of the Algerian League for Human Rights, who had argued publicly that detention of some 9,000 FIS members in roofless prison buildings deep in the Sahara violates their constitutional rights. In 1996, GIA militants turned on foreigners, kidnapping and murdering seven Trappist monks and the Christian bishop of Oran. Altogether, the civil insurrection had caused some 40,000 casualties by 1996.

WHAT PRICE DIALOGUE?
On its side, the regime pursued its chosen policy of brutal repression, tempered with small steps toward a genuine dialogue with the opposition as urged by Ben Bella and other moderate, non-Islamist leaders. In May 1996, President Zeroual announced a referendum on revisions to the Constitution. The key points of revision were a ban on political parties based on religion, language, regionalism, or gender; presidential terms of office limited to 5 years and renewable just once; and the requirement that the president declare his assets. Islam would be confirmed as the state religion and Arabic as the official language. The revised Constitution would establish a bicameral Legislature, with one third of its members appointed by the president (in the upper house, called the Council of Nations) and two thirds elected under a system of proportional representation.

The referendum was held on November 28, with 85.8 percent of registered voters casting "yes" ballots. However, most of the opposition parties urged a boycott of the referendum on the grounds that it would strengthen the powers of an already too-powerful president.

Zeroual next set June 5, 1997, for elections for an enlarged 380-seat National Assembly, the lower house of the Legislature. It was Algeria's first multiparty election since the abortive 1992 one, and increased violence beforehand kept the turnout low—65.5 percent as opposed to the 85-plus percent turnout for the referendum. The National Democratic Rally, a new party organized in April by supporters

Ferhat Abbas issues the Manifesto of the Algerian People
1943

Civil war, ending with Algerian independence
1954–1962

Ben Bella is overthrown by Boumedienne
1965

The National Charter commits Algeria to revolutionary socialist development
1976

President Boumedienne dies
1978

Land reform is resumed with the breakup of 200 large farms into smaller units; the last street and shop signs in French Algiers are replaced by Arabic ones, in an Arabization campaign
1980s

1990s

President Bendjedid steps down; the Islamic Salvation Front becomes a force and eventually is banned

The economy undergoes an austerity program

Civil war

of Zeroual, won 115 seats. Together with the 64 seats won by the resuscitated FLN, the Zeroual government dominated the Assembly, with a 57 percent majority.

Two "moderate" Islamist parties (so called because they reject violence) also participated in the elections. The Movement for a Peaceful Society ran second to the government party, with 69 seats; and An-Nahdah won 34 seats, giving at least a semblance of opposition in the Assembly. The trend continued in the 1997 elections for local and municipal offices, held in October under massive military protection. Pro-government candidates won the great majority of the 1,500 contested offices. However, the voter turnout of 55 percent underlined public fears of continued violence and apathy about Algeria's future in its struggle toward democratic government.

In the long run, not only must violence be brought under control but some form of accommodation between democracy and Islam must also be developed if Algeria is to develop a healthy society to match its economic strength. Following the June election, the GIA shifted its tactics to rural areas, visiting horror upon horror in remote villages, with beheadings of entire families and burning of homes. Some observers argued that it was the last gasp of desperate men fighting a lost cause—although the random slaughter of 1,000 villagers in July and August 1997 alone underscored the continuing effectiveness of the guerrillas. In any case, Algeria, having been a one-party state through most of its independence, clearly needs time and patience to adjust to the requirements of a new multiparty democracy.

NOTES

1. See William Spencer, *Algiers in the Age of the Corsairs* (Norman, OK: University of Oklahoma Press, 1976), Centers of Civilization Series. "The corsair, if brought to justice in maritime courts, identified himself as *corsale* or *Korsan,* never as fugitive or criminal; his occupation was as clearly identifiable as that of tanner, goldsmith, potter or tailor," p. 47.

2. Raphael Danziger, *Abd al-Qadir and the Algerians* (New York: Holmes and Meier, 1977), notes that Turkish intrigue kept the tribes in a state of near-constant tribal warfare, thereby preventing them from forming dangerous coalitions, p. 24.

3. The usual explanation for the quick collapse of the regency after 300 years is that its forces were prepared for naval warfare but not for attack by land. *Ibid.,* pp. 36–38.

4. Quoted in Harold D. Nelson, *Algeria, A Country Study* (Washington, D.C.: American University, Foreign Area Studies, 1979), p. 31.

5. Marnia Lazreg, *The Emergence of Classes in Algeria* (Boulder, CO: Westview Press, 1976), p. 53.

6. For Algerian Muslims to become French citizens meant giving up their religion, for all practical purposes, since Islam recognizes only Islamic law and to be a French citizen means accepting French laws. Fewer than 3,000 Algerians became French citizens during the period of French rule. Nelson, *op. cit.,* pp. 34–35.

7. John E. Talbott, *The War Without a Name: France in Algeria, 1954–1962* (New York: Alfred A. Knopf, 1980).

8. Georges Suffert, in *Esprit,* 25 (1957), p. 819.

9. Nelson, *op. cit.,* p. 68.

10. Robert Mortimer, "Algeria: The Dialectic of Elections and Violence," *Current History* (May 1997), p. 232.

11. Frank Ruddy, who was assigned to Tindouf by the United Nations as a member of the observer group monitoring the referendum in the Western Sahara, comments on the town's natural-history museum, "the one cultural attraction." However, "most of its space is devoted to especially grisly photos of terrible things the French did to Algerians during the Algerian war of independence." *The World & I* (August 1997), p. 138.

12. Robert Fisk, The *Independent* (London) (March 16, 1995).

13. Ahmed Ben Bella, "A Time for Peace in Algeria," *The World Today* (November 1995), p. 209.

DEVELOPMENT

Political turmoil and violence have not yet affected the important hydrocarbons sector of the economy. Discoveries in 1995 and 1996 have increased both oil and gas reserves. The completion of the trans-Mediterranean undersea pipeline to Spain in 1997 will increase exports significantly.

FREEDOM

Suspension of civil and political rights by the military regime due to the civil uprising has brought great hardship to the civilian population. The 1996 constitutional revisions provide for a bicameral Legislature, with political parties allowed officially as long as they do not campaign on the basis of religion, language, regionalism, or gender.

HEALTH/WELFARE

The 1984 Family Law improved women's rights in marriage and educational and work opportunities. But professional women and more recently rural women and their children have become special targets of Islamic violence. Some 400 professional women were murdered in 1995 and more than 400 killed in a one-day rampage in January 1998.

ACHIEVEMENTS

The government levied extra taxes on beer, gasoline, and cigarettes in 1996, raising 10.3 million dinars to fund a 6,000-unit, low-income housing project in Constantine along with a job-creation program for unemployed youths. The project will help reduce the high unemployment rate.

Bahrain (State of Bahrain)

GEOGRAPHY
Area in Square Kilometers (Miles): 678 (260) (about 4 times the size of Washington, D.C.)
Capital (Population): Manama (151,000)
Climate: hot and humid, April–October; temperate, November–March

PEOPLE

Population
Total: 590,100
Annual Growth Rate: 2.6%
Rural/Urban Population Ratio: 12/88
Ethnic Makeup: 63% Bahraini; 13% Asian; 10% other Arab; 8% Iranian; 6% others
Major Languages: Arabic; English; Farsi; Urdu

Health
Life Expectancy at Birth: 71 years (male); 76 years (female)
Infant Mortality Rate (Ratio): 18/1,000
Average Caloric Intake: n/a
Physicians Available (Ratio): 1/991

Religions
70% Shia Muslim; 30% Sunni Muslim

Education
Adult Literacy Rate: 84%

COMMUNICATION
Telephones: 100,000
Newspapers: 7 Arabic; 2 English language (one weekly, one daily)

Pearling: An Ancient Industry

Pearl diving dates back 5,000 years; the ancient *Epic of Gilgamesh* describes a diver tying stones to his feet to descend to the bed of the sea and pluck the magic flowers. Before the discovery of oil, pearl fishing was the main occupation and source of income of Bahrain. As recently as the 1930s, there were 900 dhows in Bahrain, with 20,000 pearl divers and crew. The pearling industry slumped with the introduction of cheaper Japanese cultured pearls, and oil development finished it. But Bahraini pearls are still highly valued, and a few dhows continue to bring them in, using methods unchanged for centuries.

TRANSPORTATION
Highways—Kilometers (Miles): 2,670 (1,666)
Railroads—Kilometers (Miles): none
Usable Airfields: 4

GOVERNMENT
Type: traditional monarchy (cabinet–executive system)
Independence Date: August 15, 1971
Head of State/Government: Emir Isa bin Salman al-Khalifa; Prime Minister Khalifa bin Salman al-Khalifa
Political Parties: none permitted
Suffrage: not provided since the National Assembly was suspended in 1975

MILITARY
Number of Armed Forces: 8,000
Military Expenditures (% of Central Government Expenditures): 5.5%
Current Hostilities: none

ECONOMY
Currency ($ U.S. Equivalent): 0.37 Bahrain dinar = $1 (fixed rate)
Per Capita Income/GDP: $12,100/$7.1 billion
Inflation Rate: 2%
Total Foreign Debt: $2.6 billion
Natural Resources: oil; associated and nonassociated natural gas; fish
Agriculture: eggs; vegetables; dates; dairy and poultry farming
Industry: petroleum processing and refining; aluminum; ship repair; natural gas; shrimping and fishing

FOREIGN TRADE
Exports: $3.7 billion
Imports: $3.8 billion

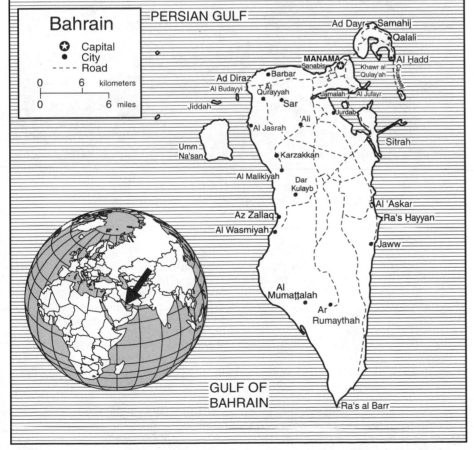

BAHRAIN

Bahrain is the smallest Arab state. It is also the only Arab island state, consisting of an archipelago of 33 islands, five of them inhabited. The largest island, also named Bahrain (from the Arabic *bahr-ayn,* or "two seas"), has an area of 216 square miles. This island contains the capital, Manama, and two thirds of the population. Bahrain's population density is thus one of the highest in the Middle East.

Although it is separated from the Arabian mainland, Bahrain is not far away; it is just 15 miles from Qatar and the same distance from Saudi Arabia. A causeway linking Bahrain with mainland Saudi Arabia opened in 1986, technically ending its insular status. The causeway has given strong stimulus to Bahraini business, much of it brought by Saudi visitors who drive across it to take advantage of the facilities of the freer Bahraini society, such as movie theaters and bar lounges.

Bahrain is unusual among the Persian Gulf states in that it started to develop its economy early. Oil was discovered there in 1932. Its head start in exportation of oil enabled the government to build up an industrial base over a long period and to build a large, indigenous, skilled labor force. As a result, today, Bahrain has a native majority of the population; 63 percent are native-born Bahrainis.

HISTORY

Archaeologists believe that, in ancient times, Bahrain was the legendary Dilmun, the land of immortality of the Sumerians of Mesopotamia. Dilmun was an important trade center between Mesopotamian cities and the cities of the Indus Valley in western India.

During the centuries of Islamic rule in the Middle East, Bahrain (it was renamed by Arab geographers) became wealthy from the pearl-fishing industry. By the fourteenth century, it had 300 villages. Bahraini merchants grew rich from profits on their large, lustrous, high-quality pearls. Bahraini sea captains and pearl merchants built lofty palaces and other stately buildings on the islands.

The Portuguese were the first Europeans to land on Bahrain, which they seized in the early sixteenth century as one of a string of fortresses along the coast to protect their monopoly over the spice trade. They ruled by the sword in Bahrain for nearly a century before they were ousted by Iranian invaders. The Iranians, in turn, were defeated by the al-Khalifas, a clan of the powerful Anaizas. In 1782, the clan leader, Shaykh Ahmad al-Khalifa, established control over Bahrain and founded the dynasty that rules the state today. (The

(UN photo/Ian Steele)

Bahrain may be the first of the Gulf states to get out of the oil business, due to its dwindling reserves. Other income-generating industries are being explored, and diversification of the economy along with political stability make Bahrain a stable regional business center. The need for an effective educational system to supply an informed labor force is paramount, as these children and their teacher at a nursery school near Manama attest.

al-Khalifas belong to the same clan as the al-Sabahs, the rulers of Kuwait, and are distantly related to the Saudi Arabian royal family.)

A British Protectorate

In the 1800s, Bahrain came under British protection in the same way as other Gulf states. The ruler Shaykh Isa, whose reign was one of the world's longest (1869–1932), signed an agreement making Britain responsible for Bahrain's defense and foreign policy. He also agreed not to give any concessions for oil exploration with-

out British approval. The agreement was important because the British were already developing oil fields in Iran. Control of oil in another area would give them an added source of fuel for the new weaponry of tanks and oil-powered warships of World War I. The early development of Bahrain's oil fields and the guidance of British political advisers helped prepare the country for independence.

INDEPENDENCE

Bahrain became fully independent in 1971. The British encouraged Bahrain to join with Qatar and seven small British-protected Gulf states, the Trucial States, in a federation. However, Bahrain and Qatar felt that they were more advanced economically, politically, and socially than were the Trucial States and therefore did not need to federate.

A mild threat to Bahrain's independence came from Iran. In 1970, Shah Mohammed Reza Pahlavi claimed Bahrain, on the basis of Iran's sixteenth-century occupation plus the fact that a large number of Bahrainis were descended from Iranian emigrants. The United Nations discussed the issue and recommended that Bahrain be given its independence, on the grounds that "the people of Bahrain wish to gain recognition of their identity in a fully independent and sovereign state."[1] The shah accepted the resolution, and Iran made no further claims on Bahrain during his lifetime.

The gradual development of democracy in Bahrain reached a peak after independence. Shaykh Khalifa (now called emir) approved a new Constitution and a law establishing an elected National Assembly of 30 members. The Assembly met for the first time in 1973; but, only 2 years later, it was dissolved by the emir.

What Had Happened?
Bahrain is an example of a problem common in the Middle East: the conflict between traditional authority and popular democracy. Fuad Khuri describes the problem as one of a "tribally controlled government that rules by historical right, opposed to a community-based urban population seeking to participate in government through elections. The first believes and acts as if government is an earned right, the other seeks to modify government and subject it to a public vote."[2]

Governmental authority in Bahrain is defined as hereditary in the al-Khalifa family, according to the 1973 Constitution. The succession passes from the ruling emir to his eldest son. Since Bahrain has no tradition of representative government or political parties, the National Assembly was set up to broaden the political process without going through the lengthy period of conditioning necessary to establish a multiparty system. Members were expected to debate laws prepared by the Council of Ministers and to assist with budget preparation. But as things turned out, Assembly members spent their time arguing with one another or criticizing the ruler instead of dealing with issues. When the emir dissolved the Assembly, he said that it was preventing the government from doing what it was supposed to do.

Since that time, government in Bahrain has reverted to its traditional patriarchal-authority structure. But the country's increased involvement in regional affairs after the Gulf War brought about some changes in the structure. In 1993, the emir formed a Shura (Council of State), whose function is to "initiate debate" on national social, educational, cultural, and health issues before they are codified into law. In addition to members of the ruling family, the Council includes business and industry representatives.

FOREIGN RELATIONS
Bahrain's strategic location in the Persian Gulf and its British-built naval base have been key factors in U.S. Middle East policy for some years, notably during the Iran–Iraq War, when the base became a staging point for U.S. convoy escort vessels. U.S. involvement in the region was greatly expanded in the aftermath of the Gulf War, and Bahrain became a "frontline state" in the American government's containment policy toward Iran and Iraq. In 1995, Manama was designated as permanent headquarters for the newly constituted U.S. Fifth Fleet. However, the U.S. presence, coupled with Bahrain's homegrown Shia fundamentalist movement (encouraged by Iran), has caused considerable friction. In May 1997, concern over possible attacks on Americans in the emirate led the U.S. Navy to put Manama off limits as a liberty port and establish a curfew for land-based personnel, some 1,000 of whom are stationed there.

Bahrain's only serious foreign-policy problem since independence has involved neighboring Qatar. In 1992, the Qatari ruler unilaterally extended Qatar's territorial waters to include an area offshore in the Gulf controlled by Bahrain since the 1930s under a British-arranged border-demarcation agreement. Bahrain responded with a claim to territory on the Qatari mainland that had been under Bahrain's control prior to the twentieth century. Finally, the two countries agreed to refer their dispute to the International Court of Justice. The ICJ agreed to hear the case, but Qatar's ruler said that he would not be bound by its verdict.

The dispute with Qatar has hampered the effectiveness of the Gulf Cooperation Council, which was established in 1981 as a mutual defense organization by the Gulf states. In addition to Bahrain, the members are Kuwait, Oman, Qatar, Saudi Arabia, and the United Arab Emirates. The GCC was formed not only to coordinate defense policies but also to promote greater economic cooperation. However, the dispute between Bahrain and Qatar caused the former to boycott the GCC summit meeting in 1996 due to the "unfriendly attitude" of the latter.

THREATS TO NATIONAL SECURITY
The 1979 Revolution in Iran caused much concern in Bahrain. The new Iranian government revived the old territorial claim, and a Teheran-based Islamic Front for the Liberation of Bahrain called on Shia Muslims in Bahrain to overthrow the Sunni regime of the emir. In 1981, the government arrested a group of Shia Bahrainis and others and charged them with a plot against the state, backed by Iran. The plotters had expected support from the Shia population, but this did not materialize. After seeing the results of the Iranian Revolution, few Bahraini Shia Muslims wanted the Iranian form of fundamentalist Islamic government. In 1982, 73 defendants were given sentences ranging from 7 years to life imprisonment. Bahrain's prime minister told a local newspaper that the plot didn't represent a real danger, "but we are not used to this sort of thing so we had to take strong action."[3]

For some time thereafter, the Shia community was inactive politically. Some 100 exiled Shia activists were pardoned by the emir and allowed to return. Fundamentalist activities elsewhere, however, have had a spin-off effect on the island nation. In Bahrain's case, opposition demands are essentially political—reinstatement of the National Assembly, multiparty elections, and greater representation of Shia in government. Some 700 demonstrators were arrested in March 1995 after a protest march, and a shadowy organization called Hezbollah Bahrain (said to have ties with the Iran-backed Hezbollah in Lebanon) has carried on a low-level campaign of violence since 1994 that has claimed some 30 lives.

AN OIL-LESS ECONOMY?
Bahrain was an early entrant in the oil business and may be the first Gulf state to face an oil-less future. Current production from its own oil fields is 42,000 barrels per day. The Bahrain Petroleum Company (Bapco) controls all aspects of production, refining, and export. However, Bapco must import 70,000 b/d from Saudi Arabia to keep its refinery operating efficiently.

The country's economic management is characterized by a lack of dynamism and conservative policies, in keeping with its patriarchal political system. This policy has begun to change in recent years; and, although oil exports still account for 80 percent of exports and 60 percent of revenues, the government is aggressively expanding production of other mineral resources. Expansion of liquified-natural-gas plant facilities increased production in

| Periodic occupation of Bahrain by Iran after the Portuguese ouster 1602–1782 | The al-Khalifa family seizes power over other families and groups 1783 | Bahrain becomes a British protectorate 1880 | Independence 1971 | The new Constitution establishes a Constituent Assembly, but the ruler dissolves it shortly thereafter 1973–1975 | 1990s |

Territorial disputes with Qatar

Bahrain takes aggressive steps to revive and diversify its economy

1992 to 170 million cubic feet per day; known reserves are 9 billion cubic feet.

In 1997, Aluminum Bahrain was enlarged to make it the world's biggest smelter, with an output of 500,000 tons yearly, representing 50 percent of non-oil exports.

Bahrain's ship-repair facilities were expanded during the Iran–Iraq War and have continued to grow. The Arab Shipbuilding and Repair Yard, built in 1968 by the Organization of Arab Oil Exporting Countries, refitted 113 ships in 1996, providing revenues of $72.6 million, a 10.8 percent increase over 1995.

INTERNATIONAL FINANCE

During the Civil War in Lebanon, Bahrain encouraged the establishment of Offshore Banking Units in order to replace Lebanon as a regional finance center. OBUs are set up to attract deposits from governments or large financial organizations such as the World Bank as well as to make loans for development projects. OBUs are "offshore" in the sense that a Bahraini cannot open a checking account or borrow money. However, OBUs bring funds into Bahrain without interfering with local growth or undercutting local banks.

The drop in world oil prices in the 1980s and the Iraqi occupation of Kuwait seriously disrupted the OBU system, and a number of offshore banks were closed. However, recent changes in government and a more aggressive posture on the part of Bahraini financiers have renewed interest in OBUs, mainly by specialized investment banks buying into companies in the growing markets of East Asia and the Pacific.

Bahrain's recovery from economic doldrums and the Gulf War has been strengthened by the Bahrain Development Company, formed in 1992, which has already generated the opening of about 20 new manufacturing plants representing foreign investors. Each plant is required by law to hire 60 percent local labor. And the Bahrain stock exchange was opened to foreign firms in June 1992, under new regulations designed to attract foreign investment in the Bahraini economy.

THE FUTURE

One key to Bahrain's future may be found in a Koranic verse (*Sura XIII, II*):

Lo! Allah changeth not the condition of a people until they first change what is in their hearts.

For a brief time after independence, the state experimented with representative government. But the hurly-burly of politics, with its factional rivalries, trade-offs, and compromises found in many Western democratic systems, did not suit the Bahraini temperament or experience. Democracy takes time to mature. Emile Nakhleh reminds us that "any serious attempt to democratize the regime will ultimately set tribal legitimacy and popular sovereignty on a collision course."[4]

Due to its small size and proximity to other patriarchally governed states, Bahrain is unlikely to move rapidly to establish representative government with popular participation beyond the steps already taken. In any case, the system of holding weekly *majlises* (public assemblies) gives Bahrainis ready access to the ruler.

However, pressure for greater democratization, particularly from the educated professional classes, brought results in 1995, as the ruling family's hold over the authority structure lessened. In June, the first cabinet shakeup in 20 years reduced the number of family members holding ministerial posts to seven, with four of the remaining nine posts allotted to Sunnis and five to Shias. But the longevity of the emir's rule—4 decades at the head of a patriarchal family system deeply embedded in Bahraini society—suggested that any major changes in the system lay well in the future.

NOTES

1. UN Security Council *Resolution 287*, 1970. Quoted from Emile Nakhleh, *Bahrain* (Lexington, KY: Lexington Books, 1976), p. 9.

2. Fuad I. Khuri, *Tribe and State in Bahrain* (Chicago: University of Chicago Press, 1981), p. 219.

3. *Gulf Daily News* (May 15, 1982).

4. Nakhleh, *op. cit.*, p. 11.

DEVELOPMENT

Expansion of non-oil industries has compensated to some degree for the decline in oil and gas production. In 1996, this sector of the economy accounted for just 18% of GDP. However, Bahrain's share of output from the Abu Saafa oil field owned jointly with Saudi Arabia was increased by mutual agreement.

FREEDOM

With the 1973 Constitution and the National Assembly both suspended, political rights for Bahrainis remain in limbo. For its continued detention of opposition leaders, particularly Shia clerics, and the death of one of them while in police custody, Bahrain was criticized by the U.S. State Department for violation of human rights in a 1996 report.

HEALTH/WELFARE

A 1993 labor law allows unions to organize and bargain with their employers and guarantees equal pay for all workers, male and female alike.

ACHIEVEMENTS

Bahrain's chronic freshwater shortage has been partially solved by expansion in 1997 of its two desalination plants to a capacity of 35 million gallons per day, meeting 50% of domestic needs. The island nation's importance as a hub of international finance was underscored in 1996, when Citibank opened the first Islamic bank there.

Egypt (Arab Republic of Egypt)

GEOGRAPHY
Area in Square Kilometers (Miles):
1,001,258 (386,258) (about the size of
Oregon and Texas combined)
Capital (Population): Cairo (more than
11 million in greater Cairo area)
Climate: dry, hot summers; moderate
winters

PEOPLE

Population
Total: 63,575,000
Annual Growth Rate: 1.9%
Rural/Urban Population Ratio: 55/45
Ethnic Makeup: 99% Eastern Hamitic
(Egyptian, Bedouin, Arab, Nubian); 1%
Greek, Italian, Syro-Lebanese
Major Languages: Arabic; English

Health
Life Expectancy at Birth: 59 years
(male); 63 years (female)
Infant Mortality Rate (Ratio): 75/1,000
Average Caloric Intake: 116% of FAO
minimum
Physicians Available (Ratio): 1/1,698

Religions
94% Muslim (mostly Sunni); 6%
Coptic Christian and others

Education
Adult Literacy Rate: 62%

COMMUNICATION
Telephones: 600,000
Newspapers: 11 dailies in Cairo, 6 in
Alexandria

TRANSPORTATION
Highways—Kilometers (Miles): 47,387
(29,569)

Railroads—Kilometers (Miles): 4,895
(3,054)
Usable Airfields: 91

GOVERNMENT
Type: republic
Independence Date: February 28, 1922
Head of State/Government: President
Mohammed Hosni Mubarak; Prime
Minister Kamal al-Ganzouri
Political Parties: National Democratic
Party; Socialist Labor Party; Socialist
Liberal Party (main opposition parties);
New Wafd Party; National Progressive
Unionist Grouping; Democratic
Unionist Party; Umma Party;
Democratic People's Party; Social
Justice Party; others
Suffrage: universal and compulsory at 18

MILITARY
Number of Armed Forces: 370,000
*Military Expenditures (% of Central
Government Expenditures):* 8.2%
Current Hostilities: none

ECONOMY
Currency ($ U.S. Equivalent): 3.39
Egyptian pounds = $1
Per Capita Income/GDP: $2,490/$151.5
billion
Inflation Rate: 7%
Total Foreign Debt: $30 billion
Natural Resources: petroleum and
natural gas; iron ore; phosphates;
manganese; limestone; gypsum; talc;
asbestos; lead; zinc
Agriculture: cotton; rice; onions; beans;
citrus fruits; wheat; corn; barley;
sugarcane
Industry: textiles; food processing;
chemicals; petroleum; construction;
cement; light manufacturing

FOREIGN TRADE
Exports: $4.9 billion
Imports: $13.8 billion

Rebuilding Egypt's Ancient Wonders

Some 2,500 years ago, Ptolemy I, founder of the Egyptian imperial line
that ended with Cleopatra, built a magnificent library at Alexandria, his
capital. The Alexandria library held half a million manuscripts and drew
scholars from the entire Mediterranean world to its portals. Seventeen
centuries ago, it was destroyed by fire; the exact site is unknown today.
But completion of a new high-tech Alexandria Library by Egyptian architects and builders in 1998 will again focus attention on the grandeur of
Egypt's storied past. The building is designed as a huge circle tilted toward
the sky, with a diaphragm foundation 3 feet thick and 100 feet deep to
keep seawater from entering (part of it is below sea level).

EGYPT

The Arab Republic of Egypt is located at the extreme northeastern corner of Africa, with part of its territory—the Sinai Peninsula—serving as a land bridge to Southwest Asia. The country's total land area is approximately 386,000 square miles. However, 96 percent of this area is uninhabitable desert. Except for a few scattered oases, the only settled and cultivable area is a narrow strip along the Nile River. The vast majority of Egypt's population is concentrated in this strip; thus, real population density is very high. Urban density is also very high. The combination of rapid population growth and limited arable land presents serious obstacles to national development.

Modern Egypt identifies itself as an Arab nation and has taken an active part in the development of other Arab states. Not one of the wealthier Arab countries in natural resources, it has a higher level of education and more skilled professionals than do most other Arab countries. Egyptian teachers, doctors, nurses, engineers, and agricultural specialists have contributed significantly to the development of Arab countries that are wealthier but do not have many skilled workers, such as Libya, Kuwait, and Saudi Arabia.

HISTORY

Although Egypt is a twentieth-century nation in terms of independence from foreign control, it has a distinct national identity and a rich culture that date back thousands of years. The modern Egyptians take great pride in their brilliant past; this sense of the past gives them patience and a certain fatalism that enable them to withstand misfortunes that would crush most peoples. The Egyptian peasants, the *fellahin,* are as stoic and enduring as the water buffaloes they use to do their plowing. Since the time of the pharaohs, Egypt has been invaded many times, and it was under foreign control for most of its history. When Gamal Abdel Nasser, the first president of the new Egyptian republic, came to power in 1954, he said that he was the first native Egyptian to rule the country in nearly 3,000 years.

It is often said that Egypt is the "gift of the Nile." The mighty river, flowing north to the Mediterranean with an enormous annual spate that deposited rich silt along its banks, attracted nomadic peoples to settle there as early as 6000 B.C. They developed a productive agriculture based on the river's seasonal floods. They lived in plastered mud huts in small, compact villages. Their villages were not too different from those one sees today in parts of the Nile Delta.

Each village had its "headman," the head of some family more prosperous or industrious (or both) than the others. The arrival of other nomadic desert peoples gradually brought about the evolution of an organized system of government. Since the Egyptian villagers did not have nearby mountains or wild forests to retreat into, they were easily governable.

The institution of kingship was well established in Egypt by 2000 B.C., and in the time of Ramses II (1300–1233 B.C.), Egyptian monarchs extended their power over a large part of the Middle East. All Egyptian rulers were called pharaohs, although there was no hereditary system of descent and many different dynasties ruled during the country's first 2,000 years of existence. The pharaohs had their capital at Thebes, but they built other important cities on the banks of the Nile. Using simple yet accurate measuring instruments and much human labor, the pharaohs built such extraordinary structures as the Pyramids, the Sphinx, and royal tombs and temples. In 1996, archaeologists discovered the world's oldest paved canal, built more than 4,500 years ago near Pharaoh Chephren's pyramid at Giza. Lined with limestone, it probably carried water from the Nile for ritual washing of the pharaoh before burial.

In the first century B.C., Egypt became part of the Roman Empire. The city of Alexandria, founded by Alexander the Great, became a center of Greek and Roman learning and culture. Later, it became a center of Christianity. The Egyptian Cop-

(UN photo/John Isaac)

These pyramids at Giza are among the most famous mementos of Egypt's past.

tic Church was one of the earliest organized churches. The Copts, direct descendants of the early Egyptians, are the principal minority group in Egypt today. When Arab invaders brought Islam to Egypt, they were welcomed by the Copts. In return, Arab Islamic rulers protected the Copts, respecting their Christian faith and not requiring conversion to Islam, although some Copts did convert. The Copts have been useful to Islamic governments in Egypt ever since, because of their high level of education and management skills.

Egypt also had, until very recently, a small but long-established Jewish community that held a similar position under various Muslim rulers. Most of the Jews emigrated to Israel after 1948. Eleven thousand were deported in 1956 after the Israeli invasion of the Suez Canal Zone.

THE INFLUENCE OF ISLAM

Islam was the major formative influence in the development of modern Egyptian society. Islamic armies from Arabia invaded Egypt in the seventh century A.D. Large numbers of nomadic Arabs followed, settling the Nile Valley until, over time, they became the majority in the population. Egypt was under the rule of the caliphs ("successors" of the Prophet Muhammad) until the tenth century, when a Shia group broke away and formed a separate government. The leaders of this group also called themselves caliphs. To show their independence, they founded a new capital in the desert south of Alexandria. The name they chose for their new capital was prophetic: al-Qahira—"City of War"—the modern city of Cairo.

In the sixteenth century, Egypt became a province of the Ottoman Empire. It was then under the rule of the Mamluks, originally slaves or prisoners of war who were converted to Islam. Many Mamluk leaders had been freed and then acquired their own slaves. They formed a military aristocracy, constantly fighting with one another for land and power. The Ottomans found it simpler to leave Egypt under Mamluk control, merely requiring periodic tribute and taxes.

EGYPT ENTERS THE MODERN WORLD

At the end of the eighteenth century, rivalry between Britain and France for control of trade in the Mediterranean and the sea routes to India involved Egypt. The French general Napoleon Bonaparte led an expedition to Egypt in 1798. However, the British, in cooperation with Ottoman forces, drove the French from Egypt. A confused struggle for power followed. The victor was Muhammad Ali, an Albanian

officer in the Ottoman garrison at Cairo. In 1805, the Ottoman sultan appointed him governor of Egypt.

Although he was not an Egyptian, Muhammad Ali had a vision of Egypt under his rule as a rich and powerful country. He began by forming a new army consisting of native Egyptians instead of mercenaries or slave-soldiers. This army was trained by European advisers and gave a good account of itself in campaigns, performing better than the regular Ottoman armies.[1]

Muhammad Ali set up an organized, efficient tax-collection system. He suppressed the Mamluks and confiscated all the lands that they had seized from Egyptian peasants over the years, lifting a heavy tax burden from peasant backs. He took personal charge of all Egypt's exports. Cotton, a new crop, became the major Egyptian export and became known the world over for its high quality. Dams and irrigation canals were dug to improve cultivation and expand arable land. Although Muhammad Ali grew rich in the process of carrying out these policies, he was concerned for the welfare of the peasantry. He once said, "One must guide this people as one guides children; to leave them to their own devices would be to render them subject to all the disorders from which I have saved them."[2]

Muhammad Ali's successors were named *khedives* ("viceroys"), in that they ruled Egypt in theory on behalf of their superior, the sultan. In practice, they acted as independent rulers. Under the khedives, Egypt was again drawn into European power politics, with unfortunate results. The Suez Canal was opened in 1869, during the reign of Khedive Ismail. Ismail was the most ambitious of Muhammad Ali's descendants. The Suez Canal was only one of the grandiose public-works projects by which he intended to make Egypt the equal of any European power. But he used up Egypt's revenues and finally had to sell the Egyptian government's share in the company that had built the canal to the British government in order to pay his debts.

Ismail's successors were forced to accept British control over Egyptian finances. In 1882, a revolt of army officers threatened to overthrow the khedive. The British intervened and established a de facto protectorate, keeping the khedive in office in order to avoid conflict with the Ottomans.

EGYPTIAN NATIONALISM

The British protectorate lasted from 1882 to 1956. An Egyptian nationalist movement gradually developed in the early 1900s, inspired by the teachings of religious leaders and Western-educated officials in the khedives' government. They advocated a revival of Islam and its strengthening to enable Egypt and other Islamic lands to resist European control.

During World War I, Egypt was a major base for British campaigns against the Ottoman Empire. The British formally declared their protectorate over Egypt in order to "defend" the country, since legally it was still an Ottoman province. The British worked with Arab nationalist leaders against the Turks and promised to help them form an independent Arab nation after the war. Egyptian nationalists were active in the Arab cause, and although at that time they did not particularly care about being a part of a new Arab nation, they wanted independence from Britain.

At the end of World War I, Egyptian nationalist leaders organized the *Wafd* (Arabic for "delegation"). In 1918, the Wafd presented demands to the British for the complete independence of Egypt. The British rejected the demands, saying that Egypt was not ready for self-government. The Wafd then turned to violence, organizing boycotts, strikes, and terrorist attacks on British soldiers and on Egyptians accused of cooperating with the British.

Under pressure, the British finally abolished the protectorate in 1922. But they retained control over Egyptian foreign policy, defense, and communications as well as the protection of minorities and foreign residents and of Sudan, which had been part of Egypt since the 1880s. Thus, Egypt's "independence" was a hollow shell.

Egypt did regain control over internal affairs. The government was set up as a constitutional monarchy under a new king, Fuad. Political parties were allowed, and in elections for a Parliament in 1923, the Wafd emerged as the dominant party. But neither Fuad nor the son who succeeded him, Farouk, trusted Wafd leaders. They feared that the Wafd was working to establish a republic. For their part, the Wafd leaders did not believe that the rulers were seriously interested in the good of the country. So Egypt waddled along for 2 decades with little progress.

THE EGYPTIAN REVOLUTION

During the years of the monarchy, the Egyptian Army gradually developed a corps of professional officers, most of them from lower- or middle-class Egyptian backgrounds. They were strongly patriotic and resented what they perceived to be British cultural snobbery as well as Britain's continual influence over Egyptian affairs.

The training school for these young officers was the Egyptian Military Academy, founded in 1936. Among them was Gamal Abdel Nasser, the eldest son of a village postal clerk. Nasser and his fellow officers were already active in anti-British demonstrations by the time they entered the academy. During World War II, the British, fearing a German takeover of Egypt, reinstated the protectorate. Egypt became the main British military base in the Middle East. This action galvanized the officers into forming a revolutionary movement. Nasser said at the time that it roused in him the seeds of revolt. "It made [us] realize that there is a dignity to be retrieved and defended."[3]

When Jewish leaders in Palestine organized Israel in May 1948, Egypt, along with other nearby Arab countries, sent troops to destroy the new state. Nasser and several of his fellow officers were sent to the front. The Egyptian Army was defeated; Nasser himself was trapped with his unit, was wounded, and was rescued only by an armistice. Even more shocking to the young officers was the evident corruption and weakness of their own government. The weapons that they received were inferior and often defective, battle orders were inaccurate, and their superiors proved to be incompetent in strategy and tactics.

Nasser and his fellow officers attributed their defeat not to their own weaknesses but to their government's failures. When they returned to Egypt, they were determined to overthrow the monarchy. They formed a secret organization, the Free Officers. It was not the only organization dedicated to the overthrow of the monarchy, but it was the best disciplined and had the general support of the army.

On July 23, 1952, the Free Officers launched their revolution. It came 6 months after "Black Saturday," the burning of Cairo by mobs protesting the continued presence of British troops in Egypt. The Free Officers persuaded King Farouk to abdicate, and they declared Egypt a republic. A nine-member Revolutionary Command Council (RCC) was established to govern the country.

EGYPT UNDER NASSER

In his self-analytical book *The Philosophy of the Revolution,* Nasser wrote, " I always imagine that in this region in which we live there is a role wandering aimlessly about in search of an actor to play it."[4] Nasser saw himself as playing that role. Previously, he had operated behind the scenes, but always as the leader to whom the other Free Officers looked up. By 1954, Nasser had emerged as Egypt's leader. When the monarchy was formally abolished in 1954, he became president,

prime minister, and head of the RCC. Cynics said that Nasser came along when Egypt was ready for another king; the Egyptians could not function without one!

Nasser came to power determined to restore dignity and status to Egypt, to eliminate foreign control, and to make his country the leader of a united Arab world. It was an ambitious set of goals, and Nasser was only partly successful in attaining them. But in his struggles to achieve these goals, he brought considerable status to Egypt. The country became a leader of the "Third World" of Africa and Asia, developing nations newly freed from foreign control.

Nasser was successful in removing the last vestiges of British rule from Egypt. British troops were withdrawn from the Suez Canal Zone, and Nasser nationalized the canal in 1956, taking over the man-

agement from the private foreign company that had operated it since 1869. That action made the British furious, since the British government had a majority interest in the company. The British worked out a secret plan with the French and the Israelis, neither of whom liked Nasser, to invade Egypt and overthrow him. British and French paratroopers seized the canal in October 1956, but the United States and the Soviet Union, in an unusual display of cooperation, forced them to withdraw. It was the first of several occasions when Nasser turned military defeat into political victory. It was also one of the few times when Nasser and the United States were on the same side of an issue.

Between 1956 and 1967, Nasser developed a close alliance with the Soviet Union—at least, it seemed that way to the United States. Nasser's pet economic pro-

(UN photo)

In 1952, the Free Officers organization persuaded Egypt's King Farouk to abdicate. The monarchy was formally abolished in 1954, when Gamal Abdel Nasser became Egypt's president, prime minister, and head of the Revolutionary Command Council.

ject was the building of a high dam at Aswan, on the upper Nile, to regulate the annual flow of river water and thus enable Egypt to reclaim new land and develop its agriculture. He applied for aid from the United States through the World Bank to finance the project, but he was turned down, largely due to his publicly expressed hostility toward Israel. Again Nasser turned defeat into a victory of sorts. The Soviet Union agreed to finance the dam, which was completed in 1971, and subsequently to equip and train the Egyptian Army. Thousands of Soviet advisers poured into Egypt, and it seemed to U.S. and Israeli leaders that Egypt had become a dependency of the Soviet Union.

The lowest point in Nasser's career came in June 1967. Israel invaded Egypt and defeated his Soviet-trained army, along with those of Jordan and Syria, and occupied the Sinai Peninsula in a lightning 6-day war. The Israelis were restrained from marching on Cairo only by a United Nations cease-fire. Nasser took personal responsibility for the defeat, calling it *al-Nakba* ("The Catastrophe"). He announced his resignation, but the Egyptian people refused to accept it. The public outcry was so great that he agreed to continue in office. One observer wrote, "The irony was that Nasser had led the country to defeat, but Egypt without Nasser was unthinkable."[5]

Nasser had little success in his efforts to unify the Arab world. One attempt, for example, was a union of Egypt and Syria, which lasted barely 3 years (1958–1961). Egyptian forces were sent to support a new republican government in Yemen after the overthrow of that country's autocratic ruler, but they became bogged down in a civil war there and had to be withdrawn. Other efforts to unify the Arab world also failed. Arab leaders respected Nasser but were unwilling to play second fiddle to him in an organized Arab state. In 1967, after the Arab defeat, Nasser lashed out bitterly at the other Arab leaders. He said, "You issue statements, but we have to fight. If you want to liberate [Palestine] then get in line in front of us."[6]

Inside Egypt, the results of Nasser's 18-year rule were also mixed. Although he talked about developing representative government, Nasser distrusted political parties and remembered the destructive rivalries under the monarchy that had kept Egypt divided and weak. The Wafd and all other political parties were declared illegal. Nasser set up his own political organization to replace them, called the Arab Socialist Union (ASU). It was a mass party, but it had no real power. Nasser and a few close associates ran the government and

controlled the ASU. The associates took their orders directly from Nasser; they called him El-Rais—"The Boss."

As he grew older, Nasser, plagued by health problems, became more dictatorial, secretive, and suspicious. The Boss tolerated no opposition and ensured tight control over Egypt with a large police force and a secret service that monitored activities in every village and town.

Nasser died in 1970. Ironically, his death came on the heels of a major policy success: the arranging of a truce between the Palestine Liberation Organization and the government of Jordan. Despite his health problems, Nasser had seemed indestructible, and his death came as a shock. Millions of Egyptians followed his funeral cortege through the streets of Cairo, weeping and wailing over the loss of their beloved Rais.

ANWAR AL-SADAT

Nasser was succeeded by his vice president Anwar al-Sadat, in accordance with constitutional procedure. Sadat had been one of the original Free Officers and had worked with Nasser since their early days at the Military Academy. In the Nasser years, Sadat had come to be regarded as a lightweight, always ready to do whatever The Boss wanted.

Many Egyptians did not even know what Sadat looked like. A popular story was told of an Egyptian peasant in from the country to visit his cousin, a taxi driver. As they drove around Cairo, they passed a large poster of Nasser and Sadat shaking hands. "I know our beloved leader, but who is the man with him?" asked the peasant. "I think he owns that café across the street," replied his cousin.

When Sadat became president, however, it did not take long for the Egyptian people to learn what he looked like. Sadat introduced a "revolution of rectification," which he said was needed to correct the errors of his predecessor.[7] These included too much dependence on the Soviet Union, too much government interference in the economy, and failure to develop an effective Arab policy against Israel. He was a master of timing, taking bold action at unexpected times to advance Egypt's international and regional prestige. Thus, in 1972 he abruptly ordered the 15,000 Soviet advisers in Egypt to leave the country, despite the fact that they were training his army and supplying all his military equipment. His purpose was to reduce Egypt's dependence on one foreign power, and as he had calculated, the United States now came to his aid.

A year later, in October 1973, Egyptian forces crossed the Suez Canal in a surprise attack and broke through Israeli defense

lines in occupied Sinai. The attack was coordinated with Syrian forces invading Israel from the east, through the Golan Heights. The Israelis were driven back with heavy casualties on both fronts, and, although they eventually regrouped and won back most of the lost ground, Sadat felt he had won a moral and psychological victory. After the war, Egyptians believed that they had held their own with the Israelis and had demonstrated Arab ability to handle the sophisticated weaponry of modern warfare.

Anwar al-Sadat's most spectacular action took place in 1977. It seemed to him that the Arab–Israeli conflict was at a stalemate. Neither side would budge from its position, and the Egyptian people were angry at having so little to show for the 1973 success. In November, he addressed a hushed meeting of the People's Assembly and said, "Israel will be astonished when it hears me saying . . . that I am ready to go to their own house, to the Knesset itself, to talk to them."[8] And he did so, becoming for a second time the "Hero of the Crossing,"[9] but this time to the very citadel of Egypt's enemy.

Sadat's successes in foreign policy, culminating in the 1979 peace treaty with Israel, gave him great prestige internationally. Receipt of the Nobel Peace Prize, jointly with Israeli prime minister Menachem Begin, confirmed his status as a peacemaker. His pipe-smoking affability and sartorial elegance endeared him to U.S. policymakers.

The view that more and more Egyptians held of their world-famous leader was less flattering. Religious leaders and conservative Muslims objected to Sadat's luxurious style of living. The poor resented having to pay more for basic necessities. The educated classes were angry about Sadat's claim that the political system had become more open and democratic when, in fact, it had not. The Arab Socialist Union was abolished and several new political parties were allowed to organize. But the ASU's top leaders merely formed their own party, the National Democratic Party, headed by Sadat. For all practical purposes, Egypt under Sadat was even more of a single-party state under an authoritarian leader than it had been in Nasser's time.

Sadat's economic policies also worked to his disadvantage. In 1974, he announced a new program for postwar recovery, *Infitah* ("Opening"). It would be an open-door policy, bringing an end to Nasser's state-run socialist system. Foreign investors would be encouraged to invest in Egypt, and foreign experts would bring their technological knowledge to help develop industries. Infitah, properly applied, would bring an economic miracle to Egypt.

Rather than spur economic growth, however, Infitah made fortunes for a few, leaving the great majority of Egyptians no better off than before. Chief among those who profited were the Sadat family. Corruption among the small ruling class, many of its members newly rich contractors, aroused anger on the part of the Egyptian people. In 1977, the economy was in such bad shape that the government increased bread prices. Riots broke out, and Sadat was forced to cancel the increase.

On October 6, 1981, President Sadat and government leaders were reviewing an armed-forces parade in Cairo to mark the eighth anniversary of the Crossing. Suddenly, a volley of shots rang out from one of the trucks in the parade. Sadat fell, mortally wounded. The assassins, most of them young military men, were immediately arrested. They belonged to *Al Takfir Wal Hijra* ("Repentance and Flight from Sin"), a secret group that advocates the reestablishment of a pure Islamic society in Egypt—by violence, if necessary. Their leader declared that the killing of Sadat was an essential first step in this process.

Islamic fundamentalism developed rapidly in the Middle East after the Iranian Revolution. The success of that revolution was a spur to Egyptian fundamentalists. They accused Sadat of favoring Western capitalism through his Infitah policy, of making peace with the "enemy of Islam" (Israel), and of not being a good Muslim. At their trial, Sadat's assassins said that they had acted to rid Egypt of an unjust ruler, a proper action under the laws of Islam.

Sadat may have contributed to his early death (he was 63) by a series of actions taken earlier in the year. About 1,600 people were arrested in September 1981 in a massive crackdown on religious unrest. They included not only religious leaders but also journalists, lawyers, intellectuals, provincial governors, and leaders of the country's small but growing opposition parties. Many of them were not connected with any fundamentalist Islamic organization. It seemed to most Egyptians that Sadat had overreacted, and at that point, he lost the support of the nation. In contrast to Nasser's funeral, few tears were shed at Sadat's. His funeral was attended mostly by foreign dignitaries. One of them said that Sadat had been buried without the people and without the army.

MUBARAK IN POWER

Vice President Hosni Mubarak, former Air Force commander and designer of Egypt's

(UN photo/Muldoon)

Nasser died in 1970 and was succeeded by Vice President Anwar al-Sadat. Sadat, virtually unknown by the Egyptian people, took many bold steps in cementing his role as leader of Egypt.

1973 success against Israel, succeeded Sadat without incident. Mubarak dealt firmly with Islamic fundamentalism at the beginning of his regime. He was given emergency powers and approved death sentences for five of Sadat's assassins in 1982. But he moved cautiously in other areas of national life, in an effort to disassociate himself from some of Sadat's more unpopular policies. The economic policy of Infitah, which had led to widespread graft and corruption, was abandoned; stiff sentences were handed out to a number of entrepreneurs and capitalists, including Sadat's brother-in-law and several associates of the late president.

Mubarak also began rebuilding bridges with other Arab states that had been damaged after the peace treaty with Israel. Egypt was readmitted to membership in the Islamic Conference, the Islamic Development Bank, the Arab League, and other Arab regional organizations. In 1990 the Arab League headquarters was moved from Tunis back to Cairo, its original lo-

cation. Egypt backed Iraq with arms and advisers in its war with Iran, but Mubarak broke with Saddam Hussein after the invasion of Kuwait, accusing the Iraqi leader of perfidy. Some 35,000 Egyptian troops served with the UN–U.S. coalition during the Gulf War; and, as a result of these efforts, the country resumed its accustomed role as the focal point of Arab politics.

Despite the peace treaty, relations with Israel continued to be difficult. One bone of contention was removed in 1989 with the return of the Israeli-held enclave of Taba, in the Sinai Peninsula, to Egyptian control. It had been operated as an Israeli beach resort.

The return of Taba strengthened the government's claim that the 10-year-old peace treaty had been valuable overall in advancing Egypt's interests. The sequence of agreements between the Palestine Liberation Organization and Israel for a sovereign Palestinian entity, along with Israel's improved relations with its other

Arab neighbors, contributed to a substantial thaw in the Egyptian "cold peace" with its former enemy. In March 1995, a delegation from Israel's Knesset arrived in Cairo, the first such parliamentary group to visit Egypt since the peace treaty.

But relations worsened after the election in 1996 of Benjamin Netanyahu as head of a new Israeli government. Egypt had strongly supported the Oslo accords for a Palestinian state, and it had set up a free zone for transit of Palestinian products in 1995. The Egyptian view that Netanyahu was not adhering to the accords led to a "war of words" between the two countries. Israeli group tours were advised that they were unwelcome in Egypt. The Egyptian newspaper *Al-Ahram* halted publication of cartoons by a popular Israeli-American cartoonist because he had served in the Israeli Army; and, in 1997, Egyptian opposition newspapers accused Israel of defiling the virtue of Egyptian young women through sales of an aphrodisiac "sex gum"!

Internal Politics
Although Mubarak's unostentatious lifestyle and firm leadership encouraged confidence among the Egyptian regime, the system that he inherited from his predecessors remained largely impervious to change. The first free multiparty national elections held since the 1952 Revolution took place in 1984, although they were not entirely free, because a law requiring political parties to win at least 8 percent of the popular vote limited party participation. Mubarak was reelected easily for a full 6-year term (he was the only candidate), and his ruling National Democratic Party won 73 percent of seats in the Assembly. The New Wafd Party was the only party able to meet the 8 percent requirement.

New elections for the Assembly in 1987 indicated how far Egypt's embryonic democracy had progressed under Mubarak. This time, four opposition parties aside from his own party presented candidates. Although the National Democratic Party's plurality was still a hefty 69.6 percent, 17 percent of the electorate voted for candidates from a coalition of the Socialist Labor and Liberal Socialist Parties plus members of the newly respectable Muslim Brotherhood, who were running as independents. The New Wafd's percentage of the vote rose to 10.9 percent. A huge banner in downtown Cairo on election day proclaimed: "Citizens: The Phony Parliament Is Over. The Future Is Up To You." Although charges of voting irregularities—a longstanding Egyptian tradition—were made by the opposition, the ruling party's success and the fact that the National Unionist Progressive Party (Tagammu), the major leftist group, failed to win a seat, indicated a broad national preference for Mubarak's brand of secular representation.

AT WAR WITH FUNDAMENTALISM
Egypt's seemingly intractable social problems—high unemployment, an inadequate job market flooded annually by new additions to the labor force, chronic budgetary deficits, and a bloated and inefficient bureaucracy, to name a few—have played into the hands of Islamic fundamentalists, those who would build a new Egyptian state based on the laws of Islam. Although they form part of a larger fundamentalist movement in the Islamic world, one that would replace existing secular regimes with regimes that adhere completely to spiritual law and custom (*Shari'a*), Egypt's fundamentalists do not harbor expansionist goals. Their goal is to replace the Mubarak regime with a more purely "Islamic" one, faithful to the laws and principles of the religion and dominated by religious leaders.

Egypt's fundamentalists are broadly grouped under the organizational name Al-Gamaa al-Islamiya, with the more militant ones forming subgroups such as the Vanguard of Islam and Islamic Jihad, itself an outgrowth of al-Takfir wal-Hijra, which had been responsible for the assassination of Anwar Sadat. Al-Gamaa differs from the mainstream Muslim Brotherhood (which the Mubarak regime tolerates as an opposition although refusing to recognize it as a political party) in advocating violence as necessary to establish a true Islamic government in the country. During Mubarak's early years in power, he kept a tight lid on violence. But in the 1990s, the growing strength of the fundamentalist movement, along with the government's failure to improve the economy, led to an upsurge of violence that has destabilized Egypt to a greater degree than any other Islamic country except Algeria.

Initially, violence was aimed at the security forces, but from 1992 on, the fundamentalists' strategy shifted to attacks on vulnerable targets such as foreign tourists and the Coptic Christian minority. Several dozen Copts were killed, and bearded young Gamaa militants forced Copt business owners to pay "protection money" in order to continue operating their various businesses.

In 1993, foreign tourists became the target as the militants stepped up their campaign. Four tourists were killed by a gunman in the lobby of a plush Cairo hotel in October, and tourist buses were attacked at several popular sites. As a result, many tour operators abroad cancelled their bookings, leading to a 30 percent decline in tourism revenues. However, the government's successful handling of security at the 1994 UN Population Conference in Cairo, which brought some 15,000 visitors to Egypt, gave a boost to the important tourism industry.

One important reason for the rise in fundamentalist violence stemmed from the government's ineptness in meeting social crises. After the disastrous earthquake of October 1992, Islamic fundamentalist groups were first to provide aid to the victims, distributing $1,000 to each family made homeless, while the cumbersome, multilayered government bureaucracy took weeks to respond to the crisis. Similarly, the Gamaa established a network of Islamic schools, hospitals, clinics, day-care centers, and even small industries in poor districts such as Cairo's Imbaba quarter.

The Mubarak government's response to rising violence has been one of extreme repression. Tough new antiterrorism laws passed by the Assembly established the death penalty for antistate activities and extended the detention period indefinitely. Some 770 members of the Vanguard of Islam were tried and convicted of subversion in 1993. The crackdown left Egypt almost free from violence for several years. But in 1996, al-Gamaa al-Islamiya and two other hitherto unknown Islamic militant groups, Assiut Terrorist Organization and Kotbion (named for a Muslim Brotherhood leader executed in 1966 for an attempt to kill President Nasser), resumed terrorist activities. Eighteen Greek tourists were murdered in April, and the State Security Court sentenced five Assiut members to death for killing police and civilians in a murderous rampage. At their trial, they chanted "God make a staircase of our skulls to Your glory," waving Korans in their prisoner cage in an eerie replay of the trials of Sadat's assassins.

An unfortunate result of government repression of the militants is that Egypt, traditionally an open and tolerant society, has become a totalitarian state, one in which civil rights are routinely suspended. Arbitrary arrest and detention without charges for indefinite periods, trials of militants before military courts with no defense lawyers present, and the use of torture to extract "confessions" are so widespread that international human rights organizations such as Amnesty International have lodged protests with the United Nations. In 1995, the regime cast its net over the Muslim Brotherhood, arresting 28 of its leaders despite the Brotherhood's formal renunciation of violence and commitment to peaceful change.

| Period of the pharaohs 2500–671 B.C. | The Persian conquest, followed by Macedonians and rule by Ptolemies 671–30 B.C. | Egypt becomes a Roman province 30 B.C. | Invading Arabs bring Islam A.D. 641 | The founding of Cairo 969 | Egypt becomes an Ottoman province 1517–1800 | Napoleon's invasion, followed by the rise to power of Muhammad Ali 1798–1831 |

Due to the extremism of methods employed by both sides, the conflict between the regime and the fundamentalists has begun to polarize Egyptian society. As a prominent judge noted, "Islam has turned from a religion to an ideology. It has become a threat to Egypt, to civilization and to humanity."[10] In their struggle to overthrow the regime, the fundamentalists have either enlisted the support of or have declared war on scholars, journalists, teachers, and other secular intellectuals who do not openly advocate the fundamentalists' views. A celebrated case involved a Cairo University professor who was charged with apostasy by Islamist lawyers, on the grounds that his academic writings defamed the religion. The professor, Nasr Abu Zaid, was tried under *hisba,* a provision in Islamic law that permits legal action against Muslims for apostasy or heresy. A lower court dismissed the case; but on appeal to a higher court, the decision was overturned. Abu Zaid was then ordered to divorce his wife, because an apostate could not be married to a Muslim woman. However, in 1996, the Peoples' Assembly passed a law outlawing hisba as inappropriate to the modern world, paving the way for reinstatement of Abu Zaid and reconstitution of his marriage.

With the Egyptian middle and professional classes increasingly polarized between fundamentalism and secularism, the regime moved in 1995 to buttress its position with new restrictions on political life. A law passed by the Assembly in June eliminated freedom of the press; any criticism of the government or the dissemination of any information "harmful to the state, public officials or the economy" is punishable by a $3,000 fine and/or a 5-year jail term. Fear of an Algerian-type scenario was clearly uppermost in government thinking. However, elections for a new National Assembly in November 1995 indicated increased support for the government and the ruling National Democratic Party. Its candidates won 317 of 444 seats—to just 14 for all opposition parties. The remaining seats went to progovernment independent candidates. Opposition leaders charged the government with massive vote fraud, including vote buying, intimidation of voters at polling stations, and stuffing of ballot boxes. Leading Islamist party candidates boycotted the elections. But the government declared them "free and fair," arguing that the ruling party's popularity obviated any need for fraud.

A STRUGGLING ECONOMY

Egypt's economy rests upon a narrow and unstable base, due to rapid demographic growth and limited arable land and because political factors have adversely influenced national development. The country has a relatively high level of education and, as a result, is a net exporter of skilled labor to other Arab countries. But the overproduction of university graduates has produced a bloated and inefficient bureaucracy, as the government is required to provide a position for every graduate who cannot find other employment.

Agriculture is the most important sector of the economy, accounting for 30 percent of national income. The major crops are long-staple cotton and sugarcane. Egyptian agriculture since time immemorial has been based on irrigation from the Nile River. In recent years, greater control of irrigation water through the Aswan High Dam, expansion of land devoted to cotton production, and improved planting methods have begun to show positive results.

A new High Dam at Aswan, completed in 1971 upstream from the original one built in 1906, resulted from a political decision by the Nasser government to seek foreign financing for its program of expansion of cultivable land and generation of electricity for industrialization. When Western lending institutions refused to finance the dam, also for political reasons, Nasser turned to the Soviet Union for help. By 1974, 3 years after its completion, revenues had exceeded construction costs. The dam has made possible the electrification of all of Egypt's villages as well as a fishing industry at Lake Nasser, its reservoir. It proved valuable in providing the agricultural sector with irrigation water during the prolonged 1980–1988 drought, although at sharply reduced levels. However, the increased costs of land reclamation and loss of the sardine fishing grounds along the Mediterranean coast have made the dam a mixed blessing for Egypt.

Egypt was self-sufficient in foodstuffs as recently as the 1970s but now must import 60 percent of its food requirements. Such factors as rapid population growth, rural-to-urban migration with consequent loss of agricultural labor, and Sadat's open-door policy for imports combined to produce this negative food balance. Subsidies for basic commodities, which cost the government nearly $2 billion a year, are an important cause of inflation, since they keep the budget continuously in deficit. Fearing a recurrence of the 1977 Bread Riots, the government kept prices in check. In 1995, however, inflation (30 percent in 1990) dropped to 8 percent as a result of International Monetary Fund–induced stabilization policies. These policies included the elimination of certain basic subsidies (notably fertilizers), the lifting of food-price controls, and other actions.

Egypt has important oil and gas reserves and is a major oil producer. Proven reserves in 1994 were 3.3 billion barrels, with natural gas reserves being 500 million cubic meters. New oil discoveries in the Gulf of Suez and the Western Desert will enable the country to maintain the current level of production of 895,000 barrels per day. Two important natural-gas discoveries in 1996 by Amoco and the Spanish company Repsol increased gas production by 95 million cubic feet per day, placing Egypt on the threshold of being one of the world's top producers.

Egypt also derives revenues from Suez Canal tolls and user fees, from tourism, and from remittances from Egyptian workers abroad, mostly working in Saudi Arabia and other oil-producing Gulf states. The flow of remittances from the approximately 4 million expatriate workers was reduced and then all but cut off with the Iraqi invasion of Kuwait. Egyptians fled from both countries in panic, arriving home as penniless refugees. With unemployment already at 20 percent and housing in short supply, the government faced an enormous assimilation problem apart from its loss of revenue. The United States helped by agreeing to write off $4.5 billion in Egyptian military debts. By 1995, the expatriate crisis caused by returning workers had eased somewhat, with 1 million Egyptian workers employed in Saudi Arabia and smaller numbers in other Arab countries.

One encouraging sign of brighter days is the expansion of local manufacturing

| The Suez Canal opens to traffic 1869 | The United Kingdom establishes a protectorate 1882 | The Free Officers overthrow the monarchy and establish Egypt as a republic 1952 | Nationalization of Suez Canal 1956 | Union with Syria into the United Arab Republic 1958–1961 | The Six-Day War with Israel ends in Israel's occupation of the Gaza Strip and the Sinai Peninsula 1967 | Gamal Abdel Nasser dies; Anwar Sadat succeeds as head of Egypt 1970 | A peace treaty is signed at Camp David between Egypt and Israel 1979 | Sadat is assassinated; he is succeeded by Hosni Mubarak; a crackdown on Islamic fundamentalists results in arrests of several religious leaders 1980s |

1990s

The government employs totalitarian tactics in its battle with fundamentalists

Deep social and economic problems persist

industrics, in line with government efforts to reduce dependence upon imported goods. A 10-year tax exemption plus remission of customs duties on imported machinery have encouraged a number of new business ventures, notably in the clothing industry.

In 1987, Mubarak gained some foreign help for Egypt's cash-strapped economy when agreement was reached with the International Monetary Fund for a standby credit of $325 million over 18 months to allow the country to meet its balance-of-payments deficit. The Club of Paris, a group of public and private banks from various industrialized countries, then rescheduled $12 billion in Egyptian external debts over a 10-year period.

Large-scale foreign aid and more liberal domestic policies have brought about a significant economic recovery in the late 1990s. With agricultural production deregulated and an extensive land reclamation program underway, Egypt's farmers set production records in 1996 in wheat, rice, and corn. These crops covered 50 percent of domestic food needs, with resulting savings in foreign exchange. The cotton harvest for 1996 was 350,000 tons, a 35 percent increase, with 50,000 tons exported as compared with 19,000 tons in 1995.

However, these economic successes must be balanced against Egypt's chronic social problems and the lack of an effective representative political system. The head of the Muslim Brotherhood made the astute observation in a 1993 speech that "the threat is not in the extremist movement. It is in the absence of democratic institutions." Until such institutions are firmly in place, with access to education, full employment, broad political participation, civil rights, and the benefits of growth spread evenly across all levels of society, unrest and efforts to Islamize the government by force are likely to continue.

In this context, the July 1997 declaration by several imprisoned Al-Gamaa leaders that they were discontinuing the use of violence to bring about the "Islamization" of the government suggested that the security forces had finally won their struggle against fundamentalist militants. Leader of Islamic Jihad also endorsed the rejection of violence. However, a massacre of foreign tourists visiting Luxor, in southern Egypt, in November not only hit hard at Egypt's important tourist industry but also indicated that fundamentalist violence was far from dead. Al-Gamaa claimed responsibility for the attack, which killed 58, saying that it was intended to obtain hostages for the release of Shaykh Omar Abdel-Rahman, the leader of its organization now jailed in the United States for complicity in the 1995 bombing of the World Trade Center.

To its credit, the Mubarak government has begun to deal seriously with the economic and social deprivation that is the root cause of Islamic militancy. New development projects have focused on the Western Desert and southern Egypt, traditionally neglected in favor of Cairo and northern Egypt.

NOTES

1. An English observer said, "In arms and firing they are nearly as perfect as European troops." Afaf L. Marsot, *Egypt in the Reign of Muhammad Ali* (Cambridge, England: Cambridge University Press, 1984), p. 132.

2. *Ibid.*, p. 161.

3. Quoted in P. J. Vatikiotis, *Nasser and His Generation* (New York: St. Martin's Press, 1978), p. 35.

4. Gamal Abdel Nasser, *The Philosophy of the Revolution* (Cairo: Ministry of National Guidance, 1954), p. 52.

5. Derek Hopwood, *Egypt: Politics and Society 1945–1981* (London: George Allen and Unwin, 1982), p. 77.

6. Quoted in Vatikiotis, *op. cit.*, p. 245.

7. Hopwood, *op. cit.*, p. 106.

8. David Hirst and Irene Beeson, *Sadat* (London: Faber and Faber, 1981), p. 255.

9. "Banners slung across the broad thoroughfares of central Cairo acclaimed The Hero of the Crossing (of the October 1973 War)." *Ibid.*, pp. 17–18.

10. Said Ashmawy, quoted in "In God He Trusts," *Jerusalem Post Magazine* (July 7, 1995).

DEVELOPMENT

New gas discoveries, which have given the Nile Delta the title "world-class gas basin," along with new oil discoveries, should enable Egypt to keep production at 800,000 b/d and reserves at 3.3 billion barrels. Another positive economic development has been the deepening of the Suez Canal to 58 feet to allow passage of supertankers.

FREEDOM

Egypt's political system is similar to that of France, with extensive powers reserved to the president. Opposition parties are allowed as long as they are not "Islamic" by definition or in scope. But the campaign against fundamentalists has caused the suspension of civil rights and press freedom.

HEALTH/WELFARE

A new project called "Reading for All," sponsored by first lady Suzanne Mubarak, makes books available for all Egyptian youngsters at very low prices. Previously school libraries were so poorly stocked and books so expensive that most youngsters had little exposure to new ideas except through Islamic preaching. The regime has made a strong commitment to education as a means of countering the Islamists.

ACHIEVEMENTS

The Social Fund for Development, set up in 1991 to channel funding to people adversely affected by the changeover to a market-oriented economy, has had considerable success in helping to establish new businesses or expand existing ones. The fund has generated some 70,000 jobs at a cost of $1,400 per job created, a very low outlay.

Iran (Islamic Republic of Iran)

GEOGRAPHY

Area in Square Kilometers (Miles):
1,648,000 (636,294) (about the size of
Alaska and Pennsylvania combined)
Capital (Population): Teheran (6,500,000)
Climate: semiarid; subtropical along
Caspian coast

PEOPLE

Population

Total: 65,780,000
Annual Growth Rate: 1.8%
Rural/Urban Population Ratio: 42/58
Ethnic Makeup: 51% Persian; 24%
Azerbaijani; 7% Kurd; 8%
Mazandarani; 10% others
Major Languages: Farsi; Azeri Turkish;
Kurdish

Health

Life Expectancy at Birth: 66 years
(male); 68 years (female)
Infant Mortality Rate (Ratio): 55/1,000
Average Caloric Intake: 114% of FAO
minimum
Physicians Available (Ratio): 1/1,600

Religions

95% Shia Muslim; 4% Sunni Muslim;
1% Zoroastrian, Jewish, Christian, and
Bahai

Education

Adult Literacy Rate: 78%

COMMUNICATION

Telephones: 2,143,000
Newspapers: 17 dailies (circulation of
two largest: 570,000)

TRANSPORTATION

Highways—Kilometers (Miles): 140,200
(87,485)
Railroads—Kilometers (Miles): 5,330 (3,198)
Usable Airfields: 261

GOVERNMENT

Type: theocratic republic
Independence Date: February 1, 1979
Head of State: Supreme Guide
Ayatollah Ali Hoseini-Khamenei;
President Mohamed Khatami
Political Parties: currently banned;
candidates for political office must be
approved by the Council of
Constitutional Guardians
Suffrage: universal at 15

MILITARY

Number of Armed Forces: 640,000
*Military Expenditures (% of Central
Government Expenditures):* 13.6%
Current Hostilities: territorial dispute
with the United Arab Emirates

ECONOMY

Currency ($ U.S. Equivalent): 3,000
rials = $1 (official rate); 4,500 rials =
$1 (unofficial rate)
Per Capita Income/GDP: $4,720/$310
billion
Inflation Rate: 23%
Total Foreign Debt: $30 billion
Natural Resources: petroleum; natural
gas; sulfur; bauxite; rare minerals
Agriculture: rice; barley; wheat; sugar
beets; cotton; dates; raisins; tea;
tobacco; sheep; goats
Industry: crude-oil production and
refining; textiles; cement; food
processing; metal fabricating

FOREIGN TRADE

Exports: $16.86 billion
Imports: $11.6 billion

Magic Strength, Magic Carpets

Iranians have made many contributions both to Islamic and to Western culture over the centuries, drawn from their own rich cultural heritage and their location as a bridge between East and West. They were the first to develop formal landscaped gardens, the earliest laid out by the Emperor Cyrus at his palace in Persepolis. Iranians also developed rose cultivation, bridge and the game of polo, and instruments such as the sitar, ancestor of the guitar. The *zur khaneh* ("House of Strength"), where Iranian men meet to do exercises, juggle clubs, and wrestle in mud, is the predecessor of our modern fitness centers. The "magic carpets" woven by young girls in nomad tents or tiny city ateliers and dyed with natural dyes such as rose petals, pistachio shells, and vine leaves, not only fetch prices as high as $200,000 but are the inspiration for Iranian films like the prize-winning Iranian film *Gabbeh,* which tells a story drawn from the designs on a nomad's carpet.

Iran
⊛ Capital
● City
River
Road

IRAN

Iran is in many respects a subcontinent, ranging in elevation from Mount Demavend (18,386 feet) to the Caspian Sea, which is below sea level. Most of Iran consists of a high plateau ringed by mountains. Much of the plateau is covered with uninhabitable salt flats and deserts, the Dasht-i-Kavir and Dasht-i-Lut, the latter being one of the most desolate and inhospitable regions in the world. The climate is equally forbidding. The so-called Wind of 120 Days blows throughout the summer in eastern Iran, bringing dust and extremely high temperatures.

Most of the country receives little or no rainfall. Settlement and population density are directly related to the availability of water. The most densely populated region is along the Caspian Sea coast, which has an annual rainfall of 80 inches. The province of Azerbaijan in the northwest, the province of Khuzestan along the Iraqi border, and the urban areas around Iran's capital, Teheran, are also heavily populated.

Water is so important to the Iranian economy that all water resources were nationalized in 1967.[1] Lack of rainfall caused the development of a sophisticated system of underground conduits, called *qanats,* to carry water across the plateau from a water source, usually at the base of a mountain. Many qanats were built thousands of years ago and are still in operation. They make existence possible for much of Iran's rural population.

Until the twentieth century, the population was overwhelmingly rural; but, due to rural–urban migration, the urban population has increased steadily. Nearly all of this migration has been to Teheran.[2] Yet the rural population has increased overall. This fact has had important political consequences for Iran, as a monarchy as well as a republic. Attachment to the land, family solidarity, and high birth rates have preserved the strong rural element in Iranian society as a force for conservatism and loyalty to religious leaders, who then are able to influence whatever regime is in power. Indeed, the rural population strongly supported the Khomeini regime and contributed much of the volunteer manpower recruited to defend the country after the invasion by Iraqi forces in 1980.

ETHNIC AND RELIGIOUS DIVERSITY

Due to Iran's geographic diversity, the population is divided into a large number of separate and often conflicting ethnic groups. Ethnic Iranians constitute the majority. The Iranians (or *Persians,* from Parsa, the province where they first settled) are an Indo-European people whose original home was probably in Central Asia. They moved into Iran around 1100 B.C. and gradually dominated the entire region, establishing the world's first empire (in the sense of rule over various unrelated peoples in a large territory). Although the Persian Empire eventually broke up, the Persian language (Farsi), system of government, and cultural/historical traditions have given Iran an unbroken national identity to the present day.

The largest ethnic minority group is the Azeri (or Azerbaijani) Turks. The Azeris live in northwestern Iran. Their ethnic origin dates back to the ancient Persian Empire, when Azerbaijan was known as Atropene. The migration of Turkish peoples into this region in the eleventh and twelfth centuries A.D. encouraged the spread of the Turkish language and of Islam. These were reinforced by centuries of Ottoman rule, although Persian remained the written and literary language of the people.

Turkish dynasties originating in Azerbaijan controlled Iran for several centuries and were responsible for much of premodern Islamic Iran's political power and cultural achievements. In the late nineteenth and early twentieth centuries, Azeris were in the forefront of the constitutional movement to limit the absolute power of Iranian monarchs. They formed the core of the first Iranian Parliament. The Azeris have consistently fought for regional autonomy from the central Iranian government in the modern period and refer to their province as "Azadistan, Land of Freedom."[3]

The Kurds are another large ethnic minority. Iran's Kurd population is concentrated in the Zagros Mountains along the Turkish and Iraqi borders. The Kurds are Sunni Muslims, as distinct from the Shia majority. The Iranian Kurds share a common language, culture, social organization, and ethnic identity with Kurds in Iraq, Turkey, and Syria. Kurds are strongly independent mountain people who lack a politically recognized homeland and who have been unable to unite to form one. The Kurds of Iran formed their own Kurdish Republic, with Soviet backing, after World War II. But the withdrawal of Soviet troops, under international pressure, caused its collapse. Since then, Iranian Kurdish leaders have devoted their efforts toward greater regional autonomy. Kurdish opposition to the central Iranian government was muted during the rule of the Pahlavi dynasty (1925–1979), but it broke into the open after the establishment of the Islamic republic. The Kurds feared that they would be oppressed under the Shia Muslim government headed by Ayatollah Khomeini and boycotted the national referendum approving the republic.[4] Central-government authority over the Kurds was restored in 1985. In 1992, Iraqi Kurdish leaders made an agreement with the Iranian government for deliveries of fuel and spare parts for their beleaguered enclave; in return, they pledged that the enclave would not be used by the Peoples' Mojahideen or any other antigovernment group for military actions against Iran.

The Arabs are another important minority group (Iran and Turkey are the two Middle Eastern Islamic countries with a non-Arab majority). The Arabs live in Khuzestan Province, along the Iraqi border. The Baluchi, also Sunni Muslims, are located in southeast Iran and are related to Baluchi groups in Afghanistan and Pakistan. They are seminomadic and have traditionally opposed any form of central-government control. The Baluchi were the first minority to oppose openly the fundamentalist Shia policies of the Khomeini government.

Lesser non-Muslim minorities include the Armenians; Jews; Assyrians (an ancient Christian sect); and Zoroastrians, followers of the major religion of the Persian and Sassanid empires, who worshipped Ahura Mazda, the god of light, and regarded fire as sacred because it was a purifier of life. The Bahais, a splinter movement from Islam founded by an Iranian mystic named the *Bab* ("Door," i.e., to wisdom) and organized by a teacher named Baha'Ullah in the nineteenth century, are the largest non-Muslim minority group. Although Baha'Ullah taught the principles of universal love, peace, harmony, and brotherhood, his proclamations of equality of the sexes, ethnic unity, the oneness of all religions, and a universal rather than a Muslim God aroused the hostility of Shia religious leaders. The Bahais were tolerated and prospered under the Pahlavis; but the republican government, due to its strong insistence on Shia authoritarianism, undertook a campaign of violent persecution that some observers called the "genocide of a noncombatant people."[5] By 1987, this campaign had resulted in the execution of more than 200 Bahais. Nearly 800 more were in prison, most of them charged with espionage. Amnesty International reported a case in 1985 in which a court ruled that an Iranian Muslim who had killed a Bahai with a "premeditated blow" should not be prosecuted and the victim's family could not claim compensation, because they were Bahais. Out of a total pre-1979 Bahai population of 350,000, some 30,000 had fled the country by 1987. Despite pressure from international human-rights organizations that have been allowed to monitor

(UN photo/John Isaac)

Iranian society today has a considerable level of cultural conformity. Shia Islam is the dominant religion of Iran, and observance of this form of Islam permeates society, as this prayer meeting at Teheran University attests.

the Bahais' situation, the government continues to mistreat them, although allowing them "the means to live." For example, Bahais are automatically passed over for high-level professional jobs and are denied access to higher education.

CULTURAL CONFORMITY
Despite the separatist tendencies in Iranian society caused by the existence of these various ethnic groups and religious divisions, there is considerable cultural conformity. Most Iranians, regardless of background, display distinctly Iranian values, customs, and traditions. Unifying features include the Farsi language, Islam as the overall religion, the appeal (since the sixteenth century) of Shia Islam as an Iranian nationalistic force, and a sense of nationhood derived from Iran's long history and cultural continuity.

Iranians at all levels have a strongly developed sense of class structure. It is a three-tier structure, consisting of upper, middle, and lower classes. However, some scholars distinguish two lower classes: the urban wage earner, and the landed or landless peasant. The basic socioeconomic unit in this class structure is the patriarchal family, which functions in Iranian society as a tree trunk does in relation to its branches. The patriarch of each family is not only disciplinarian and decisionmaker but also guardian of the family honor and inheritance.

The patriarchal structure, in terms of the larger society, has defined certain behavioral norms. These include the seclusion of women, ceremonial politeness *(ta'aruf)*, hierarchical authoritarianism with domination by superiors over subordinates, and the importance of face *(aberu)*—maintaining "an appropriate bearing and appearance commensurate with one's social status."[6] Under the republic, these norms have been increasingly Islamized as religious leaders have asserted the primacy of Shia Islam in all aspects of Iranian life.

HISTORY
Modern Iran occupies a much smaller territory than that of its pre-Islamic and some of its Islamic predecessors. The Persian Empire included nearly all of the current Middle East. The Sassanid kings, contemporaries of Roman emperors (A.D. 226–651) and heirs to much of the territory of Cyrus and Darius, made Zoroastrianism the official state religion under a powerful priestly caste. The Sassanid system of administration was taken over by the Arabs when they brought Islam to Iran.

The establishment of Islam brought significant changes into Iranian life. Arab armies defeated the Sassanid forces at the Battle of Qadisiya (A.D. 637) and the later Battle of Nihavand (A.D. 641), which resulted in the death of the last Sassanid king and the fall of his empire. The Arabs gradually established control over all the former Sassanid territories, converting the

inhabitants to Islam as they went. But the well-established Iranian cultural and social system provided refinements for Islam that were lacking in its early existence as a purely Arab religion. The Iranian converts to Islam converted the religion from a particularistic Arab faith to a universal faith. Islamic culture, in the broad sense—embracing literature, art, architecture, music, certain sciences and medicine—owes a great deal to the contributions of Iranian Muslims such as the poets Hafiz and Sa'di, the poet and astronomer Omar Khayyam, and many others.

Shia Muslims, currently the vast majority of the Iranian population and represented in nearly all ethnic groups, were in the minority in Iran during the formative centuries of Islam. Only one of the Twelve Shia Imams—the eighth, Reza—actually lived in Iran. (His tomb at Meshed is now the holiest shrine in Iran.) *Taqiya* ("dissimulation" or "concealment")—the Shia practice of hiding one's beliefs to escape Sunni persecution—added to the difficulties of the Shia in forming an organized community.

In the sixteenth century, the Safavids, who claimed to be descendants of the Prophet Muhammad, established control over Iran with the help of Turkish tribes. The first Safavid ruler, Shah Ismail, proclaimed Shiism as the official religion of his state and invited all Shias to move to Iran, where they would be protected. Shia domination of the country dates from this period. Shia Muslims converged on Iran from other parts of the Islamic world and became a majority in the population.

The Safavid rulers were bitter rivals of the Sunni Ottoman sultans and fought a number of wars with them. The conflict was religious as well as territorial. The Ottoman sultan assumed the title of caliph of Islam in the sixteenth century after the conquest of Egypt, where the descendants of the last Abbasid caliph of Baghdad had taken refuge. As caliph, the sultan claimed the right to speak for, and rule, all Muslims. The Safavids rejected this claim and called on Shia Muslims to struggle against him. In more recent years, the Khomeini government issued a similar call to Iranians to carry on war against the Sunni rulers of Iraq, indicating that Shia willingness to struggle and, if necessary, incur martyrdom was still very much alive in Iran.

King of Kings

The Qajars, a new dynasty of Turkish tribal origin, came to power after a bloody struggle at the end of the eighteenth century. They made Teheran their capital. Most of Iran's current borders were defined in the nineteenth century by treaties with foreign powers—Britain (on behalf of India), Russia, and the Ottoman Empire. Due to Iran's military weaknesses, the agreements favored the outside powers and the country lost much of its original territory.

Despite Iran's weakness in relation to foreign powers, the Qajar rulers sought to revive the ancient glories of the monarchy at home. They assumed the old Persian title *Shahinshah,* "King of Kings." At his coronation, each ruler sat on the Peacock Throne, the gilded, jewel-encrusted treasure brought to Iran by Nadir Shah, conqueror of northern India and founder of the short-lived Iranian Afshar Dynasty. They assumed other grandiose titles, such as "Shadow of God on Earth" and "Asylum of the Universe." A shah once told an English visitor, "Your King, then, appears to be no more than a first magistrate. I, on the other hand, can elevate or degrade all the high nobles and officers you see around me!"[7]

Qajar pomp and power, however, masked serious internal weaknesses. The shahs ruled by manipulating ethnic and communal rivalries to their own advantage. When they were faced with dangerous opposition, they retreated, and they made concessions, only to retract them once the danger was past. Marriages helped to establish a network of power radiating outward from the royal family to leading upper-class families; one shah married 192 times and married off 170 sons and daughters to cement alliances.[8]

Nasr al-Din Shah, Iran's ruler for most of the nineteenth century, was responsible for a large number of concessions to European bankers, promoters, and private companies. His purpose was to demonstrate to European powers that Iran was becoming a modern state and to find new revenues without having to levy new taxes, which would have aroused more dangerous opposition. The various concessions helped to modernize Iran, but they bankrupted the treasury in the process. The shah also wanted to prove to the European powers that Iran had a modern army. A contract was signed with Russia for officers from the Cossacks, a powerful Russian group, to train an elite Iranian military unit, the Cossack Brigade.

In the mid-nineteenth century, the shah was encouraged by European envoys to turn his attention to education as a means of creating a modern society. In 1851, he opened the Polytechnic College, with European instructors, to teach military science and technical subjects. The graduates of this college, along with other Iranians who had been sent to Europe for their education and a few members of aristocratic families, became the nucleus of a small but influential intellectual elite. Along with their training in military subjects, they acquired European ideas of nationalism and progress. They were "government men" in the sense that they worked for and belonged to the shah's government.

But they also came to believe that the Iranian people needed to unite into a nation, with representative government and a European-style educational system, in order to become a part of the modern world. The views of these intellectuals put them at odds with the shah, who cared nothing for representative government or civil rights, only for tax collection. The intellectuals also found themselves at odds with the religious leaders *(mullahs),* who controlled the educational system and feared any interference with their superstitious, illiterate subjects.

The intellectuals and mullahs both felt that the shah was giving away Iran's assets and resources to foreigners. For a long time, the intellectuals were the only group to complain; the illiterate Iranian masses could not be expected to protest against actions they knew nothing about. But in 1890, the shah gave a 50-year concession to a Briton named Talbot for a monopoly over the export and distribution of tobacco. Faced with higher prices for the tobacco they grew themselves, Iranians staged a general strike and boycott, and the shah was forced to cancel the concession. The pattern of local protest leading to mass rebellion, with all population groups uniting against an arbitrary ruler, was to be duplicated in the Constitutional Revolt of 1905 and again in the 1979 Revolution.

By the end of the nineteenth century, the people were roused to action, the mullahs had turned against the ruler, and the intellectuals were demanding a constitution that would limit his powers. One of the intellectuals wrote, "It is self-evident that in the future no nation—Islamic or non-Islamic—will continue to exist without constitutional law. . . . The various ethnic groups that live in Iran will not become one people until the law upholds their right to freedom of expression and the opportunity for [modern] education."[9] One century and two revolutions later, Iran is still struggling to put this formula into operation.

According to Roy Mottahedeh, "the bazaar and the mosque are the two lungs of public life in Iran."[10] The bazaar, like the Greek agora and the Roman forum, is the place where things are bought, deals are consummated, and political issues are aired for public consideration or protest. The mosque is the bastion of religious opinion; its preachers can, and do, mobilize the faithful to action through thundering denunciations of rulers and government officials. Mosque and bazaar came together in 1905 to bring about the first Iranian Revolution, a forerunner, at least in pattern, of the 1979 revolt. Two sugar merchants were bastinadoed (a punishment, still used in Iran, in which the soles of the feet are beaten with a cane) because they refused to lower their prices; they complained that high import prices set by the government gave them no choice. The bazaar then closed down in protest. With commercial activity at a standstill, the shah agreed to establish a "house of justice" and to promulgate a constitution. But 6 months later, he still had done nothing. Then a mullah was arrested, shot, and killed for criticizing the ruler in a Friday sermon. Further protests were met with mass arrests and then gunfire; "a river of blood now divided the court from the country."[11]

In 1906, nearly all of the religious leaders left Teheran for the sanctuary of Qum, Iran's principal theological-studies center. The bazaar closed down again, a general strike paralyzed the country, and thousands of Iranians took refuge in the British Embassy in Teheran. With the city paralyzed, the shah gave in. He granted a Constitution that provided for an elected *Majlis* (Parliament), the first limitation on royal power in Iran in its history. Four more shahs would occupy the throne, two of them as absolute rulers, but the 1906 Constitution and the elected Legislature survived as brakes on absolutism until the 1979 Revolution. In this sense, the Islamic Republic is the legitimate heir to the constitutional movement.

The Pahlavi Dynasty

Iran was in chaos at the end of World War I. British and Russian troops partitioned the country, and after the collapse of Russian power due to the Bolshevik Revolution, the British dictated a treaty with the shah that would have made Iran a British protectorate. Azeris and Kurds talked openly of independence; and a Communist group, the Jangalis, organized a "Soviet Republic" of Gilan along the Caspian coast.

The only organized force in Iran at this time was the Cossack Brigade. Its commander was Reza Khan, a villager from an obscure family who had risen through the ranks on sheer ability. In 1921, he seized power in a bloodless coup, but he did not overthrow the shah. The shah appointed him prime minister and then left the country for a comfortable exile in Europe, never to return.

Turkey, Iran's neighbor, had just become a republic, and many Iranians felt that Iran should follow the same line. But the religious leaders wanted to keep the monarchy, fearing that a republican system would weaken their authority over the illiterate masses. The religious leaders convinced Prime Minister Reza that Iran was not ready for a republic. In 1925, Reza was crowned as shah, with an amendment to the Constitution that defined the monarchy as belonging to Reza Shah and his male descendants in succession. Since he had no family background to draw upon, Reza chose a new name for his dynasty: Pahlavi. It was a symbolic name, derived from an ancient province and language of the Persian Empire.

Reza Shah was one of the most powerful and effective monarchs in Iran's long history. He brought all ethnic groups under the control of the central government and established a well-equipped standing army to enforce his decrees. He did not tamper with the Constitution; instead, he approved all candidates for the Majlis and outlawed political parties, so that the political system was entirely responsible to him alone.

Reza Shah's New Order

Reza Shah wanted to build a "new order" for Iranian society, and he wanted to build it in a hurry. He was a great admirer of Mustafa Kemal Ataturk, founder of the

Turkish Republic. Like Ataturk, Reza Shah believed that the religious leaders were an obstacle to modernization, due to their control over the masses. He set out to break their power through a series of reforms. Lands held in religious trust were leased to the state, depriving the religious leaders of income. A new secular code of laws took away their control, since the secular code would replace Islamic law. Other decrees prohibited the wearing of veils by women and the fez, the traditional brimless Muslim hat, by men. When religious leaders objected, Reza Shah had them jailed; on one occasion, he went into a mosque, dragged the local mullah out in the street, and horsewhipped him for criticizing the ruler during a Friday sermon.

In 1935, a huge crowd went to the shrine of Imam Reza, the eighth Shia Imam, in Meshad, to hear a parade of mullahs criticize the shah's ruthless reform policies. Reza Shah ringed the shrine with troops. When the crowd refused to disperse, they opened fire, killing a hundred people. It was the first and last demonstration organized by the mullahs during Reza Shah's reign. Only one religious leader, a young scholar named Ruhollah al-Musavi al-Khomeini, consistently dared to criticize the shah, and he was dismissed as being an impractical teacher.

Iran declared its neutrality during the early years of World War II. But Reza Shah was sympathetic to Germany; he had many memories of British interference in Iran. He allowed German technicians and advisers to remain in the country, and he refused to allow war supplies to be shipped across Iran to the Soviet Union. In 1941, British and Soviet armies simultaneously occupied Iran. Reza Shah abdicated in favor of his son, Crown Prince Mohammed, and was taken into exile on a British warship. He never saw his country again.

Mohammed Reza Pahlavi

When the new shah came to the throne, few suspected that he would rule longer than his father and hold even more absolute power. Mohammed Reza Pahlavi was young (22) and inexperienced, and he found himself ruling a land occupied by British and Soviet troops and threatened by Soviet-sponsored separatist movements in Azerbaijan and Kurdistan. Although these movements were put down, with U.S. help, a major challenge to the shah developed in 1951–1953.

A dispute over oil royalties between the government and the Anglo-Iranian Oil Company (AIOC) aroused intense national feeling in Iran. Mohammed Mossadegh, a long-time Majlis member and

ardent nationalist, was asked by the shah in 1951 to serve as prime minister and to implement the oil-nationalization laws passed by the Majlis. The AIOC responded by closing down the industry, and all foreign technicians left the country. The Iranian economy was not affected at first, and Mossadegh's success in standing up to the company, which most Iranians considered an agent of foreign imperialism, won him enormous popularity.[12]

Mossadegh served as prime minister from 1951 to 1953, a difficult time for Iran due to loss of oil revenues and internal political wrangling. Although his policies embroiled him in controversy, Mossadegh's theatrical style—public weeping when moved, fainting fits, a preference for conducting public business from his bed while dressed in pajamas, and a propensity during speeches to emphasize a point by ripping the arm from a chair—enhanced his appeal to the Iranian people. His radio "fireside chats" soon won him a mass following; he became more popular than the shy, diffident young shah, and for all practical purposes he ruled Iran.

However, by 1953, economic difficulties and Mossadegh's repressive measures had cost him most of his popularity. A contest of wills between the shah and his prime minister followed, ending as the shah left the country. However, the United States, through its Central Intelligence Agency (CIA), which feared that a Communist plot to take over Iran was behind Mossadegh, helped to mobilize mass demonstrations against Mossadegh. Fortunately for the shah, the prime minister's support base was shallow, coming mostly from leftist intellectuals and members of the Tudeh (Masses), a pro-Soviet political party. The army officer corps, the middle class, and the *bazaaris* (the powerful community of merchants and small-business owners in city bazaars) stood firm behind their ruler, while CIA agents with discreet use of minimal funds mobilized the masses in huge street parades. In August 1953, the shah returned to his country in triumph. He then gradually gathered all authority in his hands and developed the vast internal security network that eliminated parliamentary opposition.[13]

By the 1960s, the shah felt that he was ready to lead Iran to greatness. In 1962, he announced the Shah-People Revolution, also known as the White Revolution. It had these basic points: land reform, public ownership of industries, nationalization of forests, voting rights for women, workers' profit sharing, and a literacy corps to implement compulsory education in rural areas. The plan drew immediate opposition from landowners and religious leaders. But only one spoke out forcefully against the shah: Ayatollah Ruhollah Khomeini, now the most distinguished of Iran's religious scholars. "I have repeatedly pointed out that the government has evil intentions and is opposed to the ordinances of Islam," he said in a public sermon.[14] His message was short and definite: The shah is selling out the country; the shah must go.

Khomeini continued to criticize the shah, and in June 1963, he was arrested. Demonstrations broke out in various cities. The shah sent the army into the streets, and again a river of blood divided ruler from country. Khomeini was released, re-arrested, and finally exiled to Iraq. For the next 15 years, he continued attacking the shah in sermons, pamphlets, and broadsides smuggled into Iran through the "bazaar network" of merchants and village religious leaders. Some had more effect than others. In 1971, when the shah planned an elaborate coronation at the ancient Persian capital of Persepolis to celebrate 2,500 years of monarchy, Khomeini declared, "Islam is fundamentally opposed to the whole notion of monarchy. The title of King of Kings . . . is the most hated of all titles in the sight of God. . . . Are the people of Iran to have a festival for those whose behavior has been a scandal throughout history and who are a cause of crime and oppression . . . in the present age?"[15]

Yet, until 1978, the possibility of revolution in Iran seemed to be remote. The shah controlled all the instruments of power. His secret service, SAVAK, had informers everywhere. The mere usage of a word such as "oppressive" to describe the weather was enough to get a person arrested. Whole families disappeared into the shah's jails and were never heard from again.

The public face of the regime, however, seemed to indicate that Iran was on its way to wealth, prosperity, and international importance. The shah announced a 400 percent increase in the price of Iranian oil in 1973 and declared that the country would soon become a "Great Civilization." Money poured into Iran, billions of dollars more each year. The army was modernized with the most sophisticated U.S. equipment available. A new class of people, the "petro-bourgeoisie," became rich at the expense of other classes. Instead of the concessions given to foreign business firms by penniless Qajar shahs, the twentieth-century shah became the dispenser of opportunities to businesspeople and bankers to develop Iran's great civilization with Iranian money—an army of specialists imported from abroad.

In 1976, the shah seemed at the pinnacle of his power. His major adversary, Khomeini, had been expelled from Iraq and was now far away in Paris. U.S. president Jimmy Carter visited Iran in 1977 and declared, "Under your leadership (the country) is an island of stability in one of the more troubled areas of the world."[16] Yet, just a month later, 30,000 demonstrators marched on the city of Qum, protesting an unsigned newspaper article (reputed to have been written by the shah) that had attacked Khomeini as being anti-Iranian. The police fired on the demonstration, and a massacre followed.

Gradually, a cycle of violence developed. It reflected the distinctive rhythm of Shia Islam, wherein a death in a family is followed by 40 days of mourning and every death represents a martyr for the faith. Massacre followed massacre in city after city. In spite of the shah's efforts to modernize his country, it seemed to more and more Iranians that he was trying to undermine the basic values of their society by striking at the religious leaders. Increasingly, marchers in the streets were heard to shout, "Death to the shah!"

Even though the shah held absolute power, he seemed less and less able or willing to use his power to crush the opposition. It was as if he were paralyzed. He wrote in his last book, "A sovereign may not save his throne by shedding his countrymen's blood. . . . A sovereign is not a dictator. He cannot break the alliance that exists between him and his people."[17] The shah vacillated as the opposition intensified. His regime was simply not capable of self-reform or of accepting the logical consequences of liberalization, of free elections, a return to constitutional monarchy, and the emergence of legitimate dissent.[18]

THE ISLAMIC REPUBLIC

The shah and his family left Iran for good in January 1979. Ayatollah Ruhollah Khomeini returned from exile practically on his heels, welcomed by millions who had fought and bled for his return. The shah's Great Civilization lay in ruins. Like a transplant, it had been an attempt to impose a foreign model of life on the Iranian community, a surgical attachment that had been rejected.

In April 1979, Khomeini announced the establishment of the Islamic Republic of Iran. He called it the first true republic in Islam since the original community of believers was formed by Muhammad. Khomeini said that religious leaders would assume active leadership, serve in the Majlis, even fight Iran's battles as "warrior mullahs." A Council of Guardians was set up to interpret laws and ensure that they were in conformity with the sacred law of Islam. Although the republic is governed under a Constitution with an elected president and Legislature, final authority is reserved to a Velayat-e-Faqih ("Supreme Guide"), who is responsible only to God.

Khomeini, as the first Supreme Guide, embodied the values and objectives of the republic. Because he saw himself in that role, he consistently sought to remain above factional politics yet to be accessible to all groups and render impartial decisions. But the demands of the war with Iraq, the country's international isolation, conflicts between radical Islamic fundamentalists and advocates of secularization, and other divisions forced the aging Ayatollah into a day-to-day policy-making role. It was a role that he was not well prepared for, given his limited experience beyond the confines of Islamic scholarship. Quite possibly the war with Iraq, for example, could have been settled earlier if it were not for Khomeini's vision of a pure Shia Iran fighting a just war against the atheistic secular regime of Saddam Hussein.

A major responsibility of the Council of Guardians was to designate—with Khomeini's approval—a successor to Khomeini as Supreme Legal Guide. In 1985, the Council chose Ayatollah Hossein Ali Montazeri, a former student and close associate of the bearded patriarch. Montazeri, although politically inexperienced and lacking Khomeini's charisma, had directed the exportation of Iranian Islamic fundamentalist doctrine to other Islamic states after the Revolution, with some success. This responsibility had identified him abroad as the architect of Iranian-sponsored terrorist acts such as the taking of hostages in Lebanon. But, during his brief tenure as Khomeini's designated successor, he helped make changes in prison administration, revamped court procedures to humanize the legal system and reduce prisoner mistreatment, and urged a greater role for opposition groups in political life. However, Montazeri resigned in March 1989 after publishing an open letter, which aroused Khomeini's ire, criticizing the mistakes made by Iranian leaders during the Revolution's first decade.

The Islamic Republic staggered from crisis to crisis in its initial years. Abol Hassan Bani-Sadr, a French-educated intellectual who had been Khomeini's right-hand man in Paris, was elected president in 1980 by 75 percent of the popular vote. But it was one of the few postrevolutionary actions that united a majority of Iranians. Although the United States, as the shah's supporter and rescuer in his hour of exile, became Iran's "Great Satan" and thus helped to maintain revolutionary fervor, the prolonged crisis over the holding of American hostages by guards who would take orders from no one but Khomeini embarrassed Iran and damaged its credibility more than any gains made from tweaking the nose of a superpower.

Revolutions historically often seem to end by devouring those who carry them out. A great variety of Iranian social groups had united to overthrow the shah. They had different views of the future; an "Islamic republic" meant different things to different groups. The Revolution first devoured all those associated with the shah, in a reign of terror intended to compensate for 15 years of repression. Islamic tribunals executed thousands of people—political leaders, intellectuals, and military commanders.

The major opposition to Khomeini and his fellow religious leaders came from the radical group Mujahideen-i-Khalq. The Mujahideen favored an Islamic socialist republic and were opposed to too much government influence by religious leaders. However, the Majlis was dominated by the religious leaders, many of whom had no experience in government and knew little of politics beyond the village level. As the conflict between these groups sharpened, bombings and assassinations occurred almost daily.

The instability and apparently endless violence during 1980–1981 suggested to the outside world that the Khomeini government was on the point of collapse. Iraqi president Saddam Hussein thought so, and, in September 1980, he ordered his army to invade Iran—a decision that proved to be a costly mistake. President Bani-Sadr was dismissed by Khomeini after an open split developed between him and religious leaders over the conduct of the war; he subsequently escaped to France. A series of bombings carried out by the Mujahideen in mid-1981 killed a number of Khomeini's close associates, including the newly elected president of the republic.

The Khomeini regime showed considerable resilience in dealing with its adversaries. The Mujahideen were ruthlessly repressed in 1983. This organization had been in the vanguard of the struggle against the shah, but once the republic had been established, the religious leaders came to view its Marxist, and therefore atheist, members as their major internal enemy. The Mujahideen's principal leader, Massoud Rajavi, escaped to France, but many of his associates were hunted down

and killed. In 1986, the French expelled him, along with about a thousand of his supporters, as part of an effort to cultivate better relations with Iran. The Iraqi government granted him asylum.

Toward the end of the Iran–Iraq War, the Mujahideen took advantage of Iraqi successes to seize several towns inside Iran, freeing political prisoners and executing minor officials, such as prison wardens, without trial. But the organization had little internal support in the country. Its Marxist views were not shared by the majority of people, and Mujahideen claims of 90,000 executions and more than 150,000 political prisoners held by the regime were believed to be wildly exaggerated.

However, the government of Ali Akbar Hashemi Rafsanjani, who became president in 1989, was as ruthless as the shah's was in hunting down its opponents. In 1990, Rajavi's brother was killed by unknown gunmen in Geneva, Switzerland. In August 1991, Shahpour Bakhtiar, the last prime minister under the monarchy, was murdered under similar circumstances in Paris, where he had been living in exile. Although the elderly Bakhtiar had been opposed to the shah as well as to Khomeini, fellow exile and former Iranian president Bani-Sadr charged that the regime had a "hit list" of opponents, including himself and the former prime minister, slated for execution.

The other main focus of opposition was the Tudeh (Masses) Party. Although considered a Communist party, its origins lay in the constitutional movement of 1905–1907, and it had always been more nationalistic than Soviet oriented. The shah banned the Tudeh after an assassination attempt on him in 1949, but it revived during the Mossadegh period of 1951–1953. After the shah returned from exile in 1953, the Tudeh was again banned and went underground. Many of its leaders fled to the Soviet Union. After the 1979 Revolution, the Tudeh again came out into the open and collaborated with the Khomeini regime. It was tolerated by the religious leaders for its nationalism, which made its Marxism acceptable. Being militarily weak at that time, the regime also wished to remain on good terms with its Soviet neighbor. However, the rapprochement was brief. In 1984, top Tudeh leaders were arrested in a series of surprise raids and given long prison terms.

PROSPECTS
The Revolution that overturned one of the most ruthless authoritarian regimes in history has been in effect long enough to provide some clues to its future direction.

One clue is the continuity of internal politics. Despite wreaking savage vengeance on persons associated with the shah's regime, Khomeini and his fellow mullahs preserved most of the Pahlavi institutions of government. The Majlis, civil service, secret police, and armed forces were continued as before, with minor modifications to conform to strict Islamic practice. The main addition was a parallel structure of revolutionary courts, paramilitary Revolutionary Guards (Pasdaran), workers' and peasants' councils, plus the Council of Guardians as the watchdog over legislation.

In the first years of the Revolution, the mullah, in his somber robe and turban, inspired more respect among Iranians than the "Mr. Engineer" type in his Western business suit (the symbol of modernization in the shah's time). Later, however, political institutions, and particularly the Majlis, began to show a growing secular configuration. The 1984 Majlis, for example, included more professionals and technicians than its predecessor and fewer religious leaders.

The 1985 presidential election in Iran continued this secular trend. The ruling Islamic Republican Party (since dissolved) nominated President Ali Khamenei for a second term, against token opposition. However, Mehdi Bazargan, the republic's first prime minister, who subsequently went into opposition and founded the Freedom Movement, announced that he would be a candidate. The Council of Guardians vetoed his candidacy on the grounds that his opposition to the war with Iraq, although well publicized, would be damaging to national solidarity if he ran for president. Khamenei won re-election handily, but nearly 2 million votes were cast for one of the two opposition candidates, a religious leader. The relatively high number of votes for this candidate reflected increasing dissatisfaction with the Khomeini regime's no-quarter policy toward Iraq, rather than opposition to the regime itself.

In its foreign relations, the regime remained unpredictable. It played an active behind-the-scenes role in the release of Western hostages in Lebanon in 1990 and 1991, possibly reflecting a desire for improved relations with Western countries, both for economic reasons and to enable Iran to resume its important role in regional affairs. Balancing these efforts was a determined campaign to eliminate opponents even at the risk of alienating other nations, as shown by the murder of former prime minister Bakhtiar and the issuance of a death sentence for Salman Rushdie, the author of the novel *The Satanic Verses*.

This campaign underscored the division in the government between the "pragmatists," who sought accommodation with the West, and the "hard-liners," who wanted no accommodation at all.

The division emphasized the regime's difficulties in ensuring popular support and making use of its majority in the fractious Majlis to carry out necessary economic reforms. In the 1992 Majlis elections, two political groups presented candidates: the Society of Radical Clergy (*Ruhaniyat,* loosely but incorrectly translated as "moderates") and the Combatant Religious Leaders (*Ruhaniyoun,* "hard-liners"). All candidates had to be approved by the Council of Constitutional Guardians (CCG), a 12-member body of senior religious scholars, to ensure that their views were compatible with Islam.

In the 1996 Majlis elections, the distinction between Ruhaniyat and Ruhaniyoun became even more blurred, reflecting the arcane nature of Iranian politics. The former, renamed the Conservative Combatant Clergy Society, was now opposed by the Servants of Iran's Construction, a coalition of centrist supporters of then—president Rafsanjani. (The Freedom Movement, headed by former prime minister Ibrahim Yazdi, had been banned by the CCG.) The election results underscored the shift in Iran's political leadership from religious "combatants" to economic "constructionists." The latter won a majority of Majlis seats. Combined with the election of 65 independent candidates, the defeat of a number of prominent religious leaders, and the entry of women into the political arena, the change was clearly visible.

IRAN AFTER KHOMEINI

In June 1989, Ayatollah Ruhollah Khomeini died of a heart attack in a Teheran hospital. He was 86 years old and had struggled all his life against the authoritarianism of two shahs.

The Imam left behind a society reshaped by his uncompromising Islamic ideals and principles. Every aspect of social life in republican Iran is governed by these principles, from prohibition of the production and use of alcohol and drugs to a strict dress code for women outside the home, compulsory school prayers, emphasis on theological studies in education, and required fasting during Ramadan. One positive result of this Islamization program has been a renewed awareness among Iranians of their cultural identity and pride in their heritage.

Khomeini also bequeathed many problems to his country. The most immediate problem concerned the succession to him

as Supreme Guide. Earlier, he had appointed an Expediency Council to resolve differences between the Majlis and the Council of Constitutional Guardians.

A separate body of senior religious leaders and jurists, the Assembly of Experts, resolved the succession question by electing President Khamenei as Supreme Guide. However, the choice emphasized Khomeini's unique status as both political and spiritual leader. As a *Hojatulislam* (lower-ranking cleric), Khamenei lacked the credentials to replace the Ayatollah. But he was an appropriate choice, having served as a part of the governing team. Also, he was the most available religious leader. He had completed two terms as president and was ineligible for re-election.

THE PRESIDENCY

The chief executive's powers in the Iranian system were greatly strengthened by a constitutional amendment abolishing the office of prime minister, approved by voters in a July 1989 referendum. But concern for a smooth transfer of power after Khomeini's death prompted the government to advance the date for electing a new president to succeed Ali Khamenei from October to July. There were only two candidates: Majlis speaker Ali Akbar Hashemi Rafsanjani, Khomeini's right-hand man almost from the start of the Revolution; and agriculture minister Abbas Sheibani, a political unknown. As anticipated, Rafsanjani won handily, with 95 percent of the 14.1 million votes cast.

Rafsanjani's first cabinet consisted mostly of technocrats, suggesting some relaxation of the policy of exporting the revolution and supporting revolutionary Islamic groups outside the country. At home, there was also a slight relaxation of the strict enforcement of Islamic codes of behavior enforced by the morals squads and security police. But the easing was temporary. In 1992, the new Supreme Guide issued an edict, ordering these codes reinforced. A similar edict was issued for the arts, after conservative Majlis members argued that Iranians had become "too permissive" in their use of non-Islamic models. As a result, the minister of culture and Islamic guidance, a lower-ranking cleric, was dismissed.

Rafsanjani was elected for a second term in 1993. However, his margin of victory was far less in this election—63 percent, compared with 24 percent for his closest rival. The decline was attributed not so much to a loss of popularity as to the lack of success of his regime in solving Iran's economic problems and lessening the country's international isolation.

FOREIGN POLICY

During Rafsanjani's first term, Iran began to improve its relations with its neighbors. It remained neutral during the Gulf War, and it provided sanctuary for Iraqi pilots and their aircraft, which were flown to Iranian bases. Iran and Iraq restored diplomatic relations in 1990. A tentative agreement to settle some of the outstanding issues of their 8-year war was reached in 1995, with the partial return of Iraqi and Iranian prisoners of war. The "dual containment" policy of the United States in the Gulf, designed to contain both Iran and Iraq in the manner of containment of the Soviet Union during the cold war, seems to have encouraged a rapprochement between the two former enemies; in 1997, they signed a formal peace agreement.

The unwillingness of European countries to go along with secondary sanctions on Iran, due to its economic and trade importance to them, brought an improvement in Iranian–European relations in the mid-1990s. In July 1996, Total of France was given a concession to develop newly discovered oil fields near Sirri Island in the Gulf. The concession had been granted previously to the U.S. Conoco Oil Company, but Conoco withdrew under pressure from the Clinton administration to comply with sanctions regulations.

Despite their opposition to U.S. sanctions, however, the support of European governments for the U.S. position increased in 1997, when a German court convicted four Iranians for the 1992 murders of Iranian Kurdish opposition leaders in Berlin. The court's decision directly implicated the Rafsanjani government, stating that the assassination order had been given a "Committee for Special Operations" charged with the elimination of opponents of the regime. In Teheran, more than 100,000 people marched on the German Embassy to protest the decision, and the European Union suspended the "critical dialogue" that was Europe's alternative to U.S. sanctions. Further actions to chastise Iran were not forthcoming—the Iranian market offered too great an attraction for European companies, and Iranian oil remained essential to European economies.

Iran's relationship with the United States, however, remains glacially frozen. After the 1979 Revolution and the end of the hostage crisis, the only contact between the two former allies was through the U.S.–Iran Claims Tribunal, set up in The Hague, Holland, to arbitrate U.S. claims against the Iranian regime. The tribunal also dealt with Iranian claims against U.S. companies for work contracted but not completed with the shah's government and U.S. equipment ordered but never delivered. The tribunal did its work outside the glare of publicity and with great efficiency. By 1996, some $6 billion had been awarded to U.S. claimants and $4 billion awarded to Iran for undelivered equipment. (The Tribunal rejected an Iranian claim for $136 million for use of its railroads to supply U.S. military equipment to the Soviet Union during World War II, on grounds that no contractual agreement existed.)

The Clinton administration's rigid stance toward Iran has yet to allow for changing political circumstances within the country or to take advantage of growing fluidity in Iranian foreign policy. The administration imposed a trade embargo unilaterally in 1995. Subsequently, Congress involved itself in foreign-policy directives, with passage of a bill that penalizes companies that invest $40 million or more in the Iranian oil and gas industry. The ban applied equally to U.S. and foreign companies. Foreign companies affected would be barred from doing business with the U.S. government or exporting their products to U.S. markets.

The congressional action aroused fierce opposition in Europe. Total, the French company that had taken over the Conoco concession, said that it would not be bound by the restrictions. The European Union threatened to bring suit against the United States in the World Trade Organization for violation of free-trade agreements (at this writing, it has not yet done so).

In any case, the U.S. "secondary boycott" has had little effect on Iran. Through increased oil production and broadened trade relations with the rest of the world, the country has been able to accumulate record hard-currency reserves. It has also moved to establish trade and economic development links with the newly independent republics of former Soviet Central Asia. A rail link from the port of Bandar Abbas to Turkmenistan was completed in 1996, giving that landlocked country access to Gulf ports and opening a new "Silk Road" to the Far East. Also in 1996, a barter agreement was reached with Kazakhstan to import 40,000 barrels per day of Kazakh crude; the oil is brought to Iranian refineries via pipelines through Russia and under the Caspian Sea, and a matching amount of Iranian crude is exported with cash payments to Kazakhstan. A $23 billion agreement to provide natural gas to Turkey and a pact with Russia for completion of Iran's nuclear reactor at Bushire further demonstrated the country's determination to play an important role in West Asian regional affairs.

AN ELECTION SURPRISE

In May 1997, Iranian voters went to the polls to elect a new president. Four candidates had been cleared and approved by the CCG: a prominent judge; an ex-intelligence-agency director; Majlis speaker Ali Akbar Nalegh-Nouri; and Mohammed Khatami, the former minister of culture and Islamic guidance, a more or less last-minute candidate, since had been out of office for 5 years and was not well known to the public. Speaker Nalegh-Nouri was the choice of the religious leaders and the Majlis and was expected to win easily.

In Iranian politics, though, the devil is often in the details; the unexpected may be the rule. With 25 million out of Iran's 33 million potential voters casting their ballots, Khatami emerged as the winner in a startling upset, with 69 percent of the votes as compared to 25 percent for Nalegh-Nouri. Support for the new president came mainly from women, but he was also backed by the large number of Iranians under age 25, who grew up under the republic but have become deeply dissatisfied with economic hardships and Islamic restrictions on their personal freedom.

Khatami took office in August. Despite some opposition in the Majlis, all 22 of the ministers in his cabinet were approved.

Despite Khatami's election success, the deep divisions in Iranian society between liberalizing elements and those who would preserve the system of direct rule by clerical leaders continued to hamper the reform program that had won him widespread support. These divisions were intensified when Ayatollah Montazeri, originally named as Khomeini's successor but out of politics since his 1989 resignation after a disagreement with his former mentor, denounced the Velayat-e-Faqih system of governance in a November 1997 speech. Montazeri said that unelected religious leaders should only supervise and not involve themselves directly in government affairs.

Despite his popularity and legitimacy as a member of the religious establishment, Khatami's options as a change agent for Iran remained limited. Ultimate authority remains firmly in the hands of the Supreme Legal Guide, and the latter's control over the Revolutionary Guards, the urban masses, and a sizable bloc of Majlis deputies would seem to indicate that any reform program that moves away from the orthodox Shia Islamic platform laid out by Khomeini has little chance for success.

In the first months after his formal installation, however, Khatami made some bold moves. He steered all his cabinet

(UN photo)

Iran has a long Islamic tradition. This worshipper is praying at the Shah Mosque, which makes up one side of the magnificent Royal Square of Shah Abbas in Isfahan.

The Persian Empire under Cyrus the Great and his successors includes most of ancient Near East and Egypt **551–331** B.C.

The Sassanid Empire establishes Zoroastrianism as the state religion A.D. **226–641**

Islamic conquest at the Battles of Qadisiya and Nihavard **637–641**

The Safavid shahs develop national unity based on Shia Islam as the state religion **1520–1730**

nominees through the Majlis, removed cultural restrictions on the printing of books and magazines previously banned, and restored good relations with various nations in the region and the outside world. During a December 1997 Islamic conference in Teheran, Khatami even held out an olive branch to the Great Satan.

THE ECONOMY

Iran's bright economic prospects during the 1970s were largely dampened by the 1979 Revolution. Petroleum output was sharply reduced, and the war with Iraq crippled industry as well as oil exports. Khomeini warned Iranians to prepare for a decade of grim austerity before economic recovery would be sufficient to meet domestic needs. After the cease-fire with Iraq, Khomeini enlarged upon his warning, saying that the world would be watching to see if the Revolution would be destroyed by postwar economic difficulties.

Iran's remarkable turnaround since the end of the war with Iraq, despite the U.S.–imposed trade restrictions, suggests that the late Imam was a better theologian than economist. The country's foreign debts were paid up by 1990, although new debts of $30 billion had been incurred by 1993 through loans for development projects and purchases of military equipment. About $12 billion of these debts have been rescheduled, and drastic reductions in imports since 1994 resulted in a balance-of-payments surplus of $6.5 billion in 1997.

Iran was self-sufficient in food until 1970. The White Revolution redistributed a considerable amount of land, most of it from estates that Reza Shah had confiscated from their previous owners. But the new owners, most of them former tenant farmers, lacked the capital, equipment, and technical knowledge needed for productive agriculture. The revolutionary period caused another upheaval in agriculture, as farmers abandoned their lands to take part in the struggle, and fighting between government forces and ethnic groups disrupted production. Production dropped 3.5 percent in 1979–1980, the first full year of the Islamic Republic of Iran, and continued to drop at the same rate through 1982. The onset of the war with Iraq caused another upheaval. The majority of recruits came from villages, the rural population having been Khomeini's most fervent supporters. Rural youths joined the Bassijis in large numbers, resulting in severe attrition in the able-bodied male farm population.[19]

These difficulties, plus large-scale rural–urban migration, have hampered development of the agricultural sector, which accounts for 20 percent of gross domestic product. Formerly self-sufficient in food, Iran is now the world's biggest wheat importer; some 6.6 million tons were imported in 1996. Iran does have some non-oil exports—carpets, fruit, and pistachio nuts. One other important export is caviar. In 1995–1996, the country exported $33 million worth of caviar from its share of the Caspian Sea sturgeon industry.

Petroleum is Iran's major resource and the key to economic development. Oil was discovered there in 1908, making the Iranian oil industry the oldest in the Middle East. Until 1951, the Anglo-Iranian Oil Company produced, refined, and distributed all Iranian oil. After the 1951–1953 nationalization period, when the industry was closed down, a consortium of foreign oil companies—British, French, and American—replaced the AIOC. In 1973, the industry was again nationalized and was operated by the state-run National Iranian Oil Company.

After the Revolution, political difficulties affected oil production, as the United States and its allies boycotted Iran due to the hostage crisis and other customers balked at the high prices ($37.50 per barrel in 1980 as compared to $17.00 per barrel a year earlier). The war with Iraq was a further blow to the industry. Japan, Iran's biggest customer, stopped purchases entirely in 1981–1982. War damage to the important Kharg Island terminal reduced Iran's export capacity by a third, and the Abadan refinery was severely crippled. Periodic Iraqi raids on other Iranian oil terminals in more distant places such as Lavan and Qeshm, reachable by longer-range aircraft, seriously decreased Iran's export output. Recovery from war damages has not only helped oil production and export but has also benefited other sectors of the oil industry. The Abadan refinery, the country's oldest, resumed full production in 1989 after a 9-year lapse and by 1996 was producing 300,000 barrels per day, half its prewar output. In 1996, a new petrochemical complex went into operation in Tabriz. It produces 400,000 tons a year of ethylene, polyethylene, and benzine.

In addition to its oil and gas reserves, Iran has important bauxite deposits, and in 1994, it reported the discovery of 400 million tons of phosphate rock to add to its mineral resources. It is now the world's sixth-largest exporter of sulfur. However, oil and gas remain the mainstays of the economy. Oil reserves are 88 billion barrels; with new gas discoveries each year, the country sits astride 70 percent of the world's reserves.

Iran's great natural resources, large population, and strong sense of its importance in the region have fueled its drive to become a major industrial power. The country is self-sufficient in cement, steel, petrochemicals, and hydrocarbons (as well as sugar—Iranians are heavy users). Production of electricity meets domestic needs, and the projected completion of nuclear plants will add to the supply. Iran now has its own small weapons program, producing, among other items, a battle tank, the Zolfaqar.

One factor hampering development is the control over the economy exercised by bazaaris. Their support was instrumental to the success of the 1979 Revolution. The bazaaris have received preferential treatment in all commercial transactions as a result. In 1994, President Rafsanjani introduced Refah, a 1,000-store discount chain similar to Wal-Mart, with low prices on its products guaranteed by the government. The chain is funded by the Islamic Republic's first bond, which is projected to raise $370 million through the Teheran stock exchange. Refah was intended to break the bazaari stranglehold over the commercial sector of the economy. However, the U.S. economic embargo has discouraged private investment in new ventures. As a result, the bazaaris and the *bonyads* (Islamic Foundations for the Oppressed, set up originally to help families displaced or forced into poverty by the deaths in the war of their main breadwinners) have come to dominate Iranian business and commerce.

WHITHER THE REPUBLIC?

Two decades after the Revolution that brought the first Islamic republic into existence, a debate is under way to deter-

| The constitutional movement limits the power of the shah by the Constitution and Legislature 1905–1907 | The accession of Reza Shah, establishing the Pahlavi Dynasty 1925 | The abdication of Reza Shah under Anglo–Soviet pressure; he is succeeded by Crown Prince Mohammed Reza Pahlavi 1941 | The oil industry is nationalized under the leadership of Prime Minister Mossadegh 1951–1953 | The shah introduces the White Revolution 1962 | Revolution overthrows the shah; Iran becomes an Islamic republic headed by the Ayatollah Khomeini 1979–1980 | The Kohmeini regime rejects a UN Security Council resolution for a cease-fire and peace talks with Iraq | The war with Iraq comes to an end; Khomeini dies 1980s | 1990s |

| Iran's economy begins to recover; foreign relations improve | The government takes steps to strengthen the economy further | Debate emerges over how Islamic the Islamic Republic should be |

mine how "Islamic" Iranian society should be. The debate is between those who advocate strict adherence to Islamic law and those who would open up the society to diverse social behavior and norms. As noted earlier in this chapter, Iran's new president was the choice of women and young people, two groups who feel they have benefited little from the Revolution. As their candidate, he may expect to come under increasing pressure from this new and largely disadvantaged constituency. As one Iranologist notes, "Having united religion and politics, the regime now has to face antagonisms directed at the clerics for failing to deliver on lofty promises. Pressure from Islamic radicals to push for further purification of social and political practices has alienated important elements in society."[20]

Young people in Iran today feel this alienation strongly. One young professional told a reporter: "Everywhere you go, someone is telling you what to do, your family, your school, the police, the *Komiteh* [plainclothes neighborhood morals squads], all enforcing Islamic social codes of behavior."[21] Two decades ago, Iranian young people were at the forefront of the Revolution—manning the street barricades, marching and demonstrating and being killed. It is this constituency—no longer bound by the ideals of religious ideology and faced with a world of uncertainties not unlike those of youths elsewhere—that the regime must take seriously in addressing its needs.

NOTES

1. Richard F. Nyrop, ed., *Iran, A Country Study* (Washington, D.C.: American University, Foreign Area Studies, 1978), p. 12.

2. Teheran is a relatively new city for Iran. It was founded in the early nineteenth century and was chosen as the capital due to its central location. In 1900 its population was 200,000. *Ibid.*, p. 77.

3. Byron J. Good, "Azeri," in R. V. Weekes, ed., *Muslim Peoples: A World Ethnographic Survey,* 2nd ed. (Westport, CT: Greenwood Press, 1984), p. 69.

4. Daniel G. Bates, "Kurds," in *Ibid.*, p. 425.

5. *cf. The New Yorker* (February 4, 1985), p. 31. The writer notes that "merely being a member of that Bahai community is now, in effect, a crime."

6. Golamreza Fazel, "Persians," in Weekes, *op. cit.*, p. 610. "Face-saving is in fact one of the components of *Ta'aruf,* along with assertive masculinity *(gheyrat)*."

7. John Malcolm, *History of Persia,* 2 vols. (London: John Murray, 1829), Vol. II, p. 303.

8. Ervand Abrahamian, *Iran Between Two Revolutions* (Princeton, NJ: Princeton University Press, 1982), p. 48.

9. Roy Mottahedeh, *The Mantle of the Prophet* (New York: Simon & Schuster, 1985), p. 52.

10. *Ibid.,* p. 34.

11. Abrahamian, *op. cit.,* p. 83.

12. "Oil is our blood!" the crowds in Teheran chant enthusiastically. Ryszard Kapuscinski, "Reflections—Iran, Part I," *The New Yorker* (March 4, 1985), p. 82.

13. Robert Graham, *Iran: The Illusion of Power* (New York: St. Martin's Press, 1978), pp. 61–62.

14. Imam Khomeini, *Islam and Revolution,* transl. by Hamid Algar (Berkeley, CA: Mizan Press, 1981), p. 175.

15. *Ibid.,* p. 202.

16. Mohammed Reza Pahlavi, Shah of Iran, *Answer to History* (New York: Stein and Day, 1980), pp. 152–153.

17. *Ibid.,* p. 167.

18. Sepehr Zabih, *Iran's Revolutionary Upheaval: An Interpretive Essay* (San Francisco: Alchemy Books, 1979), pp. 46–49.

19. "They [the Bassijis] usually advanced ahead of the regular Iranian troops in human wave attacks. Wearing red headbands and inspired by professional chanters before battle, their heads were filled with thoughts of death and martyrdom and going to Paradise." V. S. Naipaul, "After the Revolution," *The New Yorker* (May 26, 1997), pp. 46—69.

20. Farhad Kazemi, "The Iranian Enigma," *Current History* (January 1997), p. 40.

21. Colin Barraclough, in *The Christian Science Monitor* (April 2, 1997), p. 18.

DEVELOPMENT

The 1996—1997 budget, approved by the Majlis in November is a balanced $108 billion, a record. The major source of revenue, $17.5 billion, comes from oil exports. Drastic cuts in subsidies for basic commodities brought the budget into balance, with deficit financing not required.

FREEDOM

Although Iran's human-rights record has been described as "appalling" by Amnesty International, the 1996 presidential election was conducted in conformity with democratic procedures. Upon taking office, President Khatami stated that his priorities were legalization of political parties, an end to press censorship, and limits on the power of komitehs and police to interfere in people's private lives.

HEALTH/WELFARE

Women have become increasingly visible and influential in national politics, due largely to the involvement of the wives and daughters of prominent clerical leaders who use their positions to obtain beneficial legislation for families.

ACHIEVEMENTS

The railroad between Turkmenistan and Iranian Gulf ports has been called the new Silk Road Railroad, since it links landlocked Central Asia, site of the original Silk Road, with the sea.

Iraq (Republic of Iraq)*

GEOGRAPHY
Area in Square Kilometers (Miles):
434,924 (167,924) (larger than
California)
Capital (Population): Baghdad
(3,400,000)
Climate: mostly hot and dry

PEOPLE

Population
Total: 21,422,000
Annual Growth Rate: 3.7%
Rural/Urban Population Ratio: 30/70
Ethnic Makeup: 75–80% Arab; 15–20%
Kurdish; 5% Turkish, Assyrian, and others
Major Languages: Arabic; Kurdish

Health
Life Expectancy at Birth: 66 years
(male); 68 years (female)
Infant Mortality Rate (Ratio): 62/1,000
Average Caloric Intake: below FAO
minimum
Physicians Available (Ratio): 1/1,922

Religions
62% Shia Muslim; 35% Sunni Muslim;
3% Christian and others

Education
Adult Literacy Rate: 89%

Ancient Wonder, Modern Monument

The roots of ancient Babylon reach far back into history. The Garden of Eden
supposedly was nearby, in fertile, well-watered Mesopotamia. Nebuchadnezzar, Babylonia's greatest king, built a great city there 2,500 years ago, with a
vast palace and the Hanging Gardens created on an artificial hill to please his
queen, who was homesick for her northern mountains. Saddam Hussain,
who fancies himself as a modern-day Nebuchadnezzar defending Iraq against
Iranian, U.S., and other intruders, ordered Babylon rebuilt in the 1980s. Much
of it was restored, using some 15 million bricks baked by the method used
in ancient Babylonia. Every 100th brick bears the Arabic inscription "in the
era of President Saddam Hussain, who rebuilt Babylon as protector of the
great Iraq and the builder of civilization." Towering over the Babylon skyline,
from Saddam Hill, is a gleaming white palace built after the Gulf War as a
monument to Iraq's modern-day Nebuchadnezzar.

COMMUNICATION
Telephones: 632,000
Newspapers: 4 main dailies in Baghdad
(one in English with 200,000 circulation)

TRANSPORTATION
Highways—Kilometers (Miles): 45,550
(28,423)
Railroads—Kilometers (Miles): 2,457 (1,582)
Usable Airfields: 121

GOVERNMENT
Type: officially a republic; in reality a
single-party secular state with an
absolute ruler
Independence Date: October 3, 1932,
as kingdom; July 14, 1958, as republic
Head of State/Government: President
Saddam Hussain, who is also the prime
minister and the head of the
Revolutionary Command Council
Political Parties: Ba'th (Iraqi branch of
Arab Socialist Resurrection Party), only
legal party
Suffrage: universal at 18

MILITARY
Number of Armed Forces:
350,000–400,000 (down from 1 million
before the Gulf War)
*Military Expenditures (% of Central
Government Expenditures):* n/a
Current Hostilities: border dispute with
Iran

ECONOMY
Currency ($ U.S. Equivalent): 1,000
Iraqi dinars = $1 (official rate)
Per Capita Income/GDP: n/a
Inflation Rate: n/a
Total Foreign Debt: $85 billion
Natural Resources: oil; natural gas;
phosphates; sulfur; lead; gypsum
Agriculture: wheat; barley; rice; cotton;
dates; poultry
Industry: petroleum; petrochemicals;
textiles; cement

FOREIGN TRADE
Exports: $11.4 billion
Imports: $11.0 billion

*Note: The effects of Iraq's isolation from the
world community since its 1990 invasion of Kuwait still may not be accurately reflected in these
statistics. Those noted here are the most current
available.

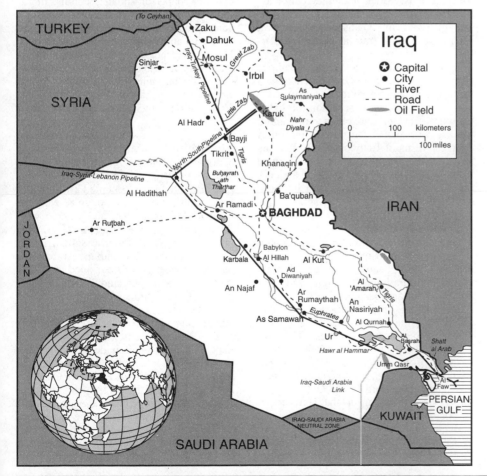

IRAQ

The Republic of Iraq is a young state in a very old land. In ancient times, its central portion was called Mesopotamia, meaning "land between the rivers." The rivers are the Tigris and the Euphrates, which originate in the highlands of Turkey and flow southward for more than a thousand miles to join in an estuary called the Shatt al-Arab, which carries their joint flow into the Persian (or, to Iraqis, the Arab) Gulf.

The fertility of the land between the rivers encouraged human settlement and agriculture from an early date. The oldest farming community yet discovered anywhere was unearthed near Nineveh, capital of the Assyrian Empire, in 1989; it dates back to 9000 B.C. Other settlements grew in time into small but important cities with local governments, their economies based on trade and crafts production in addition to agriculture. And the process of using a written alphabet with characters rather than symbols probably originated here.

Present-day Iraq (an Arabic word meaning "cliff" or, less glamorously, "mud bank") occupies a much larger territory than the original Mesopotamia. Its current land area is about the size of California. Iraqi territory also includes a Neutral Zone on the border with Saudi Arabia. Iraq's other borders are with Turkey, Syria, Jordan, Kuwait, and Iran. These borders were established by the British on behalf of the newly formed Iraqi government, which they controlled after World War I. Disagreement with Kuwait over oil production and allocation from their shared Rumaila field was a factor in the 1990 Iraqi invasion of Kuwait.

In 1994, Iraq accepted the UN border demarcated under *Resolutions 687, 773, and 883,* formally relinquishing its claims to Kuwait and the islands of Bubiyan and Warbah. The new border, re-aligned northward by an international commission, removed 1,870 feet from Iraqi jurisdiction.

Iraq's other border in question, disputed with Iran, is in the Shatt al-Arab (Arab Delta), a broad, navigable estuary extending from the confluence of the Tigris and Euphrates Rivers down to the Persian Gulf. During the years of the British mandate and early independence, Iraq claimed ownership from the west to east banks. Iran's claim extended from its own (east) bank to mid-channel. Iraq recognized the Iranian claim in a 1975 agreement; in return, Iran withdrew support from Kurds in northern Iraq who were seeking autonomy within the Iraqi state. The unilateral abrogation of this agreement by Saddam Hussain was one factor in the 1980–1988 Iran–Iraq War.

HISTORY

During its long and rich history, the "land between the rivers" has seen many empires rise and fall. Assyrians, Babylonians, Chaldeans, Persians, and others contributed layer upon layer to Mesopotamian civilization. In 1989, archaeologists digging at the site of Nimrud, a major Assyrian city, uncovered the 2,700-year-old tomb of a royal princess within the grounds of the palace of King Ashurnasirpal II, containing a vast store of her jewelry—55 pounds in all.

Despite the many varied influences, the most important influence in Iraqi social and cultural life today comes from the conquest of the region by Islamic Arabs. In A.D. 637, an Arab army defeated the Persians, who were then rulers of Iraq, near the village of Qadisiya, not far from modern Baghdad, a victory of great symbolic importance for Iraqis today. Arab peoples settled the region and intermarried with the local population, producing the contemporary Iraqi-Arab population.

During the early years of Islam, Iraq played an important role in Islamic politics. It was a center of Shia opposition to the Sunni Muslim caliphs. The tombs of Ali, Muhammad's son-in-law and the fourth and last leader of a united caliphate, and his son Husayn, martyred in a power struggle with his Damascus-based rival Yazid, are both in Iraq (at Najaf and Karbala, respectively).

In the period of the Abbasid caliphs (A.D. 750–1258), Iraq was the center of a vast Islamic empire stretching from Morocco on the west to the plains of India. Caliph al-Mansur laid out a new capital for the world of Islam, some 60 miles from the ruins of Babylon. He named his new capital Baghdad, possibly derived from a Persian word for "garden," and, according to legend, laid bricks for its foundations with his own hand. Baghdad was a round city, built in concentric circles, each one walled, with the caliph's green-domed palace and mosque at the center. It was the world's first planned city, in the sense of having been laid out in a definite urban configuration and design. Under the caliphs, Baghdad became a center of science, medicine, philosophy, law, and the arts, at a time when London and Paris were mud-and-wattle villages. The city became wealthy from the goods brought by ships from Africa, Asia, and the Far East, since it was easily reachable by shallow-draught boats from the Gulf and the Indian Ocean moving up the Tigris to its harbor.

Baghdad was destroyed by an invasion of Central Asian Mongols in A.D. 1258. The Mongols overran most of the Middle East. In addition to ravaging cities, they ruined the complex irrigation system that made agriculture possible and productive. Modern Iraq has yet to reach the level of agricultural productivity of Abbasid times, even with the use of sophisticated technology.

After the fall of Baghdad, Iraq came under the rule of various local princes and dynasties. In the sixteenth century, it was included in the expanding territory of the Safavid Empire of Iran. The Safavid shah championed the cause of Shia Islam; as a result, the Ottoman sultan, who was Sunni, sent forces to recover the area from his hated Shia foe. Possession of Iraq went back and forth between the two powers, but the Ottomans eventually established control until the twentieth century.

Iraq was administered as three separate provinces under appointed Ottoman governors. The governors paid for their appointments and were interested only in recovering their losses. The result was heavy taxation and indifference to social and economic needs. The one exception was the province of Baghdad. It was governed by a man whom today we would call an enlightened administrator. This governor, Midhat Pasha, set up a provincial newspaper, hospitals, schools, munitions factories, and a fleet of barges to carry produce downriver to ports on the Gulf. His administration also ensured public security and an equitable taxation system. Midhat Pasha later became the grand vizier (prime minister) of the Ottoman Empire and was the architect of the 1876 Constitution, which limited the powers of the sultan.

The British Mandate

World War I found England and France at war with Germany and the Ottoman Empire. British forces occupied Iraq, which they rechristened Mesopotamia, early in the war. British leaders had worked with Arab leaders in the Ottoman Empire to launch a revolt against the sultan; in return, they promised to help the Arabs form an independent Arab state once the Ottomans had been defeated. A number of prominent Iraqi officers who were serving in the Ottoman Army then joined the British and helped them in the Iraqi campaign.

The British promise, however, was not kept. The British had made other commitments, notably to their French allies, to divide the Arab provinces of the Ottoman Empire into British and French "zones of influence." An independent Arab state in those provinces was not in the cards.

The most that the British (and the French) would do was to organize protectorates, called mandates, over the Arab provinces, promising to help the population become self-governing within a specified period of time. The arrangement was approved by the new League of Nations in 1920. Iraq became a British mandate, with a government under British advisers, but was headed by its own monarch, King Faisal I.

The British kept their promise with the mandate. They worked out a Constitution for Iraq in 1925 that established a constitutional monarchy with an elected Legislature and a system of checks and balances. Political parties were allowed, although most of them were groupings around prominent personalities and had no platform other than independence of Britain.[1] In 1932, the mandate formally ended, and Iraq became an independent kingdom under Faisal. The British kept the use of certain air bases, and their large capital investment in the oil industry was protected through a 25-year treaty. Otherwise, the new Iraqi nation was on its own.

The Iraqi Monarchy: 1932–1958
The new kingdom cast adrift on perilous international waters was far from being a unified nation. It was more of a patchwork of warring and competing groups. The Muslim population was divided into Sunni and Shia, as it is today, with the Sunnis forming a minority but controlling the government and business and dominating urban life. The Shia, although a majority, were mostly rural peasants and farmers, many of them migrants to the cities, where they formed a large underclass. The Kurds, the largest non-Arab Muslim group, had been incorporated arbitrarily into the kingdom by the League of Nations when it confirmed the British mandate. The Kurds bitterly resented both Arab and British administration.

The country also had large Christian and Jewish communities, the latter tracing its origins back several thousand years to the exile of Jews from Palestine to Babylonia after the conquest of Jerusalem by Nebuchadnezzar. The Christians made up several denominational groups, such as Chaldeans (Assyrians), pre-Islamic residents of Mesopotamia, Yazidis ("devil-worshippers"), and Sabeans, lineal descendants of the ancient Babylonians. The Christians were protected and favored by the British, especially in the police and civil services; the British found them more cooperative than the Sunni Arabs.

These social and ethnic divisions, plus the economic and educational gaps between rural peasants and urban merchants and landowners, made the new state all but impossible to govern, let alone to develop politically.[2]

King Faisal I was the single stabilizing influence in Iraqi politics. His untimely death in 1933 was critical. His son and successor, Ghazi, was more interested in racing cars than anything else and was killed at the wheel of one in 1939. Ghazi's infant son succeeded him as King Faisal II, while Ghazi's first cousin became regent until the new ruler came of age.

Lacking a strong leader who could bring together the diverse groups in Iraqi society in national unity, the country was governed by a shifting coalition of landowners, politicians, wealthy merchants, and tribal leaders. They controlled the Legislature and the cabinet to such an extent that, during the period 1932–1936, there were 22 different cabinets. Nuri al-Said, one of the few real "strongmen" who served many times as prime minister, once compared the Iraqi governing system to a pack of cards. You must shuffle them often, he said, because the same faces keep turning up.[3]

THE REVOLUTION OF 1958
To its credit, the king's ministers kept the country's three broad social divisions—the Kurdish north, the Sunni Arab center, and the Shia Arab south—in relative balance and harmony. Oil revenues were channeled into large-scale development projects. Education was promoted strongly, which may explain why Iraq has a much higher literacy rate than most other Middle Eastern countries. The press was free, and, though it had a small and ingrown political elite, there was much participation in legislative elections. Despite its legitimate Arab credentials as one of the successor states fashioned by the British after World War I, however, a new generation of pan-Arab nationalist Iraqis viewed the royal regime as a continuation of foreign rule, first Turkish and then British.

Resentment crystallized in the Iraqi Army. On July 14, 1958, a group of young officers overthrew the monarchy in a swift, predawn coup. The king, regent, and royal family were killed. Iraq's new leaders proclaimed a republic that would be reformed, free, and democratic, united with the rest of the Arab world and opposed to all foreign ideologies, "Communist, American, British or Fascist."[4]

Iraq has been a republic since the 1958 Revolution, and July 14 remains a national holiday. But the republic has passed through many different stages, with periodic coups, changes in leadership, and political shifts, most of them violent. Continuing sectarian and ethnic hatreds, maneuvering of political factions, ideological differences, and lack of opportunities for legitimate opposition to express

itself without violence have created a constant sense of insecurity among Iraqi leaders. A similar paranoia affects Iraq's relations with its neighbors. The competition for influence in the Arab world and the Persian/Arab Gulf and other factors combine to keep the leadership constantly on edge.

This pattern of political instability showed itself in the coups and attempted coups of the 1960s. The republic's first two leaders were overthrown after a few years. Several more violent shifts in the Iraqi government took place before the Ba'th Party seized control in 1968. Since that time, the party has dealt ruthlessly with internal opposition. A 1978 decree outlawed all political activity outside the Ba'th for members of the armed forces. Many Shia clergy were executed in 1978–1979 for leading antigovernment demonstrations after the Iranian Revolution; and following Saddam Hussain's election to the presidency, he purged a number of members of the Revolutionary Command Council (RCC), on charges that they were part of a plot to overthrow the regime.

THE BA'TH PARTY IN POWER
The Ba'th Party in Iraq began as a branch of the Syrian Ba'th founded in the 1940s by two Syrian intellectuals: Michel Aflaq, a Christian teacher, and Salah al-Din Bitar, a Sunni Muslim. Like its Syrian parent, the Iraqi Ba'th was dedicated to the goals of Arab unity, freedom, and socialism. However, infighting among Syrian Ba'th leaders in the 1960s led to the expulsion of Aflaq and Bitar. Aflaq went to Iraq, where he was accepted as the party's true leader. Eventually, he moved to Paris, where he died in 1989. His body was brought back to Iraq for burial, giving the Iraqi Ba'th a strong claim to legitimacy in its struggle with the Syrian Ba'th for hegemony in the movement for Arab unity.

The basis of government under the Ba'th is the 1970 Provisional Constitution, issued unilaterally by the Revolutionary Command Council, the party's chief decision-making body. It defines Iraq as a sovereign peoples' democratic republic. The Constitution provides for an "elected" National Assembly with responsibility for ratification of laws and RCC decisions.

An abortive coup in 1973, which pitted a civilian faction of the Ba'th against the military leadership headed by President Ahmad Hasan al-Bakr, stirred party leaders to attempt to broaden their base of popular support. They reached agreement with the Iraqi Communist Party to set up a Progressive National Patriotic Front. Other organizations and groups joined the Front later. Although the Iraqi Communist

Party had cooperated with the Ba'th on several occasions, the agreement marked its first legal recognition as a party. However, distrust between the two organizations deepened as Ba'th leaders struggled to mobilize the masses. The Communists withdrew from the Front in 1979 and refused to participate in parliamentary elections. Their party was declared illegal in 1980 and has not been reinstated, largely due to its support for Iran during the Iran–Iraq War.

SADDAM HUSSAIN

Politics in Iraq since the 1958 overthrow of the monarchy has been marked by extreme secrecy. The intrigues and maneuvers of factions within the Ba'th take place off-screen, and there is no tradition of public pressure to bring them to account. In assessing the strengths, capabilities, and prospects for survival of Iraq's Ba'th leaders, a good question beyond "Who are they?" is "Will the Iraqi ruling class please stand up?"[5] But, in the late 1970s and early 1980s, one of its leaders, Saddam Hussain, emerged from the pack to become an absolute ruler.

Saddam Hussain's early history did not suggest such an achievement. He was born in 1937 in the small town of Tikrit, on the Tigris halfway between Baghdad and Mosul. Tikrit's chief claim to fame, until the twentieth century, was that it was the birthplace of Saladin, hero of the Islamic world in the Middle Ages against the Crusaders. (The Iraqi leader has at times identified himself with Saladin as another great Tikriti, although Saladin was a Kurd and Saddam Hussain's distrust of Kurds is well known.) His family belonged to the Begat of the Al Bu Nasser tribe and farmed about 12 acres of land near Tikrit. While still in school, he became a founding member of the Iraqi branch of the Ba'th Party and took part in its struggles against rival groups, surviving endless internal conflicts to work his way up to vice-chair of the Revolutionary Command Council and finally to chair the body, after his elderly predecessor had retired due to ill health. As chairman, he automatically became president of Iraq under the 1970 Constitution. In 1990, as there are no constitutional provisions limiting the terms of office for the position, the National Assembly named him president-for-life.

Saddam Hussain is a somewhat unusual head of state, in that he holds supreme elective offices although he has never stood as a candidate in an election and serves as commander of the armed forces although he has never served in the military. He does have considerable leadership assets, such as personal courage, a gam-

(Homer Sykes/Katz/Woodfin)

The image of Saddam Hussain has become part of the Iraqi landscape; his portrait appears in public buildings, at the entrances to cities, in homes, even on billboards along highways.

bler's instinct in decision-making, personal magnetism, and charisma. But his major asset is his control over the party, the army, and secret services, and the absolute loyalty of his supporters. Until recently, family solidarity paid off; so many of Saddam's relatives held high positions that his government was called "the Tikriti regime."[6]

The Iran–Iraq War of the 1980s was a severe test for the Ba'th and its leader. A series of Iraqi defeats with heavy casualties in the mid-1980s suggested that the Iranian demand for Hussain's ouster as a precondition for peace might ignite a popular uprising against him. But Iranian advances into Iraqi territory, and in particular the capture of the Fao Peninsula and the Majnoon oil fields, united the Iraqis behind Saddam Hussain. For one of the few times in its history, the nation coalesced around a leader and a cause.

The Iraqi leader used this support to cultivate a more popular public image. He visited the war front regularly, traveled to villages for whistle-stop appearances, helped with the harvests, and mingled with the people. Portraits of Saddam Hussain in field marshal's uniform, Bedouin robes, Ba'th Party green fatigues, and Italian designer suits, often complete with the peasant *keffiyeh* (headscarf) of his native region, are common everywhere in Iraq.

RECENT DEVELOPMENTS

The end of the war with Iran and Saddam Hussain's popularity as the heroic defender of the Iraqi Arab nation against the Shia Iranian enemy prompted a certain lifting of Ba'thist repression and authoritarian rule. Emergency wartime regulations in force since 1980 were relaxed in

1989, and an amnesty was announced for all political exiles except "agents of Iran."[5]

In July 1990, the RCC and the Arab Ba'th Regional Command, the party's governing body, approved a draft constitution to replace the 1970 provisional one. The new Constitution "legalized" the formation of political parties other than the Ba'th, as long as they conformed to Ba'thist principles. It also established freedom of the press and other civil rights, although again in conformity with Ba'thism.

The 1990 Iraqi occupation of Kuwait and the ensuing Gulf War halted even these small steps toward representative government. The draft Constitution remained in suspension; it was not issued unilaterally by the regime nor submitted to voters in a referendum. However, Saddam Hussain has taken it upon himself in recent years to open up the political process, presumably to solidify his image as the "Great Savior." He approved holding of elections for a new Majlis al-Watani in 1996, followed by local and municipal council elections. All candidates were required to be either Ba'th members or bona fide independents. These councils have the authority under a 1995 law to administer programs in health, education, and economic development in their respective localities.

Iraq's difficulties due to the United Nations embargo imposed to force Iraq to divest itself of its nuclear, biological, and chemical war-making capability have tightened party control and discipline. In 1995, the ban on political parties other than the Ba'th was confirmed by amendments to the Constitution; those based on religion, race, or ties with foreign governments were specifically excluded.

THE KURDS

The Kurds, the largest non-Arab minority in Iraq today, form a relatively compact society in the northern mountains. Kurdish territory was included in the British mandate after World War I. British troops were already there, and the territory was known to have important oil resources. The Kurds agitated for self-rule periodically during the monarchy; for a few months after World War II, they formed their own republic in Kurdish areas straddling the Iraq–Iran and Iraq–Turkey borders.

In the 1960s, the Kurds rebelled against the Iraqi government, which had refused to meet their three demands (self-government in Kurdistan, use of Kurdish in schools, and a greater share in oil revenues). The government sent an army to the mountains but was unable to defeat the Kurds, masters of guerrilla warfare. Conflict continued intermittently into the 1970s. Although the 1970 Constitution named Arabs and Kurds as the two nationalities in the Iraqi nation and established autonomy for Kurdistan, the Iraqi government had no real intention of honoring its pledges to the Kurds.

A major Iraqi offensive in 1974 had considerable success against the Kurdish *Pesh Merga* ("Resistance"), even capturing several mountain strongholds. At that point, the shah of Iran, who had little use for Saddam Hussain, began to supply arms to the Pesh Merga. The shah also kept the Iraq–Iran border open as sanctuary for the guerrillas.

In 1975, a number of factors caused the shah to change his mind. He signed an agreement with Saddam Hussain, redefining the Iran–Iraq border to give Iran control over half the Shatt al-Arab. In return, the shah agreed to halt support for the Kurds. The northern border was closed and, without Iranian support, Kurdish resistance collapsed. For more than a decade, the Kurdish region was relatively quiet. In 1986, however, Iran, in another twist of policy, resumed support for Kurdish resistance groups. The main group—the Patriotic Union of Kurdistan (PUK)—agreed to put its fighters under Iranian command, and in turn, the Khomeini regime renounced its goal of an Islamic republic in Iraq.

But with the end of the war with Iran, the Iraqi Army turned on the Kurds in a savage and deliberate campaign of genocide. Operation *Anfal* ("spoils," in Arabic) involved the launching of chemical attacks on such villages as Halabja and the forced deportation of Kurdish villagers from their mountains to detention centers in the flatlands. The campaign received international exposure when 18 tons of Iraqi state documents detailing Operation Anfal were captured by Kurdish partisans during the abortive uprising that followed the Gulf War. The documents, prepared with Nazi-like thoroughness, indicated that approximately 180,000 Kurds, mostly old men, women, and children, had died or disappeared during the operation.

A second exodus of Kurdish refugees took place in 1991, after uprisings of Kurdish rebels in northern Iraq were brutally suppressed by the Iraqi Army, which had remained loyal to Saddam Hussain. The United States and its allies sent troops and aircraft to the Iraqi–Turkish border and barred Iraq from using its own air space north of the 36th Parallel, the main area of Kurdish settlement. Several hundred thousand refugees subsequently returned to their homes and villages.

Under this umbrella of air protection and the exclusion of Iraqi forces from the Kurdish region, the Iraqi Kurds moved toward self-rule in their region. The two main factions—the Kurdish Democratic Party (KDP), led by Massoud al-Barzani, and the Patriotic Union of Kurdistan (PUK) of Jalal al-Talabani—agreed to the formation of a joint Parliament elected by the Kurdish population. This new Parliament, which was divided equally between KDP and PUK members, approved a law defining a federal relationship with Iraq, providing for internal autonomy for the Kurdish region. Kurdish was confirmed as the official language, and a Kurdish university established.

But the tragedy of the Kurds has always been their inability to unite unless there is an external threat. With the Iraqi regime effectively removed from Kurdistan, the traditional cleavages and inner conflicts of Kurdish society came to the surface. A new Kurdish Parliament was scheduled to be elected in September 1995. However, clashes between the two factions broke into open conflict before the elections could take place. By 1996, the PUK controlled two thirds of the region, including the major cities of Irbil and Sulaymaniyah. Barzani's KDP, although it controlled only one third, held an economic advantage over its rival because of its control over the main source of Kurdish revenues. The lion's share of these revenues came from trade (and smuggling) across the Turkish border.

The bell rang for another tragic hour in Iraqi Kurdistan in September 1996. Barzani's KDP struck a deal with Saddam Hussain to help him unseat the rival PUK; and KDP forces, backed by 30,000 to 40,000 Iraqi troops with tanks and artillery, swept down on Irbil and Sulaymaniyah to drive the PUK from its strongholds. KDP success was brief; the PUK withdrew into the mountains to regroup and then launched a counteroffensive, which recovered all its lost territories, except Irbil, by mid-October. Saddam Hussain withdrew his forces after a blunt U.S. warning, but not before rounding up opposition dissidents who had remained there after the Gulf War and were supported by the U.S. Central Intelligence Agency to form the anti-Saddam Iraqi National Congress.

The U.S. warning to Saddam Hussain regarding the violation of the Kurdish "safe haven" protected under Operation Provide Comfort was emphasized by a missile strike that destroyed air defense installations at four Iraqi bases in southern Iraq. But the action had little effect beyond the withdrawal of Iraqi forces from Kurdistan. As one scholar has observed, the Kurds are caught in a double bind—one internal, the other international. Massoud Barzani, son of the legendary Kurdish leader Mulla Mustafa Barzani, "has always assumed that leadership of the Kurds is his birthright. [He is] unable to see the larger interest of Iraqi Kurds outside the parochial concerns of his tribal and family alliances. . . . Talabani owes his support to the growing segment [of Kurdish society] which has become urban and modern." The "international bind" for the Kurds, both those in Iraq and in neighboring countries, is that they have always been manipulated by outside powers, always for reasons of self-interest.[7]

THE OPPOSITION

Opposition to Saddam Hussain has always been fragmented. Those of his political opponents who escaped the leader's firing squads lacked a power base inside the country; they also often disagreed among themselves and preferred a comfortable exile to the ordeal of attempting the overthrow of a well-entrenched despot. But the Iraqi defeat in the Gulf War, followed by the Kurdish and Shia popular uprisings—although they were unsuccessful—suggested that there was more internal resistance to Saddam's rule than had been suspected. The success of Iraq's Kurds in establishing de facto autonomy under UN–U.S. protection also encouraged the opposition, as did the continuing UN-imposed limitations on Iraqi sovereignty. In June 1992, representatives of some 30 opposition groups met in Vienna, Austria, to form the Iraq National Congress (INC), the first anti-Saddam organization in history. Delegates elected a 174-member Assembly and an Executive Committee headed by Ahmed Chalabi, former chairman of Jordan's Petra Bank. A second meeting, in

Iraqi Kurdistan in September 1992, brought together leaders of both Kurdish parties plus representatives of the Syrian Ba'th Party (which is anathema to the Iraqi Ba'th), the Communist Party, the Islamic fundamentalist organization al-Dawa, and the Sunni and Shia communities.

The INC's purpose is the overthrow of Saddam Hussain and the Ba'th regime and their replacement by a federal secular Islamic state, with constitutional guarantees of human rights, protection of minorities, a multiparty political system, and a free market economy that would end "years of corruption, mismanagement and waste." The United States provided the INC with funds channeled through the CIA and helped to set up an INC office in Irbil. However, due to its Kurdish identification, the organization failed to generate opposition to the Iraqi leader among the largely Sunni officer corps. With the capture of Irbil by joint Kurdish–Iraqi forces, the INC was effectively destroyed, with most of its leaders either killed or missing. A similar fate befell the Iraqi National Accord, a Turkmen opposition group based in the Kurdish city of Zakho.

OTHER COMMUNITIES

The Shia community, which forms approximately 62 percent of the total population, has been ruled by the Sunni minority since independence. Shias have been consistently underrepresented in successive Ba'thist governments and are the most economically deprived component of the population. However, they remained loyal to the regime (or at least quiescent) during the war with Iran. In a belated attempt to undo decades of deprivation and assure their continued loyalty, the government invested large sums in the rehabilitation of Shia areas in southern Iraq after the war ended. Roads were built, and sacred Shia shrines were repaired.

Long-held Shia grievances against Ba'thist rule erupted in a violent uprising after Iraq's defeat in the Gulf War. The uprising was crushed, however, as Iraqi troops remained loyal to Saddam Hussain. Some 600 troops were killed in an Alamo-type siege of the sacred shrines, which were badly damaged. Some rebels escaped to the almost impenetrable marshlands of southern Iraq, and resistance there has continued. The pursuit of these rebels

prompted the United Nations to declare another no-fly zone south of the 32nd Parallel; like the Kurdish no-fly zone, it is off limits to Iraqi aircraft and is considered by the Iraqis, with some justification, as a limitation on their sovereignty.

The rebels' retreat into the marshlands served as an excuse for the Iraqi regime to bring another distinctive community—the Marsh Arabs—under centralized government control. This community, believed by some to be descended from the original inhabitants of southern Iraq and by others to be descended from slaves, has practiced for centuries a unique way of life based on fishing and hunting in the marshes, living in papyrus-and-mud houses and traveling in reed boats through the maze of unmarked channels of their watery region. Prior to 1990, they numbered about 750,000. Previous Iraqi governments had ignored them, but Saddam Hussain was determined to bring all Iraq under centralized government control. Using their support for Shia rebels hiding in the marshes as his excuse, he declared that their culture was "primitive, debased and non-Iraqi." Iraqi troops encircled a 3,800-

(UN photo/H. Arvidsson)

UN Security Council Resolution 687 called for the disposal of Iraq's weapons of mass destruction. Saddam Hussain had stockpiled enormous quantities of chemical munitions, and while many of these insidious weapons were indeed destroyed, large quantities remained hidden. Iraq's refusal to cooperate with international inspection teams continued to be a problem and has caused sanctions to remain in place.

square-mile area of marshlands in June 1992, rounding up the population for resettlement elsewhere and killing those who resisted, while artillery barrages leveled their villages.

At the same time, the government began a massive effort to reclaim the marshes. Aside from destroying the way of life of the Marsh Arabs, it would reclaim the area and convert millions of acres to productive farmland. A "third river," in the form of a canal between the Tigris and the Euphrates, was completed in 3 months early in 1993 by 6,000 workers drawn from Iraq's huge labor surplus. Some 350 miles in length, it was intended to drain salt water from approximately 330 million acres of marshland for conversion to agriculture. By June 1993, the water level in parts of the marshes had dropped by more than 3 feet; some 46 Arab villages were left high and dry. The no-fly exclusion zone had little effect on the campaign against the Marsh Arabs and their Shia allies, since it did not extend to artillery bombardments or infantry attacks. The canal does not affect Tigris or Euphrates waters, since it flows directly into the Gulf; it thus has significant value for agriculture, as it drains excess salinity from the soil. Also, it is deep enough to compensate for loss of upstream water from Syrian and Turkish dams. But the cost in terms of destruction of habitat and way of life of a unique Iraqi society is enormous.

THE ECONOMY
Iraq's economy is based on oil production and exports, but it has a well-developed agriculture (Iraq is the world's leading exporter of dates), due to the fertile soil and water resources of the Tigris and Euphrates Rivers. It also has a large population and a skilled labor force available for industrial development.

Since the Ba'th Party took control in 1968, its economic policies have emphasized state control and guidance of the economy, under the Ba'thist rubric of guided socialism. In 1987, the regime began a major economic restructuring program. More than 600 state organizations were abolished, and young technocrats replaced many senior ministers. In 1988, the government began selling off state-run industries, reserving only heavy industry and hydrocarbons for state operation. Light industries such as breweries and dairy plants would henceforth be run by the private sector.

The oil industry was developed by the British during the mandate but was nationalized in the early 1970s. Nationalization and price increases after 1973 helped to accelerate economic growth. The bulk of Iraqi oil shipments are exported via pipelines across Turkey and Syria. During the war with Iran, the Turkish pipeline proved essential to Iraq's economic survival, since the one across Syrian territory was closed and Iraq's own refineries and ports were put out of commission by Iranian attacks. Turkey closed this pipeline during the 1990–1991 Gulf crisis, a decision that proved a severe strain for the Iraqi economy (not to mention a huge sacrifice for coalition-member Turkey).

Iraq has proven oil reserves of some 100 billion barrels, the fifth largest in the world, and new discoveries continue to augment the total. Oil output was cut to 2 million barrels per day in 1986–1987, in accordance with quotas set by the Organization of Petroleum Exporting Countries, but was increased to 4.5 million b/d in 1989 as the country sought to recover economically from war damage.

The country also has important natural-gas reserves and significant deposits of phosphate rock, sulfur, lead, gypsum, and iron ore.

The economic impact of the 8-year Iran–Iraq War was heavy, causing delays in interest payments on foreign loans, defaults to some foreign contractors, and postponement of major development projects except for dams, deemed vital to agricultural production. The war also was a heavy drain on Iraqi finances; arms purchases between 1981 and 1985 cost the government $23.9 billion. By 1986, the external debt was $12 billion. By 1988, the debt burden had gone up to nearly $60 billion, although half this total had been given by the Arab Gulf states as war aid and was unlikely ever to be repaid. Today, the foreign debt is about $85 billion.

Iraq's economic recovery after the war with Iran, despite heavy external debts, suggested rapid growth in the 1990s. Gross domestic product was expected to rise by 5 percent a year due to increasing oil revenues. Even in 1988, Iraq's GDP of $50 billion was the highest in the Arab world, after Saudi Arabia's. With a well-developed infrastructure and a highly trained workforce, Iraq appeared ready to move upward into the ranks of the developed nations.

THE UN EMBARGO
Iraq's invasion and occupation of Kuwait and the resulting Gulf War drew a red line through these optimistic prospects. Bombing raids destroyed much of the country's infrastructure, knocking out electricity grids, bridges, and sewage and water-purification systems. Although much of this infrastructure has been repaired, the oil industry and water and sanitation systems in particular have been operating at only about 40 percent of capacity.

The UN embargo that was imposed on Iraq after the Gulf War to force compliance with resolutions ordering the country to dismantle its weapons program has not only brought development to a halt but has also caused untold suffering for the Iraqi population. The resolutions in question were *Resolution 687,* which required the destruction of all missile, chemical, and nuclear facilities; *Resolution 713,* which established a permanent UN monitoring system for all missile test sites and nuclear installations; and *Resolution 986,* which allowed Iraq to sell 700,000 barrels of oil per day for 6 months, in return for its compliance with the first two resolutions. Of the $1.6 billion raised through oil sales, $300 million would be paid into a UN reparations fund for Kuwait. Another $300 million would be put aside to finance the UN monitoring system as well as providing aid for the Kurdish population. The remainder would revert to Iraq to be used for purchases of food and medical supplies.

Resolution 986 was rejected by Saddam Hussain as an infringement on Iraqi national sovereignty. But, after a number of years of political standoff, with the Iraqi people edging closer and closer to destitution, the regime agreed in 1996 to UN terms for oil sales in return for food and essential medical supplies. The agreement came none too soon for the people. A 1995 Food and Agriculture Organization report had stated that 4 million Iraqis were destitute, including 600,000 women and nursing mothers. Another UN report indicated that 750,000 Iraqi children were severely malnourished, with 4,500 dying each month due to malnutrition and the weakened resistance to disease that developed as a result.[8]

GLORIOUS LEADER
OR GREAT SURVIVOR?
Until very recently, army support and a ruthlessly efficient security service, with informers literally at every street corner, assured Saddam Hussain's continuation in power. In any case, internal opposition is nonexistent. Aside from a small (mostly Sunni) elite dependent upon the ruler and thus isolated from the impact of sanctions, potential opponents have been silenced or are in exile. The once prosperous and well-educated Iraqi middle class, the backbone of national development, has been reduced to near starvation, so survival has taken precedence over any form of political activity for those who have remained in the country.

An additional factor keeping Saddam in power is his deliberate propagation of the

Border province of the Ottoman Empire **1520–1920**	British mandate **1920–1932**	Independent kingdom under Faisal I **1932**	The monarchy is overthrown by military officers **1958**	The Ba'th Party seizes power **1968**	The Algiers Agreement between the shah of Iran and Hussein ends Kurdish insurrection **1975**	Iraqi forces invade Iran, initiating war; diplomatic relations are restored with the United States after a 17-year break **1980s**	A pipeline is completed from Iraqi oil fields to Port Yanbu on the Red Sea, bypassing the Gulf; the war with Iran comes to an end after 8 bitter years

1990s

Iraq invades and occupies Kuwait, leading to the brief but intense Gulf War; Saddam Hussein retains power	UN sanctions squeeze the Iraqi masses; army uprising and defections occur, but Saddam remains firmly in control	Saddam Hussain's obstacles to UN weapons inspectors precipitate an international crisis

cult of the "Glorious Leader." Wherever one goes in the country, there are larger-than-life posters of him looking down from bridge abutments, storefronts, public buildings, highway billboards, even a gigantic poster welcoming the occasional visitor to Baghdad's international airport. This high visibility has paid off in minor humanitarian gestures to ward off potential mass unrest. Thus, after his "re-election" in October 1995 to another 7-year term by a 99.96 percent vote in a nationwide referendum, Saddam Hussain approved a small increase in the monthly flour and vegetable ration for Iraq's hard-pressed population, effective December 1.

Despite his apparently secure hold on power, the Glorious Leader was threatened briefly by internal opposition in 1995. An army uprising led by a general of the Dulaimi clan, traditional rivals of Saddam's Tikriti clan, was put down with some difficulty in June. A more serious potential threat developed later in the summer, when two of the leader's sons-in-law, their wives, and a number of Sunni army officers defected to Jordan. One son-in-law, Hussein Kamel, had headed the Iraqi weapons program and was a member of the inner circle surrounding the president. While in Jordan, he talked openly of leading a campaign to overthrow his former chief. But, in time, the Iraqi exiles became an embarrassment to Jordan's King Hussein, in part because their former association with the regime rendered them suspect in the eyes of the Jordanian-based

Iraqi opposition group (the Iraqi National Accord). In February 1996, the Jordanian government declared them persona non grata, and they returned to Iraq. Saddam Hussain promised that they would be pardoned as repentant sinners, but shortly after their return, the sons-in-law were killed in a gun battle with members of Saddam's clan, their traditional rivals.

Thus far, neither external pressures nor internal opposition has been able to shake Saddam Hussain loose from his control over Iraq. As an Arab leader who is perceived as "standing up to the West," he enjoys considerable popularity in the region, and more often than not his game of thrust-and-parry with U.S. administrations has worked in his favor. Former U.S. congressman Bill Richardson, who mediated with him for the release of two American technicians, observed, "You cannot have a personal connection with him, because he tries to intimidate you—by the way he looks at you, by his rhetoric, his uniform and his weapon and his security. I convinced him that by releasing the Americans, he helped with his image in the world. He was also trying to send a signal to the U.S. that he was a reasonable person on a humanitarian basis."[9]

NOTES

1. The parties had names like "Free," "Awakening," "Nationalists," and "National Independence." Richard F. Nyrop, *Iraq: A Country Study* (Washington, D.C.: American University, Foreign Area Studies, 1979), p. 38.

2. " . . . sectors were divided within themselves, politicians working against their colleagues, shaykhs perpetuating traditional rivalries . . . fellahin resenting the exploitation of urban landlords and tribal shaykhs alike. . . ." Mohammad A. Tarbush, *The Role of the Military in Politics: A Case Study of Iraq to 1941* (London: Kegan Paul, 1982), p. 50.

3. *Ibid.,* p. 50.

4. Nyrop, *op. cit.,* pp. 48–49.

5. Joe Stork, "State Power and Economic Structure . . . ," in Tim Niblock, ed., *Iraq: The Contemporary State* (London: Croom Helm, 1982), p. 44.

6. See Milton Viorst, "Letter from Baghdad," *The New Yorker* (June 24, 1991), p. 61.

7. Henri J. Barkey, "Kurdish Geopolitics," *Current History* (January 1997), p. 2.

8. Yasmine Bahrani, "Iraq, the Human Cost of the Embargo," *The Washington Post Weekly* (October 14–20, 1996), p. 23.

9. Interview in *Parade* magazine (September 14, 1997), p. 7.

DEVELOPMENT

As of June 1997, Iraq had accrued $1.75 billion in oil sales, providing some humanitarian relief for its hard-pressed people. Iraqi men were able finally to "lather up and shave" with real soap, and some 550,000 tons of food have been brought in under the oil-for-food agreement. However, the limitation on oil sales to one fifth of its pre–Gulf War sales has kept development projects at a standstill.

FREEDOM

The 1990 draft constitution allowing political parties other than the Ba'th to form and guaranteeing press freedom and civil rights has yet to be adopted. In theory, Iraq is governed by the 1970 provisional Constitution; in practice, however, it is a police state.

HEALTH/WELFARE

The start of shipments of food and medical supplies under the oil-for-food agreement with the UN has brought some relief to the population and enabled the regime to increase food rations. The monthly flour ration per family is now 18 kilos (40.6 pounds). The plan sets aside $805 million for food, $65 million for soap and detergent, $210 million for medicines, and other funds for various projects.

ACHIEVEMENTS

Iraq's Third River project, a canal dug underneath the Tigris and Euphrates Rivers to link Baghdad with the port of Basra, was completed in 1996 without any foreign aid. It is intended to drain off excess salinity from the potentially rich agricultural land. The project will also improve the water quality of these rivers. Unfortunately, the construction process involved the draining of marshes and the removal of Marsh Arabs elsewhere, destroying a way of life that had existed for centuries.

Israel (State of Israel)

GEOGRAPHY
Area in Square Kilometers (Miles): 20,325 (7,850) (about the size of Delaware)
Capital (Population): Tel Aviv (357,400) recognized as official capital by most countries; Jerusalem (567,000), claimed as capital but not internationally recognized
Climate: temperate, except in desert areas

PEOPLE

Population
Total: 5,433,200 (includes settlers in East Jerusalem, the West Bank, Gaza Strip, and Golan Heights)
Annual Growth Rate: 1.4%
Rural/Urban Population Ratio: 10/90
Ethnic Makeup: 80% Jewish; 20% non-Jewish (mostly Arab)
Major Languages: Hebrew; English; Arabic

Health
Life Expectancy at Birth: 76 years (male); 80 years (female)
Infant Mortality Rate (Ratio): 8.4/1,000
Average Caloric Intake: 115% of FAO minimum
Physicians Available (Ratio): 1/214

Religions
82% Jewish; 14% Muslim; 2% Christian; 2% Druze

Education
Adult Literacy Rate: 95%

COMMUNICATION
Telephones: 1,800,000
Newspapers: 23 dailies; 20 in Hebrew

TRANSPORTATION
Highways—Kilometers (Miles): 13,461 (8,400)
Railroads—Kilometers (Miles): 520 (324)
Usable Airfields: 57

GOVERNMENT
Type: parliamentary republic
Independence Date: May 14, 1948
Head of State/Government: President Ezer Weizman (ceremonial); Prime Minister Benjamin Netanyahu
Political Parties: Likud, which governs as majority in coalition with Tsomet, Gesher, Shas, and National Religious Party; opposition parties are Labor Party, Meretz, Democratic Front for Peace and Equality, and United Arab List; others include Yisrael Ba-Aliyah (Russian immigrants), Third Way, and United Torah
Suffrage: universal over 18

MILITARY
Number of Armed Forces: 141,000
Military Expenditures (% of Central Government Expenditures): 25.4%
Current Hostilities: ongoing conflict with the Lebanese Hizbullah; periodic clashes with Palestinians in Jerusalem and West Bank

ECONOMY
Currency ($ U.S. Equivalent): 2.88 new Israeli shekels = $1
Per Capita Income/GDP: $13,880/$70.1 billion
Inflation Rate: 11%
Total Foreign Debt: $25.9 billion
Natural Resources: copper; phosphates; bromide; potash; clay; sand; sulfur; bitumen; manganese
Agriculture: fruits; vegetables; beef, dairy, and poultry products
Industry: food processing; diamond cutting and polishing; textiles and clothing; chemicals; metal products; transport and electrical equipment; potash mining; electronics

FOREIGN TRADE
Exports: $20.5 billion
Imports: $22.5 billion

Jerusalem: Golden—and Tarnished

In 1995, Israel inaugurated a 15-month celebration of the 3,000th anniversary—not of its founding, but of King David's declaration that it was the capital of the Jewish nation. Some countries, however, boycotted the ceremonies on the grounds that the city's political status remains to be negotiated. Politics aside, this city, which is sacred to three religions and claimed by two peoples as their national capital, exerts a powerful pull on visitors and residents alike. From the golden Dome of the Rock to the Wailing Wall and the Church of the Holy Sepulchre, Jerusalem symbolizes what the Israeli poet Yehuda Amichai has called "heavenly and earthly together . . . its great accomplishment is that it has succeeded in not being a museum." To Israelis, it is their eternal capital.

Israel

- ✪ Capital
- ● City
- ∿ River
- - - - Road
- ▨ Israeli-occupied (Status to be determined)

0   50   kilometers
0   50   miles

MEDITERRANEAN SEA

LEBANON
UNDOF ZONE
GOLAN HEIGHTS
SYRIA
'Akko
Nahariyya
Haifa
Tiberias'
Nazareth'
Hadera
Netanya
Herzliyya
Nablus'
WEST BANK
TEL AVIV–YAFO
Ramla
Jericho
Ashdad
JERUSALEM
Jordan River
GAZA STRIP
Bethlehem
Ashqelon
Gaza
Hebron
DEAD SEA
Rafah
Beersheba
EGYPT
Dimona
Oron
JORDAN
Mizpe Ramon
Nahal HaArava
Yotvata
Elat
GULF OF AQABA
SAUDI ARABIA

ISRAEL

Israel, the Holy Land of Judeo–Christian tradition, is a very small state about the size of Delaware. Its population is also smaller than those of most of its neighbors', with low birth and immigration rates, which dropped 4.4 percent in 1996. Population growth within these limits would be manageable. But, until recently, the country's very existence was not accepted by its neighbors and its borders remained temporary ones under the 1949 armistice agreements that ended the first Arab–Israeli war.

The country occupies a larger land area than it held at the time of its independence in 1948, due to expansion wars with its neighbors. The border with Egypt was defined by the 1979 peace treaty; subsequently, Israel retroceded the Sinai Peninsula, which had been occupied by Israeli forces in 1973. In 1994, Israel signed a peace treaty with Jordan. Among its provisions, their common border was demarcated, and areas in the Galilee were returned to Jordan. Israel's borders with Syria and Lebanon remain provisional under the 1949 armistice agreements. In the case of Lebanon, Israeli forces occupy a 9-mile-wide self-declared security zone in Lebanese territory, along the border.

Although it is small, Israel has a complex geography, with a number of distinct regions. The northern region, Galilee, is a continuation of the Lebanese mountains, but at a lower altitude. The Galilee uplands drop steeply on three sides: to the Jordan Valley on the east, a narrow coastal plain on the west, and southward to the Valley of Esdraelon, a broad inland valley from the Mediterranean to the Jordan River. This lowland area is fertile and well watered and has become important to Israeli agriculture.

Another upland plateau extends south from Esdraelon for about 90 miles. This area contains the ancient Jewish heartland—Judea and Samaria to Israelis, the West Bank for Palestinians—which is supposed to serve as the core of the self-governing Palestinian state as defined in the 1993 Oslo agreements. This plateau gradually levels off into semidesert, the barren wilderness of Judea. The wilderness merges imperceptibly into the Negev, a desert region that comprises 60 percent of the land area but has only about 12 percent of the population.

TERRITORY CHANGES

Until 1993, Israeli territory included four areas originally excluded from its territorial limits as defined under the 1948 UN Partition Plan for Palestine. These were the Gaza Strip, seized from Egypt after the 1967 Six-Day War; the West Bank (of the Jordan River) and East Jerusalem; former Jordanian territories occupied at the same time; and the Golan Heights, along the Syrian–Israeli border, captured during the 1973 Yom Kippur (October) War. The first three territories remained under Israeli occupation, but the Golan Heights was annexed unilaterally in 1981. However, the UN maintains an observer force in a demilitarized zone along the border.

The Oslo agreements and the 1995 Israeli deployment agreement began the process of establishing Palestinian self-rule over the Gaza Strip and the West Bank. Thus far, Israeli troops have been withdrawn from Gaza and certain West Bank towns, establishing putative Palestinian sovereignty in those locations. However, the assassination of Israeli prime minister Yitzhak Rabin in November 1995, followed by Likud's victory in the 1996 Knesset (Israeli Parliament) elections, have slowed down the disengagement process. Terrorist attacks in Israel, notably a suicide bombing in the main Jerusalem market in July 1997, have brought withdrawal to a halt and in some respects reversed it, as Israel has re-invoked on security grounds the restrictions on the Palestinian population imposed over 30 years of occupation.

The issue of East Jerusalem—the "Old City" sacred to three faiths but revered especially by Jews as their spiritual, emotional, and political capital—remains a difficult one to resolve. From 1949 to 1967, it was under Jordanian control, with Jews prohibited from visiting the Wailing Wall and other sites important in the history of Judaism. Almost the only contact between the divided sectors of east and west was at the Mandelbaum Gate and the adjacent American Colony Hotel. The Six-Day War of June 1967 resulted in unification of the two sectors. Since then, Jerusalem has been governed politically by an elected mayor and council. Access by adherents of the three major faiths is guaranteed, and control over them is exercised by their respective religious authorities.[1]

THE POPULATION

The great majority of the Israeli population are Jewish. Judaism is the state religion; Hebrew, the ancient liturgical language revived and modernized in the twentieth century, is the official language, although English is widely used. Language and religion, along with shared historical traditions, a rich ancient culture, and a commitment to the survival of the Jewish state, have fostered a strong sense of national unity among the Israeli people. They are extremely nationalistic, and these feelings are increased because of hostile neighbors. Most Israelis believe that their neighbors are determined to destroy their state, and this belief has helped to develop a "siege mentality" among them. This "siege mentality" has deep roots. Nobel Peace Prize–winner Elie Wiesel has defined it as follows: "Jewish history, flooded by suffering but anchored in defiance, describes a permanent conflict between *us* [Jews] and the others. Ever since Abraham [the father of Judaism], we have been on one side and the rest of the world on the other."[2]

Except for a small population of Jews that remained in the region (the village of

(Israeli Government Tourism Administration)

Israelis regard Jerusalem as the political and spiritual capital of Israel. East Jerusalem was annexed from Jordan after the 1967 Six-Day War, and returning this part of the city to Jordan has never been seriously considered by Israel.

Peki'in in Galilee is said to be the only one with an unbroken Jewish presence over the past 2,000 years), Jews dispersed throughout the world after Jerusalem's conquest by Roman legions in A.D. 70. The dispersed Jews formed two main groups—the Ashkenazi (European) and Sephardim (Oriental)—depending on location.[3]

The two groups had little in common except their religion. They had become so isolated from each other over centuries of dispersal that they spoke different languages and could not communicate. Hebrew, until the twentieth century, was one of the few communication links among widely scattered Jewish communities, being used as a literary and liturgical language.

The diversity among incoming Jews, particularly the Sephardic communities, was so great during the early years of independence that the government developed a special orientation program of Hebrew language and culture, called Ulpan (which is still in use), to help with their assimilation. Some Sephardic groups have prospered and gained economic and political equality with Ashkenazis. However, the majority of Sephardim have yet to attain full equality, and this is a cause of tension.

Another difference among Israelis has to do with religious practice. The Chasidim or Orthodox Jews strictly observe the rules and social practices of Judaism and live in their own separate neighborhoods within cities. Reform Jews, by far the majority, are Jewish in their traditions, history, and faith, but they modify their religious practices to conform to the demands of modern life and thought. Both the Orthodox and Reform Jews have chief rabbis who sit on the Supreme Rabbinical Council, the principal interpretive body for Judaism. There are also two small Jewish communities of ancient origin, the Karaites and the Samaritans. The latter speak Arabic, reject rabbinical authority, and consider themselves Palestinians, although in religious terms they are a Jewish sect that broke away from the main body of Judaism some 2,500 years ago.

Relations between the majority Reform Jews in Israel and the much smaller Orthodox community were marked by occasional incidents of friction but overall coexistence until the rise to power of Menachem Begin's Likud Bloc. Begin's own political party, Herut, always emphasized the country's biblical heritage in its platform. But, during Begin's period in office, the small religious parties that represent the Orthodox acquired political power because they were essential to the coalition government. This fact, plus the high birth rate among haredim families, has

given political (and social) influence out of proportion to their numbers. In recent years, friction has evolved into open conflict, as religious Jews have increasingly imposed Judaic law and Orthodox Jewish behavior and practice on the larger Reform community.

Differences in historical experiences have also divided the Ashkenazis. Most lived in Eastern Europe, sometimes isolated from other Jews as well as from their Christian neighbors. At one time, "They were closed off in a gigantic ghetto called the Pale of Settlement, destitute, deprived of all political rights, living in the twilight of a slowly disintegrating medieval world."[4] However, by the nineteenth century, Jews in Western Europe had become politically tolerated and relatively well-off, and, due to the Enlightenment, found most occupations and professions open to them.[5] These "emancipated" Jews played a crucial role in the Zionist movement, but the actual return to Palestine and settlement was largely the work of Ashkenazis from Eastern Europe.

The Soviet Union, ironically, with a Jewish population of 3.5 million, did not have diplomatic relations with Israel, although consular relations were established in 1990. Soviet Jews were allowed to emigrate after 1987 under the *glasnost* ("openness") policy of Mikhail Gorbachev. A U.S. limit on entry of Soviet Jews accelerated emigration to Israel, and by 1992, some 350,000 had arrived. The majority were highly educated and professionally trained, but they were often unable to find suitable jobs and placed an added strain on housing and social services in Israel. (One reason for the Israeli request to the United States for $10 billion in loan guarantees, which was held up by the Bush administration and partially released by its successor, was to obtain funds for housing Soviet immigrants. Disillusionment with their experiences and lack of professional opportunities in Israel led the immigrants to form their own political party, Yisrael Ba'Aliya, to press for better conditions. After the 1996 Knesset elections and the ensuing jockeying for power, the party joined Benjamin Netanyahu's ruling coalition. It was encouraged to do so by a $65 million "sweetener" for jobs and housing for the Russian immigrant community.

The Aliyah policy, literally "going up" (that is, to Israel), resulted in the ingathering of Jewish communities long isolated from the mainstream of world Jewry. Yemen's Jewish community was the first to arrive, being airlifted directly from medieval conditions into a modern bustling world most of them could not have imag-

ined. (A small Jewish community remains in Yemen.) In 1991, a secret airlift brought 14,324 Ethiopian Jews to Israel, just prior to the fall of Ethiopia's Marxist government. This community, called *falashas* ("strangers") by their Christian and Muslim neighbors and accused of having *budda* (satanic powers), had been so isolated that they believed themselves to be the last surviving Jews on earth. The exodus of Ethiopian Jews to Israel continued on an intermittent basis by tacit agreement with the new Ethiopian government until 1993. At that time, it was suspended due to uncertain political conditions in Ethiopia and the establishment of independence in Eritrea, that country's predominantly Muslim province, by referendum, which contributed to Ethiopian instability. Israel also airlifted 300 Jews from Albania in 1991, after establishing diplomatic relations with that country.

Modern Israel has two important non-Jewish minorities, totaling about 1 million—20 percent of the population. The larger group consists of Muslim and some Christian Arabs who stayed after Israel achieved statehood. This Arab population was ruled under military administration from 1948 until 1966, when restrictions were lifted and the Arabs ostensibly became full citizens. However, they were not allowed to serve in the armed forces; and, until recently, they did not have parity with Israelis in job training and opportunities, access to higher education, housing, and political representation. When the Israeli state was formed in 1948, they were primarily farmers living in small villages; by the 1980s, however, some 60 percent were employed in construction and other industries and in public service. Higher educational access for Arabs also greatly improved.

The key to improvement in the economic status of Israeli Arabs is their greater political representation. The first all-Arab political party was formed in 1988; it won a seat in the Knesset in the elections of that year. A new Arab party won four seats in the Knesset in the 1996 elections, increasing Arab clout, albeit in opposition along with Peres's Labor Party. During its tenure in office, the Peres government had given city status to several Arab towns, making their residents eligible for Israeli social security and other benefits. Also, child allowances for Arab families were brought into line with those given to Jewish families. But, in most other economic respects, the Israeli Arab population lags well behind its Jewish counterpart.

A second non-Jewish minority, the Druze, live not only in Israel but also in

(UN photo/John Isaac)

The Wailing Wall, a focal point of Jewish worship, is all that remains of the ancient temple destroyed by the Roman legions led by Titus in A.D. 70. The Wailing Wall stands as a place of pilgrimage for devout Jews throughout the world.

mountain enclaves in Lebanon and Syria. They form a majority of the population in the Golan Heights, occupied by Israeli forces in the 1967 Six-Day War and annexed in 1981. They practice a form of Islam that split off from the main body of the religion in the tenth century. Most Druze have remained loyal to the Israeli state. In return, they have been given full citizenship, are guaranteed freedom to practice their faith under their religious leaders, and may serve in the armed forces. Some 233 Druze have died in Israel's wars.

At present there are about 70,000 Druze in Israel, living in 16 large villages in the Galilee and near Haifa. Another 16,000 Druze live in the Israeli-annexed Golan Heights, where they are physically separated from their families on the Syrian side by the UN demilitarized zone. These Druze have rejected Israeli citizenship. When Israel annexed the Golan Heights unilaterally in 1981, they reacted with a 6-month-long general strike; it ended only when the government agreed not to force citizenship on the Druze. In 1997, on the 15th anniversary of the strike, the villagers showed their continued defiance of Israeli rule by flying the Syrian flag over their schools.

Despite their relative freedom, the Druze living in Israel, like the Israeli Arabs, suffer from discrimination in educational and work opportunities. The discrepancy is particularly noticeable for Druze women. In 1988, the first national movement for the advancement of Druze women was formed. Called the Council of

Druze Women, it works to help them to reach the educational and social levels of Israeli women and to protect them from the abuses of what is still a patriarchal society, one in which there is even a religious ban on women driving.

There are two other small minority groups in Israel, both Sunni Muslims. The Circassians, descendants of warriors from the Caucasus brought in centuries ago to help Muslim armies drive the Christian Crusaders from Palestine, have been completely integrated into Israeli society. The second minority group, the Bedouin, formerly roamed the barren uplands of Judea and the Negev Desert. Those in Judea have been completely urbanized. But the Negev Bedouin, some 100,000 in number, maintained their traditional nomadic way of life until very recently. This way of life has come under attack from many quarters. A major one stems from the government policy of settling them in permanent homes in new towns. Thus far, seven such towns have been established. The largest, Rahat (population 30,000) was given city status in 1994. However, fewer than half of the Bedouin have accepted the government's offer of money to build homes (called *Bneh Beitcha*, "Build your own home") and a *dunam* (one quarter of an acre) of land. The remaining Bedouin continue to live in tents or illegally constructed block dwellings that are subject to demolition and eviction of residents under the 1992 building code. Like the Druze, the Bedouin are discriminated against in education and job opportunities; and restrictions on their traditional right

to roam and pasture their herds on rented, leased, or open land have driven many to become day laborers.

HISTORY

For most Jews, the establishment of the modern State of Israel is the fulfillment of God's promise of the Land of Canaan to Abraham and his descendants as their home. The original promise still stands to religious Jews. At various times in their history, Jews were carried off into captivity or dispersed into exile by invaders. Each period of exile is called a diaspora (dispersion). The most important one, in terms of modern Israel, took place in the first century A.D. When the Roman Empire expanded into the Middle East, the Jews' homeland became the province of Judea, ruled indirectly at first under such rulers as Herod the Great. Herod was given the honorary title of "King of Judea," and he did much restoration and improvement of the landscape during his reign.[6] After his death, the Romans imposed direct rule under appointed governors called procurators. The Jews proved difficult to govern, and, in A.D. 69–70, they rebelled. The forces of Roman general (later emperor) Titus then besieged Jerusalem. The city fell in A.D. 70 and Roman legions sacked and destroyed much of it. (A portion of the Western Wall of the Temple was not destroyed and stands as a place of pilgrimage for devout Jews, who come from all over the world to pray beside it. It is called the Wailing Wall.) Then, and for the next 2,000 years, Jews dispersed all over the world.

Diaspora Jews were often persecuted in the lands where they lived, and they were almost always distrusted, feared, and restricted to certain occupations. They were better off in some places than in others. During the 700-year Islamic rule in Spain (A.D. 711–1492), Jews lived at peace with their Muslim neighbors and made important contributions to Hispano–Islamic society as judges, government ministers, and financial advisers to Muslim rulers. After Spain was reconquered by Christian kings, Jews and Muslims alike suffered from mistreatment and eventually forced deportation. During this "second diaspora," many Spanish Jews fled to the lands of the Ottoman Turkish Muslim Empire. The Ottomans protected them as "People of the Book," due to their generally high level of learning and their sacred books, the Talmud and Torah.

Zionism

The organized movement for a Jewish return to Palestine to fulfill the biblical promise is called Zionism. It became, however, more of a political movement formed for a particular purpose: to establish by Jewish settlement a homeland where dispersed Jews may gather, escape persecution, and knit together the strands of traditional Jewish faith and culture. As a political movement, it differs sharply from spiritual Zionism, the age-old dream of the return. Most Orthodox Jews and traditionalists opposed *any* movement to reclaim Palestine; they believed that it is blasphemy to do so, for only God can perform the miracle of restoring the Promised Land. The reality of the establishment of the Jewish state by force of arms, with a secular political system backed by strong Jewish nationalism, has created what one author calls "an unprecedented Jewish dialogue with power, an attempt to historicize the Jewish experience as a narrative of liberation by armed Jews."[7]

Zionism as a political movement began in the late nineteenth century. Its founder was Theodore Herzl, a Jewish journalist from Vienna, Austria. Herzl had grown up in the Jewish Enlightenment period. Like other Western European Jews, he came to believe that a new age of full acceptance of the Jewish community into European life had begun. He was bitterly disillusioned by the wave of Jewish persecution that swept over Eastern Europe after the murder of the liberal Russian czar, Alexander II, in 1881. He was even more disillusioned by the trial of a French Army officer, Alfred Dreyfus, for treason. Dreyfus, who was Jewish, was convicted after a trumped-up trial brought public protests that he was part of an antigovernment Jewish conspiracy.

Herzl concluded from these events that the only hope for the long-suffering Jews, especially those from Eastern Europe, was to live together, separate from non-Jews. In his book *The Jewish State,* he wrote: "We have sincerely tried everywhere to merge with the national communities in which we live, seeking only to preserve the faith of our fathers. It is not permitted to us."[8]

Herzl had attended the Dreyfus trial as a journalist. Concerned about growing anti-Semitism in Western Europe, he organized a conference of European Jewish leaders in 1897 in Basel, Switzerland. The conference ended with the ringing declaration that "the aim of Zionism is to create a Jewish homeland in Palestine secured by public law." Herzl wrote in an appendage: "In Basel I have founded the Jewish state."[9]

The Zionists hoped to be allowed to buy land in Palestine for Jewish settlements. But the Ottoman government in Palestine would not allow them to do so. Small groups of Eastern European Jews escaping persecution made their way to Palestine and established communal agricultural settlements called *kibbutzim*. Those immigrants believed that hard work was essential to the Jewish return to the homeland. Work was sacred, and the only thing that gave the Jews the right to the soil of Palestine was the "betrothal of toil." This belief became a founding principle of the Jewish state.

The Balfour Declaration

Although the Zionist movement attracted many Jewish supporters, it had no influence with European governments, nor with the Ottoman government. The Zionists had difficulty raising money to finance land purchases in Palestine and to pay for travel of emigrants.

It appeared in the early 1900s that the Zionists would never reach their goal. But World War I gave them a new opportunity. The Ottoman Empire was defeated, and British troops occupied Palestine. During the war, a British Zionist named Chaim Weizmann, a chemist, had developed a new type of explosive that was valuable to the British war effort against Germany. Weizmann and his associates pressed the British government for a commitment to support a home for Jews in Palestine after the war. Many British leaders were sympathetic to the Zionist cause. One in particular, Foreign Secretary Arthur James Balfour, sent a letter to Lord Rothschild, a wealthy Jewish banker and Zionist sympathizer, indicating in general terms Britain's support for the proposed Jewish homeland in Palestine. Because the text had been cleared in advance with the cabinet, the letter is always referred to as the Balfour Declaration.[10]

The British Mandate

The peace settlement arranged after World War I by the new League of Nations gave Palestine to Britain as a mandate. The Zionists understood this to mean that they could now begin to build a Jewish national home in Palestine, through large-scale immigration. They established a Jewish agency under Weizmann's leadership to organize the immigration.

Most of the Zionist leaders, however, had never been to Palestine. They imagined it as an empty land waiting to be developed by industrious Jews; they did not realize that it was already inhabited by a large Arab population. The Palestinian Arabs had been there for centuries; many families still lived in the villages settled by their ancestors. They regarded Palestine as their national home. The basic conflict between the Arabs and Israel arises from the claim of two different peoples to the same land.

Palestinian Arabs were opposed to the mandate, to the Balfour Declaration, and to Jewish immigration. They turned to violence on several occasions, against the British and the growing Jewish population. In 1936, Arab leaders called a general strike to protest Jewish immigration, which led to a full-scale Arab rebellion. The British tried to steer a middle ground between the two communities. But they were unwilling (or unable) either to accept Arab demands for restrictions on Jewish immigration and land purchases or Zionist demands for a Jewish majority in Palestine. British policy reports and White Papers during the mandate wavered back and forth. Thus, in 1937, a report recommended partition, while a 1939 White Paper recommended a self-governing Arab state with an end to Jewish immigration.[7]

One important difference between the Palestinian Arab and Jewish communities was in their organization. The Jews were organized under the Jewish Agency, which operated as a "state within a state" in Palestine. Jews in Europe and the United States also contributed substantially to the agency's finances and made arrangements for immigration. The Palestinian Arabs, in contrast, were led by heads of urban families who often quarreled with one another. The Palestinian Arab cause also did not have outside Arab support; leaders of neighboring Arab states were weak and were still under British or French control.

A unique feature of Zionism that helped strengthen the Jewish pioneers in Palestine in their struggle to establish their claim to the land were the kibbutzim. Originally, there were two types, *moshavim* and *kibbutzim*. The moshavim, cooperative landholders' associations whose members worked the land under cooperative management and lived in nearby villages, have largely disappeared with urbanization. The kibbutzim, in contrast, are collective-ownership communities with self-contained, communal-living arrangements; members share labor, income, and expenses. Over the years, kibbutzim have played a role that is disproportionate to their size and numbers, not only in building an integrated Jewish community in Palestine but also in the formation of the Israeli state. David Ben-Gurion, Israel's first prime minister, lived in and retired to Kibbutz Sde Boker, in the Negev. Shimon Peres, twice prime minister and longtime public official, wrote of his youth on a kibbutz in these moving terms: "We saw it as the solution to the evils of urban industrialized society. I dreamed of my future as a brawny, sunburned kibbutz farmer, plowing the fields by day, guarding the perimeter by night on a fleet-footed horse. The kibbutz would break new ground, literally; it would make the parched earth bloom and beat back the attacks of marauders who sought to destroy our pioneering lives."[11]

Adolf Hitler's policy of genocide (total extermination) of Jews in Europe, developed during World War II, gave a special urgency to Jewish settlement in Palestine. American Zionist leaders condemned the 1939 British White Paper and called for unrestricted Jewish immigration into Palestine and the establishment of an independent, democratic Jewish state. After World War II, the British, still committed to the White Paper, blocked Palestine harbors and turned back the crowded, leaking ships carrying desperate Jewish refugees from Europe. World opinion turned against the British. In Palestine itself, Jews formed their own defense organization, Haganah. Underground Jewish terrorist groups such as the Irgun Zvai Leumi and the Stern Gang developed a campaign of murder and sabotage to force the British to end the mandate and establish Palestine as an independent Jewish state.

PARTITION AND INDEPENDENCE
In 1947, the British decided that the Palestine mandate was unworkable. They asked the United Nations to come up with a solution to the problem of "one land, two peoples." A UN Special Commission on Palestine recommended partition of Palestine into two states—one Arab, one Jewish—with an economic union between them. A minority of UNSCOP members recommended a federated Arab–Jewish state, with an elected legislature and minority rights for Jews. The majority report was approved by the UN General Assembly on November 29, 1947, by a 33–13 vote, after intensive lobbying by the Zionists. The partition plan established a Jewish state consisting of 56 percent of Palestine, and an Arab state with 43 percent of the area. The population at that time was 60 percent Arab and 40 percent Jewish. Due to its special associations for Jews, Muslims, and Christians, Jerusalem would become an international city administered by the United Nations.

Abba Eban, one of the few surviving participants in the UN debates on the partition plan, noted in his memoirs that "President Truman told me: 'Quite simply, you got your state because you made feasible proposals and your adversaries did not. If Israel had asked for a Jewish state in the whole of the land of Israel it would have come away with nothing. An Arab and a Jewish state side by side with integrated economies was something that American ethics and logic could absorb.' "[12]

(Israeli Tourist Office, NYC)

Pita bread, a staple food of the Middle East, is shown for sale outside the Old City's Damascus Gate in Jerusalem.

The Jewish delegation, led by Eban and David Ben-Gurion, accepted the partition plan approved by the UN General Assembly. But Palestinian Arab leaders, backed strongly by the newly independent Arab states, rejected the plan outright. On May 14, 1948, in keeping with Britain's commitment to end its mandate, the last British soldiers left Palestine. Ben-Gurion promptly announced the "birth of the new Jewish State of Israel. On May 15, the United States and the Soviet Union recognized the new state, even as the armies of five Arab states converged on it to "push the Jews into the sea."

INDEPENDENT ISRAEL
Long before the establishment of Israel, the nation's first prime minister, David Ben-Gurion, had come to Palestine as a youth. After a clash between Arab nomads and Jews from the kibbutz where he lived had injured several people, Ben-Gurion wrote prophetically, "It was then I realized . . . that sooner or later Jews and Arabs would fight over this land, a tragedy since intelligence and good will could have avoided all bloodshed."[13] In the 5 decades of independence, Ben-Gurion's prophecy has been borne out in five Arab–Israeli wars. In between those wars, conflict between Israel and the Palestinians has gone on more or less constantly, like a running sore.

Some 700,000 to 800,000 Palestinians fled Israel during the War for Independence. After the 1967 Six-Day War, an additional 380,000 Palestinians became refugees in Jordan. Israeli occupation of the West Bank brought a million Palestinians under military control.

The unifying factor among all Palestinians is the same as that which had united the dispersed Jews for 20 centuries: the recovery of the sacred homeland. Abu Iyad, a top Palestine Liberation Organization leader, once said, " . . . our dream . . . [is] the reunification of Palestine in a secular and democratic state shared by Jews, Christians and Muslims rooted in this common land. . . . There is no doubting the irrepressible will of the Palestinian people to pursue their struggle . . . and one day, we will have a country."[14] The land vacated by the Palestinians has been transformed in the decades of Israeli development. Those Israelis actually born in Palestine—now in their third generation—call themselves Sabras, after the prickly pear cactus of the Negev. The work of Sabras and of a generation of immigrants has created a highly urbanized society, sophisticated industries, and a productive agriculture. Much of the success of Israel's development has resulted from large contributions from Jews abroad, from U.S. aid, from reparations from West Germany for Nazi war crimes against Jews, and from bond issues. Yet the efforts of Israelis themselves should not be understated. David Ben-Gurion once wrote, "Pioneering is the lifeblood of our people. . . . We had to create a new life consonant with our oldest traditions as a people. This was our struggle."[15]

ISRAELI POLITICS: DEMOCRACY BY COALITION
Israel is unique among Middle Eastern states in having been a multiparty democracy from its beginnings. The country has

no written constitution, although one has been proposed. However, there are several laws that define the constitutional rights and obligations of government and citizenry. These include the Declaration of Establishment of the State (1948), the laws governing the Knesset (Parliament), and the 1950 Law of Return, which allows diaspora Jews to return and be granted Israeli citizenship. In 1992, the government approved an important Basic Law to permit direct election of the prime minister. Previously, that office—the key to effective leadership of this fractious country—had been filled from within the party receiving the most votes in a Knesset election.

Power in the Israeli political system rests in the unicameral Knesset. It has 120 members who are elected for 4-year terms under a system of proportional representation from party lists. The prime minister and cabinet are responsible to the Knesset, which must approve all policy actions. The new Direct Elections law also has a provision for the removal from office of a prime minister, either through a 61-member no-confidence vote or through impeachment for "crimes of moral turpitude." The possibility of this type of removal loomed large for a time in 1997 during the Bar-On affair, "Israel's Watergate."[16]

The Labor Party of David Ben-Gurion controlled the government for the first 3 decades of independence. However, the party seldom had a clear majority in the Knesset. As a result, it was forced to join in coalitions with various small parties. Israeli political parties are numerous. Many of them have merged with other parties over the years or have broken away to form separate parties. The Labor Party itself is a merger of three Socialist labor organizations. The two oldest parties are Agudath Israel World Organization (founded in 1912), which is concerned with issues facing Jews outside of Israel as well as within, and the Israeli Communist Party (Rakah, founded in 1919).

The Labor Party's control of Israeli politics began to weaken seriously after the October 1973 War. Public confidence was shaken by the initial Israeli defeat, heavy casualties, and evidence of Israel's unpreparedness. Austerity measures imposed to deal with inflation increased Labor's unpopularity. In the 1977 elections, the opposition, the Likud bloc, won more seats than Labor but fell short of a majority in the Knesset. The new prime minister, Menachem Begin, was forced to make concessions to smaller parties in order to form a governing coalition.

However, the Israeli invasion of Lebanon in 1982 weakened the coalition. It

seemed to many Israelis that, for the first time in its existence, the state had violated its own precept that wars should be defensive and waged only to protect Israeli land. The ethical and moral implications of Israel's occupation, and in particular the massacre by Lebanese Christian militiamen of Palestinians in refugee camps in Beirut who were supposedly under Israeli military protection, led to the formation in 1982 of Peace Now, an organization of Israelis who mounted large-scale demonstrations against the war and are committed to peace between Israel and its Arab neighbors.

Begin resigned in 1983, giving no reason for his action but clearly distressed not only by the difficulties in Lebanon but also by the death of his wife. He remained in seclusion for the rest of his life. He died in 1992.

RECENT INTERNAL POLITICS

The Labor Party won the majority of seats in the Knesset in the 1984 elections—but not a clear majority. As a result, the two major blocs reached agreement on a "government of national unity," the first in Israel's history. The arrangement established alternating 2-year terms for each party's leader as prime minister. Shimon Peres (Labor) held the office from 1984 to 1986 and Yitzhak Shamir (Likud) from 1986 to 1988.

In the 1988 elections, certain fundamental differences between Labor and Likud emerged. By this time the Palestinian *intifada* ("uprising") was in full swing. It would not only change the relationship between Israelis and Palestinians forever but would also alter the norms of Israeli politics. Labor and Likud differed over methods of handling the uprising, but they differed even more strongly in their views of long-term settlement policies toward the Palestinians. Labor's policy was to "trade land for peace," with some sort of self-governing status for the occupied territories and peace treaties with its Arab neighbors guaranteeing Israel's "right to exist." Likud would give away none of the sacred land; it could not be bartered for peace.

The election results underscored equally deep divisions in the population. Neither party won a clear majority of seats in the Knesset; Likud took 40 seats, Labor 39. Four minority ultra-religious parties gained the balance of power, with 15 percent of the popular vote and 18 seats. Their new-found political power encouraged the religious parties to press for greater control on the part of Orthodox Jewry over Israeli life. They submitted a bill in the Knesset that, if approved, would allow only Orthodox rabbis to determine

who is a Jew for citizenship purposes. In effect, it would amend the Law of Return. The proposal aroused a storm of protest among diaspora Jews, who are mostly Reform or Conservative and would therefore be excluded from becoming Israeli citizens if they returned to Israel. Eventually the proposal was rejected by the Knesset, but it did considerable damage to Israeli–disapora relations.

The 1992 Knesset election ended 15 years of Likud dominance. Labor returned to power, winning a majority of seats. However, the splintered, multiparty Israeli electoral system denied it an absolute majority. Concessions to minority parties enabled Labor to establish a functioning government, and party leader Yitzhak Rabin was named prime minister. With the support of these minority parties, notably Shas, an ultra-religious non-Zionist party of mostly Sephardic Jews, and the left-wing Meretz Party, the Rabin government could count on 63 votes in the Knesset. This was sufficient to approve its policies, including the 1995 autonomy agreement with the PLO.

JEWISH EXTREMISTS, ARAB EXTREMISTS

The deep divisions in Israeli society regarding future relations with the Palestinian population in the occupied territories (for many Israelis, they are simply Judea and Samaria, part of the ancestral Jewish homeland) were underscored by the uncovering in the 1980s of a Jewish underground organization that had attacked Palestinian leaders in violent attempts to keep the territories forever Jewish. The group had plotted secretly to blow up the sacred Islamic shrines atop the Dome of the Rock. A number of the plotters were given life sentences by a military court. But such was the outcry of support from right-wing groups in the population that their sentences were later commuted by then-president Chaim Herzog.

A more virulent form of anti-Arab, anti-Palestinian violence emerged in 1984 with the founding by Brooklyn, New York-born Rabbi Meir Kahane of Kach, a political party that advocated expulsion of all Arabs from Israel. Kahane was elected to the Knesset in 1984, giving him parliamentary immunity, and he began organizing anti-Arab demonstrations. The Knesset subsequently passed a law prohibiting any political party advocating racism in any form from participation in national elections. On that basis, the Israeli Supreme Court barred Kach and its founder from participating in the 1988 elections. Subsequently, Kahane was murdered while on a speaking tour of the United States. However, his party's influence continues. An Israeli woman arrested in July 1997 for circulating a poster depicting the Prophet Muhammad as a pig, appeared in court wearing a T-shirt with the emblem of Kach—a clenched fist over a Star of David (an important symbol in Judaism).

Arab extremism, or, more accurately, Palestinian extremism, has evolved in the 1990s largely as a result of Palestinian anger and disillusionment over the peace agreements with Israel, which are seen as accommodation on the part of Palestinian leaders, notably Yassir Arafat, to Israel rather than negotiations to establish a Palestinian state. The main Palestinian extremist group is Hamas (the Arabic acronym for the Islamic Resistance Movement, or IRM). Hamas developed originally as a Palestinian chapter of the Muslim Brotherhood, which has chapters in various Islamic Arab countries where it seeks to replace their secular regimes by a government ruled under Islamic law. However, Hamas broke with its parent organization over the use of violence, due largely to the lack of success of the intifada in achieving Palestinian self-rule.

A number of violent attacks on Israelis, including the murder of a border policeman in 1992, led Israel to deport 415 Hamas activists to southern Lebanon. However, the Lebanese government refused to admit them. Lebanon and other Arab countries filed a complaint with the UN Security Council. The Council passed *Resolution 799,* calling for the return of the deportees. Although Israel seldom responds to UN resolutions, in this case the 1993 Oslo peace agreements provided additional motivation; after spending a cold Christmas in temporary camps along the Lebanese border, the deportees were allowed to return to their homes.

DIASPORA RELATIONS
Israel's relationship with the United States has been close since the establishment of the Jewish state, in large part due to the large American Jewish population and its unstinting support. This friendship has been tested on two occasions. The first was in June 1967, when the U.S.S. *Liberty* was attacked by Israeli aircraft and torpedo boats while cruising in the eastern Mediterranean at the time of the Six-Day War. Some 34 American sailors were killed. No satisfactory explanation has ever been given by the Israeli government for this incident.

A second strain on U.S.–Israeli relations was the Pollard affair. It involved an American Jew, Jonathan Jay Pollard, who was arrested, tried, and convicted of spy-

Right-wing Likud Party leader Benjamin Netanyahu won election as Israel's prime minister on May 29, 1996, with 50.4 percent of the vote. Netanyahu was then just 46, making him the youngest prime minister in Israeli history. His criticism of the Middle East peace process was, at the time, thought to be a factor in Netanyahu's being able to form a government. However, his majority solidified, and, under his leadership, Israel continued redeployment of settlements on the West Bank and the unification of Jerusalem.

ing for Israel on his own country. Pollard's reports on U.S. National Security Agency intelligence-collecting methods and his duplication of military satellite photographs seriously compromised U.S. security. They also damaged Israel's image in the American Jewish community. One U.S. Jewish leader asked, "Is Israel becoming an ugly little Spartan state instead of the light of the world?"[17]

The growth of political power and influence over Israeli life of the Orthodox community has had a negative effect on diaspora relations. In 1997, the three main religious parties introduced a bill in the Knesset to ban Reform and Conservative Jews from serving on religious councils. More important, it would require that conversions to Judaism in Israel be performed by Orthodox rabbis to be legal. Since 84 percent of diaspora Jews are either Reform or Conservative, the proposed bill aroused another storm of Jewish anger outside Israel.

THE INTIFADA
The Palestinian intifada in the West Bank and Gaza Strip, which began in December 1987, came as a rude shock to Israel. Coming as it did barely $2\frac{1}{2}$ years after the trauma of the Lebanon War, the uprising found the Israeli public as well as its citizen army unprepared. The recall of middle-aged reservists and dispatch of new draftees to face stone-throwing Palestinian children created severe moral and psychological problems for many soldiers. John Freymann, an eyewitness to the first

Palestinian–Israeli conflict, wrote sadly: "Forty years later the grandsons of the refugees I saw huddled in these camps clash daily with the grandsons of the Israelis with whom I endured the siege of Jerusalem."[18]

Military authorities devised a number of methods to deal with the uprising. They included deportation of suspected terrorists, demolition of houses, wholesale arrests, and detention of Palestinians without charges for indefinite periods. However, growing international criticism of the policy of "breaking the bones" of demonstrators (particularly children) developed by then–defense minister Yitzhak Rabin brought a change in tactics, with the use of rubber or plastic dum-dum bullets, whose effect is less lethal except at close range.

The government also tried to break the Palestinian resistance through arbitrary higher taxes, arguing that this was necessary to compensate for revenues lost due to refusal of Palestinians to pay taxes, a slowdown in business, and lowered exports to the territories. A Value Added Tax imposed on olive presses just prior to the processing of the West Bank's major crop was a particular hardship. Along with the brutality of its troops, the tax-collection methods drove Palestinians and Israelis further apart, making the prospect of any amicable relationship questionable.

The opening of emigration to Israel for Soviet Jews added an economic dimension to the intifada. Increased expropriation of land on the West Bank for new immigrant families, along with the expansion of Jewish settlements there, added to Palestinian resentment. Many Palestinians felt that, because the new immigrants were unable to find professional employment, they were taking menial jobs ordinarily reserved for Palestinian workers in Israel.

In October 1990, the most serious incident since the start of the intifada occurred in Jerusalem. Palestinians stoned a Jewish group, the Temple Mount Faithful, who had come to lay a symbolic cornerstone for a new Jewish Temple near the Dome of the Rock. Israeli security forces then opened fire, killing some 20 Palestinians and injuring more than 100. The UN Security Council approved a resolution condemning Israel for excessive response (one of hundreds that the Israeli state has ignored over the years). Israel appointed an official commission to investigate the killings. The commission exonerated the security forces, saying that they had acted in self-defense.

Shamir's Election Plan

In May 1989, responding to threats by Labor to withdraw from the coalition and precipitate new elections, the government approved a plan drafted by Defense Minister Rabin for elections in the West Bank and Gaza as a prelude to "self-government." Under the plan, the Palestinians would elect one representative from each of 10 electoral districts to an Interim Council. The Council would then negotiate with Israeli representatives for autonomy for the West Bank and Gaza, as defined in the 1979 Camp David treaty. Negotiations on the final status of the territories would begin within 3 years of the signing of the autonomy agreement.

The implementation of the Rabin plan would have forced Israelis to decide between the Zionist ideal of "Eretz Israel" (the entire West Bank, along with the coast from Lebanon to Egypt, as the Jewish homeland) and the trading of "land for peace" with another nation struggling for its independence. The success of the intifada lay in demonstrating for Israelis the limits to the use of force against a population under occupation. It also served as a pointed reminder to Israelis that "incorporating the occupied territories would commit Israel to the perpetual use of its military to control and repress, not 'Arab refugees' but the whole Palestinian population living in these lands."[19]

THE PEACE AGREEMENT

Prior to September 1993, there were few indications that a momentous breakthrough in Palestinian–Israeli relations was about to take place. The new Labor government had cracked down on the Palestinians in the occupied territories harder than had its predecessor in 6 years of the intifada. In addition to mass arrests and deportations of persons allegedly associated with Hamas, the government sealed off the territories, not only from Israel itself but also from one another. With 120,000 Palestinians barred from their jobs in Israel, poverty, hunger, and unemployment became visible facts of life in the West Bank and the Gaza Strip.

However, what 11 rounds of peace talks, five wars, and 40 years of friction had failed to achieve was accomplished swiftly that September, with the signing of a peace and mutual-recognition accord between Israel and its long-time enemy. The accord was worked out in secret by Israeli and PLO negotiators in Norway and under Norwegian Foreign Ministry sponsorship. It provided for mutual recognition, transfer of authority over the Gaza Strip and the West Bank city of Jericho (but not the entire West Bank) to an elected Palestinian council that would supervise the establishment of Palestinian rule, withdrawal of Israeli forces and their replacement by a Palestinian police force, and a Palestinian state to be formed after a transitional period.

Opposition to the accord from within both societies was to be expected, given the intractable nature of Palestinian–Israeli differences—two peoples claiming the same land. Implementation of the Oslo agreements has been hampered from the start by groups opposed to any form of Palestinian–Israeli accommodation. On the Israeli side, some settler groups formed vigilante posses for defense, even setting up a "tent city" in Jerusalem to protest any giveaway of sacred Jewish land. Palestinian gunmen and suicide bombers responded with attacks on Jews, sometimes in alleyways or on lonely stretches of road outside the cities, but also in public places. One of the bloodiest incidents in this tragic vendetta was the killing of 29 Muslim worshippers in a mosque in Hebron by an American emigrant, an Orthodox Jew, during their Friday service.

Labor's return to power in 1992 suggested that, despite this virulent opposition, the peace process would go forward under its own momentum. The new government, headed by Rabin as prime minister and Peres as foreign minister, began to implement the disengagement of Israeli forces and the transfer of power over the territories to Yassir Arafat's Palestine National Authority. Due not only to his strong personality and military background but also to his association with the most ruthless phase of repression of the intifada, it seemed to many Israelis (and the outside world) that, as a realist, he would be able to accomplish the difficult task of reconciliation without sacrificing Israel's security. Thus the Gaza Strip, Jericho, and several West Bank towns were transferred to Palestinian authority. A formal peace treaty was signed with Jordan in 1994, and trade relations were established with Morocco, Tunisia, and several Arab Gulf states.

RABIN'S DEATH AND ITS CONSEQUENCES

The second stage in transfer of authority over the West Bank had barely begun when Rabin was assassinated by an Orthodox Jew, while speaking at a Peace Now rally in Jerusalem on November 4, 1995. The assassination climaxed months of increasingly ugly anti-Rabin rhetoric orchestrated by Orthodox rabbis, settlers, and right-wing groups who charged the prime minister with giving away sacred Jewish land while gaining little in return. The assassin, Yigal Amir, stated in court that God had made him act, since the agreement with the Palestinians contradicted sacred Jewish religious principles. He stated: "According to *halacha* [Judaic tradition] a Jew who like Rabin gives over his people and his land to the enemy must be killed. My whole life I have been studying the *halacha* and I have all the data."[20]

Rabin's assassination marked a watershed in the convoluted progress of Israeli democracy. Aside from its impact on the peace process, it solidified division of liberal–secular democratic and Orthodox–chauvinist Jewish blocs. Superficially, the transfer of power went smoothly. Peres was confirmed as Rabin's successor by a 111–9 vote in the Knesset in a rare show of unity, while the nation mourned the death of its leader.

This division of Israeli society into opposing groups deepened in the period leading up to the 1996 Knesset elections. Israelis who support an open, democratic, secular Jewish state found themselves pitted against hard-line, uncompromising nationalists. Peres also hurt his cause by undertaking the ill-advised "Operation Grapes of Wrath" into Lebanon. The action cost him a share of the Arab vote. Meanwhile, his opponent, Likud leader Benjamin Netanyahu, won the backing of Orthodox rabbis and ultra-religious voters by pledging stricter observance of Judaic law.

The May 1996 election—Israel's first with direct voting for the office of prime minister—was extremely close. Netanyahu won 50.3 percent of the popular vote

(AP Photo/Jerome Delay)

A bomb-squad soldier examines damaged vehicles following bomb attack in Tel Aviv in October 1994. Hamas claimed responsibility for the bombing, in which 22 were killed.

to 49.6 percent for Peres. However, Likud failed to win a majority of seats in the Knesset and was forced into another coalition with the religious parties. Labor actually won more seats than Likud (34 to 32), but support from Shas and the National Religious Party (20 seats) and the Russian-immigrant Yisrael Ba'Aliya party gave Netanyahu a narrow majority in the Knesset.

After his election, Netanyahu pledged that he would be a "better patriot, better Zionist" than Peres. He would not trade land for peace, but would offer peace for peace. Unfortunately, the fragility of his coalition government posed enormous risks, both for the peace process and for his leadership. By reaching agreement with the Palestinians to move the peace process forward, he risked alienating his right-wing supporters. But, if he met their demands, he risked losing the peace.

At 50 years of age, Israel is a bitterly divided nation. Amos Elon notes that "Zionism, as originally conceived by its founders, seemed to have successfully achieved most of its purposes. Yet in its current interpretation by nationalist hardliners and religious fundamentalists [it] has been a stumbling block to peace."[21] As the country enters its fifth decade of independent existence, the optimism of 1993, centered in the Oslo agreements, has faded under the impact of Hamas-inspired Palestinian violence and equally forceful Israeli responses against the entire Palestinian population. After a series of spectacular suicide bombings in 1997, the Israeli government announced that it was suspending the peace process and would no longer be bound by the Oslo agreements.

THE ECONOMY

In terms of national income and economic and industrial development, Israel is ahead of a number of Middle Eastern states that have greater natural resources. Agriculture is highly developed; Israeli engineers and hydrologists have been very successful in developing new irrigation and planting methods that not only "make the desert bloom" but also are exported to other nations under the country's technical-aid program. Agriculture contributes 7.5 percent of gross domestic product annually. Israel is mostly self-sufficient in food, although a number of basic commodities, such as dairy products, are heavily subsidized.

The cutting and export of diamonds and other gemstones is a small but important industry, with $5.2 billion in 1996—the largest single revenue-earner. The aircraft industry is the largest single industrial enterprise, but it has fallen on hard times. The national airline, El Al, suffered through a major strike in 1982 and was placed in receivership, although it continued to operate. The fastest-growing industry is software, reflecting the skills of army-trained computer engineers and recent Russian immigrants. Software and high-technology exports, mostly by Israeli subsidiaries of such U.S. companies as Net Manage, Technomatrix Technologies, and Geotek Communications, generated $5.5 billion in 1996, one fourth of total exports.

Israel has 34 producing oil wells and produces a very small amount of natural gas, which meets only a fraction of domestic needs. After the 1967 War and the occupation of the Sinai Peninsula, Israel was able to exploit Sinai petroleum resources as well as the Alma oil fields in the Gulf of Suez. Twenty-five percent of domestic oil needs came from the Alma fields. In accordance with the Egyptian–Israeli peace treaty, these fields were returned to Egypt, with the stipulation that Israel be able to purchase Sinai oil at less than prices set by the Organization of Petroleum Exporting Countries for Egyptian oil on the world market. Israel has also bought oil from Iran from time to time and from certain African oil-producing countries. Still, fuel imports are a huge drain on the economy. There are, however, considerable deposits of bromine, magnesium, and phosphates in the Negev and Dead Sea.

Prior to 1977, when the Likud Bloc came to power, the economy was managed largely by the state in tandem with Histadrut, the Israeli labor confederation. Histadrut functions partly as a union but also as an employer, and it is the controlling factor in many industries. It negotiates for most labor contracts through bargaining with the government. The cost-of-living increases built into these contracts and the country's high level of defense expenditures sent the inflation rate out of sight in the 1980s.

Inflation was also fueled by Likud's fiscal policies. Foreign-exchange controls were abolished, along with the travel tax and import licenses. The currency was allowed to float, and Israelis could open bank accounts in foreign currency. The results were balance-of-payments deficits and a drop in foreign-exchange reserves due to luxury imports paid for in foreign currencies. By 1985, the inflation rate had reached 800 percent.

The Labor government took office amid warnings from U.S. and other economists, plus its own advisers, that the economy was on the point of collapse. Peres introduced a package of draconian reforms. Wages and prices were frozen, and imports of all but essential goods were banned. The package included devaluation of the shekel, replacing it with the new Israeli shekel (NIS) pegged to the dollar. Cost-of-living increases were eliminated from labor contracts, and 10,000 jobs were cut from the government bureaucracy.

The Zionist movement is organized by Theodor Herzel **1897**	The Balfour Declaration **1917**	British mandate over Palestine **1922–1948**	A UN partition plan is accepted by the Jewish community; following British withdrawal, the State of Israel is proclaimed **1947–1948**	Armistices are signed with certain Arab states, through U.S. mediation **1949**	The Six-Day War; Israeli occupation of East Jerusalem, the Gaza Strip, and the Sinai Peninsula **1967**	Yom Kippur War **1973**	Peace treaty with Egypt **1979**	The Israeli invasion of Lebanon **1980s**	Coalition government and 2-year alternation of prime ministers

1990s

Withdrawal of Israeli forces from Lebanon	Israeli–Palestinian moves toward peace; violence escalates on both sides in response	Benjamin Netanyahu returns the Likud Party to power
Home-grown Palestinian resistance to Israeli occupation in the West Bank and Gaza Strip intensifies	Prime Minister Yitzhak Rabin is assassinated	Israel retaliates against Hizbullah attacks by striking targets in Lebanon

These drastic measures stabilized the economy, allowing for an average 6 percent GDP growth rate annually. The inflation rate dropped to a manageable 11 percent in 1997. But increased immigration of Russian Jews, declining tax revenues, and a drop in tourism due to conflict with the Palestinians and uncertainty about visiting conditions have affected national development. The periodic closures of the West Bank and Gaza for Palestinian workers in Israel in 1996–1997, for example, have cost the Israeli economy $42.5 million in the agricultural and construction sectors due to work stoppages.

NOTES

1. In 1997, representatives of the Greek Orthodox, Armenian, and Roman Catholic Churches, historic rivals for the right to control the Church of the Holy Sepulchre, held the first joint service ever to dedicate the new cupola over the supposed tomb of Jesus, after 68 years of renovation and centuries of controversy over the right to supervise this sacred Christian site.

2. Elie Wiesel, *Memoirs: All Rivers Run to the Sea* (New York: Knopf, 1995), p. 19.

3. Ashkenazi derived from Ashkenaz (Genesis 10:3) is the name given to Jews who lived in Europe, particularly Germany, and followed particular traditions of Judaism handed down from biblical days. Sephardim (from Sepharah, Obadiah 1:20) refers to Jews originally from Spain who were expelled and emigrated to the Middle East–North Africa. R. J. Zwi Werblowsky and Geoffrey Wigoder, eds., *The Encyclopedia of the Jewish Religion* (New York: Holt, Rinehart & Winston, 1965).

4. Dan V. Segre, *A Crisis of Identity. Israel and Zionism* (Oxford, England: Oxford University Press, 1980), p. 25.

5. The Enlightenment resulted from the French Revolution and its declaration of Liberty, Equality, and Fraternity (Brotherhood), meaning that all people are created equal. "Under the new spirit of equality, ghetto walls crumbled." Abraham Shulman, *Coming Home to Zion* (Garden City: Doubleday, 1979), p. 11.

6. Recent excavations of Herod's summer palace at Herodium near Bethlehem reveal an 18′ × 30′ indoor swimming pool, saunas, and baths adorned with mosaics and frescoes, confirming the king's achievements as the "Great Builder" of Judea in early Christian times.

7. Yaron Ezrahi, *Rubber Bullets: Power and Conscience in Modern Israel* (New York: Farrar, Straus & Giroux, 1997), p. 269.

8. Quoted in Shulman, *op. cit.,* p. 14.

9. The text is in *The Middle East and North Africa* (London: Europa Publications, 1984), "Documents on Palestine," p. 58.

10. Balfour's estate in Scotland, from whence the letter was sent to Rothschild, was used as a training farm during World War II for Jewish refugee children, to prepare them for emigration to Palestine. The estate is now for sale.

11. Shimon Peres, *Battling for Peace: A Memoir,* ed. by David Landau (New York: Random House, 1995), pp. 20–21.

12. Abba Eban, "Rebirth of a Nation," *Jerusalem Post* Supplement 5757 (May 1997), p. 2.

13. David Ben-Gurion, *Memoirs* (Cleveland: World Publishing Company, 1970), p. 58.

14. Abu Iyad with Eric Rouleau, *My Home, My Land: A Narrative of the Palestinian Struggle,* transl. by Linda Butler Koseoglu (New York: New York Times Books, 1981), pp. 225–226.

15. Ben-Gurion, *op. cit.,* p. 57.

16. The Bar-On "affair" involved Netanyahu's appointment of a "mediocre lawyer," Roni Bar-On, as attorney-general, supposedly as a favor to the leader of Shas, in return for his party's support for the coalition government. The Israeli Supreme Court ruled in June 1997 that there was insufficient evidence to prosecute Netanyahu, but the near-scandal led to a no-confidence resolution in the Knesset that the prime minister survived by a 55–50 vote. See *The New York Times* (June 24, 1997).

17. Robert Schreiber, *New Outlook* (May/June 1987), p. 42.

18. John Freymann, in *Foreign Service Journal* (May 1988), p. 30.

19. Ezrahi, *op. cit.,* pp. 274–275.

20. Quoted in Amos Elon, *A Blood-Dimmed Tale: Despatches from the Middle East* (New York: Columbia University Press, 1997) (originally appeared in *The New York Review of Books,* December 21, 1995).

21. *Ibid.,* p. 2.

DEVELOPMENT

After a 7% GDP growth in 1994 due to buoyed peace prospects and the opening of trade relations with Arab countries, Israel's development has been clouded by negative factors. GDP growth in 1997 was a bare 2%. The 1997 budget of $65.6 billion reflected drastic reductions in state spending.

FREEDOM

Israel's Basic Laws guarantee its citizens full democratic rights plus the right of Jews elsewhere to immigrate and be granted citizenship. Two new Basic Laws were approved in 1992. One provides for direct election of the prime minister. The other, Law on the Freedom and Dignity of Man, protects the individual against the excessive use of state power.

HEALTH/WELFARE

The kibbutz system has changed significantly with the increasing urbanization of the country and changes in its social makeup. Most kibbutz families now live in their own homes rather than communally and keep their children with them. The major proportion of adults are now elderly people, usually single, and mostly divorced mothers from broken urban families.

ACHIEVEMENTS

In 1997, the first factory to refine magnesium for export went into production as a joint venture of Volkswagen and Israel Chemicals. Also, Israeli experts have designed a computer-assisted irrigation system for a project to reclaim 50,000 acres of arid desert land in the Central Asian republic of Kazakhstan.

Jordan (The Hashimite Kingdom of Jordan)

GEOGRAPHY
Area in Square Kilometers (Miles):
93,740 (37,727) (slightly larger than Indiana)
Capital (Population): Amman (1,300,000)
Climate: predominantly dry

PEOPLE

Population
Total: 4,212,200
Annual Growth Rate: 2.7%
Rural/Urban Population Ratio: 22/78
Ethnic Makeup: 98% Arab; 1% Circassian; 1% Armenian
Major Language: Arabic

Health
Life Expectancy at Birth: 70 years (male); 74 years (female)
Infant Mortality Rate (Ratio): 32/1,000
Average Caloric Intake: 102% of FAO minimum
Physicians Available (Ratio): 1/574

Religions
92% Sunni Muslim; 8% Christian

"Rose-Red City Half as Old as Time"

A sunset view of the rose-red glow of the ancient Jordanian city of Petra, the capital of the Nabataeans 20 centuries ago, is a never-to-be-forgotten sight. Built at the crossroads of major caravan routes between Egypt, Arabia, and Mesopotamia, Petra was carved from the red sandstone cliffsides of a narrow valley into a city housing 30,000 people. The best-preserved building is Pharaoh's Treasury, which was probably a second-century A.D. tomb of a Nabataean king. Petra was the Nabataean capital for 4 centuries. One positive result of the Jordanian–Israeli peace treaty is that Israeli tourists may now visit Petra openly, bringing much-needed tourism revenues into the Hashimite kingdom.

Education
Adult Literacy Rate: 83%

COMMUNICATION
Telephones: 81,500
Newspapers: 4 dailies (one in English); 3 weeklies

TRANSPORTATION
Highways—Kilometers (Miles): 7,500 (4,680)
Railroads—Kilometers (Miles): 789 (492)
Usable Airfields: 17

GOVERNMENT
Type: constitutional monarchy
Independence Date: May 25, 1946
Head of State/Government: King Hussein I; Prime Minister Abdul-Karim Kabariti
Political Parties: Jordanian National Alliance; Islamic Action Front; National Constitution Party; others
Suffrage: universal at 20

MILITARY
Number of Armed Forces: 84,250
Military Expenditures (% of Central Government Expenditures): 9.1%
Current Hostilities: none

ECONOMY
Currency ($ U.S. Equivalent): 0.70 Jordanian dinar = $1
Per Capita Income/GDP: $4,280/$17 billion
Inflation Rate: 6%
Total Foreign Debt: $6 billion
Natural Resources: phosphate; potash
Agriculture: vegetables; fruits; olive oil; wheat
Industry: phosphate mining; petroleum refining; cement production; light manufacturing

FOREIGN TRADE
Exports: $1.4 billion
Imports: $3.5 billion

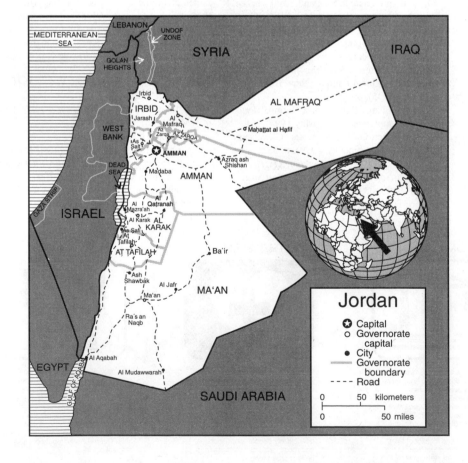

Jordan

⭐ Capital
○ Governorate capital
● City
━━ Governorate boundary
--- Road

0   50 kilometers
0   50 miles

JORDAN

The Hashimite Kingdom of Jordan (previously called Transjordan; usually abbreviated to Jordan) is one of the smaller Middle Eastern nations. The country formerly consisted of two regions: the East Bank (lying east of the Jordan River) and the West Bank of the Jordan. Israel occupied the West Bank in June 1967, although the region continued to be legally and administratively attached to Jordan and salaries of civil servants and others were paid by the Jordanian government. In 1988, King Hussein formally severed the relationship, leaving the West Bank under Israeli occupation de facto as well as de jure. Between 1948 and 1967, Jordanian-occupied territory also included the old city of Jerusalem (East Jerusalem), which was annexed during the 1948 Arab–Israeli War.

Modern Jordan is an artificial nation, the result of historical forces and events that shaped the Middle East in the twentieth century. It had no prior history as a nation and was known simply as the land east of the Jordan River, a region of diverse peoples, some nomadic, others sedentary farmers and herders. Jordan's current neighbors are Iraq, Syria, Saudi Arabia, and Israel. Their joint borders were all established by the British after World War I, when Britain and France divided the territories of the defeated Ottoman Empire between them.

Jordan's borders with Iraq, Syria, and Saudi Arabia do not follow natural geographical features. They were established mainly to keep nomadic peoples from raiding; over time, these borders have been accepted by the countries concerned. The boundary with Israel, which formerly divided the city of Jerusalem between Jordanian and Israeli control, became an artificial barrier after the 1967 Six-Day War and Israel's occupation of Jerusalem and the West Bank (of the Jordan River). The Jordan–Israel peace treaty of 1994 has resulted in a redrafting of borders. Israel returned 340 square miles captured in 1967 in the Arava Valley and south of the Galilee to Jordanian control. However, Israeli *kibbutzim* will be allowed to continue cultivating some 750 acres in the territory under a 25-year lease.

HISTORY

The territory of modern Jordan was ruled by outside powers until it became an independent nation in the twentieth century. Under the Ottoman Empire, it was part of the province of Syria. The Ottoman authorities in Syria occasionally sent military patrols across the Jordan River to "show the flag" and collect taxes, but otherwise they left the people of the area to manage their own affairs.[1]

(Jordan Information Bureau)

This sixth-century A.D. mosaic map of Palestine shows a plan for the Old City, including walls and Holy Sepulchre Church. The rare and beautiful mosaic covers a large floor section of Madabaj Greek Orthodox Church.

This tranquil existence ended with World War I. The Ottomans were defeated and their provinces were divided into protectorates, called mandates, set up by the League of Nations and assigned to Britain and/or France to administer and prepare for eventual self-government. The British received a mandate over Palestine and extended its territory to include Transjordan east of the River Jordan. Due to their commitment to help Jews dispersed throughout the world to establish a national home in Palestine, the British decided to govern Transjordan as a separate mandate.

The terms of the mandate system required the protecting power (in this case, Britain) to appoint a native ruler. During the war, the British had worked with Sharif Husayn to organize an Arab revolt against the Ottomans. Husayn was a prominent Arab leader in Mecca who held the honorary position of Protector of the Holy Shrines of Islam. Two of the sharif's sons, Faisal and Abdullah, had led the revolt, and the British felt that they owed them something. When Iraq was set up as a mandate, the British made Faisal its king. Abdullah was offered the Transjordan territory. Because the population was primarily pastoral, he chose the traditional title of emir, rather than king, considering it more appropriate.

EMIR ABDULLAH

Through his father, Abdullah traced his lineage back to the Hashim family of Mecca, the clan to which the Prophet Muhammad belonged. This ancestry gave him a great deal of prestige in the Arab world, particularly among the nomads of Transjordan, who had much respect for a person's genealogy. Abdullah used the connection assiduously to build a solid base of support among his kinspeople. When the country became fully independent in 1946, Abdullah named the new state the Hashimite Kingdom of Jordan.

Abdullah's new country had little to recommend it to outsiders except some fine Roman ruins and a great deal of empty land. It was a peaceful, quiet place, consisting entirely of what is today the East Bank of the Jordan River, with vaguely defined borders across the desert. The population was about 400,000, mostly rural peasants and nomads; the capital, Amman, was little more than a large village spread over some of those Roman ruins.

During the period of the mandate (1921–1946), Abdullah was advised by resident British officials. The British helped him draft a Constitution in 1928, and Transjordan became independent in everything except financial policy and foreign relations. But Emir Abdullah and his advisers ran the country like a private club. In traditional Arab desert fashion, Abdullah held a public meeting outside his palace every Friday; anyone who wished could come and present a complaint or petition to the emir.

Abdullah did not trust political parties or institutions such as a parliament, but he agreed to issue the 1928 Constitution as a step toward eventual self-government. He also laid the basis for a regular army. A British Army officer, John Bagot Glubb, was appointed in 1930 to train the Transjordanian Frontier Force to curb Bedouin raiding across the country's borders. Under Glubb's command, this frontier force eventually became the Arab Legion; during Emir Abdullah's last years, it played a vital role not only in defending the kingdom against the forces of the new State of Israel but also in enlarging Jordanian territory by the capture of the West Bank and East Jerusalem.[2]

When Britain gave Jordan its independence in 1946, the country was not vastly different from the tranquil emirate of the 1920s. But events beyond its borders soon overwhelmed it, like the duststorm rolling in from the desert that sweeps everything before it. The conflict between the Arab and Jewish communities in neighboring Palestine had become so intense and unmanageable that the British decided to terminate their mandate. They turned the problem over to the United Nations. In November 1947, the UN General Assembly voted to partition Palestine into separate Arab and Jewish states, with Jerusalem to be an international city under UN administration.

The partition plan was not accepted by the Palestine Arabs, and as British forces evacuated Palestine in 1947–1948, they prepared to fight the Jews for possession of all Palestine. The State of Israel was proclaimed in 1948. Armies of the neighboring Arab states, including Jordan, immediately invaded Palestine. But they were poorly armed and untrained. Only the Jordanian Arab Legion gave a good account of itself. The Legion's forces seized the West Bank, originally part of the territory allotted to a projected Palestinian Arab state by the United Nations. The Legion also occupied the old city of Jerusalem (East Jerusalem). Subsequently, Abdullah annexed both territories, despite howls of protest from other Arab leaders, who accused him of landgrabbing from his "Palestine brothers" and harboring ambitions to rule the entire Arab world.

Jordan now became a vastly different state. Its population tripled with the addition of half a million West Bank Arabs and half a million Arab refugees from Israel. Abdullah still did not trust the democratic process, but he realized that he would have to take firm action to strengthen Jordan and to help the dispossessed Palestinians who now found themselves reluctantly included in his kingdom. He approved a new Constitution, one that provided for a bicameral Legislature (similar to the U.S. Congress), with an appointed Senate and an elected House of Representatives. He appointed prominent Palestinians to his cabinet. A number of Palestinians were appointed to the Senate; others were elected to the House of Representatives.

On July 20, 1951, King Abdullah was assassinated as he entered the Al Aqsa Mosque in East Jerusalem for Friday prayers. His grandson, Hussein, was at his side and narrowly escaped death. Abdullah's murderer, who was killed immediately by royal guards, was a Palestinian. Many Palestinians felt that Abdullah had betrayed them by annexing the West Bank and because he was thought to have carried on secret peace negotiations with the Israelis (recent evidence suggests that he did so). In his *Memoirs,* King Abdullah wrote, "The paralysis of the Arabs lies in their present moral character. They are obsessed with tradition and concerned only with profit and the display of oratorical patriotism."[3]

Abdullah dealt with the Israelis because he despaired of Arab leadership. Ironically, Abdullah's proposal to Britain in 1938 for a unified Arab–Jewish Palestine linked with Jordan, if it had been accepted, would have avoided five wars and hundreds of thousands of casualties. Yet this same proposal forms the basis for discussion of the Palestinian–Israeli settlement today.[4]

KING HUSSEIN

Abdullah's son, Crown Prince Talal, succeeded to the throne. He suffered from mental illness (probably schizophrenia) and had spent most of his life in mental hospitals. When his condition worsened, his senior advisers convinced him to abdicate in favor of his eldest son, Hussein. Hussein became king in 1953.

King Hussein's is one of the longest reigns in the contemporary world, and he remains one of the few surviving examples of monarchy. He has faced and overcome a number of crises. These crises have stemmed from Jordan's involvement in the larger Arab–Israeli conflict and its pivotal location in that conflict.

Hussein faced a serious threat to his rule shortly after he became king. Elections for the new National Assembly, in 1956, resulted in a majority for parties representing the West Bank.[5] A tug-of-war between king and Assembly followed. At one point, it was rumored that Hussein had been killed. Hussein, who was very much alive, jumped into a jeep and rode out to the main army base at Zerqa, outside Amman, where he showed himself to his troops to prove that he was still in command. The army remained loyal to him, and the alleged coup never materialized.

The Zerqa incident illustrates two things about Jordanian politics. One is Hussein's sense of timing, his ability to take bold actions designed to throw his opponents off guard. The second is the importance of army support to the monarchy. The great majority of soldiers in the Arab Legion are still drawn from Bedouins. King Hussein's survival has depended on army loyalty and his own survival skills.

The June 1967 Six-Day War produced another crisis in Jordan, this one not entirely of its own making. Israeli forces occupied 10 percent of Jordanian territory, including half of its best agricultural lands. The Jordanian Army suffered 6,000 casualties, most of them in a desperate struggle to hold the Old City of Jerusalem against Israeli attack. Nearly 300,000 more Palestinian refugees from the West Bank fled into Jordan. To complicate things further, guerrillas from the Palestine Liberation Organization, formerly based in the West Bank, made Jordan their new headquarters. The PLO considered Jordan its base for the continued struggle against Israel. Its leaders talked openly of removing the monarchy and making Jordan an armed Palestinian state.

By 1970, Hussein and the PLO were headed toward open confrontation. The guerrillas had the sympathy of the population, and successes in one or two minor clashes with Israeli troops had made them arrogant. They swaggered through the streets of Amman, directing traffic at intersections and stopping pedestrians to examine their identity papers. Army officers complained to King Hussein that the PLO was really running the country. The king became convinced that unless he moved against the guerrillas, his throne would be in danger. He declared martial law and ordered the army to move against them.

The ensuing Civil War lasted until July 1971, but in the PLO annals, it is usually referred to as "Black September," because of its starting date and because it ended in disaster for the guerrillas. Their bases were dismantled and most of the guerrillas were driven from Jordan. The majority went to Lebanon, where they reorganized and in time became as powerful there as they had been in Jordan.

There have been no serious internal threats to Hussein's rule since. Jordan shared in the general economic boom in the Arab world that developed as a result of the enormous price increases in oil after the 1973 Arab–Israeli War. As a consequence, Hussein was able to turn his attention to the development of a more democratic political system. Like his grandfather, he did not entirely trust political parties or elected legislatures, and he was leery of the Palestinians' intentions toward him. He was also convinced that Jordan rather than the PLO should be the natural representative of the Palestinians.

But he realized that, in order to represent them effectively and to build the kind of Jordanian state that he could safely hand over to his successors, he would need to develop popular support in addition to that of the army. Accordingly, Hussein set up a National Consultative Council in 1978, as what he called an interim step toward democracy. The Council had a majority of Palestinians (those living on the East Bank) as members.

Hussein's arbitrary separation of Jordan from the West Bank has had important implications for internal politics in the kingdom. It enabled the king to proceed with political reforms without the need to involve the Palestinian population there. The timetable was accelerated by nationwide protests in 1989 over price increases for basic commodities. The protests turned swiftly to violence, resulting in the most serious riots in national history. Prime Minister Zaid Rifai was dismissed; he was held personally responsible for the increases and for the country's severe financial problems, although these were due equally to external factors. King Hussein appointed a caretaker government, headed by his cousin, to oversee the transitional period before national elections for the long-promised lower chamber of the Legislature.

In 1990, the king and leaders of the major opposition organization, the Jordanian National Democratic Alliance (JANDA), signed a historic National Charter, which provides for a multiparty political system. Elections were set under the Charter for an 80-member House of Representatives. Nine seats would be reserved for Christians and three for Circassians, an ethnic Muslim minority originally from the Caucasus.

In 1992, Hussein abolished martial law, which had been in effect since 1970. Henceforth, security crimes such as espionage would be dealt with by state civilian-security courts. New laws also undergird constitutional rights such as a free press, free speech, and the right of public assembly.

With political parties now legalized, 20 were licensed by the Interior Ministry to take part in Jordan's first national parliamentary election since 1956. The election was scheduled for November 1993. However, the September 13 accord between Israel and the PLO raised questions about the process. Many people in Jordan committed to democratization feared that the election would become a battle between supporters and opponents of the accord, since half the Jordanian population are of Palestinian descent. As a result, the government placed strict limits on campaigning. Political rallies were banned; the ban

was rescinded by the courts several weeks before the election. Hussein also suspended the Parliament elected in 1990; and an amendment was added to the election law stipulating that voting would be "one person, one vote" rather than by party lists.

Despite these forebodings, the election went off on schedule, with few hitches. The results were an affirmation of Hussein's policy of gradual democratization. Pro-monarchy candidates won 54 of the 80 seats in the House of Representatives to 16 for the Islamic Action Front, the political arm of the Muslim Brotherhood. The remaining seats were spread among minor parties and independents. Voter turnout was 68 percent, far higher than in the 1990 election. The electorate also surprised by choosing the first woman member, Toujan Faisal, an outspoken feminist and television personality who had been charged with apostasy by the Muslim Brotherhood in the earlier campaign.

The 1997 parliamentary elections, which took place in November, continued the trend toward Hussein's version of representative government under firm monarchical rule. Government supporters won 62 of 80 seats in the lower house; the remainder went to independent candidates and Islamists. However, the results were clouded by a partial return to authoritarian rule: A series of restrictive amendments to the press law led to the suspension of 13 newspapers prior to the election. This action plus other grievances led to an election boycott by the Muslim Brotherhood and Islamic Action Front, the major quasi opposition parties represented in the previous Parliament. Barely 50 percent of Jordan's 800,000 registered voters cast their ballots. These negative results were less due to criticism of the king than an expression of public disillusionment with the lack of benefits expected from the peace treaty with Israel and the growing gap between rich and poor in Jordan.

FOREIGN POLICY

During the 40-year cycle of hostilities between Israel and its Arab neighbors, there were periodic secret negotiations involving Jordanian and Israeli negotiators, including at times King Hussein himself, as Jordan sought to mend fences with its next-door neighbor. But in 1991 and 1992, Jordan became actively involved in the "peace process" initiated by the United States to resolve the vital issue of Palestinian self-government. As these negotiations proceeded, opponents of the process in Jordan did their best to derail them. Islamic Action Front members of the lower house of Parliament called for a vote of no-confidence in the government (but not

in Hussein's leadership) for "treachery to Jordan and the Arab nation." However, the motion failed; most Jordanians supported the peace talks, and a majority of members of the House disagreed with the motion and voted against it.

Peace with Israel became a reality in October 1994, with Jordan the second Arab nation to sign a formal treaty with the Israeli state. Subsequently, the normalization of relations has moved ahead with lightning speed. In July 1995, the Senate (the upper house of Parliament) voted to annul the last anti-Israel laws still on the books. Embassies opened in Amman and Tel Aviv under duly accredited ambassadors. As Israel's first ambassador to Jordan observed, "I don't think there have ever been two countries at war for such a long time that have moved so quickly into peaceful cooperation."[6]

In other areas of cooperation, direct mail service between Jordan and Israel went into effect in February 1995. In 1996, the maritime boundary between the two countries in the Gulf of Aqaba was formally demarcated at mid-channel. And with the border open, some 30,000 Israeli tourists flocked into Jordan to visit long-closed sites, such as Petra and Jerash. Many of them were served meals in Jordan's first kosher restaurant, opened early in 1995 under joint Israeli–Jordanian partnership.

However, the political fallout from the treaty with Israel has to a large extent offset its economic benefits. Jordan's relations with Iraq, its largest trading partner, went from bad to worse. In March 1996, the Iraqi National Accord—the main opposition group to Saddam Hussein—set up an office in Amman. As a result, the two nations traded expulsions of diplomats. Furthermore, the expected economic rewards of the treaty have yet to reach the average Jordanian.

Ironically, one result of the breakdown in the Israeli–Palestinian peace process after Benjamin Netanyahu's election in Israel and King Hussein's vocal criticism of his leadership has been an improvement in Jordan's relations with the Arab Gulf states. In 1996, Saudi Arabia began a large-scale investment program of buying Jordanian hotels and banks.

THE ECONOMY

Jordan is rich in phosphates. Reserves are estimated at 2 billion tons, and new deposits are constantly being reported. Phosphate rock is one of the country's main exports, along with potash, which is mined on the Jordanian side of the Dead Sea.

The mainstay of the economy is agriculture. The most productive agricultural

Establishment of the British mandate of Transjordan **1921**	The first Constitution is approved by the British-sponsored Legislative Council **1928**	Treaty of London; the British give Jordan independence and Abdullah assumes the title of emir **1946**	The Arab Legion occupies the Old City of Jerusalem and the West Bank during the first Arab–Israeli War **1948**	Jordanian forces are defeated by Israel in the Six-Day War; Israelis occupy the West Bank and Old Jerusalem **1967**	"Black September"; war between army and PLO guerrillas ends with expulsion of the PLO from Jordan **1970–1971**	King Hussein suspends the National Assembly **1974**

1990s

Politically, economically, and socially, Jordan is one of the primary losers in the Gulf crisis; martial law is lifted

Jordan signs a peace treaty with Israel; relations between the two countries normalize

Israel returns some territory to Jordanian control

area is the Jordan Valley. A series of dams and canals from the Jordan and Yarmuk Rivers has increased arable land in the valley by 264,000 acres and made possible production of high-value vegetable crops for export to nearby countries.

During the years of Israeli occupation of the West Bank, Jordan was estimated to have been deprived of 80 percent of its citrus crop and 45 percent of its vegetable croplands. The destruction of irrigation systems on the Yarmuk and Jordan Rivers by Israeli forces, allegedly for security reasons, and heavy use of water for Israel's agriculture have undercut Jordanian food production even further. But in June 1995, Israel completed a 2-mile-long pipeline from Lake Tiberias to Jordan's King Abdullah Canal as the first economic project of the peace treaty. However, the change of government in Israel and tension over Jordanian support for the emerging Palestine state have impeded deliveries of the water agreed upon to compensate Jordan for its water loss during the years of Israeli occupation of the West Bank.

Jordan's economy traditionally has depended on outside aid and remittances from its large expatriate skilled labor force to make ends meet. A consequence of the Gulf War was the mass departure from Kuwait of some 350,000 Jordanian and Palestinian workers. Despite the loss in remittances and the added burden on its economy, Jordan welcomed them. But their return complicated the nation's efforts to meet the requirements of a 1989 agreement with the International Monetary Fund for austerity measures as a prerequisite for further aid. The government reduced subsidies, but the resulting increase in bread prices led to "bread riots" throughout the country. The subsidies were restored; but they were again reduced in 1991, this time with basic commodities (including bread) sold at fixed low prices under a rationing system. In 1996, faced with a $230 million budgetary deficit, the government eliminated all subsidies and doubled the price of bread. The lack of protest on this occasion indicated how far the process of democratization linking government and people had proceeded.

Jordan has backed strongly the development of a Palestinian state governed by the Palestine National Authority. Initially, the Jordanian government set up a preferential tax and customs exemption system for 25 Palestinian export products. A transit agreement reached in 1996 allows Palestinian exporters direct access to Aqaba port.

The year 1998 marked King Hussein's 45th year of rule in Jordan—the longest of any Middle Eastern head of state. Aside from his survival—in itself no mean accomplishment given the instability of regional politics—Hussein's great achievement has been to steer Jordan gradually toward finding its identity as a nation and thereafter to endow it with representative political institutions.

NOTES

1. The Ottomans paid subsidies to nomadic tribes to guard the route of pilgrims headed south for Mecca. Peter Gubser, *Jordan: Crossroads of Middle Eastern Events* (Boulder, CO: Westview Press, 1983).

2. Years later, Glubb wrote, "In its twenty-eight years of life it had never been contemplated that the Arab Legion would fight an independent war." Quoted in Harold D. Nelson, ed., *Jordan, A Country Study* (Washington, D.C.: American University, Foreign Area Studies, 1979), p. 201.

3. King Abdullah of Jordan, *My Memoirs Completed,* translated by Harold W. Glidden (London: Longman, 1951, 1978), preface, xxvi.

4. The text of the proposal is in Abdullah's *Memoirs,* pp. 89–90.

5. The party with the largest number of seats, the National Socialists, openly opposed most of Hussein's policies. See Naseer Aruri, *Jordan: A Study in Political Development (1925–1965)* (The Hague: Martinus Nijhoff, 1967), p. 159.

6. Quoted in *Middle East Economic Digest* (June 16, 1995).

DEVELOPMENT

International donor commitments of $18 billion to Jordan as a consequence of the peace treaty with Israel have buoyed the country's general economic prospects. Meanwhile, the United States, in addition to its regular aid program, gave $100 million to the country for water-purification and related projects. The funds were taken from the Israel and Egypt aid programs.

FREEDOM

The 1990 National Charter provides for a bicameral Legislature with an elected lower house and an appointed upper house. In May 1996, 9 small opposition parties merged to form the National Constitution Party as a rival to the Islamic Action Front, the main opposition party. The National Charter guarantees full civil and political rights to all Jordanians.

HEALTH/WELFARE

In 1996, Saudi Arabia hired 2,500 Jordanian teachers for its schools on an expatriate basis, thus helping to reduce Jordan's high unemployment rate. The government of Qatar also helped by increasing the number of permits issued to Jordanian workers there.

ACHIEVEMENTS

In 1997, Jordan was approved as an associate member of the European Union. Membership provides duty-free access for Jordanian exports to EU states, and imports of EU industrial goods will enter Jordan free of duty. Jordan's government-sponsored family-planning programs have reduced the once astronomical birth rate.

Kuwait (State of Kuwait)

GEOGRAPHY
Area in Square Kilometers (Miles):
17,818 (6,880) (slightly smaller than
New Jersey)
Capital (Population): Kuwait (454,000)
Climate: intensely hot and dry in
summer; short, cool winters

PEOPLE

Population
Total: 1,950,100
Annual Growth Rate: 3.9%
Rural/Urban Population Ratio: 4/96
Ethnic Makeup: 45% Kuwaiti; 35%
other Arab; 9% South Asian; 4%
Iranian; 7% others
Major Language: Arabic

Health
Life Expectancy at Birth: 73 years
(male); 78 years (female)
Infant Mortality Rate (Ratio): 12/1,000
Average Caloric Intake: n/a
Physicians Available (Ratio): 1/855

Religions
85% Muslim; 15% Christian, Hindu,
Parsi, and others

Education
Adult Literacy Rate: 74%

COMMUNICATION
Telephones: 500,000
Newspapers: 5 Arabic and 2 English
dailies; 418,000 combined circulation

Drinking Water from the Sea

There is almost no fresh water in Kuwait, and less than 1 percent of the land
is arable. Rainfall is rare—less than 4 inches annually. Aridity was manageable
while the population was small, but the demands of growth have put a severe
strain on the water supply. For this reason, the Kuwaiti government has
become a world leader in the desalination of seawater to provide fresh water.
It pioneered in the 1950s with a seawater distillation plant producing 80,000
gallons of fresh water daily.

But the resumption of oil production after the Gulf War and the capping of
burning oil wells may be causing serious damage to the water table. According
to some experts, as Kuwait drills new wells in a frantic search to expand
production, the saltwater aquifer beneath the oil tends to move upward into
reservoirs that previously were filled with oil. The result is that new wells
"water out" as they go on stream, reducing reserves and putting a heavier
strain than in the past on desalination plants.

TRANSPORTATION
Highways—Kilometers (Miles): 4,270
(2,664)
Railroads—Kilometers (Miles): none
Usable Airfields: 8

GOVERNMENT
Type: constitutional monarchy
Independence Date: June 19, 1961
Head of State/Government: Emir
Shaykh Jabir al-Ahmad al-Jabir
al-Sabah; Prime Minister (Crown
Prince) Saad al-Abdullah
Political Parties: none legal
Suffrage: limited to adult males resident
before 1920 and their descendants,
excluding women

MILITARY
Number of Armed Forces: 20,300
*Military Expenditures (% of Central
Government Expenditures):* 13.3%
Current Hostilities: none

ECONOMY
Currency ($ U.S. Equivalent): 0.30
Kuwaiti dinar = $1
Per Capita Income/GDP: $16,900/$30.7
billion
Inflation Rate: 3%
Total Foreign Debt: $7.2 billion
Natural Resources: petroleum; fish;
shrimp
Agriculture: virtually none
Industry: petroleum; petrochemicals;
desalination plants; food processing;
building materials; salt

FOREIGN TRADE
Exports: $10.5 billion
Imports: $6.6 billion

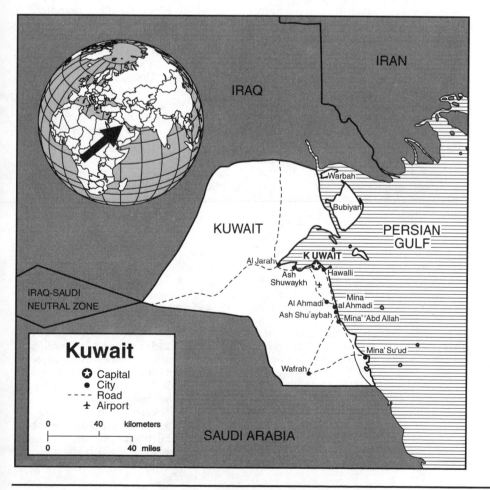

Kuwait
- ✪ Capital
- ● City
- --- Road
- ✈ Airport

0   40   kilometers

0   40 miles

KUWAIT

The State of Kuwait consists of a wedge-shaped, largely desert territory located near the head of the Persian Gulf and just southwest of the Shatt al-Arab. Kuwaiti territory includes the islands of Bubiyan and Failaka in the Gulf, both of them periodically claimed by Iraq. Kuwait also shares a Neutral Zone, consisting mainly of oil fields, which it administers jointly with Iraq and Saudi Arabia; oil production is supposedly divided equally among them. The Iraqi accusation that Kuwait was taking more than its share was one of the points of contention between the neighbors that led to Iraq's invasion of Kuwait in 1990.

Kuwait's location has given the country great strategic importance in the modern rivalries of regional powers and their outside supporters. The country played a major role in the Iran–Iraq War, supporting Iraq financially and serving as a conduit for U.S. naval intervention through the reflagging of Kuwaiti tankers. The Iraqi invasion reversed roles, with Iraq the aggressor and Kuwait both the victim and the target of UN/U.S.–led military action during the brief Gulf War in 1991.

HISTORY

Kuwait was inhabited entirely by nomadic peoples until the early 1700s. Then a number of clans of the large Anaiza tribal confederation settled along the Gulf in the current area of Kuwait. They built a fort for protection from nomadic raids—*Kuwait* means "little fort" in Arabic—and elected a chief to represent them in dealings with the Ottoman Empire, the major power in the Middle East at that time. The ruling family of modern Kuwait, the al-Sabah, traces its power back to this period.

Kuwait prospered under the al-Sabahs. Its well-protected natural harbor became headquarters for a pearl-fishing fleet of 800 dhows (boats). The town (also called Kuwait) became a port of call for British ships bound for India.

In the late 1700s and early 1800s, Kuwait was threatened by the Wahhabis, fundamentalist Muslims from central Arabia. Arab piracy also adversely affected Kuwait's prosperity. Kuwait's ruling shaykhs paid tribute to the Ottoman sultan in return for protection against the Wahhabis. However, the shaykhs began to fear that the Turks would occupy Kuwait, so they turned to the British. In 1899, Shaykh Mubarak, who reigned from 1896 to 1915, signed an agreement with Britain for protection. In return, he agreed to accept British political advisers and not to have dealings with other foreign governments.

In this way, Kuwait became a self-governing state under British protection.

Shaykh Mubarak's reign was important for another reason. During the 1890s, Kuwait had given refuge to Ibn Saud, a leader from Central Arabia whose family had been defeated by its rivals. Ibn Saud left Kuwait in 1902, traveled in secret to Riyadh, the rivals' headquarters, and seized the city in a surprise raid. Kuwait thus indirectly had a hand in the founding of its neighbor state, Saudi Arabia.

INDEPENDENCE

Kuwait continued its peaceful ways under the paternalistic rule of the al-Sabahs until the 1950s. Then oil production increased rapidly. The small pearl-fishing port became a booming modern city. In 1961, Britain and Kuwait jointly terminated the 1899 agreement, and Kuwait became fully independent under the al-Sabahs.

A threat to the country's independence developed almost immediately, as Iraq refused to recognize Kuwait's new status and claimed the territory on the grounds that it had once been part of the Iraqi Ottoman province of Basra. Iraq was also interested in controlling Kuwaiti oil resources. The ruling shaykh, now called emir, asked Britain for help, and British troops rushed back to Kuwait. Eventually, the Arab League agreed that several of its members would send troops to defend Kuwait—and, incidentally, to ensure that the country would not revert to its previous protectorate status. The Arab contingents were withdrawn in 1963. A revolution had overthrown the Iraqi government earlier in the year, and the new government recognized Kuwait's independence. However, the Ba'thist Party's concentration of power in Saddam Hussein's hands in the 1970s led to periodic Iraqi pressure on Kuwait, culminating in the 1990 invasion and occupation. After the expulsion of Iraqi forces, Kuwait requested a re-alignment of its northern border; and in 1992, the United Nations Boundary Commission approved the request, re-aligning the border approximately 1,880 feet northward. The change gave Kuwait full possession of the Rumaila oil fields and a portion of the Iraqi Umm Qasr naval base. Kuwait had argued that the existing border deprived it of its own resources and access to its territorial waters as specified in the 1963 agreement. Some 3,600 UN observers were assigned to patrol the new border; and Kuwaiti workers dug a 130-mile trench, paid for by private donations, as a further protection for the emirate.

REPRESENTATIVE GOVERNMENT

Kuwait differs from other patriarchally ruled Arabian Peninsula states in having a Constitution that provides for an elected National Assembly. Its 50 members are elected for 4-year terms.

Friction developed between the Assembly and the ruling family soon after independence. Assembly members criticized Shaykh Abdullah and his relatives, as well as the cabinet, for corruption, press censorship, refusal to allow political parties, and insufficient attention to public services. Since all members of the ruling family were on the government payroll, there was some justification for the criticism.

Abdullah died in 1965, but his successor, Shaykh al-Sabah, accepted the criticism as valid. Elections were held in 1971 for a new Assembly. The voting was hardly representative, however, since only adult male Kuwaiti citizens had the franchise; only 58,000 Kuwaitis were eligible to vote. Since there are no political parties in the country, candidates were elected by profession.

Unfortunately for democracy in Kuwait, the new Assembly paid more attention to criticism of the government than to law making. In 1976, it was suspended by Shaykh al-Sabah. He died the following year, but his successor, Shaykh Jabir, re-affirmed the ruling family's commitment to the democratic process. A new Assembly was formed in 1981, with a different membership. The majority were traditional patriarchs loyal to the rulers, along with technical experts in various fields, such as industry, agriculture, and engineering. But the new Assembly fared little better than its predecessor in balancing freedom of expression with responsible leadership. The ruler suspended it, along with the Constitution, in 1986.

Pressures to reinstate the Assembly have increased in recent years. Just prior to the Iraqi invasion, the ruler had convened a 75-member National Council "to appraise our parliamentary experiment." The process was halted during the Iraqi occupation; but, after the Iraqi withdrawal and the return to Kuwait of the ruling family, the emir pledged to hold elections for a new Assembly in October 1992. The vote was limited to males over age 21 who could trace their residence in Kuwait back to 1920 or earlier. Under these rules, some 82,000 voters would elect two candidates from each of 25 constituencies to the 50-member Assembly.

The emir kept his pledge, and, on October 5, 1992, the election took place. With political parties banned, candidates ran as representatives of coalitions or groups. Somewhat surprisingly, the campaign was marked by vigorous debate over franchise limits, accountability for the ruling family to the public, and women's rights. Government critics won more than half the seats in the Assembly; nine of them represented Islamic groupings, and seven were independents with Islamic leanings, as compared to 15 seats won by representatives from traditional pro-ruling family constituencies.

Elections were held for a new Assembly in October 1996; 250 candidates competed for the 50 seats. As in previous elections, pro-royal-family, pro-government candidates won the majority of seats.

Opposition deputies in the new Assembly wasted no time in calling for a crackdown on public corruption and nepotism in government appointments. The Crown Prince then appointed a cabinet, which included nine new ministers. The key ministries of oil, defense, interior, and commerce and industry were given to non-Sabah family members.

VULNERABILITY

Kuwait's location and its relatively open society make the country vulnerable to external subversion. In the early 1970s, the rulers were the target of criticism and threats from other Arab states because they did not publicly support the Palestinian cause. For years afterward, Kuwait provided large-scale financial aid not to only the Palestine Liberation Organization but also to Arab states such as Syria and Jordan that were directly involved in the struggle with Israel because of their common borders.

A new vulnerability surfaced with the Iranian Revolution of 1979, which overthrew the shah. Kuwait has a large Shia Muslim population, while its rulers are Sunni. Kuwait's support for Iraq and the development of closer links with Saudi Arabia (and indirectly the United States) angered Iran's new fundamentalist rulers. Kuwaiti oil installations were bombed by Iranian jets in 1981, and in 1983, truck bombs severely damaged the American and French Embassies in Kuwait City. The underground organization Islamic Jihad claimed responsibility for the attacks and threatened more if Kuwait did not stop its support of Iraq. Kuwaiti police arrested 17 persons; they were later jailed for complicity in the bombings. Since Islamic Jihad claimed links to Iran, the Kuwaiti government suspected an Iranian hand behind the violence and deported 600 Iranian workers.

Tensions with Iran intensified in the mid-1980s, as Iranian jets and missile-powered patrol boats attacked Kuwaiti tankers in the Gulf and pro-Iranian terrorists carried

(UN photo/B. Cirone)

Before the advent of tremendous oil revenues, most Kuwaitis relied on traditional livelihoods that revolved around a nomadic life. The nomadic population has now dwindled to a small segment of the population. The need to cope with new surroundings is typified by this Bedouin family confronting city life.

out a series of hijackings. A 1988 hijacking caused international concern when a Kuwaiti Airways 747 jet with several members of the royal family aboard was seized and its passengers held for 16 days while being shuttled from airport to airport. The hijackers demanded the release of the 17 truck bombers as the price for hostage freedom. The Kuwaiti government refused to negotiate; after the hostages were released through mediation by other Arab states, it passed a law making hijacking punishable by death.

Fear of Iran led Kuwait to join the newly formed Gulf Cooperation Council in 1981. The country also began making large purchases of weapons for defense, balancing U.S. with Soviet equipment. Its arms buildup made it the world's third-highest defense spender, at $3.1 billion, an average of $2,901 per capita.

During the Iran–Iraq War, Kuwait loaned 13 tankers to the United States that were reflagged and given U.S. naval escort protection to transit the Gulf. After the United States assumed a major role in the region due to the Iraqi invasion and the resulting Gulf War, Kuwait signed a 10-year mutual-defense pact, the first formal agreement of its kind for the Gulf states.

THE IRAQI OCCUPATION

The 7 months of Iraqi occupation (August 1990–February 1991) had a devastating effect on Kuwait. Some 5,000 Kuwaitis were killed, and the entire population was held hostage to Iraqi demands. Oil production stopped entirely. Iraqi forces opened hundreds of oil storage tanks as a defense measure, pouring millions of gallons of oil into the sea, thus creating a serious environmental hazard. (As they retreated, the Iraqis also set 800 oil wells afire, destroying production capabilities and posing enormous technical and environmental problems. These conflagrations were not extinguished for nearly a year.) In Kuwait City, basic water, electricity, and other services were cut off; public buildings were damaged; shops and homes were vandalized; and more than 3,000 gold bars, the backing for the Kuwaiti currency, were taken to Iraq. Nearly half the population fled the country during the occupation. In June 1992, the government approved payments of $17,000 per family in compensation for people's suffering.

Iraq's continuing efforts to destabilize Kuwait were underscored by an alleged plot to assassinate former U.S. president George Bush during his April 1993 visit to the emirate. Some 13 persons were arrested, and six Iraqis were convicted and sentenced to death. In 1995, a Kuwait appeals court upheld two of the death sentences while commuting those of four other defendants to life imprisonment.

Iraqi maneuvers near the Kuwait border and the incursion of Iraqi forces into UN–protected Kurdistan led the United States in 1996 to invoke the mutual-defense pact by sending an additional 5,000 ground troops to Kuwait to take part in a new attack on Iraq. However, the Kuwaiti gov-

Establishment of
the al-Sabah
family as the
rulers of Kuwait
1756

Agreement with
Great Britain
making Kuwait a
protectorate
1899

Independence,
followed by Iraqi
claim and
British/Arab
League
intervention
1961–1963

Elections for a
new National
Assembly
1971

The ruler
suspends the
Assembly on the
grounds that it is
a handicap to
effective
government
1976

Bombings of public
installations by
Islamic Jihad;
massive deportation
of Iranians after public
buildings and oil
installations are
sabotaged
1980s

The government
places the tanker fleet
under U.S. protection
by reflagging ships
and providing naval
escorts in the Gulf

1990s

Iraqi forces
occupy Kuwait;
Kuwait is
liberated by
U.S.–led coalition
forces in the Gulf
War; Kuwait
struggles to
recover from the
war

Tension between
the government
and the
Assembly
intensifies

Women win
suffrage and the
right to run for
and serve in
public office

ernment, which had not been consulted, agreed to accept only 3,500. With the threat from Iraq receding, 2000 U.S. troops joined with Kuwaiti forces in Operation Intrinsic Action, a war-game scenario near the Iraqi border.

THE PEOPLE

Kuwait has a very high birth rate, and, until the economic recession in the region, the country had a high rate of immigration. As a result, there are more non-Kuwaitis than Kuwaitis in the population, though dislocation resulting from the Iraqi occupation has changed the balance. Today, approximately 45 percent of the population are native Kuwaitis.

About one third of the total population, both citizens and noncitizens, are Shia Muslims. After the 1979 Revolution in Iran, they were blamed for much of the unrest in the country; Shia terrorists were charged directly with the 1983 truck bombings of embassies in Kuwait City. Two of the jailed terrorists were released and deported in 1989. The improvement in Kuwait–Iran relations that followed the end of the Iran–Iraq War lessened this Shia antigovernment activity, and Shia and Sunni residents suffered equally under the Iraqi occupation.

Before the Gulf War, the largest non-native population group was Palestinian. Although the Palestinians were denied citizenship, they were generally better educated and more industrious than the native Kuwaitis. Palestinians formed the nucleus of opposition to the ruling family,

and a number of them collaborated with the Iraqi occupation forces. After the war, more than 600 Palestinians were tried and sentenced to prison terms for collaboration, in some cases for nothing more than wearing a Saddam Hussain T-shirt. As a result of uncertain economic conditions, plus the government's resolve to reduce its dependence on foreign workers, thousands of Palestinians lost their jobs. Some 300,000 out of the 400,000 Palestinians in Kuwait emigrated to Jordan in 1991.

THE ECONOMY

Kuwait's only abundant resource is petroleum. Less than 1 percent of the land can be cultivated, and there is almost no fresh water. Drinking water comes from seawater converted to fresh water by huge desalination plants.

Kuwait's oil reserves of 94 billion barrels are the world's third largest, comprising 10 percent of global reserves. According to a 1996 study by the International Monetary Fund, the oil industry—and, with it, the economy—have recovered "impressively" from the effects of the Iraqi occupation. Oil production in 1997 reached 2 million barrels per day. The 1995–2000 5-Year Plan approved by the Assembly projects a balanced budget by the end of the plan, largely through privatization of state enterprises, increased oil and non-oil revenues, and expansion of petrochemical industries.

Kuwait's economic recovery following the Iraqi occupation was hampered not

only by the damage to its oil industry but also by an overstaffed public-service sector, huge welfare subsidies, and other adverse factors. In 1995, the World Bank recommended a number of reforms. These included an end to state subsidies for water, gas, and telephone services; and to the welfare benefits that made Kuwait society one of the most privileged in the world. Despite some opposition in the Assembly, mainly on procedural grounds, the government went ahead with the reforms.

As a result, the Kuwaiti economy has rebounded to such an extent that, in 1996, Kuwait became the first Gulf state to receive an "A" rating from the London-based International Banking Credit Association, an organization that evaluates countries for prospective lenders on the basis of short and long-term risks.

DEVELOPMENT

The Kuwait Fund for Arab Economic Development, formed in 1961, has been the conduit for aid to Arab and some African and Asian less-developed countries from Kuwait's vast oil revenues. Most of the funds are provided for transportation, electricity, and agricultural projects.

FREEDOM

As a constitutional monarchy, Kuwait is governed by the provisions of the 1962 Constitution. Only 15% of the population can vote. Women, naturalized Kuwaitis, and members of the armed forces are excluded, although those naturalized for 30 years were allowed to vote in 1996. In 1996, 300 Kuwaiti women staged a 1-day strike to protest their exclusion from the political process.

HEALTH/WELFARE

In order to balance the budget and reduce persistent deficits, the government in 1996 ended free health care for all citizens as well as non-natives. Hospitals are required to charge a $13 entrance fee, private rooms cost $17 per day, and surgery rates range from $167 to $500 for an operation.

ACHIEVEMENTS

Kuwait became a major producer of petrochemicals in 1997 with the inauguration of the new Shuaiba complex, a joint venture of the government and Union Carbide. Its ethane cracker has a production capacity of 650,000 tons annually, and the polyethylene component produces 450,000 tons a year.

Lebanon (Republic of Lebanon)

GEOGRAPHY

Area in Square Kilometers (Miles):
10,452 (4,015) (smaller than
Connecticut)
Capital (Population): Beirut (1,100,000)
Climate: Mediterranean (hot, humid
summers; cool, damp winters)

PEOPLE

Population

Total: 3,776,400
Annual Growth Rate: 2.1%
Rural/Urban Population Ratio: 14/86
Ethnic Makeup: 95% Arab; 4%
Armenian; 1% others
Major Languages: Arabic; French and
English are widely spoken

Health

Life Expectancy at Birth: 65 years
(male); 69 years (female)
Infant Mortality Rate (Ratio): 38/1,000
Average Caloric Intake: 99% of FAO
minimum
Physicians Available (Ratio): 1/407

Religions

70% Muslim; 30% Christian (Maronite,
Greek Orthodox; Melkite, Armenian,
and Protestant)

Rediscovering Lebanese Culture

With the end of the Civil War and reconstruction of their country, the
Lebanese have begun to "rediscover" their past, revitalizing their rich and
vibrant 3,000-year-old cultural heritage. In 1997, the Baalbek Festival reopened in this ancient Phoenician–Greek–Roman city, with world famous
dancers, opera stars, and classical and jazz musicians performing against a
backdrop of classical ruins and statuary.

Education

Adult Literacy Rate: 76%

COMMUNICATION

Telephones: the system was severely
damaged in the Civil War; it is now
being rebuilt
Newspapers: 37 dailies—30 in Arabic;
4 in Armenian; 2 in French; 1 in
English

TRANSPORTATION

Highways—Kilometers (Miles): 7,370
(4,580)
Railroads—Kilometers (Miles): 222
(139) (system considered inoperable)
Usable Airfields: 9

GOVERNMENT

Type: parliamentary republic
Independence Date: November 22, 1943
Head of State: President Ilyas Hrawi;
Prime Minister Rafiq Hariri
Political Parties: various parties are
identified with religious or
denominational groups; each group
nominates candidates for the
128-member Chamber of Deputies
(Parliament)
Suffrage: compulsory for males over
21; authorized for women over 21 with
elementary-school education

MILITARY

Number of Armed Forces: 21,800
*Military Expenditures (% of Central
Government Expenditures):* 5.5%
Current Hostilities: the Lebanese Army
has disarmed all militias and controls
the country, with the exception of
Israel's self-proclaimed "security zone"
along the southern Lebanese border;
some 30,000–35,000 Syrian troops still
occupy northeast Lebanon; a 1,000-man
Israeli brigade occupies a "security
zone" along Lebanon's southern border
and engages in periodic conflict with
Lebanese Hizbullah militias

ECONOMY

Currency ($ U.S. Equivalent): 1,533
Lebanese pounds = $1
Per Capita Income/GDP: $4,360/$15.8
billion
Inflation Rate: 9%
Total Foreign Debt: $765 million
Natural Resources: limestone
Agriculture: citrus fruit; wheat; corn;
barley; potatoes; tobacco; olives; onions
Industry: food processing; cement; oil
refining; light industry; textiles;
chemicals

FOREIGN TRADE

Exports: $1.1 billion
Imports: $7.8 billion

LEBANON

The Republic of Lebanon is located at the eastern end of the Mediterranean Sea. The coastal plain, which contains the capital, Beirut, and all the other important cities, is narrow, rising just a few miles east of Beirut to a rugged mountain range, Mount Lebanon. Beyond Mount Lebanon is the Biqa', a broad, fertile valley that is the country's main wheat-growing region. At the eastern edge of the Biqa', the land rises again abruptly to the snow-capped Anti-Lebanon Range, which separates Lebanon from Syria.

Lebanon's location has always been important strategically as well as commercially. Many invaders passed through it over the centuries on their conquests—Egyptians, Assyrians, Persians, Crusaders, Arabs, and Turks. However, they were seldom able to control Mount Lebanon. For this reason, the mountain served as a refuge for ethnic and religious minorities, and it became in time the nucleus of the modern Lebanese state.

Lebanon's Mediterranean ports, although small and not well protected, have traditionally served as an outlet for goods from the region's interior, notably Syria. Lebanese merchants have profited for centuries by being middlemen for this trade. However, its strategic location and its role as a commercial entrepot have hampered Lebanon's unification as a nation in the twentieth century. Unification and the establishment of a national identity have also been blocked by religious divisions and territorial rivalries by various clans. A Lebanese scholar described the country's political system as "a feudal hierarchy with fluctuating political influence, as powerful families asserted themselves to acquire power and prominence."[1]

(UN photo/J. K. Isaac)

Invasions have played an important role in the history of Lebanon. This view of Ayta az Zutt, in the southeastern area of Lebanon, shows the remains of a Crusaders' castle on the distant hill.

HISTORY

In ancient times, Lebanon was known as Phoenicia. The Phoenicians were great traders who traveled throughout the Mediterranean and probably out into the Atlantic Ocean as far north as Cornwall in England, in search of tin, copper, and iron ore, which were valued in the ancient world for their many uses. Phoenician merchants established trading posts, some of which eventually grew into great cities.

No central government was ever established in Phoenicia itself. Phoenician towns like Byblos, Tyre, Sidon, and Tripoli were independent states, often in conflict or rivalry over trade with one another. This city–state rivalry has always been a feature of Lebanese life and is another reason for today's lack of a national Lebanese sense of unity.

Lebanon began to develop a definite identity much later, in the seventh century A.D., when a Christian group, the Maronites, took refuge in Mount Lebanon after they were threatened with persecution by the government of the East Roman or Byzantine Empire because of theological disagreements over the nature of Christ. The Muslim Arabs brought Islam to coastal Lebanon at about the same time, but they were unable to dislodge or convert the Maronites. Mount Lebanon's sanctuary tradition attracted other minority groups, Muslim as well as Christian. Shia Muslim communities moved there in the ninth and tenth centuries A.D. to escape persecution from Sunni Muslims, the Islamic majority. In the eleventh century, the Druze, an offshoot of Islam, who followed the teachings of an Egyptian mystic and also faced persecution from Sunni Muslims, established themselves in the southern part of Mount Lebanon. These communities were originally quite separate. In the modern period of Lebanese history, however, they have tended to overlap, a fact, David Gordon says, "that makes both for unity and in troubled times for a dangerous struggle for turf."[2]

Lebanon acquired a distinct political identity under certain powerful families in the sixteenth and seventeenth centuries. The Ottoman Turks conquered it along with the rest of the Middle East, but they were content to leave local governance in the hands of these families in return for tribute. The most prominent was the Ma'an family, who were Druze. Their greatest leader, Fakhr al-Din (1586–1635), established an independent principality including all of present-day Lebanon, Israel, and part of Syria. It was during al-Din's rule that French religious orders were allowed to establish missions in the country, which facilitated later European intervention in Lebanon.

The Ma'ans were succeeded by the Shihabs, who were Maronites. Their descendants continue to hold important positions in the country, underscoring the durability of the extended-family system, which still dominates Lebanese politics. They also allied the Maronite Church with the Roman Catholic Church, an action that had great consequences in the twentieth century, when the Maronites came to view Lebanon as "a Christian island in a Muslim sea," preserving its unique Lebanese identity only through Western support.

European countries began to intervene directly in Lebanon in the nineteenth century, due to conflict between the Maronite and Druze communities. Mount Lebanon was occupied by Egyptian armies of the Ottoman khedive (viceroy) of Egypt, Muhammad Ali, in the 1830s. Egyptian development of Beirut and other coastal ports for trade purposes, particularly exports of Lebanese silk (still an important cash crop) at the expense of Mount Lebanon, and heavy taxes imposed by the khedive's overseers led to peasant uprisings in 1840 and 1857. By then the Ottomans had re-established their authority, with European help. However, the European powers refused to allow the sultan to change Mount Lebanon's special status as an autonomous province. Ottoman governors resorted to intrigues with Maronite and Druze leaders, playing one against the other. The result was a Maronite–Druze civil war, which broke out in 1860. The cause was insignificant—"an affray between two boys, the shooting of a partridge or the collision of two pack animals," asserts one author; but whatever the spark, the two communities were ready to go for each other's throats.[3]

Although the Maronite fighters greatly outnumbered the Druze, the latter had better leadership. The Druze massacred 12,000 Christians and drove 100,000 from their homes during a 4-week period. At that point, the European powers intervened to protect their coreligionists. French troops landed in Beirut and moved on to occupy Damascus. France and England forced the Ottoman sultan to establish Mount Lebanon as a self-governing province headed by a Christian governor. The province did not include Beirut. Although many Lebanese emigrated during this period, because Mount Lebanon was

small, rather poor, and provided few job opportunities, those who stayed (particularly the Maronites) prospered. Self-government under their own leader enabled them to develop a system of small, individually owned farms and to break their former dependence on absentee landowners. A popular saying among Lebanese at the time was, "Happy is he who has a shed for one goat in Mount Lebanon."[4]

The French Mandate

After the defeat of Ottoman Turkey in World War I, Lebanon became a French mandate. The French had originally intended the country to be included in their mandate over Syria; but, in 1920, due to pressure from Maronite leaders, they separated the two mandates. "New" Lebanon was much larger than the old Maronite–Druze territory up on Mount Lebanon. The new "Greater Lebanon" included the coast—in short, the area of the current Lebanese state. The Maronites found themselves linked not only with the Druze but also with both Sunni and Shia Muslims. The Maronites already distrusted the Druze, out of bitter experience. Their distrust was caused by fear of a Muslim majority and fear that Muslims, being mostly Arabs, would work to incorporate Lebanon into Syria after independence.

France gave Lebanon its independence in 1943, but French troops stayed on until 1946, when they were withdrawn due to British and American pressure on France. The French made some contributions to Lebanese development during the mandate, such as the nucleus of a modern army, development of ports, roads, and airports, and an excellent educational system dominated by the Université de St. Joseph, training ground for many Lebanese leaders. The French language and culture served until recently as one of the few things unifying the various sects and providing them with a sense of national identity.

THE LEBANESE REPUBLIC

The major shortcoming of the mandate was the French failure to develop a broad-based political system with representatives from the major religious groups. The French very pointedly favored the Maronites. The Constitution, originally issued in 1926, established a republican system under an elected president and a Legislature. Members would be elected on the basis of six Christians to five Muslims. The president would be elected for a 6-year term and could not serve concurrently. (The one exception was Bishara al-Khuri [1943–1952], who served during and after the transition period to independence. The

Constitution was amended to allow him to do so.) By private French–Maronite agreement, the custom was established whereby the Lebanese president would always be chosen from the Maronite community.

In the long term, perhaps more important to Lebanese politics than the Constitution is the National Pact, an oral agreement made in 1943 between Bishara al-Khuri, as head of the Maronite community, and Riad al-Sulh, his Sunni counterpart. The two leaders agreed that, first, Lebanese Christians would not enter into alliances with foreign (i.e., Christian) nations and Muslims would not attempt to merge Lebanon with the Muslim Arab world; and second, that the six-to-five formula for representation in the Assembly would apply to all public offices. The pact has never been put in writing, but in view of the delicate balance of sects in Lebanon, it has been considered by Lebanese leaders, particularly the Maronites, as the only alternative to anarchy.

Despite periodic political crises and frequent changes of government due to shifting alliances of leaders, Lebanon functioned quite well during its first 2 decades of independence. The large extended family, although an obstacle to broad nation building, served as an essential support base for its members, providing services that would otherwise have to have been drawn from government sources. These services included education, employment, bank loans, investment capital, and old-age security. Powerful families of different religious groups competed for power and influence but also coexisted, having had "the long experience with each other and with the rules and practices that make coexistence possible."[5] The freewheeling Lebanese economy was another important factor in Lebanon's relative stability. Per capita annual income rose from $235 in 1950 to $1,070 in 1974, putting Lebanon on a level with some of the oil-producing Arab states, although the country does not have oil.

The private sector was largely responsible for national prosperity. A real-estate boom developed, and many fortunes were made in land speculation and construction. Tourism was another important source of revenues. Many banks and foreign business firms established their headquarters in Beirut because of its excellent communications with the outside world, its educated, multilingual labor force, and the absence of government restrictions.

THE 1975–1976 CIVIL WAR

The titles of books on Lebanon in recent years have often contained adjectives such as "fractured," "fragmented," and "precarious." These provide a generally accurate description of the country's situation as a result of the Civil War of 1975–1976. The main destabilizing element, and the one that precipitated the conflict, was the presence and activities of Palestinians.

In some ways, the Palestinians have contributed significantly to Lebanese national life. The first group, who fled there after the 1948 Arab–Israeli War, consisted mostly of cultured, educated, highly urbanized people who gravitated to Beirut and were absorbed quickly into the population. Many of them became extremely successful in banking, commerce, journalism, or as faculty members at the American University of Beirut. A second Palestinian group arrived as destitute refugees after the 1967 Six-Day War. They have been housed ever since in refugee camps run by the United Nations Relief and Works Agency. The Lebanese government provides them with identity cards but no passports. For all practical purposes, they are stateless persons.

Neither group was a threat to Lebanese internal stability until 1970, although Lebanon backed the Palestine Liberation Organization cause and did not interfere with guerrilla raids from its territory into Israel. After the PLO was expelled from Jordan, the organization made its headquarters in Beirut. This new militant Palestinian presence in Lebanon created a double set of problems for the Lebanese. Palestinian raids into Israel brought Israeli retaliation, which caused more Lebanese than Palestinian casualties. Yet the Lebanese government could not control the Palestinians. To many Lebanese, especially the Maronites, their government seemed to be a prisoner in its own land.

In April 1975, a bus carrying Palestinians returning from a political rally was ambushed near Beirut by the Kata'ib, members of the Maronite Phalange Party. The incident triggered the Lebanese Civil War of 1975–1976. The war officially ended with a peace agreement arranged by the Arab League.[6] But the bus incident also brought to a head conflicts derived from the opposing goals of various Lebanese power groups. The Palestinians' goal was to use Lebanon as a springboard for the liberation of Palestine. The Maronites' goal was to drive the Palestinians out of Lebanon and preserve their privileged status. Sunni Muslim leaders sought to reshape the National Pact to allow for equal political participation with the Christians. Shia leaders were determined to get a better break for the Shia community, generally the poorest and least represented in the Lebanese government.[7] The Druze, also interested in greater rep-

resentation in the system and traditionally hostile to the Maronites, disliked and distrusted all of the other groups.

Like most civil wars, the Lebanese Civil War was fought by Lebanon's own people. But Lebanon's location; its international importance as a trade, banking, and transit center; and the various factions' need for financial backing ensured outside involvement in the conflict. Syrian troops intervened, at the request of the Arab League, first to enforce the 1976 cease-fire and then to crush the Palestinians. The Israelis helped a Lebanese renegade officer to set up an "independent free Lebanon" adjoining the Israeli border. The complexity of the situation was described in graphic terms by a Christian religious leader:

The battle is between the Palestinians and the Lebanese. No! It is between the Palestinians and the Christians. No! It is between Christians and Muslims. No! It is between Leftists and Rightists. No! It is between Israel and the Palestinians on Lebanese soil. No! It is between international imperialism and Zionism on the one hand, and Lebanon and neighboring states on the other.[8]

THE ISRAELI INVASION

The immediate result of the Civil War was to divide Lebanon into separate territories, each controlled by a different faction. The Lebanese government, for all practical purposes, could not control its own territory. Israeli forces, in an effort to protect northern Israeli settlements from constant shelling by the Palestinians, established control over southern Lebanon. The Lebanese–Israeli border, ironically, became a sort of "good fence" open to Lebanese civilians for medical treatment in Israeli hospitals.

In March 1978, PLO guerrillas landed on the Israeli coast near Haifa, hijacked a bus, and drove it toward Tel Aviv. The hijackers were overpowered in a shootout with Israeli troops, but 35 passengers were killed along with the guerrillas. Israeli forces invaded southern Lebanon in retaliation and occupied the region for 2 months, eventually withdrawing after the United Nations, in an effort to separate Palestinians from Israelis, set up a 6,000-member "Interim Force" in Lebanon, made up of units from various countries, in the south. But the Interim Force was not able to do much to control the Palestinians; most Lebanese and Israelis referred sarcastically to the Force as the "United Nothings."

The Lebanese factions themselves continued to tear the nation apart. Political as-

sassinations of rival leaders were frequent. Many Lebanese settlements became ghost towns; they were fought over so much that their residents abandoned them. Some 300,000 Lebanese from the Israeli-occupied south fled to northern cities as refugees. In addition to the thousands of casualties, a psychological trauma settled over Lebanese youth, the "Kalashnikov generation" that knew little more than violence, crime, and the blind hatred of religious feuds. (The Kalashnikov, a Soviet-made submachine gun, became the standard toy of Lebanese children.)[9]

The Israeli invasion of Lebanon in June 1982 was intended as a final solution to the Palestinian problem. It didn't quite work out that way. The Israeli Army surrounded Beirut and succeeded with U.S. intervention in forcing the evacuation of PLO guerrillas from Lebanon. Some of the Lebanese factions were happy to see them go, particularly the Maronites and the Shia community in the south. But they soon discovered that they had exchanged one foreign domination for another. The burden of war, as always, fell heaviest on the civilian population. A Beirut newspaper estimated almost 50,000 civilian casualties in the first 2 months of the invasion. Also, the Lebanese discovered that they were not entirely free of the Palestinian presence. The largest number of PLO guerrillas either went to Syria and then returned secretly to Lebanon or retreated into the Biqa' Valley to take up new positions under Syrian Army protection.

Israeli control over Beirut enabled the Christians to take savage revenge against the remaining Palestinians. In September 1983, Christian Phalange militiamen entered the refugee camps of Sabra and Shatila in West Beirut and massacred hundreds of people, mostly women and children. The massacre led to an official Israeli inquiry and censure of Israeli government and military leaders for indirect responsibility. But the Christian-dominated Lebanese government's own inquiry failed to fix responsibility on the Phalange.

The Lebanese Civil War supposedly ended in 1976, but it was not until 1990 that the central government began to show results in disarming militias and establishing its authority over the fragmented nation. Until then, hostage taking and clan rivalries underlined the absence in Lebanon of a viable national identity.

The 1982 Israeli invasion brought a change in government, with the Phalange leader, Bashir Gemayel, elected to head a "government of national salvation." Unfortunately for Bashir, his ruthlessness in his career had enabled him to compile an impressive list of enemies. He was killed by a bomb explosion at Phalange headquarters before he could take office. Gemayel was succeeded by his older brother, Amin. The new president was persuaded by U.S. negotiators to sign a troop-withdrawal agreement with Israel. However, the agreement was not supported by leaders of the other Lebanese communities, and, in March 1984, Gemayel unilaterally repudiated it. The Israelis then began working their way out of the "Lebanese quagmire" on their own, and in June 1985, the last Israeli units left Lebanon. (However, the Israelis did reserve a "security zone" along the border for necessary reprisals for attacks by PLO or Shia guerrillas.)

The Israelis left behind a country that had become almost ungovernable. Gemayel's effort to restructure the national army along nonsectarian lines came to nothing, since the army was not strong enough to disband the various militias. The growing power of the Shia Muslims, particularly the Shia organization Amal, presented a new challenge to the Christian leadership, while the return of the Palestinians brought bloody battles between Shia and PLO guerrillas. As the battles raged, cease-fire followed cease-fire and conference followed conference, but without noticeable success.

The Israeli withdrawal left the Syrians as the major power brokers in Lebanon. In 1985, Syrian president Hafez al-Assad masterminded a comprehensive peace and reform agreement with Elie Hobeika, the commander of the Christian Lebanese Forces, with Shia Muslim and Druze leaders concurring. The agreement would provide for the election of an enlarged Parliament, with equal representation for Christians and Muslims, and would change the Lebanese National Pact to apportion greater power in the government and the army to Muslims. But before the pact could be put into effect, one of Hobeika's rivals, privately encouraged by President Gemayel, overthrew him. Hobeika fled into exile in Syria. With his departure, the Civil War resumed, fueled by seemingly endless factional conflicts.

SYRIA INTERVENES

The collapse of peace efforts led Syria to send 7,000 heavily armed commandos into west Beirut in 1987 to restore law and order. They did restore a semblance of order to that part of the capital and opened checkpoints into east Beirut. But the Syrians were unable, or perhaps unwilling, to challenge the powerful Hizbullah faction (reputed to have held most Western hostages), which controlled the rabbit warren of narrow streets and tenements in the city's southern suburbs.

Aside from Hizbullah, Syria's major problem in knitting Lebanon together under its tutelage was with the Maronite community. With President Gemayel's 6-year term scheduled to end in September 1988, the Syrians lobbied hard for a candidate of their choice. (Under the Lebanese parliamentary system, the president is elected by the Chamber of Deputies.) Unfortunately, due to the Civil War, only 72 of the 99 deputies elected in 1972, when the last elections were held, were still in office. They rejected Syria's candidate, former president Suleiman Franjieh (1970–1976), because of his identification with the conflict and his ties with the Assad regime. When the Chamber failed to agree on an acceptable candidate, the office became vacant. Gemayel's last act before leaving office was to appoint General Michel Aoun, the commander of Christian troops in the Lebanese Army, to head an interim government. But the Muslim-dominated civilian government of Prime Minister Salim al-Hoss contested the appointment, declaring that it remained the legitimate government of the country.

BREAKDOWN OF A SOCIETY

The assassination in 1987 of Prime Minister Rachid Karami (a bomb hidden in the army helicopter in which he was traveling blew up) graphically underlined the mindless rejection of law and order of the various Lebanese factions. The only show of Lebanese unity in many years occurred at the funeral of former president Camille Chamoun, dead of a heart attack at age 87. Chamoun's last public statement, made the day before his death, was particularly fitting to this fractured land. "The nation is headed toward total bankruptcy and famine," he warned. The statement brought to mind the prophetic observations of a historian, written 30 years ago: "Lebanon is too conspicuous and successful an example of political democracy and economic liberalism to be tolerated in a region that has turned its back on both systems."[10]

The death of the Mufti (the chief religious leader) of the Sunni Muslim community in a car-bomb attack in 1989 confirmed Chamoun's gloomy prediction. The Mufti had consistently called for reconciliation and nonviolent coexistence between Christian and Muslim communities. The political situation remained equally chaotic. Rene Moawwad, a respected Christian lawyer, was elected by the Chamber to fill the presidential vacancy. However, he was murdered after barely 17 days in office. The Chamber then elected Elias Hrawi, a Christian politician from the Maronite stronghold of Zahle, as president. General Aoun contested the election, declaring himself the legitimate president of Lebanon, and holed up in the presidential palace in east Beirut, defended strongly by his Maronite militiamen.

But the Maronite community was as fragmented as the larger Lebanese community. Aoun's chief Christian rival, Samir Geagea, rejected his authority, and early in 1990, a renewed outbreak of fighting between their militias left east Beirut in shambles, with more than 3,000 casualties. After another shaky cease-fire had been reached, Syrian Army units supporting the regular Lebanese Army surrounded the Christian section. Aoun's palace became an embattled enclave, with supplies available only by running the Syrian blockade or from humanitarian relief organizations.

Aoun's support base eroded significantly in the spring, when his rival recognized the Hrawi government as legitimate and endorsed the Taif Accord.[11] In October, Hrawi formally requested Syrian military aid for the Lebanese Army. After an all-out assault on the presidential palace by joint Syrian–Lebanese forces, the general surrendered, taking refuge in the French Embassy and then going into exile.

Aoun's departure enabled the Hrawi government to begin taking the next step toward rebuilding a united Lebanon. This involved disarming the militias. The continued presence of Syrian forces was a major asset to the reconstituted Lebanese Army as it undertook this delicate process. A newspaper publisher observed that "the Syrian presence is a very natural fact for the Lebanese," echoing the Syrian president's statement to an interviewer: "Lebanon and Syria are one nation and one people, but they are two distinct states."[12] It was the first clear statement from any Syrian leader that Lebanon had a legitimate existence as a state.

Following the re-establishment of central-government authority, a new transitional Council of Ministers (cabinet) was appointed by President Hrawi in 1992. Its responsibilities were to stabilize the economy and prepare for elections for a new Chamber of Deputies. The election law was amended by decree in June to enlarge the Chamber from 108 to 128 seats, to establish a better confessional balance.

The first national elections since the start of the Civil War were held in 1992. Due in part to a boycott by Christian parties, which had demanded Syrian withdrawal as their price for participation, Shia candidates won 30 seats. Shia Amal leader

Nibih Berri was elected speaker; Rafiq Hariri, a Sunni Muslim and millionaire (who had made his fortune as a contractor in Saudi Arabia) was named prime minister.

In any case, the growing demographic imbalance of Muslims and Christians indicated that, in the not too distant future, Lebanon would no longer be "a Christian island in a Muslim sea." By 1997, Christians numbered at most 30 percent of the population (composed of 800,000 Maronites, 400,000 Greek Orthodox, 300,000 Greek Catholics or Melkites, and 75,000 Armenians). Half a million Christians had left the country during the Civil War, along with top leaders such as Michel Aoun, Amin Gemayel, and Raymond Edde, in exile in Paris. A government decision in 1997 to grant citizenship to Palestinians and other immigrant Muslims has further diminished Christian influence. The Kata'ib—the strongest Christian political party—failed to win a seat in the last parliamentary elections.

Despite the loss of Christian influence, political stability has largely been restored under Hariri's forceful leadership. In June 1996, the cabinet approved a new election law that would redistrict the country to provide greater representation for Christian and Druze populations. The elections were held in August; Hariri ran as a Sunni candidate from West Beirut. The new law allocated 57 seats to Muslims and 63 to various Christian sects. The low voter turnout—52 percent—contrasted sharply with publicly demonstrated enthusiasm on the part of the Lebanese people for democracy.

By 1993, the only remaining armed militia in the country was that of Hizbullah. With the tacit support of the government, it was allowed to keep its arms in order to resist Israeli forces in Israel's self-proclaimed "security zone" along the border. With arms and training provided by Iran and Syria, the Hizbullah developed into a formidable guerrilla force, ambushing Israeli units in a number of battles and causing sufficient casualties to generate a major debate within Israel about withdrawing from the security zone. A top Hizbullah commander noted that "resistance is a sacred thing for us," and Shaykh Hossein Fadlallah, chief religious leader (Imam) of Lebanese Shias, told an interviewer that "the occupation has provoked an embarrassment for the occupiers. Instead of shielding Israel it is turning out to be a threat and a danger."[13]

LEBANON AND THE WORLD
Aside from its vulnerability to international and inter-Arab rivalries because of internal conflicts, Lebanon drew world attention in the 1980s for its involvement in hostage taking. Lebanese militias such as Hizbullah, a Shia group backed by Iran as a means of exporting the Islamic Revolution, and shadowy organizations like the Islamic Jihad, Revolutionary Justice, and Islamic Jihad for the Liberation of Palestine kidnapped foreigners in Beirut. The conditions set for their release were rarely specific, and the refusal of the U.S. and other Western governments to "deal with terrorists" left them languishing in unknown prisons for years, seemingly forgotten by the outside world.

The changing Middle East situation and Lebanon's slow return to normalcy in the 1990s began to move the hostage-release process forward. Release negotiations were pursued by then–UN general-secretary Javier Pérez de Cuéllar. The UN team worked on two levels: Pérez de Cuéllar ran a high-profile diplomatic campaign by repeatedly visiting Iran, Syria, and Israel, while his long-time associate Giandomenico Picco conducted behind-the-scenes talks with Shia operatives in the Biqa' Valley located in the eastern part of Lebanon. Their efforts began to bear fruit: within a few months, British journalist John McCarthy, Jesse Turner, Thomas Sutherland, and British church envoy Terry Waite were freed, as were Americans Joseph Cicippio, Alan Steen, and Terry Anderson. Two German relief workers, the last Western hostages in Lebanon, were freed in 1992.

THE ECONOMY
In the mid-1970s, the Lebanese economy began going steadily downhill. The Civil War and resulting instability caused most banks and financial institutions to move out of Beirut to more secure locations, notably Jordan, Bahrain, and Kuwait. Aside from the cost in human lives, Israeli raids and the 1982 invasion severely damaged the economy. The cost of the invasion in terms of damages was estimated at $1.9 billion. Remittances from Lebanese emigrants abroad dropped significantly. The Lebanese pound, valued at 4.74 to U.S. $1 in 1982, reached a record low of 3,000 to $1 in 1992. (In early 1998, the Lebanese pound was valued at 1,533 to the dollar.)

Yet, by a strange irony of fate, some elements of the economy continued to display robust health. Most middle-class Lebanese had funds invested abroad, largely in dollar accounts, and thus were protected from economic disaster.

The expansion of the Civil War in 1989–1990 and the intervention of Syrian troops tested the survival techniques of the Lebanese people as never before. But they adjusted to the new "Battle of Beirut" with great inventiveness. A newspaper advertisement announced: "Civilian fortifications, 24-hour delivery service. Sandbags and barrels, full or empty." With the Syrian–Christian artillery exchanges concentrated at night, most residents fled the city then, returning after the muezzin's first call for morning prayers had in effect silenced the guns, to shop, to stock up on fuel smuggled ashore from small tankers, or to sample the luxury goods that in some mysterious way had appeared on store shelves.

Except for the most fortunate people, the general population began to feel the economic impact of the years of the Civil War for the first time in 1986 and 1987. A Lebanese filmmaker summed up the situation with devastating accuracy: "We are getting divided into the very poor and the very rich, and the middle class is getting squeezed out. The poor, you can see them everywhere now, for the first time."[14] The long, drawn-out civil conflict badly affected Lebanese agriculture, the mainstay of the economy. Both the coastal strip and the Biqa' Valley are extremely fertile, and in normal times produce crop surpluses for export. Lebanese fruit, particularly apples (the most important cash crop) and grapes, is in great demand throughout the Arab world. But these crops are no longer exported in quantity. Israeli destruction of crops, the flight of most of the farm labor force, and the blockade by Israeli troops of truck traffic from rural areas into Beirut had a devastating effect on production.

Lebanon produces no oil of its own, but before the Civil War and the Israeli invasion, the country derived important revenues from transit fees for oil shipments through pipelines across its territory. The periodic closing of these pipelines and damage to the country's two refineries sharply reduced revenues. The well-developed manufacturing industry, particularly textiles, was equally hard hit.

Yet the resourceful Lebanese show a remarkable resilience in adapting to difficult political and economic circumstances. Prime Minister Hariri won broad support for his policy of refusing to admit the 400 Islamic fundamentalists deported by Israel from the Gaza Strip in December 1992. On his direct orders, the Lebanese Army blocked them from entering Lebanese territory north of the Israeli self-declared security zone in southern Lebanon.

Hariri also cracked down on economic corruption, which had become a fact of life during the Civil War. During a 2-week campaign in November 1992, dozens of

Establishment of Mount Lebanon as a sanctuary for religious communities
9th–11th centuries

The first Civil War, between Maronites and Druze, ending in foreign military intervention
1860–1864

French mandate
1920–1946

Internal crisis and the first U.S. military intervention
1958

Civil War, ended (temporarily) by an Arab League–sponsored cease-fire and peacekeeping force of Syrian troops
1975–1976

Israeli invasion and occupation of Beirut; massacre of Palestinians in refugee camps by Christian militiamen

Syrian troops re-occupy Beirut, restore order, but are unable to reconcile warring factions
1980s

Foreigners are seized in a new outbreak of hostage taking; the economy nears collapse as the currency is devalued and banks halt trading

1990s

The withdrawal of Israeli forces from Lebanon is completed

All foreign hostages are released

Lebanon begins rebuilding; Israel makes air strikes in retaliation of Hizbullah attacks

stores were closed or received heavy fines (or both) for selling outdated medicines, for illegal price fixing, or for nonpayment of taxes. Some 6,000 government employees lost their jobs in a massive purge in November 1993 as Hariri carried out his promise to "clean and energize" the government. Ironically, the purge coincided with Lebanon's 50th anniversary as a state.

Under Hariri, Lebanon has also moved toward full economic recovery from the destruction of the Civil War. Soldiers, a locally based company, has rebuilt much of war-damaged Beirut, expanded airport facilities, and encouraged foreign investment. The currency was stabilized, and some progress was made in 1996–1997 toward slimming down the obese Lebanese bureaucracy, including the overuse of *wasta* (bribes), which had required the use of an intermediary for every service from police protection to tax relief to telephones.

Lebanon's economic and political vulnerability was severely tested in April 1996 by a massive Israel air and artillery bombardment. Officially named "Operation Grapes of Wrath" by the Israelis, the attack came ostensibly in response to Hizbullah shelling and escalation of violence against Israeli soldiers in the security zone. But many observers believed that Israel's response was well in excess of the provocation. Israeli warplanes knocked out the main power stations serving Beirut; and Israeli artillery destroyed a UN base in southern Lebanon, killing scores of women and children. Some

300,000 Lebanese from the south found themselves refugees again in their own country as they fled north to escape the bombardment. Ultimately, the crisis was defused through mediation by France. French technicians repaired the damage, and Hizbullah pledged to refrain from launching rocket attacks on Israeli settlements. But, without an Israeli withdrawal from the security zone, the cycle could be expected to resume its violent course in the near future.[15]

NOTES

1. Abdo Baaklini, *Legislative and Political Development: Lebanon 1842–1972* (Durham, NC: Duke University Press, 1976), pp. 32–34.

2. David C. Gordon, *The Republic of Lebanon: Nation in Jeopardy* (Boulder, CO: Westview Press, 1983), p. 4.

3. Samir Khlaf, *Lebanon's Predicament* (New York: Columbia University Press, 1987), p. 69.

4. Gordon, *op. cit.*, p. 19.

5. *Ibid.*, p. 25. See also Baaklini, *op. cit.*, pp. 200–202, for a description of the coexistence process as used by Sabri Hamadeh, for many years head of the assembly.

6. Whether the Civil War ever really ended is open to question. A cartoon in a U.S. newspaper in August 1982 shows a hooded skeleton on a television screen captioned "Lebanon" saying, "And now we return to our regularly scheduled civil war." Gordon, *op. cit*, p. 113.

7. Shia religious leader Imam Musa al-Sadr's political organization was named Harakat al-Mahrumin ("Movement of the Disinherited") when it was founded in 1969–1970. See Marius

Deeb, *The Lebanese Civil War* (New York: Praeger, 1980), pp. 69–70.

8. Gordon, *op. cit.*, p. 110.

9. *Ibid.*, p. 125.

10. Charles Issawi, "Economic Development and Political Liberalism in Lebanon," in Leonard Binder, ed., *Politics in Lebanon* (New York: John Wiley, 1966), pp. 80–81.

11. The Taif Accord, signed under Arab League auspices in Taif, Saudi Arabia, changes the power-sharing arrangement in the Lebanese government from a 6:5 Christian–Muslim ratio to one of equal representation in the government. The powers of the president are also reduced.

12. *Middle East Economic Digest* (October 10, 1990).

13. Scott Peterson, in *The Christian Science Monitor* (October 1, 1997), p. 18.

14. Quoted in *The Christian Science Monitor* (March 3, 1987).

15. In the aftermath of Operation Grapes of Wrath, Hizbullah leader Shaykh Nabil Kaouh told a visitor: "Those who were killed must be avenged. We believe the Israeli politicians will not feel the pain until their people have wept as our people have wept." Edward Cody, in *The Washington Post Weekly* (June 24–30, 1996), p. 19.

DEVELOPMENT

Considerable progress has been made since 1994 in rebuilding Lebanon's infrastructure. In 1995, GDP was $11.4 billion, almost double the 1994 level. However, the 1997 budget anticipates revenues of only $6.19 billion, with a deficit of $1.5 billion.

FREEDOM

Since independence, Lebanon has functioned as a "confessional democracy"—a democracy in which representation in the Legislature and the government are based on religious affiliation. The Taif Accord set up a 50/50 division between Christian and Muslim/Druze representatives, reflecting changes in the country's demographic composition.

HEALTH/WELFARE

An important source of Lebanese labor is Syrian workers. Some 1.3 million Syrians are currently employed in Lebanon, most in low-level construction and road jobs. Their presence is shifting Lebanon's confessional balance in favor of Muslims over Christians.

ACHIEVEMENTS

During Beirut's reconstruction, workers uncovered an 8,000-year-old mosaic floor in the heart of the city, indicating that this urban center was much older and more important in Phoenician times than had been generally believed. The floor has been preserved by archaeologists as a monument to Lebanon's rich past.

Libya (Socialist People's Libyan Arab Jamahiriya)

GEOGRAPHY
Area in Square Kilometers (Miles):
1,758,610 (679,536) (larger than Alaska)
Capital (Population): Tripoli (990,700)
Climate: arid

PEOPLE

Population
Total: 5,445,500
Annual Growth Rate: 3.7%
Rural/Urban Population Ratio: 15/85
Ethnic Makeup: 97% Berber and Arab;
3% Southern European and Southern
Asian
Major Languages: Arabic; English and
Italian widely understood

Health
Life Expectancy at Birth: 62 years
(male); 67 years (female)
Infant Mortality Rate (Ratio): 61/1,000
Average Caloric Intake: 147% of FAO
minimum
Physicians Available (Ratio): 1/948

Religions
97% Sunni Muslim; 3% others

Education
Adult Literacy Rate: 60% (males 77%,
females 42%)

COMMUNICATION
Telephones: 370,000
Newspapers: 1 daily in Tripoli

Toward Self-Sufficiency in Agriculture

The Great Man-Made River (GMR) is the showplace of Libyan leader
Muammar al-Qadhafi's goal of achieving self-sufficiency in food. The GMR
is a network of pipelines, wells, and reservoirs intended to bring water
from underground Sahara Desert aquifers to the Mediterranean coast,
bringing potable water for Libyan cities and irrigation to expand crop
production. By 1997, despite a series of technical difficulties and such
problems as excess salinity and collapsed wells, the first phase of construction had been completed, with a dependable supply of potable water
available in Tripoli and Benghazi. The water for those cities flows through
the world's largest pipeline, $15\frac{1}{2}$ *feet* in diameter.

TRANSPORTATION
Highways—Kilometers (Miles): 19,300
(12,043)
Railroads—Kilometers (Miles): none
Usable Airfields: 146

GOVERNMENT
Type: officially an "Arab" republic
(*Jamahiriya*), with authority vested in a
General People's Congress, with
members elected by popular vote
Independence Date: December 24,
1951 (kingdom); September 1, 1969
(republic)
Head of State: Revolutionary Leader
Colonel Muammar al-Qadhafi, (serves
also as secretary general of the GPC)
Political Parties: none
Suffrage: universal and compulsory
at 18

MILITARY
Number of Armed Forces: 85,000
*Military Expenditures (% of Central
Government Expenditures):* 6.1%
Current Hostilities: none

ECONOMY
Currency ($ U.S. Equivalent): 0.36
Libyan dinar = $1
Per Capita Income/GDP: $6,510/$32.9
billion
Inflation Rate: 5.8%
Total Foreign Debt: $3.5 billion
Natural Resources: petroleum;
natural gas
Agriculture: wheat; barley; olives;
dates; citrus fruits; peanuts; livestock
Industry: food processing;
petrochemicals; textiles; fishing

FOREIGN TRADE
Exports: $11.4 billion
Imports: $6.8 billion

*Note: Other commonly used spellings of
Colonel Qadhafi's name include Qaddafi,
Gaddafi, and Khadafy.

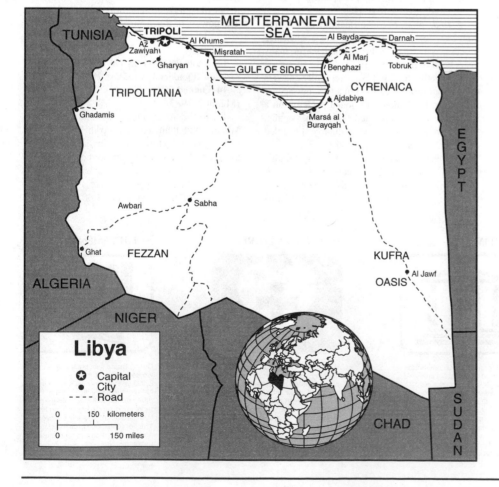

LIBYA

The Socialist People's Libyan Arab Jama-hiriya (Republic), commonly known as Libya, is the fourth largest of the Arab countries. Since it became a republic in 1969, it has played a role in regional and international affairs more appropriate to the size of its huge territory than to its small population.

Libya consists of three geographical regions: Tripolitania, Cyrenaica, and the Fezzan. Most of the population live in Tripolitania, the northwestern part of the country, where Tripoli, the capital and major port, is located. Cyrenaica, in the east along the Egyptian border, has a narrow coastline backed by a high plateau (2,400-feet elevation) called the Jabal al-Akhdar ("Green Mountain"). It contains Libya's other principal city, Benghazi. The two regions are separated by the Sirte, an extension of the Sahara Desert that reaches almost to the Mediterranean Sea. Most of Libya's oil fields are in the Sirte.

The Fezzan occupies the central part of the country. It is entirely desert, except for a string of widely scattered oases. Its borders are with Chad, Algeria, Niger, and Sudan. The border with Chad, established during French colonial rule in sub-Saharan Africa, was once disputed by Libya. The matter was settled through international mediation, with the border formally demarcated in 1994.

HISTORY

Until modern times, Libya did not have a separate identity, either national or territorial. It formed a part of some other territorial unit and in most cases was controlled by outsiders. However, control was usually limited to the coastal areas. The Berbers of the interior were little affected by the passing of conquerors and the rise and fall of civilizations.

Libya's culture and social structure have been influenced more by the Islamic Arabs than by any other invaders. The Arabs brought Islam to Libya in the early seventh century. Arab groups settled in the region and intermarried with the Berber population to such an extent that the Libyans became one of the most thoroughly Arabized peoples in the Islamic world.

Coastal Libya, around Tripoli, was an outlying province of the Ottoman Empire for several centuries. Like its neighbors Tunis and Algiers, Tripoli had a fleet of corsairs who made life dangerous for European merchant ships in the Mediterranean. When the United States became a Mediterranean trading nation, the corsairs of Tripoli included American ships among their targets. The USS *Philadelphia* was sent to Tripoli to "teach the corsairs a lesson" in 1804, but it got stuck on a sandbar and was captured. Navy Lieutenant Stephen Decatur led a commando raid into Tripoli harbor and blew up the ship, inspiring the words to what would become the official U.S. Marine hymn: "From the halls of Montezuma to the shores of Tripoli. . . ."

The Sanusiya Movement

At various stages in Islam's long history, new groups or movements have appeared committed to purifying or reforming Islamic society and taking it back to its original form of a simple community of believers led by just rulers. Several of these movements, such as the Wahhabis of Saudi Arabia, were important in the founding of modern Islamic states. The

(UN photo/pcd)

The Fezzan occupies the central part of Libya and is entirely desert, except for widely scattered oases. This oasis is called Bu Gheilan.

(UN photo/Rice)

After the 1969 Revolution, the government strove to develop many aspects of the country. These local chiefs are meeting to plan community development.

movement called the Sanusiya was formed in the nineteenth century. In later years, it became an important factor in the formation of modern Libya.

The founder, the Grand Sanusi, was a religious teacher from Algeria. He left Algeria after the French conquest and settled in northern Cyrenaica. The Grand Sanusi's teachings attracted many followers. He also attracted the attention of the Ottoman authorities, who distrusted his advocacy of a strong united Islamic world in which Ottomans and Arabs would be partners. In 1895, to escape from the Ottomans, the Grand Sanusi's son and successor moved Sanusiya headquarters to Kufra, a remote oasis in the Sahara.

The Sanusiya began as a peaceful movement interested only in bringing new converts to Islam and founding a network of *zawiyas* ("lodges") for contemplation and monastic life throughout the desert. But when European countries began to seize territories in North and West Africa, the Sanusi became warrior-monks and fought the invaders.

Italy Conquers Libya

The Italian conquest of Libya began in 1911. The Italians needed colonies, not only for prestige but also for the resettlement of poor and landless peasants from Italy's crowded southern provinces. The Italians expected an easy victory against

a weak Ottoman garrison; Libya would become the "Fourth Shore" of a new Roman Empire from shore to shore along the Mediterranean. But the Italians found Libya a tougher land to subdue than they had expected. Italian forces were pinned to Tripoli and a few other points on the coast by the Ottoman garrison and the fierce Sanusi warrior-monks.

The Italians were given a second chance after World War I. The Ottoman Empire had been defeated, and Libya was ripe for the plucking. The new Italian government of swaggering dictator Benito Mussolini sent an army to occupy Tripolitania. When the Italians moved on Cyrenaica, the Grand Sanusi crossed the Egyptian border into exile under British protection. The Italians found Cyrenaica much more difficult to control than Tripolitania. It is ideal guerrilla country, from the caves of Jabal al-Akhdar to the stony plains and dry, hidden *wadis* (river beds) of the south. It took 9 years (1923–1932) for Italy to overcome all of Libya, despite its vast superiority in troops and weapons. Sanusi guerrilla bands harried the Italians, cutting supply lines, ambushing patrols, and attacking convoys. Their leader, Shaykh Omar Mukhtar, became Libya's first national hero.

The Italians finally overcame the Sanusi by the use of methods that do not surprise us today but seemed unbelievably brutal

at the time. Cyrenaica was made into a huge concentration camp, with a barbed-wire fence along the Egyptian border. Nomadic peoples were herded into these camps, guarded by soldiers to prevent them from aiding the Sanusi. Sanusi prisoners were pushed out of airplanes, wells were plugged to deny water to the people, and flocks were slaughtered. In 1931, Omar Mukhtar was captured, court-martialed, and hanged in public. The resistance ended with his death.

The Italians did not have long to cultivate their Fourth Shore. During the 1930s, they poured millions of lire into the colony. A paved highway from the Egyptian to the Tunisian border along the coast was completed in 1937; in World War II, it became a handy invasion route for the British. A system of state-subsidized farms was set up for immigrant Italian peasants. Each was given free transportation, a house, seed, fertilizers, a mule, and a pair of shoes as inducements to come to Libya. By 1940, the Italian population had reached 110,000, and about 495,000 acres of land had been converted into productive farms, orchards, vineyards, and olive groves.[1]

Independent Libya

Libya was a major battleground during World War II, as British, German, and Italian armies rolled back and forth across the desert. The British finally defeated the Germans and occupied northern Libya, while a French army occupied the Fezzan. The United States later built an important air base, Wheelus Field, near Tripoli. Thus the three major Allied powers all had an interest in Libya's future. But they could not agree on what to do with occupied Libya.

Italy wanted Libya back. France wished to keep the Fezzan as a buffer for its African colonies, while Britain preferred self-government for Cyrenaica under the Grand Sanusi, who had become staunchly pro-British during his exile in Egypt. The Soviet Union favored a Soviet trusteeship over Libya, which would provide the Soviet Union with a convenient outlet in the Mediterranean. The United States waffled but finally settled on independence, which would at least keep the Soviet tentacles from enveloping Libya.

Due to lack of agreement, the Libyan "problem" was referred to the United Nations General Assembly. Popular demonstrations of support for independence in Libya impressed a number of the newer UN members; in 1951, the General Assembly approved a resolution for an independent Libyan state, a kingdom under the Grand Sanusi, Idris.

THE KINGDOM OF LIBYA

Libya has been governed under two political systems since independence: a constitutional monarchy (1951–1969); and a Socialist republic (1969–), which has no constitution because all power "belongs" to the people. Monarchy and republic have had almost equal time in power. But Libya's spectacular economic growth and aggressive foreign policy under the republic need to be understood in relation to the solid, if unspectacular, accomplishments of the regime that preceded it.

At independence, Libya was an artificial union of the three provinces. The Libyan people had little sense of national identity or unity. Loyalty was to one's family, clan, village, and, in a general sense, to the higher authority represented by a tribal confederation. The only other loyalty linking Libyans was the Islamic religion. The tides of war and conquest that had washed over them for centuries had had little effect on their strong, traditional attachment to Islam.[2]

Political differences also divided the three provinces. Tripolitanians talked openly of abolishing the monarchy. Cyrenaica was the home and power base of King Idris; the king's principal supporters were the Sanusiya and certain important traditional families. The distances and poor communication links between the

(Gamma-Liaison/Christian Vioujard)

Muammar al-Qadhafi led a group of army officers in the military coup of 1969 that deposed King Idris. In later years, Qadhafi gained worldwide notoriety for his apparent sanction of terrorism.

provinces contributed to the impression that they should be separate countries. Leaders could not even agree on a choice between Tripoli and Benghazi for the capital. For his part, the king distrusted both cities as being corrupt and overly influenced by foreigners. He had his administrative capital at Baida, in the Jabal al-Akhdar.

The greatest problem facing Libya at independence was economic. Per capita income in 1951 was about $30 per year; in 1960, it was about $100 per year. Approximately 5 percent of the land was marginally usable for agriculture, and only 1 percent could be cultivated on a permanent basis. Most economists considered Libya to be a hopeless case, almost totally dependent on foreign aid for survival. (It is interesting to note that the Italians were seemingly able to force more out of the soil, but one must remember that the Italian government poured a great deal of money into the country to develop the plantations, and credit must be given to the extremely hard-working Italian farmer.)

Despite its meager resources and lack of political experience, Libya was valuable to the United States and Britain in the 1950s and 1960s, because of its strategic location. The United States negotiated a long-term lease on Wheelus Field in 1954, as a vital link in the chain of U.S.

bases built around the southern perimeter of the Soviet Union due to the cold war. In return, U.S. aid of $42 million sweetened the pot, and Wheelus became the single largest employer of Libyan labor. The British had two air bases and maintained a garrison in Tobruk.

Political development in the kingdom was minimal. King Idris knew little about parliamentary democracy, and he distrusted political parties. The 1951 Constitution provided for an elected Legislature, but a dispute between the king and the Tripolitanian National Congress, one of several Tripolitanian parties, led to the outlawing of all political parties. Elections were held every 4 years, but only property-owning adult males could vote (women were granted the vote in 1963). The same legislators were re-elected regularly. In the absence of political activity, the king was the glue that held Libya together.

THE 1969 REVOLUTION

At dawn on September 1, 1969, a group of young army officers abruptly carried out a military coup in Libya. King Idris, who had gone to Turkey for medical treatment, was deposed, and a "Libyan Arab Republic" was proclaimed by the unknown officers. These officers, whose names were not known to the outside world until weeks after the coup, were led by Captain Muammar Muhammad al-Qadhafi. He went on Benghazi radio to announce to a startled Libyan population: "People of Libya . . . your armed forces have undertaken the overthrow of the reactionary and corrupt regime. . . . From now on Libya is a free, sovereign republic, ascending with God's help to exalted heights."[3]

Qadhafi's new regime made a sharp change in policy from that of its predecessor. Wheelus Field and the British bases were evacuated and returned to Libyan control. Libya took an active part in Arab affairs and supported Arab unity, to the extent of working to undermine other Arab leaders whom Qadhafi considered undemocratic or unfriendly to his regime.[4]

REGIONAL POLICY

However, Qadhafi's efforts to unite Libya with other Arab states have not been successful. A 1984 agreement for a federal union with Morocco, which provided for separate sovereignty but a federated Assembly and unified foreign policies, was abrogated unilaterally by Morocco's King Hassan II after Qadhafi accused the king of "Arab treason" for meeting with Israeli leader Shimon Peres. Undeterred, Qadhafi tried again in 1987 with neighboring Algeria, receiving a medal from Algerian president Chadli Bendjedid but no other encouragement.

Although distrustful of the mercurial Libyan leader, other North African heads of state have continued to work with him on the basis that it is safer to have Qadhafi inside the circle than isolated outside. Tunisia restored diplomatic relations in 1987, and Qadhafi agreed to compensate the Tunisian government for lost wages of Tunisian workers expelled from Libya during the 1985 economic recession. Qadhafi also accepted International Court of Justice arbitration over Libya's dispute with Tunisia over oil rights in the Gulf of Gabes. In 1989, Libya joined with other North African states in the Arab Maghrib Union, which was formed to coordinate their respective economies. However, continued conflict between Algeria and Morocco over ownership of the Western Sahara continues to block economic integration.

Libya's relations with its neighbors have improved markedly in the 1990s. Qadhafi continues to press periodically for a union of Libya with other Arab states. In 1996, he proposed union with Egypt and Sudan in an "Arab republic of northern Africa" but was rebuffed by Egyptian president Hosni Mubarak. In any case, the advent to power in Sudan of a regime dominated by Islamic fundamentalists makes such a union unlikely, given Qadhafi's repression of fundamentalists in his own country.

SOCIAL REVOLUTION

Qadhafi's desert upbringing and Islamic education gave him a strong, puritanical moral code. In addition to closing foreign bases and expropriating properties of Italians and Jews, he moved forcefully against symbols of foreign influence. The Italian cathedral in Tripoli became a mosque, street signs were converted to Arabic, nightclubs were closed, and the production and sale of alcohol were prohibited.

But Qadhafi's revolution went far beyond changing names. In a three-volume work entitled *The Green Book,* he described his vision of the appropriate political system for Libya. Political parties would not be allowed, nor would constitutions, legislatures, even an organized court system. All of these institutions, according to Qadhafi, eventually become corrupt and unrepresentative. Instead, "people's committees" would run the government, business, industry, and even the universities. Libyan embassies abroad were renamed "people's bureaus" and were run by junior officers. (The takeover

of the London bureau in 1984 led to counterdemonstrations by Libyan students and the killing of a British police officer by gunfire from inside the bureau. The Libyan bureau in Washington, D.C., was closed by the U.S. Federal Bureau of Investigation and the staff deported on charges of espionage and terrorism against Libyans in the United States.) The country was renamed the Socialist People's Libyan Arab Jamahiriya, and titles of government officials were eliminated. Qadhafi became "Leader of the Revolution," and each government department was headed by the secretary of a particular people's committee.

Qadhafi then developed a so-called Third International Theory, based on the belief that neither capitalism nor communism could solve the world's problems. What was needed, he said, was a middle way that would harness the driving forces of human history—religion and nationalism—to interact with each other to revitalize humankind. Islam would be the source of that middle way, because "it provides for the realization of justice and equity, it does not allow the rich to exploit the poor."[5]

THE ECONOMY

Modern Libya's economy is based almost entirely on oil exports. Concessions were granted to various foreign companies to explore for oil in 1955, and the first oil strikes were made in 1957. Within a decade, Libya had become the world's fourth-largest exporter of crude oil. During the 1960s, pipelines were built from the oil fields to new export terminals on the Mediterranean coast. The lightness and low sulfur content of Libyan crude oil make it highly desirable to industrialized countries, and, with the exception of the United States, differences in political viewpoint have had little effect on Libyan oil sales abroad.

After the 1969 Revolution, Libya became a leader in the drive by oil-producing countries to gain control over their petroleum industries. The process began in 1971, when the new Libyan government took over the interests of British Petroleum in Libya. The Libyan method of nationalization was to proceed against individual companies rather than to take on the "oil giants" all at once. It took more than a decade before the last company, Exxon, capitulated. However, the companies' $2 billion in assets were left in limbo in 1986, when the administration of U.S. president Ronald Reagan imposed a ban on all trade with Libya to protest Libya's involvement in international terrorism. President George Bush extended the ban

for an additional year in 1990, although he expressed satisfaction with reduced Libyan support for terroristic activities, one example being the expulsion from Tripoli of the Palestine Liberation Front, a radical opponent of Yassir Arafat's Palestine Liberation Organization.

New discoveries in recent years have increased Libya's oil reserves 30 percent, to 29.5 billion barrels, and recoverable gas reserves to 1.6 billion cubic meters. With oil production reaching a record of 1.4 million barrels per day, Libya has been able to build a strong petrochemical industry. The Marsa Brega petrochemical complex is one of the world's largest producers of urea, although a major contract with India was canceled in 1996 due to UN sanctions on trade with Libya.

Until recently, industrial-development successes based on oil revenues enabled Libyans to enjoy an ever-improving standard of living, and funding priorities were shifted from industry to agricultural development in the budget. But a combination of factors—mismanagement, lack of a cadre of skilled Libyan workers, absenteeism, low motivation of the workforce, and a significant drop in revenues (from $22 billion in 1980 to $7 billion in 1988)—cast doubts on the effectiveness of Qadhafi's *Green Book* socialistic economic policies.

In 1988, the leader began closing the book. As production incentives, controls on both imports and exports were eliminated and profit sharing for employees of small businesses was encouraged. In 1990, the General People's Congress (GPC), prodded strongly by Qadhafi, approved a major shake-up in the government. Eleven new secretaries (equivalent to cabinet ministers) were appointed to spur economic development, and new secretariats (ministries) were formed to promote cooperation with Libya's neighbors. The oil industry, criticized for its inefficiency, was placed under a new Secretariat for Petroleum Affairs, superseding the National Oil Company, which had previously managed production.

Libya also started developing its considerable uranium resources. A 1985 agreement with the Soviet Union provided the components for an 880-megawatt nuclear power station in the Sirte region. Libya has enough uranium to meet its foreseeable domestic peacetime needs. Intelligence reports suggested later that a pharmaceutical complex at Rabta built by German technicians was actually producing mustard gas and other outlawed chemical weapons. The plant was destroyed subsequently in a mysterious fire. However, similar charges have been made about an underground tunnel being built through Tarhuna Mountain, south of Tripoli, which Libya claims to be part of the Great Man-Made River (GMR). Thus far, however, Libya has refused to sign the 1993 UN Convention outlawing chemical weapons or to open Tarhuna to international inspection.

In the long run, the key to self-sufficiency and a higher standard of living for Libyans lies in increased food production. In 1990, the self-declared "Year of Agriculture," the country became self-sufficient in poultry, vegetables, and cereals.

Development in Qadhafi's Libya is tied to the successful completion of the Great Man-Made River, which will bring water from aquifers deep in the Sahara to the Mediterranean coastal belt, where Libya's arable land is located. Construction has proceeded in three phases. Phase One, now completed, furnishes potable water to Benghazi and supplies irrigation water to Cyrenaican farms. Phase Two began providing potable water to Tripoli in January 1996. When Phase Three is complete, the GMR will be the world's largest water-supply project.

AN UNCERTAIN FUTURE
The revolutionary regime's major success has been some redistribution of wealth to bring the benefits of oil revenues to all Libyans. Annual per capita income rose to $2,168 in 1970 and reached a peak of $10,900 in 1980. In 1995, per capita income was down to about $6,800. This undreamed-of wealth has brought great benefits to Libyans in less than 3 decades. Seminomadic tribes such as the Qadadfas of the Sirte (Qadhafi's kin) have been provided with permanent homes, for example. Extensive social-welfare programs such as free medical care, free education, and low-cost housing have greatly enhanced the lives of many Libyans. However, this wealth has yet to be spread evenly across society. The economic downturn of the 1990s has produced a thriving black market, along with price gouging and corruption in the public sector. In 1996, Libya organized "purification committees," mostly staffed by young army officers, to monitor and report instances of black market and other illegal activities.

Until recently, opposition to Qadhafi was confined almost entirely to exiles abroad, centered on former associates living in Cairo, Egypt, who had broken with the Libyan leader for reasons either personal or related to economic mismanagement. But economic downturns and dissatisfaction with the leader's wildly unsuccessful foreign policy ventures increased popular discontent at home. In

1983, Qadhafi introduced two domestic policies that also generated widespread resentment: He called for the drafting of women into the armed services, and he recommended that all children be educated at home until age 10. The 200 basic people's congresses, set up in 1977 to recommend policy to the national General People's Congress (which in theory is responsible for national policy), objected strongly to both proposals. Qadhafi then created 2,000 more people's congresses, presumably to dilute the opposition, but withdrew the proposals. In effect, suggested one observer, *The Green Book* theory had begun to work, and Qadhafi didn't like it.

Qadhafi's principal support base rests on the armed forces and the Revolutionary Committees, formed of youths whose responsibility is to guard against infractions of *The Green Book* rules. "Brother Colonel" also relies upon a small group of collaborators from the early days of the Revolution, and his own relatives and members of the Qadadfa form part of the inner power structure. This structure is highly informal, and it may explain why Qadhafi is able to disappear from public view from time to time, as he did after the United States conducted an air raid on Tripoli in 1986, and emerge having lost none of his popularity and charismatic appeal.

In recent years, disaffection within the army has led to a number of attempts to overthrow Qadhafi. The most serious coup attempt took place in 1984, when army units allied with the opposition Islamic Front for the Salvation of Libya, based in Cairo and headed by several of Qadhafi's former associates, attacked the central barracks in Tripoli where he usually resides. The attackers were defeated in a bloody gun battle. Other attempts were reported in 1993 and 1994. The most bizarre plot was reported in 1996. A new opposition group, Vanguards of the Liberation of Libya, based in Geneva, Switzerland, said that it was planning to poison the camel's milk that Qadhafi drinks while eating dates on his desert journeys! However, the failure of opposition groups either to unite or to develop a support base inside Libya suggests that Qadhafi will not only continue to enjoy his camels' milk in safety but supplement it with sweet water from the GMR.

INTERNAL CHANGES
Qadhafi has a talent for the unexpected that has made him an effective survivor. In 1988, he ordered the release of all political prisoners and personally drove a bulldozer through the main gate of Tripoli prison to inaugurate "Freedom Day." Exiled opponents of the regime were invited

to return under a promise of amnesty, and a number did so.

In June of that year, the GPC approved a "Charter of Human Rights" as an addendum to *The Green Book*. The charter outlaws the death penalty, bans mistreatment of prisoners, and guarantees every accused person the right to a fair trial. It also permits formation of labor unions, confirms the right to education and suitable employment for all Libyan citizens, and places Libya on record as prohibiting production of nuclear and chemical weapons. In March 1995, the country's last prison was destroyed and its inmates freed in application of the charter's guarantees of civil liberty.

THE WAR WITH CHAD
Libyan forces occupied the Aouzou Strip in northern Chad in 1973, claiming it as an integral part of the Libyan state. Occupation gave Libya access also to the reportedly rich uranium resources of the region. In subsequent years, Qadhafi played upon political rivalries in Chad to extend the occupation into a de facto one of annexation of most of its poverty-stricken neighbor.

But in late 1986 and early 1987, Chadian leaders patched up their differences and turned on the Libyans. In a series of spectacular raids on entrenched Libyan forces, the highly mobile Chadians, traveling mostly in Toyota trucks, routed the Libyans and drove them out of northern Chad. Chadian forces then moved into the Aouzou Strip and even attacked nearby air bases inside Libya. The defeats, with casualties of some 3,000 Libyans and loss of huge quantities of Soviet-supplied military equipment, exposed the weaknesses of the overequipped, undertrained, and poorly motivated Libyan Army.

In 1989, after admitting his mistake, Qadhafi signed a cease-fire with then–Chadian leader Hissène Habré and agreed to submit the dispute over ownership of Aouzou to the International Court of Justice for arbitration. The ICJ awarded the region to Chad in 1994, re-affirming Chadian sovereignty on the basis of a 1955 agreement. Libyan occupation forces withdrew in May 1994, and a subsequent friendship treaty ended one of North Africa's last remaining territorial conflicts.

FOREIGN POLICY
Libya resumed its old role of pariah state in 1992 by refusing to extradite two officers of its intelligence service suspected of complicity in the 1988 bombing of a Pan American jumbo jet over Lockerbie, Scotland. The United States, France, and

| Establishment of the Regency of Tripoli 1711 | Tripoli becomes an Ottoman province with the Sanusiya controlling the interior 1835 | The first Italian invasion 1911 | Libya becomes an Italian colony, Italy's "Fourth Shore" 1932 | An independent kingdom is set up by the UN under King Idris 1951 | The Revolution overthrows Idris; the Libyan Arab Republic is established 1969 | Qadhafi decrees a cultural and social revolution with government by people's committees 1973–1976 | A campaign to eliminate Qadhafi's exiled opponents abroad; the United States imposes economic sanctions in response to suspected Libya-terrorist ties 1980s | U.S. planes attack targets in Tripoli and Benghazi; Libyan troops are driven from Chad, including the Aouzou Strip |

1990s

Libya's relations with its neighbors improve; the UN votes to impose sanctions on Libya for terrorist acts

An army coup is put down

Qadhafi takes steps to forestall Islamic militance

Britain had demanded the officers' extradition and introduced a resolution to that effect in the UN Security Council; in the event of noncompliance on Libya's part, sanctions would be imposed on the country. *Resolution 748* passed by a 10-to-0 vote, with 5 abstentions. A concurrent ruling by the ICJ ordered Libya to turn over the suspects or explain in writing why it was not obligated to do so.

When Libya refused to comply with *Resolution 748*, the Security Council imposed partial sanctions on the country. Qadhafi argued that the suspects could be turned over to a neutral country, where they would presumably receive a fair trial, but he ruled out their extradition to Britain or the United States. Libya's continued defiance of *Resolution 748* led the Security Council in November 1993 to expand sanctions under the new *Resolution 883*. This resolution banned all sales of spare parts and industrial equipment to Libya and freezes Libyan bank deposits abroad. Sales of Libyan crude oil, Libya's main source of revenue, were not affected, since that would also harm its main customers in Western Europe, notably Britain.

In November 1997, the Security Council again extended the sanctions established under *Resolution 883,* but only for 60 days. The action reflected the deep division between the United States and its European allies over the effectiveness of the embargo. European countries, particularly Britain and Germany, not only depend on Libyan oil but have established no legal restrictions on nonmilitary sales to Libya. Furthermore, evidence has been presented to U.S. courts in several trials involving European subsidiaries of American companies that indicates that U.S. goods have been and continue to be sold to Libya by these subsidiaries, as a means of evading the sanctions.

PROSPECTS
The tide of fundamentalism sweeping across the Islamic world and challenging secular regimes has largely spared Libya thus far, although there were occasional clashes between fundamentalists and police in the 1980s, and in 1992, some 500 fundamentalists were jailed briefly. However, the bloody civil uprisings against the regimes in neighboring Algeria and Egypt caused Qadhafi in 1994 to reemphasize Libya's Islamic nature. New laws passed by the General People's Congress would apply Islamic law (Shari'a) and punishments in such areas as marriage and divorce, wills and inheritance, crimes of theft and violence (where the Islamic punishment is cutting off a hand), and for apostasy. But despite these measures intended to forestall Islamic militance by stressing the country's attachment to the fundamental laws of the religion, it appears that Qadhafi's rejection of Islam as a legitimate instrument of government and his unorthodox interpretations of Islamic issues such as women's rights and control of criminals by the society itself rather than penal institutions has begun to alienate more conservative Muslims.

Aside from relative political stability, Libya's oil wealth and lack of debt problems enable the country to undertake major infrastructure projects despite decreasing revenues and international political isolation. Such projects as expansion of the Misurata iron and steel complex, the GMR, and enlargement of the power grid by 1,000 megawatts promised continuing benefits to Libyans from the "Qadhafi revolution."

NOTES
1. "[I]rrigation, colonization and hard work have wrought marvels. Everywhere you see plantations forced out of the sandy, wretched soil." A. H. Broderick, *North Africa* (London: Oxford University Press, 1943), p. 27.

2. Religious leaders issued a *fatwa* ("binding legal decision") stating that a vote against independence would be a vote against religion. Omar el Fathaly et al., *Political Development and Bureaucracy in Libya* (Lexington, KY: Lexington Books, 1977).

3. See the *Middle East Journal,* vol. 24, no. 2 (Spring 1970), Documents Section.

4. John Wright, *Libya: A Modern History* (Baltimore, MD: Johns Hopkins University Press, 1982), pp. 124–126. Qadhafi's idol was former Egyptian president Nasser, a leader in the movement for unity and freedom among the Arabs. While he was at school in Sebha, in the Fezzan, he listened to Radio Cairo's Voice of the Arabs and was later expelled from school as a militant organizer of demonstrations.

5. *The London Times* (June 6, 1973).

DEVELOPMENT

Despite the UN embargo and U.S. "secondary sanctions" on foreign companies doing business in Libya, the country's oil production increased 3.5% in 1996, the first increase since sanctions were imposed. New discoveries have increased both oil and gas reserves. The new Murzuk oilfield went into production in 1997.

FREEDOM

The General People's Congress has the responsibility for passing laws and appointing a government. In 1994, the GPC approved laws making Islamic law applicable in the country. They concerned retribution and blood money; rules governing wills, crimes of theft and violence, protection of society from things banned in the Koran, marriage, and divorce; and a ban on alcohol use.

HEALTH/WELFARE

Qadhafi ordered the expulsion of 1,000 Palestinian workers to protest the Palestinian–Israeli peace agreements. He later reversed himself, inviting people from all Arab countries to work in Libya. However, expatriate Arab workers would not be permitted to send home their earnings—the main reason for expatriate labor—and Palestinians were specifically excluded.

ACHIEVEMENTS

A chain of small fishing harbors built in 1995 has begun to revive the Libyan coastal-fishing industry. In 1996, in another sign of change, the first privately owned bank in this nominally Socialist country began operations, with capital of $24.7 million.

Morocco (Kingdom of Morocco)

GEOGRAPHY
Area in Square Kilometers (Miles):
446,300 (172,272) (larger than
California)
Capital (Population): Rabat (1,200,000)
(metropolitan area)
Climate: Mediterranean and desert

PEOPLE

Population
Total: 29,779,000
Annual Growth Rate: 2%
Rural/Urban Population Ratio: 53/47
Ethnic Makeup: 64% Arab; 35%
Berber; 1% non-Moroccan and Jewish
Major Languages: Arabic; various
Berber dialects

Health
Life Expectancy at Birth: 67 years
(male); 71 years (female)
Infant Mortality Rate (Ratio): 46/1,000
Average Caloric Intake: 115% of FAO
minimum
Physicians Available (Ratio): 1/3,361

Religions
99% Sunni Muslim; 1% Christian and
Jewish

Education
Adult Literacy Rate: 50% (males 61%,
females 32%)

COMMUNICATION
Telephones: 280,000
Newspapers: 12 dailies; 18 weeklies

The Urban Influence in Islam

Cities have always held great importance in Islam. The Prophet Muhammad was an urban merchant, and although the design of the Islamic system owes much to the desert influence, its forms and obligations are urban. The impact of urban Islam is still visible in Moroccan cities such as Rabat, Marrakesh, and especially Fez, the world's largest intact medieval city. Fez is the first Islamic–Arab city designated by UNESCO as a world heritage site, joining Venice and Havana, among others. Restoration under UNESCO auspices is under way to preserve its medieval monuments and unique architectural style.

TRANSPORTATION
Highways—Kilometers (Miles): 59,474
(37,112)
Railroads—Kilometers (Miles): 1,893
(1,181)
Usable Airfields: 74

GOVERNMENT
Type: constitutional monarchy
Independence Date: March 2, 1956
Head of State: King Hassan II
Political Parties: National Rally of
Independents; Popular Movement;
National Democratic Party;
Constitutional Union; Socialist Union
of Popular Forces; Istiqlal; Kutla Bloc;
Party of Progress and Socialism; others
Suffrage: universal at 20

MILITARY
Number of Armed Forces: 195,500
*Military Expenditures (% of Central
Government Expenditures):* 3.8%
Current Hostilities: rule over Western
Sahara is contested by Polisario

ECONOMY
Currency ($ U.S. Equivalent): 8.25
dirhams = $1
Per Capita Income/GDP: $3,060/$87.5
billion
Inflation Rate: 4.5%
Total Foreign Debt: $20.5 billion
Natural Resources: phosphates; iron;
manganese; lead; cobalt; silver; copper;
shale oil; fish
Agriculture: wheat; barley; livestock;
wine; vegetables; olives; fishing
Industry: phosphate mining; mineral
processing; food processing; textiles;
construction

FOREIGN TRADE
Exports: $4.1 billion
Imports: $7.5 billion

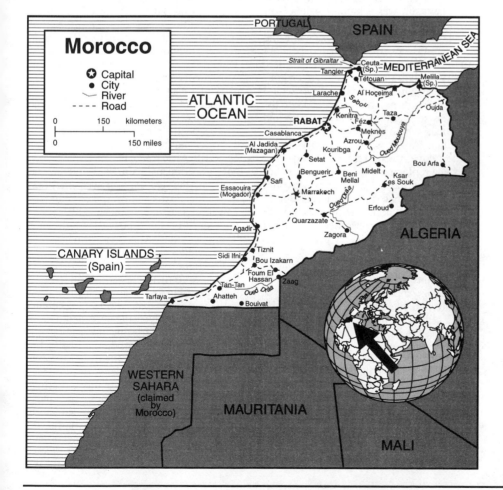

MOROCCO

The Kingdom of Morocco is the western-most country in North Africa. Morocco's population is the second largest (after Egypt) of the Arab states. Moroccan territory includes at present the Western Sahara, a former Spanish colony annexed in 1976 after the withdrawal of the Spanish administration. The annexation was opposed by a Saharan nationalism movement, Polisario. If Morocco acquires permanent control over the Western Sahara, the country's land area will be increased by 102,000 square miles, a territory the size of Colorado.

Two other territories physically within Morocco remain outside Moroccan control. They are the cities of Ceuta and Melilla, both located on rocky peninsulas that jut out into the Mediterranean Sea. They have been held by Spain since the fifteenth century. (Spain also owns several small islands off the coast in Moroccan territorial waters.) The economic advantages to Morocco of the free-port status of Ceuta and Melilla, plus the fact that they employ a large expatriate Moroccan labor force, have thus far outweighed the desire among Moroccan leaders to press hard for their return. Morocco's King Hassan II speaks periodically of the need for their retrocession, and in 1986, a new Spanish law effectively excluding Muslim residents of both cities from many of the benefits of Spanish citizenship, even if they have lived there all their lives, spawned conflict between them and Spanish police and generated a pro-Moroccan nationalist movement. In 1988, the question of ownership became moot, when the Spanish Parliament passed a law formally incorporating Ceuta and Melilla into Spain as Spanish cities with locally elected legislatures. As a sweetener for the action, Spain loaned Morocco $1.1 billion at low interest rates and supported Morocco's successful request to the European Union for preferential treatment for its citrus and fish exports to EU countries.

Morocco is a rugged land, dominated by several massive mountain ranges. The Rif Range, averaging 7,000 feet in elevation, runs parallel to the Mediterranean, isolating the northern region from the rest of the country. The Atlas Mountains dominate the interior of Morocco. The Middle Atlas begins south of the Rif, separated by the Taza Gap (the traditional gateway for invaders from the east), and extends from northeast to southwest to join the High Atlas, a snowcapped range containing North Africa's highest peak. A third range, the Anti-Atlas, walls off the desert from the rest of Morocco. These ranges and the general inaccessibility of the

country have isolated Morocco throughout most of its history, not only from outside invaders but internally as well, because of the geographical separation of peoples.

Moroccan geography explains the country's dual population structure. About 35 percent of the population are Berbers, descendants of the original North Africans. The Berbers were, until recently, grouped into tribes, often taking the name of a common ancestor, such as the Ait ("Sons of") 'Atta of southern Morocco.[1] Invading Arabs converted them to Islam in the eighth century but made few changes in Berber life. Unlike the Berbers, the majority of the Arabs who settled in Morocco were, and are, town dwellers. To a much greater degree than the Arab, the Berber was conditioned by traditional family structure and values; "a web of kinship bound the rural individual to his tribal territory, to his immediate family, and to his more distant kin."[2]

The fact that the Arabs were invaders caused the majority of the Berbers to withdraw into mountain areas. They accepted Islam but held stubbornly to their independence. Much of Morocco's past history consisted of efforts by various rulers, both Berber and Arab, to control Berber territory. The result was a kind of balance-of-power political system. The rulers had their power bases in the cities, while the rural groups operated as independent units. Moroccan rulers made periodic military expeditions into Berber territory to collect tribute and if possible to secure full obedience from the Berbers. When the ruler was strong, the Berbers paid up and submitted; when he was weak, they ignored him. At times Berber leaders might invade "government territory," capturing cities and replacing one ruler with another more to their liking. When they were not fighting with urban rulers, different Berber groups fought among themselves, so the system did little for Moroccan national unity.

HISTORY

Morocco has a rich cultural history, with many of its ancient monuments more or less intact. It has had a ruling monarchy for 12 centuries, in one form or another. The ancestors of the current monarch, King Hassan II, came to power in the seventeenth century. One reason for their long rule is the fact that they were descended from the Prophet Muhammad. Thus, Moroccans have a real sense of Islamic traditions and history through their ruler.

The first identifiable Moroccan "state" was established by a descendant of Muhammad named Idris, in the late eighth century. Idris had taken refuge in the far

west of the Islamic world to escape civil war in the east. Because of his piety, learning, and descent from Muhammad, he was accepted by a number of Berber groups as their spiritual and political leader. His son and successor, Idris II, founded the first Moroccan capital, Fez. Father and son established the principle whereby descent from the Prophet was an important qualification for political power as well as social status in Morocco.

The Idrisids ruled over only a small portion of the current Moroccan territory, and, after the death of Idris II, their "nation" lapsed into decentralized family rule. In any case, the Berbers had no real idea of nationhood; each separate Berber group thought of itself as a nation. But, in the eleventh and twelfth centuries, two Berber confederations developed that brought imperial grandeur to Morocco. These were the Almoravids and the Almohads. Under their rule, North Africa developed a political structure separate from that of the eastern Islamic world, one strongly influenced by Berber values.

The Almoravids began as camel-riding nomads from the Western Sahara who were inspired by a religious teacher to carry out a reform movement to revive the true faith of Islam. (The word *Almoravid* comes from the Arabic *al-Murabitun,* "men of the ribat," rather like the crusading religious orders of Christianity in the Middle Ages.) Fired by religious zeal, the Almoravids conquered all of Morocco and parts of western Algeria.

A second "imperial" dynasty, the Almohads, succeeded the Almoravids but improved on their performance. They were the first, and probably the last, to unite all of North Africa and Islamic Spain under one government. Almohad monuments, such as the Qutubiya tower, the best-known landmark of Marrakesh, and the Tower of Hassan in Rabat, still stand as reminders of their power and the high level of the Almohads' architectural achievements.

The same fragmentation, conflicts, and Berber/Arab rivalries that had undermined their predecessors brought down the Almohads in the late thirteenth century. From then on, dynasty succeeded dynasty in power. An interesting point about this cyclical pattern is that, despite the lack of political unity, a distinctive Moroccan style and culture developed. Each dynasty contributed something to this culture, in architecture, crafts, literature, and music. The interchange between Morocco and Islamic Spain was constant and fruitful. Poets, musicians, artisans, architects, and others traveled regularly between Spanish and Moroccan cities. One can visit the city of Fez today and be instantly transported back into the Hispano-Moorish way of life of the Middle Ages.

Mulay Ismail

In the late 1600s, the Alawis, the dynasty currently ruling Morocco, came to power. The Alawis were originally from Arabia and were descended from the Prophet Muhammad. They used this ancestral prestige to win the support of both Arabs and Berbers. The real founder of the dynasty was Mulay Ismail, one of the longest-reigning and most powerful monarchs in Morocco's history. Mulay Ismail unified the Moroccan nation. The great majority of the Berber groups accepted him as their sovereign. The sultan built watchtowers and posted permanent garrisons in Berber territories to make sure they continued to do so. He brought public security to Morocco also; it was said that, in his time, a Jew or an unveiled woman could travel safely anywhere in the land, which was not the case in most parts of North Africa, the Middle East, and Europe.

Mulay Ismail was a contemporary of Louis XIV, and the reports of his envoys to the French court at Versailles convinced him that he should build a capital like it. He chose Meknes, not far from Fez. The work was half finished when he died of old age. The slaves and prisoners working on this "Moroccan Versailles" threw down their shovels and ran away. The enormous unfinished walls and arched Bab al-Mansur ("Gate of the Victorious") still stand today as reminders of Mulay Ismail's dream.

Mulay Ismail had many wives and left behind 500 sons but no instructions as to which should succeed him. After years of conflict, one of his grandsons took the throne as Muhammad II. He is important for giving European merchants a monopoly on trade from Moroccan ports (in wool, wax, hides, carpets, and leather) and for being the first non-European monarch to recognize the United States as an independent nation, in 1787.[3]

The French Protectorate

In the 1800s and early 1900s, Morocco became increasingly vulnerable to outside pressures. The French, who were established in neighboring Algeria and Tunisia, wanted to complete their conquests. The nineteenth-century sultans were less and less able to control the mountain Berbers and were forced to make constant expeditions into the "land of dissidence," at great expense to the treasury. They began borrowing money from European bankers, not only to pay their bills but also to finance arms purchases and the development of ports, railroads, and industries to

(Hamilton Wright/Government of Morocco)

Morocco has a rich history. The Karawiyyin Mosque at Fez was founded in the ninth century A.D. and is the largest mosque in North Africa. It is also the seat of one of Africa's oldest universities.

create a modern economy and prove to the European powers that Morocco could manage its own affairs. Nothing worked; by 1900, Morocco was so far in debt that the French took over the management of its finances. (One sultan, Abd al-Aziz, had bought one of everything he was told about by European salesmen, including a gold-plated toy train that carried food from the kitchen to the dining room of his palace.) Meanwhile, the European powers plotted the country's downfall.

In 1904, France, Britain, Spain, and Germany signed secret agreements partitioning the country. The French would be given the largest part of the country, while Spain would receive the northern third as a protectorate plus some territory in the Western Sahara. In return, the French and Spanish agreed to respect Britain's claim to Egypt and Germany's claim to East African territory.

The ax fell on Morocco in 1912. French workers building the new port of Casablanca were killed by Berbers. Mobs attacked foreigners in Fez, and the sultan's troops could not control them. French troops marched to Fez from Algeria to restore order. The sultan, Mulay Hafidh (Hafiz), was forced to sign the Treaty of Fez, establishing a French protectorate over southern Morocco. The sultan believed that he had betrayed his country

and died shortly thereafter, supposedly of a broken heart. Spain then occupied the northern third of the country, and Tangier, the traditional residence of foreign consuls, became an international city ruled by several European powers.

The French protectorate over Morocco covered barely 45 years (1912–1956). But, in that brief period, the French introduced significant changes into Moroccan life. For the first time, southern Morocco was brought entirely under central government control, although the "pacification" of the Berbers was not complete until 1934. French troops also intervened in the Spanish Zone to help put down a rebellion in the Rif led by Abd al-Krim, a *Qadi* ("religious judge") and leader of the powerful Ait Waryaghar tribe.[4]

The organization of the protectorate was largely the work of the first French resident-general, Marshal Louis Lyautey. Lyautey had great respect for Morocco's past and its dignified people. His goal was to develop the country and modernize the sultan's government while preserving Moroccan traditions and culture. He preferred the Berbers to the Arabs and set up a separate administration under Berber-speaking French officers for Berber areas.[5]

Lyautey's successors were less respectful of Moroccan traditions. The sultan, supposedly an independent ruler, became a figurehead. French *colons* (settlers) flocked to Morocco to buy land at rock-bottom prices and develop vineyards, citrus groves, and orchards. Modern cities sprang up around the perimeters of Rabat, Fez, Marrakesh, and other cities. In rural areas, particularly in the Atlas Mountains, the French worked with powerful local chiefs *(qaids)*. Certain qaids used the arrangement to become enormously wealthy. One qaid, al-Glawi, as he was called, strutted about like a rooster in his territory and often said that he was the real sultan of Morocco.[6]

Morocco's Independence Struggle
The movement for independence in Morocco developed slowly. The only symbol of national unity was the sultan, Muhammad ibn Yusuf. But he seemed ineffectual to most young Moroccans, particularly those educated in French schools, who began to question the right of France to rule a people against their will.

The hopes of these young Moroccans got a boost during World War II. The Western Allies, Great Britain and the United States, had gone on record in favor of the right of subject peoples to self-determination after the war. When U.S. president Franklin D. Roosevelt and British prime minister Winston Churchill came to Casablanca for an important wartime conference, the sultan was convinced to meet them privately and get a commitment for Morocco's independence. The leaders promised their support.

However, Roosevelt died before the end of the war, and Churchill was defeated for reelection. The French were not under any pressure after the war to end the protectorate. When a group of Moroccan nationalists formed the Istiqlal ("Independence") Party and demanded the end of French rule, most of them were arrested. A few leaders escaped to the Spanish Zone or to Tangier, where they could operate freely. For several years, Istiqlal headquarters was the home of the principal of the American School at Tangier, an ardent supporter of Moroccan nationalism.

With the Istiqlal dispersed, the sultan represented the last hope for national unity and resistance. Until then, he had gone along with the French; but, in the early 1950s, he began to oppose them openly. The French began to look for a way to remove him from office and install a more cooperative ruler.

In 1953, the Glawi and his fellow qaids decided, along with the French, that the time was right to depose the sultan. The qaids demanded that he abdicate; they said that his presence was contributing to Moroccan instability. When he refused, he was bundled into a French plane and sent

into exile. An elderly uncle was named to replace him.

The sultan's departure had the opposite effect from what was intended. In exile, he became a symbol for Moroccan resistance to the protectorate. Violence broke out, French settlers were murdered, and a Moroccan Army of Liberation began battling French troops in rural regions. Although the French could probably have contained the rebellion in Morocco, they were under great pressure in neighboring Algeria and Tunisia, where resistance movements were also under way. In 1955, the French abruptly capitulated. Sultan Muhammad ibn Yusuf returned to his palace in Rabat in triumph, and the elderly uncle retired to potter about in his garden in Tangier.

INDEPENDENCE
Morocco became independent on March 2, 1956. (The Spanish protectorate ended in April, and Tangier came under Moroccan control in October, although it kept its free-port status and special banking and currency privileges for several more years.) It began its existence as a sovereign state with a number of assets—a popular ruler, an established government, and a well-developed system of roads, schools, hospitals, and industries inherited from the protectorate. Against these assets were the liabilities of age-old Arab–Berber and inter-Berber conflicts, little experience with political parties or democratic institutions, and an economy dominated by Europeans.

The sultan's goal was to establish a constitutional monarchy. His first action was to give himself a new title, King Muhammad V, symbolizing the end of the old autocratic rule of his predecessors. He also pardoned the Glawi, who crawled into his presence to kiss his feet and crawled out backwards as proof of penitence. (He died soon thereafter.) However, the power of the qaids and pashas ended; "they were compromised by their association with the French, and returned to the land to make way for nationalist cadres, many . . . not from the regions they were assigned to administer."[7]

Muhammad V did not live long enough to reach his goal. He died unexpectedly in 1961 and was succeeded by his eldest son, Crown Prince Hassan. Hassan II has ruled Morocco since then. While he fulfilled his father's promise immediately with a Constitution, in most other ways he has set his own stamp on Morocco.

The Constitution provided for an elected Legislature and a multiparty political system. In addition to the Istiqlal, a number of other parties were organized,

including one representing the monarchy. But the results of the French failure to develop a satisfactory party system soon became apparent. Berber–Arab friction, urban–rural distrust, city rivalries, and inter-Berber hostility all resurfaced. Elections failed to produce a clear majority for any party, not even the king's.

In 1965, riots broke out in Casablanca. The immediate cause was labor unrest, but the real cause lay in the lack of effective leadership by the parties. The king declared a state of emergency, dismissed the Legislature, and assumed full powers under the Constitution.

For the next dozen years, Hassan II ruled as an absolute monarch. He continued to insist that his goal was a parliamentary system, a "government of national union." But he depended on a small group of cronies, members of prominent merchant families, the large Alawi family, or powerful Berber leaders as a more reliable group than the fractious political parties. The dominance of "the king's men" led to growing dissatisfaction and the perception that the king had sold out to special interests. Gradually, unrest spread to the army, previously loyal to its commander-in-chief. In 1971, during a diplomatic reception, cadets from the main military academy invaded the royal palace near Rabat. A number of foreign diplomats were killed and the king held prisoner briefly before loyal troops could crush the rebellion. The next year, a plot by air-force pilots to shoot down the king's plane was narrowly averted. The two escapes helped confirm in Hassan's mind his invincibility under the protection of Allah. But they also prompted him to reinstate the parliamentary system. A new Constitution issued in 1972 defined Morocco "as a democratic and social constitutional monarchy in which Islam is the established religion."[8] However, the king holds broad constitutional powers. Royal power is based on the leadership of the Alawi family, the king's spiritual role as "Commander of the Faithful," and his control of patronage. When Hassan puts on an army uniform, or rides to the mosque on Fridays in the traditional white jellaba under an umbrella symbolizing royalty, or meets with his cabinet dressed in a business suit, he symbolizes these three roles of leadership.

INTERNAL POLITICS
Morocco's de facto annexation of the Western Sahara has important implications for future national development due to the territory's size, underpopulation, and mineral resources, particularly shale oil and phosphates. But the annexation has

(Hamilton Wright/Government of Morocco)

Tangier, Morocco, was once a free city and port. It now is Morocco's northern metropolis just across the Strait of Gibraltar from Spain.

been equally important to national pride and political unity. The "Green March" of 350,000 unarmed Moroccans into Spanish territory in 1975 to dramatize Morocco's claim was organized by the king and supported by all segments of the population and the opposition parties. In 1977, opposition leaders agreed to serve under the king in a "government of national union." The first elections in 12 years were held for a new Legislature; several new parties took part.

The 1984 elections continued the national unity process. The promonarchist Constitutional Union (UC) party won a majority of seats in the Chamber of Representatives (Parliament). A new party, the National Rally of Independents (RNI), formed by members with no party affiliations, emerged as the chief rival to the UC.

New elections were scheduled for 1989 but postponed three times; the king said that the postponements were needed to give time for the economic-stabilization program to show results and generate public confidence. The elections finally took place in two stages in 1993: the first for election of party candidates; and the second, in September, for trade-union and professional-association candidates. The final tally showed 195 seats for center-right (royalist) candidates to 120 for the Democratic-bloc opposition. As a result, coalition government became necessary. The two leading opposition parties, however—the Socialist Union of Popular

Forces (USFP) and the Istiqlal—refused to participate, claiming election irregularities. Opposition from members of these parties plus the Kutla Bloc, a new party formed from the merger of several minor parties, blocked legislative action until 1994. At that point, the entire opposition bloc walked out of the Legislature and announced a boycott of government. In late 1994, the king moved to resolve the stalemate by appointing USFP leader Abdellatif Filali as the new prime minister, and the opposition ended its year-long boycott.

Previously, in 1992, voters had approved a new Constitution in a referendum. Its main provisions are a stated commitment to human rights, transfer of responsibility for cabinet appointments from the king to the prime minister, and the establishment of a Constitutional Council with the power to arbitrate parliamentary disputes. Also, 20 was set as the minimum voting age.

Several important amendments to the Constitution were approved in a referendum in 1996. A bicameral Legislature replaced the unicameral one. Members of the lower chamber are to be elected directly, while the upper chamber is to be two thirds elected and one third appointed. The November 1997 parliamentary elections reflected little change. Royalist parties increased their majority in the lower house, while the opposition USFP and Istiqlal together lost one third of the seats they had held in the previous Parliament.

FOREIGN POLICY
In 1984, King Hassan signed an agreement with Libyan leader Muammar al-Qadhafi for a Moroccan–Libyan federal union. Under the agreement, the countries would keep their separate governing structures but form a federal Parliament with shared responsibilities. But the king had second thoughts almost immediately, and he unilaterally abrogated the agreement. Subsequently, Libya suspended aid to Polisario along with Algeria, signaling their desire to improve relations with Morocco by forming the Arab Maghrib Union, with Tunisia and Mauritania, in 1990.

In September 1994, Morocco opened low-level diplomatic relations with Israel, establishing a liaison office in Tel Aviv. A similar office was set up in Gaza to emphasize Moroccan support for Palestinian sovereignty.

In October 1994, Hassan sponsored a conference of Israeli, Palestinian, Turkish, and Arab industrial leaders to lay plans for a Middle East–North African trading bloc. Such an alliance would establish an economic union "from Morocco to Mesopotamia," comparable in many respects to the European Union and underscoring the "Peace of the Brave" between Israel and the Palestinians.

Concern about Morocco's poor human rights record and its continued delays in implementing the projected UN referendum in the Western Sahara caused the European Union in 1992 to suspend the fourth installment of an agreed-on $580 million in aid to the country. The aid was restored after Hassan released long-term political prisoners and pardoned 150 accused Islamic militants. In 1995, Morocco became the second African country after Tunisia to be granted associate status with the European Union. A new Trade and Fisheries Agreement with the EU was signed in 1996. It phases out Moroccan customs duties on imports of EU–manufactured goods, in return for financial aid to help local Moroccan industries adapt to the increased competition.

THE ECONOMY
Morocco has many of certain resources but too little of other, critical ones. It has two thirds of the world's known reserves of phosphate rock and is the top exporter of phosphates. The major thrust in industrial development is in phosphate-related industries. Collapse of the global phosphates market in the mid-1980s was an important factor in Morocco's debt crisis. However, phosphate exports rose sharply in the late 1980s, as world prices stabilized.

The country also has important undeveloped iron-ore deposits and a small but

The foundations of Moroccan nation are established by Idris I and II, with the capital at Fez **788–790**	The Almoravid and Almohad dynasties, Morocco's "imperial period" **1062–1147**	The current ruling dynasty, the Alawi, establishes its authority under Mulay Ismail **1672**	Morocco is occupied and placed under French and Spanish protectorates **1912**	Independence under King Muhammad V **1956**	The accession of King Hassan II **1961**	Unsuccessful attempts by army officers to overthrow Hassan **1971, 1972**	The Green March into the Western Sahara dramatizes Morocco's claim to the area **1975**

Bread riots; agreement with Libya for a federal union; the king unilaterally abrogates the 1984 treaty of union with Libya **1980s**

1990s

Completion of the sixth section of the Sand Wall around Western Sahara; an exchange of prisoners with Algeria; Morocco joins the Arab Maghrib Union	Morocco accepts a UN plan for a cease-fire in the Western Sahara and amnesties Sahrawi exiles and Polisario members	Elections establish parliamentary government

significant production of rare metals such as mercury, antimony, nickel, and lead. A major obstacle to large-scale economic development is the lack of oil. Morocco has some 80 billion tons of shale-oil deposits near Tarfaya in the far south; until recently, however, extraction using existing technology has not been commercially feasible. An agreement with an Israeli oil-technology firm in 1995 to extract 400 tons from the Tarfaya deposit by use of experimental new techniques may change the country's economic situation.

The austerity program and economic reforms required by the World Bank in the 1980s as a prerequisite for further loans have been instrumental to Morocco's economic progress. Unfortunately, several years of drought earlier in the 1990s had a bad effect on agriculture—one of the main elements in the economy, with 20 percent of gross domestic product. The rains finally came in 1996, and, as a result, the wheat harvest was a record 9 million tons.

PROSPECTS
In March 1997, King Hassan II completed 36 years on the throne, the second-largest reign among Arab rulers, and one of the longest in the world. Other than a brief period of hospitalization for pneumonia, he is in good health. But strains within the political system (due in part to the broadening of party activity) and society itself continue to affect development. Some 70 percent of Moroccans are under age 25,

and the downsizing of government and public enterprises to reduce budgetary deficits has resulted in a 30 percent unemployment rate for this age group. The king has always shown great skill in balancing factions; and his role as "Commander of the Faithful," a lineal descendent of the Prophet Muhammad, gives him a special status and charisma in the eyes of his subjects. He also has a talent for the unexpected. In 1994, following up his statement that "democracy is for everyone to be involved and for everyone to take his turn," he resolved a year-long political crisis with the opposition USFP leader as prime minister. He has also gone on record as personally guaranteeing that abuses in the new electoral system will not be tolerated. As Morocco's voters prepared for the momentous November 1997 elections that would establish parliamentary government (in the Western sense of the term), it appeared that the national leadership was in good hands.

NOTES
1. See David M. Hart, *Dadda 'Atta and His Forty Grandsons* (Cambridge: Menas Press, 1981), pp. 8–11. Dadda 'Atta was a historical figure, a minor saint or marabout.

2. Harold D. Nelson, ed., *Morocco, A Country Study* (Washington, D.C.: American University, Foreign Area Studies, 1978), p. 112.

3. The oldest property owned by the U.S. government abroad is the American Consulate in Tangier; a consul was assigned there in 1791. *Ibid.*, p. 40.

4. See David Woolman, *Rebels in the Rif: Abd 'al Krim and the Rif Rebellion* (Palo Alto, CA: Stanford University Press, 1968). On the Ait Waryaghar, see David M. Hart, *The Ait Waryaghar of the Moroccan Rif: An Ethnography and a History* (Tucson, AZ: University of Arizona Press, 1976). Abd 'al Krim had annihilated a Spanish army and set up a Republic of the Rif (1921–1926).

5. For a detailed description of protectorate tribal administration, see Robin Bidwell, *Morocco Under Colonial Rule* (London: Frank Cass, 1973).

6. He once said: "Morocco is a cow, the Qaids milk her while France holds the horns." Nelson, *op. cit.*, p. 53.

7. Mark Tessler, "Morocco: Institutional Pluralism and Monarchical Dominance," in W. I. Zartman, ed., *Political Elites in North Africa* (New York: Longman, 1982), p. 44.

8. Nelson, *op. cit.*, p. 205.

DEVELOPMENT

Increased privatization of state-owned enterprises—notably the telecommunications system and the national airline—and the end of the prolonged drought argue well for Morocco's development. In 1996, GDP was 9%.

FREEDOM

Amendments to the 1992 Constitution have set up a bicameral Legislature with a lower house elected directly by the voters and an upper house two thirds elected and one third appointed from municipal councils. Another important amendment commits the country to full observance of human rights. Previously, its poor human-rights record had deterred the European Union from granting it associate status.

HEALTH/WELFARE

The Moroccan family-planning program, begun in the 1980s, has achieved a 50% reduction in its once astronomical birth rate. The rate is now 2% per year.

ACHIEVEMENTS

The 1996 Fisheries agreement with the EU and a supplemental 3-year pact with Russia will bring a much greater return to the Moroccan fishing industry than was thought possible in the years of open competition in Morocco's fishing grounds. Under the agreement, Moroccan trawlers have exclusive rights to offshore fishing grounds along the Western Sahara.

Oman (Sultanate of Oman)

GEOGRAPHY

Area in Square Kilometers (Miles):
212,460 (82,009) (about the size of
New Mexico)
Capital (Population): Muscat (85,000)
Climate: coast, hot and humid; interior,
hot and dry

PEOPLE

Population
Total: 2,186,600
Annual Growth Rate: 3.7%
Rural/Urban Population Ratio: 88/12
Ethnic Makeup: almost entirely Arab;
small Baluchi, Zanzibari, and Indian
groups
Major Language: Arabic

Health
Life Expectancy at Birth: 68 years
(male); 72 years (female)
Infant Mortality Rate (Ratio): 34.3/1,000
Average Caloric Intake: n/a
Physicians Available (Ratio): 1/910

Religions
75% Ibadi Muslim; remainder Sunni
Muslim, Shia Muslim, some Hindu

Education
Adult Literacy Rate: 40%

COMMUNICATION
Telephones: 50,000
Newspapers: 3 dailies; 2 weeklies

"Atlantis of the Sands"

The development boom initiated nearly 3 decades ago by Sultan Qabus when he came to power has changed Oman almost beyond recognition. Muscat, Oman's once sleepy capital, is now a bustling city, with modern government buildings, a university, hospitals, and office towers, all painted gleaming white by order of the sultan. Beyond the modern facade, however, lie the ruins of Oman's rich and storied ancient past. The fortress-city of Ubar, on the frankincense route near the "Empty Quarter" (Rub al-Khali), in desolate southeastern Oman, was recently discovered by using satellite-imaging techniques. The technology showed where to look for a water table large enough to support a city. Archaeologists are now at work digging up the ruins of the lost "Atlantis of the Sands," a vital link in the trade routes of the ancient world.

TRANSPORTATION
Highways—Kilometers (Miles): 26,000
(16,224)
Railroads—Kilometers (Miles): none
Usable Airfields: 140

GOVERNMENT
Type: monarchy; the monarch's
absolute power is limited by the 1996
Basic Law
Independence Date: 1951
Head of State: Sultan and Prime
Minister Qabus ibn Said Al Said
Political Parties: none
Suffrage: none

MILITARY
Number of Armed Forces: 25,500
*Military Expenditures (% of Central
Government Expenditures):* 14.2%
Current Hostilities: border disputes
with Saudi Arabia and Yemen

ECONOMY
Currency ($ U.S. Equivalent): 0.39
Omani rial = $1
Per Capita Income/GDP: $10,020/$17
billion
Inflation Rate: 1.2%
Total Foreign Debt: $3 billion
Natural Resources: crude petroleum;
natural gas; coal; chromite; copper;
gypsum
Agriculture: dates; alfalfa; wheat;
bananas; coconuts; limes; vegetables;
fish
Industry: oil refining; fisheries; copper
smelting; butane; cement

FOREIGN TRADE
Exports: $4.8 billion
Imports: $4.1 billion

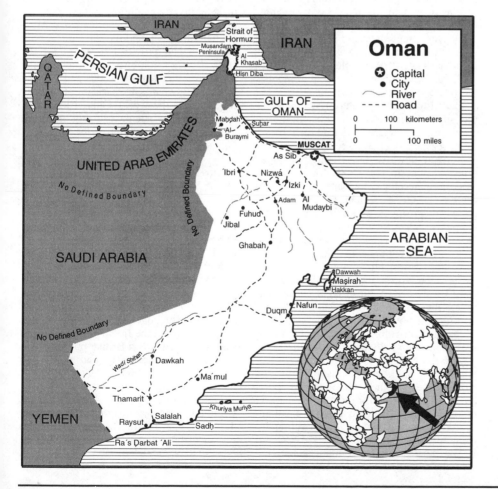

OMAN

The Sultanate of Oman was, at least until about 1970, one of the least-known countries in the world. Yet it is a very old country with a long history of contact with the outside world. Merchants from Oman had a near monopoly on the trade in frankincense and myrrh. Oman-built, shallow-draught, broad-beamed ships called dhows crisscrossed the Indian Ocean, trading with India and the Far East.

In the twentieth century, Oman has become important to the outside world for two reasons. First, it has been producing oil since the 1960s; and second, it has a strategic location on the Strait of Hormuz, the passageway for supertankers carrying Middle Eastern oil to the industrialized nations. Eighty percent of Japan's oil needs passes through Hormuz, as does 60 percent of Western Europe's. A Swiss journalist called the Omanis "sentinels of the Gulf" because they watch over this vital traffic.

GEOGRAPHY

Oman is the second-largest country in the Arabian Peninsula. However, the population is small, and large areas are uninhabited or sparsely populated. The geographic diversity—rugged mountains, vast gravelly plains, and deserts—limits large-scale settlement. Prior to the discovery of oil, Oman's geography was an obstacle to its agricultural development. The bulk of the population lives in the coastal area around Muscat, the capital, and on the Batinah coast on the Persian Gulf opposite Iran. Here an ingenious system of underground irrigation channels *(falaj)* makes intensive agriculture feasible. Another important area of development is the southwestern coast of Dhofar Province, source of the legendary frankincense tree—still an important Omani export.

Behind Oman's coast is a spine of rugged mountains, the Jabal al-Akhdar ("Green Mountain"), with peaks over 10,000 feet. The mountains form several disconnected chains, interspersed with deep, narrow valleys where village houses hang like eagles' nests from the mountaintops, above terraced gardens and palm groves.

Most of Oman's oil wells are located in the interior of the country. The interior is a broad, hilly plain dotted with oasis villages, each one a fortress with thick walls to keep out desert raiders. The stony plain eventually becomes the Rub al-Khali ("Empty Quarter"), the great uninhabited desert of southeastern Arabia.

Omani territory includes the Musandam Peninsula, at the northeastern tip of Arabia projecting into the Strait of Hormuz. The peninsula is separated from the rest of Oman by the Union of Arab Emirates. In 1995, the Omani border with Yemen was formally demarcated in accordance with a UN–sponsored 1992 agreement. The oasis of Buraimi, on the Oman/Saudi Arabia/ U.A.E. border, is currently under U.A.E. control, although it is claimed by both Saudi Arabia and Yemen. The surrounding desert hinterland is shared by the three states and remains undefined.

HISTORY

As was the case elsewhere in Arabia, the early social structure of Oman consisted of a number of tribal groups. Many of them were and still are nomadic (Bedouin), while others became settled farmers and herders centuries ago. The groups spent much of their time feuding with one another. Occasionally, several would join in an alliance against others, but none of them recognized any higher authority than their leaders.

In the seventh century A.D., the Omanis were converted to Islam. They developed their own form of Islam, however, called Ibadism, meaning "Community of the Just," a branch of Shia Islam. The Ibadi peoples elect their own leader, called an Imam. The Ibadi Imams do not have to be descendants of the prophet Muhammad, as do the Imams in the main body of Shia Muslims. The Ibadi community believes that anyone, regardless of background, can be elected Imam, as long as the individual is pious, just, and capable. If no one is available who meets those requirements, the office may remain vacant.

Ibadi Imams ruled interior Oman with the support of family shaykhs until the eighteenth century. Well before then, however, coastal Oman was being opened up to foreign powers. The Portuguese captured Muscat in the 1500s for use as a stopping place for their ships on the trade route to India. (An Omani served as navigator to Portuguese admiral Vasco da Gama in his voyage across the Indian Ocean to India.) They built two great forts guarding the entrance to Muscat harbor, forts that still stand, giving the town its picturesque appearance. The Portuguese were finally driven out in 1650. Since that time, Oman has not been ruled directly by any foreign power.

The current ruling dynasty in Oman is the Al Bu Said Dynasty. It has been in power since 1749, when a chief named Ahmad ibn Said defeated an Iranian invasion and established his authority over most of Oman. But, for most of the period, Oman actually had two rulers—a sultan ruling in Muscat and an Imam ruling in the interior at the same time.

The most successful Omani sultan before the twentieth century was Said ibn Sultan (1804–1856). He added Dhofar Province and Zanzibar, on the East African coast, to Omani territory. Sultan Said had good relations with Britain. He signed a treaty with the British that stated, "the friendship between our two states shall remain unshook to the end of time." The sultan also signed a friendship treaty with the United States in 1833; and in 1836, to the surprise of the New York Port authorities, an Omani ship docked in New York harbor. Its captain said that the sultan had sent him to get to know the Americans whom he had heard so much about and to arrange trade contacts. Friendship between the United States and Oman operates on a different basis today. Now it is the Omanis who allow the Americans the use of the British-built Masirah Island base and share responsibility for patrolling the Strait of Hormuz, the strategic entrance point for the strife-ridden Persian Gulf. But this friendship has its roots in Sultan Said's mission.

After Said's death, a number of ethnic, tribal, and religious differences re-asserted themselves, and Oman lost its importance in regional affairs. Its territory was again restricted to its small corner of southeastern Arabia. The opening of the Suez Canal in 1869 diverted shipping to new Red Sea routes, and ships no longer called at Muscat harbor. Piracy and the slave trade, both of which had provided revenues for the sultan, were prohibited by international law. For the rest of the 1800s and most of the 1900s, Oman sank back into isolation, forgotten by the world. Only Britain paid the Omanis any attention, giving the sultan a small monthly subsidy in the event that Oman might be of some future use to it.

In the early twentieth century, the Imams of inner Oman and the sultans ruling in Muscat came to a complete parting of the ways. In 1920, a treaty between the two leaders provided that the sultan would not interfere in the internal affairs of inner Oman. Relations were reasonably smooth until 1951, when Britain recognized the independence of the Sultanate of Muscat-Oman, as it was then called, and withdrew its advisers. Subsequently, the Imam declared inner Oman to be a separate state from the sultanate. A number of Arab states supported the Imam, on the grounds that the sultan was a British puppet. Conflict between the Imam and the sultan dragged on until 1960, when the sultan finally re-established his authority.

Oman's ruler for nearly 4 decades in the twentieth century was Sultan Said ibn Taimur (1932–1970). The most interesting aspect of his reign was the way in which he stopped the clock of modernization. Oil was discovered in 1964 in inland Oman;

within a few years, wealth from oil royalties began pouring in. But the sultan was afraid that the new wealth would corrupt his people. He refused to spend money except for the purchase of arms and a few personal luxuries such as an automobile, which he liked to drive on the only paved road in Salalah, his southern capital in Dhofar Province. He would not allow the building of schools, houses, roads, or hospitals for his people. Before 1970, there were only 16 schools in all of Oman. The sole hospital was the American mission in Muscat, established in the 1800s by Baptist missionaries; and all 10 of Oman's qualified doctors were practicing abroad, because the sultan did not trust modern medicine. The few roads were rough caravan tracks; many areas of the country, such as the Musandam Peninsula, were inaccessible.

The sultan required the city gates of Muscat to be closed and locked 3 hours after sunset; no one could enter or leave the city after that. Flashlights were prohibited, since they were a modern invention; so were sunglasses and European shoes. Anyone found on the streets at night without a lighted kerosene lantern was liable to imprisonment. In the entire country, there were only about 1,000 automobiles; to import an automobile, one had to have the sultan's personal permission. On the darker side, slavery was still a common practice. Women were almost never seen in public and had to be veiled from head to foot if they so much as walked to a neighbor's house to visit. Prisoners could be locked up in the old Portuguese fort at Muscat on the slightest pretext and left to rot.

As the 1960s came to an end, there was more and more unrest in Oman. The opposition centered around Qabus ibn Said, the sultan's son. Qabus had been educated in England. When he came home, his father shut him up in a house in Salalah, a town far from Muscat, and refused to give him any responsibilities. He was afraid of his son's "Western ideas."

On July 23, 1970, supporters of Crown Prince Qabus overthrew the sultan, and Qabus succeeded him. Sultan Qabus brought Oman into the twentieth century in a hurry. The old policy of isolation was reversed. In 1981, worried about a possible spread of the Iran–Iraq War, Oman joined the Gulf Cooperation Council and allowed the U.S. military to use the facilities on Masirah Island in return for $200 million in aid.

Qabus also ended a long-running rebellion in Dhofar. The rebellion had developed originally from the social and economic neglect of the province by the

(UN photo/A221)

Boys study the Koran at a village in Oman. When Qabus ibn Said came to power in 1970, replacing his father, he targeted education, health care, and transportation as prime development areas.

Taimur government. The Dhofar rebels were supported and armed by the then–People's Democratic Republic of Yemen, Oman's neighbor. Relations between the two countries remained poor even after the sultan had crushed the rebellion in 1975, with the help of troops from Britain and Iran. The unification of the two Yemens in 1990 improved prospects for an Omani–Yemeni reconciliation, which was confirmed by the 1992 border agreement and the 1995 demarcation.

OMANI SOCIETY

Today, Omanis typically live in two worlds. They may wear both a *kanjar,* the traditional curved dagger, and a digital watch; travel by car; dress in *dishdasha* and skullcap, yet do business by telephone in English; and spend holidays abroad. The pace of modernization is dizzying. Yesterday, Muscat had a small dirt airstrip; today, a huge industrial park with shops, factories, and high-rise apartments covers the old runway. Broad paved highways

curve along the coast and branch inland to the Imam's old fortress towns and oasis villages, where only camel tracks existed before 1970.

Sultan Qabus set education, health care, and transportation as his top priorities. The results have been astonishing. Within 2 decades, there were 490 schools, with 7,700 teachers and 150,000 students—one third of them girls. In 1996, the sultan announced the expansion of the *Majlis al-Shura* (Council of State) to 80 members, "to enhance constructive cooperation between government and people." He also issued a Basic Law defining the succession. Since he is not married and has no male heir, the Basic Law stipulates that the succession must be retained within the bin Said family, which must agree on any successor he designates.

The sultan also set out to blanket his country with roads and health clinics. By the mid-1980s, all but a few remote Musandam villages were served by graded roads. Medical services used to be pro-

The Portuguese seize Muscat and build massive fortresses to guard the harbor
1587–1588

The Al Bu Said Dynasty is established; extends Omani territory
1749

The British establish a de facto protectorate; the slave trade is supposedly ended
late 1800s

Independence
1951

Sultan Said ibn Taimur is deposed by his son, Prince Qabus
1970

With British and Iranian help, Sultan Qabus ends the Dhofar rebellion
1975

An agreement with the United States allows the American military the use of Masirah air base
1980s

Sultan Qabus sets up a Consultative Assembly as an advisory body as the first step toward democratization

1990s

The sultan focuses on expanding Oman's industrial base

The Consultative Assembly is enlarged

vided by local traditional doctors; today, however, the health team comes to the villages fully equipped in a Land Rover.

THE ECONOMY

Oman began its production and export of oil in 1967. There are two main fields, one near Muscat, the other in Dhofar province in the south. Production in 1997 was 857,522 barrels per day (b/d), while reserves were 5.2 billion b/d. Oil revenues provide 96 percent of national revenues.

Prior to oil development, Oman and the then–Yemen Arab Republic were the only two Arabian Peninsula countries where agriculture was extensively practiced. Some 40 percent of the labor force are engaged in agriculture (including fisheries). However, the agricultural sector accounts for only 4 percent of gross domestic product. Farming is largely subsistence oriented, due to limited arable land and undependable rainfall. However, the country's varied geography and range of climate allow cultivation of many different crops. These include dates and limes, grown on the Batinah coast, bananas and papayas from Dhofar (which receives extensive rainfall from Indian Ocean monsoon winds), and market garden vegetables grown in interior oases.

Oman also produces natural gas. Discoveries in the 1990s have increased known reserves to 14 billion cubic feet. The geology of the gas fields makes extraction difficult, however, which adds to the cost.

The fishing industry employs 10 percent of the working population, but obsolete equipment and lack of canning and freezing plants have severely limited the catch in the past. Another problem is the unwillingness of Omani fishermen to move into commercial production; most of them catch just enough fish for their own use. The Oman Fish Company was formed in 1987 to develop fishery resources, financing the purchase by fishermen of aluminum boats powered by outboard motors to replace the seaworthy but slow traditional wooden dhows. The company has also set up processing and cold-storage plants inland for preparation and marketing of the catch.

The search for ways to add to its oil income led Oman to form a consortium in 1992 with the former Soviet republics of Russia, Kazakhstan, and Azerbaijan to build a pipeline linking the Caspian and Black Seas. In 1996, a second consortium, comprising Russia, Kazakhstan, and Oman, was formed for joint construction of a pipeline from the Kazakh Tengiz oil field to Black Sea ports, whence it would connect with the Oman refinery via a pipeline across Turkey and various Arab states.

PROSPECTS

Omanis celebrated Sultan Qabus's silver jubilee in November 1995 in full confidence that the future would bring them continued prosperity and meet their rising expectations. Long known as the Gulf's "best kept secret," with its close-knit expatriate community and an elite that is more like an extended family, Oman in the 1990s began attracting tourists along with potential foreign investors. In preparation for his jubilee, the sultan began laying the groundwork for a broadening of political leadership in 1990. His first step was to form the Council of State as an advisory body. In 1996, the Council was enlarged from 59 to 80 members, representing each of Oman's 59 *wilayas* (provinces), plus two representatives each from wilayas of more than 30,000. Qabus's commitment to female education and the advancement of women professionally was underscored by his appointment of two women members to that body.

Oman has begun to play a more active role in regional affairs than in the past, due to its strategic location. U.S. involvement in the Persian Gulf after the Iraqi invasion of Kuwait and the Gulf War, and the evolution of U.S. policy in the region, dictated a closer relationship with the Arab Gulf states. In 1980, Oman agreed to the use of Omani bases by U.S. naval and military personnel. In return, the United States supplied tanks and other vehicles to the Omani armed forces and built extensive base housing for personnel assigned to Omani bases.

DEVELOPMENT

The 1995–2000 5-Year Plan for Omani development projects total expenditures of $26.3 billion. With new fields in operation and the arrangement with Kazakh-crude to use Oman's refineries for processing, oil revenues are expected to increase to $6.8 billion under the plan.

FREEDOM

In 1995 the Majlis al-Shura (Consultative Council), formed in 1990 to advise the ruler, was enlarged from 59 to 80 members to provide for better representation of Oman's growing urban population. Two women were included in the membership, for the first time.

HEALTH/WELFARE

Improved health services and greater coverage of rural areas and villages by mobile health clinics reduced the infant mortality rate to 34.3 deaths per 1,000 live births by 1995.

ACHIEVEMENTS

The discovery of important gold and high-grade copper deposits in inner Oman in 1996 should provide an important addition to its non-oil revenue sources. Oman is self-sufficient in cement and textiles, the latter made in textile plants in the Rusail industrial free-trade zone near Muscat. The 60 factories now located in this zone generate $51.9 million in finished goods, 40% exported.

Qatar (State of Qatar)

GEOGRAPHY
Area in Square Kilometers (Miles): 11,000 (4,427) (about the size of Connecticut)
Capital (Population): Doha (313,600)
Climate: hot and dry

PEOPLE

Population
Total: 547,800
Annual Growth Rate: 2.7%
Rural/Urban Population Ratio: 9/91
Ethnic Makeup: 40% Arab; 18% Pakistani; 18% Indian; 10% Iranian; 14% others
Major Languages: Arabic; English widely used

Health
Life Expectancy at Birth: 70 years (male); 75 years (female)
Infant Mortality Rate (Ratio): 20/1,000
Average Caloric Intake: n/a
Physicians Available (Ratio): 1/671

Religions
95% Muslim; 5% others

Education
Adult Literacy Rate: 76%

COMMUNICATION
Telephones: 110,000
Newspapers: 4 dailies; 2 weeklies

A Vanishing Lifestyle

A century ago, an English traveler described Qatar as "miles and miles of low barren hills, with hardly a single tree." Bedouin tents pitched in a palm grove were the only signs of human life. Today, one is more likely to pass a marquee set up beside a paved highway, a city family from Doha under it, although a shiny BMW or Toyota parked nearby guarantees a quick return to urban life.

TRANSPORTATION
Highways—Kilometers (Miles): 1,190 (743)
Railroads—Kilometers (Miles): none
Usable Airfields: 6

GOVERNMENT
Type: traditional monarchy
Independence Date: September 3, 1971
Head of State/Government: Emir Shaykh Hamad bin Khalifa; Prime Minister Shaykh Abdullah al-Thani
Political Parties: none
Suffrage: none

MILITARY
Number of Armed Forces: 7,000
Military Expenditures (% of Central Government Expenditures): 25%
Current Hostilities: dispute with Bahrain over ownership of Hawar Islands

ECONOMY
Currency ($ U.S. Equivalent): 3.64 riyals = $1
Per Capita Income/GDP: $20,820/$10.7 billion
Inflation Rate: 3%
Total Foreign Debt: $1.5 billion
Natural Resources: petroleum; natural gas; fish
Agriculture: farming on small scale
Industry: oil production and refining; natural gas development; fishing; cement; petrochemicals; steel; fertilizer

FOREIGN TRADE
Exports: $3.13 billion
Imports: $1.75 billion

QATAR

Qatar is a shaykhdom on the eastern (Gulf) coast of Arabia, a peninsula 4,427 square miles in area. It is the second-smallest Middle Eastern state, after Bahrain; but, due to its oil wealth, it has an extremely high per capita annual income. Before 1949, when its oil exports began, there were about 20,000 Qataris, all descendants of peoples who had migrated to the coast centuries ago in search of a dependable water supply. Since then, rapid economic growth has attracted expatriate workers and immigrants from other Arab countries and distant Muslim states such as Pakistan. As a result, Qatar has a high number of immigrants and expatriates, which makes for some tension.

HISTORY

Although the peninsula has been inhabited since 4000 B.C., little is known of its history before the nineteenth century. At one time, it was ruled by the al-Khalifa family, the current rulers of Bahrain. It became part of the Ottoman Empire formally in 1872, but the Turkish garrison was evacuated during World War I. The Ottomans earlier had recognized Shaykh Qassim al-Thani, head of the important al-Thani family, as emir of Qatar, and the British followed suit when they established a protectorate after the war.

The British treaty with the al-Thanis was similar to ones made with other shaykhs in Arabia and the Persian Gulf in order to keep other European powers out of the area and to protect their trade and communications links with India. In 1916, the British recognized Shaykh Abdullah al-Thani, grandfather of the current ruler, as ruler of Qatar and promised to protect the territory from outside attack either by the Ottomans or overland by hostile Arabian groups. In return, Shaykh al-Thani agreed not to enter into any relationship with any other foreign government and to accept British political advisers.

Qatar remained a tranquil British protectorate until the 1950s, when oil exports began. Since then, the country has developed rapidly, though not to the extent of producing the dizzying change visible in other oil-producing Arab states.

INDEPENDENCE

Qatar became independent in 1971, and the ruler, Shaykh Ahmad al-Thani, took the title of emir. Disagreements within the ruling family led the emir's cousin, Shaykh Khalifa, to seize power in 1972. Khalifa made himself prime minister as well as ruler and initiated a major program of social and economic development, which his cousin had opposed.

Shaykh Khalifa limited the privileges of the ruling family. There were more than 2,000 al-Thanis, and most of them had been paid several thousand dollars a month whether or not they worked. Khalifa reduced their allowances and appointed some nonmembers of the royal family to the Council of Ministers, the state's chief executive body. In 1992, he set up a Consultative Council of 30 members to advise the cabinet on proposed legislation and budgetary matters. Subsequently, the cabinet itself was enlarged, with new ministries of Islamic affairs, finance, economy, and industry and trade. While the majority of cabinet and Consultative Council members belonged to the royal family, the appointment of a number of nonfamily members to both these organizations heralded the "quiet revolution" toward power sharing to which Shaykh Khalifa was committed.

FOREIGN RELATIONS

Because of its small size, great wealth, and proximity to regional conflicts, Qatar is vulnerable to outside intervention. The government fears especially that the example of the Iranian Shia Revolution may bring unrest to its own Shia Muslim population. After the discovery of a Shia plot to overthrow the government of neighboring Bahrain in 1981, Qatari authorities rounded up and deported several hundred Shia Qataris of Iranian origin. But, thus far, the government has avoided singling out the Shia community for heavy-handed repression, preferring to concentrate its efforts on economic and social progress. On the 10th anniversary of Qatar's independence, the emir said that "economic strength is the strongest guarantee that safeguards the independence of nations, their sovereignty, rights and dignity."[1]

Fears of a possible attack by Iran led the country to sign a bilateral defense agreement with Saudi Arabia in 1982. The Iraqi invasion of Kuwait exposed Saudi military weakness as regards Iraq, and, as a result, Qatar turned to the United States for its defense. A Qatar official noted, "Saudi Arabia was the protector, but the war showed that the emperor had no clothes."[2] Qatar has subsequently become the "linchpin" of U.S. Gulf security policy, according to U.S. secretary of defense William Perry. In 1997, 30 F-15E and F-16 fighter planes were sent to a new, U.S.-built Qatari base, along with tanks and sufficient equipment for an entire armored brigade.

However, U.S. insistence on the "dual containment" of Iraq and Iran as threats to regional security has drawn some opposition in Qatar. During his official visit

to Washington, D.C., in June 1997, Emir Shaykh Hamad bin Khalifa urged the Clinton administration to change its policy toward those countries, arguing that the Iraqi people had suffered enough from sanctions and that the new leadership in Iran was ready for dialogue.

Qatar's main foreign policy concerns involve borders. Ownership of the Hawar Islands has been disputed with Bahrain for years. In 1992, Qatar unilaterally extended its territorial waters to 12 nautical miles, bringing the islands and the adjacent seabed into Qatari territory. Bahrain protested and then submitted a complaint to the International Court of Justice asking for its decision on jurisdiction. Both countries at various times have said that they would not accept the Court's decision, but, in 1996, they accepted an offer by Saudi Arabia to mediate.

Qatar's fear that it would be the next target of Iraqi expansionism after Kuwait led the country to take an active role in regional affairs. U.S. aircraft were based there during the Gulf War (as they are today), and the small Qatari Army was beefed up by 7,500 troops from Tunisia. Palestinian workers in Qatar were expelled in response to the Palestine Liberation Organization's endorsement of the Iraqi invasion. (However, Qatar was the first Gulf state to endorse the 1993 Palestinian–Israeli peace agreements.)

THE ECONOMY

The Qatari economy is currently based on oil, but, in the very near future, oil will be replaced by natural gas as its major mineral resource.

Until recently, the Qatari oil industry was considered to be in a state of terminal decline, with dwindling reserves and low production. New discoveries and production-sharing agreements have revived the industry. Production has reached a milestone of 500,000 barrels per day (b/d) due to government initiatives and greater participation by foreign oil companies under favorable concession terms.

Natural gas is the major prospect for long-term development. Production from the existing North Field began in 1991. With 350 trillion metric tons of reserves—none associated with oil deposits (which make recovery more costly and complicated)—its output could meet the heating needs of all U.S. homes for the next 60 years.

Depletion of water supplies due to heavy demand and dependence on outdated desalination plants for its fresh water has prompted the country to undertake some innovative food-production projects. One such project, begun in 1988,

Britain recognizes Shaykh Abdullah al-Thani as emir
1916

The start of oil production in Qatar
1949

An abortive federation with Bahrain and the Trucial States (U.A.E.), followed by independence
1971

The ruler is deposed by Shaykh Khalifa
1972

1990s

Qatar condemns the Iraqi invasion of Kuwait and expels resident Palestinians

Border conflicts continue

Crown Prince Hamad al-Thani deposes his father and takes over as emir

uses solar energy and seawater to cultivate food crops on sand. As a result of such projects, Qatar produces sufficient food both to meet domestic needs and to export vegetables to neighboring states.

SOCIETAL CHANGES

Qatar was originally settled by nomadic peoples, and their influence is still strong. Traditional Bedouin values, such as honesty, hospitality, pride, and courage when faced with adversity, have carried over into modern times.

Most Qataris belong to the strict puritanical Wahhabi sect of Islam, which is also dominant in Saudi Arabia. They are similar to Saudis in their conservative outlook, and Qatar generally defers to its larger neighbor in foreign policy. Thus, in resolving a border dispute in 1996, the government accepted Saudi demarcation, although the redesigned border gave Saudi Arabia a larger territory.

There are, however, significant social differences between Qataris and Saudis. Western movies are shown in Qatar, for example, but not in Saudi Arabia. Furthermore, Qatar does not have religious police or "morals squads" to enforce Islamic conventions, and foreigners may purchase alcoholic beverages legally.

The most significant societal change in Qatar involves the position of women. The first school for girls opened there in 1956. But change in women's rights and roles has accelerated in recent years. By 1997, the ratio of women to men was 3 to 1. Approximately 30 percent of Qatari women work outside the home, and many of them drive their own cars—something forbidden in Saudi Arabia.

Despite their new freedoms and the prospects of voting in the country's first municipal elections in late 1997, Qatari women continue to base their behavior on Islam while savoring their options. A well-known fashion designer once expressed the prevailing mood: "We hold to our traditions. What I want is for us to change, but wisely. Change should take place within the framework of our habits and traditions."[3] Thus, in Qatar, a woman may drive herself to work; but, when she leaves her home, she wears the black head-scarf, face veil, and shapeless black *abaya* considered the correct costume for women in public under Wahhabi Islamic strictures. "They are part of our religion," a woman bank manager told a reporter. "Working and studying are not forbidden by Islam, but going to mixed parties and having contact with foreign men—these things cannot be done."[4]

INTERNAL POLITICS

In July 1995, Crown Prince Shaykh Hamad bin Khalifa deposed his father, the ruling emir, while the latter was on vacation in Switzerland. The "palace coup" was bloodless, although, since then, several attempts by supporters of the deposed ruler to overthrow his son have been thwarted. (Shaykh Khalifa also made off with some $3.7 billion in government revenues that he had squirreled away over the years in personal accounts in various countries. The Qatari government pressed claims for recovery of the funds, and, in October 1996, Shaykh Khalifa agreed to return $2 billion, saying that it represented the full amount due. The new emir in return declared that his father would be welcome to come back to Qatar as the honorary "father of the nation.")

Qatar's new ruler has undertaken a "quiet revolution" since his accession to the throne. Thus he scheduled municipal elections for late 1997, with women permitted to vote—both firsts for Qatar. In 1996, the emir named his brother Shaykh Abdullah prime minister, relinquishing the post he had held as heir apparent. He also broke with tradition by naming the eldest son of his third wife as crown prince.

NOTES

1. Qatar News Agency (November 23, 1981).
2. Douglas Jehl, *The New York Times International* (July 20, 1997).
3. Helga Graham, *Arabian Time Machine: Self-Portrait of an Oil State* (London: Heinemann, 1978), p. 207.
4. Jehl, *op. cit.*

DEVELOPMENT

The 1997 budget anticipates revenues of $3.6 billion and expenditures of $3.76 billion. However, the huge expense of developing the Ras Laffan gas field may unbalance this budget, although revenues should net $7 billion by 2002, when the project is in full production.

FREEDOM

Qatar has a provisional Constitution, enacted in 1970. But, in practice, the country is an absolute monarchy. In 1996, the emir decreed universal adult suffrage in preparation for the 1997 municipal elections. Press censorship is now at an end.

HEALTH/WELFARE

In 1996, the country's first private hospital opened its doors. It has 7 pediatric units, plus special-care clinics and an emergency room. Qatar's national health system is increasingly staffed by Qatari doctors and nurses, and it has the highest ratio of medical personnel per population of any Arab state.

ACHIEVEMENTS

Completion of the huge Ras Laffan natural-gas project will make Qatar one of the major gas exporters in the world, along with Indonesia and Malaysia. By 2002, exports to fill current orders will reach 10 million metric tons per year.

Saudi Arabia (Kingdom of Saudi Arabia)

GEOGRAPHY

Area in Square Kilometers (Miles):
2,331,000 (899,770) (about ¼ the size of the continental United States)
Capital (Population): Riyadh (1,500,000)
Climate: arid, with great extremes of temperature

PEOPLE

Population
Total: 19,409,100
Annual Growth Rate: 3.7%
Rural/Urban Population Ratio: 21/79
Ethnic Makeup: 90% Arab; 10% Afro-Asian
Major Language: Arabic; English widely used

Health
Life Expectancy at Birth: 67 years (male); 70 years (female)
Infant Mortality Rate (Ratio): 49/1,000
Average Caloric Intake: 116% of FAO minimum
Physicians Available (Ratio): 1/523

Religion
100% Muslim

Education
Adult Literacy Rate: 79%

COMMUNICATION
Telephones: 1,624,000
Newspapers: 8 dailies in Arabic; 3 dailies in English

The Changing Face of Mecca

Mecca, 45 miles inland from the Red Sea and set in a dusty bowl surrounded by barren mountains, is Saudi Arabia's spiritual capital and the site of the holiest shrines of Islam. The Prophet Muhammad's first revelations from God (the Koran) were given him in a cave on nearby Mount Hira. The annual Hajj (Great Pilgrimage) to Mecca draws some 2 million pilgrims to the city. In 1997, the Saudi government completed a 10-year plan to enlarge the Great Mosque and its courtyard to allow 190,000 pilgrims to circumnavigate the Ka'ba, the central focus of Islamic worship. The plan also provides improved facilities and services for pilgrims. There is even a McDonald's just outside the mosque; in accordance with Islamic dietary laws, it serves only *halal* (ritually slaughtered) beef in its burgers.

TRANSPORTATION
Highways—Kilometers (Miles): 151,530 (94,555)
Railroads—Kilometers (Miles): 1,390 (867)
Usable Airfields: 211

GOVERNMENT
Type: hereditary monarchy in the al-Saud family
Independence Date: September 23, 1932 (unification)
Head of State/Government: King and Prime Minister Fahd
Political Parties: none; prohibited
Suffrage: none

MILITARY
Number of Armed Forces: 67,500
Military Expenditures (% of Central Government Expenditures): 13.8%
Current Hostilities: unresolved border disputes with the United Arab Emirates

ECONOMY
Currency ($ U.S. Equivalent): 3.75 Saudi rials = $1
Per Capita Income/GDP: $9,510/$173.1 billion
Inflation Rate: 4.9%
Total Foreign Debt: $18.9 billion
Natural Resources: hydrocarbons; iron ore; gold; copper
Agriculture: dates; grain; livestock
Industry: petroleum production; petrochemicals; cement; fertilizer; light industry

FOREIGN TRADE
Exports: $39.4 billion
Imports: $28.9 billion

Note: "Makkah" and "Madinah" are the *Board of Geographic Names*–approved spellings for Mecca and Medina, respectively.

SAUDI ARABIA

The Kingdom of Saudi Arabia is the giant of the Arabian Peninsula, with an area of nearly 900,000 square miles. It is also a giant in the world economy, because of its oil. To many people, the name *Saudi Arabia* is a synonym for oil wealth. Indeed, its huge oil reserves, large financial surpluses from oil production, and its ability to use oil as a political weapon (as in the 1973 embargo) enable the country to play an important part in regional as well as international affairs.

Saudi Arabia's population is small in relation to the country's size and is heavily urbanized. Urban growth has been very rapid, since only 1 percent of the land can be used for agriculture and all employment opportunities are in the cities or in the oil-producing regions. Due to its small population, the country has traditionally relied upon foreign labor, both skilled and unskilled, in its development. However, the recession of the 1980s and the economic and political dislocation resulting from the Gulf War led to the expulsion of several hundred thousand foreign workers.

The country contains three main geographical regions: the Hejaz, along the Red Sea; the Nejd, a vast interior plateau that comprises the bulk of Saudi territory; and the Eastern Province. The kingdom's largest oases, al-Hasa Safwa, are located in this third region, along with the major oil fields and industrial centers. The Empty Quarter (al-Rub' al-Khali), an uninhabited desert where rain may not fall for a decade or more, occupies the entire southeastern quadrant of the country.

THE WAHHABI MOVEMENT

In the eighteenth century, most of the area included in present-day Saudi Arabia was the home of nomads, as it had been for centuries. These peoples had no central government and owed allegiance to no one except their chiefs. They spent much of their time raiding one another's territories in the struggle for survival. Inland Arabia was a great blank area on the map, a vast, empty desert.

The only part of modern Saudi Arabia under any government control in the eighteenth century was the Hejaz, which includes the Islamic holy cities of Mecca and Medina. It was a province of the Ottoman Empire, the major power in the Middle East at that time.

Saudi Arabia became a nation, in the modern sense of the word, in 1932. But the origins of the Saudi nation go back to the eighteenth century. One of the tribes that roamed the desert beyond Ottoman control was the tribe of Saud. Its leader, Muhammad ibn Saud, wanted to gain an advantage over his rivals in the constant search for water and good grazing land for animals. He approached a famous religious scholar named Abd al-Wahhab, who lived in an oasis near the current Saudi capital, Riyadh (then a mud-walled village). Abd al-Wahhab promised Allah's blessing to ibn Saud in his contests with his rivals. In return, the Saudi leader agreed to protect al-Wahhab from threats to his life by opponents of the strict doctrines he taught and preached, and he swore an oath of obedience to these doctrines. The partnership between these two men gave rise to a crusading religious movement called Wahhabism.

Wahhabism is basically a strict and puritanical form of Sunni Islam. The Wahhabi code of law, behavior, and conduct is modeled on that of the original Islamic community established in Mecca and Medina by the Prophet Muhammad. Although there has been some relaxation of the code due to the country's modernization, it remains the law of Saudi Arabia today. As a result, Saudi society is not only more conservative and puritanical than many other Islamic societies, but it also is governed much more strictly. A Ministry of Public Morals Enforcement, for example, has the responsibility to ensure that women (including foreigners) are dressed and veiled in accordance with Islamic modesty, and its squads patrol the streets to guarantee compliance.

Recently, the Committee to Promote Virtue and Prevent Vice, a private organization of young Muslims who wear robes and short beards, has taken to enforcing the rules more vigorously. Their leader, the Shaykh Bin Baz (noted for his public statements that the world is flat) is also the head of the Saudi *ulema* (religious leaders), giving the organization the needed aura of Islamic respectability. Wahhabi strictures were tested in November 1990, when a group of women from prominent families defied the ban on women driving and drove their cars on public streets in Riyadh. Fearing a religious backlash, the interior minister issued a decree formalizing the ban.

Due to the Wahhabi–Saud partnership, religious leaders in the country (many of whom are descendants of Abd al-Wahhab) have a great deal of influence in the government. They may delay or even annul government actions that they believe are contrary to Islamic principles. Thus, they have successfully prevented the opening of movie theaters in the kingdom.

In the late 1700s, the puritanical zeal of the Wahhabis led them to declare a "holy war" against the Ottoman Turks, who were then in control of Mecca and Med-ina, in order to restore these holy cities to the Arabs. In the 1800s, Wahhabis captured the cities. Soon the Wahhabis threatened to undermine Ottoman authority elsewhere. Wahhabi raiders seized Najaf and Karbala in Iraq, centers of Shia pilgrimage, and desecrated Shia shrines. In Mecca, they removed the headstones from the graves of members of the Prophet's family, because in their belief system, all Muslims are supposed to be buried unmarked.

The Ottoman sultan did not have sufficient forces at hand to deal with the Wahhabi threat, so he called upon his vassal, Muhammad Ali, the khedive (viceroy) of Egypt. Muhammad Ali organized an army equipped with European weapons and trained by European advisers. In a series of hard-fought campaigns, the Egyptian Army defeated the Wahhabis and drove them back into the desert.

Inland Arabia reverted to its old patterns of conflict. The only difference between the Saudis and their rivals was the bond of Wahhabism. It did not help them in their conflicts, and in the 1890s, the Saudis' major rivals, the Rashidis, seized Riyadh. The Saudi chief escaped across the desert to Kuwait, a town on the Persian Gulf that was under British protection. He took along his young son, Abd al-Aziz ibn Saud.

IBN SAUD

Abd al-Aziz ibn Saud, or Ibn Saud, as he is usually known in history, was the father of his country, in both a political and a literal sense.[1] He grew up in exile in Kuwait, where he brooded and schemed about how to regain the lands of the Saudis. When he reached age 21, in 1902, he decided on a bold stroke to reach his goal. Crossing the desert with a small band of followers, he scaled the walls of Riyadh at night and seized the fortress by surprise at daybreak. This daring exploit won him the support of the people of Riyadh, who drove the Rashidis out of the town.

Over the next 3 decades, Ibn Saud steadily expanded his territory. He said that his goal was "to recover all the lands of our forefathers."[2] In World War I, he became an ally of the British, fighting the Ottoman Turks in Arabia. In return, the British provided arms for his followers and gave him a monthly allowance. The British continued to back Ibn Saud after the war, and, in 1924, he entered Mecca in triumph. His major rival, Sharif Husayn, who had been appointed by the Ottoman government as the "Protector of the Holy Places," fled into exile. (Sharif Husayn was the great-grandfather of King Hussein I of Jordan.)

(Aramco photo)

The Great Mosque at Mecca, in Saudi Arabia, is the holiest of shrines to Muslims. Historically, Mecca was the site at which Islam was founded, in the seventh century A.D., by the Prophet Muhammad. Pilgrims today flock to the Great Mosque to fulfill their Muslim duties as set down by the Five Pillars of Islam.

Ibn Saud's second goal, after recovering his ancestral lands, was to build a modern nation under a central government. He used as his motto the Koranic verse, "God changes not what is in a people until they change what is in themselves" *(Sura XIII, 2).* The first step was to gain recognition of Saudi Arabia as an independent state. Britain recognized the country in 1927, and other countries soon followed suit. In 1932, the country took its current name of Saudi Arabia, a union of the three provinces of Hejaz, Nejd, and al-Hasa.

INDEPENDENCE

Ibn Saud's second step in his "grand design" for the new country was to establish order under a central government. To do this, he began to build settlements and to encourage the nomads to settle down, live in permanent homes, and learn how to grow their own food rather than relying on the desert. Those who settled on the land were given seeds and tools, were enrolled in a sort of national guard, and were paid regular allowances. These former Bedouin warriors became in time the core of the Saudi armed forces.

Ibn Saud also established the country's basic political system. The basis for the system was the Wahhabi interpretation of Islamic law. Ibn Saud insisted that "the laws of the state shall always be in accordance with the Book of Allah and the Sunna (Conduct) of His Messenger and the ways of the Companions."[3] He saw no need for a written constitution, and as yet Saudi Arabia has none. Ibn Saud decreed that the country would be governed as an absolute monarchy, with rulers always chosen from the Saud family. He was unfamiliar with political parties and distrusted them in principle; political organizations were therefore prohibited in the kingdom. Yet Ibn Saud was himself democratic, humble in manner, and spartan in his living habits. He remained all his life a man of the people and held every day a public assembly *(majlis)* in Riyadh at which any citizen had the right to ask favors or present petitions. (The custom of holding a daily majlis has been observed by Saudi rulers ever since.) More often than not, petitioners would address Ibn Saud not as Your Majesty but simply as Abd al-Aziz (his given name), a dramatic example of Saudi democracy in action.

Ibn Saud died in 1953. He had witnessed the beginning of rapid social and economic change in his country due to oil revenues. Yet his successors have presided over a transformation beyond the imaginations of the warriors who scaled the walls of Riyadh half a century earlier. Almost the only building left in Riyadh from that period is the Masmak Fort, headquarters of the Rashidi leader, still standing in the midst of tall modern buildings, a reminder to young Saudis of the epic age in their nation's history.

Ibn Saud was succeeded by his eldest surviving son, Crown Prince Saud. A number of royal princes felt that the second son, Faisal, should have become the new king because of his greater experience in foreign affairs and economic management. Saud's only experience was as governor of Nejd.

Although he was large and corpulent and lacked Ibn Saud's forceful personality, the new king was like his father in a number of ways. He was more comfortable in a desert tent than running a bureaucracy or meeting foreign dignitaries. Also, like his father, he had no idea of the value of money. Ibn Saud would carry a sackful of rials (the Saudi currency) to the daily majlis and give them away to petitioners. His son, Saud, not only doled out money to petitioners but also gave millions to other members of the royal family. One of his greatest extravagances was a palace surrounded by a bright pink wall.[4]

By 1958, the country was almost bankrupt. The royal family was understandably nervous about a possible coup supported by other Arab states, such as Egypt and Syria, which were openly critical of Saudi Arabia because of its lack of political institutions. The senior princes issued an ultimatum to Saud: First he would put Faisal in charge of straightening out the kingdom's finances, and, when that had been done, he would abdicate. When the financial overhaul was complete, with the kingdom again on a sound footing, Saud abdicated in favor of Faisal.

This incident offers a good example of how the Saudi monarchy operates in crisis situations. Decisions are made collectively, and although the king is an absolute monarch to his subjects, he serves as "head of the family" and in reality must consult with the senior princes on all matters of policy. Decisions are also made in secret in order to give the impression of family unity to the outside world. The reasons for a decision must always be guessed at; the Saudis never explain them. It is a system very different from the open, freewheeling one of Western democracies, yet it has given Saudi Arabia stability and leadership on occasions when crises threatened the kingdom.

FAISAL AND HIS SUCCESSORS

In terms of state-building, the reign of King Faisal (1964–1975) is second in importance only to that of Ibn Saud. One author wrote of King Faisal during his reign, "He is leading the country with gentle insistence from medievalism into the jet age."[5] Faisal's gentle insistence showed itself in many different ways. Encouraged by his wife, Queen Iffat, he introduced education for girls into the kingdom. Before Faisal, the kingdom had had no systematic development plans. In introducing the first 5-year development plan, the king said that "our religion requires us to progress and to bear the burden of the highest tradition and best manners."[6]

In foreign affairs, Faisal ended the Yemen Civil War on an honorable basis for both sides; took an active part in the Islamic world in keeping with his role as Protector of the Holy Places; and, in 1970, founded the Organization of the Islamic Conference, which has given the Islamic nations of the world a voice in international affairs. Faisal laid down the basic

(UPI/Corbis-Bettman)

King Faisal Ibn Abdul Aziz Al Saud was instrumental in bringing Saudi Arabia into the world's international community and in establishing domestic plans that brought his country into the twentieth century. Faisal established the basic strategies that his successors have followed. It was a tragic loss to Saudi Arabia when he was assassinated in 1975.

strategy that his successors have followed, namely, avoidance of direct conflict, mediation of disputes behind the scenes, and use of oil wealth as a political weapon when necessary. The king never understood the American commitment to Israel, any more than his father had. (Ibn Saud had met U.S. president Franklin D. Roosevelt in Egypt during World War II. Roosevelt, already motivated by American Jewish leaders to help in the establishment of a Jewish homeland in Palestine, sought to convince Ibn Saud, as head of the only independent Arab state at that time, to moderate Arab opposition to the project.) But Faisal's distrust of communism was equally strong. This distrust led him to continue the ambivalent yet close Saudi alliance with the United States that has continued up to the present.

Faisal was assassinated in 1975 by a deranged nephew while he was holding the daily majlis. The assassination was another test of the system of rule by consensus in the royal family, and the system held firm. Khalid, Faisal's eldest half-brother, his junior by 6 years, succeeded him without incident and ruled until 1982. King Khalid, who was already in poor

health, delegated most of his powers to his half-brother Fahd. He died suddenly in 1982, and Crown Prince Fahd, the current ruler, succeeded him.

THE MECCA MOSQUE SIEGE

One of the most shocking events in Saudi Arabia since the founding of the kingdom was the seizure of the Great Mosque in Mecca, Islam's holiest shrine, by a group of fundamentalist Sunni Muslims in November 1979. The leader of the group declared that one of its members was the *Mahdi* (in Sunni Islam, the "Awaited One") who had come to announce the Day of Judgment. The group occupied the mosque for 2 weeks. The siege was finally overcome by army and national guard units, but with considerable loss of life on both sides. No one knows exactly what the group's purpose was, nor did it lead to any general expressions of dissatisfaction with the regime. But the incident reflects the very real fear of the Saudi rulers of a coup attempted by the ultra-religious right.

Although the Saudi government remains staunchly conservative, it has before it the example of Iran, where a similar Islamic fundamentalist movement overthrew a well-established monarchy. Furthermore, the Shia Muslim population of the country is concentrated in al-Hasa Province, where the oil fields are located. The government's immediate fear after the Great Mosque seizure was of an outside plot inspired by Iran. When this plot did not materialize, the Saudis feared Shia involvement. Outside of increased security measures, the principal result of the incident has been a large increase in funding for the Shia community to ease socioeconomic tensions.

THE ECONOMY

Oil was discovered in Saudi Arabia in 1938, but exports did not begin until after World War II. Reserves in 1997 were 261 million barrels, 26 percent of the world's oil supply. The oil industry was controlled by Aramco (Arabian–American Oil Company), a consortium of four U.S. oil companies. In 1980, it came under Saudi government control, but Aramco continued to manage marketing and distribution services. The last American president of Aramco retired in 1989 and was succeeded by a Saudi.

King Faisal's re-organization of finances and development plans in the 1960s set the kingdom on an upward course of rapid development. The economy took off after 1973, when the Saudis, along with other Arab oil-producing states, reduced production and imposed an export embargo on Western countries as a gesture of support to Egypt in its war with Israel. After 1973, the price per barrel of Saudi oil continued to increase, to a peak of $34.00 per barrel in 1981. (Prior to the embargo, it was $3.00 per barrel; in 1979, it was $13.30 per barrel.) The outbreak of the Iran–Iraq War in 1980 caused a huge drop in world production. The Saudis took up the slack.

The huge revenues from oil made possible economic development on a scale undreamed of by Ibn Saud and his Bedouin warriors. The old fishing ports of Yanbu, on the Red Sea, and Jubail, on the Persian Gulf, were transformed into new industrial cities, with oil refineries, cement and petrochemical plants, steel mills, and dozens of related industries. Riyadh experienced a building boom; Cadillacs bumped into camels on the streets, and the shops filled up with imported luxury goods. Every Saudi, it seemed, profited from the boom through free education and health care, low-interest housing loans, and guaranteed jobs.

The economic boom also lured workers from many poor countries, who were attracted by the high wages and benefits available in Saudi Arabia. Most came from such countries as Pakistan, Korea, and the Philippines, but the largest single contingent was from Yemen, next door. However, the bottom dropped out of the Saudi economy in the late 1980s. Oil prices fell, and the kingdom was forced to draw heavily on its cash reserves. Yemen's support for Iraq during the Gulf War was the last straw; the government deported 850,000 Yemeni workers, seriously disrupting the Yemeni economy with the shutdown in remittances.

In recent years, the economy has regained much of its lost momentum. This is due partly to increase oil production and higher oil prices but also to steep cuts in government spending and reduction of unprofitable grain subsidies. These subsidies, which averaged $2 billion annually, were paid to farmers to encourage them to grow wheat and barley, to establish self-sufficiency in flour, and to increase non-oil exports. But the cost to the treasury far exceeded the benefits. Also, the expansion of production of these crops has seriously depleted the water table.

THE FUTURE
Its size, distance from major Middle Eastern urban centers, and oil wealth historically have insulated Saudi Arabia from the winds of political change. Domestic and foreign policy alike evolve from within the ruling family. Officials who undertake independent policy actions are quickly brought into line (an example being the

freewheeling former oil minister Shaykh Zamani). The ruling family is also closely aligned with the ulema; Saudi rulers since Ibn Saud's time have held the title "Guardians of the Holy Mosques" (of Mecca and Medina), giving them a preeminent position in the Islamic world. Except for the army, the ulema form the only organized group in the kingdom outside of the royal family, and they help to legitimize the government, although at a price.

Saudi Arabia marked its Diamond Jubilee as a nation in 1992, but with a society vastly changed since 1932, when Riyadh was a remote, walled town deep in the desert, reachable only by camelback along faint, dusty tracks. Today, Riyadh is a sprawling metropolis of 1.5 million. Yet, since 1932, the political system has changed hardly at all, in a country still ruled by the sons of Ibn Saud through an extended-family decision-making structure. Pressures to broaden this structure have increased markedly in recent years with the spread of education and the economic modernization of society. While agreeing in principle to changes, the House of Saud, strongly supported by the religious leaders, has held fast to its patriarchal system.

Given these strictures, it was somewhat surprising in 1991 when the ulema submitted a list of 11 "demands" to King Fahd. The most important one was the formation of a *Majlis al-Shura* (Consultative Council), which would have the power to initiate legislation and advise the government on foreign policy. The king's response, developed in deliberate stages with extensive behind-the-scenes consultation, in typical Saudi style, was to issue in February 1992 an 83-article "Organic Law," comparable in a number of respects to a Western constitution. The law sets out the basic rules for Saudi government; it went into effect by royal decree in August 1993. It defines the Saudi governing system as comprising the Majlis al-Shura; the Council of Ministers (cabinet); and regional, provincial, and local councils. The first Majlis was appointed in 1993 for a 4-year term. At the time of expiration of its term, the speaker stated that the new Shura would be appointed rather than elected as requested by groups interested in broadening the political process. However, nonpartisan "elections" for the 18-member Riyadh Chamber of Commerce were held in 1996, with similar elections in other Saudi cities scheduled for late 1997.

Saudi Arabia is defined in the Organic Law as an Arab Islamic sovereign state (Article 5), with Islam the state religion (Article 1), and as a monarchy under the

rule of Ibn Saud's descendants. Other articles establish an independent judiciary under Islamic law (*shari'a*) and define the powers and responsibilities of the ruler.

Aside from some internal pressures, mainly from intellectuals, the main reason for Fahd's decision to broaden the political process was the Gulf War, which exposed the Saudi system to international scrutiny and pointed up the risks of patriarchal government. A major difference between the Saudi Organic Law and Western-style constitutions is the absence of references to political, civil, and social rights. Political parties as such remain illegal; but, in 1993, the first human-rights organization in the country, the Committee for the Defense of Legitimate Rights, was formed by a group of academics, tribal leaders, and government officials. Its members included the second-ranking religious scholar, Shaykh Abdullah al-Jubrien, and the former head of Diwan al-Mazalem, the Saudi equivalent of ombudsman. The Committee's goal was the elimination of oppression and injustice, which is considered an important part of its members' religious duty. But its emergence was perceived as a threat to the ulema. An edict condemned it, stating that there was no need for such an organization in a country ruled by Islamic law.

In May 1993, the government arrested Muhammad al-Masari, a distinguished Islamic scholar as well as a theoretical physicist, on charges of publicly criticizing the regime for its human-rights record and lack of progress toward broadening political representation. Masari was later released and deported to England. However, his continued attacks on the Saudi regime led the British government to deport him to the Caribbean island of Dominica in 1996, on the grounds that his presence was damaging to British–Saudi trade relations. After his deportation, he was dismissed as head of the Committee.

Under the circumstances, King Fahd's statement introducing the Organic Law was of little comfort to Westernized Saudis concerned with the lack of human rights, government corruption, and authoritarian rule by the royal family. The transfer of power in January 1996 from the ailing King Fahd to his half-brother Crown Prince Abdullah opened a window to political reform for a brief time. But, within a year, the ruler had recovered and was back at work.

FOREIGN POLICY
The Iraqi invasion and occupation of Kuwait caused a major shift in Saudi policy, away from mediation in regional conflicts and bankrolling of popular causes (such

Wahhabis seize Mecca and Medina
1800

Ibn Saud captures Riyadh in a daring commando raid
1902

Ibn Saud is recognized by the British as the king of Saudi Arabia
1927

Oil exports get under way
1946

King Saud, the eldest son and successor of Ibn Saud, is deposed in favor of his brother Faisal
1963

Faisal is assassinated; succession passes by agreement to Khalid
1975

The Great Mosque in Mecca is seized by a fundamentalist Muslim group
1979

King Khalid dies; succession passes to Crown Prince Fahd; Saudi jets shoot down an Iranian jet for violation of Saudi air space
1980s

1990s

Saudi Arabia hosts foreign troops and shares command in the Gulf War

The Saudi government clamps down on criticism

The Saudi economy stabilizes

as the Palestinian) to one of direct confrontation. For the first time in its history, the Saudi nation felt directly threatened by the actions of an aggressive neighbor. Diplomatic relations were broken with Iraq and subsequently with Jordan and Yemen, due to their support of the Iraqi occupation. Yemeni workers were rounded up and expelled, and harsh restrictions were imposed on Yemeni business owners in the kingdom. Establishment of the UN/U.S.–led coalition against Iraq led to the stationing of foreign non-Muslim troops on Saudi soil, also a historic first.

The failure of the Gulf War to topple the Iraqi regime has led to huge Saudi weapons purchases, mostly from its U.S. ally. This fact, plus the stationing of 5,000 American troops in the country (another historic first, seen by one Arab leader in these terms: "Kuwait and Saudi Arabia are not really independent states, they are part of the U.S. Saudi Arabia only buys weapons to be manned by Americans.")[7] The risks inherent in this American presence were underlined by a June 1996 bomb explosion at a U.S. military housing complex at King Abd al-Aziz Air Base near al-Khobar. The attack killed 19 Americans and injured more than 100.[8]

The country's often difficult relationship with Iran underwent another change in 1991. The fall of the Iranian monarchy and establishment of the Islamic Republic had initially been welcomed by Saudi rulers because of the new regime's fidelity to Islamic principles. But, in 1987, Iranian pilgrims attending the pilgrimage to Mecca undertook anti-Saudi demonstra-

tions that led to a violent confrontation with police, resulting in more than 400 casualties. The two countries broke diplomatic relations; and, in 1988, Saudi Arabia established a quota system for pilgrims on the basis of 1 pilgrim per 1,000 population. The quota system was described as necessary to reduce congestion on the annual pilgrimages, but in fact it would limit Iran to 50,000 pilgrims and limit Iranian-inspired political activism. Iran boycotted the pilgrimage in 1988 and 1989 as a result.

Relations with neighboring Gulf states have also improved. Long-time border disputes with Qatar and Yemen have been resolved amicably, with demarcation through largely featureless desert territory. In the Yemeni case, the border was demarcated by a joint arbitration commission to extend from Jebel Thar to the Omani border, on the basis of the 1934 Treaty of Taif.

After a less violent incident in 1992, the Saudi government banned all parades and demonstrations for the foreseeable future. Subsequent pilgrimages passed without incident. In 1997, the government increased the Iranian pilgrim quota to 100,000.

NOTES

1. He had 24 sons by 16 different women during his lifetime (1880–1953). See William Quandt, *Saudi Arabia in the 1980's* (Washington, D.C.: Brookings Institution, 1981), Appendix E, for a genealogy.

2. George Rentz, "The Saudi Monarchy," in Willard A. Beling, ed., *King Faisal and the Mod-*

ernization of Saudi Arabia (Boulder, CO: Westview Press, 1980), pp. 26–27.

3. *Ibid.,* p. 29.

4. The wall was torn down by his successor, King Faisal. Justin Coe, in *The Christian Science Monitor* (February 13, 1985).

5. Gordon Gaskill, "Saudi Arabia's Modern Monarch," *Reader's Digest* (January 1967), p. 118.

6. Ministry of Information, Kingdom of Saudi Arabia, *Faisal Speaks* (n.d.), p. 88.

7. Quoted in Scott Peterson, "Peace in the Balance," *The Christian Science Monitor* (August 6, 1997), p. 9.

8. Earlier, four Muslim militants convicted of a 1995 car bombing at a U.S. training facility in Riyadh, which killed five Americans, were beheaded under Saudi law. But, despite a $2.7 million reward offered by King Fahd for the arrest of those responsible, the reward remains unclaimed.

DEVELOPMENT

The 1997 budget anticipated a $4.5 billion deficit, 3.3% of GDP. However, an increase in oil revenues to $43.7 billion and a highly favorable balance of trade were expected to offset the deficit. Saudi Arabia is the United States' largest oil supplier, with exports of 1.32 million b/d.

FREEDOM

Despite international criticism of its poor human-rights record, Saudi Arabia continues to observe strict Islamic law. Political freedom and Western-style civil rights do not exist. In 1995 there were 141 beheadings, compared to 53 in 1994. Most of them were for drug trafficking, and a number involved foreigners, mainly Turks.

HEALTH/WELFARE

New quotas were set in 1996 to put limits on the employment of expatriate workers and thus encourage Saudi participation in economic development. The quotas were coupled with higher salary levels for Saudi workers over expatriates ($1,600 to $2,133 for Saudi engineers, as compared with $1,200 to $1,600 for foreign engineers, for example).

ACHIEVEMENTS

As part of the "rediscovery" of its desert heritage, Saudi Arabia has taken the lead in the region in wildlife preservation and restoration of the natural environment. Some 14 protected wildlife areas have been set up, covering 10 percent of the country; and state-of-the-art captive breeding programs have re-introduced several species to the wild, where they are safe from jeep-riding hunters.

Sudan (Democratic Republic of Sudan)

GEOGRAPHY

Area in Square Kilometers (Miles):
2,504,530 (967,500) (about ¼ the size
of the continental United States)
Capital (Population): Khartoum
(1,000,000 est.)
Climate: dry in the north to tropical in
the south

PEOPLE

Population

Total: 31,065,000
Annual Growth Rate: 2.35%
Rural/Urban Population Ratio: 73/27
Ethnic Makeup: 52% black; 39% Arab;
6% Beja; 3% others
Major Languages: Arabic; Dinka;
Nubian; Nuer; others

Health

Life Expectancy at Birth: 54 years
(male); 56 years (female)
Infant Mortality Rate (Ratio): 78/1,000
Average Caloric Intake: 99% of FAO
minimum
Physicians Available (Ratio): 1/10,000

Religions

70% Sunni Muslim in north; 25%
indigenous beliefs; 5% Christian

Education

Adult Literacy Rate: 32%

COMMUNICATION

Telephones: 68,500
Newspapers: 2 dailies in English, 2 in
Arabic; party newspapers

TRANSPORTATION

Highways—Kilometers (Miles): 20,703
(12,919)
Railroads—Kilometers (Miles): 5,516
(3,428)
Usable Airfields: 70

GOVERNMENT

Type: formerly under military rule but
reverted to nominal civilian authority in
1993
Independence Date: January 1, 1956
Head of State: President Omar Hassan
al-Bashir
Political Parties: suspended since 1989;
the National Islamic Front, a
quasi-political organization dominates
political life
Suffrage: universal adult

MILITARY

Number of Armed Forces: 74,500
*Military Expenditures (% of Central
Government Expenditures):* 7.3%
Current Hostilities: civil war

ECONOMY

Currency ($ U.S. Equivalent): 980
Sudanese dinars = $1
Per Capita Income/GDP: $870/$23.7
billion
Inflation Rate: 70%
Total Foreign Debt: $17 billion
Natural Resources: oil; iron ore;
copper; chrome; other industrial metals
Agriculture: cotton; peanuts; sesame;
gum arabic; sorghum; wheat
Industry: textiles; cement; cotton
ginning; edible oils; distilling;
pharmaceuticals

FOREIGN TRADE

Exports: $419 million
Imports: $1.7 billion

A Divided Land

Sudan is really two nations, a Muslim Arab north ("Brown") and a Christian
or animistic south ("Black"), peopled by various sub-Saharan groups. One of
these is the Dinka, very tall, spear-carrying cattle herders. A young Dinka,
7-foot, 6-inch Manute Bol, was the star center on the University of Bridgeport,
Connecticut, basketball team during the 1984–1985 season, although he had
never played the game before coming to the United States.

The traditional separation of north and south deepened after independence, as southerners fought for greater autonomy and a share in economic development. The imposition of strict Islamic law over the
non-Muslim population in 1983 led to a renewal of the Civil War, a conflict
that has yet to be resolved.

Sudan
- ✪ Capital
- ⊙ Region Capital
- ● City
- — River
- --- Road

0   150 kilometers
0   150 miles

SUDAN

Sudan is the largest nation in Africa. The bulk of the population is concentrated in the province of Khartoum (also the name of the capital) and in the central region, which includes the Blue Nile and the White Nile, the country's principal rivers.

The name of the country underscores its distinctive social structure. Centuries ago, Arab geographers named it *Bilad al-Sudan,* "Land of the Blacks." The northern half, including Khartoum, is Arabic in language, culture, and traditions, and Islamic in religion. The southern half is sub-Saharan African, made up of a number of black African peoples—the Shilluk, Dinka, Nuer, Azande, and many others. Some of them are Christian due to the efforts of European mission schools established during the British occupation. Others practice traditional religions.

The two halves of Sudan have little or nothing in common. The country's basic political problem is how to achieve unity between these two different societies, which were brought together under British rule to form an artificial nation.

HISTORY

The ancient history of Sudan, at least of the northern region, was always linked with that of Egypt. The pharaohs and later conquerors of Egypt—Persians, Greeks, Romans, and eventually the Arabs, Turks, and British—periodically attempted to extend their power farther south. The connection with Egypt became very close when the Egyptians were converted to Islam by invading armies from Arabia, in the seventh century A.D. As the invaders spread southward, they converted the northern Sudanese people to Islam, developing in time an Islamic Arab society in northern Sudan. Southern Sudan remained comparatively untouched, because it was isolated by the geographical barriers of mountain ranges and the great impassable swamps of the Nile.

The two regions were forcibly brought together by conquering Egyptian armies in the nineteenth century. The conquest became possible after the exploration of sub-Saharan Africa by Europeans. After the explorers and armies came slave traders and then European fortune hunters, interested in developing the gold, ivory, diamonds, timber, and other resources of sub-Saharan Africa.

The soldiers and slave traders were the most brutal of all these invaders, particularly in southern Sudan. In fact, many of the slave traders were Muslim Sudanese from the north. The Civil War between the Islamic north and the Christian/animist south, which began in 1955 and is still

going on, had its roots in the nineteenth-century experiences of the southerners, as "memories of plunder, slave raiding and suffering" at the hands of slavers and their military allies were passed down from generation to generation.[1]

THE ORIGINS OF THE SUDANESE STATE

The first effort to establish a nation in Sudan began in the 1880s, when the country was ruled by the British as part of their protectorate over Egypt. The British were despised as foreign, non-Muslim rulers. The Egyptians, who made up the bulk of the security forces assigned to Sudan, were hated for their arrogance and mistreatment of the Sudanese.

In 1881, a religious leader in northern Sudan announced that he was the *Mahdi,* the "Awaited One," who, according to Sunni Islamic belief, would appear on Earth, sent by God to rid Sudan of its foreign rulers. The Mahdi called for a jihad (struggle or holy war) against the British and the Egyptians.

Sudanese by the thousands flocked to join the Mahdi. His warriors, fired by revolutionary zeal, defeated several British-led Egyptian armies. In 1885, they captured Khartoum, and, soon thereafter, the Mahdi's rule extended over the whole of present-day Sudan. For this reason, the Mahdi is remembered, at least in northern Sudan, as Abu al-Istiqlal, the "Father of Independence."[2]

The Mahdi's rule did not last long; he died in 1886. His chief lieutenant and successor, the Khalifa Abdallahi, continued in power until 1898, when a British force armed with guns mowed down his spear-carrying, club-wielding army. Sudan was ruled jointly by Britain and Egypt from then until 1955. Since the British already ruled Egypt as a protectorate, for all practical purposes, joint rule meant British rule.

Under the British, Sudan was divided into a number of provinces, and British university graduates staffed the country's first civil service.[3] But the British followed two policies that have created problems for Sudan since it became independent. One was "indirect rule" in the north. Rather than developing a group of trained Sudanese administrators who could take over when they left, the British governed indirectly through local chiefs and religious leaders. The second policy was to separate southern from northern Sudan through "Closed Door" laws, which prohibited northerners from working in, or even visiting, the south.

Sudan became independent on New Year's Day 1956, as a republic headed by

a civilian government. The first civilian government lasted until 1958, when a military group seized power "to save the country from the chaotic regime of the politicians."[4] But the military regime soon became as "chaotic" as its predecessors. In 1964, it handed over power to another civilian group. The second civilian group was no more successful than the first had been, as the politicians continued to feud, and intermittent conflict between government forces and rebels in the southern region turned into all-out civil war.

In 1969, the Sudanese Army carried out another military coup, headed by Colonel Ja'far (or Gaafar) Nimeiri. Successive Sudanese governments since independence, including Nimeiri's, have faced the same basic problems: the unification of north and south, an economy hampered by inadequate transportation and few resources, and the building of a workable political system. Nimeiri's record in dealing with these difficult problems is one explanation for his longevity in power. A written Constitution was approved in 1973. Although political parties were outlawed, an umbrella political organization, the Sudan Socialist Union (SSU), provided an alternative to the fractious political jockeying that had divided the nation before Nimeiri.[5]

Nimeiri's firm control through the military and his effectiveness in carrying out political reforms were soon reflected at the ballot box. He was elected president in 1971 for a 6-year term and was re-elected in 1977. Yet broad popular support did not generate political stability. There were a number of attempts to overthrow him, the most serious in 1971 and 1976, when he was actually captured and held for a time by rebels.

One reason for his survival may be his resourcefulness. After the 1976 coup attempt, for example, instead of having his opponents executed, he invited them and other opposition leaders to form a government of national unity. One of Nimeiri's major opponents, Sadiq al-Mahdi, a great grandson of the Mahdi and himself an important religious leader, accepted the offer and returned from exile.

Nimeiri's major achievement was to end temporarily the Civil War between north and south. An agreement was signed in 1972 in Addis Ababa, Ethiopia, mediated by Ethiopian authorities, between his government and the southern Anya Anya resistance movement. The agreement provided for regional autonomy for the south's three provinces, greater representation of southerners in the National People's Assembly, and integration of Anya Anya units into the armed forces without restrictions.

THE COUP OF 1985

Nimeiri was re-elected in 1983 for a third presidential term. Most of his political opponents had apparently been reconciled with him, and the army and state security forces were firmly under his control. It seemed that Sudan's most durable leader would round out another full term in office without too much difficulty. But storm clouds were brewing on the horizon. Nimeiri had survived for 16 years in power largely through his ability to keep opponents divided and off balance by his unpredictable moves. From 1983 on, however, his policies seemed designed to unite rather than divide them.

The first step in Nimeiri's undoing was his decision to impose Islamic law (Shari'a) over the entire country. The impact fell heaviest on the non-Muslim southern region. In a 1983 interview, Nimeiri explained his reasons for the action. His goal from the start of his regime, he said, was "to raise government by the book [i.e., the Koran] from the level of the individual to that of government." If the Sudanese, with their numerous ethnic and cultural differences and the country's vast size, were governed properly by God's Book, they would provide an example of peace and security to neighboring countries.[6]

In Nimeiri's view, the application of Islamic restrictions on alcohol, tobacco, and other prohibited forms of behavior was appropriate to Sudanese Muslims and non-Muslims alike, since "Islam was revealed to serve man and all its legislation has the goal of regulating family, social, and individual life and raising the level of the individual."[7]

The new draconian measures were widely resented, but particularly in the south, where cigarettes and home-brewed beer were popular palliatives for a harsh existence. When Nimeiri continued his "Islamic purification" process with a reorganization of Sudanese administration into several large regions in order to streamline the cumbersome bureaucracy inherited from the British, the southerners reacted strongly. Consolidation of three autonomous provinces into one directly under central-government control was seen by them as a violation of the commitment made to regional autonomy that had ended the Civil War. An organized guerrilla army, the Sudan People's Liberation Army (SPLA), resumed civil war under the expert leadership of U.S.–trained colonel John Garang. The rebels' new strategy was not only to oppose government troops but also to strike at development projects essential to the economy.

Foreign workers in the newly developed oil fields in southwestern Sudan were kidnapped or killed; as a result, Chevron Oil Company halted all work on the project.

A crackdown on Islamic fundamentalist groups, particularly the Muslim Brotherhood, added to Nimeiri's growing list of opponents. Members of the Brotherhood had been active in implementing Islamic law as the law of the land, but Nimeiri felt that they had gone too far. By late 1984, it appeared that the president had angered or alienated everybody in the country, all for different reasons.

In the end, it was the failure of his economic policies rather than anything else that brought about Nimeiri's fall. The International Monetary Fund imposed strict austerity requirements on Sudan in 1984 as a prerequisite to a $90 million standby loan to enable the country to pay its mounting food and fuel bills. The food bills were aggravated by famine, the fuel bills by the necessity to import almost all fuel requirements. The IMF insisted on drastic budget cuts, devaluation of currency, and an end to subsidies on basic commodities. If Nimeiri had been able to carry out these reforms, he would have stood a chance of restoring the country to solvency and his own rule to respectability. Protests turned to riots, mainly over the end of price subsidies and a consequent 33 percent increase in the prices of such necessities as bread, sugar, and cooking oil. Other protests erupted over the application of Islamic law, especially the ban on alcohol, which brought thousands of Sudanese into the streets shouting "We want beer! We want beer!"

Nimeiri's departure for the United States to seek further economic help triggered a general strike in 1985. A genuine national movement arose, uniting students and professionals with the urban poor, all demanding that Nimeiri resign. Fearing anarchy or an uprising by young army officers, the senior military leaders moved quickly, took over the government, and ordered Nimeiri deposed. Crowds in Khartoum shouted, "Nimeiri the butcher is finished; the country belongs to the people." "He's nothing, let him sell lemons," cried one demonstrator, and others tore Nimeiri's picture from devalued banknotes.[8]

The new military government, headed by General Abd al-Rahman Swareddahab, a highly respected senior officer, promised to hold elections within a year to restore civilian rule and to revive political parties. That promise was kept: In 1986, elections were held for a new People's Assembly. Two revived pre-Nimeiri parties, the Umma and the Democratic Unionist Party

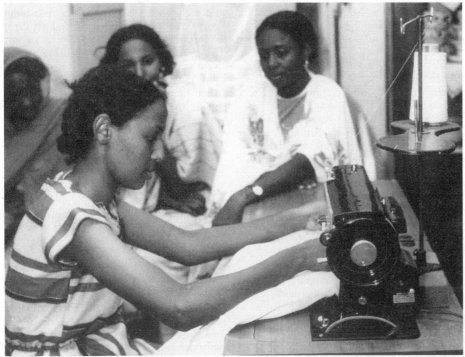

(UN photo/Louise Gubb)

The attainment of political stability is important to Sudanese development, but it will be a strong economy that makes for lasting peace. Job training is extremely important. This woman in a sewing class in Khartoum represents the need for creating a skilled labor pool.

(DUP), won the majority of seats, with the fundamentalist National Islamic Front emerging as a strong third party. Sadiq al-Mahdi, head of the Umma, automatically became prime minister; his principal rival, DUP leader Ahmed Ali al-Mirghani, was chosen as president. The new prime minister chose a coalition cabinet to begin the arduous process of restoring the democratic process to Sudan after 15 years of Nimeiri.

But the euphoria over the departure of "Nimeiri the Butcher" soon gave way to the realization that the problems that had daunted him remained unresolved. They included heavy foreign indebtedness, a weak economy, inefficient agricultural production, an inadequate transportation system, party and personal rivalries, and extreme distrust between north and south in the divided Sudanese nation.

INTERNAL PROBLEMS
The al-Mahdi government had no more success than its predecessors in resolving Sudan's endemic political disunity. Efforts to limit the application of Islamic law throughout the country were blocked by

the National Islamic Front (NIF) in 1988. The Civil War then heated up. SPLA success in capturing the principal towns in the south led the DUP to sign a separate agreement with the rebels for a cease-fire. The People's Assembly rejected the agreement, and the DUP then withdrew from the government.

Faced with the imminent collapse of civilian authority, the armed forces again seized power, in Sudan's fourth military coup since independence. The army moved after food shortages and soaring inflation, fed by war costs of $1 million a day, led to riots in Khartoum and other cities. A Revolutionary Council, headed by Lieutenant General Omar Hassan al-Bashir, suspended the Constitution and arrested government leaders.

In 1992, Bashir appointed a 300-member National Transitional Assembly to lay the groundwork—at least in theory—for a return to civilian rule. Its members included military leaders (those who sat on the ruling Revolutionary Council), provincial (state) governors, and some former government leaders. Its primary function was to implement Council decrees; during

the transitional period, however, it could develop legislation.

The regime also sought to broaden its popular base through the establishment of local elections. The elections were held in two stages, the first stage being the election of people's congresses (at the village and town level); in the second stage of the process, the congresses then elected provincial legislatures. Due to the Civil War, the southern region remained unrepresented.

The regime's increasing economic difficulties and its international isolation as a "rogue" Islamic state committed to terrorism led Bashir to take steps toward restoring civilian government in 1995, mainly in order to regain the country's respectability and thus invite foreign investors. By then, the ruling Revolutionary Council had already been abolished; the Transitional National Assembly was to oversee the transition. In 1996, the first national elections in a decade were held to elect a president and a 400-member Parliament to replace the Transitional Assembly. Not surprisingly, Bashir was elected president, garnering 75.5 percent of the 5.5 million voters (the south was excluded). Hassan al-Turabi, head of the powerful National Islamic Front, which has ruled Sudan indirectly through the military regime since the coup, was elected speaker of the new Parliament. Bashir and Turabi described the election system as a political innovation, a non-party system with universal participation under Islam, which obviated any need for political parties.

The "new" civilian government also undertook an administrative reorganization. Sudan was divided into 26 states (10 in the southern region), along with a federal district around Khartoum. Each state would have full executive and legislative authority over its territory.

THE CIVIL WAR
The government gained some ground against rebels in the Civil War in late 1991, when the SPLA split into contending factions. One faction, led by Lieutenant Rick Machar, accused SPLA commander John Garang of a dictatorial reign of terror within the organization. The split became tribal when Nuer troops of Machar's faction invaded Dinka territory; the Dinkas are Garang's main supporters. Some 100,000 Dinka fled their homeland during the fighting. Sudan government forces took advantage of internal SPLA rivalry to capture several important southern towns during an offensive in March 1992.

The ethnic killings of Nuer and Dinka, along with famine (which has been intensified by the SPLA infighting) led other

(UN photo 157681/Milton Grant)

The lives of millions of people in Sudan have been disrupted by the Civil War and years of drought. This displaced mother and her child are waiting for medical attention in Nasir.

African states and, in late 1993, the United States to attempt to mediate and bring the two factions together as a prelude to ending the Civil War. But even the presence of former U.S. president Jimmy Carter as mediator failed to bridge the differences separating the two SPLA leaders. And the major differences between southerners and northerners—imposition of Islamic law on non-Muslims, revenue sharing among regions, states' rights and powers versus those of the national government—seemed insurmountable.

The hardline positions of the SPLA and the regime in regard to these differences were intensified in the 1990s by the success of the National Islamic Front in gaining control over the Revolutionary Council. The security forces, the judiciary, and the universities were purged of moderate or liberal staff members and replaced by NIF fundamentalists. In 1991, the regime bowed to NIF pressure and issued an edict making Islamic law the "law of the land" in both north and south Sudan. As a result, the Civil War intensified.

PEACE AT LAST?

Africa's longest war seemed to have run its course in 1997 with the signing of peace agreements between the government and the various SPLA factions. The agreements followed a series of SPLA victories.

As reported by a U.S. team of Africa specialists who attended the signing of the agreements, southern Sudan is to be governed by a coordinating council made up of the president of the republic, the cabinet, and the governors of the 10 southern states. At the end of a 4-year interim period, these states would hold a referendum to enable the southern Sudanese to choose between independence and full integration with the north. Other provisions guaranteed freedom of religion, belief, and worship; the establishment of Islamic law as the basis for legislation but with recognition of the south's non-Islamic cultural and ethnic distinctness; and the creation of an independent Supreme Court with final authority over constitutional interpretation.

In principle, the agreements seemed to meet the basic demands of both sides. But government forces used the cease-fire lull to rebuild. A patriotic fervor swept over the Islamic north, with women in Khartoum selling their jewelry to pay for the war effort. Former U.S. president Jimmy Carter revisited the country in July in a vain effort to convince the warring sides to extend the cease-fire and honor the peace agreements, but he came away empty-handed. It seemed that Africa's longest war was destined to continue until all participants were exhausted.

THE ECONOMY

Although the attainment of political stability is important to Sudanese development, it depends in the long run on the economy—creating jobs, educating youths, building a future for the country's population that will keep pace with population growth. Unfortunately, the Sudanese economy is still a weak reed to lean on. The economy is largely dependent on agriculture. The most important crop is cotton, and cotton exports are affected by world demand and resulting price fluctuations. Until recently, the only other Sudanese export crop of importance was gum arabic.

Because Sudan has great agricultural potential, due to its rivers, alluvial soils, and vast areas of unused arable land, Nimeiri had set out in the 1970s to develop the country into what experts told him could be the "breadbasket" of the Middle East. Enough food could be grown through the expansion of agriculture, he was told, to meet all domestic needs, raise the country's low standard of living, and cover the food needs of all the Arab countries, most of which are not self-sufficient and must import food. To reach this ambitious goal, cotton plantations were converted to production of grain crops. The huge Kenana sugar-refinery complex was started with joint foreign and Sudanese management; the long-established Gezira cotton scheme was expanded; and work began on the Jonglei Canal, intended to drain a vast marshy area called the Sudd (swamp) in the south, in order to bring hundreds of thousands of acres of marshlands under cultivation.

But the breadbasket was never filled. It was as if the Sudanese government had had a good idea but had implemented it from the wrong end. Mismanagement and lack of skilled labor delayed some projects, while others languished because the roads and communications systems needed to implement them did not exist. The most critical need was for domestic sources of oil. Oil was discovered in the southwest in the early 1980s by Chevron Oil Company. Early projections were for production of 50,000 barrels per day by 1986. But the work came to a halt in 1984 due to the resumption of the Civil War. Although production has resumed, on a small scale, most of Sudan's oil needs must be met through imports. Thus far, Iran, Libya, and Iraq (before the Gulf War) have provided the country with oil on favorable terms, at below world-market rates. And in 1995, new discoveries in the Greater Heglig oil field being developed by a Canadian firm indicated reserves of 50 million barrels.

However, the aid needed for the country's development has yet to materialize. The United States suspended aid in 1991, the result of Sudan's support for Iraq during the Gulf War. In 1993, the World Bank cut off *all* funding after the Bashir government failed to pay $37 million in arrears for project loans.

The government claimed in 1992 that a 3-year salvation program "based on Islam" had generated considerable growth; good wheat and sorghum crops had eliminated the need for imports, and the country was now self-sufficient in food. But it offered no proof. Exports of cotton, Sudan's only significant crop, brought in revenues of $96 million in 1995, far below expenditures, which included $1 million a day for the Civil War.

A major problem with oil development, apart from the Civil War, stems from lack of transport facilities. The nearest refinery is at Port Sudan, 840 miles from the oil fields on the Red Sea. Rather than build a new on-site refinery, the Nimeiri government decided to construct a $1 billion pipeline from the fields to the refinery. The southern Sudanese objected to the proposed pipeline, on the grounds that it would take away oil revenues that were rightfully theirs. The pipeline project along with Nimeiri's imposition of Islamic law were the main causes for the renewal of the Civil War.

FAMINE

The Sudanese people traditionally have lived on a barter economy, with little need for money. Huge budget deficits and high prices for basic commodities hardly affect the mass of the population. But the Civil War and a 12-year drought cycle in the sub-Saharan Sahel region, which includes Sudan, have changed their subsistence way of life into one of destitution.

The drought became critical in 1983, and millions of refugees from Ethiopia and Chad, the countries most affected, moved into temporary camps in Sudan. Then it was Sudan's turn to suffer. Desperate families fled from their villages as wells dried up, cattle died, and crops wilted. By 1985, an estimated 9 million persons, half of them native Sudanese, were dying of starvation. Emergency food supplies from many countries poured into Sudan; but, due to inadequate transportation, port delays, and diversion of shipments by incompetent or dishonest officials, much of this relief could not be delivered to those who most needed it. Bags of grain lay on the docks, waiting

An Egyptian province under Muhammad Ali
1820

Mahdi rebellion against the British and Egyptians
1881

The British recapture Khartoum; establishment of joint Anglo-Egyptian control
1898

The Civil War begins
1955

Sudan becomes an independent republic
1956

Nimeiri seizes power
1969

Nimeiri is overthrown in a bloodless coup; millions of people die of starvation; the Civil War resumes in the south
1980s

1990s

Sudan remains ravaged by the Civil War

The Bashir regime fails to resolve the war or deal with the country's chronic economic problems

The regime institutes systematic slavery

for trucks that did not come because they were immobilized somewhere else, stuck in the sand or mired in the mud of one of Sudan's few passable roads.

Equally distressing things were happening along Sudan's one railroad. While refugees starved in Darfur Province, heavy rains to the east washed out track sections. Out of one shipment of 6,000 tons, half vanished before arrival at Nyala. "Use your imagination," a UN distribution official told a reporter, indicating corruption or theft, or both.[9] Meanwhile, at the far end of this thin lifeline, children grew weaker daily from malnutrition. Hassan Atiya, Sudanese deputy commissioner for refugees, estimated the death rate for children at 2,000 per day, in the worst famine of this century.

Sudan's political instability compounded the hunger problem. SPLA control of the south had forced the government to suspend the April 1986 elections there, so the region was unrepresented in the National Assembly. The rebels refused to allow delivery of relief supplies on government planes and shot one down to make their point.

The end of the drought in 1987 and improved food production sharply reduced the number of Sudanese needing emergency relief, from 4.3 million to 1.2 million by 1994. But the endless Civil War continues to affect the population of the southern region. By 1994, some 400,000 Sudanese were refugees in neighboring African countries. Apart from war-related deaths, malnutrition, and water-borne diseases, the conflict led to an epidemic of sleeping sickness in Western Equatoria, a province isolated from the rest of the country since 1990 and totally lacking in medical care as a result.[10]

Apart from the devastation of the Civil War, Sudan suffered a severe economic blow when its backing of Iraq in the Gulf War resulted in the expulsion of 300,000 Sudanese expatriate workers from the Arab Gulf states. The country lost the $445 million annually in remittances accrued from this source of revenue. Then, in 1996, the UN Security Council passed *Resolution 1044,* imposing an economic embargo on the country for its failure to extradite three Sudanese nationals to Egypt; they were charged with the attempt to assassinate Egyptian president Mubarak during his official visit to Ethiopia. In 1997, the United States imposed sweeping economic sanctions on Sudan due to its poor human-rights record, support of international terrorism, and the involvement of Sudanese nationals in attempted bombings of the United Nations and other New York buildings. Sudanese assets in the United States were frozen, and exports to the country were banned under the International Emergency Economic Powers Act.

NOTES

1. Dunstan Wai, *The African-Arab Conflict in the Sudan* (New York: Africana Publishing Co., 1981), p. 32.

2. Southerners are not so favorable; in the south, the Mahdi's government was as cruel as the Egyptian. *Ibid.,* p. 31.

3. Peter M. Holt, in *The History of the Sudan,* 3rd ed. (London: Weidenfeld and Nicolson, 1979), p. 123, quotes the British governor as saying that they were recruited on the basis of "good health, high character and fair abilities."

4. *Ibid.,* p. 171.

5. The SSU is defined as "a grand alliance of workers, farmers, intellectuals, business people and soldiers." Harold D. Nelson, ed., *Sudan, A Country Study* (Washington, D.C.: American University, Foreign Area Studies, 1982), p. 199.

6. Quoted in Tareq Y. Ismael and Jacqueline S. Ismael, *Government and Politics in Islam* (New York: St. Martin's Press, 1985), Appendix, pp. 148–149.

7. *Ibid.,* p. 150.

8. *The Christian Science Monitor* (April 16, 1985).

9. David K. Willis, in *The Christian Science Monitor* (July 11, 1985).

10. James C. McKinley, Jr., in *The New York Times International* (July 18, 1997).

DEVELOPMENT

The Civil War, large foreign debts, and the loss of foreign remittances continue to block development in Sudan. The only recent development project completed is a sewage system for Khartoum.

FREEDOM

Elections were held for a 400-member National Assembly in 1996 as a step toward the restoration of civilian government and, with it, constitutional freedoms. However, Islamic law remains in force for both Muslim and non-Muslim regions.

HEALTH/WELFARE

The UN embargo and sanctions imposed for Sudan's noncompliance with the order for extradition for Sudanese implicated in the assassination attempt on Egyptian president Mubarak have imposed severe hardships on the nation. In 1996, the government set up 35 distribution centers to sell basic commodities to the public at subsidized prices to lessen the impact of the embargo.

ACHIEVEMENTS

Agriculture, which employs 80% of the labor force, improved in 1994, with bumper crops in cotton, wheat, and gum arabic, Sudan's main crops. As a result, GDP grew 7% in that year.

Syria (Syrian Arab Republic)

GEOGRAPHY
Area in Square Kilometers (Miles):
185,170 (71,500) (about the size of
North Dakota)
Capital (Population): Damascus
(1,600,000)
Climate: predominantly dry, but
considerable variation between the
interior and coastal regions

PEOPLE

Population
Total: 15,609,000
Annual Growth Rate: 3.4%
Rural/Urban Population Ratio: 49/51
Ethnic Makeup: 90% Arab; 10%
Kurdish, Armenian, and others
Major Languages: Arabic; Kurdish;
Armenian

Health
Life Expectancy at Birth: 66 years
(male); 68 years (female)
Infant Mortality Rate (Ratio): 41/1,000
Average Caloric Intake: 120% of FAO
minimum
Physicians Available (Ratio): 1/966

Religions
74% Sunni Muslim; 16% Alawite and
other Muslim sects; 10% Christian and
Jewish

Education
Adult Literacy Rate: 64%

COMMUNICATION
Telephones: 512,600
Newspapers: 3 dailies in Damascus;
others in other major cities

TRANSPORTATION
Highways—Kilometers (Miles): 31,569
(19,699)

Railroads—Kilometers (Miles): 1,998
(1,247)
Usable Airfields: 107

GOVERNMENT
Type: republic under a left-wing
military regime
Independence Date: April 17, 1946
Head of State: President Hafez al-Assad
Political Parties: Ba'th (Arab Socialist
Resurrection Party), dominant; various
minor parties, several forming token
opposition in the People's Assembly
Suffrage: universal at 18

MILITARY
Number of Armed Forces: 346,000
*Military Expenditures (% of Central
Government Expenditures):* 6%
Current Hostilities: maintains troops in
Lebanon; ongoing disputes with Turkey
over water sharing and with Israel over
Golan Heights

ECONOMY
Currency ($ U.S. Equivalent): 41.9
Syrian pounds = $1 (free-market rate)
Per Capita Income/GDP: $850/$14
billion
Inflation Rate: 16.3%
Total Foreign Debt: $19.4 billion
Natural Resources: crude oil; natural
gas; phosphates; chrome; iron;
manganese ores; asphalt; rock salt;
marble; gypsum
Agriculture: cotton; wheat; barley; sugar
beets; tobacco; sheep and goat raising
Industry: petroleum; mining;
manufacturing; textiles; food
processing; construction

FOREIGN TRADE
Exports: $4.8 billion
Imports: $5.8 billion

Ancient Civilizations

In Syria, as in other areas of the Middle East, the visitor is surrounded by the ruined monuments of many long-vanished civilizations. Some are not only visible but still in use. The Roman waterwheels of Hama, for example, turn creakingly, bringing water up from the Orontes River for thirsty citizens as they have for centuries. One comes upon signs of other civilizations suddenly. Palmyra (Tadmor), "Bride of the Desert," appears abruptly at the edge of the ferocious Syrian desert like a mirage of Roman civilization, with its broken columns and arches. Damascus, often considered the world's oldest continuously inhabited city, combines Roman walls, Corinthian columns, Islamic mosques, and colorful Arab *suqs* (markets) in a vivid pageant of diverse civilizations, marred ironically by jarring symbols of the modern world: traffic jams and satellite dishes.

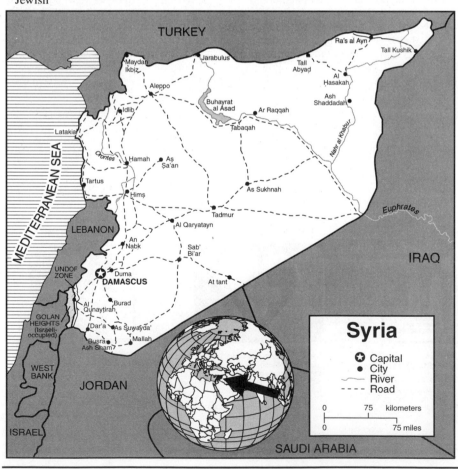

SYRIA

The modern Syrian state is a pale shadow of the Syria that existed centuries ago. In the time of Christ, ancient Syria was a powerful kingdom stretching from the Euphrates River to the Mediterranean Sea. It included the modern countries of Israel, Jordan, Lebanon, Iraq, and southern Turkey. During the first 2 centuries of Islam, the caliphs ("successors" of Muhammad) ruled a vast empire from their capital at Damascus. Arab geographers viewed Syria as a large geographical unit, Bilad ash-Sham.

Modern Syria is a nation of artificial boundaries. Its borders were determined by agreement between France and Britain after World War I. The country's current boundaries are with Turkey, Iraq, Jordan, Israel, and Lebanon. (The only one of these boundaries in dispute is the Golan Heights, which was seized and annexed unilaterally by Israel in the 1970s.) The border with Turkey is defined by a single-track railroad, perhaps the only case in the world of a railroad put to that use. Syria's other borders are artificial lines established by outside powers for convenience.

Syria is artificial in another sense: Its political system was established by outside powers. Since becoming independent in 1946, the Syrians have struggled to find a political system that works for them. The large number of coups and frequent changes in government are evidence of this struggle. The most stable government in Syria's independent history is the current one, which has been in power since 1970.

Syrian political instability stems from the division of the population into separate ethnic and religious groups. The Syrians are an amalgamation of many different ethnoreligious groups that have settled the region over the centuries. The majority of the population are Sunni Muslim Arabs. The Alawis form the largest minority group. Although the Alawis are nominally Shia Muslims, the Sunni Muslims distrust them—not primarily because of religion, but because of the secret nature of their rituals and because as a minority they are very clannish. A second large minority is the Druze, who are distrusted by both Sunni Muslims and Alawis because their religion, an offshoot of Islam, has Christian and Jewish elements and secret rituals. There are a number of Christian denominations, the most important being the Armenians, and a community of Jews with ancient origins. Syria also has a number of groups that are distinguished from the rest of the population by language or origin, the largest group being the Kurds (who are Sunni Muslims).

Although Syrian cities are slowly becoming more homogeneous in population,

(The Bettmann Archive)

A view of Damascus, probably the oldest city in the world.

the different communities still constitute a majority in certain areas. Thus, the Alawis make up 60 percent of the population of the northern coast, the Druze are dominant in the Jabal Druze area in southwestern Syria, and the Kurds live predominantly in the mountains north of Aleppo.

HISTORY

Syria's greatest period was probably that of the Umayyad caliphs (A.D. 661–750). These caliphs were rulers of a vast Islamic empire. The first Umayyad caliph, Muawiya, is considered one of the political geniuses of Islam. He described his political philosophy to a visitor as follows:

> I apply not my lash where my tongue suffices, nor my sword where my whip is enough. If there be one hair binding me to my fellow men I let it not break. If they pull I loosen; if they loosen I pull.[1]

During this period of Umayyad rule, Damascus became a great center of learning and culture. But later Umayyad caliphs were no more successful than their modern Syrian counterparts in developing effective government. They ruled by fear, repression, and heavy taxation. They also made new non-Arab converts to Islam pay a special tax from which Arab Muslims were exempted. They were finally overthrown by non-Arab Muslim invaders from Iraq. From that time until Syria became an independent republic, its destiny was determined by outsiders.

Syria was ruled by the Ottoman Turks for 4 centuries as a part of their empire. It was divided into provinces, each governed by a pasha whose job it was to collect taxes and keep order (with the help of an Ottoman garrison). In mountain areas such as Lebanon, then part of Syria, the Ottomans delegated authority to the heads of powerful families or leaders of religious communities. The Ottomans recognized each of these communities as a *millet,* a Turkish word meaning "nation." The religious head of each millet represented the millet in dealings with Ottoman

(UPI/Bettmann)

Following the successful expulsion of the Ottoman government from Syria in 1918, Emir Faisal (pictured above) was proclaimed king of Syria in 1920.

officials. The Ottomans, in turn, allowed each millet leader to manage the community's internal affairs. The result was that Syrian society became a series of sealed compartments. The millet system has disappeared, but its effects have lingered to the present, making national unity difficult.

The French Mandate

In the nineteenth century, as Ottoman rule weakened and conflict developed among Muslim, Christian, and Druze communities in Syria, the French began to intervene directly in Syria to help the Maronite Christians. French Jesuits founded schools for Christian children. In 1860, French troops landed in Lebanon to protect the Christian Maronites from massacres by the Druze. French forces were withdrawn after the Ottoman government agreed to establish a separate Maronite region in the Lebanese mountains. This arrangement brought about the development of Leba-

non as a nation separate from Syria. The Christians in Syria were less fortunate. About 6,000 of them were slaughtered in Damascus before Ottoman troops restored order.[2]

In the years immediately preceding World War I, numbers of young Syrian Christians and some Muslims were exposed through mission schools to ideas of nationalism and human rights. A movement for Arab independence from Turkish rule gradually developed, centered in Damascus and Beirut. After the start of World War I, the British, with French backing, convinced Arab leaders to revolt against the Ottoman government. The Arab army recruited for the revolt was led by Emir Faisal, the second son of Sharif Husayn of Mecca, leader of the powerful Arab Hashimite family, and the Arab official appointed by the Ottomans as "Protector of the Holy Shrines of Islam." Faisal's forces, along with a British army, drove the Ottomans out of Syria. In 1918, the emir entered Damascus as a conquering hero, and, in 1920, he was proclaimed king of Syria.

Faisal's kingdom did not last long. The British had promised the Arabs independence in a state of their own, in return for their revolt. However, they had also made secret agreements with France to divide the Arab regions of the defeated Ottoman Empire into French and British protectorates. The French would have Syria and Lebanon; the British would have Palestine and Iraq. The French now moved to collect their pound of flesh. They sent an ultimatum to Faisal to accept French rule. When he refused, a French army marched to Damascus, bombarded the city, and forced him into exile. (Faisal was brought back by the British and later was installed as the king of Iraq under a British protectorate.)

What one author calls the "false dawn" of Arab independence was followed by the establishment of direct French control over Syria.[3] The Syrians reacted angrily to what they considered betrayal by their former allies. Resistance to French rule continued throughout the mandate period (1920–1946), and the legacy of bitterness over their betrayal affects Syrian attitudes toward outside powers, particularly Western powers, to this day.[4]

The French did some positive things for Syria. They built schools, roads, and hospitals, developed a productive cotton industry, and established order and peaceful relations among the various communities. But the Syrians remained strongly attached to the goals of Arab unity and Arab independence, first in Syria, then in a future Arab nation.[5]

INDEPENDENT SYRIA

Syria became independent in 1946. The French had promised the Syrians independence during World War II but delayed their departure after the war, hoping to keep their privileged trade position and military bases. Eventually, pressure from the United States, the Soviet Union, and Britain forced the French to leave both Syria and Lebanon.

The new republic began under adverse circumstances. Syrian leaders had little experience in government; the French had not given them much responsibility and had encouraged personal rivalries in their divide-and-rule policy. The Druze and Alawi communities feared that they would be under the thumb of the Sunni majority. In addition to these problems, the establishment in 1948 of the State of Israel next door in Palestine caused great instability in Syria. The failure of Syrian armies to defeat the Israelis was blamed on weak and incompetent leaders.

For 2 decades after independence, Syria had the reputation of being the most unstable country in the Middle East. There were four military coups between 1949 and 1954 and several more between 1961 and 1966. There was also a brief union with Egypt (1958–1961), which ended in an army revolt.

One reason for Syria's chronic instability is that political parties, at least until the 1960s, were simply groups formed around leading personalities. At independence, the country had many such parties. Other parties were formed on the basis of ideology, such as the Syrian Communist Party. In 1963, one party, the Ba'th, acquired control of all political activities. Since then, Syria has been a single-party state.

THE BA'TH

The Ba'th Party (the Arabic word *ba'th* means "resurrection") began in the 1940s as a political party dedicated to Arab unity. It was founded by two Damascus schoolteachers, both French-educated: Michel Aflaq, a Greek Orthodox Christian, and Salah Bitar, a Sunni Muslim. In 1953, the Ba'th merged with another political party, the Arab Socialist Party. Since then, the formal name of the Ba'th has been the Arab Socialist Resurrection Party.

The Ba'th was the first Syrian political party to establish a mass popular base and to draw members from all social classes. Its program called for freedom, Arab unity, and socialism. The movement for Arab unity led to the establishment of the branches of the party in other Arab countries, notably Iraq and Lebanon. The party appealed particularly to young officers in the armed forces; and it attracted strong support from the Alawi community, because it called for social justice and the equality of all Syrians.

The Ba'th was instrumental in 1958 in arranging a merger between Syria and Egypt as the United Arab Republic (U.A.R.). The Ba'thists had hoped to undercut their chief rival, the Syrian Communist Party, by the merger. But they soon decided that they had made a mistake. The Egyptians did not treat the Syrians as equals but as junior partners in the firm. Syrian officers seized control and expelled the Egyptian advisers. It was the end of the U.A.R.

For the next decade, power shifted back and forth among military and civilian factions of the Ba'th Party. The process had little effect on the average Syrian, who liked to talk about politics but was wary, with good reason, of any involvement. Gradually, the military faction got the upper hand; and, in 1970, Lieutenant General Hafez al-Assad, the defense minister of one of the country's innumerable previous governments, seized power in a bloodless coup.[6]

THE ASSAD REGIME

Hafez al-Assad has been head of Syria longer than any of his predecessors since independence. He was elected president for a 7-year term in 1971 and was reelected in 1978, in 1985, and in 1991 for a fourth term. He was hospitalized in 1983 after a heart attack and underwent successful prostate surgery in January 1997. But these health problems have had little effect on his ability to remain in power.

Syria can be called a presidential republic, in the sense that the head of state has extensive powers, which are confirmed in the Constitution approved in 1973. He decides and executes policies, appoints all government officials, and commands the armed forces. He is also head of the Ba'th Party. Under the Constitution, he has unlimited emergency powers "in case of grave danger threatening national unity or the security . . . of the national territory" (Article 113), which only the president can determine.

Another important difference between Assad and most of his predecessors is that he has made some effort to broaden the governing process and thereby make his regime more popular. Several small Socialist parties whose programs are acceptable to the Ba'th have been allowed to function as token opposition, and national elections were held for a People's Assembly in 1986 and again in 1990. The Ba'th won 60 percent of seats in the Assembly

(Reuters/Bettmann)

President Hafez al-Assad waves to students in Damascus in 1990 at an opening session of the Syrian Students Union.

in 1986; but, in 1990, the party's margin was less in an enlarged, 250-member Legislature. The difference was because candidates were allowed to run as independents. They won 84 seats to 132 for the Ba'th and 32 for the opposition parties, now grouped into a Progressive National Front. However, the extent of the Assembly's power is the approval of laws issued by the Ba'th Central Committee and concurrent approval of the national budget.

SYRIA'S ROLE IN LEBANON

Assad's position was strengthened domestically in the 1970s due to his success (or perceived success) in certain foreign policy actions. The Syrian Army fought well against Israel in the October 1973 War, and Syria subsequently received both military and financial aid from the Soviet Union as well as its Arab brothers. The invitation by the Arab League for Syria to intervene in Lebanon, beginning with the 1975–1976 Lebanese Civil War, was widely popular among Syrians. They never fully accepted the French action of separating Lebanon from Syria during the mandate period, and they continue to maintain a proprietary attitude toward Lebanon. Assad's determination to avoid conflict with Israel led him in past years to keep a tight rein on Syrian-based Palestine Liberation Organization operations. The al-Saiqa Palestinian Brigade was integrated into the Syrian Army, for example. However, Assad's agreement to join a Middle East conference with other Arab states and Israel in 1991 resulted in the

release of all PLO activists held in detention in Syria.

When the Lebanese Civil War broke out, Assad pledged that he would control the Palestinians in Lebanon. He sent about 2,000 al-Saiqa guerrillas to Beirut in early 1976. The peacekeeping force approved by the Arab League for Lebanon included 30,000 regular Syrian troops. For all practical purposes, this force maintained a balance of power among Lebanese factions until the Israeli invasion of June 1982. It then withdrew to the eastern Biqa' Valley, avoiding conflict with Israeli forces and providing sanctuary to Palestinian guerrillas escaping from Beirut.

From this vantage point, Syria made a number of attempts to broker a peace agreement among the various Lebanese factions. However, all of them failed, owing in large measure to the intractable hostility separating Muslim from Christian communities and intercommunal rivalries among the militias. In 1987, faced with a near-total breakdown in public security, Assad ordered 7,000 elite Syrian commandos into West Beirut. Syrian forces maintained an uneasy peace in the Lebanese capital until 1989, when they were challenged directly by the Christian militia of General Michel Aoun, who refused to accept Syrian authority and declared himself president. Syrian forces surrounded the Christian enclave and, early in 1990, mounted a massive assault, backed by heavy artillery, that finally broke the Christian resistance. Aoun took refuge in the French Embassy and then went into exile.

With the end of civil war in Lebanon, Syrian forces were reduced to 30,000–35,000 and withdrawn to bases in the northeast. They have remained there as a sort of brooding presence, a Syrian eagle "appointed by the international community to oversee the emergence of Lebanon into a phase of peace and reconstruction of the Lebanese state."[7]

INTERNAL OPPOSITION

Opposition to the Assad regime has lessened in recent years, due largely to economic improvement but also to liberalization of the system. A major cause for resentment among rank-and-file Syrians is the dominance of the Alawi minority over the government, armed forces, police, and intelligence services. The main opposition group—the Syrian branch of the Muslim Brotherhood (a Sunni organization spread throughout the Arab world)—has opposed Assad since he came to power, because of his autocratic style of leadership and his favoring of Alawi interests over those of the Sunni majority. Its main stronghold was the ancient city of Hama, famed for its Roman waterwheels. In 1982, Assad's regular army moved against Hama after an ambush of government officials there. The city was almost obliterated by tanks and artillery fire, with an estimated 120,000 casualties. Large areas were bulldozed as a warning to other potentially disloyal elements in the population.[8]

Memories of Hama, along with an unwritten "mutual cooperation pact" between the regime and the country's large merchant class, have kept potential opposition under control in recent years. It is a control admittedly reinforced by the presence of some 15 intelligence and paramilitary agencies, the mukhabarat, which keeps close tabs on the population. But, despite the narrow support base provided by his status as member of a minority group, Assad has given Syria the stability that his predecessors did not provide. His most recent election victory, in December 1991, was marked by huge rallies honoring "our savior, hero of the people."

Assad's Alawi background continues to render him suspect among Sunnis—it is often whispered that Alawis are not true Muslims.[9] But Assad's ability to play a waiting game in the on-going Middle Eastern political configuration has won him considerable national support, particularly in the 1990s, as other Arab states have moved toward an accommodation with Israel. As a result, he has begun to loosen the reins. After his election in 1991 as president for a fourth 7-year term, he appointed a cabinet that included a number of Sunni ministers. In June 1992, he released 3,000 political prisoners, most of them Muslim Brotherhood members. An additional 1,000 members were freed in 1995 and the head of the Syrian branch, Abu Ghadda, allowed to return to his home in Damascus. The Brotherhood subsequently declared that the organization would not resume secret political action "while the door to public participation remains open." In 1997, the Brotherhood also disclaimed any connection with scattered acts of violence occurring within the country.

THE ECONOMY

At independence, Syria was primarily an agricultural country, although it had a large merchant class and a free enterprise system with considerable small-scale industrial development. When it came to power, the Ba'th Party was committed to state control of the economy. Agriculture was collectivized, with land expropriated from large landowners and converted into state-managed farms. Most industries were nationalized in the 1960s. The free-enterprise system all but disappeared.

Cotton was Syria's principal export crop and money earner until the mid-1970s. But, with the development of oil fields, petroleum became the main export. Syria produced enough oil for its own needs until 1980. However, the changing global oil market and the reluctance of foreign oil companies to invest in Syrian oil exploration under the unfavorable concession terms set by the government have hampered development. The Gulf War brought Syria a $5 billion windfall from various donors in return for its contribution of 20,000 troops to Allied forces in Operation Desert Storm. This funding has facilitated oil and gas exploration. In 1996–1997, oil production from existing fields reached 580,000 barrels per day. New gas discoveries signaled the country's emergence as a major gas producer. Initial gas production was 3 million cubic feet per day; it was expected to reach 12.5 million cubic feet per day by the end of 1997.

Agricultural production has shown marked improvement in the 1990s. It accounts for 30 percent of gross domestic product and employs one third of the country's 4.3 million labor force. The cotton harvest was 725,000 tons in 1996, a record, due in large part to expansion of cultivable lands and improved irrigation methods.

The end of Syria's special relationship with the Soviet Union due to the breakup of that country in 1991 has encouraged a modest liberalization of the Ba'thist economic system. A prominent exiled businessman who had been one of Assad's bitterest critics returned in 1993 to set up a retail store chain similar to London's Marks & Spencer, taking advantage of new tax exemptions and other incentives. The Assad regime has moved steadily away from state control of economic development; a 1991 law encourages private investment by allowing industries to import needed machinery duty-free and gives a 7-year tax exemption to companies developing projects of benefit to national development.

In the final analysis, not only economic but also political and, to some extent, social change in Syria emanates—if at all—from one man: Assad. A European diplomat has called Assad's influence an example of old-think and new-think emerging at the same time as Syria develops a new relationship with its neighbors and the region. "Old-think" for many years was the view of most Syrians confronted by constant and chronic electricity shortages. "New-think" may represent the Syrian leader's sudden awareness of the problem while pondering new directions for his country. Thus, one evening Assad observed from his palace window that Damascus was dark. He demanded an explanation, and, in 1993, he ordered a crash program to provide every Syrian with "a secure supply of electricity, which is his right."

FOREIGN RELATIONS

Syria's often prickly relations with its neighbors and its rigid opposition to Israel have made the country the "odd man out" in the region at various times. Periodic disagreements with the rival Ba'thist regime in Iraq have caused the latter to suspend oil shipments through Syrian pipelines to refineries on the Mediterranean coast. (These shipments stopped entirely after the UN embargo on Iraqi oil sales abroad.) The income from use of its pipelines for transit purposes earned more for Syria than its own oil production, so the shutdown has been a blow to the Syrian economy.

Syria's role as an alleged major sponsor of international terrorism has adversely affected its relations with Western countries for years. In 1986, a number of these countries broke diplomatic relations after the British discovered a Syrian-funded plot to blow up an Israeli airliner at Heathrow Airport in London, England. Relations were restored after the Assad regime disassociated itself from terrorist actions, and the image of Syria as a terrorist sponsor largely disappeared after the country sent troops to aid in the expulsion of Iraq from Kuwait. In 1997, the U.S.

| The capital of Umayyads is removed to Damascus; Syria becomes the center of the Islamic world
661–750 | Ottoman province
1517–1917 | An independent Arab Kingdom of Syria is proclaimed under Faisal; shot down by French
1920 | French mandate, followed by independence
1920–1946 | Union with Egypt into the United Arab Republic
1958–1961 | Hafez al-Assad takes control of the government; later he is elected president
1971 | Syrian troops are sent to Lebanon as a peacekeeping force
1976 | Syria's association with international terrorism leads some European countries to break relations and some to impose economic sanctions
1980s | **1990s** |

| Assad approves amnesty for members of the Muslim Brotherhood, formerly the main opposition to his rule | Assad's efforts to gain the release of hostages in Lebanon leads the United States and other countries to resume aid and diplomatic relations | President Assad has role in mediating dispute between Israel and Hizbullah |

State Department removed Syria from its list of global-terrorism sponsors, enabling U.S. companies to do business there legally.

The dramatic PLO–Israeli peace agreement of September 1993 put Assad in an awkward position, not only because of his personal dislike for PLO chairman Yassir Arafat but also because the proposed autonomy for the Gaza Strip and Jericho seemed to undercut Assad's goal of recovering the Golan Heights from Israel. The earlier rounds of talks in Madrid for a comprehensive Middle East peace settlement had produced little progress toward this goal.

Prospects for a "peace of the brave" between Israel and the Palestinians in 1993 encouraged Assad to begin serious negotiations with Israel for settlement of the Golan Heights issue. Talks began under U.S. sponsorship between Israeli and Syrian representatives in 1995. At base, the issue was simple: Israel would withdraw its forces, and Syria would sign a peace treaty. But, as always in the Middle East, "the devil is in the details." The talks were suspended in 1996 after Assad failed to condemn Hamas suicide bombings in Israel, and the election of Benjamin Netanyahu as Israel's new prime minister halted all negotiations toward a settlement of the long-running issue.

PROSPECTS

As is usually the case with states ruled by a single nondynastic leader, Syria must deal eventually with the question of a successor to Hafez al-Assad. Not only does Assad belong to a distrusted minority, but feuding within his own family has also limited his options. One brother, Rifaat, who spent several years in exile for his part in an attempted coup in 1983, was placed under house arrest for unspecified reasons in 1996. Another brother, Jamil, was exiled in December 1996 for involvement in public corruption. Assad's oldest son and heir-apparent, Basil, was killed in a traffic accident in 1994, leaving the younger son, Bashar (an opthalmologist by training), as the sole surviving potential successor within the family.

Fortunately for the Assad regime, although it lacks legitimacy in terms of majority Sunni support, it has firmly established the legitimacy of the Syrian state. In this respect, Syria may well follow the examples of Tunisia and Egypt, where the death or retirement of a charismatic leader resulted in the orderly transfer of power to a constitutionally accepted successor regime.

NOTES

1. The statement is found in many chronicles of the Umayyads. See Richard Nyrop, ed., *Syria, A Country Study* (Washington, D.C.: American University, Foreign Area Studies, 1978), p. 13.

2. Philip Khoury, *Urban Notables and Arab Nationalism: The Politics of Damascus 1860–1920* (Cambridge, England: Cambridge University Press, 1983), pp. 8–9.

3. Umar F. Abd-Allah, *The Islamic Struggle in Syria* (Berkeley, CA: Mizan Press, 1983), p. 39.

4. A. H. Hourani, *Syria and Lebanon, A Political Essay* (London: Oxford University Press,

1954), p. 54, notes that "His [Faisal's] government had more solid foundations in popular consent than any perhaps since Umayyad times."

5. "Syrians had long seen themselves as Arabs . . . who considered the Arab world as rightly a single entity." John F. Devlin, *Syria: Modern State in an Ancient Land* (Boulder, CO: Westview Press, 1983), p. 44.

6. He was barred from attending a cabinet meeting and then surrounded the meeting site with army units, dismissed the government, and formed his own. *Ibid.*, p. 56.

7. Adnan Iskandar, quoted in "Why Lebanon Follows the Road to Damascus," by John Battersby, *The Christian Science Monitor* (August 1, 1995).

8. Thomas L. Friedman, in *From Beirut to Jerusalem*, coined the phrase "Hama rules" to describe Assad's domestic political methods. "Hama rules" are no rules at all.

9. Abd-Allah, *op. cit.*, pp. 42–48, describes them as believing in a Trinity, worshipping natural objects, giving less than absolute obedience to the Koran as the word of God, and following a religious teacher who claimed to be a Prophet and messenger 200 years after Muhammad.

DEVELOPMENT

The 1996–1997 budget sets expenditures at $4.46 billion, a 13.5% increase over 1995–1996. In 1996, Syria settled long-standing debt problems with France, its main aid supplier, by rescheduling $370 million in arrears obligations. Also, the economic liberalization program economic development has generated $3 billion in foreign investment since it was enacted.

FREEDOM

The 1973 Constitution defines Syria as a Socialist, populist democracy. In practice, Assad and the Ba'th dominate national life. A free press, representative political parties, civil rights, and other features of a democratic consensual political system do not exist in the country.

HEALTH/WELFARE

The new comprehensive waste-water treatment plant in Damascus, completed in 1993, is the first of a series of projects designed to upgrade Syrian urban-waste systems, after years of neglect. It is being financed by Kuwait.

ACHIEVEMENTS

Ghada Shonaa brought honor and glory to Syria when she became the first Syrian to win an Olympic gold medal. She won the women's heptathlon at the 1996 Olympic Games in Atlanta, Georgia.

Tunisia (Republic of Tunisia)

GEOGRAPHY

Area in Square Kilometers (Miles):
164,149 (63,378) (about the size of
Missouri)
Capital (Population): Tunis (1,000,000)
Climate: hot, dry summers; mild, rainy
winters

PEOPLE

Population

Total: 9,020,000
Annual Growth Rate: 1.7%
Rural/Urban Population Ratio: 40/60
Ethnic Makeup: 98% Arab–Berber; 1%
European; 1% others
Major Languages: Arabic; French

Health

Life Expectancy at Birth: 71 years
(male); 75 years (female)
Infant Mortality Rate (Ratio): 32/1,000
Average Caloric Intake: 116% of FAO
minimum
Physicians Available (Ratio): 1/1,799

Religions

98% Muslim; 1% Christian; less than
1% Jewish

Education

Adult Literacy Rate: 57%

Peace at Last

In 1985, after 2,000 years, the mayors of Rome and Carthage (now a Tunis
suburb) signed a treaty symbolically ending the state of war between their
ancestor city-states. The treaty was a reminder of the great days of Roman
Africa with its capital at Carthage. The Bardo Museum in Tunis houses the
world's finest collection of Roman African mosaics.

Students went there to work under mosaic masters from Alexandria (Egypt)
in the first century A.D. They soon developed their own distinct impression-
istic style, incorporating native themes, showing rural hunting and harvest-
ing scenes, fishing expeditions with boat models of the period, and family
picnics. One of the largest mosaics, showing the triumph of Neptune, covers
1,465 square feet.

COMMUNICATION

Telephones: 233,000
Newspapers: 2 Arabic dailies; 4 French
dailies

TRANSPORTATION

Highways—Kilometers (Miles): 29,183
(18,210)
Railroads—Kilometers (Miles): 2,241
(1,389)
Usable Airfields: 31

GOVERNMENT

Type: republic
Independence Date: March 20, 1956
Head of State/Government: President
Zine el-Abidine Ben Ali; Prime
Minister Hamed Karoui
Political Parties: Constitutional
Democratic Rally; Movement of
Democrats; Socialists; Movement for
Renewal; other opposition parties
Suffrage: universal at 20

MILITARY

Number of Armed Forces: 38,000
*Military Expenditures (% of Central
Government Expenditures):* 5.7%
Current Hostilities: none

ECONOMY

Currency ($ U.S. Equivalent): 0.98
Tunisian dinar = $1
Per Capita Income/GDP: $4,200/$37.1
billion
Inflation Rate: 4.5%
Total Foreign Debt: $7.7 billion
Natural Resources: oil; phosphates;
iron ore; lead; zinc
Agriculture: wheat; barley; olives; citrus
fruits; grapes; vegetables; fish
Industry: mining (phosphates);
petroleum; olive oil; textiles; food
processing; construction

FOREIGN TRADE

Exports: $4.9 billion
Imports: $6.8 billion

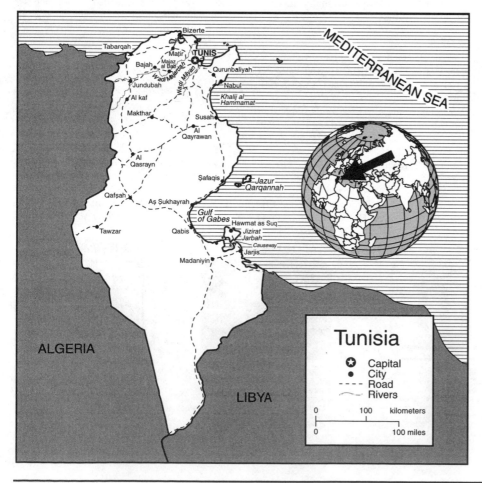

TUNISIA

Tunisia, the smallest of the four North African countries, is less than one tenth the size of Libya, its neighbor to the east. However, its population is nearly twice the size of Libya's.

Tunisia's long coastline has exposed it over the centuries to a succession of invaders from the sea. The southern third of the country is part of the Sahara Desert, and the central third consists of high, arid plains. Only the northern region has sufficient rainfall for agriculture; this region contains Tunisia's single permanent river, the Madjerda.

The country is predominantly urban. There is almost no nomadic population, and there are no high mountains to provide refuge for independent mountain peoples opposed to central government. The Tunis region and the Sahel, a coastal plain important in olive production, are the most densely populated areas. Tunis, the capital, is not only the dominant city but also the hub of government, economic, and political activity.

HISTORY

Tunisia has an ancient history that is urban rather than territorial. Phoenician merchants from what is today Lebanon founded a number of trading posts several thousand years ago. The most important one was Carthage, founded by tradition in 814 B.C. It grew wealthy through trade and developed a maritime empire. Its great rival was Rome; after several wars, the Romans defeated the Carthaginians and destroyed Carthage. Later, the Romans rebuilt the city, and it became great once again, the capital of the Roman province of Africa. Rome's African province was one of the most prosperous in the empire. The wheat and other commodities shipped to Rome from North African farms were vitally needed to feed the Roman population. When the ships from Carthage were late due to storms, lost at sea, or seized by pirates, the Romans suffered hardship. Modern Tunisia has yet to reach the level of prosperity it had under Roman rule.

The collapse of the Roman Empire in the fifth century A.D. affected Roman Africa as well. Cities were abandoned; the irrigation system that had made the farms prosperous fell into ruin. A number of these Roman cities, such as Dougga, Utica, and Carthage itself, which is now a suburb of Tunis, have been preserved as historical monuments of this period.

Arab armies from the east brought Islam to North Africa in the late seventh century. After some resistance, the population accepted the new religion, and from that time on, the area was ruled as the Arab–Islamic province of *Ifriqiya*. The Anglicized form of this Arabic word, "Africa," was eventually applied to the entire continent.

The Arab governors did not want to have anything to do with Carthage, since they associated it with Christian Roman rule. They built a new capital on the site of a village on the outskirts of Carthage, named Tunis. The fact that Tunis has been the capital and major city in the country for 14 centuries has contributed to the sense of unity and nationhood that most Tunisians have.[1]

The original Tunisian population consisted of Berbers, a people of unknown origin. During the centuries of Islamic rule, many Arabs settled in the country. Other waves of immigration brought Muslims from Spain, Greeks, Italians, Maltese, and many other nationalities. Tunisia also had until recently a large community of Jews, most of whom emigrated to the State of Israel when it was founded in 1948. The blending of ethnic groups and nationalities over the years created a relatively homogeneous and tolerant society, with few of the conflicts that marked other societies in the Islamic world.

From the late 1500s to the 1880s, Tunisia was a self-governing province of the Ottoman Empire. It was called a regency because its governors ruled as "regents" on behalf of the Ottoman sultan. Tunis was already a well-established, cosmopolitan city when it became the regency capital. Its rulers, called beys, were supported by an Ottoman garrison and a corsair fleet of fast ships that served as auxiliaries to the regular Ottoman navy. The corsairs, many of them Christian renegades, ruled the Mediterranean Sea for 4 centuries, raiding the coasts of nearby European countries and preying on merchant vessels, seizing cargoes and holding crews for ransom.[2]

In the nineteenth century, European powers, particularly France and Britain, began to interfere directly in the Ottoman Empire and to seize some of its outlying provinces. France and Britain had a "gentleman's agreement" about Ottoman territories in Africa—the French were given a free hand in North Africa and the British in Egypt. In 1830, the French seized Algiers, capital of the Algiers Regency, and began to intervene in neighboring Tunisia in order to protect their Algerian investment.

The beys of Tunis worked very hard to forestall a French occupation. In order to do this, they had to satisfy the European powers that they were developing modern political institutions and rights for their people. Ahmad Bey (1837–1855) abolished slavery and piracy, organized a modern army (trained by French officers), and established a national system of tax collection. Muhammad al-Sadiq Bey (1859–1882) approved in 1861 the first written Constitution in the Islamic world. This Constitution had a declaration of rights and provided for a hereditary (but not an absolute) monarchy under the beys. The Constitution worked better in theory than in practice. Provincial landowners and local chiefs opposed it because it undermined their authority. The peasants, whom it supposedly was designed to protect, opposed it because it brought them heavy new taxes, collected by government troops sent from Tunis. In 1864, a popular rebellion broke out against the bey, and he was forced to suspend the Constitution.

In 1881, a French army invaded and occupied all of Tunisia, almost without firing a shot. The French said that they had intervened because the bey's government could not meet its debts to French bankers and capitalists, who had been lending money for years to keep the country afloat. There was concern also about the European population. Europeans from many countries had been pouring into Tunisia, ever since the bey had given foreigners the right to own land and set up businesses.

The bey's government continued under the French protectorate, but it was supplemented by a French administration, which held actual power. The French collected taxes, imposed French law, and developed roads, railroads, ports, hospitals, and schools. French landowners bought large areas and converted them into vineyards, olive groves, and wheat farms. For the first time in 2,000 years, Tunisia exported wheat, corn, and olive oil to the lands on the other side of the Mediterranean.

Because Tunisia was small, manageable, and urban, its society, particularly in certain regions, was influenced strongly by French culture. An elite developed whose members preferred the French language to their native Arabic and who sent their children to French high schools and to colleges or universities in France. The Tunisian Nationalist Movement was developed largely from members of this group, who had matured enough to feel that a friendly association of the two countries as equals would be of mutual benefit. The movement began in the 1920s.[3] The French allowed a certain amount of political freedom, and the nationalists took the name *Destour* (in Arabic, *Dustur*), meaning "Constitution."

In the 1930s, a new generation of Tunisians began to talk seriously of independence. Most of them had been educated in France. The youths of the new generation became convinced that nationalism, "in order to be effective against the French, had to break loose from its traditional power base in the urban elite and mobilize mass support."[4] In 1934, a group of young nationalists quit the Destour and formed a new party, the Neo-Destour. The goal of the Neo-Destour Party was independence from France. From the beginning, its principal leader was Habib Bourguiba.

HABIB BOURGUIBA

Bourguiba, born in 1903, once boasted that he had "invented" Tunisia. In a sense, he was right. The Neo-Destour Party, under his leadership, became the country's first mass political party. It drew its membership from shopkeepers, craftspeople, blue-collar workers, and peasants, along with French-educated lawyers and doctors. The party became the vanguard of the nation, mobilizing the population in a campaign of strikes, demonstrations, and violence in order to gain independence. It was a long struggle. Bourguiba spent many years in prison. But eventually, the Neo-Destour tactics succeeded. On March 20, 1956, the French ended the protectorate and Tunisia became an independent republic led by Habib Bourguiba.

One of the problems facing Tunisia today is that its political organization has changed very little since independence. A Constitution was approved in 1959 that established a "presidential republic"—that is, a republic in which the elected president has very great power. Habib Bourguiba was elected president in 1957.

Bourguiba was also the head of the Neo-Destour Party, the country's only legal political party. The Constitution provides for a National Assembly, which is responsible for enacting laws. But, to be elected to the Assembly, a candidate had to be a member of the Neo-Destour Party. Bourguiba's philosophy and programs for national development in his country were often called Bourguibism. It was tailored to the particular historical experience of the Tunisian people. Since ancient Carthage, Tunisian life has been characterized by the presence of some strong central government able to impose order and bring relative stability to the people. The predominance of cities and villages over nomadism reinforced this sense of order. The experience of Carthage, and even more so that of Rome, set the pattern. "The Beys continued the pattern of strong order while the French developed a strongly bourgeois, trade-oriented society, adding humanitarian and some authoritarian values contained in French political

philosophy."[5] Bourguiba always considered himself the tutor of the Tunisian people, guiding them toward moral, economic, and political maturity.

In 1961, Bourguiba introduced a new program for Tunisian development that he termed "Destourian Socialism." It combined Bourguibism with government planning for economic and social development. The name of the Neo-Destour Party was changed to Destour Socialist Party (PSD) to indicate its new direction. Destourian Socialism worked for the general good, but it was not Marxist; Bourguiba stressed national unanimity rather than class struggle and opposed communism as the "ideology of a godless state." Bourguiba took the view that Destourian Socialism was directly related to Islam. He said once that the original members of the Islamic community (in Muhammad's time in Mecca) "were socialists . . . and worked for the common good."[6] For many years after independence, Tunisia appeared to be a model among new nations because of its stability, order, and economic progress. Particularly notable were Bourguiba's reforms in social and political life. Islamic law was replaced by a Western legal system with various levels of courts. Women were encouraged to attend school and enter occupations previously closed to them and were given equal rights with men in matters of divorce and inheritance.

Bourguiba strongly criticized those aspects of Islam that seemed to him to be obstacles to national development. He was against women veiling, polygyny, and ownership of lands by religious leaders, which kept the lands out of production. He even encouraged people not to fast during Ramadan, because their hunger made them less effective in their work.

There were few challenges to Bourguiba's leadership. His method of alternately dismissing and reinstating party leaders who disagreed with him effectively maintained Destourian unity. But in later years, Bourguiba's periodic health problems, the growth of Islamic fundamentalism, and the disenchantment of Tunisian youth with the single-party system raised doubts about Tunisia's future under the PSD.

The system was provided with a certain continuity by the election of Bourguiba as president-for-life in 1974, when a constitutional amendment was approved specifying that, at the time of his death or in the event of his disability, the prime minister would succeed him and hold office pending a general election. One author observed: "Nobody is big enough to replace Bourguiba. He created a national libera-

tion movement, fashioned the country and its institutions."[7] Yet he failed to recognize or deal with changing political and social realities in his later years.

The new generation now coming of age in Tunisia is deeply alienated from the old. Young Tunisians (half the population are under age 15) increasingly protest their inability to find jobs, their exclusion from the decision-making process, the unfair distribution of wealth, and the lack of political organizations. It seems as if there are two Tunisias: the old Tunisia of genteel politicians and freedom fighters; and the new one of alienated youths, angry peasants, and frustrated intellectuals. Somehow the two have gotten out of touch with each other.

The division between these groups has been magnified by the growth of Islamic fundamentalism, which in Bourguiba's view was equated with rejection of the secular, modern Islamic society that he created. The Islamic Tendency Movement (MTI) emerged in the 1980s as the major fundamentalist group. MTI applied for recognition as a political party after Bourguiba agreed to allow political activity outside of the Destour Party and had licensed two opposition parties. But the application was rejected.

THE END OF AN ERA

Riots over an increase in the price of bread in 1984 signaled a turning point for the regime. For the first time in the republic's history, an organized Islamic opposition challenged Bourguiba, on the grounds that he had deformed Islam to create a secular society. Former Bourguiba associates urged a broadening of the political process and formed political movements to challenge the Destour monopoly on power. Although they were frequently jailed and their movements proscribed or declared illegal, they continued to press for political reform.

However, Bourguiba turned a deaf ear to all proposals for political change. Having survived several heart attacks and other illnesses to regain reasonably good health, he seemed to feel that he was indestructible. In 1986 and 1987, he not only assumed direct control over party and nation but also turned against most of his long-term friends and colleagues. These included senior officials; his son Habib, Jr.; his wife Wassila, whom he divorced and accused of urging changes in the succession amendment; and members of her family. The two legal opposition parties were forced out of local and national elections by arrests of leaders and a shutdown of opposition newspapers. The Tunisian Labor Confederation (UGTT) was disbanded, and the government launched a massive purge of fundamentalists.

The purge was directed by General Zine el-Abidine Ben Ali, the minister of the interior, regarded by Bourguiba as one of the few people he could trust. There were mass arrests of Islamic militants, most of them belonging to the outlawed Islamic Tendency Movement. In 1987, a trial of MTI activists ended with seven death sentences and long prison terms for others, including the leader of the movement, Rachid Ghannouchi. But Bourguiba intervened, demanding a new trial and the death sentence for Ghannouchi.

Increasingly, it seemed to responsible leaders that Bourguiba was becoming senile as well as paranoid. "The government lacks all sense of vision," said a long-time observer. "The strategy is to get through the day, to play palace parlor games." A student leader was more cynical: "There is no logic to [Bourguiba's] decisions; sometimes he does the opposite of what he did the day before."[8]

A decision that would prove crucial to the needed change in leadership was made by Bourguiba in September 1987, when he named Ben Ali as prime minister. Six weeks later, Ben Ali carried out a bloodless coup, removing the aging president under the 1974 constitutional provision that allows the prime minister to take over in the event of a president's "manifest incapacity" to govern. Seven prominent Tunisian doctors signed such a statement. "Perhaps I should have given up sooner," said the former president-for-life in a moment of sad lucidity as he was gently taken away to temporary house arrest.[9] Recognizing Bourguiba's "historic role" in the building of the Tunisian state, the Ben Ali government in 1990 allowed him to receive visitors and to move freely about his hometown of Monastir.

NEW DIRECTIONS
President Ben Ali (elected to a full 5-year term in April 1989) initiated a series of bold reforms designed to wean the country away from the one-party system. Political prisoners were released under a general amnesty. Prodded by Ben Ali, the Destour-dominated National Assembly passed laws ensuring press freedom and the right of political parties to form as long as their platforms are not based exclusively on language, race, or religion. The Assembly also abolished the constitutional provision establishing the position of president-for-life, which had been created expressly for Bourguiba. Henceforth Tunisian presidents would be limited to three consecutive terms in office.

Ben Ali also undertook the major job of restructuring and revitalizing the Destour Party. In 1988, it was renamed the Constitutional Democratic Assembly (RCD). Ben Ali told delegates to the first RCD Congress that no single party could represent all Tunisians. There can be no democracy without pluralism, fair elections, and freedom of expression, he said.

Elections in 1988 underscored Tunisia's fixation on the single-party system. RCD candidates won all 141 seats in the Chamber of Deputies, taking 80 percent of the popular vote. Two new opposition parties, the Progressive Socialist Party and the Progressive Socialist Rally, participated but failed to win more than 5 percent of the popular vote, the minimum needed for representation in the Chamber. MTI candidates, although required to run as independents because of the ban on "Islamic" parties under the revised election law, dominated urban voting, taking 30 percent of the popular vote in the cities. However, the winner-take-all system of electing candidates shut them out as well.

Local and municipal elections have confirmed the RCD stranglehold on Tunisian political life; its performance was the exact opposite of that of the National Liberation Front in neighboring Algeria, where the dominant party was discredited over time and finally defeated in open national elections by a fundamentalist party. In the 1995 local and municipal council elections, RCD candidates won 4,084 out of 4,090 contested seats, with 92.5 percent of Tunisia's 1,865,401 registered voters casting their ballots.

Efforts to mobilize an effective opposition movement earlier were hampered when Ahmed Mestiri, the long-time head of the Movement of Socialist Democrats (MDS), the major legal opposition party, resigned in 1992. In the 1994 elections, the only opposition party to increase its support was the former Tunisian Communist Party, renamed Movement for Renewal. It won four seats in the Chamber as Tunisia continued its slow progress toward multiparty democracy.

Certain political developments in 1994, however, indicated a serious commitment on the part of the regime to broaden representation in government. Prior to the elections, the Chamber was enlarged from 144 to 160 members, with 19 seats reserved for deputies from the six legal opposition parties. Encouraging was the emergence of opposition to President Ben Ali after he had been nominated by the Chamber for a third presidential term. The two declared opposition candidates were the head of the Tunisian League of Human Rights (the oldest such organization in the

Arab world) and the leader of the Movement of Unionist Vanguard, an unrecognized party whose platform called for unity of all Arab nations. Both candidates stated that the constitutional provision requiring a presidential candidate to have the support of 30 deputies was undemocratic. However, their candidacies were declared invalid by the Tunisian High Court on constitutional grounds, and on March 20, Ben Ali was re-elected for a third term.

THE ECONOMY
The challenge to Ben Ali lies not only in broadening political participation but also in improving the economy. After a period of impressive expansion in the 1960s and 1970s, the growth rate began dropping steadily, largely due to decreased demand and lowered prices for the country's three main exports (phosphates, petroleum, and olive oil). Tunisia is the world's fourth-ranking producer of phosphates, and its most important industries are those related to production of superphosphates and fertilizers.

Problems have dogged the phosphate industry. The quality of the rock mined is poor in comparison with that of other phosphate producers, such as Morocco. The Tunisian industry experienced hard times in the late 1980s with the drop in global phosphate prices; one fourth of its 12,000-member workforce was laid off in 1987. However, improved production methods and higher world demand led to a 29 percent increase in exports in 1990.

Tunisia's oil reserves are estimated at 1.65 billion barrels. The main producing fields are at El Borma and offshore in the Gulf of Gabes. New offshore discoveries and a 1996 agreement with Libya for 50/50 sharing of production from the disputed Gulf of Gabes oil field have improved oil output, currently 4.3 million barrels annually.

Tunisia's associate-member status in the European Union has brought the country some economic benefits. In addition, the economic stabilization program begun in 1986 as a consequence of International Monetary Fund insistence on reforms as a prerequisite for further loans, has provided a strong stimulus to the economy. The economic growth rate averaged 5 percent annually from 1987 to 1994. In 1996, it reached a record 6.9 percent due to record cereals crops and increased oil and phosphates exports.

Tunisia's general political stability and diverse resources have made it a favored country for foreign aid. It has received more World Bank loans than any other Arab or African country in recent decades.

Wars between
Rome and
Carthage, ending
in the destruction
of Carthage and
its rebuilding as a
Roman city
264–146 B.C.

The
establishment of
Islam in Ifriqiya,
with its new
capital at Tunis
A.D. 800–900

The Hafsid
dynasty develops
Tunisia as a
highly centralized
urban state
1200–1400

Ottoman Turks
establish Tunis as
a corsair state to
control
Mediterranean
sea lanes
1500–1800

French
protectorate
1881–1956

Tunisia gains
independence,
led by Habib
Bourguiba
1956

An abortive
merger with Libya
1974

Bourguiba is
removed from
office in a "palace
coup" on grounds
of mental
incapacity; he is
succeeded by
Ben Ali
1980s

1990s

Tunisia's
economic picture
brightens

Ben Ali seeks
some social
modernization

Women's rights
are expanded

The country's goal of becoming a "Mediterranean Singapore," well run and able to absorb large amounts of foreign capital, seemed within reach.

THE FUTURE

Tunisia's progress as an "economic beacon" of stability in an unstable region has been somewhat offset by a decline in its long-established status as a successful example of a secular, progressive Islamic state. Following President Ben Ali's ouster of his predecessor in 1987, he proclaimed a new era for Tunisians, based on respect for law, human rights, and democracy. Tunisia's "Islamic nature" was re-affirmed by such actions as the reopening of the venerable Zitouna University in Tunis, a center for Islamic scholarship. But the rise of Islamic fundamentalism, in Tunisia as elsewhere in the Islamic world, has seriously damaged the country's reputation as an "oasis of openness." An attack on RCD party headquarters in February 1991 by members of An-Nahda, a fundamentalist group that advocates a Tunisian government based on Islamic law, was a turning point. Since then, the government has pursued a policy of extreme repression of An-Nahda and related groups. Parties that have an "Islamic tendency" are proscribed, several thousand persons have been arrested, and trials by military courts in 1992 and 1993 resulted in long prison terms for some 300 militants.

The regime's uncompromising hostility toward political Islam has adversely affected human rights, even extending to the suspension in 1992 of the Tunisian League for Human Rights, the oldest such organization in the Arab world, for its criticism of violations of these rights. The press is censored, and indefinite detention of suspects without trial or charges is common practice. Tunisia under Bourguiba was a beacon for human rights, leading the Arab world in such actions as ending polygamy, encouraging female education, and granting to both men and women rights unavailable elsewhere. But fears of a spillover of Islamic fundamentalist violence after 1991 have led the regime to impose drastic limitations on rights.

The regime has undertaken certain social reforms that undercut the appeal of Islamic fundamentalism, particularly among disadvantaged youths. Although schools are required to provide "Islamic" education, it is based on a twentieth-century updating of the Koran, and pilot high schools for the gifted have been established to offer a curriculum that encourages open-mindedness and development of broad interests to supplement technical skills. New laws in 1992 and 1993 also strengthened the position of women, perhaps the most vulnerable sector of society in many Islamic lands. One promising social reform was the establishment in 1993 of a Center for Social Defense in a poor section of Tunis. It is intended to provide school dropouts with training in usable skills. A component of the program provides similar training for short-term prisoners scheduled for release, prior to their return to civilian life. Thus far, some 4,000 prisoners have been trained in electrical work, joinery, agriculture, and mechanics, and many have found work in those fields.

NOTES

1. Harold D. Nelson, ed., *Tunisia: A Country Study* (Washington, D.C.: American University, Foreign Area Studies, 1979), p. 68.

2. Attacks on American shipping by Tunisian corsairs led the U.S. to sign a treaty with the bey in 1799, guaranteeing an annual tribute in return for protection. *Ibid.*, p. 27.

3. The nationalists were nearly all graduates of Sadiki College, a "high school" with a European curriculum that included courses in European politics. They also went on to complete their education in France. *Ibid.*, p. 39.

4. *Ibid.*, p. 42.

5. What Nelson means, in this case, by "authoritarianism" is that the French brought to Tunisia the elaborate bureaucracy of metropolitan France, with levels of administration from the center down to local towns and villages. *Ibid.*, p. 194.

6. *Ibid.*, p. 196.

7. Jim Rupert, in *The Christian Science Monitor* (November 23, 1984).

8. Louise Lief, in *The Christian Science Monitor* (April 10, 1987).

9. *The Economist* (November 14, 1987), p. 50.

DEVELOPMENT

A 1995 agreement with the European Union allows Tunisia free access to European industrial products for its local market and extends its quota for olive-oil exports to EU members. Newly established free-trade zones at Zarzis and Bizerte and a revised investment code for foreign investors.

FREEDOM

The crackdown on Islamic fundamentalist groups has curtailed many civil rights. Amnesty International estimates that there are nearly 2,000 political prisoners in the country. Press freedom is so restricted that the World Press Association voted in 1997 to expel the Tunisian Association of Editors from its membership.

HEALTH/WELFARE

The 1995 "pact for social peace" between the government and the Tunisian Labor Confederation establishes an escalating cycle of wage increase to offset price increase in basic commodities. The pact also sets a guaranteed minimum wage of $165 per week for workers in industry.

ACHIEVEMENTS

Tunisia's leadership in women's rights in the Arab world is based on the 1956 Personal Status Code, which outlawed polygamy, set the minimum marriageable age at 17, and made women equal to men in divorce and inheritance rights. As a result, women have entered public life as well as entering professional fields previously limited to men.

Turkey (Republic of Turkey)

GEOGRAPHY
Area in Square Kilometers (Miles): 780,580 (301,303) (about 2 times the size of California)
Capital (Population): Ankara (3,306,000)
Climate: moderate coastal areas; harsher temperatures inland

PEOPLE

Population
Total: 63,700,000
Annual Growth Rate: 1.9%
Rural/Urban Population Ratio: 37/63
Ethnic Makeup: 80% Turk; 17% Kurd (Kurds not officially recognized as separate ethnic group); 3% others
Major Languages: Turkish; Kurdish

Health
Life Expectancy at Birth: 69 years (male); 74 years (female)
Infant Mortality Rate (Ratio): 46/1,000
Average Caloric Intake: 122% of FAO minimum
Physicians Available (Ratio): 1/1,108

Religions
99% Muslim (about 79% Sunni, 20% Shia); 1% others (mostly Christian and Jewish)

Education
Adult Literacy Rate: 79%

Turkish Delights

The so-called Turkish delight, a jelly-like confection cut into small cubes and dusted with sugar, is one of many components of Turkish culture whose presence in Turkish life today recall the country's storied past, particularly the long period of the Ottoman Empire when Turkey was a major world power. Another is the *narghile* (water pipe). In cafés by the Bosporus, it offers a release from the day's cares for Turkish smokers; sultans used to smoke a mixture of opium, perfume, and crushed pearls in their narghiles. Another "delight" is drawn from the Hoca stories, tales told by the witty *Kadi* (religious judge) Nasreddin Hoca centuries ago and preserved today by Turkish writers, artists, and musicians in drama, music, cartoons, and even comic strips. And, although modern Turkey is a secular state, the stately dances of the Whirling Dervish Sufi order remain enormously popular with Turkish and international audiences.

COMMUNICATION
Telephones: 3,400,000
Newspapers: 54 dailies

TRANSPORTATION
Highways—Kilometers (Miles): 320,611 (200,061)
Railroads—Kilometers (Miles): 10,413 (6,498)
Usable Airfields: 116

GOVERNMENT
Type: republican parliamentary democracy
Independence Date: October 29, 1923
Head of State/Government: President Suleyman Demirel; Prime Minister Mesut Yilmaz
Political Parties: True Path; People's Republican Party; Motherland Party; Islamic Welfare Party (Refah); Democratic Left; Republican People's Party; others
Suffrage: universal at 18

MILITARY
Number of Armed Forces: 647,400
Military Expenditures (% of Central Government Expenditures): 11.7%
Current Hostilities: civil strife in southeast with Kurdish separatist movement; Turkey maintains occupation force in Cyprus

ECONOMY
Currency ($ U.S. Equivalent): 172,605 Turkish lira = $1
Per Capita Income/GDP: $4,910/$182 billion
Inflation Rate: 80%
Total Foreign Debt: $66.6 billion
Natural Resources: coal; chromite; copper; boron
Agriculture: cotton; tobacco; cereals; sugar beets; fruits; nuts; livestock products
Industry: textiles; food processing; mining; iron and steel; cement; petroleum; leather goods

FOREIGN TRADE
Exports: $27 billion
Imports: $47 billion

TURKEY

Except for a small area in extreme South-eastern Europe called Thrace, the Republic of Turkey comprises the large peninsula of Asia Minor (Anatolia), which forms a land bridge between Europe and Asia. Asiatic Turkey is separated from European Turkey by the Bosporus, a narrow strait connecting the Black Sea with the Aegean Sea and the Mediterranean Sea via the Sea of Marmara. Throughout history the Bosporus and the Dardanelles, at the Mediterranean end, have been important strategic waterways, fought over by many nations.

Except for the Syrian border, Asiatic Turkey's borders are defined by natural limits, with seas on three sides and rugged mountains on the fourth. European Turkey's frontiers with Greece and Bulgaria are artificial; they fluctuated considerably in the nineteenth and twentieth centuries before the Republic of Turkey was established.

Modern Turkey occupies a much smaller area than did its predecessor, the Ottoman Empire. The Ottoman Turks were the dominant power in the Middle East for more than 5 centuries. After the defeat of the empire in World War I, Turkey's new leader, Mustafa Kemal Ataturk,

turned away from the imperial past, limiting the new republic to territory with a predominantly Turkish population. Since then, Turkey has not attempted to annex land beyond its natural Anatolian borders—with two exceptions. One was the Hatay, formerly a province of Syria that was ceded to Turkey by the French (who then controlled Syria under mandate from the League of Nations). The annexation was considered justified since the majority of the population was Turkish. The second exception was Cyprus. This island republic has a Greek majority in the population, but a significant minority (20 percent) are Turkish Cypriots, descended from Turkish families that settled there when Cyprus was Ottoman territory. Although it is a sovereign state, fears of violence against the Cypriot Turks led Turkish forces to occupy the northern third of the island in 1974. They have been there since then, with no agreement as yet on re-unification of Cyprus. Some years ago, the Turkish government officially recognized the area under its control as the Republic of Northern Cyprus, but no other country has done so.

Asia Minor has an ancient history of settlement. Most of the peninsula is a plateau ringed by mountains. The mountains are close to the coast; over the centuries,

due to volcanic action, the coastline became cracked, with deep indentations and islands just offshore. The inland plateau has an area of arid steppe with dried-up salt lakes at the center, but most of it is rolling land, well suited to agriculture. Consequently, people settled in small, self-contained villages at an early period and began to cultivate the land. Over the centuries, nomadic peoples migrated into Asia Minor, but the geographical pattern there did not encourage them to remain nomadic.

In terms of national unity, the modern Turkish state has not had the thorny problem of ethnic conflicts—with two important exceptions. One is the Armenians, an ancient Christian people who ruled over a large part of what is now eastern Turkey many centuries ago. The great majority were forced to leave their homeland during World War I, because the Turkish government suspected them of aiding the invading Russian armies. Hundreds of thousands of Armenians died or were killed during this series of forced emigrations. Although the republican government has consistently disclaimed responsibility for all wartime actions of its Ottoman predecessor, including the massacres of Armenians, Armenian terrorist groups car-

(UN photo/Rice)

Turkey has been populated for thousands of years by a myriad of peoples, including Hittites, Greeks, and Romans. This ancient Turkish artifact is mute evidence of one of these many bygone civilizations.

ried out a number of attacks on Turkish diplomats abroad in the 1970s and 1980s, in an effort to force the government to admit at least a measure of guilt. The violence refocused international attention on the Armenian "question." The Armenian community in the United States has regularly lobbied Congress to pressure the modern Turkish government to admit its Ottoman predecessor's responsibility for Armenian genocide. Thus far, the Turks have refused to do so, on grounds that they cannot be held responsible for actions by the government of a state that is no longer in existence. However, in 1996, congressional amendments were added to the U.S. foreign-aid appropriations bill that would sharply reduce aid to Turkey until such admission had been made. In response, Turkey declined all economic and military aid for 1997. In October 1996, the amendments were deleted from the bill; opponents called them a gratuitous insult to a loyal and important ally.

The other exception to Turkish homogeneity is the Kurds, who make up about 17 percent of the population. The Kurds are an ancient people of unknown origin who have lived for 2,000 years or more in the mountainous areas where modern Turkey, Iran, Iraq, and Syria meet. Turkey's Kurds, who number somewhere between 8 million and 12 million, form the largest component of this "people without a nation." Their clannish social structure and fierce spirit of independence have led to periodic Kurdish uprisings against the governments that rule them. In Turkey, the Ataturk regime crushed Kurdish rebellions in the 1920s, and from then on, Kurds were referred to officially as "Mountain Turks." Until the 1980s, Turkey's Kurds were considered an unimportant, albeit economically deprived, population group. Many emigrated to the cities or abroad, mainly to Germany and the Netherlands. Those remaining are concentrated in southeastern Anatolia and adjoining mountain regions, living in compact villages and working as farmers or herders.

In addition to those in Cyprus, there are two other important populations of ethnic Turks outside of Turkey. They are in Bulgaria and western (Greek) Thrace. Those in Bulgaria make up about 10 percent of the population. In the 1980s, they were suppressed by the Communist Bulgarian regime as foreigners and as Muslims, although they had lived in peace with their neighbors for centuries. About one third fled to Turkey as refugees. This forced assimilation policy was reversed after the fall of the Communist regime, and most of them have now returned to their Bulgarian homes.

There are also about 120,000 ethnic Turks in Greek Thrace, left over from the forced exchange of Greek and Turkish populations in 1922. However, they have never been granted Greek citizenship and are discriminated against in various ways. In 1990, the Greek government unilaterally abrogated the 1923 Treaty of Lausanne, which, among other things, guaranteed the Turkish minority the right to choose its own religious leaders. The issue is one of many that continue to cause friction between Greece and Turkey—North Atlantic Treaty Organization allies but long-term rivals for control of the eastern Mediterranean.

An estimated 20 percent of Turkey's population are *Alevis,* a blanket term for various Muslim communities whose Islamic rituals and beliefs differ from those of the Sunni majority. Some are Shias; others, particularly in the Hatay and southern Turkey, are ethnically related to the Alawis, who currently rule Syria; still others speak Kurdish or Azerbaijani Turkish and are related to the Azeris of northwestern Iran. The Alevi practice of Islam differs in many respects from that of Sunni Islam. Thus "instead of adherence to the Shari'a [Islamic Law], they profess obedience to a set of simple moral norms; they claim to live according to the inner (*batin*) meaning of religion rather than its external (*zahir*) demands," and "prayer, the fast in Ramazan, *zakat* and *hajj* are alien practices to most Alevi communities."[1]

HISTORY: A PARADE OF PEOPLES

The earliest political unit to develop in the peninsula was the Empire of the Hittites (1600–1200 B.C.), inventors of the two-wheeled chariot and one of the great powers of the ancient Near East. Various peoples succeeded the Hittites. One, the Lydians, invented money as a means of exchange in the time of the Lydian king Croesus. The modern expression "rich as Croesus" comes from this king's habit of panning gold from a nearby river, which he pressed into coins to pay for his kingdom's purchases. According to legend, Midas, another early Anatolian king, had the gift of turning anything he touched into gold.

The Greeks settled Asia Minor still later, followed by the Romans. When Christianity developed as a religion, many cities on the peninsula became important centers of Christian faith, such as Ephesus, Antioch, and Nicaea. A Roman citizen from Tarsus named Saul became the greatest missionary of the new Christian Church, as the Apostle Paul.

Following the collapse of the Roman Empire in the fifth century A.D., Asia Minor became the largest part of the East Roman or Byzantine Empire, named for its capital, Byzantium. The city was later renamed Constantinople, in honor of the Roman emperor Constantine, after he had become Christian. For a thousand years, this empire was a center and fortress of Christianity against hostile neighbors and later against the forces of Islam.

The Ottoman Centuries[2]

Various nomadic peoples from Central Asia began migrating into Islamic lands from the ninth century onward. Among them were the ancestors of the Turks of today. They settled mostly along the borders between Christian and Islamic powers in Asia Minor and northwest Iran. Although divided into families and clans and often in conflict, the Turks had a rare sense of unity as a nation. They were also early converts to Islam. Its simple faith and requirements appealed to them more than did Christian ritual, and they readily joined in Islam's battles as Ghazis, "warriors for the faith." Asia Minor, having been wrested from the Greeks by the Turks, also gave the Turks a strong sense of identification with that particular place. To them it was Anadolu (Anatolia), "land of the setting sun," a "sacred homeland" giving the Turks a strong sense of national identity and unity.

The Ottomans were one of many Turkish clans in Anatolia. They took their name from Osman, a clan leader elected because of certain qualifications considered ideal for a Ghazi chieftain—wisdom, prudence, courage, skill in battle, and justice, along with a strong belief in Islam.[3] Osman's clan members identified with their leader to such an extent that they called themselves *Osmanlis,* "sons of Osman," rather than *Turks,* a term they equated with boorish, unwashed peasants.

Although the Ottomans started out with a small territory, they were fortunate in that Osman and his successors were extremely able rulers. Osman's son, Orkhan, captured the important Greek city of Bursa across the Sea of Marmara from Constantinople. It became the first Ottoman capital. Later Ottoman rulers took the title of sultan to signify their temporal authority over expanding territories. A series of capable sultans led the Ottoman armies deep into Europe. Constantinople was not surrounded, and on May 29, A.D. 1453, Mehmed II, the seventh sultan, captured the great city amid portents of disaster for Christian Europe.[4]

Ottoman power continued to expand after the death of Mehmed II. By the 1600s, it included most of Central/Eastern Europe, North Africa, and the Middle East. This large territory was headed by the sultan, who was also the caliph of Islam, ensuring him the spiritual authority over Muslims that supplemented his temporal authority. The Ottomans developed a strong army and fleet that were more than a match for European Christian powers for several centuries. The core of the army was the Janissaries, an elite body of soldiers recruited from Christian villages, forced to convert to Islam and given special privileges as the sultan's personal guard. Janissary garrisons were assigned to important cities in the empire; in certain cities, notably the North African provinces, they ran the government, ignoring the sultan's appointed governors.

Another factor that made the Ottoman system work was the religious organization of non-Muslim minority groups as self-governing units called *millets,* a Turkish word meaning "nations." Each millet was headed by its own religious leader, who was responsible to the sultan for the leadership and good behavior of his people. The three principal millets in Turkey were the Armenians, Greek Orthodox Christians, and Jews. Although Christians and Jews were not considered equal to freeborn Muslims, they were under the sultan's protection. They usually were not interfered with, and Greek and Jewish merchants in particular rendered important services to the Ottoman government as intermediaries in trade with European countries.

The "Sick Man of Europe"

In the eighteenth and nineteenth centuries, the Ottoman Empire gradually weakened, while European Christian powers grew stronger. European countries improved their military equipment and tactics and began to defeat the Ottomans regularly. The sultans were forced to sign treaties and lost territories, causing great humiliation, since they had never treated Christian rulers as equals before. To make matters worse, the European powers helped the Greeks and other Balkan peoples to win their independence from the Ottomans.

The European powers also took advantage of the millet system to intervene directly in the Ottoman Empire's internal affairs. French troops invaded Lebanon in 1860 to restore order after civil war broke out there between the Christian and the Druze communities. The European powers claimed the right to protect the Christian minorities from mistreatment by the Muslim majority, saying that the sultan's troops could not provide for their safety.

One or two sultans in the nineteenth century tried to make reforms in the Ottoman system. They suppressed the Janissaries, who by then had become an unruly mob, and organized a modern army equipped with European weapons, uniforms, and advisers. One sultan issued a charter stating that all of his subjects would have equal rights "regardless of religion, race or language, in matters such as taxation, education, property rights and encouragement of good citizenship."[5] In 1876, Sultan Abdul-Hamid II, prodded by the British, issued a Constitution providing for a Grand National Assembly, representing all classes, races, and creeds within the empire, and limiting the ruler's absolute powers "to the counsel and will of the nation, on the model of the British system of government."[6]

Unfortunately, the forces of reaction, represented by the religious leaders, the sultan's courtiers, and the sultan himself, were stronger than the forces for reform. Abdul-Hamid had no real intention of giving up the absolute powers that Ottoman sultans had always had. Thus, when the first Grand National Assembly met in 1877 and the members ventured to criticize the sultan's ministers, he dissolved the Assembly.

The European powers became convinced that the Ottomans were incapable of reform. European rulers compared the healthy state of their economies and the growth of representative government in their countries to the grinding poverty and lack of rights for Ottoman subjects, as a healthy person looks at an ill one in a hospital bed. The European rulers referred to the sultan as the "Sick Man of Europe" and plotted his death.[7]

However, the Sick Man's death was easier to talk about than to carry out. The main reason was that the European rulers distrusted one another almost as much as they disliked the sultan. If one European ruler seemed to be getting too much territory, trade privileges, or control over the sultan's policies, the others would band together to block that ruler.

World War I: Exit Empire, Enter Republic

During World War I, the Ottoman Empire was allied with Germany against Britain, France, and Russia. Ottoman armies fought bravely against heavy odds but were eventually defeated. A peace treaty signed in 1920 divided up the empire into British and French protectorates, except for a small part of Anatolia that was left to the sultan. The most devastating blow of all was the occupation by the Greeks of western Anatolia, under the provisions

of a secret agreement that brought Greece into the war. It seemed to the Turks that their former subjects had become their rulers.

At this point in the Turkish nation's fortunes, however, a new leader appeared. He would take it in a very different direction. His name was Mustafa Kemal. During the war, Mustafa Kemal was one of the few successful Ottoman military commanders, organizing brilliant tactical retreats and defeating the British in 1915 when they attempted to capture the Dardanelles.

Mustafa Kemal took advantage of Turkish anger over the occupation of Anatolia by foreign armies, particularly the Greeks, to launch a movement for independence. It would be a movement not only to recover the sacred Anatolian homeland but also for independence from the sultan.

The Turkish independence movement began in the interior, far from Constantinople. Mustafa Kemal and his associates chose Ankara, a village on a plateau, as their new capital. They issued a so-called National Pact stating that the "New Turkey" would be an independent republic. Its territory would be limited to areas where Turks were the majority of the population. The nationalists resolutely turned their backs on Turkey's imperial past.

The Turkish War of Independence lasted until 1922. It was fought mainly against the Greeks. The nationalists were able to convince other occupation forces to withdraw from Anatolia by proving that they controlled the territory and represented the real interests of the Turkish people. The Greeks were defeated in a series of fierce battles; and eventually France and Britain signed a treaty recognizing Turkey as a sovereign state headed by Mustafa Kemal.

THE TURKISH REPUBLIC

The Turkish republic has passed through several stages of political development since it was founded. The first stage, dominated by Mustafa Kemal, established its basic form. "Turkey for the Turks" meant that the republic would be predominantly Turkish in population; this was accomplished by rough surgery, with the expulsion of the Armenians and most of the Greeks. Mustafa Kemal also rejected imperialism and interference in the internal affairs of other nations. He once said, "Turkey has a firm policy of ensuring [its] independence within set national boundaries."[8] Peace with Turkey's neighbors and the abandonment of imperialism enabled Mustafa Kemal to concentrate on internal changes. By design, these changes would be far-reaching, in order to break what he viewed as the dead hand of Islam on Turk-

(UPI/Corbis-Bettmann)

Mustafa Kemal Ataturk was the driving force behind the establishment of Modern Turkey. Ataturk positioned Turkey as a secular democratic state, developed a Constitution in 1924, and made sweeping changes in the social and cultural life that have brought Turkey into the twentieth century. He died on November 10, 1938, a date that, even today, is observed by all Turks.

ish life. Turkey would become a secular democratic state on the European model. A Constitution was approved in 1924, the sultanate and the caliphate were both abolished, and the last Ottoman sultan went into exile. Religious courts were also abolished, and new European law codes were introduced to replace Islamic law. An elected Grand National Assembly was given the responsibility for legislation, with executive power held by the president of the republic.

The most striking changes were made in social life, most bearing the personal stamp of Mustafa Kemal. The traditional Turkish costume and polygyny were outlawed. Women were encouraged to work, allowed to vote (in 1930), and given equal rights with men in divorce and inheritance. Turks were required to have surnames; Mustafa Kemal took the name *Ataturk,* meaning "Father of the Turks."

Mustafa Kemal Ataturk died on November 10, 1938. His hold on his country had been so strong, his influence so pervasive, that a whole nation broke down and wept when the news came. The anniversary of his death is still observed by a moment of silence.

Ismet Inonu, Ataturk's right-hand man, succeeded Ataturk and served as president until 1950. Ataturk had distrusted political parties; his brief experiment with a two-party system was abruptly cancelled when members of the officially sponsored "loyal opposition" criticized the Father of the Turks for his free lifestyle. The only political party he allowed was the Republican People's Party (RPP). It was not dedicated to its own survival or to repression, as are political parties in many single-party states. The RPP based its program on six principles, the most important, in terms of politics, being *devrim-*

cilik ("revolutionism" or "reformism"). It meant that the party was committed to work for a multiparty system and free elections. One author noted, "The Turkish single party system was never based on the doctrine of a single party. It was always embarrassed and almost ashamed of the monopoly [over power]. The Turkish single party had a bad conscience."[9]

Agitation for political reforms began during World War II. Later, when Turkey applied for admission to the United Nations, a number of National Assembly deputies pointed out that the UN Charter specified certain rights that the government was not providing. Reacting to popular demands and pressure from Turkey's allies, Inonu announced that political parties could be established. The first new party in the republic's history was the Democratic Party, organized in 1946. In 1950, the party won 408 seats in the National Assembly, to 69 for the Republican People's Party. The Democrats had campaigned vigorously in rural areas, winning massive support from farmers and peasants. Having presided over the transition from a one-party system with a bad conscience to a two-party one, President Inonu stepped down to become head of the opposition.

MILITARY INTERVENTIONS

Modern Turkey has struggled for decades to develop a workable multiparty political system. An interesting point about this struggle is that the armed forces have seized power three times, and three times they have returned the nation to civilian rule. This fact makes Turkey very different from other Middle Eastern nations, whose army leaders, once they have seized power, have been unwilling to give it up.

Ataturk deliberately kept the Turkish armed forces out of domestic politics. He believed that the military had only two responsibilities: to defend the nation in case of invasion and to serve as "the guardian of the reforming ideals of his regime."[10] Since Ataturk's death, military leaders have seized power only when they have been convinced that the civilian government had betrayed the ideals of the founder of the republic.

The first military coup took place in 1960, after a decade of rule by the Democrats. Army leaders charged them with corruption, economic mismanagement, and repression of the opposition. After a public trial, the three top civilian leaders were executed. Thus far, they have been the only high-ranking Turkish politicians to receive the death sentence. (After the 1980 coup, a number of civilian leaders were arrested, but the most serious sentence imposed was a ban on political activity for the next 10 years for certain party chiefs.)

The military leaders re-instated civilian rule in 1961. The Democratic Party was declared illegal, but other parties were allowed to compete in national elections. The new Justice Party, successor to the Democrats, won the elections but did not win a clear majority. As a result, the Turkish government could not function effectively. More and more Turks, especially university students and trade union leaders, turned to violence as they became disillusioned with the multiparty system. As the violence increased, the military again intervened, but it stopped short of taking complete control.

In 1980, the armed forces intervened for the third time, citing three reasons: failure of the government to deal with political violence; the economic crisis; and the revival of Islamic fundamentalism, which they viewed as a total surrender of the secular principles established by Ataturk. (The National Salvation Party openly advocated a return to Islamic law and organized huge rallies in several Turkish cities in 1979–1981.) The National Assembly was dissolved, the Constitution was suspended, and martial law was imposed throughout the country. The generals said that they would restore parliamentary rule—but not before terrorism had been eliminated.

RETURN TO CIVILIAN RULE

The military regime approved a new Constitution in 1982. It provided for a multiparty political system, although pre-1980 political parties were specifically excluded. (Several were later re-instated, notably the Republican People's Party, or RPP. Three new parties were allowed to present candidates for a new Grand National Assembly (GNA), and elections were scheduled for 1983. However, the party least favored by the generals, the Motherland Party (ANAP), ran an American-style political campaign, using the media to present its candidates to the country. It won handily. Its leader, Turgut Ozal, became the first prime minister in this phase of Turkey's long, slow progress toward effective multiparty democracy.

Ozal, an economist by profession, had served as minister of finance under the military government in 1980–1982. In that capacity, he developed a strict austerity program that stabilized the economy. But the prime ministership was another matter, especially with five generals looking over his shoulder. The Motherland Party's popularity declined somewhat in 1986–1987, a decline that owed more to a broad-

ening of the political process than to voter disenchantment.

On September 6, 1987, the nation took a significant step forward—although some analysts viewed it as sideways—toward full restoration of the democratic process. Voters narrowly approved the restoration of political rights to about 100 politicians who had been banned from party activity for 10 years after the 1980 coup: The vote was 50.23 percent "yes" to 49.77 percent "no" in a nationwide referendum, a difference of fewer than 100,000 votes. The results surprised many observers, particularly the most prominent political exiles, former prime ministers Suleyman Demirel of the Justice Party and Bulent Ecevit, leader of the banned Republican People's Party. They had expected a heavy vote in their favor. Prime Minister Ozal's argument that the nation should not return to the "bad old days" before the 1980 coup, when a personal vendetta between these two leaders had polarized politics and paralyzed the economy and there were several dozen murders a day, had clearly carried weight with the electorate.[11]

Thus encouraged, Ozal scheduled new elections for November 1, 1987, a year ahead of schedule. But, in October, the Constitutional Court ruled that a December 1986 electoral law was invalid, because it had eliminated the primary system, thereby undermining the multiparty system. The elections were held on November 29 under new electoral guidelines. The Motherland Party won easily, taking 292 of 450 seats in the GNA. The Social Democratic Populist Party (SHP), a newcomer to Turkish politics, ran second, with 99 seats; while True Path (DYP), founded by Demirel to succeed the Justice Party, ran a distant third, with 59.

The Motherland Party's large parliamentary majority enabled Ozal to have himself elected president to succeed General Evren in 1989, at the end of the latter's term in office. Although the Turkish presidency is largely a ceremonial office, Ozal continued to run the nation as if it were not, with less successful results than those he had attained during his prime ministership. As a result, popular support for his party continued to erode. In the October 1991 elections for a new National Assembly, candidates of the opposition True Path Party won 180 seats to 113 for the Motherland Party, taking 27 percent of the popular vote, as compared to 24 percent for the majority party. The Social Democratic Populist Party garnered 20 percent of the vote, followed by Islamic Welfare Party (Refah), whose growing strength was reflected in its 16 percent support from voters.

Lacking a majority in the Assembly, the DYP formed a coalition government with the SHP in November 1991. Party leader Suleyman Demirel became prime minister. The DYP–SHP coalition improved its political position in local elections early in 1992, when its candidates won a majority of urban mayorships. In July of that year, the ban on political parties existing before the 1980 military coup was lifted; most of them had been incorporated into new parties, but the Republican People's Party, founded by Ataturk, reentered the political arena. It drew a number of defections from Assembly members, due in large part to the charismatic appeal of its leader, Deniz Baykal; as a result, the coalition was left with a shaky six-vote majority in the Legislature.

President Ozal died in April 1993, abruptly ending the long political feud between him and Demirel that had weakened government effectiveness. Demirel succeeded him as president. The DYP elected Tansu Ciller, a U.S.–trained economist and university professor, as Turkey's first woman prime minister, one of two in the Muslim world (the other was Benazir Bhutto of Pakistan).

Ciller's first 2 years in office were marked by economic difficulties, growing tendencies toward Islamic fundamentalism spearheaded by Refah, and intensified violence by Kurdish separatists of the Workers' Party of Kurdistan (PKK), in the southeastern region. Nevertheless, her government, a coalition of the DYP and the Republican People's Party, representing the center left and the center right respectively in the political spectrum, seemed to be governing effectively. By early 1995, the army had regained control of much of the southeast from PKK forces, and in March, agreement was reached for a customs union with the European Union. Municipal elections in June also favored the ruling coalition. It won 61.7 percent of Council seats against 17.4 percent for Refah candidates and 13.4 percent for those of ANAP.

Thus, the collapse of the coalition government in September came as a surprise to most observers. Republican People's party head Deniz Baykal had set certain terms for continuation of his party's alliance with DYP. These included repeal of a strict antiterrorism law, which had drawn international condemnation for its lack of rights for detained dissidents; tighter controls over Islamic fundamentalists; and pay raises of 70 percent for public workers to offset inflation. When these terms were rejected, he withdrew his party from the coalition.

Elections in December 1995 brought another shock, with Refah winning 158 seats to 135 for True Path and 132 for ANAP. For the first time in modern Turkish history, an Islamic-oriented party had won more seats in the Grand National Assembly than its rivals. Refah leader Necmettin Erbakan was named Turkey's first "Islamist" prime minister, taking office in April 1996. However, his party lacked a clear majority in the Assembly. As a result, coalition government became necessary. Erbakan's cabinet included ministers from the three major parties, and Ciller became foreign minister.

Initially, Erbakan and his party brought a breath of fresh air into Turkish politics. The prime minister's vision of a "Just Order" for Turkey, which would involve withdrawal from NATO and closer relations with other Islamic nations, produced several economic rewards. Erbakan's concern with "honest government" and improved living standards for the less-fortunate classes brought some relief to a people conditioned to corruption in government.

But these positive elements were outweighed by determined efforts on the part of Turkey's military leaders to oust Erbakan. Although Refah represents the moderate end of the Islamic fundamentalist spectrum and many of its members are solid middle-class conservatives, some of its policies sowed distrust among these leaders as to the party's real intentions. Thus closer ties with Islamic Iran, expanded "Islamic" education, and mandatory dress and veiling requirements for Turkish school girls were viewed as efforts to undermine Turkish secular values. Although traditionally the Turkish military has sought to stay clear of internal politics, as guardians of the Ataturk revolution, its leaders feared that Refah's victory at the polls presaged the replacement of the secular government by a fundamentalist Islamic regime.

In March 1997, Erbakan's government survived a censure motion in the Assembly by a mere six votes. Subsequently, the state prosecutor filed suit with the Constitutional Court, asking the court to outlaw Refah on the grounds that it threatened the basic tenets of the secular state. (In January 1998, the Court acted to outlaw Refah as a threat to democracy.) Things went rapidly downhill thereafter for the embattled prime minister. After several ultimatums from military leaders, he resigned in June. President Demirel then named Mesut Yilmaz, leader of ANAP, to succeed him, bypassing Ciller—who would normally have been appointed—because she was, and is, under investigation for corruption during her earlier period in office. Yilmaz was confirmed when two dozen members of True Path joined ANAP, giv-

ing the new prime minister a 25-vote majority. But there was no guarantee that the colorless Yilmaz would do better than his flamboyant rivals in governing his fractious country. In its 74th year as a secular republic, Turkey seemed pulled in two directions, "with those who have inherited Ataturk's secularism and those in search of an Islamic revival gazing at each other across a gulf of incomprehension."[12]

THE KURDISH PROBLEM INTENSIFIES

Until recently, the almost total exclusion of the Kurdish population from national life aroused little resistance. However, the breakdown of law and order throughout the country in the 1970s led to a revival of Kurdish nationalism. The Workers' Party of Kurdistan, founded in 1978 as a Marxist–Leninist party, took part in the general violence but went further than other left-wing groups (or, for that matter, the Kurdish mainstream) in demanding a separate Kurdish state. The PKK was outlawed after the 1980 military takeover; several of its leaders were executed, and 1,500 members were arrested and jailed.

The PKK shifted to guerrilla operations in 1984. Since then, more than 6,000 persons have been killed, including a large number of Kurdish civilians as well as guerrillas and members of the Turkish Army and police. The government imposed martial law in 1991, after a series of PKK raids on police posts and remote villages.

With the outbreak of the Gulf War, the Kurdish problem intensified. The PKK set up bases in northern Iraq to supplement its main base in northern Lebanon, where the guerrillas came under Syrian protection. Cross-border infiltration from Iraq created a dilemma for Iraqi Kurdish leaders. On the one hand, they were committed to the Kurdish nationalist cause that they shared with their "blood brothers"; on the other hand the raids invited Turkish retaliation and endangered their own hard-won autonomy from the government of Saddam Hussein. After Turkish forces launched a series of attacks on PKK bases inside Iraqi Kurdistan, Kurdish leaders there said that they did not support the PKK and would not permit use of their territory for raids into Turkey proper.

An agreement with Syria reached in late 1992 also closed the Lebanese border, under Syrian control, to PKK penetration into Turkey. The border closures seriously hampered the organization's effectiveness; and in April 1993, the PKK leader, Abdullah Ocalan, announced a unilateral 25-day cease-fire. However, the government insisted that it would not deal with "ter-

rorists." Ocalan then declared an "all-out war," promising "the bloodiest summer ever" for the Turkish people. PKK militants and their sympathizers seized hostages and held demonstrations at Turkish consulates and embassies in Europe.

In 1995 and again in 1997, Turkish forces invaded Iraqi Kurdistan, in hot pursuit of PKK rebels who have used the area as a safe haven for launching attacks into Turkish territory. Although it was criticized by the United Nations for violations of Iraqi sovereignty, the Turkish government insisted on its right to self-defense in view of PKK provocations form inside Iraqi territory.

The Ciller government's commitment to democratic reforms was also tested severely by social unrest. In March 1995, the Alawite population in several cities went on a rampage after Alawite coffeehouses in Istanbul were firebombed by unknown persons.

At its base, this social unrest, affecting both Kurds and Alawis, rests on economic deprivation. Both communities have been bypassed in national development over the years in favor of the Turkish majority. In the 1990s, the government has made some effort to improve Kurdish economic circumstances and to recognize their distinct culture. The use of Kurdish in official documents relative to their region was authorized in 1991. Also, the Southeast Anatolia Project and its centerpiece, the gigantic Ataturk Dam on the Euphrates, has begun the process of turning Turkey's most arid and deprived region into a fertile garden.

FOREIGN POLICY

Although Turkey's efforts to crush Kurdish irredentism have drawn criticism from the international community and its human-rights record has been much criticized, the country has played a positive role in regional affairs in recent years. Operation Provide Comfort, initiated after the Gulf War to protect Iraqi Kurds from reprisals by Saddam Hussein's Iraqi army, established a no-fly zone patrolled by aircraft from Britain, France, and the United States operating out of Turkish air bases. This agreement has been extended regularly by the Turkish Grand National Assembly, most recently in July 1997.

Turkey's increasingly independent posture in foreign policy was marked by the 1996 agreement with Iran and a pact with Israel for joint training of air-force pilots. The country has also cultivated links with the newly independent Muslim republics of Central Asia. It loaned $2 billion to Kazakhstan for oil development, becoming in the process the latter's top creditor. Turkey was also the first country to rec-

The founding of Constantinople as the Roman Christian capital, on the site of ancient Byzantium **330**	The capture of Constantinople by Sultan Mehmed II; the city becomes the capital of the Islamic Ottoman Empire **1453**	The Ottoman Empire expands deep into Europe; the high-water mark is the siege of Vienna **1683**	The defeat of Ottomans and division of territories into foreign protectorates **1918–1920**	Turkey becomes a republic **1925**	The first military coup **1960**	Military coup; civilian rule later returns **1980s**	The government imposes emergency rule

1990s

Turkey strongly supports coalition efforts in the Gulf War	The Kurdish problem intensifies; Alawi and Kurdish social unrest	The economy improves; Turkey moves toward European Union membership

ognize the independence (from the former Soviet Union) of Kazakhstan and Azerbaijan.

THE ECONOMY

Turkey has a relatively diversified economy, with a productive agriculture and considerable mineral resources. Cotton is the major export crop, but the country is the world's largest producer of sultana raisins and hazelnuts. Other important crops are tobacco, wheat, sunflower seeds, sesame and linseed oils, and cotton-oil seeds. Opium was once an important crop, but, due to illegal exportation, poppy growing was banned by the government in 1972. The ban was lifted in 1974 after poppy farmers were unable to adapt their lands to other crops; production and sale are now government-controlled.

Mineral resources include bauxite, chrome, copper, and iron ore, and there are large deposits of lignite. Turkey is one of the world's largest producers of chromite (chromium ore). Another important mineral resource is meerschaum, used for pipes and cigarette holders. Turkey supplies 80 percent of the world market for emery, and there are rich deposits of tungsten, perlite, boron, and cinnabar, all important rare metals.

Turkey has no significant oil or gas deposits, but agreements for natural-gas imports signed in 1996 with Iran, Yemen, and Egypt will meet domestic power station and household needs. With the reopening of the pipeline to Iraqi oil fields in December 1996, Turkey began receiving 75,000 barrels per day of crude oil for refining plus $130 million in transit fees.

A landmark customs agreement with the European Union was approved by the EU in 1996. The agreement eliminates EU import quotas on Turkish textiles, and on customs duties and excise taxes on iron and steel-manufactured products that the country must import from Europe. However, Turkey's poor human-rights record caused the EU to suspend $6 million in European Currency Unit aid.

The country does have a fairly large skilled labor force, and Turkish contractors have been able to negotiate contracts for development projects in oil-producing countries, such as Libya, with partial payment for services in oil shipments at reduced rates. The large Turkish expatriate labor force, much of it in Germany, provided an important source of revenue through worker remittances. Prospects for the 1.8 million Turks living and working in Germany, however, deteriorated sharply in 1993 as neo-Nazi "skinheads" carried out a series of violent attacks on them as part of the campaign of the German far right to force foreigners to leave the country.

NOTES

1. Martin van Bruinessen, "Kurds, Turks and the Alevi Revival in Turkey," *Middle East Report* (July–Sept 1996), p. 7.

2. Cf. Lord Kinross, *The Ottoman Centuries: The Rise and Fall of the Turkish Empire* (New York: William Morrow, 1977).

3. *Ibid.,* p. 25.

4. An American astronomer, Kevin Pang, has advanced the proposal that the fall of the Byzantine capital was preceded by a "darkening of the skies" and other portents of doom related to the eruption of the volcano Kuwae, in the New Hebrides, in 1453. See Lynn Teo Simarski, "Constantinople's Volcanic Twilight," *Aramco World* (November/December 1996), pp. 8–13.

5. *Op. cit.,* Kinross, p. 501.

6. *Ibid.,* p. 511.

7. British prime minister William Gladstone said in 1880 that the Ottoman government was "a bottomless pit of fraud and falsehood." *Ibid.,* p. 538.

8. V. A. Danilov, "Kemalism and World Peace," in A. Kazancigil and E. Ozbudun, eds., *Ataturk, Founder of a Modern State* (Hamden, CT: Archon Books, 1981), p. 110.

9. Maurice Duverger, *Political Parties* (New York: John Wiley, 1959), p. 277.

10. C. H. Dodd, *Democracy and Development in Turkey* (North Humberside, England: Eothen Press, 1979), p. 135.

11. *The Economist* (August 22, 1987) noted that ballots would be colored orange (for "yes") and blue (for "no") to simplify the process for rural voters, who make up half of the electorate and are mostly illiterate.

12. "Generals and Politics," *The Economist* (July 19, 1997), p. 23.

DEVELOPMENT

The 1997 fiscal-reform package sets as its goal a balanced budget, the first in 36 years. Some $10 billion is to be raised by increased taxes, leasing of 6 thermal power plants, and sale of other state-owned enterprises to private investors.

FREEDOM

Constitutional amendments approved in 1995 formally ended all restrictions on civil rights imposed after the 1980 military coup. In August, the Assembly approved an amnesty for some newspaper editors imprisoned for violating Turkey's restrictive press laws. But the laws remain in force for future violators.

HEALTH/WELFARE

The Southeast Anatolia Project, centered in the ancient Biblical city of Harran, has already begun to improve the living standards of the largely Kurdish population of this neglected region.

ACHIEVEMENTS

The village of Narlica drew world attention when it rejected in a 1997 referendum the proposal of a French mining company to develop the country's first gold mine. Villagers, fearing the impact on local tourism, joined with environmentalists to protest its development.

United Arab Emirates

GEOGRAPHY
Area in Square Kilometers (Miles): 83,600 (42,498) (about the size of Maine)
Capital (Population): Abu Dhabi (363,400)
Climate: hot, dry desert; cooler in eastern mountains

PEOPLE

Population
Total: 3,057,400
Annual Growth Rate: 4.6%
Rural/Urban Population Ratio: 18/82
Ethnic Makeup: 19% Emirian; 23% other Arab; 50% South Asian; 8% East Asian and Westerner
Major Languages: Arabic; several others

Health
Life Expectancy at Birth: 70 years (male); 75 years (female)
Infant Mortality Rate (Ratio): 22/1,000
Average Caloric Intake: n/a
Physicians Available (Ratio): 1/694

Religions
96% Muslim (80% Sunni, 16% Shia); 4% Hindu, Christian, and others

Education
Adult Literacy Rate: 71%

COMMUNICATION
Telephones: 386,600
Newspapers: 2 notable dailies; 1 weekly

Dubai Diversions

Falconry, the traditional sport of desert shaykhs, and sand skiing, popular not only with U.A.E. residents but also with U.S. sailors on leave from their ships patrolling the Persian Gulf, have been displaced in recent years by camel racing. Subsidized by the Dubai government as a community service, the sport boasts a huge racetrack, a training center that treats prize racing camels like royalty, and an artificial-insemination center for breeding purposes. The world's first frozen embryo camel baby was born there in 1995. The sport costs the Dubai government some $45 million a year, but officials refuse to put a price tag, in terms of ticket charges or membership fees, on what has been a tradition among Bedouin for centuries and is only now becoming something of a tourist attraction.

TRANSPORTATION
Highways—Kilometers (Miles): 2,000 (1,248)
Railroads—Kilometers (Miles): none
Usable Airfields: 41

GOVERNMENT
Type: federation of emirates
Independence Date: December 2, 1971
Heads of State/Government: Supreme Council of Rulers of the 7 emirates: Shaykh Zayed bin Sultan al-Nuhayyan, president; Shaykh Maktum bin Rashid al-Maktoum, vice president
Political Parties: none
Suffrage: none

MILITARY
Number of Armed Forces: 44,000
Military Expenditures (% of Central Government Expenditures): 4.3%
Current Hostilities: territorial dispute with Iran and border dispute with Oman; internal border disputes

ECONOMY
Currency ($ U.S. Equivalent): 3.67 dirhams = $1 (fixed rate)
Per Capita Income/GDP: $22,480/$62.7 billion
Inflation Rate: 37%
Total Foreign Debt: $11.6 billion
Natural Resources: oil; natural gas; cement aggregate
Agriculture: vegetables; dates; limes; alfalfa; tobacco
Industry: petroleum; light manufacturing

FOREIGN TRADE
Exports: $28.8 billion
Imports: $24.9 billion

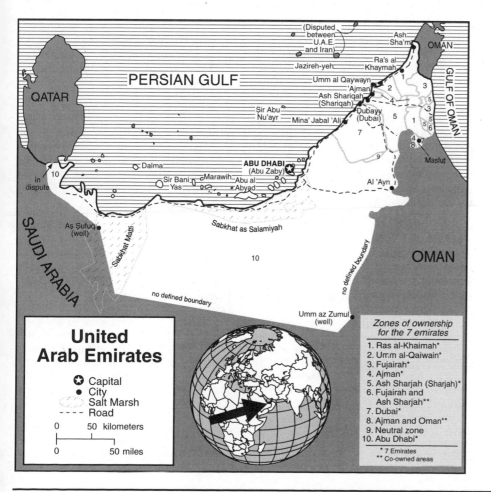

United Arab Emirates

- ⊛ Capital
- ● City
- Salt Marsh
- - - - Road

0   50 kilometers
0   50 miles

Zones of ownership for the 7 emirates
1. Ras al-Khaimah*
2. Umm al-Qaiwain*
3. Fujairah*
4. Ajman*
5. Ash Sharjah (Sharjah)*
6. Fujairah and Ash Sharjah**
7. Dubai*
8. Ajman and Oman**
9. Neutral zone
10. Abu Dhabi*

* 7 Emirates
** Co-owned areas

THE UNITED ARAB EMIRATES

The United Arab Emirates (U.A.E.) is a federation of seven independent states with a central governing Council located on the northeast coast of the Arabian Peninsula. The states—called emirates, from the title of their rulers—are Abu Dhabi, Ajman, Dubai, Fujairah, Ras al-Khaimah, Sharjah, and Umm al-Qaiwain. They came under British protection in the 1800s and were given their independence of Great Britain by treaty in 1971. At that time, they joined in the federal union. From its modest beginnings, the U.A.E. has come to play an important role in Middle East Arab affairs, because of its oil wealth.

Abu Dhabi, the largest emirate, contains 87 percent of the U.A.E. in area. Its capital, also called Abu Dhabi, is the largest city in the federation. Dubai, the second-largest emirate, has the federation's only natural harbor, which has been enlarged to handle supertankers. Abu Dhabi, Dubai, and Sharjah produce oil; Sharjah also has important natural-gas reserves and cement. Fujairah port is a major entrepôt for shipping. The other emirates have little in the way of resources and have yet to find oil in commercial quantities.

The early inhabitants of the area were fishermen and nomads. They were converted to Islam in the seventh century A.D., but little is known of their history before the sixteenth century. By that time, European nations, notably Portugal, had taken an active interest in trade with India and the Far East. Gradually, other European countries, particularly Holland, France, and Britain, challenged Portuguese supremacy. As more and more European ships appeared in Arabian coastal waters or fought one another over trade, the coastal Arabs felt threatened with loss of their territory. Meanwhile, the Wahhabis, militant Islamic missionaries, spread over Arabia in the eighteenth century. Wahhabi agents incited the most powerful coastal group, the Qawasim, to interfere with European shipping. European ships were seized along with their cargoes, and their crews were held for ransom. To the European countries, this was piracy; to the Qawasim, however, it was defense of Islamic territory against the infidels. Ras al-Khaimah was their chief port, but soon the whole coast of the present-day U.A.E. became known as the Pirate Coast.

Piracy lasted until 1820, when the British, who now controlled India and thus dominated Eastern trade, convinced the principal chiefs of the coast to sign a treaty ending pirate activities. A British naval squadron was stationed in Ras al-Khaimah to enforce the treaty. In 1853, the arrangement was changed into a "Perpetual Maritime Truce." Because it specified a *truce* between the British and the chiefs, the region became known as the Trucial Coast, and the territory of each chief was termed a trucial state. A British garrison was provided for each ruler, and a British political agent was assigned to take charge of foreign affairs. Britain paid the rulers annual subsidies; in most cases, it was all the money they could acquire. There were originally five Trucial States (also called emirates); Sharjah and Ras al-Khaimah were reorganized as separate emirates in 1966.

The arrangement between Great Britain and the Trucial States worked smoothly for more than a century, through both world wars. Then, in the 1960s, the British decided—for economic and political reasons—to give up most of their overseas colonies, including those in the Arabian Peninsula, which were technically protectorates rather than colonies. In 1968, they proposed to the Trucial Coast emirs that they join in a federation with Bahrain and Qatar, neighboring oil-producing protectorates. But Bahrain and Qatar, being larger and richer, decided to go it alone. Thus, the United Arab Emirates, when it became independent in 1971, included only six emirates. Ras al-Khaimah joined in 1972.

PROBLEMS OF INTEGRATION

Differences in size, wealth, resources, and population have hampered U.A.E. integration since it was formed. Another problem is poor communications. Until recently, one could travel from emirate to emirate only by boat, and telephone service was nonexistent. These limitations are disappearing rapidly, however, as the U.A.E. develops.

There are some internal disagreements among the emirates. Ras al-Khaimah and Umm al-Qaiwain have yet to reach agreement on demarcation of their common border, and Sharjah's border with neighboring Oman, on the Musandam Peninsula, is also in dispute. Differences in resources and allocation of revenues are another point of disagreement, separating the oil-rich emirates from the oil-poor ones.

The U.A.E. federal system is defined in the 1971 Constitution. The government consists of a Supreme Council of Rulers of the seven emirates; a Council of Ministers (cabinet), appointed by the president of the Council; and a unicameral Federal National Assembly (*Majlis Watani Ittihad*) of 40 members appointed by the ruling emirs on a proportional basis, according to size and population.

One of the strengths of the system is that Shaykh Zayed, the ruler of Abu Dhabi, has served as president of the Council of Rulers since its inception. The federal capital is located in Abu Dhabi, the largest and richest emirate. The ruler of Dubai, the second largest of the emirates, serves as vice-president. Other unifying features of the U.A.E. are a common commercial-law code, a common currency, and a common defense structure. The sharing of revenues by the wealthy emirates with the less prosperous ones has also helped to strengthen U.A.E. unity.

The 1979 Revolution in Iran, which seemed to threaten the U.A.E.'s security, accelerated the move toward centralization of authority over defense forces, abolition of borders, and merging of revenues. In 1981, the U.A.E. joined with other states in the Gulf Cooperation Council to establish a common defense policy toward their large and powerful neighbor. The U.A.E. also turned to the United States for help; the two countries signed a Defense Cooperation Agreement in 1994. Under the agreement, a force of 300 U.S. military personnel is stationed in the emirates to supervise port facilities and air refueling for American planes patrolling the no-fly zone (the 36th parallel in northern Iraq). But disagreements over the jurisdiction of U.S. personnel, notably after the 1995 conviction of an American sailor by a U.A.E. court for accidentally killing a local child, have blocked the assignment of additional U.S. military personnel there.

The governments of the emirates themselves are best described as patriarchal. Each emir is head of his own large "family" as well as head of his emirate. The ruling emirs gained their power a long time ago from various sources—through foreign trade, pearl fishing, or ownership of lands—and, in recent years, they have profited from oil royalties to confirm their positions as heads of state.

Disagreements within the ruling families have sometimes led to violence or "palace coups," there being no rule or law of primogeniture. The ruler of Umm al-Qaiwain came to power when his father was murdered in 1929. Shaykh Zayed deposed his brother, Shaykh Shakbut, in 1966, when the latter refused to approve a British-sponsored development plan for the protectorate. In 1987, Shaykh Abd al-Aziz, the elder brother of the ruler of Sharjah, attempted to overthrow his brother, on the ground that economic development was being mishandled. The U.A.E. Supreme Council mediated a settlement, and Abd al-Aziz retired to Abu Dhabi. However, he continued to demand authority over Sharjah's economic policies in his capacity as minister for National Development. In 1990, the ruler dismissed him by abolishing the position.

The U.A.E. reduces its dependence on oil revenues

The U.A.E.'s free-trade zone proves a success

Ajman and Umm al-Qaiwain are coastal ports with agricultural hinterlands. Ras al-Khaimah has continually disappointed oil seekers; its only natural resource is aggregate, which is used in making cement. Fujairah, although lacking in energy resources, has become a major oil-bunkering and -refining center. In April 1996, the new bunkering terminal in its port went into operation. Built by the Dutch-owned Van Ommeren Tank Company, the world's largest independent operator, the new facilities will double the millions of tons of cargo now being handled by the port.

AN OIL-DRIVEN ECONOMY
In the past, the people of the Trucial Coast made a meager living from breeding racing camels, some farming, and pearl fishing. Pearls were the main cash crop. But twentieth-century competition from Japanese cultured pearls ruined the Arabian pearl-fishing industry.

In 1958, Shaykh Zayed, then in his teens, led a party of geologists into the remote desert near the oasis of al-Ain, following up the first oil-exploration agreement signed by Abu Dhabi with foreign oil companies. Oil exports began in 1962, and, from then on, the fortunes of the Gulf Arabs improved dramatically. Production was 14,200 barrels per day (b/d) in 1962. In 1982, it was 1.1 million b/d, indicating how far the country's oil-driven economy had moved in just 2 decades. Oil reserves are 98.1 billion barrels, while gas reserves are 205 trillion cubic feet—10 percent of global reserves. They are expected to last well into the twenty-first century at current rates of extraction.

The bulk of hydrocarbon production and reserves is in Abu Dhabi, whose economy is almost totally dependent on oil and gas production and export. Dubai, with a more diversified economic base, inaugurated in 1997 a Strategic Development Plan intended to reach a per capita non-oil income of $20,000 by the year 2010. To reach this goal, the emirate approved generous foreign-investment and re-export rules in 1996. A free-trade zone in the port of Jebel Ali has more than 735 international companies represented there, with $3 billion in assets.

Sharjah's economic fortunes changed dramatically in 1992 with the discovery of a natural-gas field at Kahaif. Current production is 580 million cubic feet per day. Due in part to this energy source, Sharjah's manufacturing plants now account for more than a third of total U.A.E. industrial production.

Its wealth has given the U.A.E. the luxury of being able to move away from overdependence on oil. A large industrial zone opened in Abu Dhabi in 1982 with a refinery and fertilizer and other plants. Dubai took an early lead in non-oil development, setting up aluminum and petrochemical plants as well as the world's largest dry dock. In the 1980s, the extension of the Iran–Iraq War to the Gulf, with attacks on tankers by both sides and danger from floating mines, brought about a boom in the ship-repair business.

The U.A.E.'s dependence on expatriate workers, who comprise approximately 80 percent of the labor force, has been an obstacle to self-sufficiency and diversification. In October 1996, a strict new residency law governing expatriate labor was approved by the Supreme Council. The law limits both immigration numbers and length of stay; it is aimed particularly at low-level Asian workers. As a result, some 400,000 "guest workers"—approximately 15 percent of the total expatriate population—left the federation.

In December 1996, the U.A.E. celebrated its 25th birthday in grand style. The world's largest birthday cake—all 69 tons of it—was paraded through the streets of Dubai, passing under signs emblazoned in English and Arabic: "The Best of the World Is Dubai." The federation's Silver Jubilee featured world-class tennis tournaments, horse racing, and a golf course of heat-resistant turf kept lush by millions of gallons of desalinated water.

The U.A.E.'s cities now feature shopping malls, mini-trains, designer boutiques, and U.S. fast-food franchises. It is a far cry from the eastern Arabia of 25 years ago, when the Gulf Arabs traveled by camel over the desert. Sinbad the Sailor, the legendary traveler, would be amazed if he returned to his old harbor, the creek at Dubai. He would hardly know what to think of the sprawling industrial world going up on the old Trucial Coast; many of his fellow Arabs have had the same difficulty adjusting to their changing world.

DEVELOPMENT

Due largely to the global increase in oil prices, the U.A.E. economy grew 6.6% in 1994–1995 and 5.5% in 1996. The 1997 budget was nearly in balance, with $4.7 billion in revenues and $4.96 billion in expenditures.

FREEDOM

Although overall federal authority rests with the Supreme Council, the rulers of the 7 emirates have full control over their separate territories. The small population and general access of the people to national wealth militate against any changes in the current system in favor of a more democratic one.

HEALTH/WELFARE

Education and health care are available to all U.A.E. nationals at no cost, through the respective emirate governments. But they are available to foreign workers only by arrangement with their employers. Those most affected are low-paid workers from Asian countries.

ACHIEVEMENTS

Nearly 2 million acres of desert have been reclaimed for cultivation. In 1997, Shaykh Zayed, the moving spirit behind the U.A.E. drive for self-sufficiency in food and the "greening" of the desert, received the Gold Panda award from the Worldwide Fund for Nature for his services to global conservation—the first head of state to be so honored.

Yemen (Republic of Yemen)

GEOGRAPHY

Area in Square Kilometers (Miles):
527,970 (203,796) (about twice the size of Oregon)
Capital (Population): San'a (political capital) (972,000); Aden (economic capital) (562,000)
Climate: hot, with minimal rainfall except in mountain zones

PEOPLE

Population

Total: 17,300,000
Annual Growth Rate: 3.7%
Rural/Urban Population Ratio: 77/23
Ethnic Makeup: almost all ethnic Arab
Major Language: Arabic

Health

Life Expectancy at Birth: 62 years (male); 63 years (female)
Infant Mortality Rate (Ratio): 58/1,000
Average Caloric Intake: 76% of FAO minimum
Physicians Available (Ratio): 1/3,900

Religions

55% Shia Muslim; 45% Sunni Muslim

Education

Adult Literacy Rate: 38%

COMMUNICATION

Telephones: 65,000
Newspapers: n/a

TRANSPORTATION

Highways—Kilometers (Miles): 51,390 (32,067)
Railroads—Kilometers (Miles): none
Usable Airfields: 46

GOVERNMENT

Type: republic, formed by merger of former Yemen Arab Republic and People's Democratic Republic of Yemen
Independence Date: formally united May 22, 1990 (date of merger)
Head of State/Government: President Ali Abdullah Saleh; Prime Minister Faraj ibn Ghanim
Political Parties: General People's Congress; Islamic Reform Party; Yemen Socialist Party
Suffrage: universal over 18

MILITARY

Number of Armed Forces: 26,500
Military Expenditures (% of Central Government Expenditures): 7.1%
Current Hostilities: territorial dispute with Eritrea

ECONOMY

Currency ($ U.S. Equivalent): 140 Yemeni rials = $1
Per Capita Income/GDP: $1,955/$23.4 billion
Inflation Rate: 55%
Total Foreign Debt: $7 billion
Natural Resources: oil; natural gas; gold; rock salt; small deposits of coal and copper
Agriculture: cotton; fruits and vegetables; cereals; qat; livestock and poultry; coffee
Industry: oil refining; food processing; textiles; fisheries and fish processing

FOREIGN TRADE

Exports: $2.4 billion
Imports: $3.2 billion

A World of Contrasts

San'a, the capital of united Yemen, was named a world historic landmark by UNESCO in 1985. It has a skyline of minarets and mosques, multistory "skyscraper" houses, and the open-air *suq* (market) where vendors hawk spices, kohl, henna for the hands of brides, and the ubiquitous qat—the leaves of a narcotic shrub that, when chewed, give Yemenis what they call the "elixir of life." The suq, the "pedestrian mall" of San'a, with its men in flowing *galabiyas,* the customary *jambiya* (curved dagger) at the belt, and women in multicolored robes that cover them from head to toe, contrasts sharply with the traffic snarls and noises outside on the streets of San'a. Yet, along the ancient frankincense route to Ma'rib, where the Queen of Sheba once ruled, all is quiet, modern civilization subdued by the silence of the desert.

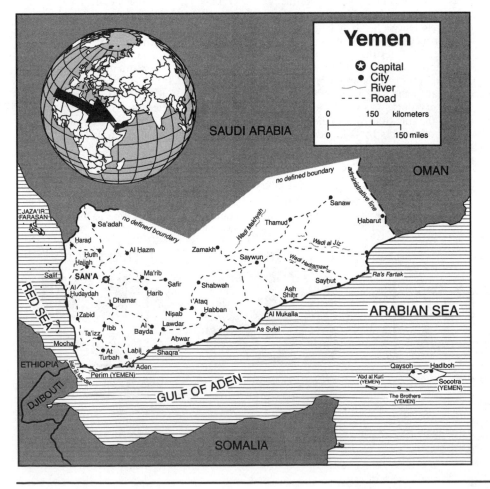

Yemen

- ★ Capital
- ● City
- ~ River
- --- Road

0   150   kilometers
0   150 miles

YEMEN

The Republic of Yemen occupies the extreme southwest corner of the Arabian Peninsula. It consists of three distinct regions, which until 1990 had been separated geographically for centuries and divided politically into two states: the Yemen Arab Republic (North Yemen, or Y.A.R.) and the People's Democratic Republic of Yemen (South Yemen, or P.D.R.Y.). Until the twentieth century, the entire area was known simply as Yemen; and with the merger of the two states, it has resumed its former geographic identity. The former Y.A.R.'s territory consists of two distinct regions: a hot, humid coastal strip, the Tihama, along the Red Sea; and an interior region of mountains and high plains that shade off gradually into the bleak, waterless South Arabian desert.

The Yemeni interior is very different not only from the Tihama but also from other parts of the Arabian Peninsula. It consists of highlands and rugged mountains ranging up to 12,000 feet. At the higher elevations, the mountain ridges are separated by deep, narrow valleys, usually with swift-flowing streams at the bottom. The ample rainfall allows extensive use of terracing for agriculture. The main crops are coffee, cereals, vegetables, and *qat,* a shrub whose leaves are chewed as a mildly intoxicating narcotic.

This part of Yemen has been for centuries the home of warlike but sedentary peoples who have formed a stable, stratified society living in villages or small cities. These groups have been the principal support for the Shia Zaidi Imams, whose rule was the political nucleus of Yemen from the ninth century A.D. to the establishment of the republic in 1962. The Yemeni political capital, San'a, is located in these northern highlands.

The former P.D.R.Y., almost twice the size of its neighbor but less favored geographically, consists of the port and hinterland of Aden (today Yemen's economic capital); the Hadhramaut, a broad valley edged by desert and extending eastward along the Arabian Sea coast; the Perim and Kamaran Islands, at the south end of the Red Sea; and Socotra Island, off the Arabian coast adjacent to the Dhofar Province of Oman.

Until the recent discoveries of oil, South Yemen was believed to have no natural resources. The dominant physical feature is the Wadi Hadhramaut. It is one of the few regions of the country with enough water for irrigation. Except for Aden, the area has little rainfall; in some sections, rain may fall only once in every 10 years. Less than 2 percent of the land is cultivable.

In ancient times, the whole of Yemen was known to the Greeks, Romans, and other peoples as Arabia Felix ("Happy Arabia"), a remote land that they believed to be fabulously wealthy. They knew it as the source of frankincense, myrrh, and other spices as well as other exotic products brought to Mediterranean and Middle Eastern markets from the East. In Yemen itself, several powerful kingdoms grew up from profits earned in this Eastern trade. One kingdom in particular, the Sabaeans, also had a productive agriculture based on irrigation. The water for irrigation came from the great Marib Dam, built around 500 B.C. Marib was a marvel of engineering, built across a deep river valley. The Sabaean economy supported a population estimated at 300,000 in a region that today supports only a few thousand herders.

The Sabaeans were followed by the Himyarites. Himyarite rulers were converted to Christianity by wandering monks in the second century A.D. The Himyarites had contacts with Christian Ethiopia across the Red Sea and for a time were vassals of Ethiopian kings. An Ethiopian army invaded South Arabia but was defeated by the Himyarites in A.D. 570, the "Year of the Elephant" in Arab tradition, so called because the Ethiopian invaders were mounted on elephants. (The year was also notable for the birth of Muhammad, the founder of Islam.)

Sabaeans and Himyarites ruled long ago, but they are still important to Yemenis as symbols of their long and rich historical past. The Imams of Yemen, who ruled until 1962, used a red dye to sign their official documents in token of their relationship to Himyarite kings. (The word *Himyar* comes from the same root as *hamra,* "red.")

The domestication of the camel and development of an underground irrigation system of channels (*falaj*) made this civilization possible. Ships and camel caravans brought the frankincense, myrrh, and musk from Socotra and silks and spices from India and the Far East to northern cities in Egypt, Persia, and Mesopotamia. Aden was an important port for this trade, due to its natural harbor and its location at the south end of the Red Sea.

Yemenis were among the first converts to Islam. The separation of the Yemenis into mutually hostile Sunni and Shia Muslims took place relatively early in Islamic history. Those living in the Tihama, which was easily accessible to missionaries and warriors expanding the borders of the new Islamic state, became Sunnis, obedient to the caliphs (the elected "successors" of Muhammad). The Yemeni mountaineers were more difficult to reach; and when

they were converted to the new religion, it was through the teachings of a follower of the Shi'at Ali, "Party of Ali," those who felt that Muhammad's son-in-law Ali and his descendants should have been chosen as the rightful leaders of the Islamic community. Yemenis in Aden and the Hadhramaut, as well as those in the Tihama, became Sunni, creating the basis for an intra-Yemeni conflict, which still exists today.

THE ZAIDI IMAMATE

In the late ninth century A.D., a feud among certain nominally Muslim groups in inland Yemen led to the invitation to a religious scholar living in Mecca to come and mediate in their dispute. (Use of an outside mediator was common in Arabia at that time.) This scholar brought with him a number of families of Ali's descendants who sought to escape persecution from the Sunnis. He himself was a disciple of Zaid, Ali's great-grandson. He settled the feud, and, in return for his services, he was accepted by both sides of the conflict as their religious leader, or Imam. His followers received lands and were given a protected status, so that in time they became a sort of theocratic aristocracy. This was the beginning of the Zaidi Imamate, a theocratic state that lasted for a thousand years (until 1962).

The first Zaidi Imam had some personal qualities that enabled him to control the unruly mountain people and bend them to his will. He was a shrewd judge of Yemeni character, using his knowledge and his prestige as a member of the family of Ali to give personal favors or to give his power of *baraka* (special powers from God) to one group or withhold it from another. He had great physical strength. It was said of him that he could grind corn with his fingers and pull a camel apart barehanded. He wrote 49 books on Islamic jurisprudence and theology, some of which are still being studied by modern Yemeni scholars. He was also said to bring good (or bad) fortune to a subject merely by a touch or a glance from his piercing black eyes.[1]

In a reversal of the ancient process whereby South Arabian merchants carried goods to the far-flung cities of the north, from the late 1400s on, the towns of the bleak Arabian coast attracted the interest of European seafaring powers as way stations or potential bases for control of their expanding trade with the East Indies, India, and China. Aden was a potentially important base, and expeditions by Portuguese and other Europeans tried without success to capture it at the time. In 1839, a British expedition finally succeeded. It found a town of "800 miserable souls, huddled in huts of reed matting, surrounded by guns that would not fire," or so the American traveler Joseph Osgood described the scene.

Under British rule, Aden became an important naval base and refueling port for ships passing through the Suez Canal and down the Red Sea en route to India. For many British families bound for India, Aden was the last land, with the last friendly faces, that they would see before arriving many days later in the strange wonderland of India. The route through the Suez Canal and down the Red Sea past Aden was the lifeline of the British Empire. In order to protect Aden from possible attack by hostile peoples in the interior, the British signed a series of treaties with their chiefs, called shaykhs or sometimes sultans. These treaties laid the basis for the South Arabian Protectorates. British political agents advised the rulers on policy matters and gave them annual subsidies to keep them happy. One particular agent, Harold Ingrams, was so successful in eliminating feuds and rivalries that "Ingrams's Peace" became a symbol of the right way to deal with proud, independent local leaders.

The Zaidi Imams continued to rule inland Yemen until the nineteenth century, when the Ottoman Turks, who controlled the Tihama, sent an army to conquer all of Yemen (except for Aden, which remained under British protection). The Turks installed an Ottoman governor in San'a and made Yemen a province (*vilayet*) of the empire. But this action did not sit well with the mountain peoples. A Yemeni official told a British visitor: "We have fought the Turks, the tribes . . . and we are always fighting each other. We Yemenis submit to no one permanently. We love freedom and we will fight for it."[2]

The Turkish occupation sparked a revolt. Turkish forces were unable to defeat the mountain peoples, and, in 1911, they signed a treaty that recognized Imam Yahya as ruler in the highlands. In return, the Imam recognized Turkish rule in the Tihama. At the end of World War I, the Turks left Yemen for good. The British, who now controlled most of the Middle East, signed a treaty with Imam Yahya, recognizing his rule in all Yemen.

The two Yemens followed divergent paths in the twentieth century, accounting in large measure for the difficulties that they faced in incorporating into a single state. North Yemen remained largely uninvolved in the political turmoil that engulfed the Middle East after World War II. Imam Yahya ruled his feudal country as an absolute monarch with a handful of advisers, mostly tribal leaders, religious scholars, and members of his family. John Peterson notes that the Imamate "was completely dependent on the abilities of a single individual who was expected to be a competent combination of religious scholar, administrator, negotiator, and military commander."[3] Yahya was all of these, and his forceful personality and ruthless methods of dealing with potential opposition (with just a touch of magic) ensured his control over the population.

Yahya's method of government was simplicity itself. He held a daily public meeting (*jama'a*) seated under an umbrella outside his palace, receiving petitions from anyone who wished to present them and signing approval or disapproval in Himyarite red ink. He personally super-vised tax collections and kept the national treasury in a box under his bed. The Imam distrusted the Ottomans, against whom he had fought for Yemeni independence, and refused to accept their coinage. He also rejected the British currency because it represented a potential foreign influence.

Yahya was determined to keep foreign influences out of Yemen and to resist change in any form. Although Yemen was poor by the industrial world's standards, it was self-sufficient, free, and fully recognized as an independent state. Yahya hoped to keep it that way. He even refused foreign aid because he felt that it would lead to foreign occupation. But he was unable to stop the clock entirely and to keep out all foreign ideas and influences.

Certain actions that seemed to be to his advantage worked against him. One was the organization of a standing army. In order to equip and train an army that would be stronger than tribal armies, Yahya had to purchase arms from abroad and to hire foreign advisers to train his troops. Promising officers were also sent for training in Egypt, and on their return, they formed the nucleus of opposition to the Imam.

In 1948, Imam Yahya was murdered in an attempted coup. He had alienated not only army officers who resented his repressive rule but also leaders from outside the ruling family who were angered by the privileges given to the Imam's sons and relatives. But the coup was disorganized, the conspirators unsure of their goals. Crown Prince Ahmad, the Imam's eldest son and heir, was as tough and resourceful as his 80-year-old father had been.[4] He gathered support from leaders of other clans and nipped the rebellion in the bud.

Imam Ahmad (1948–1962) ruled as despotically as his father had ruled. But the walls of Yemeni isolation inevitably began to crack. Unlike Yahya, Ahmad was willing to modernize a little. Foreign experts came to design and help build the roads, factories, hospitals, and schools that the Imam felt were needed. Several hundred young Yemenis were sent abroad for study. Those who had left the country during Imam Yahya's reign returned. Many Yemenis emigrated to Aden to work for the British and formed the nucleus of a "Free Yemen" movement.

In 1955, the Imam foiled an attempted coup. Other attempts, in 1958 and 1961, were also unsuccessful. The old Imam finally died in 1962 of emphysema, leaving his son, Crown Prince Muhammad al-Badr, to succeed him.

THE MARCH TO INDEPENDENCE

The British wanted to hold on to Aden as long as possible because of its naval base

(UN photo/Kay Muldoon)

Yemen has long been an important trade center. Over time, warring tribes and alternate trade routes greatly diminished the economic strength of the country. Agriculture is an important element in its economy, but modern technology has not yet caught up with this industry, as this picture illustrates.

and refinery. It seemed to them that the best way to protect British interests was to set up a union of Aden and the South Arabian Protectorates. This was done in 1963, with independence promised for 1968. However, the British plan proved unworkable. In Aden, a strong anti-British nationalist movement developed in the trade unions among the dock workers and refinery employees. This movement organized a political party, the People's Socialist Party, strongly influenced by the socialist, anti-Western, Arab nationalist programs of President Gamal Abdel Nasser in Egypt.

The party had two branches: the moderate Front for the Liberation of Occupied South Yemen (FLOSY) and the leftist Marxist National Liberation Front (NLF). About all they had in common was their opposition to the British and the South Arabian sultans, whom they called "lackeys of imperialism." FLOSY and the NLF joined forces in 1965–1967 to force the British to leave Aden. British troops were murdered; bombs damaged the refinery. By 1967, Britain had had enough. British forces were evacuated, and Britain signed a treaty granting independence in South Yemen under a coalition government made up of members of both FLOSY and the NLF.

Muhammad al-Badr held office for a week and then was overthrown by a military coup. Yemen's new military leaders formed a Revolution Command Council and announced that the Imam was dead. Henceforth, they said, Yemen would be a republic. It would give up its self-imposed isolation and would become part of the Arab world. But the Revolution proved to be more difficult to carry out than the military officers had expected. The Imam was not dead, as it turned out, but had escaped to the mountains. The mountain peoples rallied to his support, helping him to launch a counterrevolution. About 85,000 Egyptian troops arrived in Yemen to help the republican army. The coup leaders had been trained in Egypt, and the Egyptian government had not only financed the Revolution but also had encouraged it against the "reactionary" Imam.

For the next 8 years, Yemen was a battleground. The Egyptians bombed villages and even used poison gas against civilians in trying to defeat the Imam's forces. But they were unable to crush the people hidden in the wild mountains of the interior. Saudi Arabia also backed the Imam with arms and kept the border open. The Saudi rulers did not particularly like the Imam, but he seemed preferable to an Egyptian-backed republican regime next door.

After Egypt's defeat by Israel in the 1967 Six-Day War, the Egyptian position in Yemen became untenable, and Egyptian troops were withdrawn. It appeared that the royalists would have a clear field. But they were even more disunited than the republicans. A royalist force surrounded San'a in 1968 but failed to capture the city. The Saudis then decided that the Imam had no future. They worked out a reconciliation of royalists and republicans that would reunite the country. The only restriction was that neither the Imam nor any of his relatives would be allowed to return to Yemen.

Thus, as of 1970, two "republics" had come into existence side by side. The Yemen Arab Republic was more of a tribal state than a republic in the modern political sense of the term. Prior to 1978, its first three presidents either went into exile or were murdered, victims of rivalry within the army. Colonel Ali Abdullah Saleh, a career army officer, seized power in that year and was subsequently chosen as the republic's first elected president. He was re-elected in 1983 and again in 1988 for consecutive 5-year terms. (With unification, he became the first head of state of all Yemen.)

Saleh provided internal stability and allowed some broadening of the political process in North Yemen. A General People's Congress (GPC) was established in 1982. A Consultative Council, elected by popular vote, was established in 1988 to provide some citizen input into legislation. Saleh displayed great skill in balancing tribal and army factions and used foreign aid to develop economic projects such as dams for irrigation to benefit highland and Tihama Yemenis alike.

SOUTH YEMEN: A MARXIST STATE

With the British departure, the South Arabian Federation collapsed. Aden and the Hadhramaut were united under Aden political leadership in 1970 as the People's Democratic Republic of Yemen. It began its existence under adverse circumstances: Britain ended its subsidy for the Aden refinery, and the withdrawal of British forces cut off the revenues generated by the military payroll.

But the main problem was political. A power struggle developed between FLOSY and the NLF. The former favored moderate policies, good relations with other Arab states, and continued ties with Britain. The NLF were leftist Marxists. By 1970, the Marxists had won. FLOSY leaders were killed or went into exile. The new government set its objectives as state ownership of lands, state management of all

business and industry, a single political organization with all other political parties prohibited, and support for antigovernment revolutionary movements in other Arab states, particularly Oman and Saudi Arabia.

During its 2 decades of existence, the P.D.R.Y. modeled its governing structure on that of the Soviet Union, with a Presidium, a Council of Ministers, a Supreme People's Legislative Council, and provincial and district councils, in descending order of importance. The ruling (and only legal) political party took the name Yemen Socialist Party in 1978 to emphasize its Yemeni makeup.

Although the P.D.R.Y. government's ruthless suppression of opposition enabled it to establish political stability, rivalries and vendettas among party leaders led to much instability within the ruling party. The first president, Qahtan al-Sha'bi, was overthrown by pro-Soviet radicals within the party. His successor, Salim Rubayyi Ali, was executed after he had tried and failed to oust his rivals on the party Central Committee. Abd al-Fattah Ismail, the country's third president, resigned in 1980 and went into exile due to a dispute over economic policies. Ali Nasir Muhammad, the fourth president, seemed to have consolidated power and to have won broad party support, until in 1986, he also tried to purge the Central Committee of potential opponents. The peoples of the interior, who formed Muhammad's original support base, stayed out of the fighting. After 10 days of bloody battles with heavy casualties, the president's forces were defeated. He then went into exile and was convicted of treason in absentia. He returned to Yemen in November 1996 after the end of the Civil War and the re-unification of the "two Yemens."

UNIFICATION

Despite their natural urge to unite in a single Yemeni nation, the two Yemens were more often at odds with each other than united in pursuing common goals. This was due in part to the age-old highland–lowland, Sunni–Shia conflict that cut across Yemeni society. But it was also due to their very different systems of government. There were border clashes in 1972, 1975, and 1978–1979, when the P.D.R.Y. was accused of plotting the overthrow of its neighbor. (A P.D.R.Y. envoy brought a bomb hidden in a suitcase to a meeting with the Y.A.R. president, and the latter was killed when the bomb exploded.)

Improved economic circumstances and internal political stability in both Yemens revived interest in unity in the 1980s, especially after oil and natural-gas discoveries in border areas promised advantages

Collapse of the Marib Dam, destroying the flourishing Himyarite civilization	Establishment of the Zaidi Imamate in highland Yemen	Yemen is occupied by the Ottoman Turks; it eventually becomes an Ottoman province		The capture of Aden by a British naval expedition
500	**890**	**1517, 1872**		**1839**
●	●	●		●

to both governments through joint exploitation. In May 1988, President Saleh and Prime Minister al-Attas of the P.D.R.Y. signed the May Unity Pact, which ended travel restrictions and set up a Supreme Yemeni Council of national leaders to prepare a constitution for the proposed unitary state.

From then on, the unity process snowballed. In 1989, the P.D.R.Y. regime freed supporters of former President Ali Nasir Muhammad. Early in 1990, the banks, postal services, ports administration, and customs of the two republics were merged, followed by the merger under joint command of their armed forces.

Formal unification took place on May 22, 1990, with approval by both governments and ratification of instruments by their legislative bodies. Ali Abdullah Saleh was unanimously chosen as the republic's first president, with a four-member Presidential Council formed to oversee the transition. The draft constitution of the new republic established a 39-member Council of Ministers headed by P.D.R.Y. prime minister al-Attas, with ministries divided equally between North and South. In a national referendum in May 1991, voters approved a new all-Yemen Constitution. (The Constitution was opposed by the newly formed Islah Party, representing the tribes and Islamic fundamentalists, on the grounds that it did not conform fully to Islamic law.)

The Constitution provides for elections to a 301-member Parliament. Elections were scheduled for November 1992 but were postponed until April 1993 after the elections committee protested that insufficient time had been allocated for voter registration, preparation of candidate lists, drawing of constituency borders, and campaigning.

The campaign itself was marred by violence, much of it directed at officials of the Yemen Socialist Party by tribal opponents of unification or others who feared that the election would result in greater influence for the more liberal, ex-Marxist Southerners in the government. In December 1992, an economic crisis also hit the country; people took to the streets protesting price increases and a 100 percent inflation rate.

Despite the disruption, the elections were held on schedule, on April 27, 1993.

President Saleh's General People's Congress won 147 seats in Parliament, just shy of a majority. The elections were carried out in open democratic fashion, with women and the small Yemenite Jewish community allowed to vote, in sharp contrast to election practice in other parts of the Middle East.

A coalition government was formed in May 1993 between the General People's Congress, the Yemen Socialist Party, and Islah, which ran third in the balloting. But rivalry between the former political elites of North and South, plus differences in outlook, continued to impede progress toward full unification. Early in 1994, Ali al-Beidh, Yemen Socialist Party (YSP) leader and vice president of the ruling coalition, presented a set of 18 demands whose acceptance was a prerequisite for his return to the government. They were rejected by President Saleh, and civil war broke out in May 1994. Initially, the South Yemeni forces had the better of it, but the more numerous and better-equipped army of the North, moving slowly southward, surrounded Aden and captured the city after a brief siege. Vice President al-Beidh fled into exile, effectively depriving the rebellion of its chief leader, and his Yemen Socialist Party was excluded from the governing coalition, although it was allowed to continue as a political party.

The end of the civil war, more or less on North Yemen's terms, offered Saleh another opportunity to unify the nation. The first step would be the restoration of representative government. A 1992 law was re-instated to require political parties to have 5,000 or more members, plus offices in each governorate, in order to present candidates in the forthcoming national elections. The elections, for a 301-member House of Representatives, were scheduled for April 1997.

The election was held on April 27. Some 2,300 candidates vied for the 301 seats in the unicameral Yemeni national Legislature. As expected, the GPC won a large majority: 239 seats to 62 for Islah, the main opposition party. The Yemen Socialist Party, which boycotted the elections, was shut out of legislative participation entirely.

What struck outside observers about the election was its faithful adherence to political democracy. The entire process was

supervised by the Supreme Election Commission, established by law as an independent body with balanced political representation. Despite having one of the lowest literacy rates in the world, Yemenis participated with enthusiasm and in great numbers, illiterate voters being assisted by literate volunteers to mark their ballots inside the curtained polling booths. Ballots were tabulated by hand by representatives of the Supreme Election Council, prompting an American observer to ask why "they didn't use voting machines and computers; they said they would not trust such a system because it would not be transparent."[5] Despite the fact that most Yemenis are armed and tribalism is close to the surface, the election took place without violence, as 3 million out of 6 million eligible voters cast their ballots.

THE ECONOMY

Discoveries of significant oil deposits in the 1980s should have augured well for Yemen's economic future. Reserves are estimated at 1 billion barrels in the Marib basin and 3.3 billion in the Shabwa field northeast of Aden, with an additional 5.5 billion in the former neutral zone shared by the two Yemens and now administered by the central government. Yemen also has large deposits of natural gas, with reserves estimated at 5.5 trillion cubic feet.

Unfortunately, the political conflicts of the 1990s have had a negative effect on these rosy prospects. The Gulf War, in which Yemen supported Iraq against the UN–U.S.–Saudi coalition, caused Saudi Arabia to deport some 850,000 Yemeni workers. This resulted in a loss of expatriate remittances that had made up 20 to 25 percent of Yemen's national budget. And the Civil War in 1994 seriously damaged the infrastructure, requiring some $200 million in repairs to schools, hospitals, roads, and power stations.

Despite the gloomy forecasts of 1995— when foreign-exchange reserves were down to $144.6 million, expatriate remittances dropped 42 percent, and unemployment reached 50 percent of the labor force—the Yemeni economy has made a remarkable turnaround. The main reasons are the stabilization of the currency and drastic price increases on basic commodities. As a result, donor countries, who had demanded these reforms as the price for

South Arabian Protectorates are established by the British
1882–1914

Yemen is recognized as an independent nation under Imam Yahya
1934

A revolution overthrows Imam al-Badr; a military group proclaims a republic in North Yemen
1962

Civil war between supporters of Badr and Egyptian-backed republicans; protectorates merge with Aden Crown Colony
1962–1969

British forces withdraw from Aden; the National Liberation Front proclaims South Yemen an independent republic
1967

Major oil and natural-gas discoveries
1980s

1990s

The two Yemens unite on May 22, 1990; the border with Saudi Arabia is undemarcated and disputed

Free elections are held on April 27, 1993

A coalition of North Yemeni parties takes over the government

further aid, have pledged $500 million and agreed to restructure Yemen's $7 billion in external debts.

Both Yemens until very recently were among the poorest and least-developed countries in the Middle East. This description is somewhat misleading in North Yemen's case, however, since the highland regions have traditionally supported a sizable population, due to fertile soil, dependable and adequate rainfall, and effective use of limited arable land. South Yemen's resources were mostly unexploited during the 130 years of British rule, except for a small local fishing industry and the Aden port and refinery. During its brief period of independence, the P.D.R.Y.'s budget came mostly (70 percent) from the former Soviet Union and other Communist countries. The reduction in Soviet aid from $400 million in 1988 to $50 million in 1989 was one of the economic factors that encouraged re-unification from the South Yemen side.

The Yemen Arab Republic's economy was also altered drastically in the 1980s. One development was the emigration of more than 1 million Yemenis to work in Saudi Arabia and other Arab oil-producing states. Remittances from expatriate workers generated a cash economy in the country, resulting in inflation, a huge increase in imports of consumer goods, and depreciation of the currency.

In ancient times, Yemen, particularly in the South, had a flourishing agriculture based on monsoon rains, supplemented by a sophisticated system of small dams and canals and centered in the Wadi Hadh-ramaut. But long neglect and 2 decades of disastrous Soviet-style state-farm management adversely affected agricultural production.

Since re-unification, most state-owned lands in the Hadhramaut have been privatized. And oil drilling in the region has resulted in discovery of important underground water resources. As a result, and with aid from the World Bank, the region has recovered much of its former agricultural productivity, as date-palm groves, fields of corn, orchards, and beehives flourish.

FOREIGN RELATIONS

Prior to unification with South Yemen, North Yemen's geographical isolation and tribal social structure limited its contact with other Arab states. South Yemen's Marxist regime, in contrast, actively attempted to subvert the governments of its neighbors. Re-unification has brought better and closer relations with these states. In 1995, the flags of Yemen and Oman flew side by side on their newly demarcated common border, based on a 1992 agreement to accept UN adjudication.

Yemen's relations with Saudi Arabia have been more difficult. A dispute over their common northwestern border resulted in several skirmishes in 1995, after Saudi troops barred oil-company geologists prospecting in the area under concessions from the Yemeni government. Subsequent mediation by Syria resulted in a "Memorandum of Understanding" based on the 1934 Treaty of Taif between Imam Yahya and Ibn Saud. The Memorandum recognizes Saudi sovereignty over the provinces of Asir, Najran, and Jizan, which had been part of Yemen before 1934. In return, Saudi Arabia recognized Yemeni sovereignty over the Marib oil fields and agreed to the return of Yemeni expatriate workers to their jobs without having to have a Saudi sponsor.

NOTES

1. Robin Bidwell, *The Two Yemens* (Boulder, CO: Westview Press, 1983), p. 10.

2. Quoted in Robert Stookey, *Yemen: The Politics of the Yemen Arab Republic* (Boulder, CO: Westview Press, 1978), p. 168.

3. John Peterson, "Nation-building and Political Development in the Two Yemens," in B. R. Pridham, ed., *Contemporary Yemen: Politics and Historical Background* (New York: St. Martin's Press, 1985), p. 86.

4. Yemenis believed that he slept with a rope around his neck to terrify visitors, that he could turn twigs into snakes, and that he once outwrestled the devil. Bidwell, *op. cit.,* p. 121.

5. William A. Rugh, "A (Successful) Test of Democracy in Yemen," *The Christian Science Monitor* (May 28, 1997), p. 19.

DEVELOPMENT

The return of political stability and drastic fiscal reforms buoyed economic prospects in 1996—1997. The inflation rate was reduced to a manageable 55%. The 1996–2000 5-Year-Plan projects annual GDP growth at 7.7%, compared with a 3.7% annual average for 1990–1995.

FREEDOM

The 1991 Constitution established a parliamentary republic in unified Yemen. Elections in 1997 for the national Legislature resulted in a two-party division of power, with majority (GPC) and minority (Islah) parties represented. The press is free, and women enjoy full civil rights and may run for public office.

HEALTH/WELFARE

Faced with an astronomical birth rate, the government has adopted an indirect approach to family planning. Its strategy includes raising the marriageable age to at least 18 and emphasizing the Koran's recommendations for small families, along with encouragement of spaced births for women.

ACHIEVEMENTS

YemenInvest, a company founded by a Saudi family of Yemeni origin, set up a $500 million fund in 1997 to revitalize Aden and make it one of the world's leading ports. The fund establishes an Aden free-trade zone and industrial complex to provide 25,000 jobs, helping to reduce the 30% unemployment rate.

Articles from the World Press

Topic Guide to Articles

TOPIC AREA	TREATED IN	TOPIC AREA	TREATED IN
Nationalism	4. Islamic and Western Values 9. God That Did Not Fail 10. If I Forget Thee	**Roots**	1. How the Modern Middle East Map Came to Be Drawn 2. Islam: Sunnis and Shiites 3. What Is Islam?
Natural Resources	6. Dubai Puts Politics Aside		4. Islamic and Western Values 5. Islam's Shame: Lifting the Veil of Tears
Palestine	10. If I Forget Thee 12. Life with the Enemy: The One-State Solution		9. God That Did Not Fail 10. If I Forget Thee 11. Atlantis of the Sands 12. Life with the Enemy: The One-State Solution 13. Digging in the Land of Magan 16. On Ancient Terraced Hills
Pilgrimages	3. What Is Islam?		
Political Reform	8. Eighteen Years Later: Assessing the Islamic Republic of Iran 14. Wild Card in Mideast Peace: Syria 15. Increasing Loneliness of Being Turkey	**Social Reform**	4. Islamic and Western Values 5. Islam's Shame: Lifting the Veil of Tears 7. Cairo's Poor: Dilemmas of Survival and Solidarity
Politics	1. How the Modern Middle East Map Came to Be Drawn 4. Islamic and Western Values 8. Eighteen Years Later: Assessing the Islamic Republic of Iran 10. If I Forget Thee 14. Wild Card in Mideast Peace: Syria 15. Increasing Loneliness of Being Turkey	**Standard of Living**	6. Dubai Puts Politics Aside
		Sunnis/Shiites	2. Islam: Sunnis and Shiites 8. Eighteen Years Later: Assessing the Islamic Republic of Iran
		War	14. Wild Card in Mideast Peace: Syria
Poverty	7. Cairo's Poor: Dilemmas of Survival and Solidarity	**Women's Rights**	5. Islam's Shame: Lifting the Veil of Tears
Refugees	7. Cairo's Poor: Dilemmas of Survival and Solidarity	**Zionism**	9. God That Did Not Fail 10. If I Forget Thee
Religion	2. Islam: Sunnis and Shiites 3. What Is Islam? 4. Islamic and Western Values 5. Islam's Shame: Lifting the Veil of Tears 8. Eighteen Years Later: Assessing the Islamic Republic of Iran 9. God That Did Not Fail 10. If I Forget Thee 12. Life with the Enemy: The One-State Solution		

Article 1   *Smithsonian*, May 1991

How the modern Middle East map came to be drawn

When the Ottoman Empire collapsed in 1918, the British created new borders (and rulers) to keep the peace and protect their interests

David Fromkin

Lawyer-historian David Fromkin is the author of a prizewinning book entitled A Peace to End All Peace.

The dictator of Iraq claimed—falsely—that until 1914 Kuwait had been administered from Iraq, that historically Kuwait was a part of Iraq, that the separation of Kuwait from Iraq was an arbitrary decision of Great Britain's after World War I. The year was 1961; the Iraqi dictator was Abdul-Karim Qasim; and the dispatch of British troops averted a threatened invasion.

Iraq, claiming that it had never recognized the British-drawn frontier with Kuwait, demanded full access to the Persian Gulf; and when Kuwait failed to agree, Iraqi tanks and infantry attacked Kuwait. The year was 1973; the Iraqi dictator was Ahmad Hasan al-Bakr; when other Arab states came to Kuwait's support, a deal was struck, Kuwait made a payment of money to Iraq, and the troops withdrew.

August 2, 1990. At 2 A.M. Iraqi forces swept across the Kuwaiti frontier. Iraq's dictator, Saddam Hussein, declared that the frontier between Iraq and Kuwait was invalid, a creation of the British after World War I, and that Kuwait really belonged to Iraq.

It was, of course, true, as one Iraqi dictator after another claimed, that the exact Iraq-Kuwait frontier was a line drawn on an empty map by a British civil servant in the early 1920s. But Kuwait began to emerge as an independent entity in the early 1700s—two centuries before Britain invented Iraq. Moreover, most other frontiers between states of the Middle East were also creations of the British (or the French). The map of the Arab Middle East was drawn by the victorious Allies when they took over

these lands from the Ottoman Empire after World War I. By proposing to nullify that map, Saddam Hussein at a minimum was trying to turn the clock back by almost a century.

A hundred years ago, when Ottoman governors in Basra were futilely attempting to assert authority over the autonomous sheikdom of Kuwait, most of the Arabic-speaking Middle East was at least nominally part of the Ottoman Empire. It had been so for hundreds of years and would remain so until the end of World War I.

The Ottomans, a dynasty, not a nationality, were originally a band of Turkish warriors who first galloped onto the stage of history in the 13th century. By the early 20th century the Ottoman Empire, which once had stretched to the gates of Vienna, was shrinking rapidly, though it still ruled perhaps 20 million to 25 million people in the Middle East and elsewhere, comprising perhaps a dozen or more different nationalities. It was a ramshackle Muslim empire, held together by the glue of Islam, and the lot of its non-Muslim population (perhaps 5 million) was often unhappy and sometimes tragic.

In the year 1900, if you traveled from the United States to the Middle East, you might have landed in Egypt, part of the Ottoman Empire in name but in fact governed by British "advisers." The Egyptian Army was commanded by an English general, and the real ruler of the country was the British Agent and Consul-General—a position to which the crusty Horatio Herbert Kitchener was appointed in 1911.

The center of your social life in all likelihood would have been the British enclave in Cairo, which possessed (wrote one of Lord Kitchener's aides) "all the narrowness and provincialism of

an English garrison town." The social schedule of British officials and their families revolved around the balls given at each of the leading hotels in turn, six nights out of seven, and before dark, around the Turf Club and the Sporting Club on the island of El Gezira. Throughout Egypt, Turkish officials, Turkish police and a Turkish army were conspicuous by their absence. Outside British confines you found yourself not in a Turkish-speaking country but in an Arabic-speaking one. Following the advice of the *Baedeker,* you'd likely engage a dragoman—a translator and guide—of whom there were about 90 in Cairo ("all more or less intelligent and able, but scarcely a half of the number are trustworthy").

On leaving Egypt, if you turned north through the Holy Land and the Levant toward Anatolia, you finally would have encountered the reality of Ottoman government, however corrupt and inefficient, though many cities—Jerusalem (mostly Jewish), Damascus (mostly Arab) and Smyrna, now Izmir (mostly Greek)—were not at all Turkish in character or population.

Heading south by steamer down the Red Sea and around the enormous Arabian Peninsula was a very different matter. Nominally Ottoman, Arabia was in large part a vast, ungoverned desert wilderness through which roamed bedouin tribes knowing no law but their own. In those days Abdul Aziz ibn Saud, the youthful scion of deposed lords of most of the peninsula, was living in exile, dreaming of a return to reclaim his rights and establish his dominion. In the port towns on the Persian Gulf, ruling sheiks paid lip service to Ottoman rule but in fact their sheikdoms were protectorates of Great Britain. Not long after you passed Kuwait you reached Basra, in what is now Iraq, up a river formed by the union of the great Tigris and Euphrates.

A muddy, unhealthy port of heterogeneous population, Basra was then the capital of a province, largely Shiite Arab, ruled by an Ottoman governor. Well north of it, celebrated for archaeological sites like Babylon and Nippur, which drew tourists, lay Baghdad, then a heavily Jewish city (along with Jerusalem, one of the two great Jewish cities of Asia). Baghdad was the administrative center of an Ottoman province that was in large part Sunni Arab. Farther north still was a third Ottoman province, with a large population of Kurds. Taken together, the three roughly equaled the present area of Iraq.

Ottoman rule in some parts of the Middle East clearly was more imaginary than real. And even in those portions of the empire that Turkish governors did govern, the population was often too diverse to be governed effectively by a single regime. Yet the hold of the Turkish sultan on the empire's peoples lingered on. Indeed, had World War I not intervened, the Ottoman Empire might well have lasted many decades more.

In its origins, the war that would change the map of the Middle East had nothing to do with that region. How the Ottoman Empire came to be involved in the war at all—and lost it—and how the triumphant Allies found themselves in a position to redesign the Middle Eastern lands the Turks had ruled, is one of the most fascinating stories of the 20th century, rich in consequences that we are still struggling with today.

The story begins with one man, a tiny, vain, strutting man addicted to dramatic gestures and uniforms. He was Enver Pasha, and he mistook himself for a sort of Napoleon. Of modest origins, Enver, as a junior officer in the Ottoman Army, joined the Young Turks, a secret society that was plotting against the Ottoman regime. In 1913, Enver led a Young Turk raiding party that overthrew the government and killed the Minister of War. In 1914, at the age of 31, he became the Ottoman Minister of War himself, married the niece of the sultan and moved into a palace.

As a new political figure Enver scored a major, instant success. The Young Turks for years had urgently sought a European ally that would promise to protect the Ottoman Empire against other European powers. Britain, France and Russia had each been approached and had refused; but on August 1, 1914, just as Germany was about to invade

Belgium to begin World War I, Enver wangled a secret treaty with the kaiser pledging to protect the Ottoman domains.

Unaware of Enver's coup, and with war added to the equation, Britain and France began wooing Turkey too, while the Turks played off one side against the other. By autumn the German Army's plan to knock France out of the war in six weeks had failed. Needing help, Germany urged the Ottoman Empire to join the war by attacking Russia.

Though Enver's colleagues in the Turkish government were opposed to war, Enver had a different idea. To him the time seemed ripe: in the first month of the war German armies overwhelmingly turned back a Russian attack on East Prussia, and a collapse of the czar's armies appeared imminent. Seeing a chance to share in the spoils of a likely German victory over Russia, Enver entered into a private conspiracy with the German admiral commanding the powerful warship *Goeben* and its companion vessel, the *Breslau*, which had taken refuge in Turkish waters at the outset of hostilities.

During the last week of October, Enver secretly arranged for the *Goeben* and the *Breslau* to escape into the Black Sea and steam toward Russia. Flying the Ottoman flag, the Germans then opened fire on the Russian coast. Thinking themselves attacked by Turks, the Russians declared war. Russia's allies, Britain and France, thus found themselves at war with the Ottoman Empire too. By needlessly plunging the empire into war, Enver had put everything in the Middle East up for grabs. In that sense, he was the father of the modern Middle East. Had Enver never existed, the Turkish flag might even yet be flying—if only in some confederal way—over Beirut and Damascus, Baghdad and Jerusalem.

Great Britain had propped up the Ottoman Empire for generations as a buffer against Russian expansionism. Now, with Russia as Britain's shaky ally, once the war had been won and the Ottomans overthrown, the Allies would be able to reshape the entire Middle East. It would be one of those magic moments in history when fresh starts beckon and dreams become realities.

"What is to prevent the Jews having Palestine and restoring a real Judaea?" asked H. G. Wells, the British novelist, essayist and prophet of a rational future for mankind. The Greeks, the French and the Italians also had claims to Middle East territory. And naturally, in Cairo, Lord Kitchener's aides soon be-

gan to contemplate a future plan for an Arab world to be ruled by Egypt, which in turn would continue to be controlled by themselves.

At the time, the Allies already had their hands full with war against Germany on the Western Front. They resolved not to be distracted by the Middle East until later. The issues and ambitions there were too divisive. Hardly had the Ottoman Empire entered the war, however, when Enver stirred the pot again. He took personal command of the Ottoman Third Army on the Caucasus frontier and, in the dead of winter, launched a foolhardy attack against fortified positions on high ground. His offensive was hopeless, since it was both amateurishly planned and executed, but the czar's generals panicked anyway. The Russian government begged Lord Kitchener (now serving in London as Secretary of State for War) to stage a more or less instant diversionary action. The result was the Allied attack on the Dardanelles, the strait that eventually leads to Constantinople (now Istanbul).

Enver soon lost about 86,000 of his 100,000 men; the few, bloodied survivors straggled back through icy mountain passes. A German observer noted that Enver's army had "suffered a disaster which for rapidity and completeness is without parallel in military history." But nobody in the Russian government or high command bothered to tell the British that mounting a Dardanelles naval attack was no longer necessary. So on the morning of February 19, 1915, British ships fired the opening shots in what became a tragic campaign.

Initially, the British Navy seemed poised to take Constantinople, and Russia panicked again. What if the British, having occupied Constantinople, were to hold onto it? The 50 percent of Russia's export trade flowing through the strait would then do so only with British permission. Czar Nicholas II demanded immediate assurance that Constantinople would be Russia's in the postwar world. Fearing Russia might withdraw from the war, Britain and France agreed. In return, Russia offered to support British and French claims in other parts of the Middle East.

With that in mind, on April 8, 1915, the British Prime Minister appointed a committee to define Britain's postwar goals in the Middle East. It was a committee dominated by Lord Kitchener through his personal representative, 36-year-old Sir Mark Sykes, one of many remarkable characters, including Winston Churchill and T. E. Lawrence, to be involved in the remaking (and remapping) of the Middle East.

A restless soul who had moved from school to school as a child, Sykes left college without graduating, and thereafter never liked to stay long in one spot. A Tory Member of Parliament, before the war he had traveled widely in Asiatic Turkey, publishing accounts of his journeys. Sykes' views tended to be passionate but changeable, and his talent for clever exaggeration sometimes carried over into his politics.

As a traditional Tory he had regarded the sultan's domains as a useful buffer protecting Britain's road to India against Britain's imperial rivals, the czar chief among them. Only 15 months earlier, Sykes was warning the House of Commons that "the disappearance of the Ottoman Empire must be the first step towards the disappearance of our own." Yet between 1915 and 1919, he busily planned the dismantling of the Ottoman Empire.

The Allied attack on the Dardanelles ended with Gallipoli, a disaster told and retold in books and films. Neither that defeat, nor the darkest days of 1916–17, when it looked for a while as though the Allies might lose the war, stopped British planning about how to cut up the Turkish Middle East. Steadily but secretly Sykes worked on. As the fight to overthrow the Ottoman Empire grew more intense, the elements he had to take into account grew more complex.

It was clear that the British needed to maintain control over the Suez Canal, and all the rest of the route to their prized colonial possession, India. They needed to keep the Russians and Germans and Italians and French in check. Especially the French, who had claims on Syria. But with millions of men committed to trench warfare in Europe, they could not drain off forces for the Middle East. Instead, units of the British Indian Army along with other Commonwealth forces attacked in the east in what are now Iraq and Iran, occupying Basra, Baghdad and eventually Mosul. Meanwhile, Allied liaison officers, including notably T. E. Lawrence, began encouraging the smallish group of Arabian tribesmen following Emir (later King) Hussein of the Hejaz, who had rebelled against the Turks, to fight a guerrilla campaign against Turkish forces.

Throughout 1917, in and near the Hejaz area of Arabia, the Arabs attacked the railway line that supported Turkish troops in Medina. The "Arab Revolt" had little military effect on the outcome

of the war, yet the fighting brought to the fore, as British clients and potential Arab leaders, not only Hussein of the Hejaz, but two of his sons, Faisal and Abdullah. Both were deadly rivals of Ibn Saud, who by then had become a rising power in Arabia and a client of the British too.

British officials in Cairo deluded themselves and others into believing that the whole of the Arabic-speaking half of the Ottoman Empire might rise up and come over to the Allied side. When the time came, the Arab world did not follow the lead of Hussein, Abdullah and Faisal. But Arab aspirations and British gratitude began to loom large in British, and Arab, plans for the future. Sykes now felt he had to take Arab ambitions into account in his future planning, though he neglected those of Ibn Saud (father of today's Saudi king), who also deserved well of Britain.

By 1917 Sykes was also convinced that it was vital for the British war effort to win Jewish support against Germany, and that pledging support for Zionism could win it. That year his efforts and those of others resulted in the publication of a statement by Arthur James Balfour, the British Foreign Secretary, expressing Britain's support for the establishment of a Jewish national home in Palestine.

The year 1917 proved to be a turning point. In the wake of its revolution Russia pulled out of the war, but the entrance by the United States on the Allied side insured the Allies a victory—if they could hold on long enough for U.S. troops to arrive in force. In the Middle East, as British India consolidated its hold on areas that are now part of Iraq, Gen. Edmund Allenby's Egyptian-based British army began fighting its way north from Suez to Damascus. Lawrence and a force of Arab raiders captured the Red Sea port of Aqaba (near the point where Israel and Jordan now meet). Then, still other Arabs, with Faisal in command, moved north to harass the Turkish flank.

By October 1918, Allenby had taken Syria and Lebanon, and was poised to invade what is now Turkey. But there was no need to do so, because on October 31 the Ottoman Empire surrendered.

As the Peace Conference convened in Paris, in February 1919, Sykes, who had been rethinking Britain's design for the Middle East, suddenly fell ill and died. At first there was nobody to take his place as the British government's overall Middle East planner. Prime Minister David Lloyd George took personal

charge in many Middle East matters. But more and more, as the months went by, Winston Churchill had begun to play a major role, gradually superseding the others.

Accordingly, early that year the ambitious 45-year-old politician was asked by the Prime Minister to serve as both War Minister and Air Minister. ("Of course," Lloyd George wrote Churchill, "there will be but one salary!") Maintaining the peace in the captured—and now occupied—Arab Middle East was among Churchill's new responsibilities.

Cheerful, controversial and belligerent, Churchill was not yet the revered figure who would so inspire his countrymen and the world in 1940. Haunted by the specter of a brilliant father, he had won fame and high office early, but was widely distrusted, in part for having switched political parties. Churchill's foresighted administration of the Admiralty in the summer of 1914 won universal praise, but then the botched Dardanelles campaign, perhaps unfairly, was blamed on him. As a Conservative newspaper put it, "we have watched his brilliant and erratic course in the confident expectation that sooner or later he would make a mess of anything he undertook." In making Churchill minister of both War and Air in 1919, Lloyd George was giving his protégé a try at a political comeback.

By the end of the war, everyone was so used to the bickering among the Allies about who was going to get what in the postwar Middle East that the alternative—nobody taking anything—simply didn't enter into the equation. Churchill was perhaps the only statesman to consider that possibility. He foresaw that many problems would arise from trying to impose a new political design on so troubled a region, and thought it unwise to make the attempt. Churchill argued, in fact, for simply retaining a reformed version of the Ottoman Empire. Nobody took him seriously.

After the war, a British army of a million men, the only cohesive military force in the region, briefly occupied the Middle East. Even as his real work began, however, Churchill was confronted with demands that the army, exhausted from years of war, be demobilized. He understood what meeting those demands meant. Relying on that army, Prime Minister Lloyd George had decided to keep the whole Arab Middle East under British influence; in the words he once used about Palestine: "We shall be there by conquest and shall remain." Now Churchill repeatedly warned that once British troops were withdrawn, Britain would not be able to impose its terms.

Lloyd George had predicted that it would take about a week to agree on the terms of peace to be imposed on the defeated Ottoman Empire. Instead it took nearly two years. By then, in Churchill's words, the British army of occupation had long since "melted away," with the dire consequences he predicted.

In Egypt, demonstrations, strikes and riots broke out. In Arabia, Ibn Saud, though himself a British client, defeated and threatened to destroy Britain's protégé Hussein. In Turkey, the defeated Enver had long since fled the country to find refuge in Berlin. From there he journeyed to Russia, assumed leadership of Bukhara (in what is now the Uzbek Republic of the USSR) in its struggle for independence from Moscow, and was killed in battle against the Red Army of the Soviet Union in 1922. Turkish nationalists under the great Ottoman general Mustafa Kemal (later known as Kemal Ataturk) rebelled against the Allied-imposed treaty and later proclaimed the national state that is modern Turkey.

In Palestine, Arabs rioted against Jews. In what is now Saddam Hussein's Iraq, armed revolts by the tribes, sparked in the first instance by the imposition of taxes, caused thousands of casualties. "How much longer," the outraged London *Times* asked, "are valuable lives to be sacrificed in the vain endeavour to impose upon the Arab population an elaborate and expensive administration which they never asked for and do not want?"

By the end of 1920, Lloyd George's Middle East policy was under attack from all sides. Churchill, who had warned all along that peacetime Britain, in the grip of an economic collapse, had neither the money, the troops, nor the will to coerce the Middle East, was proved right—and placed even more directly in charge. On New Year's Day 1921 he was appointed Colonial Secretary, and soon began to expand his powers, consolidating within his new department responsibility for all Britain's domains in Arabic-speaking Asia.

He assembled his staff by combing the government for its ablest and most experienced officials. The one offbeat appointment was T. E. Lawrence. A young American journalist and promoter named Lowell Thomas, roaming the Middle East in search of a story, had found Lawrence dressed in Arab robes, and proceeded to make him world-famous as "Lawrence of Arabia." A complex personality, Lawrence was chronically insubordinate, but Churchill admired all the wonderful stories he'd heard of Lawrence's wartime exploits.

Seeking to forge a working consensus among his staff in London and his men in the field, Churchill invited them all to a conference that opened in Cairo on March 12, 1921. During the ten-day session held in the Semiramis Hotel, about 40 experts were in attendance. "Everybody Middle East is here," wrote Lawrence.

Egypt was not on the agenda. Its fate was being settled separately by its new British proconsul, Lord Allenby. In 1922 he established it as an independent kingdom, still largely subject to British control under terms of a unilateral proclamation that neither Egypt's politicians nor its new king, Fuad, accepted.

All Britain's other wartime conquests—the lands now called Israel, the West Bank, Jordan and Iraq—were very much on the agenda, while the fate of Syria and Lebanon, which Britain had also conquered, was on everybody's mind. In the immediate aftermath of the war, it was control of Syria that had caused the most problems, as Lloyd George tried to keep it for Britain by placing it under the rule of Lawrence's comrade-in-arms, Prince Faisal, son of Hussein. After Syria declared its independence, the French fought back. Occupying all of Syria-Lebanon, they drove Faisal into exile. The French also devised a new frontier for Lebanon that invited eventual disaster, as would become evident in the 1970s and '80s. They refused to see that the Muslim population was deeply hostile to their rule.

Churchill, meanwhile, was confronted by constant Arab disturbances in Palestine. West of the Jordan River, where the Jewish population lived, Arabs fought against Jewish immigration, claiming—wrongly, as the future was to show—that the country was too barren to support more than its existing 600,000 inhabitants. Churchill rejected that view, and dealt with the Arab objections to a Jewish homeland by keeping—though redefining—Britain's commitment to Zionism. As he saw it, there was to be a Jewish homeland in Palestine, but other homelands could exist there as well.

The 75 percent of Palestine east of the Jordan River (Transjordan, as it was called, until it became Jordan in 1950) was lawless. Lacking the troops to police it and wanting to avert additional causes of strife, Churchill decided to forbid Jews from settling there, temporarily at least.

Fittingly while still War and Air Minister, Churchill had devised a strategy for controlling the Middle East with a minimum number of British troops by using an economical combination of airpower and armored cars. But it would take time for the necessary units to be put in place. Meanwhile tribal fighting had to be contained somehow. As the Cairo conference met, news arrived that Abdullah, Faisal's brother, claiming to need "a change of air for his health," had left Arabia with a retinue of bedouin warriors and entered Transjordan. The British feared that Abdullah would attack French Syria and so give the French an excuse to invade Transjordan, as a first step toward taking over all Palestine.

As a temporary expedient Churchill appointed Abdullah as governor of a Transjordan to be administratively detached from the rest of Palestine. He charged him with keeping order by his prestige and with his own bedouin followers—at least until Britain's aircraft and armored cars were in place. This provisional solution has lasted for seven decades and so have the borders of Transjordan, now ruled over by Abdullah's grandson, Hussein, the Hashemite King of Jordan.

The appointment of Abdullah seemed to accomplish several objectives at once. It went partway toward paying what Lawrence and others told Churchill was Britain's wartime debt to the family of King Hussein, though Hussein himself was beyond help. Too stubborn to accept British advice, he was losing the battle for Arabia to his blood rival, Ibn Saud. Meanwhile Prince Faisal, Britain's preferred Arab ruler, remained in idle exile.

Other chief items on the Cairo agenda were the Ottoman territories running from the Persian Gulf to Turkey along the border of Persia, which make up present-day Iraq. Including what were suspected—but not proved—to be vast oil reserves, at a time when the value of oil was beginning to be understood, these territories had been the scene of the bloodiest postwar Arab uprisings against British rule. They caused so many difficulties of every sort that Churchill flirted with the idea of abandoning them entirely, but Lloyd George would have none of it. If the British left, the Prime Minister warned, in a year or two they might find that they had "handed over to the French and Americans some of the richest oil fields in the world."

As a matter of convenience, the British administered this troubled region as a unit, though it was composed of the three separate Ottoman provinces—Mosul, Baghdad and Basra, with their incompatible Kurdish, Assyrian Christian, Jewish, Sunni Muslim, and Shiite populations. In making it into a country, Churchill and his colleagues found it convenient to continue treating it as a single unit. (One British planner was warned by an American missionary, "You are flying in the face of four millenniums of history . . .") The country was called Iraq—"the well-rooted country"—in order to give it a name that was Arabic. Faisal was placed on the throne by the British, and like his brother Abdullah in Transjordan, he was supposed to keep Iraq quiet until the British were ready to police it with aircraft and armored cars.

One of the leftover problems in 1921 was just how to protect Transjordan's new governor, Abdullah, and Iraq's new king, Faisal, against the fierce warriors of Ibn Saud. In August 1922 Ibn Saud's camel-calvary forces invading Transjordan were stopped outside Amman by British airplanes and armored cars. Earlier that year, the British forced Ibn Saud to accept a settlement aimed at protecting Iraq. With this in mind, the British drew a frontier line that awarded Iraq a substantial amount of territory claimed by Ibn Saud for Arabia: all the land (in what is now Iraq) west of the Euphrates River, all the way to the Syrian frontier. To compensate Ibn Saud's kingdom (later known as Saudi Arabia) the British transferred to it rights to two-thirds of the territory of Kuwait, which had been essentially independent for about two centuries. These were valuable grazing lands, in which oil might exist too.

It is this frontier line between Iraq, Kuwait and Arabia, drawn by a British civil servant in 1922 to protect Iraq at the expense of Kuwait, that Iraq's Saddam Hussein denounced as invalid when he invaded.

In 1922, Churchill succeeded in mapping out the Arab Middle East along lines suitable to the needs of the British civilian and military administrations. T. E. Lawrence would later brag that he, Churchill and a few others had designed the modern Middle East over dinner. Seventy years later, in the tense deliberations and confrontations of half the world over the same area, the question is whether the peoples of the Middle East are willing or able to continue living with that design.

Article 2   *Social Education*, October 1994

Islam: Sunnis and Shiites

Muhammad Hanif

Muhammad Hanif is an associate professor in the Early and Middle Childhood Education Department at the University of Louisville, Kentucky.

Islam is one of the world's fastest growing religions, and is the principal faith in large parts of the Third World. There are currently over 970 million Muslims concentrated mainly in the Middle East, North Africa, and South and South-East Asia (*World Almanac 1994*, 727). Of these, eighty-three percent are Sunnis and sixteen percent Shiites. Shiites constitute the majority of the population in Iran, Iraq, and Bahrain, and are the largest Muslim population group in Lebanon.

In addition to its religious vitality, Islam is an increasingly important political force on the world scene. In the last twenty years, there has been a surge in the activities of political movements that define themselves as Islamic. A watershed event was the Islamic revolution in Iran engineered by the now deceased Shiite Ayatollah Khomeini, which ousted the Shah in 1979. Clerical rule initiated radical changes in different facets of life in Iran, and the foreign relations of the Middle East.

The war between Iran and Iraq that took place soon after and lasted from 1980 to 1988 highlighted some of the differences between Sunni and Shiite Muslims. Iran is a Persian Shiite country; while the leadership of Iraq is predominantly Sunni Muslim and Arab.[1] Most Sunni Muslim governments supported Iraq during the war.

In many Middle East states, Islamic movements are the main opposition force, and there has been increased activity by Islamic revolutionary groups. In Lebanon, militant Shiites supported by Iran took an active part in the country's civil war, and engaged in spectacular acts of violence, including taking a number of western citizens hostage. Radical Sunni Muslim movements in countries such as Egypt and Algeria have also engaged in violence against government and western targets.

This article will furnish background information on Sunni and Shiite Islam, highlighting their historical, religious, and ideological differences, and pointing out what both have in common as well as what divides them. It will also outline some of the reasons for the recent strength of Islamic political movements.

Beliefs Shared by Sunnis and Shiites

There is a substantial common denominator between Sunni and Shiite Islam. All Muslims believe that Allah chose a man named Muhammad as the Prophet of Islam, and that, with Allah's blessings and continuous revelations, Muhammad guided the Muslims to lead life according to the Koran, a collection of divine revelations, and the "Hadith" (the sayings, teachings, and practices of the Prophet Muhammad, which serve as a supplement to the Koran). In a short period of 22 years, from 610 to 632 A.D he succeeded in leaving a great political and spiritual legacy that ultimately led to the establishment of Islamic civilization.

All Muslims believe that piety, righteous observance of the principles of the Koran, and striving for goodness in daily life are the greatest virtues of human beings. Both Sunni and Shiite Muslims agree on the need for a strong ethical and moral code to regulate human behavior in all its manifestations. Social justice is also believed to be a fundamental right.

Sunnis and Shiites share the belief that there are five pillars of Islam: (1) the unity of Allah and the prophethood of Muhammad, (2) the five obligatory prayers, (3) fasting, (4) charity, and (5) the pilgrimage to Mecca. Both groups also believe that the Koran has a Divine source, and that Allah's prophetic missions concluded with Muhammad.

The Sunni-Shiite Split

The differences between Sunni and Shiite Islam originated in a historical dispute over the succession to the Prophet Muhammad. On Muhammad's death in 632 A.D., the "Majlis al-Shura"[2] (assembly of advisors), comprising the most devoted and highly knowledgeable Muslims, selected Abu Bakr as the first Caliph, or leader, of the Muslims. Abu Bakr was one of the close companions of Muhammad, and the father of Muhammad's second wife. This action by the assembly indicated that leaders were to be selected by Muslims on the basis of their piety and merit, and ruled out the idea of a bloodline succession to the Prophet in the religious and political governance of Islam.

Most Muslims accepted the selection of Abu Bakr as the first legitimate Caliph, who would rule according to the practices established by the Prophet. On major worldly issues concerning which there was no direct reference in the Koran, the Prophet had taken advice from the assembly of advisors, so it seemed the appropriate body to decide the issue of the succession.

The first Shiites were a small group of Muslims who opposed the selection of Abu Bakr as the first Caliph. They rallied around the person of Ali, the Prophet's cousin and son-in-law, who had married the Prophet's daughter, Fatima. They supported Ali and the concept of a legitimate bloodline succession to the Prophet Muhammad in both religious and temporal matters. Ali had, in fact, been one of the prominent members of the consulting body which selected Abu Bakr as the first Caliph of Islam. But given the tribal traditions of the Arabian Peninsula, the selection of Abu Bakr was regarded by some Muslims as denying the right of Ali to succeed the Prophet and serve as a leader or Imam in religious and political matters.

Who Is a Shiite?

The schism led to the creation of two major branches of Islam, the Sunnis and the Shiites. The supporters of Ali were called Shiites. Distinguished authorities on the Arabic language define the word "Shiite" as meaning a group of people that develops consensus on an issue. Etymologically, the word's meaning is confined to the helpers, supporters, and partisans of a person but, by and large, the word is applied to the followers of Ali and his eleven male descendants. The word "Sunni," which means "orthodox," is applied to Muslims who are part of the main branch of Islam and belong to one of the four schools of jurisprudence, Hanafi, Hanbali, Maliki, and Shaf'i. Although Ali is highly regarded by Sunni Muslims, they reject the Shiite conception of the succession to Muhammad.

After the selection of Abu Bakr as the first Caliph, the Shiites grew in number and became a political group supporting Ali as the successor of the Prophet. They vehemently rejected the Caliphate, and instead advocated the concept of the "Imamate,"[3] a religious and political ideology based on guidance by Imams. Etymologically, the word "Imam" means "he who stands before," a guide and a leader. It is used to describe men of religion today, as well as to refer to the Twelve Imams who followed Muhammad. The Imamate concept reflects a belief that humanity is at all time in need of a divinely ordained leader, an authoritative teacher in all religious matters, who is endowed with full immunity from sin and error.

The predominant trend in Shiism is that described as "Twelver Shiism,"[4] which is centered in Iran and is the principal form of Shiism in Iraq, Lebanon, and Bahrain. This Shiism holds that Muhammad was succeeded by twelve divinely ordained Imams directly descended from him through Ali and his wife Fatima, and that rejection of and disobedience to any of the twelve Imams constitutes infidelity equal to rejection of the Prophet Muhammad (Donaldson 1933, 344). Shiites consider Ali and his descendants the rightful successors of the Prophet, entitled to lead the Muslims by divine and infallible inspiration. This issue is not, of course, simply a genealogical matter, because it raises the vital issue of knowing from which authority to obtain guidance as to the will of Allah and its exercise on earth.

In support of this belief, Shiites refer to certain sayings of Muhammad debated by the Sunnis, such as: "I am the city of knowledge and Ali is my gate" (Bayat 1982, 4).

The distinctiveness of Twelver Shiism lies in its belief that the Twelfth Imam, Muhammad al-Mahdi, disap-

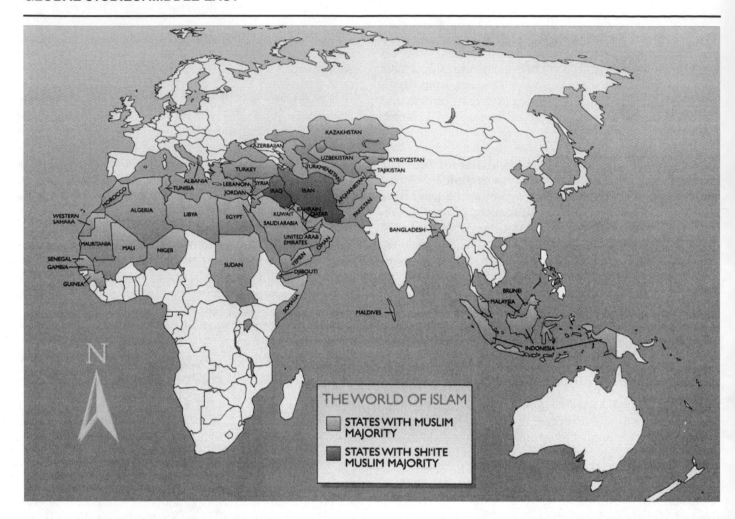

THE WORLD OF ISLAM

STATES WITH MUSLIM MAJORITY

STATES WITH SHI'ITE MUSLIM MAJORITY

peared and will reappear one day to inaugurate a reign of justice that will presage the final judgment.

Those Shiites who are not Twelver Shiites also believe that Ali was the rightful Imam, in succession to Muhammad, but differ on the importance of some of the succeeding Imams. The Isma'ilis accept the first six Twelver Imams, but hold that the son of the sixth Imam, Isma'il, whose descendants continue to the present day, was the rightful succeeding Imam. The present Aga Khan is the Imam of the best-known subsection of the Isma'ilis. The Zaydis believe that the Imams received divine guidance, but do not believe in their infallibility or share the commitment to all twelve Imams, and reject the doctrine about the hidden Imam.

Sunni-Shiite Doctrinal Differences

Of the Sunni and Twelver Shiite differences, some of the most important relate to the issue of the Imamate; the question of intercession between Allah and human beings; matters not delineated by the Koran; the means of attaining paradise; and the role of present-day Imams, or religious leaders.

1. The Concept of the Imamate

In the Shiite view, the twelve Imams inherited their positions as the exclusive leaders of the Muslims through the authority of the Prophet Muhammad and divine ordination. They are considered to have been not only Muhammad's temporal successors but also the inheritors of the prerogatives of closeness to Allah, and the interpreters of the Koran.

According to Shiism, the "Imam" has three functions: to rule over the Islamic community, to explain the religious sciences and law, and to be a spiritual guide to lead human beings to an understanding of the inner meaning of things. Because of these functions, he cannot possibly be elected by a public assembly. As a spiritual guide he receives his authority only from on "high." Therefore, each Imam is appointed through the designation of the previous "Imam" by Divine Command.

The Imam is to be concerned with daily matters as well as the spiritual and unmanifested world. His functions are at once human and cosmic (Nasr 1978, 278). The "Twelve Imams" are mediators for mankind (Donaldson 1933, 343).

Sunni Muslims. The above beliefs of the "Twelvers," which give legitimacy to the verbal and written comments of "The Twelve Imams," are categorically rejected by the Sunnis, who do not consider the institution of hereditary "Imamate" as part of the Islamic faith. All the prophets of Allah recognized by Islam, such as Adam, Noah, Abraham, Moses, Christ, and Muhammad, are seen as having been divinely ordained to guide human beings to worship Allah and seek His mercy. However, even the progeny of prophets are considered to be denied the privilege of the closeness and the blessings of Allah if they fail to practice His commandments. A typical expression of this belief is the Koranic passage,

And remember that Abraham was tried by his Lord with certain commands which he fulfilled. Allah said: I will make thee Imam to the Nations. Abraham pleaded: "And also Imams from my offspring!" Allah said, "But my promise is not within the reach of evil doers (Koran 2:124).

The Sunni Muslims do not place any human being, including the Twelve Shiite Imams, on a level equal to or even close to the prophets. The Sunni view is that nowhere in the Koran is it mentioned that the twelve Shiite Imams are divinely ordained to lead Muslims after the death of Muhammad. Muslims should be guided by words such as those in Muhammad's last "Hajj" sermon, known as the Sermon of the Mount, in which he addressed all of humanity:

- - - I am leaving behind two things; as long as you cling to them, you will not go astray. One is the "Book of Allah," and the other is my "tradition" (Zaheer 1985, 10).

2. Intercession between Allah and Human Beings
Sunni Muslims. The Sunni Muslims believe that no one can intercede between Allah and human beings.

Say: To God belongs exclusively [the right to grant] intercession. To Him belongs the dominion of the heavens and the earth. In the End, it is to Him that ye shall be brought back (Koran 39:44).

Shiite Muslims. According to Shiism, the Twelve Imams can intercede between mankind and Allah.
The Apostle of Allah said to Ali:

"- - - You and your descendants are mediators for mankind as they [human beings] will not be able to know God except through your introduction" (Donaldson 1933, 343).

"- - - Shi'i Muslims must know their Imam in order to be saved, and the Imams, as well as the Prophets, of course, can and do intercede for believers before God at the hour of judgment - - -" (Nasr 1987, 261).

3. Matters not Addressed by the Koran

Sunni Muslims. The four Sunni schools of jurisprudence accept with different degrees of emphasis the use of the consensus of the Muslim community and analogy (the application of the principles of the Koran and Hadith) as sources for legal decisions where the Koran and the Traditions ("Hadith") of the Prophet do not provide direct guidance.
"Ijma"[5] (consensus) guarantees the authority of the Koran and the traditions as records of divine revelation.
Consensus and analogy can be applied by those scholars who are highly knowledgeable in the Koran, the traditions of the prophet, and Islamic law, and practice the faith in every facet of their lives.
Shiite Muslims. The sources of Muslim law in Shiism are somewhat similar to those in Sunni Islam, namely the Koran, Muhammad's practices, consensus, and analogy. However, the determination of consensus is related to the views of the Imams, and more freedom is given to analogy than in Sunni Islam (Nasr 1978, 278).

4. Paradise and Hell on the Day of Judgment
Sunni Muslims. Sunni Muslims strongly believe that the redemption of human beings is dependent on faith in Allah, His prophets, acceptance of Muhammad as the final prophet, and belief in righteous deeds as explained in the Koran. The mercy of Allah will determine the redemption of all human beings. Even the prophet Muhammad is at the mercy of Allah.

I would, if I disobeyed my Lord, Indeed have fear of the penalty of a Mighty Day (Koran 39:13).

There are many other verses in the Koran which enumerate that the basis of paradise is the mercy of Allah and the righteous deeds of human beings according to the Koran and Hadith.
Shiite Muslims. Shiite Muslims are guaranteed paradise if they obey and follow Muhammad and the Twelve Imams. Ibn Babuwaihi, a Shiite scholar, quoted Ibn-i-Sadiq, the sixth Imam, in reference to Muhammad's address to Ali.

- - - that you present to God those who may enter Paradise, i.e., those who recognize you and those whom you recognize. - - - that you are the absolute mediator, for those who will go to Hell will only be those who do not recognize you and whom you do not recognize (Donaldson 1933, 343).

5. The Role and Status of Present-Day Imams
Sunni Muslims. For Sunnis, the "Twelve Imams" and the present-day Shiite Imams (e.g., "Ayatollahs," or the "shadows of Allah") are humans without any divine powers. They are considered righteous Muslims, and the Twelve Imams are particularly respected because of their relationship to Ali and his wife Fatima, the daughter of

Muhammad. Sunnis believe that Ali and his two sons, Hassan and Hussain, were highly respected by the first three Caliphs and the companions of Muhammad. Any righteous and knowledgeable Sunni Muslim can serve as an Imam with the prime function of leading the prayers and interpreting the Koran and Hadith provided he is well versed in these subjects. Sunnis also consider it heretical to impute to human beings attributes of Divine nature such as infallibility and the knowledge of all temporal and cosmic matters.

Shiite Muslims. The highest ranking present-day Imams (Ayatollahs) are believed to receive their guidance and spiritual enlightenment directly from the "Twelve Imams," who stay in continuous contact with their followers on earth every day through contemporary spiritual leaders. The Ayatollahs thus play a vital mediatory role. Because of their spiritual role, Ayatollahs cannot be appointed by governments, but only by consensus of other Ayatollahs.

Differences in Religious Organization

The differences between Sunni and Shiite Islam are more than theological and historical. They are embedded in the social and political structure of the Middle East. Sunnis and Shiites form distinct communities. Conversions from Shiism to Sunnism and vice versa are rare, and Sunnis and Shiites are expected to marry members of their own community. The vital moments of life—marriage, birth, and death—are commemorated within the framework of the rituals of the community. Members of each community learn about Islam within the traditions of their own faith, and under the guidance of their faith's religious teachers.

Despite these traditions, the political loyalties of Sunnis and Shiites are affected by their country of citizenship and nationality. In 1980, Iran, a Shiite country whose language and culture are Farsi (Persian), was invaded by Iraq, an Arab country with a Sunni leadership but a Shiite majority in the population. Despite Iranian appeals, most Iraqi Shiites remained loyal to Iraq, performing military service when required during the 1980–88 Iran-Iraq war.

Both Sunni and Shiite Islam are organized in ways that reflect their beliefs. In view of the emphasis of mainstream Shiism on the role of the Imamate, it is not surprising that the Shiites have a more elaborate religious hierarchy than Sunni Muslims. With the exception of post-revolutionary Iran, the Shiite clergy has been more independent of the government than religious officials have been in Sunni Muslim countries. Shiite religious officials have had less need to rely on secular governments for money to finance their activities, since they control substantial religious endowments.

In the Shiite communities, the most important appointments to senior religious positions are made by Shiite religious officials, not by the state. In Sunni countries, in contrast, it is typical for governments to exercise control over the appointment of senior religious officials. These governments have also assumed the right to allocate large religious endowments through government ministries created for that purpose. This makes high-ranking Sunni clergy more dependent on the government than their Shiite counterparts. Sunnis are also more open than Shiites to the idea that the leading of prayers and preaching can be done by lay persons without formal clerical training.

In view of the power of the Shiite clergy, it is not surprising that they play an important political role. Led by the Ayatollah Khomeini, the clergy organized the revolution that overthrew the Shah of Iran in 1978–79 and turned the country into an Islamic Republic. Shiite clergy have also been prominent in opposition movements in Iraq and Lebanon.

Islamic Political Movements

Both Shiite and Sunni Muslim political movements have as a primary objective the establishment of Islamic law as the sole basis of government. They reject secularism as an imported western idea, and are opposed to several kinds of social change that use the west as a model, such as changes in the status of women.

Political movements with a religious message have a popular appeal in many Muslim countries. This is partly because of the religious outlook of the people. But it is also because the leaders of these movements are addressing the political issues of the day.

One of the reasons for the fall of the Shah of Iran was that his secularizing policies alienated the religious establishment. In contrast, the monarchs of oil-rich Sunni Muslim countries have made a greater effort to keep their policies in line with religious sensitivities.

Another very important reason for the fall of the Shah was the widespread discontent with his development policies favoring rich and westernized groups. The Shah spent a great deal of the country's oil wealth on military and civilian projects thought by many to be poorly conceived. Iran was a more populous country than other oil-rich Middle Eastern states, so its oil wealth spread less widely among the people. The effect of the Shah's westernizing development policies was to produce a new bourgeois class that was a target of hatred and resentment for poor people. In addition, like nationalist and leftist Iranian parties, the clergy vehemently attacked the Shah's ties to the West.

In spite of their religious orientation, many of the issues addressed by the Islamic movements are the same political or social issues that concern secular politicians. The movements attack government corruption and the gulf between rich and poor. In Iraq and Lebanon, where Shiite communities are poorer than the Sunni and Christian communities, resentment at perceived discrimination has also allowed Shiite movements to mobilize grassroots support. Problems of corruption and poverty are also invoked by Sunni movements in countries such as Egypt and Algeria, though these movements have so far not been able to obtain support from high-level religious leaders of a stature comparable to the Ayatollah Khomeini before the Iranian revolution.

The opposition to the West is derived from historic resentment in many parts of the Muslim world at western colonialism earlier this century. In addition to problems arising from that period, a number of more recent American and western policies are often cited by Muslim movements: western attempts to incorporate Muslim countries in alliances against the Soviet Union during the Cold War; political interventions such as the CIA-backed coup d'etat of 1953 that restored the Shah after a nationalist government led by Mohammed Massadegh had taken power in Iran; western military and political support for Israel against the Arab world; and western military and political support for unrepresentative governments.

Some of the most dramatic anti-western acts have been carried out by Shiite political groups in Lebanon, where the central government collapsed following the outbreak of civil war in 1975. The fighting led to foreign intervention by Syrian, Israeli, and American forces. Radical Shiite movements such as the Hizballah ("Party of God") flourished in the period following the dramatic western military intervention in Lebanon in 1982, when Israeili troops expelled the PLO from Beirut, and American peace-keeping forces were sent to Lebanon (to be withdrawn in 1984). Militant Shiites taking advantage of the lack of a central authority in the country attacked western and Israeli targets, and took hostages, some of whom were killed. Sunni opposition movements in Egypt and Algeria have also recently been increasingly violent in their anti-government, anti-western tactics.

These tactics have caused a major debate in the Islamic world. There is no justification in Islamic scriptures and juriprudence for indiscriminate killings or assassinations of local or foreign citizens by either Sunni or Shiite Muslims. Many intellectuals, however, cite the shortcomings of governments as a reason for these acts. "These bomb-throwers and wild men," writes the well-known Egyptian journalist Muhammad Hassanein Haykal, "are the result of almost unimaginably corrupt and mediocre governments" (*New York Times* Magazine, November 21, 1993, 65).

Violent anti-civilian acts are not Islamic in origin. In fact, radical violence seems to be a worldwide phenomenon. Radical groups, whether religious or not, often flourish in non-democratic environments where injustice, repression, and inappropriate foreign influence are widely believed to be dominant characteristics of the existing order.

Notes

1. The majority of the Iraqi population consists of Arab Shiites, but Sunni Arabs form a large minority group in the country.
2. "Majlis" is the Arabic word for assembly, and "Shura" means counsel or advice. "Majlis-al-Shura" thus designates the body of Muslims selected for consultation on all matters in Islam.
3. "Imamate" is the Arabic noun form of Imam, which means "he who stands before."
4. "Ithna 'Ashariyya" is the Arabic name for the branch of Shiism that believes in twelve Imams beginning with Ali and ending with Muhammad Al-Mahdi.
   Their names are
   a. Ali bin Abi Talib
   b. Al-Hassan bin Ali
   c. Al-Hussain bin Ali
   d. Ali bin al-Hussain
   e. Muhammad al-Bakir
   f. Jafar-al-Sadik
   g. Musa al-Kazim
   h. Ali al-Riza
   i. Muhammad Jawad al-Taki
   j. Ali al-Naki
   k. Al-Hassan al-Askari
   l. Muhammad al-Mahdi
5. "Ijma" is an Arabic word for the consensus of Muslim opinion, and is applied to matters not covered by the Koran and Hadith. According to the well-known jurist, Al-Shaf'i, Ijma is the third source of Islamic jurisprudence.

References

Bayat, M. *Mysticism and Dissent*. Syracuse, New York: Syracuse University Press, 1982.

Donaldson, M. *The Shi'ite Religion: A History of Islam in Persia and Iraq*. London: Luzac & Company, 1933.

Ismaeel, S. *The Difference Between the Shi'ite and the Majority of Muslim Scholars*. Carbondale, IL: A Muslim Group, 1983.

Khateeb, M. *Broad Aspects of Shi'ite Religion*. Riyadh: National Offset Printing Press, 1986.

Khomeini, Ayatollah Ruhallah, *Islam and Revolution: Writings and Declarations of Imam Khomeini*. Berkeley, CA: Mizan Press, 1981.

Kohlberg, E., "Imam and Community in the Pre-Ghayba Period." In *Authority and Political Culture in Shi'ism*. New York: New York State University Press, 1988.

Nasr, S. H. "Ithna Ashariyya." In *Encyclopedia of Islam*, vol. 4, 277–278. 1978.

____. "Ithna Ashariyya." In *Encyclopedia of Religion*, vol. 13, 260–270. 1987.

Tabatabai, S. H. N. *Shi'ite Islam*. Houston: Free Islamic Literatures, Inc., 1979.

World Almanac, the World Almanac and Book of Facts 1994. New York: Pharos Books, 1993.

Zaheer, Ehsan E. *Shias and the House of Ali*. Lahore, Pakistan: Javed Riaz Printers, 1985.

Article 3   *The World & I*, September 1997

TAKING THE MYSTERY OUT OF ISLAM

WHAT IS ISLAM?

*Islam, a great monotheistic religion, provides spiritual and moral life,
and cultural and sometimes national identity, to more than a billion people.*

ABDULAZIZ SACHEDINA

In the mass media, Islam and Muslims are frequently depicted as the "other" in global politics and cultural warfare. The Iranian revolution under Ayatollah Khomeini in 1978–79, the tragic death of 241 marines near Beirut airport in 1983, and the bombing of the World Trade Center in New York in 1993 are among the violent images associated with Muslims. But those images resonate poorly with the majority of Muslims. Most Muslims, like other human beings, are engaged in their day-to-day life in this world, strug-

gling to provide for their usually large extended families, working for peaceful resolution to the conflicts that face them, and committed to honor universal human values of freedom and peace with justice.

Muslims in general take their religion seriously. For many it is the central focus of their spiritual and moral life. For others, less religiously inclined, it remains a source of their cultural and sometimes national identity. So the word *Islam* carries broader ramifications than is usually recognized in the media. As the name of the religion, *Islam* means "submission to God's will." It is also applied to cultures and civilizations that developed under its religious impulse.

Historically as well as psychologically, Islam shares the monotheistic religious genome with Judaism and Christianity. Islamic civilization has acted as the repository of the Hebrew, Persian, Indian, and Hellenistic intellectual traditions and cultures.

Historical Development

Islam was proclaimed by Muhammad (570–632), the Prophet of Islam and the founder of Islamic polity, in Arabia. Seventh-century Arabia was socially and politically ripe for the emergence of new leadership. When Muhammad was growing up in Mecca, by then an important center of flourishing trade between Byzantium and the Indian Ocean, he was aware of the social inequities and injustices that existed in the tribal society dominated by a political oligarchy. Before Islam, religious practices and attitudes were determined by the tribal aristocracy, who also upheld tribal values—bravery in battle, patience in misfortune, persistence in revenge, protection of the weak, defiance of the strong, generosity, and hospitality—as part of their moral code. The growth of Mecca as a commercial center had weakened this tribal moral code and concern

for the less fortunate in society, leaving them without any security. It was in the midst of a serious socioeconomic imbalance between the rich and the poor, between extreme forms of individualism and tyrannical tribal solidarity, that Islam came to proclaim an ethical order based on interpersonal justice.

The founder and his community

Muhammad's father died before he was born, and his mother died when he was only six years old. In accordance with Arab tribal norms, he was brought

---

Islam: One of the World's Great Religions

Islam was proclaimed by Muhammad (570–632), the Prophet of Islam and the founder of Islamic polity.

After Muhammad's death, the Islamic community divided into the Sunni ("people of tradition") and the Shiites ("partisans").

The Sunni have mostly a quietist and authoritarian stance, while the Shiites tend to be more activist and radical.

The Muslim faith is built on Five Pillars.

Islam today continues to inspire more than a billion people to go beyond a self-centered existence to establish a just society.

up first by his grandfather and then, following his grandfather's death, by his uncle. As a young man he was employed by a wealthy Meccan woman, Khadija, as her trade agent. He was twenty-five when he accepted a marriage offer from Khadija, who was fifteen years his senior. When Muhammad received his prophetic call at the age of forty, Khadija was the first person to become "Muslim" ("believer in Islam").

Meccan leadership resisted Muhammad and persecuted him and his followers, who were drawn mainly from among the poor and disenfranchised. Muhammad decided to emigrate to Medina, an oasis town in the north. This emigration in 622 marks the beginning of the Muslim calendar, as well as the genesis of the first Islamic polity. (Muslims marked their new year, 1418, on May 8, 1997.)

Muhammad as a statesman instituted a series of reforms to create his community, the Umma, on the basis of religious affiliation. This also established a distinctive feature of Islamic faith, which does not admit any separation between the religious and temporal spheres of human activity and has insisted on the ideal unity of civil and moral authority under the divinely ordained legal system, the Shari'ah.

At Muhammad's death, he had brought the whole of Arabia under the Medina government, but he apparently left no explicit instruction regarding succession to his religious-political authority. The early Muslim leaders who succeeded him as caliph (meaning political and spiritual "successor") exercised Muhammad's political authority, making political and military decisions that led to the expansion of their domain beyond Arabia. Within a century Muslim armies had conquered the region from the Nile in North Africa to the Amu Darya in Central Asia east to India.

This phenomenal growth into a vast empire required an Islamic legal system for the administration of the highly developed political systems of the conquered Persian and Byzantine regions. Muslim jurists therefore formulated a comprehensive legal code, using the ethical and legal principles set forth in the Qur'an.

Differences of opinion on certain critical issues emerged as soon as Muhammad died. The question of succession was one of the major issues that divided the community into the Sunni and the Shiites. Those supporting the candidacy of Abu Bakr (ca. 573–634), an elderly associate of the Prophet, as caliph formed the majority of the community and gradually came to be known as the Sunni ("people of tradition"); those who acclaimed 'Ali (ca. 600–661), Muhammad's cousin and son-in-law, as the "imam" (religious and political leader) designated by the Prophet formed the minority group, known as the Shiites ("partisans").

The civil strife in Muslim polity gave rise to two distinct, and in some ways contradictory, attitudes among Muslims that can be observed even today: quietist and activist. Those upholding a quietist posture supported an authoritarian stance, to the point of feigning unquestioning and immediate obedience to almost any nominally Muslim political authority. Exponents of an activist posture supported radical politics and taught that under certain circumstances people had the right to revolt against evil Muslim rulers.

Gradually the quietist and authoritarian stance became associated with the majority Sunni Muslims, although every now and then they had their share of radicalism, as seen in the assassination of Egyptian President Anwar Sadat in 1981. The activist-radical stance came to be associated with Shiite Islam, represented by Iran today.

The Muslim community has continued to live in the shadow of the idealized history of early Islam, when religious and secular authority was united under pious caliphs. Efforts to actualize this ideal today give rise to radical politics among a number of religious-minded Muslim groups, usually designated pejoratively as "fundamentalists," who regard *jihad* (war) against their corrupt rulers as a legitimate tool for change.

What Do Muslims believe?

Muslims derive their religious beliefs and practices from two sources: the Qur'an, which they regard as the "Book of God," and the Sunna, or the exemplary conduct of the Prophet. The Qur'an consists of the revelations Muhammad received intermittently over the twenty-two years from the time of his calling in 610 until his death. Muslims believe that the Qur'an was directly communicated by God through the archangel Gabriel, and accordingly, it is regarded as inerrant and immutably preserved. It has served as the normative source for deriving principal theological, ethical, and legal doctrines. The Sunna (meaning "trodden path") has functioned as the elaboration of the Qur'anic revelation. It provides details about each and every precept and deed attributed to Muhammad. The narratives that carried such information are known as *hadith*. In the ninth century, Muslim scholars developed an elaborate system for the theological and legal classification of these hadith to derive certain beliefs and practices.

In this connection it is relevant to remember the Rushdie affair of the 1980s. Salman Rushdie's novel *The Satanic Verses* was directed toward discrediting both the Qur'an and the Prophet as the normative sources for Muslim religiosity, which, understandably, enraged more than a billion Muslims around the world. And while many Muslims may not have endorsed the death sentence passed on Rushdie by the Ayatollah Khomeini, they unanimously condemned the novel for its profanity in connection with the founder of Islam and Muslim scriptures.

The Five Pillars of Islam

The Muslim faith is built upon Five Pillars, as follow:

The First Pillar is the *shahada*, the profession of faith: "There is no deity but God, and Muhammad is the messenger of God." This is the formula through which a person converts to Islam. Belief in God constitutes the integrity of human existence, individually and as a member of society. The Qur'an speaks about God as the being whose presence is felt in everything that exists; everything that happens is an indicator of the divine. God is the "knower of the Unseen and the Visible; . . . the All-merciful, the All-compassionate, . . . the Sovereign Lord, the All-holy, the Giver of peace, the Keeper of faith, the All-preserver, the All-mighty, the All-powerful, the Most High" (Qur'an, 59:23). Faith in God results in being safe, well integrated, sound, and at peace.

Human beings are not born in sin, but they are forgetful. To help them realize their potential God sends prophets to "remind" humanity of their covenant with God (7:172). Noah, Abraham, Moses, Jesus, and Muhammad are regarded as "messengers" sent to organize their people on the basis of the guidance revealed by God.

The Second Pillar is daily worship (*salat*), required five times a day: at dawn, midday, afternoon, evening, and night. These prayers are short and require bowing and prostrations. Muslims may worship anywhere, preferably in congregation, facing Mecca. They are re-

Islam and the Arabic Language

By Tamara Sonn

Those are the verses of the glorious book. We have revealed it as an Arabic recitation, so that you will understand. (Qur'an, 12:2)

These words from Islamic scripture, and others like them, reveal the integral relationship between the Arabic language and Islam. Muslims believe that all revelation comes from the same divine source, so there is no need to be concerned that the Jews have their Torah and the Christians have their Gospels, for example. The Qur'an is simply divine revelation sent to speakers of Arabic, according to this sacred book. "Yet before it was the Book of Moses for a model and a mercy; and this is a book confirming in Arabic, to warn the evil-doers and bring good tidings to the good-doers" (46:11–12). The Qur'an, therefore, is essentially Arabic. But that does not mean Islam is only for Arabs.

According to the Qur'an, no one can be forced to convert. "In matters of religion there is no compulsion" (2:256). But those who choose to become Muslim must pray five times a day, reciting from the Qur'an in Arabic. The role of the Arabic language in Islam, therefore, remains central, despite the fact that the vast majority of Muslims are neither Arab nor Arabic speaking.

The majority of Muslims worldwide today "read" Arabic for prayer the way Roman Catholics used to "read" Latin at mass. They can make out the words but know the general ideas represented primarily through vernacular interpretations. Yet there is no movement to substitute the vernacular for the original language, as there was in Catholicism before the Second Vatican Council. On the contrary, emphasis on the importance of studying Arabic is increasing.

Only one country has ever authorized a translation of the Qur'an. Turkey, created after the breakup of the Ottoman Empire in World War I, stressed the Turkish language in an effort to distinguish itself from the rest of the Muslim world. Even in Turkey, however, prayer continued to be in Arabic, and today there is a strong movement to return to Arabic as the universal language of Islam.

Part of the contemporary stress on Arabic results from the worldwide movement of rebirth (*al-nahda*) in Islam. After centuries of eclipse and Euro-Christian domination, the Muslim world entered the twentieth century with a renewed commitment to its roots as a means of reviving both cultural strength and political independence. Formal independence from colonial control, however, left most of the Muslim world afflicted with severe economic and political underdevelopment. Experiments with European-style social and political models have been judged failures, benefiting only a few. The result has been a populist call for "the Islamic solution," religiously based cultural and political identity. Renewed emphasis on the Qur'an—and with it, Arabic—is an integral part of this "Islamist" movement. As a result, the Arabic language is being studied more widely than ever.

The Islamist stress on Islamic and therefore Arabic studies, however, should not be confused with another modern movement known as Arabism (*'urubah*). Arabism stresses not only the centrality of the Arabic language to Islamic identity but the dominance of Arab culture. Early proponents described Islam as "the highest moment of consciousness" of Arab culture. Therefore, as people become Muslim, they actually become Arab as well, at least to a certain degree. Some see Arabism as simply a religiously oriented version of the Arab nationalist movement.

A controversial movement from the outset, Arabism has declined in popularity with the rise of Islamism, although its echoes can still be heard. In a recent speech, Sadek Jawad Sulaiman, former ambassador of Oman to the United States, stressed the centrality of Arabism to Islam: "Outside its repository of Arabic culture, Islam is left with little form or substance."

The majority of those who stress the importance of Arabic believe they are simply following the Qur'an's own teaching. The Qur'an repeatedly refers to the power and beauty of its language. It tells of Prophet Muhammad being an illiterate (or unlettered) orphan and yet producing a work of such splendor that it challenges his detractors to match it (10:38–9, 11:13–16, 28:49). Even today, non-Muslim Arabic speakers are awed by its beauty. Undoubtedly, the book's inherent beauty and power would suffer in translation. Beyond aesthetic concerns, however, is recognition of the insidious effect of translation on understanding.

Even so, Muslims agree that fluency in Arabic is no guarantee that one will be moved by the Qur'an or be a good Muslim. As the Qur'an teaches, "God summons to the abode of peace and guides whomsoever he will to a straight path" (3:27). Islam enters "through the heart," according to Qur'anic metaphor. It is primarily a turning of the will toward God, an inner transformation. This transformation may or may not be prompted by the power of the Qur'an. The Qur'an counts among the believers anyone—including Jews and Christians—who believes in God and does good deeds. For at its core, Islam is a matter of behavior rather than words: "Woe betide those who pray, yet are neglectful of their prayers—those who pray for show and yet refuse charity" (107:1–7).

Tamara Sonn is a professor in the Department of Religious Studies at the University of South Florida, Tampa.

quired to worship as a community on Fridays at midday and on two major religious holidays.

The Third Pillar is the mandatory "alms-levy" (*zakat*). The obligation to share what one possesses with those less fortunate is stressed throughout the Qur'an. The Muslim definition of the virtuous life includes charitable support of widows, wayfarers, orphans, and the needy. Although zakat has for the most part been left to the conscience of Muslims, the obligation to be charitable and contribute to the general welfare of the community continues to be emphasized. In a number of poor Muslim countries this benevolence provided by wealthy individuals has underwritten badly needed social services for those who cannot afford them.

The Fourth Pillar is the fast during the month of Ramadan, observed according to the Muslim lunar calendar, which has been in use since the seventh century. Since the lunar year is some ten days shorter than the solar year, the fasting and all Muslim festivals occur in different seasons. During the fast, which lasts from dawn to dusk, Muslims are required not only to refrain from eating, smoking, and drinking; they are also to refrain from sexual intercourse and acts leading to sensual behavior. The end of the month is marked by a festival, Eid al-Fitr, after which life returns to normal.

The Fifth Pillar is the *hajj*, or pilgrimage to Mecca, which all Muslims are required to undertake once in their lives, provided they have the financial means. The pilgrimage brings together Muslims of diverse cultures and nationalities to achieve a purity of existence and a communion with God that will exalt the pilgrims for the rest of their lives.

The Islamic ethical-legal system, known as the Shari'ah, was developed to determine normative Islamic conduct.

Muslim moral and legal guidance

The Islamic ethical-legal system, known as the Shari'ah, was developed to determine normative Islamic conduct.

The Shari'ah is the divinely ordained blueprint for human conduct, which is inherently and essentially religious. The juridical inquiry in discovering the Shari'ah code was comprehensive because it necessarily dealt with every case of conscience covering God-human relations, as well as the ethical content of interpersonal relations in every possible sphere of human activity. Most of the legal activity, however, went into settling more formal interpersonal activities that affected the morals of the community. These activities dealt with the obligation to do good to Muslims and guard the interests of the community.

Islamic legal theory recognized four sources on the basis of which judicial decisions could be deduced: the Qur'an, the Sunna, consensus of the early community of Muslims, and analogical reasoning, which attempts to discover the unknown from the known precedent. Ash-Shafi'i (767–820), a rigorous legal thinker, systematically and comprehensively linked the four sources to derive the entire legal system covering all possible contingencies. The legal precedents and principles provided by the Qur'an and Sunna were used to develop an elaborate system of rules of jurisprudence. Human conduct was to be determined in terms of how much legal weight was borne by a particular rule that rendered a given practice obligatory or merely recommended.

As Islamic law became a highly technical process, disputes about method and judicial opinions crystallized into legal schools designated by the names of prominent jurists. The legal school that followed the Iraqi tradition was called "Hanafi," after Abu Hanafi (669–767), the great imam in Iraq. Those who adhered to the rulings of Malik ibn Anas (ca. 715–795), in Arabia and elsewhere, were known as "Malikis." Ash-Shafi'i founded a legal school in Egypt whose influence spread widely to other regions of the Muslim world. His followers were known as Shafi'is. Another school was associated with Ahmad ibn Hanbal (780–855), who compiled a work on traditions that became the source for juridical decisions for Hanbalis.

The Shiites developed their own legal school, whose leading authority was Imam Ja'far ibn Muhammad (ca. 702–765). Normally, Muslims accept one of the legal schools prevalent in their region. Most of the Sunni follow Hanifah or Shafi'i, whereas the Shiites follow the Ja'fari school. In the absence of an organized "church" and ordained "clergy" in Islam, determination of valid religious

practice is left to the qualified scholar of religious law known as a *mufti* (the one who issues a *fatwa*, or decree).

Muslim family law

In Islamic family law, the rights of women, children, and other dependents are protected against the male head of the family, who, on the average, is stronger than a woman and more independent, since he is free of pregnancy and immediate care of children. Islamic marital rules encourage individual responsibility by strengthening the nuclear family. The Shari'ah protects male prerogative as the one who is required to support the household, whereas a woman is protected primarily by her family. All schools give a husband one-sided divorce privileges, because for a woman to divorce a man would mean to unsettle her husband's economic investment. Under these rules a husband could divorce a wife almost at will, but a wife who wished to leave her husband had to show good reason. The main legal check upon the man in divorce is essentially financial and a matter of contract between equal parties that includes a provision about the bridal gift. The man pays part of the gift, which might be substantial, at the time of marriage; if he divorces her without special reason, he has to pay her the rest.

The Muslim woman can own property, and it cannot be touched by any male relative, including her husband, who is required to support her from his own funds. Moreover, she has a personal status that might allow her to go into business on her own. However, this potential feminine independence was curbed primarily by cultural means, keeping marriages within the extended family, so that family property would not leave the family through women marrying out.

All schools of Islam, although tending to give men an extensive prerogative, presupposed a considerable social role for women. The Qur'anic injunction to propriety was stretched by means of the Sunna to impose seclusion. The veil for women was presented simply in terms of personal modesty, the female apartments in terms of family privacy.

In the patriarchal family structures, and not necessarily in the Shari'ah, women were assigned a subordinate role in the household and community. Here, the term *Islam* is being used in the sense of culture or local tradition. And it is precisely in the confusion between normative Islam and cultural practices that

Muslims, like Christians, have raised critical questions about human responsibility in view of God's overpowering will.

we find tension in ethical and legal formulations among Muslims.

In some parts of the Muslim world women are victims of traditional practices that are often harmful to them and to their children's well-being. One controversial and persistent practice is female circumcision (*khafd or khifad*), without which it is believed that girls could not attain the status of womanhood. Islamic views of female circumcision are ambiguous. The operation was performed long before the rise of Islam, and it is not a practice in many Muslim countries, including Saudi Arabia, Tunisia, Iran, and Turkey. There is nothing in the Qur'an that sanctions female circumcision, especially its most severe form, infibulation. The Prophet opposed the custom, found among pre-Islamic Arabs, since he considered it harmful to women's sexual well-being. Yet the official position adopted by a majority of Sunni jurists is that female circumcision is sanctioned by the tradition. They concede, however, that the Shari'ah does not regard it as an obligatory requirement.

Are humans free agents of God?

Muslims, like Christians, have raised critical questions about human responsibility in view of God's overpowering will. In the first half of the eighth century, the rudiments of the earliest systematic theology were developed by a group called the Mu'tazilites. Before them, some Muslim thinkers had developed theological arguments, including a doctrine of God and human responsibility. The Mu'tazilites undertook to show that there was nothing repugnant to reason in the Islamic revelation. Their theological system was worked out under five headings: (1) belief in God's unity, which rejected anything that smacked of anthropomorphism; (2) the justice of God, which denied any ascriptions of injustice to God's judgment of human beings, with the consequence that humans alone were responsible for all their acts and thus punishable for evil actions; (3)

the impending judgment, which underscored the importance of daily righteousness and rejected laxity in matters of faith; (4) the middle position of the Muslim sinner, who, because of disobeying God's commandments was neither condemned to hell nor rewarded with paradise; and (5) the duty to command the good and forbid evil to ensure an ethical social order.

The traditionalist Ash'arites, reacting to Mu'tazilite rationalism, limited speculative theology to a defense of the doctrines given in the hadith, which were regarded as more reliable than abstract reason in deriving individual doctrines. The Ash'arites emphasized the absolute will and power of God and denied nature and humankind any decisive role. In their effort to maintain the effectiveness of a God who could and did intervene in human affairs, they maintained that good and evil are what God decrees them to be. Accordingly, good and evil cannot be known from nature but must be discovered in the Qur'an and the tradition. Ash'arite theological views have remained dominant throughout Islamic history, well into modern times, and had a profound effect upon scientific theory and practice among the Sunni.

The attitude of resignation, a by-product of belief in predestination, is summed up in the Sunni creedal confession: "What reaches you could not possibly have missed you; and what misses you could not possibly have reached you" (*Fiqh akbar*, Article 3).

The Shiite Muslims, on the other hand, have developed a rational theology and ethical doctrines resembling those of the Mu'tazilites. Hence, they believe that humans are free agents of God who are responsible for their own actions. Moreover, the justice of God requires that God provide a constant source of guidance through reason and exemplary leaders, known as imams, for human advancement toward perfection. This belief is the source of the emergence of Khomeini-like leadership in Shiite Iran today.

Mystical dimension of Islam

From the early days of the Islamic empire (eighth century) the ascetic reaction to growing worldliness in the Muslim community took the form of mysticism of personality in Islam, whose goal was spiritual and moral perfection of an individual. Sufism, as Islamic mysticism came to be known, aimed to internalize the ritual acts by emphasizing rigorous self-assessment and self-discipline. In its

early form Sufism was mainly a form of ascetic piety that involved ridding oneself of any dependence on satisfying one's desire, in order to devote oneself entirely to God. Mystical practices developed by the Sufi masters comprised a moral process to gain the relative personal clarity that comes at moments of retreat and reflection.

From daily moments of reflection the mystic experienced more intense levels of awareness, which could take ecstatic forms, including ecstatic love of God. This aspect of Sufism brought the mystics into direct conflict with the traditionalist Muslims, who emphasized active obedience to God as the highest goal of religious meaning and purpose.

By the eleventh century, the Sufi masters had developed a new form of religious orientation that brought about the acceptance of Sufism by the ordinary people in many places. Near the end of the twelfth century, the Sufi organized several formal brotherhoods or orders (*tariqa*) in which women also participated. Each order taught a pattern of invocation and meditation that used devotional practices to organize a group of novices under a master. Through special control of breath and bodily posture accompanied by invocative words or syllables, they developed more intense concentration.

These brotherhoods, however, degenerated into antisocial groups that caused much damage to the teachings of Islam about societal and familial obligations. Moreover, because of their unquestioning devotion to the Sufi masters, both living and dead, a shrine culture leading to almost saint worship took deep roots among ordinary peoples attracted to this folk Islam. This condition elicited a strong reaction against Sufism in the Muslim world in modern times. Both the traditionalist reformers, like the Wahhabis of Saudi Arabia, and the champions of secularist modernism, like the founder of modern Turkey, Kemal Atatürk (1881–1938), disbanded Sufism as being totally un-Islamic.

Although its interaction with history is not free of tension, and even contradictions, on the whole Islam has developed an enviable system of coexistence among religious communities.

Nevertheless, the formal approval of Sufism as a genuine form of Islamic piety by the great scholar Abu Hamid al-Ghazal (1058–1111), who taught Islamic law and theology in Baghdad, has been revived in many countries. There sufism continues to thrive as a bastion of religious tolerance and free-spirited religiosity.

Islam today

Islam as a religion, culture, and civilization continues to inspire a billion peo-ple worldwide to take up the challenge to go beyond one's self-centered exist-ence to establish a just society that will reflect "submission to God's will." As an Abrahamic faith, Islam has accepted the pluralism of human responses to spiri-tual guidance as a divine mystery. And although its interaction with history is not free of tension, and even contradic-tions, on the whole Islam has developed an enviable system of coexistence among religious communities. Its vision of a global community working toward the common good of humanity has been overshadowed by political upheavals in the postcolonial Muslim world. Unless the violated justice of the ordinary peo-ple is restored, like its other Abrahamic forebears Islam will continue to inspire activist response to social and political injustices in the Muslim world.

Abdulaziz Sachedina is professor of religious studies at the University of Virginia.

Article 4   *Foreign Affairs*, September/October 1997

Islamic and Western Values

Ali A. Mazrui

ALI A. MAZRUI *is Director of the Insti-tute of Global Cultural Studies at the State University of New York at Bing-hamton. He is also Ibn Khaldun Professor-at-Large at the School of Islamic and Social Sciences in Leesburg, Virginia, and Senior Scholar in Africana Studies at Cor-nell University. His books include* Cul-tural Forces in World Politics *and, with Alamin M. Mazrui, the forthcoming* The Power of Babel: Language and Govern-ance in Africa's Experience.

DEMOCRACY AND THE HUMANE LIFE

WESTERNERS TEND to think of Islamic societies as backward-looking, op-pressed by religion, and inhumanely governed, comparing them to their own enlightened, secular democracies. But measurement of the cultural distance be-tween the West and Islam is a complex undertaking, and that distance is nar-rower than they assume. Islam is not just a religion, and certainly not just a fun-damentalist political movement. It is a civilization, and a way of life that varies from one Muslim country to another but is animated by a common spirit far more humane than most Westerners realize. Nor do those in the West always recog-nize how their own societies have failed to live up to their liberal mythology.

Moreover, aspects of Islamic culture that Westerners regard as medieval may have prevailed in their own culture until fairly recently; in many cases, Islamic so-cieties may be only a few decades be-hind socially and technologically advanced Western ones. In the end, the question is what path leads to the high-est quality of life for the average citizen, while avoiding the worst abuses. The path of the West does not provide all the answers; Islamic values deserve serious consideration.

THE WAY IT RECENTLY WAS

MORES AND values have changed rap-idly in the West in the last several dec-ades as revolutions in technology and society progressed. Islamic countries, which are now experiencing many of the same changes, may well follow suit. Pre-marital sex, for example, was strongly disapproved of in the West until after World War II. There were laws against sex outside marriage, some of which are still on the books, if rarely enforced. To-day sex before marriage, with parental consent, is common.

Homosexual acts between males were a crime in Great Britain until the 1960s (although lesbianism was not outlawed). Now such acts between consenting adults, male or female, are legal in much of the West, although they remain illegal in most other countries.

Half the Western world, in fact, would say that laws against homosexual sex are a violation of gays' and lesbians' human rights.

Even within the West, one sees cul-tural lag. Although capital punishment has been abolished almost everywhere in the Western world, the United States is currently increasing the number of capital offenses and executing more death row inmates than it has in years. But death penalty opponents, including Human Rights Watch and the Roman Catholic Church, continue to protest the practice in the United States, and one day capital punishment will almost cer-tainly be regarded in America as a vio-lation of human rights.

Westerners regard Muslim societies as unenlightened when it comes to the status of women, and it is true that the gender question is still troublesome in Muslim countries. Islamic rules on sex-ual modesty have often resulted in ex-cessive segregation of the sexes in public places, sometimes bringing about the marginalization of women in public af-fairs more generally. British women, however, were granted the right to own property independent of their husbands only in 1870, while Muslim women have always had that right. Indeed, Islam is the only world religion founded by a businessman in a commercial partner-ship with his wife. While in many West-ern cultures daughters could not inherit anything if there were sons in the family, Islamic law has always allocated shares from every inheritance to both daughters and sons. Primogeniture has been illegal under the sharia for 14 centuries.

The historical distance between the West and Islam in the treatment of women may be a matter of decades rather than centuries. Recall that in almost all Western countries except for New Zealand, women did not gain the right to vote until the twentieth century. Great Britain extended the vote to women in two stages, in 1918 and 1928, and the United States enfranchised them by constitutional amendment in 1920. France followed as recently as 1944. Switzerland did not permit women to vote in national elections until 1971—decades after Muslim women in Afghanistan, Iran, Iraq, and Pakistan had been casting ballots.

Furthermore, the United States, the largest and most influential Western nation, has never had a female president. In contrast, two of the most populous Muslim countries, Pakistan and Bangladesh, have had women prime ministers: Benazir Bhutto headed two governments in Pakistan, and Khaleda Zia and Hasina Wajed served consecutively in Bangladesh. Turkey has had Prime Minister Tansu Çiller. Muslim countries are ahead in female empowerment, though still behind in female liberation.

CONCEPTS OF THE SACRED

CENSORSHIP IS one issue on which the cultural divide between the West and Islam turns out to be less wide than Westerners ordinarily assume. The most celebrated case of the last decade—that of Salman Rushdie's novel *The Satanic Verses*, published in Britain in 1988 but banned in most Muslim countries—brought the Western world and the Muslim world in conflict, but also uncovered some surprising similarities and large helpings of Western hypocrisy. Further scrutiny reveals widespread censorship in the West, if imposed by different forces than in Muslim societies.

As their civilization has become more secular, Westerners have looked for new abodes of the sacred. By the late twentieth century the freedom of the artist—in this case Salman Rushdie— was more sacred to them than religion. But many Muslims saw Rushdie's novel as holding Islam up to ridicule. The novel suggests that Islam's holy scripture, the Koran, is filled with inventions of the Prophet Muhammad or is, in fact, the work of the devil rather than communications

from Allah, and implies, moreover, that the religion's founder was not very intelligent. Rushdie also puts women characters bearing the names of the Prophet's wives in a whorehouse, where the clients find the blasphemy arousing.

Many devout Muslims felt that Rushdie had no right to poke fun at and twist into obscenity some of the most sacred symbols of Islam. Most Muslim countries banned the novel because officials there considered it morally repugnant.[1] Western intellectuals argued that as an artist, Rushdie had the sacred right and even duty to go wherever his imagination led him in his writing. Yet until the 1960s *Lady Chatterley's Lover* was regarded as morally repugnant under British law for daring to depict an affair between a married member of the gentry and a worker on the estate. For a long time after Oscar Wilde's conviction for homosexual acts, *The Picture of Dorian Gray* was regarded as morally repugnant. Today other gay writers are up against a wall of prejudice.

The Satanic Verses was banned in some places because of fears that it would cause riots. Indian officials explained that they were banning the novel because it would inflame religious passions in the country, already aroused by Kashmiri separatism. The United States has a legal standard for preventive action when negative consequences are feared—"clear and present danger." But the West was less than sympathetic to India's warnings that the book was inflammatory. Rushdie's London publisher, Jonathan Cape, went ahead, and the book's publication even in far-off Britain resulted in civil disturbances in Bombay, Islamabad, and Karachi in which some 15 people were killed and dozens more injured.

Distinguished Western publishers, however, have been known to reject a manuscript because of fears for the safety of their own. Last year Cambridge University Press turned down *Fields of Wheat, Rivers of Blood* by Anastasia Karakasidou, a sociological study on ethnicity in the Greek province of Macedonia, publicly acknowledging that it did so because of worries about the safety of its employees in Greece. If Jonathan Cape had cared as much about South Asian lives as it said it cared about freedom of expression, or as Cambridge University Press cared about its staff members in Greece, less blood would have been spilled.

Targets, sources, and methods of censorship differ, but censorship is just as much a fact of life in Western societies

as in the Muslim world. Censorship in the latter is often crude, imposed by governments, mullahs and imams, and, more recently, militant Islamic movements. Censorship in the West, on the other hand, is more polished and decentralized. Its practitioners are financial backers of cultural activity and entertainment, advertisers who buy time on commercial television, subscribers of the Public Broadcasting System (PBS), influential interest groups including ethnic pressure groups, and editors, publishers, and other controllers of the means of communication.[2] In Europe, governments, too, sometimes get into the business of censorship.

CENSORING AMERICA

THE THREAT to free speech in the United States comes not from the law and the Constitution but from outside the government. PBS , legally invulnerable on the issue of free speech, capitulated to other forces when faced with the metaphorical description in my 1986 television series "The Africans" of Karl Marx as "the last of the great Jewish prophets." The British version had included the phrase, but the American producing station, WETA, a PBS affiliate in Washington, deleted it without authorial permission so as not to risk offending Jewish Americans.

On one issue of censorship WETA did consult me. Station officials were unhappy I had not injected more negativity into the series' three-minute segment on Libya's leader, Muammar Qaddafi. First they asked for extra commentary on allegations that Libya sponsored terrorism. When I refused, they suggested changing the pictures instead—deleting one sequence that humanized Qaddafi by showing him visiting a hospital and substituting a shot of the Rome airport after a terrorist bombing. After much debate I managed to save the hospital scene but surrendered on the Rome airport addition, on condition that neither I nor the written caption implied that Libya was responsible for the bombing. But, ideally, WETA would have preferred to cut the whole segment.

WETA in those days had more in common with the censors in Libya than either side realized. Although the Libyans broadcast an Arabic version and seemed pleased with the series as a whole, they cut the Qaddafi sequence. The segment also offended Lynne Cheney, chair of the National Endowment for the Humanities, who demanded that the endowment's name be removed from the series credits. After she stepped down from her post, she called for the NEH to be abolished, citing "The Africans" as an example of the objectionable liberal projects that, she said, the endowment had tended to fund.

In another case of decentralized censorship that affected my own work, Westview Press in Boulder, Colorado, was about to go to press with my book *Cultural Forces in World Politics* when editors there announced they wanted to delete three chapters: one discussing *The Satanic Verses* as a case of cultural treason, another comparing the Palestinian intifada with Chinese students' 1989 rebellion in Tiananmen Square, and a third comparing the South African apartheid doctrine of separate homelands for blacks and whites with the Zionist doctrine of separate states for Jews and Arabs. Suspecting that I would have similar problems with most other major U.S. publishers, I decided that the book would be published exclusively by James Currey, my British publisher, and Heinemann Educational Books, the American offshoot of another British house, which brought it out in 1990. Not even universities in the United States, supposed bastions of intellectual freedom, have been free from censorship. Until recently the greatest danger to one's chances of getting tenure lay in espousing Marxism or criticizing Israel or Zionism.

The positive aspect of decentralized censorship in the West, at least with regard to books, is that what is unacceptable to one publisher may be acceptable to another; what is almost unpublishable in the United States may be easily publishable in Britain or the Netherlands. With national television, the choices are more restricted. Many points of view are banned from the screen, with the possibility of a hearing only on the public access stations with the weakest signals.

In Western societies as in Muslim ones, only a few points of view have access to the national broadcast media and publishing industry or even to university faculties. In both civilizations, certain points of view are excluded from the center and marginalized. The source of the censorship may be different, but censorship is the result in the West just as surely as in the Islamic world.

LIFE AMONG THE BELIEVERS

MANY OF the above issues are bound up with religion. Westerners consider many problems or flaws of the Muslim world products of Islam and pride their

(CORBIS-BETTMANN)

Clothes don't make the woman: Yemen, 1977

societies and their governments on their purported secularism. But when it comes to separation of church and state, how long and wide is the distance between the two cultures?

A central question is whether a theocracy can ever be democratized. British history since Henry VIII's establishment of the Church of England in 1531 proves that it can be. The English theocracy was democratized first by making democracy stronger and later by making the theocracy weaker. The major democratic changes had to wait until the nineteenth and twentieth centuries, when the vote was extended to new social classes and finally to women.[3] The Islamic Republic of Iran is less than two decades old, but already there seem to be signs of softening theocracy and the beginnings of liberalization. Nor must we forget Muslim monarchies that have taken initial steps toward liberalization. Jordan has gone further than most others in legalizing opposition groups. But even Saudi Arabia and the smaller Gulf states have begun to use the Islamic concept of *shura* (consultative assembly) as a guide to democracy.

The West has sought to protect minority religions through secularism. It has not always worked. The Holocaust in secular Germany was the worst case. And even today, anti-Semitism in Eastern Europe is disturbing, as are anti-Muslim trends in France.

The United States has had separation of church and state under the Constitution for over 200 years, but American politics is hardly completely secular. Only once has the electorate chosen a non-Protestant president—and the Roman Catholic John F. Kennedy won by such a narrow margin, amid such allegations of electoral fraud, that we will never know for certain whether a majority of Americans actually voted for him. Jews have distinguished themselves in many fields, but they have so far avoided competing for the White House, and there is still a fear of unleashing the demon of anti-Semitism among Christian fundamentalists. There are now more Muslims—an estimated six million—than Jews in the United States, yet anti-Muslim feeling and the success of appeals to Christian sentiment among voters make it extremely unlikely that Americans will elect a Muslim head of state anytime in the foreseeable future. Even the appointment of a Muslim secretary of commerce, let alone an attorney general, is no more than a distant conjecture because of the political fallout that all administrations fear. When First Lady Hillary Rodham Clinton entertained Muslim leaders at the White House last year to mark a special Islamic festival, a *Wall Street Journal* article cited that as evidence that friends of Hamas had penetrated the White House. In Western Europe, too, there are now millions of Muslims, but history is still awaiting the appointment of the first to a cabinet position in Britain, France, or Germany.

Islam, on the other hand, has tried to protect minority religions through ecu-

Muslims are criticized for not producing the best, but their ethic has avoided the worst.

menicalism throughout its history. Jews and Christians had special status as People of the Book—a fraternity of monotheists. Other religious minorities were later also accorded the status of protected minorities (*dhimmis*). The approach has had its successes. Jewish scholars rose to high positions in Muslim Spain. During the Ottoman Empire, Christians sometimes attained high political office: Suleiman I (1520–1566) had Christian ministers in his government, as did Selim III (1789–1807). The Moghul Empire integrated Hindus and Muslims into a consolidated Indian state; Emperor Akbar (1556–1605) carried furthest the Moghul policy of bringing Hindus into the government. In the 1990s Iraq has had a Chaldean Christian deputy prime minister, Tariq Aziz. And Boutros Boutros-Ghali, a Coptic Christian, would never have been appointed secretary-general of the United Nations if not for his long and distinguished service in the foreign ministry of an otherwise Muslim government in Egypt.

The Republic of Senegal in West Africa, which is nearly 95 percent Muslim, had a Roman Catholic president for two decades (1960–80). In his years presiding over that relatively open society, Léopold Sédar Senghor never once had to deal with anti-Christian disturbances in the streets of Dakar. His political opponents called him a wide range of derogatory names—hypocrite, stooge of the French, dictator, political prostitute—but virtually never taunted him for being a *kafir* (infidel).

When Senghor became the first African head of state to retire voluntarily from office, Abdou Diouf, a Muslim, succeeded him, and he remains president today. But the ecumenical story of Senegal did not end there; the first lady is Catholic. Can one imagine an American presidential candidate confessing on *Larry King Live*, "Incidentally, my wife is a Shiite Muslim?" That would almost certainly mark the end of his hopes for the White House.

One conclusion to be drawn from all this is that Westerners are far less secular in their political behavior than they think they are. Another is that Muslim societies historically have been more ecumenical, and therefore more humane, than their Western critics have recognized. Islamic ecumenicalism has sometimes protected religious minorities more effectively than Western secularism.

BETWEEN THE DAZZLING AND THE DEPRAVED

CULTURES SHOULD be judged not merely by the heights of achievement to which they have ascended but by the depths of brutality to which they have descended. The measure of cultures is not only their virtues but also their vices.

In the twentieth century, Islam has not often proved fertile ground for democracy and its virtues. On the other hand, Islamic culture has not been hospitable to Nazism, fascism, or communism, unlike Christian culture (as in Germany, Italy, Russia, Czechoslovakia), Buddhist culture (Japan before and during World War II, Pol Pot's Cambodia, Vietnam, North Korea), or Confucian culture (Mao's China). The Muslim world has never yet given rise to systematic fascism and its organized brutalities. Hafiz al-Assad's Syria and Saddam Hussein's Iraq have been guilty of large-scale violence, but fascism also requires an ideology of repression that has been absent in the two countries. And apart from the dubious case of Albania, communism has never independently taken hold in a Muslim culture.

Muslims are often criticized for not producing the best, but they are seldom congratulated for an ethic that has averted the worst. There are no Muslim equivalents of Nazi extermination camps, nor Muslim conquests by genocide on the scale perpetrated by Europeans in the Americas and Australia, nor Muslim equivalents of Stalinist terror, Pol Pot's killing fields, or the starvation and uprooting of tens of millions in the name of Five Year Plans. Nor are there Muslim versions of apartheid like that once approved by the South African Dutch Reformed Church, or of the ferocious racism of Japan before 1945, or of the racist culture of the Old South in the United States with its lynchings and brutalization of black people.

Islam brings to the calculus of universal justice some protection from the abyss of human depravity. Historically, the religion and the civilization have been resistant to forces that contributed to the worst aspects of the twentieth century's interludes of barbarism: racism, genocide, and violence within society.

First, Islam has been relatively resistant to racism. The Koran confronts the issue of national and ethnic differences head on. The standard of excellence it sets has nothing to do with race, but is instead moral and religious worth— what the Koran calls "piety" and what Martin Luther King, Jr., called "the content of one's character." An oft-quoted verse of the Koran reads:

O people! We have created you from a male and a female, and have made you nations and tribes so that you may know one another. The noblest among you is the most pious. Allah is all-knowing.

In his farewell address, delivered on his last pilgrimage to Mecca in A.D. 632, Muhammad declared: "There is no superiority of an Arab over a non-Arab, and indeed, no superiority of a red man over a black man except through piety and fear of God . . . Let those who are present convey this message to those who are absent."

Unlike Christian churches, the mosque has never been segregated by race. One of Muhammad's most beloved companions was an Ethiopian, Bilal Rabah, a freed slave who rose to great prominence in early Islam. Under Arab lineage systems and kinship traditions, racial intermarriage was not discouraged and the children were considered Arab regardless of who the mother was. These Arab ways influenced Muslim societies elsewhere. Of the four presidents of Egypt since the revolution of 1952, two had black African ancestors—Muhammad Nagib and Anwar al-Sadat.[4]

Islam has a doctrine of Chosen Language (Arabic) but no Chosen People. Since the conversion of the Roman Emperor Constantine I in A.D. 313, Christianity has been led if not dominated by Europeans. But the leadership of the Muslim world has changed hands several times: from the mainly Arab Umayyad dynasty (661–750) to the multiethnic Abbasid dynasty (750–1258) to the Ottoman Empire (1453–1922), dominated by the Turks. And this history is quite apart from such flourishing Muslim dynasties as the Moghuls of India and the Safavids of Persia or the sub-Saharan empires of Mali and Songhai. The diversification of Muslim leadership—in contrast to the Europeanization of Christian leadership—helped the cause of relative racial equality in Islamic culture.

Partly because of Islam's relatively nonracial nature, Islamic history has been free of systematic efforts to obliterate a people. Islam conquered by co-optation, intermarriage, and conversion rather than by genocide.

Incidents in Muslim history, it is true, have caused large-scale loss of life. During Turkey's attempt in 1915 to deport the entire Armenian population of about 1,750,000 to Syria and Palestine, hundred of thousands of people, perhaps up to a million, died of starvation or were murdered on the way. But—though this does not exonerate Turkey of its responsibility for the deaths—Armenians had provoked Turkey by organizing volunteer battalions to help Russia fight against it in World War I. Nor is the expulsion of a people from a territory, however disastrous its consequences, equivalent to the Nazi Holocaust, which systematically took the lives of six million Jews and members of other despised groups. Movement of people between India and Pakistan after partition in 1947 also resulted in thousands of deaths en route.

Saddam Hussein's use of poison gas against Kurdish villages in Iraq in 1988 is more clearly comparable to Nazi behavior. But Saddam's action was the use of an illegitimate weapon in a civil war rather than a planned program to destroy the Kurdish people; it was an evil incident rather than a program of genocide. Many people feel that President Harry S. Truman's dropping of atomic bombs on Hiroshima and Nagasaki was also an evil episode. There is a difference between massacre and genocide. Massacres have been perpetrated in almost every country on earth, but only a few cultures have been guilty of genocide.

Nor did Islam ever spawn an Inquisition in which the burning of heretics at the stake was sanctioned. Cultures that had condemned human beings to burn and celebrated as they died in the flames, even hundreds of years before, were more likely to tolerate the herding of a whole people of another faith into gas chambers. Islam has been a shield against such excesses of evil.

THE ORDER OF ISLAM

AGAINST WESTERN claims that Islamic a "fundamentalism" feeds terrorism, one powerful paradox of the twentieth century is often overlooked. While Islam may generate more political violence than Western culture, Western culture generates more street violence than Islam. Islam does indeed produce a dis-proportionate share of mujahideen, but Western culture produces a disproportionate share of muggers. The largest Muslim city in Africa is Cairo. The largest westernized city is Johannesburg. Cairo is much more populous than Johannesburg, but street violence is only a fraction of what it is in the South African city. Does Islam help pacify Cairo? I, along with many others, believe that it does. The high premium Islam places on *umma* (community) and *ijma* (consensus) has made for a Pax Islamica in day-to-day life.

In terms of quality of life, is the average citizen better off under the excesses of the Islamic state or the excesses of the liberal state, where political tension may be low but social violence has reached crisis proportions? Tehran, the capital of the Islamic Republic of Iran, is a city of some ten million. Families with small children picnic in public parks at 11 p.m. or midnight. Residents of the capital and other cities stroll late at night, seemingly unafraid of mugging, rape, or murder. This is a society that has known large-scale political violence in war and revolution, but one in which petty interpersonal violence is much rarer than in Washington or New York. Iranians are more subject to their government than Americans, but they are less at risk from the depredations of their fellow citizens. Nor is dictatorial government the explanation for the safe streets of Tehran—otherwise, Lagos would be as peaceful as the Iranian capital.

The Iranian solution is mainly in the moral sphere. As an approach to the problems of modernity, some Muslim societies are attempting a return to pre-modernism, to indigenous traditional disciplines and values. Aside from Iran, countries such as Sudan and Saudi Arabia have revived Islamic legal systems and other features of the Islamic way of life, aspects of which go back 14 centuries. Islamic movements in countries like Algeria, Egypt, and Afghanistan are also seeking revivalist goals. A similar sacred nostalgia is evident in other religions, such as the born-again Christian sects in the United States and Africa.

Of all the value systems in the world, Islam has been the most resistant to the leading destructive forces of the twentieth century—including AIDS. Lower levels of prostitution and of hard drug use in conservative Muslim cultures compared with other cultures have, so far, contributed to lower-than-average HIV infection rates.[5] If societies closer to the sharia are also more distant from the human immunodeficiency virus, should the rest of the world take a closer look?

One can escape modernity by striving to transcend it as well as by retreating from it into the past. Perhaps the Muslim world should explore this path, searching for postmodern solutions to its political tensions and economic woes, and pursuing the positive aspects of globalization without falling victim to the negative aspects of westernization.

THE DIALECTIC OF CULTURE

WESTERN LIBERAL democracy has enabled societies to enjoy openness, government accountability, popular participation, and high economic productivity, but Western pluralism has also been a breeding ground for racism, fascism, exploitation, and genocide. If history is to end in arrival at the ultimate political order, it will require more than the West's message on how to maximize the best in human nature. Humankind must also consult Islam about how to check the worst in human nature—from alcoholism to racism, materialism to Nazism, drug addiction to Marxism as the opiate of the intellectuals.

One must distinguish between democratic principles and humane principles. In some humane principles—including stabilizing the family, security from social violence, and the relatively nonracial nature of religious institutions—the Muslim world may be ahead of the West.

Turkey is a prime example of the dilemma of balancing humane principles with democratic principles. In times of peace, the Ottoman Empire was more humane in its treatment of religious minorities than the Turkish Republic after 1923 under the westernizing influence of Mustafa Kemal Atatürk. The Turkish Republic, on the other hand, gradually moved toward a policy of cultural assimilation. While the Ottoman Empire tolerated the Kurdish language, the Turkish Republic outlawed its use for a considerable period. When not at war, the empire was more humane than the Turkish Republic, but less democratic.

At bottom, democracy is a system for selecting one's rulers; humane governance is a system for treating citizens. Ottoman rule at its best was humane governance; the Turkish Republic at its best has been a quest for democratic values. In the final years of the twentieth century, Turkey may be engaged in reconciling the greater humaneness of the Ottoman Empire with the greater democracy of the Republic.

The current Islamic revival in the country may be the beginning of a fundamental review of the Kemalist revolution, which inaugurated Turkish secularism. In England since Henry VIII, a theocracy has been democratized. In Turkey, might a democracy be theocratized? Although the Turkish army is trying to stop it, electoral support for Islamic revivalism is growing in the country. There has been increased speculation that secularism may be pushed back, in spite of the resignation in June, under political pressure from the generals, of Prime Minister Necmettin Erbakan, the leader of the Islamist Welfare Party. Is Erbakan nevertheless destined to play in the Kemalist revolution the role that Mikhail Gorbachev or Boris Yeltsin played in the Leninist revolution? Or is Erbakan a forerunner of change? It is too early to be sure. The dialectic of history continues its conversation with the dialectic of culture within the wider rhythms of relativity in human experience.

NOTES

1. In citing the Rushdie case as evidence of Islamic society's repressive nature, Westerners point to the 1989 *fatwa*, or legal ruling, by the Ayatollah Khomeini of Iran indicting Rushdie for blasphemy and the capital crime of apostasy and sentencing him to death in absentia. Iran, however, was the only Muslim country to decree the death penalty for Rushdie. Bangladesh said that Rushdie's crime, if proved, was a capital offense, but that he would have to be tried in a Muslim country to ascertain his guilt. There is a broad consensus that the book is blasphemous (even the Vatican agrees that it is), but Iran stands alone with the *fatwa*.

2. *American writers such as Carl Bernstein, Howard Fast, Erica Jong, and Peter Maas have spoken of both overt and covert censorship; see Midge Decter, "The Rushdiad," Commentary, vol. 87, no. 6 (June 1989), pp. 20–21.*

3. See Leonard Binder, *Islamic Liberalism: A Critique of Development Ideologies*, Chicago: University of Chicago Press, 1988, especially Chapter 9, "Conclusion: The Prospects for Liberal Government in the Middle East," pp. 336–60.

4. Like most other religions and civilizations, Islam tolerated the ownership and trade of slaves for centuries. But slavery among Muslims was almost race-neutral. In contrast to the racially polarized transatlantic slave system— white masters, black slaves—slaves in the Islamic world could be white, black, brown, or other, and so could masters. Moreover, slavery among Muslims allowed for great upward social mobility. Both Muslim India and Muslim Egypt produced slave dynasties; the former slaves who became Mamluk rulers of Egypt dominated the country from 1250 to 1517.

5. Studies by researchers in Ivory Coast of Muslim countries in Africa have shown that approximately half as many Muslims as non-Muslims are likely to be infected with HIV. See Catherine Tastemain and Peter Coles, "Can a Culture Stop AIDS in its Tracks?" *New Scientist* (London), vol. 139, no. 1890 (September 11, 1993), p. 13.

Free Inquiry, Fall 1997

Islam's Shame

Lifting the veil of tears

Ibn Warraq

Islam is deeply anti-woman. Islam is the fundamental cause of the repression of Muslim women and remains the major obstacle to the evolution of their position.[1] Islam has always considered women as creatures inferior in every way: physically, intellectually, and morally. This negative vision is divinely sanctioned in the Koran, corroborated by the *hadiths,* and perpetuated by the commentaries of the theologians, the custodians of Muslim dogma and ignorance.

Far better for these intellectuals to abandon the religious argument, to reject these sacred texts, and have recourse to *reason* alone. They should turn instead to human rights. The Universal Declaration of Human Rights (adopted on December 10, 1948, by the General Assembly of the United Nations in Paris and ratified by most Muslim countries) at no point has recourse to a religious argument. These rights are based on natural rights, which any adult human being capable of choice has. They are rights that human beings have simply because they are human beings. Human reason or rationality is the ultimate arbiter of rights—human rights, the rights of women.

Unfortunately, in practice, in Muslim countries one cannot simply leave the theologians with their narrow, bigoted world view to themselves. One cannot ignore the *ulama,* those learned doctors of Muslim law who by their *fatwas* or decisions in questions touching private or public matters of importance regulate the life of the Muslim community. They still exercise considerable powers of approving or forbidding certain actions. Why the continuing influence of the *mullas*?

The Koran remains for all Muslims, not just "fundamentalists," the uncreated word of God Himself. It is valid for all times and places; its ideas are absolutely true and beyond all criticism. To question it is to question the very word of God, and hence blasphemous. A Muslim's duty is to believe it and obey its divine commands.

Ibn Warraq, who was raised as a Muslim, now devotes himself to the scholarly examination of the beliefs and practices of Islam. He is the author of Why I Am Not a Muslim *(Prometheus Books, 1995).*

> *Muslim thinkers continue to confine Muslim women to the house—to leave is against the will of God and the principles of Islam.*

Several other factors contribute to the continuing influence of the *ulama*. Any religion that requires total obedience without thought is not likely to produce people capable of *critical thought*, people capable of free and independent thought. Such a situation is favorable to the development of a powerful "clergy" and is clearly responsible for the intellectual, cultural, and economic stagnation of several centuries. Illiteracy remains high in Muslim countries. Historically, as there never was any separation of state and religion, any criticism of one was seen as a criticism of the other. Inevitably, when many Muslim countries won independence after the Second World War, Islam was unfortunately linked with nationalism, which meant that any criticism of Islam was seen as a betrayal of the newly independent country—an unpatriotic act, an encouragement to colonialism and imperialism. No Muslim country has developed a stable democracy; Muslims are being subjected to every kind of repression possible. Under these conditions healthy criticism of society is not possible, because critical thought and liberty go together.

The above factors explain why Islam in general and the position of women in particular are never criticized, discussed, or subjected to deep scientific or skeptical analysis. All innovations are discouraged in Islam—every problem is seen as a religious problem rather than a social or economic one.

PROFOUNDLY ANTI-WOMAN

Islam took the legend of Adam and Eve[2] from the Old Testament and adapted it in its own fashion. The creation of mankind from one person is mentioned in the following *suras:*

4.1. O Mankind! Be careful of your duty to your Lord who created you from a single soul and from it created its mate and from them twain hath spread abroad a multiple of men and women.

39.6. He created you from one being, then from that (being) He made its mate.

7.189. He it is who did create you from a single soul and therefrom did make his mate that he might take rest in her.

From these slender sources Muslim theologians have concluded that man was the original creation—womankind was created secondarily for the pleasure and repose of man. The legend was further developed to reinforce the supposed inferiority of women. Finally, the legend was given a sacred character so that to criticize it was to criticize the very words of God, which were immutable and absolute. Here is how Muhammad describes women in general: "Be friendly to women for womankind was created from a rib, but the bent part of the rib, high up, if you try to straighten it you will break it; if you do nothing, she will continue to be bent."

God punishes Adam and Eve for disobeying his orders. But there is nothing in the verses to show that it was Eve (as in the Old Testament) who led Adam astray. And yet Muslim exegetists and jurists have created the myth of Eve the temptress that has since become an integral part of Muslim tradition. Muhammad himself is reputed to have said: "If it had not been for Eve, no woman would have been unfaithful to her husband."

The Islamic tradition also attributes guile and deceit to women and draws its support from the Koran. Modern Muslim commentators interpret certain verses to show that guile, deceit, and treachery are intrinsic to a woman's nature. Not only is she unwilling to change, she is by nature incapable of changing—she has no choice.[3] In attacking the female deities of the polytheists, the Koran takes the opportunity to malign the female sex further.

4.1 17. They invoke in His stead only females; they pray to none else than Satan, a rebel.

53.21–22. Are yours the males and His the females That indeed were an unfair division!

53.27. Lo! it is those who disbelieve in the Hereafter who name the angels with the names of females.

Islamic Mutilation

According to the nineteenth century *Dictionary of Islam* and Richard Burton, female circumcision was widespread in Arabia, where "clitoris cutter" was a legitimate profession practiced by old women, and perhaps most other Islamic countries. According to the Minority Rights Group's Report "Female Genital Mutilation: Proposals for Change," published in 1992, the practice is still followed widely across Western, Saharan, and Eastern Africa, as well as in Yemen and Oman, by Muslims, Christians, Jews, and animists. "Tens of millions of girls are affected every year." Unlike the public nature of the boy's circumcision, female excision is practiced discreetly, and does not have the symbolic significance.

Female excision is not mentioned in the Koran and learned doctors of theology, when they deign to address the matter, spend very little time on it, simply recommending it as a pious act. What exactly does the operation involve? According to Burton, "in the babe [the clitoris] protrudes beyond the labiae and snipping off the head forms female circumcision." "Excision," continues Burton,

is universal amongst the negroids of the Upper Nile, the Somal and other adjacent tribes. The operator, an old woman, takes up the instrument, a knife or razor blade fixed into a wooden handle, and with three sweeps cuts off the labia and the head of the clitoris. The parts are then sewn up with a packneedle and a thread of sheepskin; and in Dar-For a tin tube is inserted for the passage of urine. Before marriage the bridegroom trains himself for a month on beef, honey and milk; and if he can open his bride with the natural weapon he is a sworder to whom no women in the tribe can deny herself. If he fails, he tries penetration with his fingers and by way of last resort whips out his whittle and cuts the parts open. The sufferings of the first few nights must be severe.

In modern times little seems to have changed; here is how the *Economist* describes the situation in 1992: "The procedure varies from mildly painful to gruesome, and can involve the removal of the clitoris and other organs with knives, broken glass, and razors—but rarely anesthetic. It can lead to severe problems with menstruation, intercourse and childbirth, psychological disturbances and even death."

Richard Burton, *The Book of a Thousand Nights and a Night* (London: N.D.) vol. 15.

—Ibn Warraq

Other verses from the Koran also seem of a misogynist tendency.

2.228. Women who are divorced shall wait, keeping themselves apart, three (monthly) courses. And it is not lawful for them that they should conceal that which Allah hath created in their wombs if they are believers in Allah and the Last Day. And their husbands would be better to take them back in that case if they desire a reconciliation. And they (women) have rights similar to those (of men) over them in kindness, and men are a degree above them. Allah is Mighty, Wise.

2.282. But if he who oweth the debt is of low understanding, or weak or unable himself to dictate, then let the guardian of his interests dictate in (terms of) equity. And call to witness, from among your men, two witnesses. And if two men be not (at hand) then a man and two women, of such as ye approve as witnesses, so that if the one erreth (through forgetfulness) the other will remember.

4.11. Allah chargeth you concerning (the provision for) your children: to the male the equivalent of the portion of two females.

4.34. Men are in charge of women, because Allah hath made the one of them to excel the other, and because they spend of their property (for the support of women). So good women are the obedient, guarding in secret that which Allah hath guarded. As for those from whom ye fear rebellion, admonish them and banish them to beds apart; and scourge (beat) them. Then if they obey you, seek not a way against them Lo! Allah is ever High Exalted, Great.

Equally, in numerous *hadiths* on which are based the Islamic laws, we learn of the woman's role—to stay at home, to be at the beck and call of man to obey him (which is a religious duty), and to assure man a tranquil existence. Here are some examples of these traditions:

• The woman who dies and with whom the husband is satisfied will go to paradise.

• A wife should never refuse herself to her husband even if it is on the saddle of a camel.

• Hellfire appeared to me in a dream and I noticed that it was above all peopled with women who had been ungrateful. "Was it toward God that they were ungrateful?" They had not shown any gratitude toward their husbands for all they had received from them. Even when all your life you have showered a woman with your largesse she will still find something petty to re-

proach you with one day, saying, "You have never done anything for me."

• If anything presages a bad omen it is: a house, a woman, a horse.

• Never will a people know success if they confide their affairs to a woman.

It will be appropriate to include two quotes from the famous and much revered philosopher al-Ghazali (1058–1111), whom Professor Montgomery Watt describes as the greatest Muslim after Muhammad. In his "The Revival Of The Religious Sciences," Ghazali defines the woman's role:[4]

She should stay at home and get on with her spinning, she should not go out often, she must not be well-informed, nor must she be communicative with her neighbours and only visit them when absolutely necessary; she should take care of her husband and respect him in his presence and his absence and seek to satisfy him in everything; she must not cheat on him nor extort money from him; she must not leave her house without his permission and if given his permission she must leave surreptitiously. She should put on old clothes and take deserted streets and alleys, avoid markets, and make sure that a stranger does not hear her voice or recognize her; she must not speak to a friend of her husband even in need. . . . Her sole worry should be her virtue, her home as well as her prayers and her fast. If a friend of her husband calls when the latter is absent she must not open the door nor reply to him in order to safeguard her and her husband's honour. She should accept what her husband gives her as sufficient sexual needs at any moment. . . . She should be clean and ready to satisfy her husband's sexual needs at any moment.

Such are some of the sayings from the putative golden age of Islamic feminism. It was claimed that it was the abandonment of the original teachings of Islam that had led to the present decadence and backwardness of Muslim societies. But there never was an Islamic utopia. To talk of a golden age is only to conform and perpetuate the influence of the clergy, the *mullas,* and their hateful creed that denies humanity to half the inhabitants of this globe, and further retards all serious attempts to liberate Muslim women.

WHAT RIGHTS?

The inequality between men and women[5] in matters of giving testimony or evidence or being a witness is enshrined in the Koran: *sura* 2.282 (quoted above).

How do Muslim apologists justify the above text? Muslim men and women writers point to the putative

Any religion that requires total obedience without thought is not likely to produce people capable of critical thought, people capable of free and independent thought.

psychological differences that exist between men and women. The Koran (and hence God) in its sublime wisdom knew that women are sensitive, emotional, sentimental, easily moved, and influenced by their biological rhythm, lacking judgment. But above all they have a shaky memory. In other words, women are psychologically inferior. Such are the dubious arguments used by Muslim intellectuals—male and, astonishingly enough, female intellectuals like Ahmad Jamal, Ms. Zahya Kaddoura, Ms. Ghada al-Kharsa, and Ms. Madiha Khamis. As Ghassan Ascha points out, the absurdity of their arguments are obvious.

By taking the testimony of two beings whose reasoning faculties are faulty we do not obtain the testimony of one complete person with a perfectly functioning rational faculty—such is Islamic arithmetic! By this logic, if the testimony of two women is worth that of one man, then the testimony of four women must be worth that of two men, in which case we can dispense with the testimony of the men. But no! In Islam the rule is not to accept the testimony of women alone in matters to which men theoretically have access. It is said that the Prophet did not accept the testimony of women in matters of marriage, divorce, and *hudud. Hudud* are the punishments set down by Muhammad in the Koran and the *hadith* for (1) adultery—stoning to death; (2) fornication—a hundred stripes; (3) false accusation of adultery against a married person—eighty stripes; (4) apostasy—death; (5) drinking wine—eighty stripes; (6) theft—the cutting off of the right hand; (7) simple robbery on the highway—the loss of hands and feet; robbery with murder—death, either by the sword or by crucifixion.

On adultery the Koran 24.4 says: "Those that defame honourable women and cannot produce four witnesses shall be given eighty lashes." Of course, Muslim jurists will only accept four male witnesses. These witnesses must declare that they have "seen the parties in the very act of carnal conjunction." Once an accusation of forni-

cation and adultery has been made, the accuser himself or herself risks punishment if he or she does not furnish the necessary legal proofs. Witnesses are in the same situation. If a man were to break into a woman's dormitory and rape half a dozen women, he would risk nothing since there would be no male witnesses. Indeed the victim of a rape would hesitate before going in front of the law, since she would risk being condemned herself and have little chance of obtaining justice. "If the woman's words were sufficient in such cases," explains Judge Zharoor ul Haq of Pakistan, "then no man would be safe." This iniquitous situation is truly revolting and yet for Muslim law it is a way of avoiding social scandal concerning the all-important sexual taboo. Women found guilty of fornication were literally immured, at first; as the Koran 4.15 says: "Shut them up within their houses till death release them, or God make some way for them." However this was later canceled and stoning substituted for adultery and one hundred lashes for fornication. When a man is to be stoned to death, he is taken to some barren place, where he is stoned first by the witnesses, then the judge, and then the public. When a woman is stoned, a hole to receive her is dug as deep as her waist—the Prophet himself seems to have ordered such procedure. It is lawful for a man to kill his wife and her lover if he catches them in the very act.

In the case where a man suspects his wife of adultery or denies the legitimacy of the offspring, his testimony is worth that of four men. *Sura* 24.6: "If a man accuses his wife but has no witnesses except himself, he shall swear four times by God that his charge is true, calling down upon himself the curse of God if he is lying. But if his wife swears four times by God that his charge is false and calls down His curse upon herself if it be true, she shall receive no punishment." Appearances to the contrary, this is not an example of Koranic justice or equality between the sexes. The woman indeed escapes being stoned to death but she remains rejected and loses her right to the dowry and her right to maintenance, *whatever the outcome of the trial.* A woman does not have

Islam is the fundamental cause of the repression of Muslim women and remains the major obstacle to the evolution of their position

the right to charge her husband in a similar manner. Finally, for a Muslim marriage to be valid there must be a multiplicity of witnesses. For Muslim jurists, two men form a multiplicity but not two or three or a thousand women.

In questions of heritage, the Koran tells us that male children should inherit twice the portion of female children:

> 4.11–12. A male shall inherit twice as much as a female. If there be more than two girls, they shall have two-thirds of the inheritance, but if there be one only, she shall inherit the half. Parents shall inherit a sixth each, if the deceased have a child; but if he leave no child and his parents be his heirs, his mother shall have a third. If he have brothers, his mother shall have a sixth after payment of any legacy he may have bequeathed or any debt he may have owed.

To justify this inequality, Muslim authors lean heavily In the fact that a woman receives a dowry and has the right to maintenance from her husband. It is also true that according to Muslim law the mother is not at all obliged to provide for her children, and if she does spend money on her children, it is, to quote Bousquet, "recoverable by her from her husband if he is returned to a better fortune as in the case of any other charitable person. Therefore there is no point in the husband and wife sharing in the taking charge of the household; this weighs upon the husband alone. There is no longer any financial interest between them."[6]

This latter point referred to by Bousquet simply emphasized the negative aspects of a Muslim marriage— that is to say, the total absence of any idea of "association" between "couples" as in Christianity. As to dowry, it is, of course, simply a reconfirmation of the man's claims over the woman in matters of sex and divorce. Furthermore, in reality the woman does not get to use the dowry for herself. The custom is either to use the dowry to furnish the house of the newly married couple or for the wife to offer it to her father. According to the Malekites, the woman can be obliged by law to use the dowry to furnish the house. Muslim law also gives the guardian the right to cancel a marriage—even that of a woman of legal age—if he thinks the dowry is not sufficient. Thus the dowry, instead of being a sign of her independence, turns out once more to be a symbol of her servitude.

The woman has the right to maintenance but this simply emphasizes her total dependence on her husband, with all its attendant sense of insecurity. According to Muslim jurists, the husband is not obliged under Islamic law to pay for her medical expenses in case of illness. Financial independence of the woman would of course

be the first step in the liberation of Muslim women and thus it is not surprising that it is seen as a threat to male dominance. Muslim women are now obliged to take equal responsibility for looking after their parents. Article 158 of Syrian law states "The child—male or female—having the necessary means is obliged to take responsibility for his or her poor parents." The birth of a girl is still seen as a catastrophe in Islamic societies. The system of inheritance just adds to her misery and her dependence on the man. If she is an only child she receives only half the legacy of her father; the other half goes to the male members of the father's family. If there are two or more daughters, they inherit two-thirds. This pushes fathers and mothers to prefer male children to female so that they can leave the entirety of their effects or possessions to their own descendants. "Yet when a new-born girl is announced to one of them his countenance darkens and he is filled with gloom" (*sura* 43.15). The situation is even worse when a woman loses her husband—she only receives a quarter of the legacy. If the deceased leaves more than one wife, all the wives are still obliged to share among themselves a quarter or one-eighth of the legacy.

Muslim jurists[7] are unanimous in their view that men are superior to women in virtue of their reasoning abilities, their knowledge, and their supervisory powers. And since it is the man who assumes financial responsibility for the family, it is argued, it is natural that he should have total power over the woman. These same jurists, of course, totally neglect changing social conditions where a woman may contribute her salary to the upkeep of her family—power over women remains a divine command and "natural" or "in the nature of things." Muslim thinkers continue to confine Muslim women to the house—to leave the house is against the will of God and against the principles of Islam. Confined to their houses, women are then reproached for not having any experience of the outside world!

According to theologians,[8] the husband has the right to administer corporal punishment to his wife if she

Muslim theologians have concluded that man was the original creation— womankind was created secondarily for the pleasure and repose of man.

1. Refuses to make herself beautiful for him;
2. Refuses to meet his sexual demands;
3. Leaves the house without permission or without any legitimate reason recognized by law; or
4. Neglects her religious duties.

A *hadith* attributes the following saying to the Prophet: "Hang up your whip where your wife can see it." There are a number of other *hadiths* that contradict this one. In those, Muhammad explicitly forbids men to beat their wives—in which case the Prophet himself is contradicting what the Koran, enshrining divine law, permits.

CASE HISTORIES: THE WOMEN OF PAKISTAN

In Pakistan in 1977, General Zia al-Haq took over in a military coup declaring that the process of Islamization was not going fast enough. The *mullas* had finally got someone who was prepared to listen to them.

Zia imposed martial law, total press censorship, and began creating a theocratic state, believing that Pakistan ought to have "the spirit of Islam." He banned women from athletic contests and even enforced the Muslim fast during the month of Ramadan at gunpoint. He openly admitted that there was a contradiction between Islam and democracy. Zia introduced Islamic laws that discriminated against women. The most notorious of these laws were the *Zina* and *Hudud* Ordinances that called for the Islamic punishments of the amputation of hands for stealing and stoning to death for married people found guilty of illicit sex. The term *zina* included adultery, fornication, and rape, and even prostitution. Fornication was punished with a maximum of a hundred lashes administered in public and ten years' imprisonment.

In practice, these laws protect rapists, for a woman who has been raped often finds herself charged with adultery or fornication. To prove *zina*, four Muslim adult males of good repute must be present to testify that sexual penetration has taken place. Furthermore, in keeping with good Islamic practice, these laws value the testimony of men over women. The combined effect of these laws is that it is impossible for a woman to bring a successful charge of rape against a man; instead, she herself, the victim, finds herself charged with illicit sexual intercourse, while the rapist goes free. If the rape results in a pregnancy, this is automatically taken as an admission that adultery or fornication has taken place with the woman's consent rather than that rape has occurred.

Here are some sample cases.[9]

In a town in the northern province of Punjab, a woman and her two daughters were stripped naked, beaten, and gang raped in public, but the police declined to pursue the case.

A thirteen-year-old girl was kidnapped and raped by a "family friend." When her father brought a case against the rapist, it was the girl who was put in prison and charged with *zina*, illegal sexual intercourse. The father managed to secure the child's release by bribing the police. The traumatized child was then severely beaten for disgracing the family honor.

A fifty-year-old widow, Ahmedi Begum,[10] decided to let some rooms in her house in the city of Lahore to two young veiled women. As she was about to show them the rooms, the police burst into the courtyard of the house and arrested the two girls and Ahmedi Begum's nephew, who had simply been standing there. Later that afternoon, Ahmedi Begum went to the police station with her son-in-law to inquire about her nephew and the two girls. The police told Ahmedi they were arresting her too. They confiscated her jewelry and pushed her into another room. While she was waiting, the police officers shoved the two girls, naked and bleeding, into the room and then proceeded to rape them again in front of the widow. When Ahmedi covered her eyes, the police forced her to watch by pulling her arms to her sides. After suffering various sexual humiliations, Ahmedi herself was stripped and raped by one officer after another. They dragged her outside where she was again beaten. One of the officers forced a policeman's truncheon, covered with chili paste, into her rectum, rupturing it. Ahmedi screamed in horrible agony and fainted, only to wake up in prison, charged with *zina.* Her case was taken up by a human rights lawyer. She was released on bail after three months in prison, but was not acquitted until three years later. In the meantime, her son-in-law divorced her daughter because of his shame.

Was this an isolated case? Unfortunately no. The Human Rights Commission of Pakistan said in its annual report that one woman is raped every three hours in Pakistan and one in two rape victims is a juvenile. According to Women's Action Forum, a woman's rights organization, 72% of all women in police custody in Pakistan are physically and sexually abused. Furthermore, 75% of all women in jail are there under charges of *zina*. Many of these women remain in jail awaiting trial for years.

In other words, the charge of *zina* is casually applied by any man who wants to get rid of his wife, who is immediately arrested, and kept waiting in prison, sometimes for years. Before the introduction of these laws the total number of women in prison was 70; the present number is more than 3,000. Most of these women have been charged under the *Zina* or *Hudud* Ordinances.[11]

The Western press naively believed that the election of Benazir Bhutto as Pakistan's prime minister in November 1988 would revolutionize women's role not just in Pakistan, but in the entire Islamic world. Under Islamic law of course, women cannot be head of an Islamic state, and Pakistan had become an Islamic republic under the

The United Nations on the Rights of Women

Article 1—Discrimination against women, denying or limiting as it does their equality of rights with men, is fundamentally unjust and constitutes an offence against human dignity.

Article 2—All appropriate measures shall be taken to abolish existing laws, customs, regulations and practices which are discriminatory against women, and to establish adequate legal protection for equal rights of men and women . . .

Article 3—All appropriate measures shall be taken to educate public opinion and to direct national aspirations towards the eradication of prejudice and the abolition of customary and all other practices which are based on the idea of the inferiority of women.

Article 4—All appropriate measures shall be taken to ensure to women on equal terms with men, without any discrimination:
(a) The right to vote in all elections and be eligible for election to all publicly elected bodies;
(b) The right to vote in all public referenda;
(c) The right to hold public office and to exercise all public functions. Such rights shall be guaranteed by legislation.

Article 5—Women shall have the same rights as men to acquire, change or retain their nationality. Marriage to an alien shall not automatically affect the nationality of the wife either by rendering her stateless or by forcing upon her the nationality of her husband.

Article 6—1. Without prejudice to the safeguarding of the unity and the harmony of the family, which remains the basic unit of any society, all appropriate measures, particularly legislative measures, shall be taken to ensure to women, married or unmarried, equal rights with men in the field of civil law. . . .

2. All appropriate measures shall be taken to ensure the principle of equality of status of the husband and wife, and in particular:
(a) Women shall have the same right as men as to free choice of a spouse and to enter into marriage rights with men during marriage and at its dissolution. In all cases the interest of the children shall be paramount. . . .
(c) Parents shall have equal rights and duties in matters relating to their children. In all cases the interest of the children shall be paramount.

3. Child marriage and the betrothal of young girls before puberty shall be prohibited, and effective action, including legislation, shall be taken to specify a minimum age for marriage and to make the registration of marriages in an official registry compulsory.

Article 7—All provisions of penal codes which constitute discrimination against women shall be repealed.

Article 8—All appropriate measures, including legislation, shall be taken to combat all forms of traffic in women and exploitation of prostitution of women.

Article 9—All appropriate measures shall be taken to ensure to girls and women, married or unmarried, equal rights with men in education at all levels. . . .

Article 10—1. All appropriate measures shall be taken to ensure to women, married or unmarried, equal rights with men in the field of economic and social life. . . .

2. In order to prevent discrimination against women on account of marriage or maternity and to ensure their effective right to work, measures shall be taken to prevent their dismissal in the event of marriage or maternity and to provide paid maternity leave, with the guarantee of returning to former employment, and to provide the necessary social services, including child-care facilities.

3. Measures taken to protect women in certain types of work, for reasons inherent in their physical nature, shall not be regarded as discriminatory.

Article 11—1. The principle of equality of rights of men and women demands implementation in all States in accordance with the principles of the Charter of the United Nations and of the Universal Declaration of Human Rights.

2. Governments, non-governmental organizations and individuals are urged, therefore, to do all in their power to promote the implementation of the principles contained in this Declaration. **FI**

Excerpted from the United Nations Declaration on the Rights of Women, adopted November 7, 1967.

The birth of a girl is still seen as a catastrophe in Islamic societies.

new constitution of 1956. Thus, Benazir Bhutto had defied the *mullas* and won. But her government lasted a bare 20 months, during which period Nawaz Sharif, who was the prime minister briefly in the early 1990s, is said to have encouraged the *mullas* in their opposition to having a woman as the head of an Islamic state. Benazir Bhutto's government was dismissed on charges of corruption, and her husband imprisoned in 1990.

The lot of the Muslim woman was harsh before Benazir's election, and nothing has changed. She has pandered to the religious lobby, the *mullas,* the very people who insist that a woman cannot hold power in an Islamic state, and has repeatedly postponed any positive action on the position of women.

Pakistan shows the same grim picture. Pakistan is one of only four countries in the world where female life expectancy (51 years) is lower than the male (52 years); the average female life expectancy for all poor countries is 61 years. A large number of Pakistani women die in pregnancy or childbirth, six for every 1,000 live births. Despite the fact that contraception has never been banned by orthodox Islam, under Zia the Islamic Idealogy Council of Pakistan declared family planning to be un-Islamic. Various *mullas* condemned family planning as a Western conspiracy to emasculate Islam. As a result, the average fertility rate per woman in Pakistan is 6.9. Pakistan is also among the world's bottom ten countries for female attendance in primary schools. Some people put female literacy in the rural areas as low as 2% (*Economist*, March 5, 1994). As the *Economist* put it, "Some of the blame for all this lies with the attempt of the late President Zia ul Haq to create an Islamic republic. . . . Zia turned the clock back. A 1984 law of his, for instance, gives a woman's legal evidence half the weight of a man's" (*Economist*, January 13, 1990).

Indeed a large part of the blame lies with the attitudes inculcated by Islam, which has always seen woman as inferior to man. The birth of a baby girl is the occasion for mourning. Hundreds of baby girls are abandoned every year in the gutters and dust bins and on the pavements. An organization working in Karachi to save these children has calculated that more than five hundred children are abandoned a year in Karachi alone, and that 99% of them are girls.[12]

Little did Jinnah, the founder of Pakistan, realize how literally true his words were when he said in a 1944 speech:[13] "No nation can rise to the height of glory unless your women are side by side with you. We are victims of evil customs. It is a crime against humanity that our women are shut up within the four walls of the houses as prisoners."

But we do not need to leave with a completely pessimistic picture. Pakistani women have shown themselves to be very courageous, and more and more are fighting for their rights with the help of equally brave organizations such as Women's Action Forum (WAF) and War Against Rape. WAF was formed in 1981 as women came onto the streets to protest against the *Hudud* Ordinances, and to demonstrate their solidarity with a couple who had recently been sentenced to death by stoning for fornication. In 1983, women organized the first demonstrations against martial law.

NOTES

1. Ghassan Ascha, *Du Statut Inferieur de la Femme en Islam* (Paris: 1989) p. 11.
2. Ibid., pp. 23f.
3. Ibid., pp. 29f.
4. Ibid., p. 41.
5. Ascha, op. cit., pp. 63f.
6. G. H. Bousquet, *L'Ethique sexuelle de L'Islam* (Paris: 1966) vol. 1, p. 120.
7. Ascha, op. cit. p. 89.
8. Ibid., pp. 108.
9. Kurt Schork, "Pakistan's Women in Despair," *Guardian Weekly,* September 23, 1990.
10. Jan Goodwin, *Price of Honor* (Boston: 1994) p. 49–50.
11. Schork, op. cit.
12. Goodwin, op. cit., p. 64.
13. R. Ahmed, ed., *Sayings of Quaid-i-Azam (Jinnah)* (Karachi: 1986) p. 98.

Article 6   The Christian Science Monitor, Wednesday, April 23, 1997

Dubai Puts Politics Aside, Aims To Be a Mideast 'Hong Kong'

By Scott Peterson

Staff writer of The Christian Science Monitor

DUBAI, UNITED ARAB EMIRATES

ONE look at a map explains why tiny Dubai is looking 20 years into the future and preparing for booming business as *the* hub of the Gulf.

This already thriving trade center, one of seven states that make up the United Arab Emirates, is close to the mouth of the Persian Gulf and links big markets and oil producers like Iran, Iraq, and Saudi Arabia to the rest of the world.

Dubai Arabs have been traders for centuries, remaining so despite the oil wealth that now dominates the regional economy.

Now Dubai's rulers and economists are looking to carry that history forward and turn Dubai into an indispensable hub of Middle East business. New infrastructure is being built, and trading and banking rules loosened. A campaign stretching across a quarter of the globe is under way.

Merchants do much of their import-export work with Iran and Saudi Arabia. But when international sanctions on Iraq are lifted, they expect a windfall.

Even with the sanctions—which were imposed when Iraq invaded Kuwait in 1990—Dubai merchants have been involved in smuggling everything from tires and car parts to computers.

Iraqi traders have been lining up to cash in on the oil-for-food deal approved for Iraq by the United Nations in December. Iraq would be able to sell $2 billion worth of oil for food and medicine. So far, 300,000 tons of wheat and rice have reached Iraq.

The number of Iraqi investors now in Dubai is 40 percent greater than last year, according to government statistics.

But Dubai is also casting its net much farther, often leaving politics aside in pursuit of business. A recently completed Dubai Strategic Development Plan—the first in Dubai's history—sets down a blueprint for coming decades and declares that Dubai is on the "threshold of a new era."

Among the most ambitious goals is a per capita, non-oil income of almost $20,000 by 2010. Since most [of] the UAE's oil is found in the capital state of Abu Dhabi to the south, Dubai aims for its non-oil GDP to reach nearly 90 percent of the total.

"Everyone says that we will be like Hong Kong," said Ali Ibrahim, the director of economic planning for Dubai. "We are aiming to be the regional economic center. Already we're a trade hub, but we are looking to be a financial center."

The strategic plan calls for heavy domestic investment and less reliance on foreign workers. But to be successful, it will also have to continue working without political constraints that often limit growth elsewhere. Iran, for example, barely figures as a trading partner for most Gulf states, who fear its dominance. (Iran is again flaunting its might this week, having begun military exercises April 22 code-named "Road to Jerusalem"—and which involve 200,000 troops.) But even though it is locked in a war of words with Abu Dhabi, the UAE capital, over Iran's occupation of three offshore islands, Iran accounts for 20 percent to 30 percent of Dubai's business. Everything from cosmetics to electronic goods crisscross the Persian Gulf.

"Iran is a big neighbor, a big market, and the UAE is trying not to mix the issues of economics and politics," says Abdallah Mograby, the head of economics for The Emirates Center for Strategic Studies and Research.

"The UAE will presumably provide a bridge for Iraq [as] it does for Iran."

A push for Dubai came during the Gulf War, when businesses that had been in Kuwait fled to Bahrain and Dubai. Iraq's increased interest in doing its business here is also due to a souring with its traditional trading partner, Jordan, since late 1995.

The UAE has taken advantage of this change of heart in Baghdad, spearheading a high-profile effort to ease the suffering of Iraqis by lifting sanctions. The root of the policy is economic and infu-

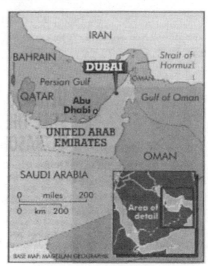

(JEWEL BECKER SIMMONS—STAFF)

riates Iraq's vulnerable neighbor, Kuwait.

"In the end, this is business," says Mr. Ibrahim of Dubai's openness to Iran and Iraq. "We are small and must look around, toward India and Pakistan and Southeast Asia. We form a natural triangle that way."

Dubai is looking for ways to make manufacture cheaper for companies in Dubai, he says, and is upgrading its communications networks with fiber-optic cable.

Speaking at a recent conference on the Emirates in Dubai, Jeffrey Sachs, the director of the Institute for International Development at Harvard University in Cambridge, Mass., said that Dubai needed a more sophisticated financial sector and a "detailed fiscal strategy" to reach its aims.

Dubai's popularity is already expanding. Russians spend more than $900 each day when they come, according to one report. Signs in Dubai markets now appear in Russian. More than 1 million people came to a shopping festival a year ago.

"This is a vision," says Ibrahim about Dubai's strategy. "Maybe we will run out of oil in 20 years, so then what will we do? We have to be ready for that day."

Article 7

Middle East Report, Winter 1997

Cairo's Poor: Dilemmas of Survival and Solidarity

The dearth of cooperative and contentious collective action on the part of the Egyptian urban poor by no means implies a lack of grassroots activism. Conditioned by political and cultural constraints, the poor instead resort to an alternative strategy—that of quiet encroachment. Qualitatively different from defensive measures or coping mechanisms, this strategy represents a silent, protracted, pervasive advancement of ordinary people—through open-ended and fleeting struggles without clear leadership, ideology or structured organization—on the propertied and powerful in order to survive.

Asef Bayat

Asef Bayat, *a guest editor of this issue, teaches sociology at the American University in Cairo. His latest book,* Street Politics: Poor People's Movements in Iran, 1977–1990, *is published in the United States by Columbia University Press (1997).*

The proliferation of more than 100 squatter communities with some six million inhabitants signifies only one, but perhaps the starkest, component of the growing socioeconomic disparity[1] in Cairo since Sadat's *infitah* ("opening up" or economic liberalization) in 1974 and the more recent implementation of the IMF's structural adjustment program. Between 1981 and 1991, rural poverty doubled and urban poverty increased more than 1.5 times.[2] By the early 1990s, more than half of Cairo and adjacent Giza were classified either as "poor" or "ultra-poor."[3] Millions of Cairenes are consumed by their constant search for adequate food, shelter, jobs and the maintenance of individual and familial dignity; most are involved in the informal economy and live in informal communities.[4]

For some time, state safety nets, in particular populist measures of protection, served to sustain low-income groups. With the dawn of neo-liberalism in Egypt in the 1980s, as in many other countries, the populist state has gradually withdrawn its protection from the popular sectors—peasants, workers and the urban poor. Although it is acknowledged that the poor will suffer in the short-term, the trickle-down of national economic growth is expected in the long run to benefit the poor as well. Thus far, however, there is no evidence to suggest that this is actually the case. If anything, every sign indicates increasing social inequality and impoverishment.

The Social Fund for Development (SFD)—a "safety net" program capitalized by the World Bank and other bilateral and multilateral donors at over $1 billion dollars and designed to offset the negative impact of structural adjustment programs on the "losers" in the Egyptian economy—has encountered innumerable problems in addressing its mandate of reaching the poor through nongovernmental organizations (NGOs).[5] The SFD and its backers nonetheless remain optimistic about the ability of NGOs to enhance structural adjustment without exacerbating poverty. Many Egyptian NGOs—spread throughout many of Cairo's poorer neighborhoods—specialize in relief work or in community development activities, including poverty alleviation, income generation and child protection. More than 100 NGOs are active in the Sayyida Zeinab neighborhood in Cairo alone. The extent of their effectiveness, however, remains unclear due largely to the fact that an in-depth and comprehensive evaluation of the NGOs' impact in Egypt has yet to be done. The few available studies do not offer a bright picture.[6] Although these NGOs provide some services, credit and financial assistance to the needy, their ability to sustain and empower the lower class remains limited. Even the more efficient Christian and Islamic NGOs limit themselves largely to the ad hoc provision of emergency services. While the activities of NGOs in Egyptian society are surely a welcome development, one should acknowledge that their meager resources cannot match the magnitude of the needs of the urban poor in Cairo.

Poor Cairenes cope with these economic realities either by stretching their resources to meet their needs or by cutting down on their consumption. Thus, breadwinners are forced to work longer hours, while other family members—primarily women and children—must also work. Some resort to selling their personal belongings for cash, begging and even prostitution. They further decrease their expenditures by sharing living spaces with relatives, purchasing low-quality food and secondhand clothes which they may share with others within the household, limiting health and education expenses, and reducing daily meals to two or one.[7] These practices are as common now in Cairo as in New Delhi, Manila or Rio de Janeiro.

Community Activism

Beneath these coping mechanisms, there is also a strong, if quiet, tide of resentment, resistance and reclamation. When opportunities arise, the poor do get involved in visible collective struggle.

Facts and Figures on Cairo

Despite the attention focused on the problems of cities around the world—most recently at the Habitat II Conference in Istanbul—surprisingly little comparable data on urban centers are available, as was found by the World Resources Institute on preparing their 1996— World Resources report. Population figures, for example, often vary depending on the definition of the urban center concerned. In the case of Cairo, estimates of its population range from a low of 9.7 million to a high of 12 million. This variation is due, in part, to the fact that Cairo can be defined at least three ways: Cairo City, metropolitan Cairo, and the Greater Cairo Region; Greater Cairo falls under at least three separate jurisdictions—Cairo, Giza, and Qalyubia—which further complicates the collection of data.

Population Density   Greater Cairo: 40,000 persons per square kilometer; up to 100,000/km^2 in older districts.

Rate of Growth   While Cairo City is now growing at a rate of less than two percent per year, other parts of Greater Cairo are growing at a rate of more than three percent. If growth were to continue at just the two percent rate, however, Cairo's population would double in 35 years.

Life Expectancy   65 years

Infant Mortality   35.1 per 1,000 live births (1991), Cairo City only. As in many developing countries, infant mortality rates are lower in urban than in rural areas. A comparison of data from the mid-1980s with that of other major cities placed Cairo on a par with Bombay and Istanbul.

Maternal Mortality   200 women die for every 100,000 live births (1992), Cairo City only. Egypt's overall maternal mortality rate of about 250 per 100,000 live births is in the range of such countries as Guatemala and Mexico, but roughly twice as high as the rate in such ME/NA countries as Tunisia, Iran and Syria.

Adult Literacy   69.3 percent total; 59.2 percent female (1992) Cairo City only.

Unemployment Rate   10 percent (1993), Cairo City only. Unemployment among women is estimated at 20.7 percent. Beyond the official unemployment rate, however, disguised unemployment or underemployment, is a severe problem in both the central and local government bureaucracy where the create of disguised unemployment may exceed 30 percent.

Income   LE 2782 per capita (1992), Cairo City only. Real GDP per capita, which is based upon purchasing power, was estimated at $2,570 for 1992/93 or about half of what the UNDP considers sufficient.

Water   About 20 percent of Cairo's population, mostly in Giza and other peripheral areas, have no access to piped water and use canals, wells and public water fountains. As much as half the water available is lost due to leaks and breaks in water pipes.

Electricity   More than 95 percent of households throughout Greater Cairo have electricity.

Sewerage   Some three million people lack adequate sewerage. In the 1970s, prior to an internationally financed upgrading of some of the sewerage system, over 100 incidents of sewerage flooding occurred daily.

Telephones   510 per 1000 households (Cairo City only, 1992).

Public Safety   In a 1990 study, the murder rate in Cairo was cited as less than five per 100,000 population per year. This was on a par with most Asian cities and similar to murder rates in cities in Britain/the United Kingdom. Murder rates in such US cities as New York; Washington, DC; and Miami were between 10 and 20 per 100,000.

—Compiled by Sally Ethelston

Sources *Egypt Human Development Report 1995,* (Cairo, Egypt: Institute of National Planning, 1995); *Cities: Life in the World's 100 Largest Metropolitan Areas,* (Washington, DC: Population Action International, 1990); United Nations Population Division, *Population growth and Policies in Mega-Cities: Cairo,* (New York: United Nations, 1990); World Resources Institute, et al., *World Resources 1996—97,* (New York: Oxford University Press, 1997).

When opportunities to engage in suitable types of social activism are unavailable, they may create them. Inaz Tewfiq's account* of the prolonged struggles of the residents of Ezbat Mekawy is one example. In this low-income neighborhood in Cairo, residents managed, through several years of collective campaigning, to close down local smelter plants which had caused major

*See "Community Participation and Environmental Change," *Middle East Report,* Winter 1997, pp. 27–28.

health and environmental problems. They used traditional strategies of communication within the community, as well as modern tactics, such as engaging the media, lobbying politicians and accessing the court system as a means of registering opposition.

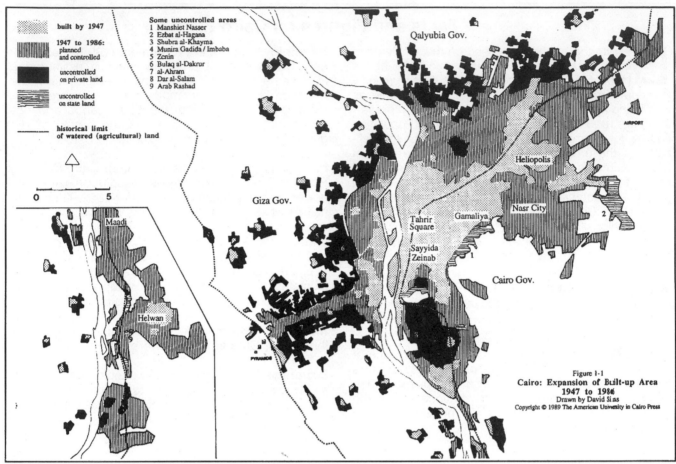

built by 1947

1947 to 1986:
planned
and controlled

uncontrolled
on private land

uncontrolled
on state land

historical limit
of watered (agricultural) land

Some uncontrolled areas
1 Manshiet Nasser
2 Ezbat al-Hagana
3 Shubra al-Khayma
4 Munira Gadida / Imbaba
5 Zenin
6 Bulaq al-Dakrur
7 al-Ahram
8 Dar al-Salam
9 Arab Rashad

Qalyubia Gov.

AIRPORT

Heliopolis

Giza Gov.

Nasr City

Tahrir
Square

Gamaliya

Sayyida
Zeinab

Cairo Gov.

Maadi

Helwan

PYRAMIDS

0   5

Figure 1-1
**Cairo: Expansion of Built-up Area
1947 to 1986**
Drawn by David Sims
Copyright © 1989 The American University in Cairo Press

Cairo.

David Sims, *A Place to Live*/The American University in Cairo Press

Compared to the poor in Latin American and South Asian cities, however, such overt and organized social activism is quite rare among Cairo's poor.[8] While the lower classes in Cairo are aware of environmental problems, they do little to address them through collective action, either through cooperative communal engagement to upgrade the community itself, or through contentious protest actions. Social networks, which extend beyond kinship and ethnicity, remain overwhelmingly casual, unstructured and nonpolitical. (The *gamaiyyat*, the informal credit system, is perhaps the most important form of neighborhood networking in Cairo.) The weakness of civic or non-kinship cooperation at the community level only reinforces traditional hierarchical, paternalistic relations with people depending more on local elders and problem solvers than on broad-based social activism.

Why are the poor of Cairo not as mobilized as their counterparts, for example, in Mexico City or Tehran? In Monterey, Mexico, shantytown dwellers were able to stop a freight train full of corn as families rushed out "to fill pots and sacks full of grain."[9] In Iran, the protests of the urban poor in the early 1990s,[10] notably the three-day riots in the neighborhood of Islamshahr in Tehran, constituted one of the most significant internal political challenges to the Islamic Republic."[11]

One major reason for the lack of mass protest in Cairo is the absence of structures that permit collective action in Egypt. Sadat's "Emergency Law" restricts contentious collective activities. Likewise, the present electoral structure in Egypt is not as conducive to group mobilization as it is, for example, in India or Turkey. In a truly competitive political system, political forces are compelled to bargain with, and thus mobilize, the poor to win their electoral support. In Egypt, this happens only in rare cases where opposition parties are involved in local disputes.[12] Although many Islamic associations are indeed involved in welfare activities, they rarely result in social mobilization and group activity. The impetus behind such institutions as Islamic clinics or associations ("social Islam"), like their Christian counterparts, is largely a combination of religious/moral, social and economic concerns. Few expound an explicit political agenda with the aim of collective mobilization.[13]

Political patronage in other impoverished countries sometimes leads inadvertently to social and political mobilization when patrons bargain with their poor clients in their pursuit of political power. The mobilization of street vendors in Mexico City is partially the result of this type of political patronage.[14] In Cairo, however, patronage appears to work more through individual channels, which rarely leads to the organization of group activities.

Today, the legacy of Nasserite populism continues to influence the political behavior of ordinary people. Nasserism established a social contract between the popular classes and the state, whereby the state agreed to provide the basic necessities in exchange for popular support, social peace and, consequently, demobilization. This was an agreement between the state and a shapeless mass, an aggregate of individuals and corporate institutions, in which the idea of a plural, independent and critical collectivity was seriously undermined. While the social contract is waning and market forces are escalating unheeded, many Egyptians still look to the government as the main source of protection as well as misfortune.

The legacy of this social contact has also contributed to the tendency of many ordinary urban Egyptians to seek individualistic solutions to their problems. At the same time, the lack of solidarity among the different strata of the poor undermines broad scale social or political mobilization. More often than not, families of different social strata tend to compete when resources are scarce. In Cairo, this is more so in the new and heterogenous communities (such as Dar al-Salam or Kafr Seif) than in the Old City neighborhoods where the relative homogeneity of inhabitants and the longevity of residence have produced a spatial identity. The coexistence of identifiable strata in a community (such as Kafr Seif where "villagers," "newcomers," "shanty-dwellers" and "tent-dwellers" live side by side) sharpens the existing competition and leads to conflicts. In Kafr Seif, "villagers" feared that "shanty-dwellers" and "tent-dwellers" would jeopardize their own insecure position; the latter groups remained silent so as to not be noticed by the municipality. Consequently, with solidarity being intangible among the many poor Cairenes, recourse to the state—the provider and the punisher—becomes an alternative way to achieve their goals. Many of them know, however, that the bureaucracy is unable or unwilling to respond formally to the growing demands of the urban poor. Thus, they tend to seek informal, individualistic and opportunistic ways of cultivating officials.

Quiet Encroachment

The dearth of cooperative and contentious collective action on the part of the Egyptian urban poor by no means implies a lack of grassroots activism. Conditioned by political and cultural constraints, the poor instead resort to an alternative strategy—that of quiet encroachment. Qualitatively different from defensive measures or coping mechanisms, this strategy represents a silent, protracted, pervasive advancement of ordinary people—through open-ended and fleeting struggles without clear leadership, ideology or structured organization—on the propertied and powerful in order to survive. While these types of grassroots activities are not social movements, they are also distinct from survival strategies or "everyday resistance" in that the struggles and gains of the agents are not at the cost of their fellow poor or themselves, but of the state, the rich and the powerful. In this type of struggle, the poor, to provide light for their shelter, tap electricity not from their neighbors, but from the municipality; or instead of putting their children to work to raise their living standard they demand higher pay from their employers. These struggles are not necessarily defensive, but cumulatively encroaching—the actors tend to expand their space by winning new positions from which to move. In this sense, they do not constitute "accommodating protest"[15] since, first, they are not conscious acts of protest, but rather represent the way people live their lives. This quiet encroachment challenges many fundamental aspects of the state's prerogatives—including the meaning of order, control of public space, the importance of modernity, and finally the state's encroachment on private property.[16]

Thus, to escape from high rents, millions of rural migrants and the urban poor in Cairo have quietly claimed state/public lands and cemeteries on the outskirts of the city, creating largely autonomous communities. Greater Cairo contains more than 111 *ashwa'iyyat* (spontaneous communities) that house over six million people who have put up their shelters unlawfully. Cairo is also characterized by another form of encroachment—the informal addition of rooms, balconies and extra space in and on buildings. Those who formally have been given housing in public projects built by the state, illegally redesign and rearrange their space to suit their needs by erecting partitions, and by adding and inventing new space. (See Farha Ghannam ["Relocation and the Use of Urban Space," *Middle East Report,* Winter 1997] in this issue.) Often whole communities emerge as a result of intense struggles and negotiations between the poor and others in their daily lives. (See Petra Kuppinger, "Giza Spaces," *MER,* Winter 1997].)

Once settled, slum dwellers try to force state authorities to extend water and electricity to their neighborhoods by tapping into them illegally.[17] A cursory look at Cairo communities such as Dar al-Salam, Ezbat Sadat, Ezbat Khairullah, Ezbat Nasr and Basaatin provides evidence of this widespread phenomenon. In late April 1996, the municipality reported that it had cut off 800 illegal electricity lines in Cairo's Dar al-Salam and Basaatin communities in one raid alone.[18]

In the domain of employment, street subsistence workers have quietly taken over public thoroughfares to conduct their business in the vast parallel economy. Well over 200,000 street vendors have occupied the streets in Cairo's main commercial centers, encroaching on favorable business opportunities created by local shopkeepers. Many streets around major shopping areas in the neighborhoods of Muski, al-Husayn, Embaba, Sayyida Zeinab, Boulaq and Abul-Alaa have been transformed into street bazaars, through some of which vehicles can no longer venture. Informality means that not only are the agents generally free from the costs of formality (taxes, regulation and so forth), they can also benefit from the piracy of import commodities and, like many others, theft of intellectual property. With six dollars of capital, a vendor can make up to 55 dollars a month.[19]

The polarization of wealth also creates opportunities for the poor. The explosion of car ownership, for instance, has meant that middle class as well as wealthy people now depend daily on the poor to park and protect their cars in the street. Thousands of Cairo's poor subsist on tips from parking cars in the streets, which they control and organize in such a way as to create maximum parking space. Many streets have thus turned into virtual parking lots controlled by working gangs with elaborate internal organization.

Quiet encroachment does not mean an absence of local networks, organizations or oppositional collective action. Indeed, networks are established, not only as a mechanism to ensure survival and encroachment, but also as a means to safeguard gains already won. Thus, without support from and cooperation among kin members who tend to reside in the same vicinity or work in similar occupations, the consolidation of the gains of the poor would be extremely difficult. For the popular classes of Cairo, kinship is the most significant source of solidarity.[20] Family connections help poor households circumvent the legal/bureaucratic constraints to securing shelter, obtaining jobs and extending governmental subsidies.

While structured neighborhood meetings are rare, widespread, albeit casual, networks ensure the flow of information among community members. Although people rarely elect their local leaders, nevertheless, charismatic leaders do emerge out of seemingly inactive communities. Similarly, in the domain of work, although the spread of street vending takes place on a largely individual basis, security is ensured by spatial networks embodied in "market sheikhs." These informal leaders, selected by their seniority, experience and skill, mediate between the vendors and the government/public. Their strategy of quiet diplomacy among the "informal market sheikhs" is probably more effective than the formal approaches of the official vendors' union.[21]

Traditional practices, solidarities and leaders thus have taken the place of and perform some of the functions of more structured neighborhood organizations found in other societies. But quiet encroachment as a type of grassroots activism has both its costs as well as its advantages. It represents a sustained, albeit silent, encroachment, that is largely unlawful and runs the constant risk of suppression. As fluid and unstructured forms of activism, these largely atomistic strategies have the advantages of flexibility and versatility; but they fall short of developing legal, technical and organizational support needed to advance the search for social justice on the broader, national level.

Endnotes

1 According to Egyptian economist Karima Korayem, the richest of urban households (the top 10 percent) which controlled about 26 percent of disposable income in 1981 had, by 1991, increased their share to 32.6 percent. See Karima Korayem, "Structural Adjustment. Stabilization Policies, and the Poor in Egypt," in Cairo Papers in Social Science 184 Winter 1995/6, table 4, p. 26.

2 *Ibid.*, p.2.

3 These data are estimated for the urban areas of the governorates of Cairo and Giza; see *ibid.*, p. 19, table 2. In this study, the expenditure poverty line for the average urban households (of 4.6 members) was considered to be LE 3347.4 annual income, and the average

rural household (with 5.2 members) was LE 3334.2. As for the urban "ultra-poor" (with 4.6 household members), the figure was LE 1933.8 and for rural areas (with 5.2 members) LE 2186.1; *ibid.*, p. 10.

4 This notion of urban poor draws on Peter Worsley's definition in his *The Three Worlds*, (London: Weidenfeld and Nicolson, 1984).

5 For analysis of the Social Fund see Korayem, *ibid.*, p. 50.

6 See, for instance, *Grassroots Participation in Egypt*, (Cairo: Ibn Khaldoun Center, 1995), sponsored by the Cairo office of UNICEF; see also Maha Mahfouz, "Community Development in Egypt," unpublished MA thesis, The American University in Cairo, 1992.

7 A compilation of these methods is available in Alyaa Shoukry, *Poverty and Adaption Mechanism: A Sociological Approach on Research in Egypt during the 1980s*, (Cairo: UNICEF, 1993).

8 See the research of [Nicholas] Hopkins and [Sohair] Mehanna in ["Pollution, Popular Perceptions and Grassroots Environmental Activism," *Middle East Report* (Winter 1997), pp. 21–25.

9 See Anthony DePalma, "Income Gap in Mexico Grows, and So Do Protests," *New York Times*, July 20, 1996, p. 3. According to the same article citing United Nations and the World Bank reports, "the richest 10 percent of Mexicans earn 41 percent of the country's income, while the bottom half of the population earns only 16 percent of all national income."

10 In 1991, the top 20 percent of the population earned about 50 percent of the country's income, while the bottom 40 percent earned only 13.4 percent; see Ali Akbar Karbasian, "The Process of Income Distribution in Iran," in *Iran-e Farda* 17, Ordiehesht 1374/1995, p. 44 (in Farsi).

11 For an analysis of these events see Asef Bayat, "Squatters and the State: Back Street Politics in the Islamic Republic," *Middle East Report* 191 (November–December, 1994), pp. 10–14.

12 For instance, when in 1960, the Cairo Governorate began to evict the settlers of today's Manshiet Nasser from

their earlier squatter community (Ezbat al-Safis, close to the Gamaliya neighborhood) deputies of the National Assembly from the district represented not the community but the government, negotiating with the local informal community leaders. See Belgin Tekce, Linda Oldham and Frederic Shorter, *A Place to Live: Families and Child Care in a Cairo Neighborhood*, (Cairo: The American University in Cairo Press, 1994), pp. 23–25.

13 For evidence of this see Amani Qandil and Sarah Ben Nafisah, *Al-Gamiyyat Al-Ahli Fi Al-Misr*, (Cairo: Al-Ahram Strategic Studies, 1995). See also Denis Sullivan, *Private Voluntary Organizations in Egypt: Islamic Developments, Private Initiative and State Control*, (Florida: University Press of Florida, 1994), pp. 64–84.

14 See John Cross, *Informal Politics: Street Vendors and the State in Mexico City*, (Palo Alto: Stanford University Press, forthcoming).

15 Arlene Macleod, *Accommodating Protest: Working Women, the New Veiling, and Change in Cairo*, (New York, Columbia University Press, 1991).

16 For a theoretical elaboration of "quiet encroachment," see Asef Bayat, "The Quiet Encroachment of the Ordinary: The Politics of the 'Informal People,'" *Third World Quarterly* 18/1, March 1997. For a more comprehensive discussion with reference to the experience of Iran see Asef Bayat, *Street Politics: Poor People's Movements in Iran, 1977–1990*, (New York: Columbia University Press, 1997, forthcoming).

17 For an interesting report see Mariz Tadros, "Unhomely Homes," *Al-Ahram Weekly*, October 17–23, 1996.

18 *Akhbar Al-Maadi*, May 1, 1996.

19 See Emad Mekay, "Necessity is the Mother of Invention," *Ru'ya* 9, Summer 1996, p. 20.

20 For a detailed study of networks in popular Cairo neighborhoods, see Diane Singerman, *Avenues of Participation: Family, Politics and Networks in Urban Quarters of Cairo*, (Princeton, NJ: Princeton University Press. 1995).

21 For more on the market sheikhs see H. Tadros, M. Fateeha and A. Hipbard, "Squatter Markets in Cairo," in *Cairo Papers in Social Science* 13/1, Spring 1990, p. 62.

Article 8

HARVARD INTERNATIONAL REVIEW, Spring 1997

Political Islam

Eighteen Years Later

Assessing the Islamic Republic of Iran

By H. E. CHEHABI

H. E. Chehabi is Associate Professor of History at the University of California at Los Angeles.

POLITICAL ISLAM BURST ONTO THE STAGE OF WORLD history with the Iranian revolution of 1979. Although the Muslim Brotherhood in the Arab Middle East and the Jama'at-i Islami in South Asia predate Ayatollah Ruhollah Khomeini's movement by a few decades, it was in Iran that political Islam first succeeded in overthrowing the existing order and establishing an Islamic state. The Shi'i branch of Islam dominant in Iran confers great importance to the legal scholars of Islam, who have thereby acquired some of the characteristics of a clergy. The Iranian/Shi'i conception of the state put power in their hands, based on the belief that Islamic rule was best ensured by those with the most expertise on Islamic laws, norms, and principles. After 1979, the Iranian adherents of political Islam attempted to translate this theocratic concept of the Islamic state into practice. Eighteen years later, their vision is challenged on not only secular but on religious grounds, although the level of support for the regime is difficult to determine.

The relative ease with which Iran's Islamists succeeded in gaining power had to do at least as much with the weaknesses of the Shah's regime as with the inherent strength of religious feeling in pre-revolutionary Iran. In the eyes of many politically articulate Iranians, the Shah lacked legitimacy because he had become the ruler of his country through a 1953 coup d'etat planned by Western intelligence. Given the circumstances of his coming to power, Iranians of vastly different ideological persuasions suspected that he put Western, and in particular American, interests above those of his own country.

But the way that the Shah exercised power, regardless of the legitimacy of its origins, also mattered. By the mid-1970s the Shah's autocratic rule had alienated people of most social strata. Traditional Iranians, whose life-styles were less affected by the regime's Westernization policies, were offended by what they perceived to be the impiety reigning at the top. The Westernized middle class yearned for political participation, and in the end even many capitalist entrepreneurs, the beneficiaries of the oil-induced economic boom, resented the corruption in the ruling circles. Thus it came to pass that when the Shah attempted to liberalize his regime in 1977, pent-up popular discontent resulted in a broad oppositional movement; by the autumn of 1978 millions of citizens were demonstrating in the streets of Teheran and other major cities to demand a change of regime. The Shah, weakened by his terminal illness, left the country in January 1979, and a few weeks later Ayatollah Khomeini returned from fifteen years of exile to oversee the change to a new order.

Building an Islamic State

The oppositional movement that brought down Iran's ancient monarchy had many distinct ideological and social components. What held it together was little more than antipathy toward the Shah; there was no consensus as to what should replace his rule. Leftists of various hues clamored for a socialist state spreading social justice by means of widespread nationalizations; moderates, both secular and Islamic, hoped for a liberal constitutional state; regionalists demanded improvements in the status of Iran's ethnic minorities; and Islamists of various types regarded Islam as the panacea for all the country's ills, although they differed on what the Islamic solutions to the problems at hand were. Ayatollah Khomeini dominated this heterogeneous coalition by the force of his charismatic personality. Even though many in the opposition had misgivings about him, they did not voice these publicly, knowing full well that in view of his followers' numerical strength and mobilizational resources, dissent would spell political irrelevance.

Upon his return to Iran in February 1979, Ayatollah Khomeini appointed Mehdi Bazargan, a veteran leader of the moderate opposition to the Shah and a pious Muslim, as prime minister of a provisional government that was to administer the country until the definitive institutions of the new state were put in place. Bazargan's cabinet included secular and Islamic moderates, but it soon came under attack by hardliners, both leftist and

Islamist, and was swept out of office in the aftermath of the seizure of the American embassy by young revolutionaries in November. In the meantime a constitution had been elaborated (and approved by plebiscite) that reflected the heterogeneity of the revolutionary coalition.

In this constitution, popular and divine sovereignty coexist uneasily in an institutional structure that combines republican and theocratic elements: a president and a parliament are elected by universal suffrage, yet the institutional edifice of the state is headed by a religious dignitary who wields supreme political and religious authority, a position created with Imam Khomeini in mind. Parliament legislates, but an appointed "council of guardians" can reject legislation it deems contrary to Islam. Leftist sensibilities are reflected in the document's endorsement of nationalizations, and regionalist aspirations are given a nod by the recognition of minority languages.

> *While it is true that Iran's political institutions provide a setting for managing factional rivalries peacefully, the institutions have themselves been manipulated and in some cases subverted by the country's leaders.*

The first elections held under the auspices of the new constitution in early 1980 resulted in a divided government, as the parliament's hard line majority opposed the policies of the more liberal president, Abolhasan Banisadr. At first, Khomeini tried to stay above the fray, but in June 1981 he came out in support of the hardliners and ousted Iran's first elected president, who fled to France. Since then Islamists committed to an Islamic state and to a thorough Islamization of public life have exercised total political control. Implementing the Islamist blueprint for good government proved more difficult than anticipated. To be sure, making citizens conform with Islamist notions of public morality was relatively easy: recalcitrance met with considerable violence. Women were forced to cover their hair and bodies in public, with whiplashes administered to those who did not. Alcohol and pork were banned. Where feasible, public spaces were segregated by sex. Walls were covered with graffiti cursing those who would not conform. But devising public policies consistent with Islamic law

(*shari'a*) proved far more difficult. The reason is that, quite simply, Islamic law does not address most of the issues and dilemmas facing a modern state. Solutions to pressing social and economic problems therefore had to be deduced from religious tenets, which led to deep disagreements within the power elite, as different political figures interpreted religious principles in line with their own predispositions.

For instance, economic conservatives would emphasize that Islam respects private property and enterprise, which would limit the role of the state in economic life. Economic radicals, in contrast, would argue that Islam mandates social justice, which could be achieved only by a redistribution of wealth and an interventionist state. The resulting public debates which took place within the institutions of the country blended political, religious, and legal arguments. Opposing views were aired in parliament, the cabinet, the council of guardians, and, of course, the press.

Through the 1980s, the war with Iraq mandated a command economy, as all resources had to be harnessed against the army of Saddam Hussein. The first three legislatures, from 1980 to 1992, were dominated by economic radicals, but their initiatives were often thwarted by the more conservative council of guardians. The conclusion of the war in 1988, Imam Khomeini's death a year later, and the accession to the presidency of the more pragmatic Ali-Akbar Hashemi Rafsanjani in the same year heralded the end of the radicals' dominance. Rafsanjani made reconstruction of the war-ravaged nation his top priority, and allied with the economic conservatives in 1992 to eliminate the radicals from parliament. But factional strife continued, as the allies found themselves on opposite sides of many issues. The conservatives were backed by Ayatollah Ali Khameini, Khomeini's successor as supreme religious and political leader, who has managed to use the resources of his office to circumscribe the president's margin of maneuver. The legislative elections of 1996 resulted in a tie between conservatives and Rafsanjani's followers, and whatever the ultimate outcome of the power struggle, it is too early to tell whether the economic policies enacted by the Rafsanjani administration will succeed.

Repressive Aspects of the Regime

This capsule history of Iran's political developments since the revolution should not be misconstrued to suggest that the leaders of the Islamic Republic have adhered to the letter and the spirit of the institutions put in place in 1979. While it is true that Iran's political institutions provide a setting for managing factional rivalries peacefully, the institutions have themselves been manipulated and in some cases subverted by the country's leaders. This applies both to the theocratic and to the republican components of the state.

The position of supreme religious and political leader was meant to embody the abolition of the separation between religion and politics, which Islamists everywhere consider harmful. It was tailor made for Imam Khomeini, who combined deep learning in religious matters with political leadership qualities proven in the course of the revolution. However, unlike its Roman Catholic counterpart, the Shi'i clergy lacks a true hierarchy: there is no Shi'i "pope." At any given moment believers have a choice between several high-ranking clerics whom they can follow in religious matters. In 1980 Khomeini was only one of half a dozen such top leaders, and his supremacy over his peers was due to his role as a political leader, not to superior religious credentials. Most of Imam Khomeini's peers did not share his vision of a theocratic state, but while he was alive, his political power silenced those among the clergy who disagreed with him.

As Imam Khomeini neared the end of his life in 1989, none of the top religious leaders who possessed the requisite religious learning to be eligible for his succession was acceptable to the regime; most did not even aspire to the position. The dilemma was eliminated by changing the constitution so that the new leader would no longer have to be a high-ranking member of the religious hierarchy. This opened the way for a smooth transition, in the course of which the country's then president, Ali Khameini, moved up to become the new political/religious leader. Although a very cultured man, Khameini lacked the religious learning and scholarly credentials to join the late Imam's peers at the top of the clerical hierarchy. Thus, a de facto bifurcation of religious authority took place, as purely "religious" religious leaders now faced a "political" religious leader—a step toward undoing in practice the unity of politics and religion so dear to Islamists.

While Shi'i clerics figure very prominently among the leaders of Iran's Islamic state, much of the clergy opposes clerical involvement in politics, considered to be undignified and prone to corruption. Since these clerics have a considerable number of followers, Iran's ruling Islamists cannot even claim to represent all Shi'is in Iran, to say nothing of Iran's Sunnis or non-Muslims. As for Iran's republican institutions, their seemingly smooth operation should not hide the fact that citizens are given a very limited choice at election time. True, there have been six presidential and five parliamentary elections, but candidates are pre-selected by the authorities, and electoral participation has consistently gone down. The fact that the constitution does not provide for a single party has made it possible for the various factions within the regime to function as quasi-parties and field candidates representing slightly different policies. This gives Iranians a more genuine choice than in the stage-managed elections that are the norm in one-party dictatorships, but is of no consolation to those citizens (very numerous among professionals and in the intelligentsia) who reject the very idea of an Islamic republic. These citizens, however, have benefited indirectly from the limited pluralism in Iran. The factionalism of political and religious life has prevented the emergence of a totalitarian state, as no group has been able to impose its will on the others. The result was an intellectual climate tolerating a considerable amount of public debate. This allowed at least some secular intellectuals to make their voices heard, too—at least until recently, for political and intellectual freedom, on the rise since Imam Khomeini's death and Rafsanjani's accession to the presidency, have been drastically curtailed since the spring of 1996.

There are probably two reasons for this recent repressive turn of the regime. First, the regime's hardliners, led by Ayatollah Khameini, felt perhaps that they were losing the struggle for ideological hegemony in Iranian society, as the foundations of political Islam have come to be questioned not only by secularists but also by Muslim dissidents. These figures, chief among them Abdolkarim Soroush, are potentially more dangerous to the current power holders than secularist critics, as they challenge the Islamic Republicans on their own grounds and thereby appeal to the regime's own social base. Second, the economic and cultural liberalization of the post-Khomeini years led both to a widening of the gap between rich and poor, a gap that had narrowed after the revolution, and to the emergence of a youth subculture that flaunted the ascetic norms of the regime. The regime may have found it convenient to channel the frustrations of economic disparity into moral outrage directed against the secular "rich," so as to create an outlet for underprivileged youth's resentment and contain it within the parameters of the regime.

The Years to Come

Whatever the causes of the recent changes may be, it is impossible to tell at this point whether they are a temporary setback or the harbinger of a more totalitarian style of governance. Much will depend on the outcome of the forthcoming presidential elections in May 1997, from which Rafsanjani is excluded as the constitution limits the presidency to two terms, but in which his brother, Mohammad Hachemi, may yet choose to run.

In the absence of genuinely free elections and scientific opinion polls, it is impossible to gauge the popularity of the regime. Travelers to Iran are likely to find much criticism and hostility toward it, but this may well reflect the type of social circles in which Westerners tend to move. There can be little doubt that the regime is unpopular among those who favor nonpolitical Shi'ism, non-observant Shi'is, non-Shi'i Muslims, and non-Muslims, but it is impossible to tell what percentage of the total population the combined weight of these groups represents. Among the rest, the omnipresentgriping and grumbling in Iran does not necessarily reflect disenchantment with the regime, for many Iranians still believe in the ideals

of the late Imam Khomeini while criticizing the policies of the men who carry on his legacy. Much will depend on whether the regime manages to retain, if not the loyalty, at least the acquiescence of the young, for given the high birth rates of the 1980s, soon over half of the country's population will have been born after the revolution, with no memory of the struggle to overthrow the Shah.

Article 9   *THE NEW REPUBLIC*, September 8 & 15, 1997

THE GOD THAT DID NOT FAIL

Martin Peretz

I

THEODOR HERZL WAS PREPARED FOR RIDICULE. ALREADY, IN 1896, on the publication of his book *Der Judenstaat*, or The Jewish State, in a first edition of 3,000 copies, he had several times been derided as "the Jewish Jules Verne." Some Jews, especially the highly placed but socially insecure, thought him more dangerous than a mere phantast, and many would not even see him. His radical Jewish politics put into question their loyalty to the states in which they lived. Newly (and precariously) accepted as citizens, they were alarmed by his assumptions: that they belonged to an old nation about to be revived; that the hostility toward them in Europe was essentially ineradicable. From their standpoint, Herzl was preaching pessimism. Would all their striving for acceptance be for naught? And what would the gentiles think? And Herzl discomfited the old-fashioned no less than the new-fashioned: many religious Jews also were threatened by his ideas. They saw in him the peril of politics, of a worldly activism that amounted to a heresy, an intrusion on God's will.

The editors of the *Neue Freie Presse*, the respectably liberal daily of the Viennese bourgeoisie, for which the boulevardier Herzl worked as a Paris correspondent, tried to prevent the publication of his little tract. They never so much as mentioned it in their columns; and other periodicals that did take note did not take great note. But Herzl would not be deflected. With a small coterie of scattered comrades, not all of the same sensibility, he prepared to convene what would come to be called the First Zionist Congress. For his manifesto had

echoed among independent Jewish intellectuals, the bulk of them children of the Enlightenment (Baruch Spinoza, too, had imagined a restored Jewish commonwealth), but some of them religious as well. And also with some of the Jewish masses—but not the masses of the German-speaking countries of Central Europe. No, Herzl's troops resided in fear in the East, living their lives in Yiddish and under the cruel regime of the czar. The book had been translated into Yiddish and other languages, including Ladino, the tongue of Sephardic Jews. So there were new constituencies for Zionism, and it was Herzl's little volume that had galvanized them.

There were also older, proto-Zionist constituencies, a bit more fragile, less grandiose, perhaps self-enclosed by doctrine or station or fright. They had been Zionists, or what would soon be called Zionists, long before the arrest of Captain Dreyfus, the event that roused Herzl from his Jewish slumber. These Jews had never believed that "the Jewish question" had really been solved. The persecution of the Jews was almost as old as the Jewish exile, and they were still in exile. These people had medieval blood libels and massacres in their very modern memories. Thus, they were not stunned, as Herzl appeared to be, by the cries of "death to the Jews!" on the streets of Paris and elsewhere in Europe.

In any case, Herzl did not invent political Zionism. Others had sown the seeds. A. D. Gordon and Leo Pinsker and Peretz Smolenskin are unknowns now, but they were titans in their time. The first "modern" Zionist was Moses Hess, who started out as a young Hegelian moving in the same revolutionary orbit as Karl Marx (who, though Jewish himself, reviled Hess because he was a Jew—worse, a Jew who was a Zionist). And there were stray Zionist organizations and Zionist publications before Herzl—and, aside from the centuries-old communities of pious Jews in Palestine, there were even Zionists returning to Zion. Between 1881 (the year the pogrom became a matter of official Russian policy) and 1896, at least a dozen new Jewish settlements, a few of them thriving, had been established in Palestine by unlikely pioneers from Eastern Europe, supported largely by a new secular version of the old religious charities and by the generous (and closely monitored) subventions of the grandees, such as the Barons Edmond de Rothschild and Maurice de Hirsch. Still, it was a pathetic migration. When the Congress actually assembled in Basel there were in attendance five delegates from the Promised Land itself, where 50,000 Jews lived, up from 25,000 twenty-five years earlier.

Five delegates among nearly 200 men, and perhaps ten women, maybe a few more. We do not have entirely reliable lists. But there are photographs. Herzl's mother sat on the dais during some of the proceedings. (A Jewish mother's fantasy if ever there was one.) Still, not counting this matriarchal vestige, one has only to look, in Roger Shattuck's *The Banquet Years*, at the famous picture of a grand banquet in Paris in the late nineteenth century, altogether without women, to grasp how sharp a break this assembly of Zionists was, not only with the past of the Jews but with the present of all Europe. Of course, the gathering had nothing to do with gender; but the participation of women was only one of the more advanced qualities of the conference.

More impressive, perhaps, was that this was a gathering across social and economic classes. None of the legendary Jewish princes came, though Otto Warburg, of the great Berlin banking family, would soon join the cause and ultimately become head of the Zionist Executive. But, among many impecunious people, there were rich men in Basel, and their impact was to put practical proposals on the docket and to get them passed. Thus, a Jewish national bank was mandated by the delegates, as was an institutional vehicle for the purchase of land for Jewish settlements. Basel was a collusion of dreamers and pragmatists. And a collision, too: there were ill feelings between the two types, and these persist in their spiritual descendants in the Zionist camp a century later.

Though it evoked ridicule from some of his critics, Herzl insisted that the delegates to the Congress wear frock coats and white ties. The delegates from Berlin and Baltimore, from The Hague and Heidelberg, certainly knew this attire, but what about those who had traveled from Bobruysk and Vitebsk, from the indigent world of carters and fiddlers that we know from the paintings of Chagall? In Herzl's view, all of those assembled had to feel that the Jewish people were in Basel asserting their collective equality with other polities, and their appearance had to evince their gravity. Some compared the Congress to the Sanhedrin assembled by Napoleon, at

which the Jews abjured their identity as a nation to become "Frenchmen of the Mosaic persuasion"; but Herzl conceived of Basel as the first Jewish parliament convened by the Jewish people themselves.

Still, the Congress, like Herzl's whole diplomatic strategy, was not a little focused on the gentiles. There were some clergymen attending as invited guests, a French baron, the founder of the Red Cross and, at one session, the president of Switzerland himself. There were great precedents for gentile enthusiasm for the Zionist project: from Julian the Apostate to Lord Shaftesbury, Lord Palmerston and the mad Lady Hester Stanhope. The romance of the Jewish return entered English fiction through George Eliot's influential *Daniel Deronda,* and through *Tancred,* the visionary novel by the convert from judaism Benjamin Disraeli. There were Christian philosemites in other countries, too; but the British ones set the cultural context for Lord Balfour, who finally gave the Zionists the charter that Herzl coveted. (Barbara Tuchman, herself an impassioned Zionist, wrote a whole book on such people, called *Bible and Sword: England and Palestine from the Bronze Age to Balfour.*)

Of course, much of this was rooted in Old Testament Protestantism. But all the European powers were looking for leverage in the Holy Land, and some saw enterprising and industrious Jews providing it. In any case, the competition between these powers for influence was intense. It was even fought out archaeologically and architecturally in Jerusalem, "the prize of contending nations," as one visitor put it: a Bavarian hospital on Mount Scopus, an Anglican church across from what was once thought to be a Davidic remain, a Scottish hospice above the Valley of Gehenna, a Russian church in Gethsemane, a French convent abutting the Mount of Olives, these and many more, jockeying against each other by height of tower and grandeur of view. Piety was an expression of empire, of the thirst for strategic advantage.

In truth, what the Zionists wanted could be granted them only by the Turkish sultan. For this to happen, however, Herzl knew they needed European interlocutors or European enforcers: the Kaiser, Pope Pius X (whose hand he declined to kiss) and a succession of cabinet ministers, primarily British. There was also an American connection to the Ottoman Empire on whom Herzl tried his arguments. But the American minister to the Divine Porte turned out to be Jewish, not Christian, and less amenable. For several decades Constantinople was the Jewish seat in the American diplomatic corps, literally the only capital to which a Jew could be posted, and it was used to ensure the security of the precariously placed Jewish community of Palestine. But it was not used to advance Zionist goals.

Herzl's labors were the first exercise in shuttle diplomacy for Zion. The diplomacy to which Jews had become accustomed was the diplomacy conducted by *Hofjuden*, "court Jews" who interceded with local princes for the benefit of Jews as a whole, mostly in efforts to vacate or to delay some draconian edict. Herzlian diplomacy aimed at ending those demeaning interactions by securing from the powers the political independence of the Jewish nation.

His intentions notwithstanding, there remained something of the court Jew in his high-level interactions. Still, for a people who had so little experience with the worldly politics of sovereign states, Herzl's palace politics, although mendicant to prince, was an improvement on the past. Didn't the Jews have to unlearn their habits of dependence? Unlearn them they did, and rather quickly. But what of their spiritual regeneration? The fact is that the heroic impulse in Herzl left little psychological space for spiritual reflection. Or for learning. He himself was an unlettered Jew, relying on his tutors for the articulation of every intrinsic Jewish thought.

Herzl's easy way in the world kept him from despair or self-pity. Indeed, every rebuff seemed simply to strengthen him. But his self-confidence did not keep him from becoming a target, especially the target of a group of Russian Zionist intellectuals led by Asher Ginsberg, who renamed himself Ahad Ha'am, or "One of the People," which he was not. Ahad Ha'am saw the new Zionists as "a rabble of youth" and attended their Basel gathering as "a mourner at a wedding feast." From the beginning, Ahad Ha'am stood as a totemic figure for the Zionist opposition, for those who found practical matters more than a bit demeaning. Churlish and resentful at seeing the leadership of the cause seized by someone whom he considered superficial and even a false messiah—he referred to Herzl more than once as Sabbatai Zvi, the false messiah of the seventeenth century—Ahad Ha'am put his words as barriers to each of his nemesis's acts. What was he not against? Migration was a distraction. Land acquisition was a chimera. A national bank was a pecuniary pettiness. Such tangibles do not build a nation.

Unfortunately, history had seen to it that by 1897 all that the Jews had, as a people, were intangibles. It was precisely the tangibles that had to be devised. When Herzl died in 1904, the imperious Odessan wrote patronizingly that his opponent "gave us the Congress, the Organization, the Bank, the National Fund. Whether these are to be reckoned great achievements we cannot yet know." Yet, in truth and certainly so early, these were everything that the Zionist movement had produced and was palpable. These, and its diplomacy. And so Ahad Ha'am reviled what he called the "romance of diplomatic embassies . . . interviews with prominent personages." Soon after the Congress, he wrote, as much to recommend himself as to diminish Herzl, "The salvation of Israel will be achieved by prophets not by diplomats." (Ahad Ha'am's biographer, Steven J. Zipperstein, has written that he was drawn to Ginsberg's life as he followed "Israeli events in the late 1980s with mounting unhappiness and some sense of tragedy." Had Ginsberg's more elevated ideas prevailed, maybe Zionism's encounter with the Arabs would have been less bitter. But Zipperstein found little support in his work for this intuition.)

Herzl could not see everyone he wished to see since many did not wish to see him. And from those he did see he rarely got what he asked. Most of them were not in the position to give. He had to make do with the Zionist fervor of the Grand Duke of Baden, who was the uncle of the Kaiser. And the Kaiser himself? That was another matter. Yet a diplomatic success was almost Zionism's undoing. This success was a strange unfolding. Herzl didn't see Joseph Chamberlain, the British Colonial Secretary, until 1902. But, when they met, various options filled the agenda: Cyprus, the Sinai, a Jewish colony in Egypt. It all came to nothing. A few months later, however, Chamberlain suggested Uganda. He didn't like Jews: "there is only one race I despise—the Jews. . . ." There were too many East European Jews coming to England. East Africa was the place to take them in.

For the first time in history, a sovereign state had negotiated with a representative Jewish body for a political solution to the Jewish problem. This was not a minor triumph. The Sixth Zionist Congress made a gesture toward the British offer of Uganda. Like the British, oblivious to the native Africans, some Zionists preferred Africa to Palestine because of the absence of hostile Arabs. Others favored Africa because it was the only place available. A place of haven now seemed more pressing: the Kishinev pogrom had just occurred, a terrible carnage leaving forty-nine dead and 500 wounded. The Hebrew poet Chaim Nahman Bialik would soon write of this atrocity:

Arise and go now to the city of slaughter;
Into the courtyard wind thy way;
There with thine own hand touch, and with the eyes of thine head
Behold on tree, on stone, on fence, on mural clay,
The spattered blood and dried brains of the dead.

Still, the vague Uganda resolution passed only because Herzl spoke eloquently for it. It was clear that almost no one would go anywhere other than to Palestine. Bitterness ran deep among the Zionist rank-and-file. Herzl's closest ally, Max Nordau, was almost assassinated by a disenchanted young Zionist.

Already at this Congress in 1903, Herzl must have felt the folly of his Uganda proposal. "If I forget thee, O Jerusalem, let my right hand wither," he swore in the words of the Psalmist as the dejected assembly adjourned. But the failed Uganda gambit defined the borders of the territorial solution to the Jewish question. To be sure, not everyone was in agreement. The idea of an independent Jewish polity didn't logically require a particular place for its fulfillment. As long as Palestine was politically remote, then, there would still be new places proposed. Some favored the Pampas in Argentina, others Manitoba, still others Australia—all of them possible sites of Jewish refuge, but without meaning for the Jewish soul. Grasping the power of the Zionist idea among the Jewish masses, the Soviets desperately contrived their own competitive version of an autonomous haven for Jews: the Jewish Autonomous Republic of Birobidzhan, nestled in the Siberian vastness, with Yiddish its official language; at last estimate, there were less than 5,000 Jews, almost all aged, in this broken Stalinist artifact. And there still exists the Jewish Territorial Organization, founded in the wake of the Sixth Congress to support the Uganda alternative and which then proceeded to other geographical panaceas.

Nothing but Palestine would do. Palestine was not only a piece of geography. Palestine was also an idea, an idea known as Zion. Said one Zionist: "To us Palestine is not a distant bread basket but a homeland." It resonated to religious devotion and historical memory. By the time Herzl had forlornly turned to Uganda, the word "Palestina" was already on the lips of millions of Jews; and for many decades thereafter, when "Palestine" was uttered, the utterance was not by Arabs but by Jews: the Palestine *Post*, the United Palestine Appeal, the Palestine Symphony Orchestra, and so on. The Zionists discovered and invented modern Palestine. It is certainly true that there were Arab *felaheen* on the spot, but they lived in villages and not beyond them, and had little or no conception of Palestine as a country. Long after there were Arab nationalists riveted on Egypt and on what would later be Iraq and Syria, Arabs did not see in Palestine the realization of any collective Arab aspirations.

For 1,500 years and more, however, that is exactly what Jews saw in Palestine, and it is exactly what Herzl and the delegates in Basel saw. Moreover, they had a finely textured sense of the land, its possibilities and its needs. The first truly practical Zionist enterprise in Palestine was established in 1870, long before the First Zionist Congress, when French Jews opened an agricultural school at Mikve Israel. These Frenchmen did not consider themselves Zionists. Nor did the others who, with funds and aggressive technical assistance from imported European experts, followed this "productivization" paradigm. Their motive, Derek J. Penslar has written, was not precisely Zionism, but "an inchoate Palestinophilia." But this sentiment quickly became a transformatory Zionist program: working the land was not simply an economic activity, it was also moral regeneration.

In a sense, of course, Basel 1897 was the consummation of small Zionist assemblies throughout Europe during the preceding decades, much as Philadelphia in 1776 was the consummation of little declarations of independence in the scattered colonies. It was Herzl's daring, however, to break out of the spare self-enclosures of virtue, to renounce abstraction and strike grand, concrete initiatives. The first session of the Congress was begun, appropriately and deliberately, with a religious practice. The believers and the unbelievers, the learned and the unlearned, the delegates from Algeria and Sweden, from Turkey and America, from everywhere, chanted together the haunting *Shehecheyanu* blessing: "Blessed art Thou, O Lord our God, Ruler of the Universe, who has kept us in life, sustained us and allowed us to witness this day." We are told that a tremor of emotion ran through the gathering. And then Herzl rose and declared: "We are here to lay the foundation stone of the house which is to shelter the Jewish nation." A few days later, he confided to his diary: "If I were to sum up the congress in a word—which I shall take care not to publish—it would be this: At Basel I founded the Jewish state. If I said this out loud today I would be greeted by universal laughter. In five years, perhaps, and certainly in fifty years, everyone will perceive it."

Are these the words of a megalomaniac? Maybe. But he was off by only nine months. Not quite fifty-one years after the First Zionist Congress, the troops of the British mandatory power withdrew, and David Ben-Gurion, the democratically elected leader of Jewish Palestine, proclaimed the independence of the State of Israel. The fifteen-minute founding ceremony ended with the resounding *Shehecheyanu* prayer, much as the Zionist odyssey of the Jews had begun with it half a century before at Basel.

Herzl had eight years in the limelight, eight years in the cause. He died in 1904, at the age of 44; and we have many testimonies to the press of Jewish humanity that massed at his funeral in Vienna. The movement that he founded went on, and on, to victory, but his own family collapsed. His embittered wife died three years later, at the age of 39. His daughter Pauline survived until her thirtieth year, when, a vagrant and a morphine addict, she expired in Bordeaux. His son Hans, uncircumcised and not a bar mitzvah either, dealt with his Jewish burdens by becoming in turn Baptist, Catholic, Lutheran, Unitarian and Quaker before returning to Judaism. When the news came that Pauline had died, he blew his brains out, just in time to be buried with her in the same coffin. Hans and Pauline's younger sister, Trude, survived, but lived for almost a quarter century of her life in a Vienna psychiatric hospital; in 1942, the Nazis transferred all of its patients to the Theresienstadt concentration camp, where she died the following year. Her son, Stephen,

Herzl's only grandchild, jumped off the Massachusetts Avenue bridge in Washington, D.C., in 1946. Herzl's most subtle biographer, Ernest Pawel, compares "the end of the Herzl bloodline" to "the inexorable fatality of a Greek tragedy." But it was Herzl's accomplishment that no inexorable fatality would any longer be the fate of his own people.

II

The odds against this extraordinary journey of a dispersed and despised people were enormous. No enterprise in nation-building is easy, but the circumstances of the Jewish nation were especially adverse. Except for the high rate of literacy among the Jews, they possessed virtually none of the common clay of modern nationalism. And their literacy did not necessarily work in favor of their ingathering. It wasn't simply that they were inordinately literate in the languages of others. It was also that they had several linguistic traditions of their own, at odds with each other historically and psychologically. These were languages of exile.

Benjamin Harshav, in *Language in Time of Revolution,* tells us that in the year of the Basel conference half the world's Jews lived in Russia and 98 percent of them declared Yiddish to be their native tongue. Yiddish was also the vernacular for many Jews living elsewhere in Europe and in America. Another 10 percent of the Jews who lived around the Mediterranean, descendants of the Iberian expulsions, communicated with each other in Ladino, an obscure but resilient language, and one which was slow to pick up modern currents like nationalism. Other Jews spoke the native languages of their places of abode. (In Iraq, where Jews had lived continually since the destruction of the First Temple in the sixth century before Jesus, they spoke Arabic, and they were intrigued by Arab nationalism and at best indifferent to emerging Zionism.) In 1880, and for two decades thereafter, no one really spoke functional Hebrew, though maybe 5,000 to 10,000 ideologically inflamed Jews read and wrote innovative versions of a tongue that had long been reserved for sacred and scholarly usage.

Of course, the contemporary convention that Hebrew had been dead before Zionism was not true. When the modernizers and the revivers embarked on their effort to get Jews to buy their groceries, give traffic directions and curse their neighbors in Hebrew, they found out just how rich and powerful this ancient language was. Literally every man (and many women as well) had studied the Hebrew holy texts and their Hebrew interpretations. Millions of Jews spoke thousands of Hebrew words in prayer three times a day. This intimacy of the time-honored Jew with Hebrew is surely one reason why the resuscitation of the language as the national tongue happened so quickly. Still, one shouldn't exaggerate. It

was not uncommon to hear, on the streets of Tel Aviv in the early decades of this century, the greatest enthusiasts of Hebrew speaking among themselves in Yiddish. In Europe, the bulk of Zionist literature and most of the movement's periodicals were published in Yiddish. The Jews who cheered Herzl in Vilna cheered him in Yiddish. And most Yiddish speakers were neither Hebraists nor Zionists.

Aside from an extraordinary and subtle literature of European materials, Yiddish had its own "isms" attached to it, one of them being the delusion of a meaningful cultural autonomy in Europe, articulated in the minority rights treaties of the League of Nations legislated just before Hitler came to power. Yiddish was also the linguistic vehicle of Jewish socialists, who were persuaded that the solution to the Jewish question had to be not a Jewish solution, but a universal one, among the cruelest mirages of the era. The language was also the vernacular with which the pious Jews of Europe ran their quotidian and hermetic lives. Everybody sensed that for Zionism to succeed it would need one usable language, and the only plausible candidate for that role was Hebrew. But Herzl himself needed to be coached whenever he wanted to express himself in a symbolic Hebrew phrase.

Language was not the only problem. In Central and Western Europe especially, the drive toward assimilation robbed Zionism of precisely those Jews who were otherwise lured by the liberal idea of the nation and its promise of the rights of citizenship. The trouble was that the nations that drew them were the likes of Germany and Austria and France, not especially welcoming to strangers and where citizenship did not do away with the toxic encrustations of Jew-hatred. Even in the East, more worldly and educated Jews from the middle and professional classes—to say nothing of the rich—somehow believed that the countries in which they lived could be the countries to which they truly belonged. Some Jews in Poland also persuaded themselves of this hopeless hope. The paradox of the emancipated Jewries, as David Feldman demonstrates, was nowhere more sharp than in England. There, Jews became nervous when men of government declared themselves sympathetic to Zionist aims. The aims of the Zionists seemed to sabotage the aims of the assimilationists, who had shed the separating practices of faith and the jarring signs of cultural difference to be like everyone else.

And more numerous than the emancipated Jews were those who, "with perfect faith," believed that they would be in exile until the coming of the Messiah. It is true that there were active religious Zionists who believed in a this-worldly return *and* in a divine redemption, and their numbers grew during the twentieth century. But the thrust of Jewish piety in the centers of Jewish population was hostile to Zionism. The pious were historically and theologically quietist, accepting God's portion as He determined it. And so the most Jewish Jews were deaf to the idea of Jewish self-determination. This barely understood but powerful strain among religious Jews persists today. In Israel itself there are fervent Jews who deny the legitimacy of the state, its creation having been, in their eyes, a blasphemous act; and their immediate ancestors kept the faithful in a state of frenzy against the Zionist heresy. Against anti-Semitism, they did virtually nothing: Jew-hatred was, in their eyes, a punishment for the sins of the people, like the exile itself. But God did not save the pious from the unimaginable, and many of them perished in the ovens.

Thus—given the upwardly mobile assimilationists, the mostly poor, "trust in the Almighty" religious and the Jews who sought relief in socialism and communism—the Zionists inevitably had to be drawn from a relatively small cohort of the Jewish population. Of course, the emergence of political Zionism drew converts away from the other political dispensations, especially among younger people. So, here and there, a city would suddenly brim with Zionist activity, and the community would never be the same. Still, Zionism was a mostly marginal venture. Did the communities in which Zionists were particularly influential behave differently from others before the catastrophe of 1939–1945? Some did. There was a particularly strong Zionist presence in Salonica, where, until the mid-'30s, some 65,000 Jews lived. In 1935 and 1936, seeing the ugly handwriting on the wall, 15,000 of these Jews emigrated to Palestine, and it was largely they who built the port of Haifa. (Of the remaining 50,000 Salonician Jews, 12,000 survived the war.) There were also many Zionists in the Free City of Danzig; and, in 1938, having experienced the depredations of Nazism despite the League of Nations' formal guarantees of freedoms in the city, the official Jewish community began the painful dissolution of its society 500 years old, an idea broached earlier by Revisionist Zionists. Braving the British blockade, some of these Jews made their way to Palestine. Other escapees to Palestine were interned by the Crown in Mauritius. Still others, seeking sanctuary in America, were on the *S.S. St. Louis*—not the only such desperate cargo—as it plied the East Coast of the U.S. Refused entry, they sailed back to Europe, to death.

Zionism did not save European Jewry. Still, as Walter Laqueur has written, Palestine would become the haven for more Jews than all other countries combined. The Holocaust seemed to bring a grim uniformity to the history of European Jewry. In death, the Jews were one. In life, the Jews had never really been one. Even in Europe, their histories varied widely. The political and cultural experiences of a Jew in Russia and of a Jew in Germany couldn't be more different, in expectations as well as in sensations. And the Jewries of the Arab world, and elsewhere in what used to be called the Orient, added to this already dizzying mix of the potential recruits to Zionism, men and women—and communities—with virtually no acquaintance with politics, no conception of rights, no knowledge of mechanized industry, no idea that Jews might be and think of themselves as secular. This, certainly, was not the case for Western Jewries. Many of these Jews had simply taken the idea of the nation out of Judaism. This, the oriental Jews had not done, although their notion of the nation was more historical legend than political intention. These Jewries were not even one racial group, at least on the physical surface. (Although three articles by Stanford Professor Samuel Karlin, et al., in *The American Journal of Human Genetics* show that, measured by fourteen genetic markers, "the Ashkenazi, Sephardi and Iraqi Jewish populations [are] consistently close in genetic constitution and, significantly, equally distant from . . . the Arabs and non-Jewish German and Russian populations." But this is another matter.) These Jewries were at different levels of economic development, scientific consciousness and political ambition. Some Jews came from environments in which a Jew had to dismount his horse when an ordinary member of the society walked by. Other Jews, from other environments, expected to be elected parliamentarians (and by gentiles, yet).

Zionism had to appeal to all these Jews and all these Jewries. No national movement ever had so intrinsically complex a constituency. Not that nationalisms everywhere didn't have to straddle economic classes and social strata. But this again was different. Each of the dispersed Jewries had its own demographic pyramid, some mostly paupers, others mostly middle-class, some top-heavy with intellectuals, others top-heavy with shoemakers. What no Jewry possessed was a landed gentry, and almost no Jewry had a real peasantry. This gave the return to the land a romantic, artificial character. Still, much Zionist rhetoric premised the idea of redemption on the idea of toil in the earth. Or, as one Zionist leader put it, "When the Jew holds the plough in Palestine, the Jewish problem will be solved." And the social problem would be solved, too. Some Zionists were convinced, in fact, that the kibbutz simultaneously dissolved the moral predicament of hierarchical societies while normalizing the Jewish condition. Kibbutzniks were an aristocracy of poverty; they both provided norms for the wider community and had a harmonious relationship with the land.

Yet the real impediment facing Zionism was the land itself. It was a land on which very few Jews lived, a land which only a few Jews had ever seen, a land which most Jews knew only from texts. And texts, however vivid, are not eyes and ears, hands and feet. Other nationalist movements struggled for political sovereignty over lands in which their nation lived but over which another nation ruled. The Jewish land required a great voyage of faith and imagination. For Zionism to succeed, the people had to move. And, to move, they had to think of two millennia of experience in exile as abnormal, for Jews as individuals and for Jews as a people.

And there was another impediment on the land. There were Arabs there. The Arabs had the moral advantage of having been there first—first, that is, in modern times. But they were not there in enormous numbers, and many of them had arrived recently. They had crossed the invisible borders of the Ottoman Empire, from one *sanjak* to the next, districts of bureaucratic convenience rather than real polities, without any sense that they were going across the frontiers of this country to that. As Jewish economic activity increased in Palestine, so did the arrival of Arabs. But no Arab who went from what is now Syria to what is now Israel thought that he was migrating to another country: he was simply moving from one part of his world to a neighboring part in order to make a living. Even after the First World War, when the League confirmed the frontiers of mandatory Palestine, which was reserved for a Jewish homeland, the borders were both psychologically and physically porous. Of course, the local Arabs did understand that the Zionist project meant that fierce competition for land would ensue, and this recognition stimulated Arab resistance to Jewish settlement. So there was Arab terror against the Jews from the very beginning, and more conventional protest as well. Yet many of the actual leaders of this resistance, called the Arab Higher Committee, sold land to the Jews. This is an index of how thin Arab national sentiment was, and how little many Arab notables cared about the real-life anxieties of ordinary Arabs. But, in Arab politics, leaders do not apologize or explain.

Hostile to the Zionist undertaking though they were, the Palestinian Arabs were in no way a threat to it. Yes, they might burn a kibbutz's crops or kill a farmer in the field, but the main obstacles to the success of the Zionists were, first, that big-power diplomacy would abandon Zionism just as it had once sponsored it, and, second, that, in the period after World War II and after the establishment of the State, the armies of the surrounding Arab states might defeat the Zionist forces in combat. But the interest in Palestine of the neighboring Arabs was their own interest. When Egypt and Syria (and Jordan) fought Israel, it was as part of their own scramble for leadership of the Arab world. They never really did battle for Arab Palestine. They used anti-Zionism as a prop in their own political pyrotechnics. Had the outside Arabs ever won a war against Israel, Palestine would have been carved up by the victors, and its name would have evaporated into history. (This is just about what happened when the West Bank was annexed by Jordan and the Gaza Strip was policed by Egypt). The Palestinian movement didn't come into its own until Egypt and Syria, whose people have yet to meet the industrial revolution, simply exhausted themselves in their ongoing conflicts with the Jews.

For the Zionists, however, the problem of Palestine had long been their encounter with the Arabs just over the next hill. There is a cliché that asserts that the Zionists did not see these Arabs in Palestine. Many of them didn't. But the truth is that Zionism was riven by internal struggles on how to see the Arabs and how to deal with them. Some of the luminaries of Jewish Palestine were bi-nationalists, Martin Buber most famously. In retrospect, a bi-national state seems merely an instance of loftiness in a tight spot. Still, the idea looked unimpeachable. That there would be one state for two nations struck roots in the Labor Zionist movement, the dominant stream among the Zionists, and even hard-liners occasionally toyed with the notion. It certainly appealed to the residual universalism of the socialist Zionists, a philosophical disposition always in tension with the exigencies of the national struggle. Since ideas were powerful weapons in Zionism, this bi-national possibility was never easily dismissible, and it tore at the Zionist heart. It also had practical consequences, most especially for the partition formula that early on seemed to be (as it does now for the West Bank) the obvious solution to the conflict. The bi-nationalists were against partition and wanted to avoid the inevitable separation of the two peoples that was its corollary. There were many Jews who favored the bi-national dispensation, and there would have been many more had there been any Arabs. Or, as one dovish Zionist wrote about bi-nationalism, "What is the point of reaching agreement between ourselves if there is no one on the other side?"

Other obstacles to Zionism included the previously prevailing standards of Jewish life. While some of these were traditional, many of them were revolutionary. Hadn't the Jews been among the most eager believers in the utopian ideas that would make the world a better place? Socialism, communism, even pacifism: moral codes from all of these worldviews had infiltrated into Zionism. (It was a Jew who, in these years, invented Esperanto.) So, despite itself, Zionism was hostage to the very ideologies from which it was trying to liberate the Jews. And it was hostage also to the idealisms that non-Jews wanted Jews to exemplify. Thorstein Veblen, for example, had written that one of the baleful normalizing consequences of Jewish nationalism would be that the world would lose its most powerful and permanent outsider critics, and some Zionists felt that this complaint struck deeply. At least one Zionist thinker took up Gandhi's counsel to the Jews of Germany that they stay in Europe to fight Nazism with *satyagraha*. Even Zionists did not completely shed the deep Jewish reluctance to act for themselves as other peoples do. Jewish history had made this reluctance seem moral.

Alas, Zionism did not bring the Jews of Europe to Palestine until more than half of them had been murdered. But at least a lesson had been learned: stateless Jews are defenseless Jews. The Jews would use force, if that is what it took to make them free. Zionism would overcome the internal odds.

III

At the very time that the Zionists were mounting their first Congress in Basel, two Jewish intellectuals were launching very different careers. In 1897, Rosa Luxemburg was on her way to Berlin to join her anti-imperialist and anti-capitalist comrades in what would later emerge as the Spartakus League. And, in 1897, Leon Trotsky—born Bronstein, but living under his first nom de guerre, Lvov—founded his original circle of clandestine revolutionaries. The utopian trajectories of these proudly un-Jewish Jews (Luxemburg once wrote in a letter that she had "no room in my heart for Jewish suffering") ended in famously dystopian ways. Shortly after the abortive putsch of the socialist revolutionaries in Berlin in 1919, Luxemburg was assassinated and became a legend. Trotsky went on to become a real and most cruel Pharaoh of the Soviet Union, and he, too, was assassinated, not by a fascist thug but by a true believer sent by Stalin to put an ice pick in his deviationist brain.

Who, in those early inflamed decades in the history of modern revolution, would have imagined that it was not the socialist revolution of the reracinated Jews, but the nationalist revolution of the reracinated Jews, that would come out on top? But the cause to which Luxemburg and Trotsky gave their lives is itself dead, and, in those redoubts where it still exists, it owes its existence increasingly to deals with the running dogs of capitalism. The cause, indeed, has become known as "the God that failed," after the title of a bitter book by six apostates from communism. In his contribution to that clarifying book, Arthur Koestler wrote that "I served the Communist Party for seven years—the same length of time Jacob tended Laban's sheep to win Rachel, his daughter. When the time was up, the bride was led into his dark tent" and turned out to be not Rachel but Leah. Jacob worked another seven years to win the hand he had first been pledged; but Koestler was spent and would do no more. He was through with Laban.

If socialism was the God that failed, then Zionism was the God that did not fail. I do not mean to say that Zionism was, or is, a God. It was too rambunctious, too contentious and too democratic to become an orthodoxy, and it consistently refused—except in a few instances of internecine violence that scandalized the entire Jewish community—to meet heterodoxy with physical force. (It was partly for these reasons, no doubt, that Koestler became an idiosyncratic Zionist). There are religious Zionists, to be sure, who regard the state, or the land, or their own chauvinism, as divine; but Zionism was not essentially a messianism. All that it insisted upon was freedom and security, which are supremely secular objectives. Indeed, if Zionism did not fail, it was not least because it was not a God. It was a morality, and a politics, of worldliness.

But Zionism was an ideology, emerging from among the high tide of ideologies; and its secular, worldly promise was certainly revolutionary. Of all the modern promises of transformation, Zionism is the only one to have accomplished what it set out to do—and to have done so with reasonable decency. The narrative of this century is cluttered with brutalized hopes, brutalized bodies, brutalized language. Socialism, communism, Third Worldism, pan-Arabism, even neutralism: all these isms, with their grandiose aims and their callous means, which conscripted many ordinary men and women and enticed so many intellectuals (and so many Jewish intellectuals) are already receding into the mists of time. Our children will scarcely know that they were; but the luck of our children will have been purchased at a fearful price.

Zionism was an ideology unlike other ideologies, even if its decolonization struggle looks very much like other decolonizations, in the Indian subcontinent, for example. The State of Israel was born when the Zionists sent the British packing (it was the Jews who sent them packing, not the Arabs); and, at that very moment, the British (and the French and the Belgians and the Dutch) were also packing elsewhere in Africa and Asia. Israel was an anti-imperialist creation. (Four imperialists were the vivid demons of my childhood in a Zionist home: Perfidious Albion, Colonel Blimp, John Bull and Ernest Bevin.) Is it still necessary to insist that the Jewish refugees who streamed into Palestine and later into Israel were not colonialists? Israel came into the world in the company of dozens of other states, some relatively homogeneous, some not, but all, unlike Israel, with their populations in place. The age of nation-building, of the great experiments in ethno-nationalism, had begun.

What happened with these great ventures in nation-building? The answer is not edifying. Most of the postcolonial states are multiple sectarian configurations. You have only to look at maps of Africa and of the Arab Middle East, to grasp that these straight lines and sharp angles follow neither nature nor population. Their boundaries splintered clans and tribes and sects into fragments across senseless frontiers, and then mixed them all up within frozen borders. Like the empires themselves, these new states seem to have been drawn in a fit of absence of mind, or of malice. States may be declared and proclaimed and celebrated into existence, but not nations. Nor is a nation formed simply because its discordant elements were once governed by a foreign power: a society must be founded on more than a collective grudge, on more than a memory of oppression. (Classical Zionism's "negation of the Diaspora," its desire to deny the Jewish experience of the dispersion, was a terrible cultural exaggeration, but it had the consequence of making this nationalism look forward as much as backward.) Elsewhere exiting imperialists' revenge on its colonials may well have been nationalism itself. It swiftly turned out that the tools of state power may serve the tribe as readily as the nation. Nigeria, the Sudan, Algeria, Iraq, Lebanon, Kenya, Pakistan, Indonesia: These are states, but are they nations? Even the fate of India is uncertain. Will it be able to weather its persistent, primal torments? Maybe; but only through a huge statist exertion. Other nation-states are withering away before us every day, right there on CNN. The former Soviet Union is an unstable prisonhouse of nations, the reality of which, for the sake of Boris Yeltsin, we dare not speak. And near the heart of Europe, a few hours from Venice and Vienna, a former nation-state has collapsed into ethnic cleansing.

So this is the background against which moral, historical and political evaluations must be made; and, against this background, who will not forgive Zionism, and the imperfect and even troubled state to which it gave birth, a centenary moment of self-congratulation?

The test that almost all the new states of the second half of the twentieth century failed is the test of pluralism. But consider the hundreds of thousands and then the millions who came to Israel. If they came for the same reason, they were not the same people. They were literate and illiterate, from liberal societies and illiberal ones, scientists and worshipers of relics, teachers of history and acolytes of wonder-rabbis, so diverse in origins, so split in habits, so different in traditions that the physical reunion of the Jews in the Land would appear more threatening to the oneness of the nation, which for so long had only been an abstract idea, than its continued dispersion. That they came to what they thought was a nation did not guarantee that a nation is what they would become, or remain. Before statehood, there was only the moral suasion of a voluntary collective to bridge the philosophical, cultural, economic and psychological gaps; and after statehood the chasms even seemed to deepen. There were dire prophecies of Israel divided, even of civil war. The thrust of all these prognoses was that the Jewish nation would not hold as a political entity, that the intrinsic and structural strains were too great for the fragile state to bear, that the prospects of Zionism would be undone by the Jews themselves. Yet none of this friction turned to real strife, even in conditions of

extreme austerity. (The same cannot be said about the conflict between certain believers and unbelievers in Israel. A virulent strain of religious nationalism put a bullet in Yitzhak Rabin's back. But such fanaticism, contained and disdained, will no more tear the Israeli polity asunder than the right-wing militias will tear up America.)

And the success of the actual state can be traced to the character of the movement which begat it. No state has been better served by its visionaries and its pioneers and its founders. Let us put this, too, into perspective. Zionism may be the one national movement of the century that condemned—that physically and politically fought against—the terrorism of its own extremes. This refusal to murder innocents—the principle of restraint that was known as *havlagah* in the Jewish defense forces before the state and as *tohar haneshek,* or "the purity of arms," in the Israel Defense Forces—provided official Zionism with the moral equanimity necessary to make difficult tactical decisions. And these Jewish soldiers were operating in, and defending their community against, a brutal place. There has always been a tension between the norms of combat and the realities of combat. Sometimes the Zionist forces, and later the Israeli forces, did not withstand this tension, and the society proceeded toward a moral reckoning; but it is not an exaggeration to say that the Zionist militia, and later the Israeli army, has been a military with a conscience. And its people have been a people with a conscience. (The official Zionists, in an operation known as the *saison,* actually cooperated with the British in rounding up terrorists of the right.)

As it happens, there was always in political Zionism a dicey encounter between the realistic and the ideal, the practical and the abstract. An encounter, but not a contradiction. This was certainly true for the agricultural settlements and the kibbutzim that dotted the cartography of Palestine with working Jewish enclaves. They could not be just Tolstoyan colonies or Zionist versions of Brook Farm if they were to be truly productive or truly defensive. But they could not be just plain farms if they were to imbue their workers with a touch of the utopian spirit, without which these former city and town dwellers could not dredge swamps, clear rock, reforest the land and plumb in a forbidding desert for precious drops of water. And they would also have to be alert to the danger of Arab marauders. The early stockade-and-watchtower settlements demanded sacrifice, and sacrifice required a transcendent meaning. In Palestine, then, socialism and Zionism met in a felicitous match.

The idealism of the Zionist pioneers had its practical refractions in the Diaspora. With its blue-and-white boxes displaying a Holy Land of indistinct borders, the Jewish National Fund, which bought land from Arabs (usually for very high prices), and also sustained a massive undertaking of the planting of trees, established an almost palpable personal tie between Jewish youth and Eretz Yisrael. Here is how the historian Simon Schama remembers this from his own English childhood: "I was gumming small leaves to a paper tree. . . . Every sixpence collected . . . merited another leaf. When the tree was throttled with foliage the whole box was sent off, and a sapling, we were promised, would be dug into the Galilean soil, the name of our class stapled to one of its green twigs. All over north London, paper trees burst into leaf . . . and the forests of Zion thickened in happy response. The trees were our proxy immigrants, the forests our implantation. . . . All that we knew was that to create a Jewish forest was to go back to the beginning of our place in the world, the nursery of the nation."

If Zionist agriculture in Palestine (and Israeli agriculture thereafter) fed more people than anyone had imagined the land could support; if it developed an export food and flower economy and eventually crated high-tech agronomic tools which, when sold abroad, made farming the land in Israel a competitively unproductive venture for Jews; if Jews came to flourish as farmers and soldiers—all this was because Jews had effected a transformation in themselves. In Palestine, and then in Israel, the self-image of the Jew as a passive actor in history was gradually retired. A new and intensely practical conception of historical agency was put in its place. How could it be otherwise? It had become a fact that Jews were writing their own history in a land of their own. This is finally what is meant by what Schama elsewhere called "the Zionist style of existentially muscular 'fact creation.'"

Even in the Diaspora, Zionism implied the appearance of a different and more assertive Jew. Zionism gave the Jews of exile the daring to fight back when anti-Semitic thugs attacked on the street. Michael Berkowitz, the cultural historian of Jewish nationalism, has shown how the credo of *Muskeljudentum,* muscular Jewry, first enunciated by Max Nordau, became a widely practiced social phenomenon in a cult of nature and through athletics and gymnastics. There were Jewish dueling societies and Jewish olympics named after Jewish heroes: King David, the Maccabees, Bar Kokhba and the generic Lion of Judah. The Jews were not only emerging from the ghetto, they were also no longer behaving as if these "gentile pursuits" were alien activities. They included even Franz Kafka, that quintessential neurasthenic artist who studied Hebrew and planned to emigrate to Palestine: his biographers trace his own frenetic physical exercise to a fashion among young Zionists in Prague. Or, as one of them writes, "By linking Zionism and body building . . . Jews could build bodies as a preparation for the settlement of Palestine." Fortunately, there were more successful enthusiasts of the healthy body in Jewry than Kafka.

Zionism began as a threat to assimilated Jews; but for many Jews it turned out to be their road back to Judaism and back to the Jewish people. This does not sound exciting or controversial these days, when there are very few anti-Zionists. But Zionism's demand of "normalcy" for Jewish life was a revolutionary demand and the occasion of a great inner struggle. The most important of the returnees to Jewish consciousness by way of Zionism was undoubtedly the "people's lawyer," Louis Dembitz Brandeis, who, even while serving as associate justice of the U.S. Supreme Court, involved himself in the political, financial and intellectual struggles of the movement, and its agricultural and industrial arcana. (The campaign against his nomination mounted by A. Lawrence Lowell, the president of Harvard, is a strikingly ugly tale.) He would not resign the court to take the official helm of the World Zionist Organization because he wanted to demonstrate that there was no contradiction, as one of his biographers has written, between remaining "attached to America while working for a Jewish homeland in Palestine." In any case, he had already headed the American Zionist movement and was a decisive participant in the crucial wording of the Balfour Declaration. (Brandeis also put an early Zionist stamp on this magazine through his friends among its editors, Felix Frankfurter in particular.) Brandeis was a territorially hard-line Zionist; and, if anybody can be said to have swung the Jewish masses of America to Zionism, it is he. His own ease with Zion became that of others.

The assimilated virtues also emigrated to Palestine with the Zionists. In their universities, before the state and after, there were rich academic programs to study the other, especially the Arabs. (Scholarship on Islam and on the world around Israel has been much deepened by scholars who for most of their lives were not allowed to see the objects of their studies.) Into the desert, surrounded by cultures hostile to the West and its values, the Zionists brought Mill and Mozart, Curie and Conrad. These affinities put the Jews at odds with their neighbors. Israel is a Levantine country, but the country and its schools measure their performance by decidedly un-Levantine standards of literacy, numeracy and sensibility. Consider a melancholy index of cultural migration: the import of pianos to Palestine. According to a social history of music in Jewish Palestine, in 1931, before Hitler, sixty-seven pianos were brought into Palestine. In 1933, the year the Nazis came to power, 216 pianos arrived; in 1934; 294; in 1935, in crushing crescendo, 372. When Jewish migration was restricted, there was little Jewish cargo: in 1939, fifty-four pianos; and in 1941, twenty-one. After that there were few European Jews alive, with pianos or without.

Zionism had foreseen this unfolding history, not in its gruesome details but in its general outlines. Europe was doomed soil for Jews, and even the well-intentioned and well-positioned liberal European polities would look away when the flames of anti-Semitism spread across the continent in their most virulent form. But it is important to understand that the Jews are not the creation of the anti-Semites. The Jews were a people before they called themselves a nation; and they called themselves a nation before the catastrophe. This is one of the oldest truths about Jewish identity: it is an autonomous self-ascription. A Jew in sixteenth-century Budapest felt that he had more in common with a Jew in sixteenth-century Cairo than with a non-Jew in sixteenth-century Budapest. No, it was not the Jewish understanding of the Jewish predicament that was transformed by the catastrophe. It was the non-Jewish understanding of the Jewish predicament. For most gentiles, it took the catastrophe to accept that their Jewish neighbors, patriotic Americans and loyal Frenchmen though they were, were not only different in some unspecified ways but belonged also to another nation.

No, that is not precise. There were many Jews who did not wake up to the Jewish difference until it was too late. The Zionist intuition of Jewish fate was tragically uncommon. "Only now," wrote Stefan Zweig, "did the bankers from their Berlin palaces and sextons from the synagogues of orthodox congregations, the philosophy professors from Paris and Rumanian cabbies, the undertakers' helpers and Nobel Prize winners . . . the just and the unjust . . . the baptised and the semi-Jews understand, only now were they forced. . . ." Forced into what? Understanding that their enemies thought they were alike? Had they grasped their kinship earlier and on their own, more Jews would have gone to Palestine when there were more Jews to go. Surely it is an incontrovertible (and heartbreaking) proposition that had more Jews recognized the essential truth of the Zionist analysis of Jewish fate the destruction of Jewish life in Europe would not have been as enormous as it was.

The terrible, terrible irony of Zionist history is that its dream was fulfilled only when there were so few European Jews to rescue. Conventional wisdom has it that, were it not for the Shoah, Israel would not have come into being. Quite to the contrary, in my view: if there had not been a Holocaust, in which some 6 million Jews perished, there would have now been in the world not 13 million Jews but scores of millions. But there would still have been anti-Semitism in Europe, even in the absence of a Judeocide. So the blockade of Palestine would have been run, and the gates of Palestine been stormed, not by thousands but by millions of Jews, from Central Europe and Eastern Europe and the countries of Islam. Instead of the more than 600,000 Jews in the Yishuv after the Second World War, there would have been many times that number. It was, in any case, not the United

Nations that brought the British Mandate to a close, but the Yishuv, or the determined and self-determined Jewish community in Palestine. It was Zionism that created the Jewish state. (And it was the Zionists who defeated the Arab armies.) The more numerous the Jews in the world and in Palestine, the more irresistible would have been the creation of the Jewish state.

Returning Jews were the psychological lifeblood of the country, an ongoing confirmation of its purpose: first, from the displaced persons' camps in Europe and the detention camps in Cyprus where the British imprisoned the survivors seeking admission to Palestine; and then the magical migrations from Yemen and Morocco and Iraq; and then the little Jewries of Bukhara and Kurdistan and India; and then the migrants from here and there, in no particular pattern; and, at the last, the transfiguring arrival of more than 750,000 Jews from the Soviet Union, Jews who would otherwise soon have been lost to their people; and these immigrants followed by the long-separated but stubbornly Jewish Jews of Ethiopia. Some of these groups are lower on the social scales than others, and too many immigrants to Israel continue to experience discrimination; and yet this state's genius for absorption is unrivaled. This has been a great romance: of a people with a country, of a people with each other. Not unlike what the delegates imagined 100 years ago at Basel.

Yet those delegates would not recognize in present-day Israel the visions that Herzl had conjured up for its future. No matter. The state is, by any contemporary standard, a success. Like Britain, without the advantage of a constitutional text, its highest court has crafted a system of justice continually at odds with the democratically subversive tyrannies of democratic majorities. When the court freed John Demjanjuk because he may have been merely a brutal guard at a concentration camp, Judge Alex Kozinski of the Ninth Circuit of the U.S. Court of Appeals wrote in these pages: "[It] will surely become a model of how a court confronting a difficult and painful subject ought to comport itself. Jews can take pride that Judaism's age-old commitment to the rule of law did not waver. . . . Subtly woven into the common law woof of the Israeli Court's opinion are the warp threads of talmudic law. The willingness to admit any evidence—even that of highly doubtful reliability—so long as it helps the accused. . . ." Kozinski writes that even our Supreme Court under Justices Warren, Brennan and Marshall would have reached a different result. This may not be prudent of Israel's judges, but it is exquisite.

It is a little tiresome, for some, to hear that Israel is the only democracy in the Middle East. But Israel is the only democracy in the Middle East. It is also the only modern society in the region. Not so long ago Israel was a pitiable place. No longer. Its per capita GDP is roughly equal to the United Kingdom's, despite the enormous burden of its military footing and the costs of immigrant integration, and despite a big drain owed to inefficient and cumbersome state-held businesses. Depending on whose numbers you use, Israel ranks on the GDP index in the mid-teens in the world. Although there is growing income disparity, Israel retains its status as a relatively egalitarian economy. In a 1993 projection of future competitiveness, for example, the Union Bank of Switzerland puts Israel third most favorable in the world, behind South Korea and China and ahead of Singapore, Japan and the United States. Israel shows the single strongest resource growth in the world, this being measured by fixed investment relative to GDP, research and development expenditures relative to GDP, and human capital growth, which is understood as a combination of spending on education relative to GDP and average school enrollment rates per capita. Indeed, according to UBS, Israel spends fully a fifth of its national output on education. (It is also, according to a recent study, among the least corrupt countries in which to do business.) On August 6, 1997, *The Wall Street Journal* reported that "Tech Takes Hold in Ancient Jerusalem. A high-technology paradise is being built on sacred ground." This is newspaper hype; but Israel is already a center for computer, communications and bio-tech research, as well as a producer of high-end products for the most advanced engineering and scientific projects in the world. The gap between Israel and its neighbors has never been greater, and it will grow because the Arab world failed to use its oil wealth to transform its economies, and it is now in no position to do so. Pity the societies in which modernity is denounced as an evil.

There is no greater measure of the success of Zionism, finally, than the phenomenon of Post-Zionism. What really gnaws at the post-Zionist scholars and writers is the spectacle of a Jewish society in which Jews are not always brooding about cosmic questions, in which they sit at cafés, dance in the moonlight, eat good food, make piles of money, chatter on cell phones, have film festivals—all of the activities of an unafraid and unanguished people. The post-Zionists claim that Israel is complacent, devoid of a self-critical temper. They want to deconstruct and to demythologize the old narrative of Zionism and its successes (the sort of narrative that I have just told). In their rage to modernize, didn't the Zionists offend the sensibilities of the Jews of the East? Didn't Jewish soldiers sometimes beat up on innocent Arab town-dwellers and even drive some of them into another part of historic Palestine? The answer to these questions, and to others, is "yes." Israel is a strong state, and it has fought wars, and it bears the responsibility of power—which is to say, Israel is not innocent. The Jewish state has committed acts that it should not have committed, just like every

other country, including the United States. But Zionism permits us to admit this without flinching. Indeed, post-Zionism is a great tribute to Zionism, for it is the natural consequence of the open, wakeful, contrarian spirit that characterized Jewish nationalism from the start. Israel is not an evil state, and the post-Zionists are not prophets without honor: what we are witnessing is the continued "normalization of the Jewish people," to use the old Zionist slogan. Israel must feel pride where pride is right and regret where regret is right; but it must feel a tinge of pride also about its regret.

Now the revisionists are embarked on a campaign to change the national anthem. Its words—and its melancholy key of C-minor—appeal, they say, only to Jews.

> *Within their hearts,*
> *Jews' souls yearn*
> *Looking eastward*
> *An eye beholds Zion . . .*

No Arab can kindle to those words. The post-Zionists say that the song known as the *Hatikvah*, or "The Hope," excludes Arabs from the national discourse. Never mind that this must be the most unwarlike anthem in the world. There is a kernel of truth in what the critics say. But they purchase their point at the price of a healthy realism about their state, about politics in general. The fact is that Israel is a Jewish state, in the way that other states are the sovereign expressions of other peoples; and it is a state that includes minorities. Those minorities may feel alienated from the national myth and the national anthem. But surely their alienation is not the whole story. There is also the matter of their civil and political enfranchisement. What a minority loses in symbols, it gains in rights. Or are we to prefer a state and a society that is ethnically and religiously homogeneous? The sensitive revisionist souls who want to do away with the Jewish national anthem live in a world in which the only alternatives are an empty universalism or a totalizing particularism. But Israel is a different kind of experiment: a democratic multiethnicity. No, Israel's democracy, from the standpoint of its Arab citizens, is not perfect. But who will be so foolish as to suggest that the experiment has failed? Anyway, the great conflict is not over yet. Despite Madrid and Oslo, the relationship between the Arabs of Palestine and Israel is still warlike. And not even a vast withdrawal of Israel from the territories will affect the conflict in its depths. It is too old, and it is sanctioned by each and every demagogue on the Arab street.

The Zionists brought to Zion at least three advantages. The first was pragmatism, practicality, a willingness to compromise. Their state is itself a monument to compromise: the Zionists took what they could get, and renounced the map of their dreams, because the Jews were in misery, and this was intolerable. Practicality is sometimes a form of morality. And at a time when population transfers were "solving" other national disputes, such as those between Turkey and Greece and between India and Pakistan, the Zionists did not for a moment think that Palestine couldn't be shared.

The second advantage was that the Zionists came with a confident notion of what their nation was, a confidence springing from the fact that this was the nation that more or less invented the idea of peoplehood. This people and the idea of this people have always been tied to one land. The Jewish attitude toward Jerusalem (and Palestine) was not merely nostalgia. Nostalgia is what some Jews may still feel about what they once had, say, in Spain or in Poland or in Baghdad. But Spain and Poland and Baghdad were addresses, not ideals, as Avi Erlich argues in his provocative book *Ancient Zionism*. Similarly, the Arabs lost much in historic Palestine and in Jerusalem; but there is no sacred Muslim ideal of these places. The fact is that, for a thousand years and more, Muslims prayed in the direction of Mecca and Jews prayed in the direction of Jerusalem. And there is no secular ideal attached to Palestine either, as there is a secular ideal of Zion.

The third advantage of Zionism was the advantage of the modern. For this reason, Zionism was a genuine revolution in its region. Was modernity a foreign, Western import, as the critics like to say? Of course. That is why it worked. It did not mistake authenticity for backwardness. And so it traumatized its neighbors not only with nationalism, but also with science, with industry, with agriculture, with the whole gleaming consumerist oasis that it devised. And these chasms will not be easily bridged, even if peace ever comes. For the fear of the modern is always accompanied by envy; and this envy fires bullets from guns and activates bombs. The fanatics of faith, the "martyrs" and those who cheer and weep for the martyrs, do not wish only to stop the advance of the Jews; they wish also to stop the advance of the moderns. But the Jews and the moderns are in the land to stay. Herzl said that the Zionist goal was to have the Jewish people "live at last as free men on our own soil, and in our homes peacefully die." The first of these aims has been achieved. The second will be a long time in coming.

Article 10   *The New Republic*, April 28, 1997

Does Jerusalem really matter to Islam?

IF I FORGET THEE

By Daniel Pipes

The architects of the Oslo peace accords understood Jerusalem's power. Fearing that even discussing the holy city's future would detonate the fragile truce between Israelis and Palestinians, they tried to defer the issue until everything else had been settled. But it is now all too clear that this approach has failed. Last September, riots met the opening of a new entrance to the ancient Hasmonean tunnel, while the recent building of apartments on an empty plot in eastern Jerusalem has brought the Netanyahu-Arafat dialogue to a bitter and bloody standstill. And so the international actors must begin to do what they had hoped to postpone: sort through the Jews' and Muslims' conflicting claims on the city King David entered three millennia ago.

DANIEL PIPES is editor of the *Middle East Quarterly* and author of *The Hidden Hand: Middle East Fears of Conspiracy* (St. Martin's Press).

The debate matters. In Jerusalem, theological and historical arguments matter, serving often as the functional equivalent of legal claims. The strength of these arguments will ultimately help determine who governs the city. Already we hear the ritual and relativistic cliché that Jerusalem is "a city holy to both peoples." But, like many clichés, this one is more false than true. Jerusalem stands as the paramount religious city of Judaism, a place so holy that not just its soil but even its air is deemed sacred. Jews pray in its direction, invoke its name at the end of each meal and close the Passover service with the wistful statement "Next year in Jerusalem."

In contrast, Jerusalem is not the place to which Muslims pray. It is not directly connected to any events in Mohammed's life. And it is not even mentioned by name in the Koran. The city never became a cultural center or served as capital of a sovereign Muslim state. Jerusalem has mattered to Muslims only intermittently over the past thirteen centuries, and when it has mattered, as it does today, it has been because of politics.

The story begins in A.D. 622, when the prophet Mohammed fled his hometown of Mecca for Medina, a city with a substantial Jewish population. He adopted a number of practices friendly to Jews—a Yom Kippur-like fast, a synagogue-like house of prayer and kosher-style dietary laws. Mohammed also adopted the Judaic practice of facing the Temple Mount in Jerusalem during prayer. "He chose the Holy House in Jerusalem in order that the People of the Book [i.e., Jews] would be conciliated," notes at-Tabari, an early Muslim commentator on the Koran, "and the Jews were glad." Modern historians agree: W. Montgomery Watt, a leading biographer of Mohammed, interprets the prophet's "far-reaching concessions to Jewish feeling" as part of his "desire for a reconciliation with the Jews."

But Jews criticized the new faith and rejected Mohammed's gestures, leading Mohammed eventually to break with them, probably early in 624. The most dramatic sign of this change came in a Koranic passage (2:142–52) ordering the faithful no longer to pray toward Syria but toward Mecca instead. (The Koran and other sources only mention the direction as "Syria"; other information makes it clear that "Syria" means Jerusalem.) This episode initiated a pattern that would be repeated many times over the succeeding centuries: Muslims have taken serious religious interest in Jerusalem at times when it has most conspicuously served them politically; and when the political climate has changed, the religious interest has flagged.

In the century after Mohammed's death, politics prompted the Damascus-based Umayyad dynasty, which controlled Jerusalem, to make the city sacred in Islam. Embroiled in fierce competition with a dissident leader in Mecca, the Umayyad rulers were seeking to diminish Arabia at Jerusalem's expense. They sponsored a genre of literature praising the "virtues of Jerusalem" and circulated accounts of the prophet's sayings or doings (called *hadiths*) favorable to Jerusalem. In 688–91, they built Islam's first grand structure, the Dome of the Rock, on top of the remains of the Jewish Temple.

They even reinterpreted the Koran to make room for Jerusalem. The Koran, describing Mohammed's Night Journey (*isra'*), reads: "[God] takes His servant [i.e., Mohammed] by night from the Sacred Mosque to the furthest mosque." When this Koranic passage was first revealed, in about 621, a place called the Sacred Mosque already existed in Mecca. In contrast, the "furthest mosque" was a turn of phrase, not a place. Some early Muslims understood it as metaphorical or as a place in heaven. And if the "furthest mosque" did exist on earth, Palestine would have seemed an unlikely location, for that region elsewhere in the Koran (30:1) was called "the closest land" (*adna al-ard*).

But, in 715, the Umayyads built a mosque in Jerusalem, again right on the Temple Mount, and called it the Furthest Mosque (*al-Masjid al-Aqsa,* or al-Aqsa Mosque). With this, the Umayyads not only inserted Jerusalem into the Koran but retroactively gave it a prominent role in Mohammed's life. For if the "furthest mosque" is in Jerusalem, then Mohammed's Night Journey and his subsequent ascension to heaven (*mi'raj*) also took place on the Temple Mount.

But Jerusalem still mattered theologically only when it mattered politically, and when the Umayyad dynasty collapsed in 750, Jerusalem fell into near-obscurity. For the next three and a half centuries, books praising the city lost favor and the construction of glorious buildings not only stopped, but existing ones fell apart (the Dome over the rock collapsed in 1016). "Learned men are few, and the Christians numerous," bemoaned a tenth-century Muslim native of Jerusalem. The rulers of the new dynasty bled Jerusalem and the surrounding country through what F. E. Peters of New York University calls "their rapacity and their careless indifference."

By the early tenth century, notes Peters, Muslim rule over Jerusalem had an "almost casual" quality with "no particular political significance." In fact, even the Crusade conquest of the city in 1099 initially aroused only a mild Muslim response: "one does not detect either shock or a sense of religious loss and humiliation," notes Emmanuel Sivan of the Hebrew University, a scholar of the era.

Only as the military effort to retake Jerusalem grew serious in about 1150 did Muslim leaders stress Jerusalem's importance to Islam. Once again, *hadiths* about Jerusalem's sanctity and books about the "virtues of Jerusalem" appeared. One *hadith* put words into the prophet Mohammed's mouth saying that, after his own death, Jerusalem's falling to the infidels is the second greatest catastrophe facing Islam.

Once safely back in Muslim hands after Saladin's reconquest, however, interest in Jerusalem dropped, to the point where one of Saladin's grandsons temporarily ceded the city in 1229 to Emperor Friedrich II in return for the German's promise of military aid against his brother. But learning that Jerusalem was back in Christian hands again provoked intense Muslim emotions. As a result, in 1244, Muslims retook the city. The psychology at work bears note: that Christian knights traveled from distant lands to make Jerusalem their capital made the city more valuable in Muslim eyes. Sivan writes, "It was a city strongly coveted by the enemies of the faith, and thus became, in a sort of mirror-image syndrome, dear to Muslim hearts."

The city then lapsed into its usual obscurity for nearly eight centuries. The Temple Mount sanctuaries were abandoned and became dilapidated. Under Ottoman rule (1516–1917), Jerusalem suffered the indignity of being treated as a tax farm for non-resident, one-year (and therefore very rapacious) officials. The Turkish authorities raised funds by gouging European visitors, and so made little effort to promote Jerusalem's economy. The tax rolls show soap as the city's only export. In 1611, George Sandys found that "Much lies waste; the old buildings (except a few) all ruined, the new contemptible." Gustav Flaubert of *Madame Bovary* fame visited in 1850 and found "ruins everywhere." Mark Twain in 1867 wrote that Jerusalem "has lost all its ancient grandeur, and [has] become a pauper village."

In modern times, notes the Israeli scholar Hava Lazarus-Yafeh, Jerusalem "became the focus of religious and political Arab activity only at the beginning of the present century, and only because of the renewed Jewish activity in the city and Judaism's claims on the Western Wailing Wall." British rule over the city, lasting from 1917 to 1948, also galvanized Muslim passion for Jerusalem. The Palestinian leader (and mufti of Jerusalem) Hajj Amin al-Husayni made the Temple Mount central to his anti-Zionist efforts, raising funds throughout the Arab world for the restoration of the Dome of the Rock. Arab politicians made Jerusalem a prominent destination; Iraqi leaders frequently turned up, where they demonstrably prayed at al-Aqsa and gave rousing speeches.

But, when Muslims retook the Old City with its Islamic sanctuaries in 1948, they quickly lost interest in it. An initial excitement stirred when the Jordanian forces took the walled city in 1948—as evidenced by the Coptic bishop's crowning of King Abdallah as "King of Jerusalem" in November of that year—but then the usual ennui set in. The Hashemites had little affection for Jerusalem, where some of their most devoted enemies lived and where Abdallah himself was shot dead in 1951. In fact, the Hashemites made a concerted effort to diminish the holy city's importance in favor of their capital, Amman. Jerusalem had once served as the British administrative capital, but now all government offices there (save tourism) were shut down. The Jordanians also closed some local institutions (e.g., the Arab Higher Committee) and moved others to Amman (the treasury of the Palestinian *waqf*, or religious endowment).

Their effort succeeded. Once again, Arab Jerusalem became an isolated provincial town, now even less important than Nablus. The economy stagnated and many thousands left Arab Jerusalem. While the population of Amman increased five-fold in the period 1948–67, Jerusalem's grew just 50 percent. Amman was chosen as the site of the country's first university as well as of the royal family's many residences. Perhaps most insulting of all,

Jordanian radio broadcast the Friday prayers not from al-Aqsa Mosque but from a mosque in Amman.

Nor was Jordan alone in ignoring Jerusalem; the city virtually disappeared from the Arab diplomatic map. No foreign Arab leader came to Jerusalem between 1948 and 1967, and even King Hussein visited only rarely. King Faisal of Saudi Arabia often spoke after 1967 of yearning to pray in Jerusalem, yet he appears never to have bothered to pray there when he had the chance. Perhaps most remarkable is that the Palestinian Liberation Organization's founding document, the Palestinian National Covenant of 1964, does not even mention Jerusalem once.

All this abruptly changed after June 1967, when the Old City came under Israeli control. As in the British period, Palestinians again made Jerusalem the centerpiece of their political program. Pictures of the Dome of the Rock turned up everywhere, from Yasir Arafat's office to the corner grocery. The PLO's 1968 Constitution described Jerusalem as "the seat of the Palestine Liberation Organization."

Nor were Palestinians alone in their renewed interest. "As during the era of the Crusaders," Lazarus-Yafeh points out, many Muslim leaders "began again to emphasize the sanctity of Jerusalem in Islamic tradition," even dusting off old *hadiths* to back up their claims. Jerusalem became a mainstay of Arab League and United Nations resolutions. The formerly stingy Jordanian and Saudi governments now gave munificently to the Jerusalem *waqf*.

As it was under the British mandate, Jerusalem has since 1967 again become the primary vehicle for mobilizing international Muslim opinion. A fire at al-Aqsa Mosque in 1969 gave Saudi King Faisal the occasion to convene twenty-five Muslim heads of state and establish the Organization of the Islamic Conference, a United Nations for Muslims. Since the Islamic Revolution, Iran's one-rial coin and 1,000-rial banknote have featured the Dome of the Rock. Iranian soldiers at war with Saddam Hussein's forces in the 1980s received primitive maps marking a path through Iraq and onto Jerusalem. Ayatollah Khomeini decreed the last Friday of Ramadan Jerusalem Day.

Since Israeli occupation, some ideologues have sought to establish the historical basis of Islamic attachment to Jerusalem by raising three main arguments, all of them historically dubious. First, they assert a Muslim connection to Jerusalem that predates the Jewish one. Ghada Talhami, a scholar at Lake Forest College, asserts that "There are other holy cities in Islam, but Jerusalem holds a special place in the hearts and minds of Muslims because its fate has always been intertwined with theirs." Always? Jerusalem's founding antedated Islam by about two millennia, so how can that be? Ibrahim Hooper, national communications director for the Washington-based Council on American-Islamic Relations, explains: "the Muslim attachment to Jerusalem does not begin with the prophet Muhammad, it begins with the prophets Abraham, David, Solomon and Jesus, who are also prophets in Islam." In other words, the central figures of Judaism and Christianity were really proto-Muslims.

Second, and equally anachronistic, is the claim that the Koran mentions Jerusalem. Hooper (and others) argue that "the Koran refers to Jerusalem by its Islamic center-piece, al-Aqsa Mosque." But this makes no sense: a mosque built a century after the Koran was delivered cannot establish what a Koranic verse originally meant.

Third, some Muslims deny Jerusalem's importance to Jews. Abd al-Malik Dahamshe, an Arab member of Israel's parliament, flatly stated last month that "the Western Wall is not associated with the remains of the Jewish Temple." A fundamentalist Israeli Arab leader went further and announced that "It's prohibited for Jews to pray at the Western Wall." Or, in the succinct wording of a recent Palestinian protest banner: "Jerusalem is Arab."

Despite the loud assertions that Jerusalem is essential to Islam, the religion does contain a recessive but persistent strain of anti-Jerusalem sentiment. Perhaps the most prominent adherent of this view was Ibn Taymiya (1263–1328), one of Islam's strictest and most influential religious thinkers. (The Wahhabis of Arabia are his modern-day successors.) In an attempt to purify Islam of accretions and impieties, Ibn Taymiya dismissed the sacredness of Jerusalem as a notion deriving from Jews and Christians, and from the long-ago Umayyad rivalry with Mecca. More broadly, learned Muslims living in the years following the Crusades knew that the great publicity given to *hadiths* extolling Jerusalem's sanctity resulted from the Countercrusade—that is, from political exigency—and treated it warily.

Recalling that God once had Muslims direct their prayers toward Jerusalem and then turned them instead toward Mecca, some early *hadiths* suggested that Muslims specifically pray facing away from Jerusalem, a rejection that still survives in vestigial form; he who prays in al-Aqsa Mosque not coincidentally shows his back to the Temple area toward which Jews pray.

In Jerusalem, these theological and historical arguments are in essence legal claims, crucial to who prevails. In this context, the fact that politics has so long fueled the Muslim attachment to Jerusalem has two implications. First, it points to the relative weakness of the Islamic connection, one that arises as much from mundane need as from the immutable claims of faith. Second, it suggests that the Muslim interest lies not so much in controlling Jerusalem as in denying control over the city to anyone else. Jerusalem will never be more than a secondary city for Muslims.

Mecca, by contrast, is the eternal city of Islam, the place where Muslims believe Abraham nearly sacrificed Isaac's brother Ishmael and toward which Muslims pray five times each day. Non-Muslims are strictly forbidden there, and the city's "very mention reverberates awe in Muslims' hearts," writes Abad Ahmad of the Islamic Society of Central Jersey. Very roughly speaking, what Jerusalem is to Jews, Mecca is to Muslims. And just as Muslims rule an undivided Mecca, so Jews should rule an undivided Jerusalem.

Article 11

ARCHAEOLOGY, May/June 1997

Atlantis of the Sands

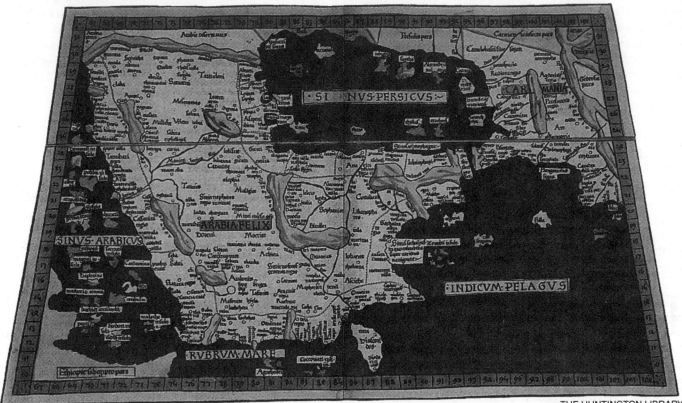

Southern Oman yields ruins of an ancient city on the fabled frankincense route.

By Juris Zarins

In 1930 the British explorer Bertram Thomas set out across the Rub al-Khali, or Empty Quarter, in central Arabia. As he approached its southern edge his guide, pointing to the faint outline of a road, remarked, "Look Sahib, there is the way to Ubar. It was a great city, rich in treasure, with date gardens and a fort of red silver. It now lies buried beneath the sands. . . ." Thomas had heard about Ubar on previous journeys through central Arabia, but no one could say where it was. He called it the "Atlantis of the Sands" and speculated that it might have been a trading center in southern Oman's Dhofar province. Herodotus, Pliny the Elder, Strabo, and other ancient authors, though not specifically mentioning Ubar, gave brief accounts of cities in southern Arabia that marketed resins from frankincense and myrrh trees.

While it is certain that people of the Dhofar area grew rich trading these commodities, it would appear that the city of Ubar was an *Arabian Nights* fantasy. Arab historians have referred to Ubar as a region, and no city of that name appears on maps of the second-century A.D. Greek geographer Ptolemy. Since 1990 I have been looking for remains of a commercial center splendid enough to inspire such a myth.

The search began with a close study of the classical sources. Herodotus, Pliny, Ptolemy, and Strabo are all fairly clear about maritime trade routes. Myrrh and frankincense resins were brought from inland areas of

Cities in center of 1482 copy of Ptolemy's map of Arabia, such as Iula, Marimatha, and Thabane, may have been settlements within Iobaritae tribal land, a region later named Ubar after this tribe.

Dhofar to the coastal towns of Moscha, modern Khor Rohri in southeastern Oman, and Syagrus, modern Ras Fartak in eastern Yemen. Land routes led from Dhofar west to cities such as Shabwah, Timna, and Marib in Yemen, then north through western Arabia to Gaza or east to Wadi Sirhan in northern Saudi Arabia. Ptolemy's maps and the *Periplus,* a collection of anonymous reports by ancient sailors, describe an Omanum Emporium, a trading center located either in Dhofar or as far east as Qatar. Ptolemy mentions frankincense trees near the territory of the Iobaritae tribe in southeastern Oman, and the area may have been named Ubar after this tribe. Other centers on Ptolemy's map such as Iula, Marimatha, and Thabane in the interior of Dhofar may have been settlements within Iobaritae tribal territory. Arab historians say these people lived in a region called Al Akhaf, perhaps modern Dhofar, and that trade cross the Rub al-Khali continued well into the nineteenth century.

Studying Ptolemy's map, Nicholas Clapp and George Hedges, the organizers of our expedition, decided to search the interior of Dhofar using the longitude and latitude recorded by Bertram Thomas for the portion of ancient road system he saw at the edge of the Rub al-Khali as a starting point. They asked for help from the Jet Propulsion Laboratory (JPL) in Pasadena, whose satellite images revealed faint traces of ancient roads. Encouraged by these images, Hedges, Clapp, the JPL's Ron Blom, the explorer Sir Ranulph Fiennes, and I visited the area in the summer of 1990. We traced some 20 miles of road between fields of dunes, but located few archaeological remains.

On subsequent visits to oases in the Dhofar region we discovered red- and black-polished ceramics of the classical period (after 300 B.C.). Based on these finds, we became convinced that the road at the edge of the Rub al-Khali was linked to ancient urban centers mentioned in classical sources and Arab histories. We chose to study Shisur, a ruined city some 90 miles northwest of Salalah on the edge of the desert. A permanent spring there had attracted people since the Neolithic (ca. 5000–2500 B.C.), and a fortress first built during the Bronze Age (2500–1300 B.C.) was in use until A.D. 1500. Bedouin still camp there year-round.

Visitors including the British explorer Wilfred Thesiger (1948) and archaeologists from Harvard University and the Danish Archaeological Survey (1972) had already noted remains of fortifications at the site. Our initial survey revealed the presence of flint materials probably from the Neolithic or Bronze Age. We found red- and black-polished, dot-and-circle, and painted ceramics of a pre-Islamic date (before A.D. 650). We also found several rough-cut stone blocks, partitions along a wall, and remains of a tower described by Thomas and Thesiger.

Between 1992 and 1994 we uncovered a fortress and administrative center that had protected the water supply from raiding bedouin tribes. A seven-and-one-half-foot-high wall surrounded the top of a collapsed cavern leading to the spring. The wall had fallen in places, especially along the western side where a large gate complex once stood. Abutments, or small walls, had been built within it, creating partitions for stalls or rooms. We found the remains of towers in corners inside the wall and just outside it. Debris covered almost the entire wall system. Further excavation revealed irregularities in the wall's height resulting from the removal of stones to build a small fort in 1950. It became clear that the fortress had formed a focal point for people in the region. Small villages that served as camps for caravans moving goods to east Arabia or south to the coast surround the site. These date to the classical or Islamic periods. Thesiger reported evidence of an extensive farming system including plow marks and irrigation channels.

The site was occupied for the first time in the Neolithic, around 5000 B.C.. Because of the construction of the fortress, little remains from this early period. We have found typical Neolithic cores, axes, blades, scrapers, and grinding stones in garbage dumps and built into the fort walls. The recovery of such material links the site with at least 60 other settlement remains concentrated on the ancient river systems in southern Dhofar. Whether or not the site was inhabited continuously after 5000 B.C. is difficult to determine since we do not yet have a clear idea when the earliest ceramics were used in the region. Northern Oman has a ceramic tradition dating back to 4500 B.C., but we know little of its relationship to Dhofar at that date. Comparison with artifacts from sites in Yemen indicate that ceramics could have been brought to the area by 2400 B.C. Some of the simple burnished bowls at Shisur may date to the second millennium B.C. The earliest walls and dwellings at the site were erected sometime after 1000 B.C., and by 500 B.C. Iron Age ceramics such as burnished red wares appear. Dot-and-circle ware is present in great quantities. We first found this type of pottery in 1993 at the site of Al Balid, located in the city of Salalah in southern Oman. Its presence there and at Shisur suggests there was a trade network between interior and coastal Dhofar. Vessels with an overturned, incised rim and constricted neck opening into a larger body are unique to Shisur. A finely burnished red ware introduced by the Parthians in northern Oman ca. 250 B.C. suggests a close tie between the northern and southern parts of the country.

The ceramic material from the Iron Age (1300–300 B.C.) and classical period (300 B.C.–A.D. 500) make it virtually certain that this was a principal city on Ptolemy's map. Ceramic ties with eastern Arabia, such as classical and Hellenistic red wares with incised and appliqué decoration, indicate a long history of trade across the Rub al-Khali, one that originated in the Neolithic with obsidian and seashells as barter items and continued until A.D. 1500. But which city on Ptolemy's map was Shisur? Based on its location within the area of the Iobaritae tribal territory, we believe it is the town of Marimatha. Late nineteenth- and early twentieth-century scholars believed Shisur might have been the Omanum Emporium mentioned in Pliny and the *Periplus*, but this name may have been used for a larger market area, not a permanent settlement. Be that as it may, Shisur was a city with ties to both Parthia in the east and the Hadramaut (modern Yemen) in the west, suggesting that it may have linked all parts of southern Arabia. The frankincense trade declined with the economic collapse of the western Roman Empire during the fifth and sixth centuries A.D. and with the subsequent Christian church prohibition of the use of frankincense for elaborate funeral rites. The Roman collapse resulted in a precipitous economic decline in the entire south Arabian area.

We believe Shisur was a key trading center that linked Dhofar to eastern Arabia and early Mesopotamian civilizations. Classical writers, such as Pliny the Elder and Ptolemy, and early Islamic sources, such as the Omani epic *Kashf al-Gumma*, refer to a people of Ad in Dhofar and describe their involvement in the incense trade. Almost certainly, this is also the period of interaction between the Ad and Arab tribes called the Omani. The Ad may have been the ancestors of modern tribes living in the Dhofar mountains: the Semitic, non-Arabic-speaking Mahra, Shahra, and others. Even today the Mahra and Shahra control much of the frankincense region, and local bedouin harvest the resin for them. One way to identify the ancestors of the modern Dhofaris is to study triliths, small, three-stone monuments set in rows in Mahra tribal territory sometime between 150 B.C. and A.D. 200. Many are inscribed with a south Arabic script that has yet to be deciphered. We think these triliths may have served ritual purposes, possibly connected with Persian-influenced Zoroastrian practices that centered on the harvest. Because many are located along caravan routes, they may have been associated with the frankincense trade. The more we learn from the triliths about the ancestors of the Mahra and Shahra, the more we will learn about Shisur's importance as a trade center.

Shisur was abandoned shortly after the Portuguese navigator Alfonso d'Albuquerque conquered Muscat in 1508, disrupting Omani ocean trade networks. Inland sites bore the brunt of the decline in trade, were gradually deserted, and were in time covered by the sands.

Juris Zarins *is a professor of archaeology at Southwest Missouri State University.*

Article 12   *The World Today*, August/September 1997

Middle East

Life With the Enemy: the one-state solution

The policy of the present Israeli government has made the option of a Palestinian state less workable and less likely. As an alternative, a single democratic state including Israelis and Palestinians might seem utopian, but it is a route to a stable region.

Ghada Karmi

As THE MIDDLE EAST PEACE PROCESS LUMBERS TO-WARDS WHAT should be its final phase, with the permanent status talks between the two sides supposedly next on the agenda, one idea for the future seems to have taken firm hold. A two-state solution for the Palestinian/Israeli conflict has become accepted dogma.

This is not a new concept, but it has never before enjoyed such credence. It was first raised in 1974, when the Palestine National Council (PNC) voted at its 12th meeting to establish a Palestinian 'authority' on any liberated part of the Palestinian homeland. Since then, the Palestinian leadership has consistently aimed for an independent state, to be set up in the West Bank and Gaza, most of which is currently under Israeli occupation, with East Jerusalem as its capital.

After the Oslo Accords were signed in 1993, this position crystallised and found support, both tacit and overt, from the Arab world and the international community—with the exception of Israel and the United States. The Arab League had in any case embraced 'Palestine' as a member state in 1976.

Although the exact boundaries of the proposed state have not been defined, even by the Palestinians, and international support has not expressed itself in terms of

GHADA KARMI is a Research Associate at the Centre of Near and Middle Eastern Studies of the School of Oriental and African Studies in London. Her book *Jerusalem Today: What Future for the Peace Process?* (London: Ithaca Press) was published last year.

square metres of land which might constitute the new state, the idea of such an entity 'alongside Israel' has been accepted. Today, it so dominates discussion about the final outcome of the peace process as to exclude all other possibilities.

POCK-MARKED BY SETTLEMENTS

Yet, it is by no means certain that the two-state solution for this intractable conflict is either feasible or desirable. If we take first the question of feasibility, we see at once that there are considerable logistical obstacles in the way of a Palestinian state. A glance at the latest map of the occupied territories explains the position. This shows a West Bank pock-marked by Jewish settlements encircling Palestinian towns and separating them from each other, criss-crossed by so-called bypass roads built for the exclusive use of Israelis and breaking up Palestinian territory even more.

Sharing the West Bank and Gaza with the Palestinians are 140,000 Jews, living in over 14 urban and 82 rural settlements. In addition there are eleven residential areas in and around East Jerusalem, giving this part of the city a Jewish population of 200,000.

When the latest development at Jabal Abu Ghoneim (Har Homa) is built to the south of Jerusalem, the separation between Jerusalem and the West Bank will be complete. The map thus shows no territorial continuity between the Palestinian areas in the West Bank, which are cut off from each other, from Gaza and from Jerusalem.

If the settlements remain, then any projected Palestinian state would have no meaningful territory on which to become established. The problem is further complicated by the lack of natural resources in the Palestinian

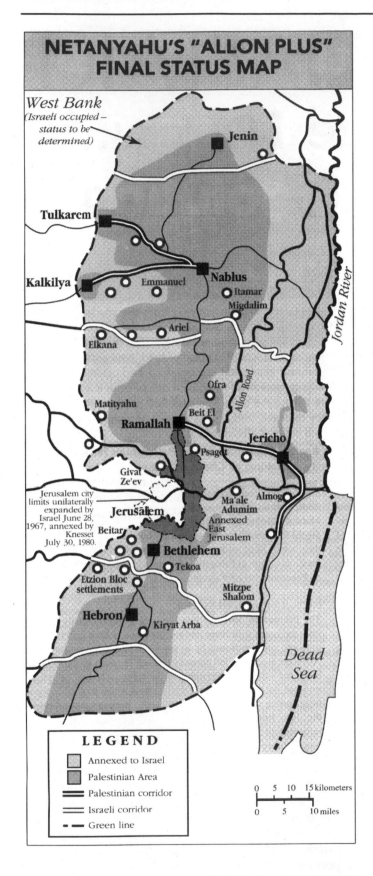

NETANYAHU'S "ALLON PLUS" FINAL STATUS MAP

West Bank
(Israeli occupied –
status to be
determined)

Jenin

Tulkarem

Kalkilya

Emmanuel

Nablus

Itamar

Migdalim

Ariel

Elkana

Ofra

Allon Road

Matityahu

Beit El

Ramallah

Jericho

Psagot

Givat
Ze'ev

Jerusalem city
limits unilaterally
expanded by
Israel June 28,
1967, annexed by
Knesset
July 30, 1980.

Jerusalem

Ma'ale
Adumim   Almog

Annexed
East
Jerusalem

Beitar

Bethlehem

Tekoa

Etzion Bloc
settlements

Mitzpe
Shalom

Hebron

Kiryat Arba

*Dead
Sea*

Jordan River

LEGEND

Annexed to Israel
Palestinian Area
Palestinian corridor
Israeli corridor
Green line

| 0 | 5 | 10 | 15 kilometers |
| 0 | 5 | | 10 miles |

(Map from the Foundation for Middle East Peace/Andy Hemstreet)

areas. One of the effects of thirty years of Israeli occupation has been a transfer of those resources from Palestinian inhabitants to the settlers. Thus, Meron Benvenisti, the former deputy mayor of Jerusalem and an expert on the West Bank, calculated in 1989 that 90 per cent of its cultivable land and 75 per cent of its water had been switched to the settlers and beyond them to Israel.[1]

Since the Palestinian economy is heavily dependent on agriculture—in 1991 it accounted for 35 per cent of the West Bank and Gaza's GDP, compared with 2 per cent for Israel—this depletion of land and water is extremely serious. To make matters worse, there was a significant lack of investment in the infrastructure of the West Bank and Gaza throughout the years of Israeli occupation.

Unskilled labouring in Israel consequently became a major economic activity for Palestinians from the Occupied Territories. In 1990, nearly 35 per cent of the Palestinian labour force was working in Israel. These factors made the already weakened Palestinian economy heavily dependent on Israel.

DETERIORATED FURTHER

Since 1993, the economic situation in the Palestinian territories has deteriorated further as a result of the Israeli closures of Gaza and the West Bank and the importation into Israel of foreign labour. The Palestinian areas are thus disadvantaged by high unemployment, trade restrictions, an undeveloped industrial base and poor natural resources. Any Palestinian state set up on this basis is obviously not viable and could only survive with a massive infusion of billions of dollars' worth of aid.

A different approach would be needed to change the situation, for example the lifting of closures and a willingness to share resources equitably. But recent events in Israel are not encouraging.

The Israeli government has instituted a vigorous programme of settlement expansion with a target to settle 500,000 Jews in the Palestinian territories by the turn of the century. It has declared East Jerusalem non-negotiable. The closures are still in place and no Israeli withdrawal under the Oslo Agreement has taken place since that from Hebron in February. On 5 June, Israel's Prime Minister, Benjamin Netanyahu, set out his vision for the final settlement with the Palestinians (see map).

According to this, Israel would keep most of the land and control all the resources. East Jerusalem would remain part of Israel's 'united capital' for ever. All Israeli settlements and their connecting roads would stay, leaving about 40 per cent of the West Bank and 60 per cent of Gaza for the Palestinians. In the West Bank, there would be three Palestinian cantons around Nablus, Hebron and Jericho, not connected with each other or with Gaza.

This plan is not new, a similar version having been put forward in 1968 by the then Labour party leader, Yigal Allon, but its significance is that it makes a nonsense of the idea of a Palestinian state. Without the removal of the settlements and a withdrawal from East Jerusalem, the formula put forward for a Palestinian state with East Jerusalem as its capital simply cannot work. To realise the aim of the two states, one would have to postulate either an Israeli renunciation of the settlements and East Jerusalem, or an external force willing to pressure Israel into this. Neither is on offer.

For these reasons, a Palestinian state as envisaged is not feasible, and the situation on the ground makes even a physical separation of the two peoples hard to achieve. Abandoning the two-state solution in favour of one state to include both peoples would seem the obvious alternative. Currently, such an idea will provoke strong opposition, but there are several good reasons why it should not be dismissed out of hand.

DEMOCRATIC PALESTINE

The history of the single-state solution goes back nearly thirty years. The proposal to create what was then called a secular democratic state in Palestine was first put forward in 1969 by the Palestine Liberation Organisation (PLO) and formally adopted in the modified version of a 'democratic state of Palestine' by the 6th PNC meeting the same year.[2] This was described as a state in all of historic Palestine wherein Muslims, Christians and Jews would enjoy the same rights, free from religious and sectarian discrimination. Hebrew and Arabic would be the official languages. The intention was to offer liberation not only for the Palestinians but for the Jews as well, whom the PLO saw as condemned by Zionism to live in the perpetual insecurity of a Jewish state.[3]

With a few exceptions, this proposal met with rejection on both sides. The Israelis considered it quite simply a recipe for their destruction, and the Palestinians thought it an unacceptable concession to the enemy and worried that in such a state the more advanced Jews would dominate. In reality, it should be seen as a remarkable psychological breakthrough on the part of the Palestinian[s], who were offering to embrace in equality the very people who had dispossessed them—an offer, incidentally, which has never been reciprocated even remotely by any Israeli leader. However, it was never followed through by either side and the idea was quietly dropped after 1974, as the option of a West Bank state began to unfold.

In recent times, and faced with the current political impasse, the idea of one state for the two peoples has begun to resurface among left-wing Israelis and diaspora Palestinians, albeit from varying perspectives and for different motives.[4] The debate centres on what form this state should take, whether binational or secular and democratic.

In a binational state Jews and Palestinians would co-exist as separate communities guaranteed the legal right to use their own language, religion and traditions. Both would participate in government—not necessarily on an equal basis. Such a state would be the homeland of both communities and could be modelled on the cantonal structure of Switzerland or the Belgian arrangement between Flemings and Walloons.[5]

The democratic secular state, on the other hand—an idea this author supports—envisages a one-man, one-vote polity without reference to ethnicity or creed. It would aim to create an equitable pluralist society on the Western democratic model. It is opposed to an arrangement of separate communities.

The details of these proposals cannot be entered into here, but irrespective of which system is chosen, the one-state solution is unlikely to find acceptance amongst the mass of Palestinians or Israelis. For the former, it means the end of the dream of a sovereign Palestinian state which had become familiar and seemed until recently so attainable. For the latter, the secular democratic state would spell the end of Zionism and force them to share with non-Jews the land they view as exclusively Jewish. For both, the prospect of life with the enemy, after decades of hatred, would seem highly unpalatable.

And yet, there is no other way forward now. Ironically enough, it is the Israeli government's annexationist policies in the Occupied Territories which have destroyed the two-state option. In fragmenting the West Bank so effectively, it has ensured that no separate state can exist there and thus opened the door to the one-state alternative.

The late Yitzhak Rabin, aware that such a danger would ensue if the Palestinians were not given their own state, tried to safeguard the Zionist ideal by entering into the Oslo agreement with the PLO. Many observers believe that the previous Israeli Labour government would ultimately have ceded enough land to make a Palestinian entity possible. Thanks to the present government's policies, however, that is no longer feasible. Nor, from a Palestinian viewpoint, is it even desirable. A two-state solution, had it ever happened, would have been unstable and ultimately unacceptable to the Palestinians for a number of reasons.

It would have given them at best a truncated entity, almost certainly demilitarised and economically dependent, on a fifth of their original homeland. Even if they were offered the whole of the West Bank, Gaza and East Jerusalem, these would form only 23 per cent of Mandate Palestine. It would be unable to absorb the four million displaced Palestinians, and would end any hope of their right to return to their homes. Most seriously, it would have set the seal of approval on the Zionist claim to Palestine as the exclusive land of the Jews, which no Palestinian has ever accepted.

RESOLVING INJUSTICE

The Palestinians' sense of injustice, which fundamentally derives from the loss of their homeland and the denial of their right to return to it, will not be redressed by an unequal arrangement of two states. And if the injustice is left unresolved, it will remain a source of instability and a cause of 'terrorism' in the region. The past cannot be reversed, but a solution even at this late stage which permits the equitable sharing of the whole land between the two peoples and repatriates the refugees will help lay the foundations for a stable future.

A secular democratic state will not be easy to achieve and may indeed seem utopian now—but surely no less so than the Zionist dream of establishing a Jewish state in someone else's country must have seemed at the first Zionist Congress in Basle exactly one hundred years ago.

NOTES

1. Quoted in the *New York Times*, 22 October 1989, p. A18.
2. Aryeh Yodafat, Yuval Arnon-Ohanna, PLO Strategy and Tactics (London, 1981) pp. 55–7.
3. David Hirst, *The Gun and the Olive Branch*. (London, 1977). p. 292.
4. Yair Sheleg, Kol Ha'ir, 31 January 1997.
5. Jenab Tutunji, Kamal Khalidi, 'A binational state in Palestine: the rational and moral choice', *International Affairs*, Vol. 73, January 1997, pp. 31–59.

Article 13

ARCHAEOLOGY, May/June 1997

Digging in the Land of Magan

Excavations yield evidence of cultures spanning some 8,000 years.

By M. Redha Bhacker and Bernadette Bhacker

Oman's early settlers were Neolithic pastoralists and seafaring people who worked trade routes from Mesopotamia to the Indus Valley. Arrowheads found in Qatar in 1960 by Danish prehistorian Holgar Kapel and ash from ancient campfires found in Muscat in 1983 are the earliest evidence of the nomads who followed their flocks south from the Levant, settling the Arabian peninsula 8,000 years ago. Remains of Neolithic camps found during the past three decades suggest that as Arabia's climate became wetter, these herders thrived, roaming in widely dispersed groups from Syria and Iraq in the north to Dhofar in southern Oman.

The resources of the Arabian Gulf supported fishing communities along the coast. In the 1970s Italian archaeologists unearthed shell and fishbone middens, evidence of a 7,000-year-old fishing village at Ras al Hamra, a rocky promontory in Qurum, then miles west of Muscat. When excavations began there in 1977, eight of the ten middens originally identified had been destroyed mostly by construction activity. One, designated RH4, was hastily studied before demolition. It yielded stone net sinkers; a necklace of shell, soapstone, and limestone beads; and finely carved shell pendants. Poorly preserved human skeletons were found in two layers of oval pit

graves, indicating different burial phases. The deceased had been placed on thick beds of oyster shells.

Excavation of nearby RH5 in the 1980s revealed a densely packed group of 57 oval pit burials with remains of 80 people in a 167-foot-square area. Turtle bones, carapaces, and egg-shaped pebbles were present in considerable quantities in most grave fills, and in several burials a turtle skull had been placed next to a human one. Sea turtles would have held a fascination, even a spiritual significance, for fishermen, who would have been impressed by the annual spectacle of thousands of females crawling onto the beaches of Ras al Hamra to lay their eggs.

Carbon dating indicates that these middens and burials were in continuous use from 6000 to 3000 B.C. A dearth of faunal remains suggests that the community was isolated from inland areas, where small game was abundant. Some characteristics of the skeletons suggest genetic inbreeding: a number exhibit spina bifida, a congenital cleft in the spinal column, and analysis showed a high frequency of the relatively uncommon A blood group. Many skeletons also display signs of inflammatory bone disease and abnormal skull thickening, often interpreted as indicative of malaria.

In the 1950s Danish archaeologists excavating grave mounds in Bahrain, northwest of Oman, found 4,200-

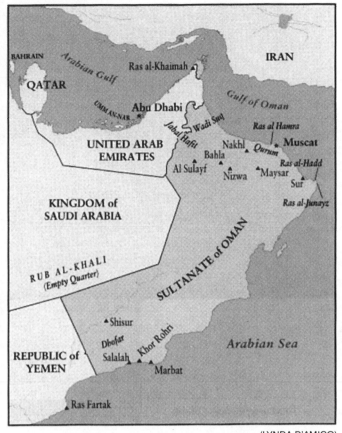

bronze pins; and stone and faience beads. The jars were the same type as those used in southern Mesopotamia around 3000 B.C. Unfortunately there is little trace of the ancient settlements associated with these tombs.

In the past 20 years, hundreds of Hafit tombs and other roughly contemporary single-chamber "beehive" tombs have been found on high ridges above wadis (dry riverbeds) in an arc from southern Oman north to Abu Dhabi. Meanwhile, some Umm an-Nar-culture tombs are now being reclassified as Hafit or beehive. There is no consensus among archaeologists on the chronology or the relationship between the cultures they represent.

Was Oman the land of Magan, which appears in Sumerian cuneiform texts ca. 2300 B.C. as a source of copper and diorite for the flourishing city-states of Mesopotamia? These texts tell us that ships with a cargo capacity of 20 tons sailed up the Arabian Gulf, stopping at Dilmun to take on fresh water before continuing to Mesopotamia. They also say that Magan lay south of Sumer and Dilmun, was frequented by Indus Valley travelers, and had high mountains from which diorite or gabro for black statues was quarried. Research since the 1970s has located significant copper deposits and more than 150 medieval islamic smelting sites. Excavations by the German Mining Museum have identified numerous Magan-period (2500–2000 B.C.) slag heaps under tons of medieval slag and third millennium remains from mining and smelting at the oasis village of Maysar in central-eastern Oman. A hoard of bun-shaped copper ingots found in a small fireplace indicates the form in which copper was traded. The excavators also identified a metal workshop. The Maysar finds leave little doubt that Oman was the land of Magan. A three-sided prism seal and pottery characteristic of the Indus Valley found at Maysar, and Harappan pottery found by an Italian-French mission at the eastern Arabian cape of Ras al-Junayz, suggests that Harappan sailors traded with inland Maysar, loading Omani wares aboard at coastal sites before sailing for Dilmun and Mesopotamian ports.

Until recently the period between 2000 and 1300 B.C. was thought to be a dark age. Finds in the grave complex at Wadi Suq in northern Oman, however, and at contemporary settlements throughout the peninsula indicate cultural continuity. The transitional culture is known as early (2000–1600 B.C.) and late (1600–1300 B.C.) Wadi Suq. Judging from the number of graves of this period, Oman was well populated. The near absence of foreign trade artifacts, however, suggests that the country was more isolated from its neighbors than before.

The Wadi Suq culture gave way to the Omani Iron Age (ca. 1300–300 B.C.), roughly contemporary with the Persian Iron Age and Achaemenid dynasty. The latter half of the Iron Age saw an unparalleled expansion of settlement and technology that is often linked to the building

year-old settlements and temples of the city-state of Dilmun, known as the city of the gods in ancient Sumerian literature. Their 1959 discovery on the island of Umm an-Nar off Abu Dhabi of a second, previously unknown culture contemporary with Dilmun was unexpected. At the site an outer wall enclosed circular graves, 15 to 40 feet in diameter and often two stories high, in which as many as 30 people were buried. During the past 30 years thousands of Umm an-Nar-style stone tombs have been identified from Ras al-khaimah in the north to Ras al-Hadd south of Muscat. Caravan routes are known to have run along a north-south axis from the incense lands of the Hadramaut (modern Yemen) and Dhofar north to Umm an-Nar. Oasis villages along these routes in Oman resembled the Umm an-Nar island settlement in their use of circular graves, and all revealed pottery and other artifacts from Iran, the Indus Valley, and Mespotamia, attesting strong trade links with those regions.

Spurred on by the discoveries at Dilmun and Umm an-Nar, Danish archaeologists excavated 200 single-chambered burial cairns in 1961 near Jabal Hafit on the Oman-United Arab Emirates border. There they discovered a culture earlier than that of Dilmun or Umm an-Nar. Excavation yielded jars with geometric designs painted in black, white, and plum red; copper and of irrigation systems known as *falaj*. These systems watered date palms and lime trees, and were the basis of Oman's subsequent prosperity and settlement patterns. Evidence from Maysar indicates that *falaj* may have been introduced by the Persians around 1000 B.C., or perhaps even earlier.

Today, oil has taken the place of copper and frankincense as the source of Oman's wealth. Development has led to the destruction of many historical and ancient sites—some before they have been identified, let alone excavated. We can only hope that the remaining sites can be saved for excavation before they are swallowed up in the country's march toward modernity.

M. REDHA BHACKER, *an Omani historian and independent scholar, is the author of* Trade and Empire in Muscat and Zanzibar *(New York: Routledge, 1992).* BERNADETTE BHACKER *is a commercial lawyer and student of Arabian Gulf history and archaeology.*

Article 14   *The Christian Science Monitor, Wednesday, September 24, 1997*

Wild Card in Mideast Peace: Syria

Damascus puts a new spin on relations with US, Israel—even Iran and Iraq

By Scott Peterson

Staff writer of The Christian Science Monitor

DAMASCUS, SYRIA

SUBTLE messages have long served as political discourse in the Middle East, and the complexity of Syria's "dialogue" with Israel and the United States about the peace process is no different.

The current peace crisis has displayed the surprisingly wide range of political cards that Syria can play.

The authoritarian regime of President Hafez al-Assad is still technically at war with Israel over capture by the Jewish state in 1967 of the strategic Golan Heights. Return of that land—now annexed by Israel, and populated by right wing Jewish settlers—is an article of faith here.

And Syria has, over the years, been the most strident in its anti-Israel rhetoric, despite the fact that US-brokered peace talks made significant progress before Israel broke them off in February 1996.

So consider these "messages" emerging from this tangled Mideast drama: After a botched Israeli commando raid in southern Lebanon earlier this month, guerrillas paraded the severed head of the one Israeli, holding it

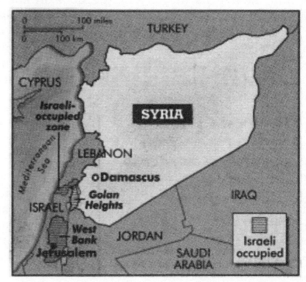

(STAFF)

aloft like a trophy. Photographs of this "triumph" were printed across the Arab and Islamic world. But Syria's press did not join in.

And footage of dead and wounded Israelis from a suicide bombing in Jerusalem on Sept. 4 was the first ever shown on Syrian television. The attacks were not called "operations," in the parlance of the Palestinian Hamas militants who claimed responsibility, but simply "explosions."

"They [the Syrians] were one step away from expressing regret," says one Western diplomat here, because of the negative consequences the bombs would have on the peace process.

Both examples appeared designed to send a message of peace and moderation to Israel.

But there are signs that point another way: Just hours after the Jerusalem bombing, leaders of various hard-line Palestinian groups that oppose the peace process met in Damascus, the first time in months that such a meeting was permitted.

Hamas was congratulated by the others for its "good work" with the Jerusalem bombings.

The continued presence of these groups keeps Syria on the US State Department list of "terrorist" states, though no act of terror is believed to have come from Syria itself for more than a decade. Several months ago these groups were warned to keep a low profile, but those orders seem to have changed.

"These are all cards in the Syrian hands, with which they manage to give signals but not, at this point, to cause a rupture," says a Western source here. "They hope the US makes good on its commitment to bring peace."

Talks with Israel's previous left-wing government foundered on details of security arrangements that would accompany an Israeli pullout. But right-wing Prime minister Benjamin Netanyahu has rejected a full withdrawal from the Golan—fearing that giving up this "strategic buffer" would jeopardize Israel's security—along with the US land-for-peace formula that underpins the peace process.

President Assad said on Friday that Mr. Netanyahu "closes the doors on all who are concerned with the peace process."

Syria's demands center on United Nations Security Council resolutions that require full Israeli withdrawal from the Golan and from southern Lebanon.

Syrian and Western analysts note that Israel's settlement policies in the Golan also violate the fourth Geneva Convention, which prohibits building on occupied territory. Israel counters that Syria does not want peace and is instead preparing for war. Western military analysts here discount such a threat.

But Syria has linked any comprehensive peace in southern Lebanon—the last "hot" front line in the Arab-Israeli conflict where Iran- and Syria-backed Hizbullah guerrillas battle occupying Israeli troops—to a Golan deal. Some 30,000 Syrian troops also remain in Lebanon after more than 20 years, making Damascus the recognized power broker in Lebanon. Without this card in Syrian hands, and in view of Israel's military superiority, observers note, Israel might have little reason to give up the Golan at all.

So Syria has lauded the "balanced" words of Secretary of State Madeleine Albright during her first Mideast trip earlier this month. Western diplomats say that, in asking for US pressure on Israel, Assad told her: "We are the most disciplined follower of US policy [of land-for-peace], but what about you?"

"Syria considers that it is the only true follower of the American peace initiative," says a Western diplomat. Further afield, however, Syria is eyeing a new axis between Israel and Turkey with anxious suspicion. Joint naval exercises—which will include the US—are to be held in November, just 20 miles off the Syrian coast.

To pressure Turkey for water resources in the past, Syria has given sanctuary to militant Kurds of the Kurdistan Workers party (PKK) who carry out armed attacks inside Turkey. But the PKK has been largely banished from Syria proper, and now operates out of Lebanon's Syria-controlled Bekaa Valley and Iran.

"Syria is doing nothing at all to antagonize Turkey now," says a Western diplomat. "They know where the balance of power lies, and have not moved one soldier to the border." Seeking to defuse the tension, Turkey has announced the exercises will only be search and rescue operations. But Syria sees them as a direct threat and has sought support outside the Western camp.

Assad—who rarely travels—visited Iran at the end of July to confer with top leaders of the Islamic republic and confirm close ties. This week, in a rare sign that Iran and Syria were in step, Iranian President Mohammad Khatami also spoke out against the planned joint exercises.

And Syria has begun improving ties with Iraq, an archenemy. A border crossing has been reopened after 17 years, and Syria has given $1 million worth of medicine to Iraqis hit by United Nations sanctions. Syrians also say they were shocked to see portraits of Assad and Iraqi strongman Saddam Hussein hanging side by side at a Damascus international fair.

Ties with Saudi Arabia have also improved, according to a Western news report. A key suspect in the bombing of US servicemen in Saudi Arabia in June 1996 was tracked down in Lebanon by the Syrians and handed over to Saudi Arabia.

"Everyone is feeling vulnerable, and that is why they want to get together," says a Syrian analyst.

Article 15   *The Economist*, July 19th, 1997

The increasing loneliness of being Turkey

A country that could be the meeting-place of democracy and Islam is in danger of becoming a no-man's-land between them. This can be prevented.

TURKEY, say the geopoliticians, is the most important member of the new, expanded Atlantic alliance; and they may well be right. This is a huge place, with the biggest land area and the second-biggest population of any NATO country east of the Atlantic. It has the biggest army of them all, including America's, and though its soldiers do not have the most modern weapons they are dogged and uncomplaining fighters: there are gentlemen in England still abed who remember Gallipoli and Kut al-Amara. Above all, Turkey stands where Germany did in the previous period of NATO's existence: on the front line, face to face with the big problem. Now that the Soviet army no longer looms over Germany, NATO's eyes have turned southward, to the bubbling mixture of oil and Islamism and decrepit authoritarian regimes called the Middle East: a bubbling which will not be kept from boiling over by diplomacy alone.

The trouble is that the alliance of the democracies needs Turkey for two different reasons, and both have been put at risk by what is now happening in Turkish politics.

The military value of Turkey is that it sits next door to Saddam Hussein's Iraq, to the mullahs' Iran and to the unpredictable dictatorship of Syria's Hafez Assad. Its own armed forces, the bases it provides for allied aircraft and warships and—not least—its quiet ability to control the flow of the Tigris and Euphrates rivers into Iraq and Syria are all weighty pieces in the regional balance of power. But Turkey has been of even greater value for a different, political reason. Until recently, it had looked like the one fairly solid example of a Muslim country that was also a working democracy. It looks less solid now.

On February 28th, Turkey's generals stuck their hand into politics again (they had three full-scale coups between 1960 and 1980) by issuing a list of instructions to the mildly Islamist government. This has made it harder to argue that Turkey was at last settling down to be a real democracy, a place where the people take the decisions. And if the generals have miscalculated—if the Koran-toting Welfare Party, which they have now pushed out of power, comes back into office at the next election on a wave of Muslim resentment—they will either have to live with a new government that will among other things be much more suspicious of their pro-western foreign policy, or do an Algeria and squash the election.

A little time was bought when Mesut Yilmaz, the beneficiary of the generals' intervention, got a rather wobbly vote of confidence last Saturday (a majority of 25 in the 550-member parliament) for a three-party coalition he has stitched together out of his own conservative Motherland Party, its old adversary the Democratic Left, and a small splinter group. The generals would have had an immediate crisis on their hands if Welfare and its ally in government since last July, the True Path Party, had beaten Mr Yilmaz. Only two weeks earlier a majority of parliament's members had signed a plea that Welfare and True Path should stay in office. The necessary votes were, in the end, cajoled or bought. But the crisis is far from over.

Even if Mr Yilmaz's majority survives the year, which is by no means certain, some hard questions have to be answered. All those involved—the generals, Mr Yilmaz and Welfare's leader, Necmettin Erbakan—have to try to work out what sort of country they want Turkey to be.

They went over the top

The generals' answer is that they want Turkey to remain the secular state created 70 years ago by their hero Mustafa Kemal Ataturk, "Father of the Turks". They went into action last February

armed with Article 118 of the constitution, under which the National Security Council—five senior officers and four civilian ministers under the chairmanship of the country's president—can say what it wants done to preserve "the independence of the state" and "the peace and security of society". They gave the prime minister a list of 18 things they wanted done to reduce Islam's influence on the workings of government.

Mr Erbakan, relying on his parliamentary majority, fudged and dodged. The generals replied with a creeping barrage.

Further demands were made on the government, including its approval for the dismissal of military officers considered too pro-Welfare. A handful of big firms that had shown sympathy for Welfare got a dressing-down. The lady in charge of True Path, Tansu Ciller, who had used her coalition with Welfare as an umbrella against the charges of corruption raining down on her, came under renewed attack. Towards the end, the newspapers suddenly revealed that a government ministry had been tapping the soldiers' telephones. Most curiously of all, the country's chief prosecutor, shortly after saying he did not think such a thing could be successfully done, brought a suit before the Constitutional Court calling for the Welfare Party to be banned.

Not all of these things were organised from military headquarters, though many of them undoubtedly were. Nor have the generals had unanimous support among secular Turks who enjoy a western-style way of life: the main businessmen's association, in a list of proposals to improve Turkish democracy, suggested abolishing the National Security Council. But eventually the pressure worked. Mr Erbakan said he would go; a vain attempt was made to get the prime ministership transferred to Mrs Ciller; President Demirel said he preferred Mr Yilmaz; Mr Yilmaz won some

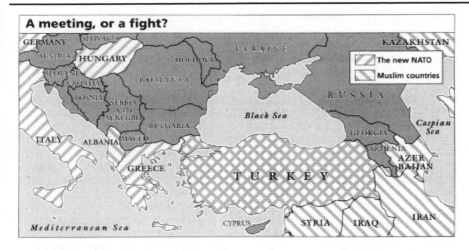

A meeting, or a fight?

The new NATO / Muslim countries

more defectors; and on July 12th he got his majority, and the generals got their way.

The problem with all this is not just that their victory could be short-lived. A sizeable chunk of Mr Yilmaz's majority last weekend consisted of the Republican People's Party, but this party has refused to join the government and would like a new election in 1997, whereas Mr Yilmaz wants to wait until next year. Motherland and the Democratic Left, the two chief parts of the new coalition, will not find it easy to run a joint government programme (the Democratic Left is keen on bigger pensions for public-sector workers, Motherland wants to cut the budget deficit and do some more privatisation).

Turkish parties are anyway much given to fragmentation; pieces regularly drop off and join other parties, and it is only half-jokingly said that the average parliamentarian's price is between $2m and $5m. Mr Yilmaz is a clever enough politician, but not the only one with the technique of making converts. He is also rather a dull dog, with little taste for big ideas and no known ability to capture people's imagination. He could have trouble holding on to that 25 majority.

But there is a bigger reason for worrying about what has happened over the past five months. When you inspect the list of accusations that are said to justify the Welfare Party's removal from government, they turn out to be remarkably vague.

Not proven

The chief prosecutor's reasons for saying that Welfare should be banned include only a couple of things actually done by Welfare during its past year in government—its attempt to insist that women should be allowed to wear head-scarves in public buildings, despite a ban dating from Ataturk's time, and Mr Erbakan's invitation to dinner at the prime minister's house of some controversial people who, good gracious, "attended in attires in violation of revolutionary laws". It is perfectly true that the Welfare-led government did encourage the wearing of scarves in schools and other buildings. But that is hardly reason enough to ban a party. It even seems a rather liberal idea, when you reflect that peasant mothers whose soldier sons have been wounded in the civil war against Kurdish rebels are made to remove their daily headgear if they want to visit their boys in a military hospital.

Probe a little deeper than the public prosecutor does, and you dig up two further charges. One is that Welfare has allowed money to be brought into the country, and has perhaps itself provided money, for Masonic-like secret societies dedicated to spreading the Islamist word. This may or may not be true. It is hard to tell, because apart from one or two clear-cut episodes—such as the arrest at Istanbul airport of a man trying to smuggle in money from Islamists in Germany—most of the evidence offered is distinctly murky. "Our control system is very good." "The information is to be found in Welfare's computer system." This is less than wholly convincing.

The other chief complaint of the defenders of secularism concerns religious education. Turkey has about 500 Imam Hatip ("Parson-Preacher") secondary and high schools—a small fraction of the total number of schools for children of that age—which offer a modest dose of Muslim education to 11-to-14-year olds on top of the regular state curriculum but a much larger dose, up to a third of the total week's work, to those above 14. The secularists' fear is that these schools will pour out a flood of fanatical young

graduates like the Taliban students of Afghanistan.

Unfortunately for the secularists, however, the Imam Hatip schools are a product of the secular regime. They were started, with the generals' blessing, back in the 1950s, and most of the existing ones were founded in the 1970s and 1980s; not one was added during Welfare's just-ended year in government. They are run, and inspected, by the state. They are also popular with parents, since they tend to be more orderly than other schools, and to get better results. The generals want to cut the ground from under them by building more non-religious secondary schools. But that would seem to clash with many parents' wishes, as well as adding to the government's overspending. If Imam Hatip graduates subsequently do illegal things, they should be arrested. But unless a disproportionate number of them do, the case against these schools does not seem to stand up.

After this, the charge-list grows even mistier. Mr Erbakan has supported the idea of building a mosque in Istanbul's Taksim Square, which is a bit like proposing a Christian revivalist centre in Piccadilly Circus. The Welfare mayor of a small town earlier this year invited the Iranian ambassador to a Muslim revivalist rally, which was provocative but no dafter than a communist mayor in cold-war Western Europe inviting the Soviet ambassador to his country to a joint denunciation of capitalism. Various Welfare people have said heated things at public meetings. A few of these are worrying (Istanbul's mayor is quoted as saying that democracy is like a tram: you take it where you want to go, and then you get off). But most were just politicians saying in the rough accent of Anatolian politics that, if they get elected, the other side had better not try keeping them out of office.

The flavour of the 1930s

To be sure, all Islamic revivalists need to be examined through narrowed eyes. Some of them are ignorantly and brutally dictatorial: look at the Taliban in Afghanistan, and the wilder specimens in Algeria, Egypt and Pakistan. But not all are like this.

The mainline revivalist parties in Tunisia, Egypt and Jordan have said that they wish to operate within a democratic system—multi-party free elections, alternation of government and all. Malaysia's Islamists, in that country's admittedly creaky semi-democracy, are obeying the rules. The heartening discovery of the past few years is that the Muslim world's revivalist movement is not a uniform entity; it is a spectrum, ranging from incurable authoritarians to devout searchers after God's will who are nevertheless prepared to accept the people's judgment. With any luck, Turkey's plump if occasionally excitable Mr Erbakan, and most of his party, are at the moderate end of the spectrum.

The fact that the leaders of the anti-Welfare campaign will have none of this says much about the psychology of Ataturk's Turkey. No, they insist, you can never trust a politician with the Koran in his hand; these people are trained to say one thing and do another; we secular Turks know in our bones that they are plotting to force a fundamentalist dictatorship on us. There is a neurotic edge to the way many secularists talk about the awkward, rather earnest, just-up-from-the-country sort of people who make up most of Mr Erbakan's following.

This may be because, when you look at it, the Ataturk definition of secularism is not quite what most other westerners mean by the word. There is still a flavour of the 1930s about today's Turkey. It is not just the self-consciously heroic statuary, the assurances that "the army knows what the people want", the still far too big state sector of industry. The Turkey that Ataturk built two-thirds of a century ago was constructed out of a now rather old-fashioned mixture of nationalism and rationalism.

The nationalism was not too bad: the Turks treat their Kurdish minority very badly, and they are stubborn about their interests in Cyprus, but Ataturkian Turkey has never been a serious threat to its neighbours. The rationalism part, alas, now feels like something out of a dusty past.

For most Europeans and Americans, a secular state is a state in which the church cannot dictate to the government and, in America at least, the symbols and ceremonies of the two are kept firmly separate. But this does not mean that for most people in the West of the 1990s the business of government can be conducted without reference to some kind of moral order.

The rational pursuit of self-interest is the necessary basis of human activity but, if a country is to be worth living in, all those competing individual self-interests have to operate within an agreed set of rules. The rules may be derived from a belief in God, or they may be constructed by a consensus of non-believers;

but in either case they will draw upon the instinctive part of the mind—the tug of compassion, the intuitive sense of right and wrong—as well as the purely rational part. Christian Democrats and Christian socialists in Europe, Christian revivalists in America and communitarians on both sides of the Atlantic would all nowadays agree on that much.

For Ataturk, though, rationalism was king. To be useful, he said, religion "has to conform . . . to science and knowledge, to logic." The phrase "a moral order" would probably have struck Ataturk, with his belief in the absolute supremacy of reason, as something murky dug out of the medieval recesses of the Islamic mind.

This is why his sort of secularism has less in common with the secularism of most of today's Europeans and Americans than it has with that of France's 19th-century rationalists. It is not merely an insistence that religious believers should keep the propagation of their ideas within the rules of the democratic system. It is a preference for excluding their ideas from the public arena altogether. It is not impartiality towards religion so much as a turning of the back upon it. And this is why in 1997 Turks who have inherited Ataturk's secularism and Turks in search of an Islamic revival find themselves gazing at each other across a gulf of incomprehension.

If they don't try

If the gulf is to be bridged, both Mr Erbakan and the generals have to stretch out a hand. Mr Erbakan can reasonably argue that in his year in the prime ministership he did not visibly break any of democracy's rules. He might add that this foreign policy, apart from a smirk towards Iran and a humiliating visit to Colonel Qaddafi's Libya, was just the sort of thing the generals wanted: his government stayed a loyal member of NATO, kept knocking on the European Union's door, and even let the Turkish army get on with its cosy new programme of military co-operation with Israel.

But Mr Erbakan could go further. He could formally commit himself to the democratic credo already voiced by open-minded Islamists in other countries. What people believe or do not believe, says this credo, is their own private business; the state should keep its nose out. But both believers and non-believers should be free to put their ideas about the government of the country, wherever in heaven or earth those ideas are said

to come from, to the country's voters. If they and their allies get the support of a majority of the voters, they can put their proposals into law, provided these laws do not clash with the country's constitution (which must itself have the voters' approval). If at the next election a different lot of people with different ideas win a majority of the votes, the first lot will stand down and accept the changes the second lot make, subject to the same proviso. Full stop. That is democracy.

In reply, the generals could say that their only concern is to preserve the rules of democracy. They do not support or oppose any particular body of ideas; they merely want to make sure that the voters can make the choice, and change their choice next time if they wish. Given Mr Erbakan's commitment to the same principal, the generals will go back to their military business and watch the next election with impartial interest. They might add, *sotto voce*, that if anybody really does break the rules they will know what to do about it.

If something like this happens, the Turks can resume normal politics. If it does not, they face an increasingly isolated future. A continuation of the army's campaign against the Welfare Party—maybe even a court order disbanding the party—will give new ammunition to the people in the European Union who say that Turkey will never be democratic enough to be a full member of the EU (even though its economic qualifications for membership are in some ways better than those of most of the EU's other current applicants). It would also make it harder for the United States to insist on Turkey's military importance to the NATO alliance, since the countries now seeking to join NATO are being told that they first have to prove they are good democrats. And Iran's mullahs will be even more anti-Turkey than they are now.

If the generals have got it wrong, on the other hand, and their harassment of Welfare wins indignant Islamists more votes in Turkey's next election, the next Turkish government is likely to be colder to NATO, less interested in Europe, and on even pricklier terms than its predecessors with the hard-nosed and ungodly men who run Iraq and Syria. Either way, a country that could have been a demonstration of the compatibility of Islam and democracy would be drifting off into a lonely limbo between the two. That is not what the democracies need, and it is not what most Turks want.

Article 16   *The New York Times*, September 2, 1997

On Ancient Terraced Hills, Urbanism Sprouted With Crops

Digs in Yemen revise views on the earliest Arabian towns.

By JOHN NOBLE WILFORD

IN the high country of Yemen, long before the reign of the legendary Queen of Sheba, farmers terraced hillsides and prospered with crops of barley, wheat and sorghum. They produced tools and weapons from obsidian, the glassy rock found in the slopes. They also settled in walled villages, perhaps the earliest experience in urbanism in all the Arabian peninsula.

Archeologists from the University of Chicago have uncovered ruins of two such towns on a 6,500-foot-high plateau about 50 miles south of Sana, the capital of Yemen. Preliminary excavations indicate that the towns were built more than 4,000 years ago, several hundred years before the frankincense trade in the region that scholars previously thought stimulated development of the first Arabian towns.

"Urbanism did not take off here because of the frankincense trade," Dr. Tony J. Wilkinson, an archeologist at the university's Oriental Institute, said in an interview. "It began much earlier and apparently was supported by advances in agricultural engineering."

In expeditions over the last three years, led by Dr. Wilkinson and R. McGuire Gibson, also of the Oriental Institute, archaeologists found the stones, sediments and other traces of ancient terraces that enabled farmers to cultivate the steep slopes and prevent erosion.

People still practice terrace farming in Yemen, but the oldest agricultural terraces, which have fallen into disrepair, probably date to 3000 B.C., making them among the oldest in the world. Other early terrace farmers were the Chinese and other cultures in the Middle East.

The region was presumably less arid at the time, the archeologists said, but the people there also enhanced farming conditions by erecting a system of dams in the mountain valleys. Using finely cut volcanic rock, the people built low dams to collect rainwater and direct it toward fields and high dams to contain and deflect flood water. The archeologists said they found evidence of sluices adjacent to the dams and in some cases, channels carved through bedrock.

"The builders of the dams had a precise understanding not only of dam construction, but also of the whole watershed system that fed the dams," Dr. Wilkinson said. "They were able to construct just the right size dam for each particular area."

While studying the ancient dams and terraces, the Chicago team came upon several dozen sites of settlement ruins, a few of which appeared to be large enough to have been towns. The archeologists have excavated two of them; Hamat al-Qa, which flourished between 2250 B.C. and 1500 B.C., and al-Sibal, which dates between 2500 B.C. and 1700 B.C.

Dr. Wilkinson, Dr. Gibson and Dr. Christopher Edens of Harvard University describe the archeology of the two towns and other remains in the current issue of the journal Arabian Archaeology and Epigraphy. "Present evidence," they wrote, "suggests that there occurred a fairly abrupt development of settlements in probably the third millennium B.C."

The two excavated towns, they reported, covered an area of 10 to 12 acres each and were characterized by "dense architecture," indicating fairly large populations and some degree of social complexity. They traced the outlines of rectangular buildings of large stone blocks that were separated by streets and open spaces. They also found ruins of a defensive wall around the settlements and gates. No large public buildings like temples or palaces have been uncovered.

The style of pottery at the towns and the absence of any trade goods from faraway led the archeologists to conclude that this ancient culture was local, with no apparent economic links to the rest of the Middle East either by sea or caravans across the desert. Although sorghum is normally considered an African crop, traces of it in the terrace fields do not necessarily reflect significant contacts at that time between Africans and the hill people of Yemen.

Many of the later towns in Yemen had contacts far and wide. They sprang up on the fringes of the Arabian desert, near the trees that were the major source of the aromatic resin for the frankincense so prized in ancient times. Camel caravans fanned out from these towns, bearing incense to cities in Mesopotamia and around the Mediterranean.

The height of the frankincense trade between southern Arabia and the Mediterranean was in the first millennium B.C., which happens to be the time that King Solomon of Israel was supposed to be having dealings with the Queen of Sheba. That part of Yemeni history is "very shadowy," Dr. Gibson said. There were queens of Sheba, or Saba, a region that is part of Yemen today, but the ones for whom there is firm documentary evidence lived later in the first millennium B.C.

In 1992, explorers and archeologists reported finding in Oman the buried ruins of one of the earliest of the caravan cities. They tentatively identified the site with the fabled lost city of Ubar, which T. E. Lawrence called "the Atlantis of the sands." Some artifacts uncovered there indicated that the ruins were some 4,000 years old, making them the oldest known settlements in southern Arabia before the older towns in Yemen came to light.

When Ubar was just beginning to trade in incense, farmers miles away on the more verdant plateau to the southwest in Yemen were tilling their terraces in virtual isolation.

Credits

Sources for Statistical Reports

U.S. State Department, *Background Notes* (1994–1997)

The World Factbook (1997)

World Statistics in Brief (1997)

World Almanac (1998)

The Statesman's Yearbook (1996–1997)

Demographic Yearbook (1996)

Statistical Yearbook (1997)

World Bank, World Development Report (1997)

Ayers Directory of Publications (1997)

Glossary of Terms and Abbreviations

Abd—Slave, servant of God (as in Gamal Abdel Nasser: Abd al-Nasir).

Alawi (Nusayri)—A Shia Muslim minority group in Syria, currently in power under President Hafez al-Assad.

Allah—God, in Islam.

Ayatollah—"Sign of God," the title of highest rank among the Shia religious leaders in Iran.

Ba'th (Arab Socialist Resurrection Party)—A Socialist political party that has two main branches, ruling in Syria and Iraq respectively, plus members in other Arab countries.

Caliph—In Arabic, *Khalifa;* agent, representative, or deputy; in Sunni Islam, the line of successors to Muhammad.

Chador—A body covering worn by some Muslim women.

Colon—Settler, colonist (French), a term used for the French population in North Africa during the colonial period (1830–1962).

Dar al-Islam—"House of Islam," territory ruled under Islam. Conversely, *Dar al-Harb,* "House of War," denotes territory not under Islamic rule.

Druze (or Druse)—An offshoot of Islam that has developed its own rituals and practices and a close-knit community structure; Druze populations are found today in Lebanon, Jordan, Syria, and Israel.

Emir (or Amir)—A title of rank, denoting either a patriarchal ruler, provincial governor, or military commander. Today it is used exclusively for rulers of certain Arabian Peninsula states.

Fatwa—A legal opinion or interpretation delivered by a Muslim religious scholar-jurist.

Fida'i (plural Fida'iyun, also Fedayeen, cf. Mujahideen)—Literally, "fighter for the faith"; a warrior who fights for the faith against the enemies of Islam.

FLN (National Liberation Front)—The resistance movement against the French in Algeria that succeeded in establishing Algerian independence.

GCC (Gulf Cooperation Council)—Established in 1981 as a mutual-defense organization by the Arab Gulf states. Membership: Bahrain, Kuwait, Oman, Qatar, Saudi Arabia, and United Arab Emirates. Headquarters: Riyadh.

Hadith—"Traditions" of the Prophet Muhammad, the compilation of sayings and decisions attributed to him that serve as a model and guide to conduct for Muslims.

Hajj—Pilgrimage to Mecca, one of the Five Pillars of Islam; also used as a title for one who has made the pilgrimage.

Hijrah (Hegira)—The Prophet Muhammad's emigration from Mecca to Medina in A.D. 622 to escape persecution; the start of the Islamic calendar.

Ibadi—A militant early Islamic group that split with the majority (Sunni) over the question of the succession to Muhammad. Their descendants form majorities of the populations in Oman and Yemen.

IBRD (International Bank for Reconstruction and Development)—Established in 1945 to make loans at conventional interest rates to countries for development projects. Headquarters: Washington, D.C. Affiliated organizations are the International Development Assistance Organization (IDA), the International Finance Corporation (IFC), and the International Monetary Fund (IMF).

Ihram—The seamless white robe worn by all Muslims making the hajj.

Ikhwan—Brothers, as in a religious confraternity. When capitalized (*i.e.,* Ikhwan al-Muslimin) it refers to the Muslim Brotherhood, a secret but widespread Sunni organization opposed to Muslim secular governments.

Imam—Religious leader, prayer-leader of a congregation. When capitalized it refers to the descendants of Ali who are regarded by Shia Muslims as the rightful successors to Muhammad.

Intifadah—Literally, "resurgence"; uprising of the Palestinians against Israeli occupation.

Islam—Submission to the will of God, as revealed in the Koran. The religion of Muslims.

Jahiliyya—The "time of ignorance" of the Arabs before Islam. Sometimes used by Islamic fundamentalists today to describe secular Muslim societies, which they regard as sinful.

Jama'a—The Friday communal prayer, held in a mosque (*jami'*). By extension, the public assembly held by Muslim rulers for their subjects in traditional Islamic states such as Saudi Arabia.

Jamahiriyya—Popular democracy (as in Libya).

Jihad—The struggle of Muslims collectively or individually to do right and defend the community; commonly, "holy war."

Khan—A title of rank in eastern Islam (Turkey, Iran, etc.) for military or clan leaders.

Kharijites—An early Muslim group who opposed the succession in Muhammad's family but also opposed the election of the first four caliphs as undemocratic. They assassinated Ali after he had negotiated a truce with his opponents upon becoming caliph; in their view, he had bartered away his right to the office.

Khedive—Viceroy, the title of rulers of Egypt in the nineteenth and twentieth centuries who ruled as regents of the Ottoman sultan.

Kibbutz—A collective settlement in Israel.

Koran—In Arabic, *Qur'an;* "Recitation," the book of God's revelations to Muhammad via the Angel Gabriel that form the basis for Islam.

League of Arab States (Arab League)—Established in 1945 as a regional organization for newly independent

Arab countries. Membership: all the Arab states except Egypt (suspended in 1979) plus the PLO.

Maghrib—"West," the hour of the sunset prayer; in Arabic, a geographical term for North Africa.

Mahdi—"The Awaited One" in both Sunni and Shia Islam; the Messiah, who will appear on earth to reunite the divided Islamic community and announce the Day of Judgment. In Shia Islam he is the Twelfth and Last Imam (al-Mahdi al-Muntazir) who disappeared 12 centuries ago but is believed to be in a state of occultation (suspended between heaven and earth).

Majlis—Assembly, parliament, legislature.

Mandates—An arrangement set up under the League of Nations after World War I for German colonies and territories of the Ottoman Empire inhabited by non-Turkish populations. The purpose was to train these populations for eventual self-government under a temporary occupation by a foreign power, which was either Britain or France.

Marabout—Particularly in North Africa, a local saint or holy man respected for his intercessory powers with God on behalf of a community.

Mawlid (Mouloud)—Birthday, usually used only for the birthday of the Prophet Muhammad, a major holiday in the Islamic world.

Millet—"Nation," a non-Muslim population group in the Ottoman Empire recognized as a legitimate religious community and allowed self-government in internal affairs under its own religious leaders, who were responsible to the sultan for the group's behavior.

Muezzin—A prayer-caller, the person who announces the five daily obligatory prayers from the minaret of a mosque.

Mufti—A legal scholar empowered to issue fatwas. Usually one mufti is designated as the Grand Mufti of a particular Islamic state or territory.

Mujahideen (*see* **Fida'i**)—A common term for resistance fighters in Afghanistan and opposition militants in Iran.

Muslim (*see* **Islam**)—One who submits (to the Will of God).

OAPEC (Organization of Arab Petroleum Exporting Countries)—Established in 1968 to coordinate oil policies—but not to set prices—and to develop oil-related inter-Arab projects, such as an Arab tanker fleet and dry-dock facilities. Membership: all Arab oil-producing states. Headquarters: Kuwait.

OIC (Organization of the Islamic Conference)—Established in 1971 to promote solidarity among Islamic countries, provide humanitarian aid to Muslim communities throughout the world, and provide funds for Islamic education through construction of mosques, theological institutions of Islamic learning, etc. Membership: all states with an Islamic majority or significant minority. Headquarters: Jiddah.

OPEC (Organization of Petroleum Exporting Countries)—Established in 1960 to set prices and coordinate global oil policies of members. A majority of its 13 member states are in the Middle East. Headquarters: Vienna.

PLO (Palestine Liberation Organization)—Established in 1964 to develop political and military strategies for the creation of a sovereign Arab state in Palestine and its liberation from Israeli control. Overall PLO authority is vested in the Palestine National Council (PNC). Fatah (the Palestine National Liberation Movement, a guerrilla military group) joined the PLO in 1968, when a charter for Palestinian Arab national independence was issued. The PNC (in theory) supervises the Palestine Liberation Army, a body of 16,000 troops dispersed since 1982 in various Arab states. The PLO holds observer status at the United Nations. Funding comes from annual contributions from the Arab states, mainly Saudi Arabia, plus a 3 to 6 percent tax levied on the incomes of all Palestinians. Headquarters (temporary): Tunis.

Polisario—A national resistance movement in the Western Sahara that opposes annexation by Morocco and is fighting to establish an independent Saharan Arab state, the Sahrawi Arab Democratic Republic (SADR).

PSD (Parti Socialiste Destourien)—The dominant political party in Tunisia since independence and until recently the only legal party.

Qaid (Caid, Kaid)—Particularly in North Africa, a native Muslim official appointed to administer a region or territory by the French during the protectorate period.

Qanat—An underground tunnel used for irrigation.

Qasba (Casbah, Kasba)—A fortified section of an Islamic city; citadel.

Qibla—The section of wall in an Islamic mosque that faces in the direction of Mecca, marked by a recess or niche *(mihrab)*.

Quraysh—The group of clans who made up Muhammad's community in Mecca.

Shari'a—"The Way," the corpus of the sacred laws of Islam as revealed to Muhammad in the Koran.

Sharif—"Holy," a term applied to members of Muhammad's immediate family and descendants through his daughter Fatima and son-in-law Ali.

Shaykh (Sheikh, Sheik)—A patriarchal leader of an Islamic community, usually elected for life; also used for certain religious leaders and community elders as a title of honor.

Shia—commonly, but incorrectly, *Shiite*. Originally meant "Party," *i.e.,* of Ali, those Muslims who supported him as Muhammad's rightful and designated successor. Today, broadly, a member of the principal Islamic minority.

Sufi—An Islamic mystic.

Sunna—Custom or procedure, the code of acceptable behavior for Muslims based on the Koran and hadith. Not to be confused with Sunni, the name for the majority group in Islam.

Suq (Souk)—A public weekly market in Islamic rural areas, always held in the same village on the same day of the week, so that the village may have the word incorporated into its name. Also refers to a section of an Islamic city devoted to the wares and work of potters, cloth merchants, wood workers, spice sellers, etc.

Taqiyya—Dissimulation, concealment of one's religious identity or beliefs (as by Shia under Sunni control) in the face of overwhelming power or repression.

Tariqas—The religious brotherhoods or orders of Sunni Islam.

U.A.R. (United Arab Republic)—The name given to the abortive union of Egypt and Syria (1958–1961).

Ulema—The corporate body of Islamic religious leaders, scholars, and jurists.

Umma—The worldwide community of Muslims.

UNHCR (United Nations High Commission for Refugees)—Established in 1951 to provide international protection and material assistance to refugees worldwide. UNHCR has several refugee projects in the Middle East.

UNIFIL (United Nations Interim Force in Lebanon)—Formed in 1978 to ensure Israeli withdrawal from southern Lebanon. After the 1982 Israeli invasion, UNIFIL was given the added responsibility for protection and humanitarian aid to the people of the area. Headquarters: Naqoura.

United Nations Peacekeeping Forces—Various military observer missions formed to supervise disengagement or truce agreements between the Arab states and Israel. They include UNDOF (United Nations Disengagement Observer Force). Formed in 1974 as a result of the October 1973 Arab-Israeli War and continued by successive resolutions. Headquarters: Damascus.

UNRWA (United Nations Relief and Works Agency for Palestine Refugees)—Established in 1950 to provide food, housing, and health and education services for Palestinian refugees who fled their homes after the establishment of the State of Israel in Palestine. Headquarters: Vienna. UNRWA maintains refugee camps in Lebanon, Syria, Jordan, the occupied West Bank, and the Gaza Strip. UNRWA has also assumed responsibility for emergency relief for refugees in Lebanon displaced by the Israeli invasion and by the Lebanese Civil War.

Wilayat al-Faqih—Supreme guardianship of the law, according to Iran's 1980 Constitution.

Bibliography

CRADLE OF ISLAM

Akbar Ahmed, *Discovering Islam: Making Sense of Muslim History and Society* (London: Routledge Kegan Paul, 1988).

Scott Appleby, ed., *Spokesmen for the Despised: Fundamentalist Leaders of the Middle East* (Chicago: University of Chicago Press, 1997).

Leonard Binder, *Islamic Liberalism: A Critique of Developmental Ideologies* (Chicago: University of Chicago Press, 1988).

John L. Esposito, *The Islamic Threat: Myth or Reality?* (New York: Oxford University Press, 1992).

Yvonne Y. Haddad, et al., *The Contemporary Islamic Revival: A Critical Survey* (New York: Greenwood Press, 1991).

Yvonne Y. Haddad and John L. Esposito, *The Islamic Revival since 1988: A Critical Survey & Bibliography* (Westport, CT: Greenwood Press, 1997).

Shireen T. Hunter, ed., *The Politics of Islamic Revivalism* (Bloomington, IN: Indiana University Press, 1988).

Martin Kramer, *The Islamism Debate* (Syracuse: Syracuse University Press, 1997).

Bernard Lewis, *The Middle East: A Brief History of the Last 2000 Years* (New York: Simon and Schuster, 1995).

Charles Lindholm, *The Islamic Middle East: An Historical Anthropology* (London: Blackwell, 1996).

Heath W. Lowry and Bernard Lewis, eds., *Shi'a Islam from Religion to Revolution* (Princeton, NJ: Markus Wiener Publishers, 1997). Originally published in German.

Fatima Mernissi, *Islam and Democracy: Fear of the Modern World* (New York: Addison-Wesley, 1992). Translated by Mary Jo Lakeland.

Olivier Roy, *The Failure of Political Islam.* Trans. Carol Volk (Cambridge, MA: Harvard University Press, 1996).

Edward Said, *Culture and Imperialism* (New York: Vintage Books, 1994).

Michael Sells, ed., *Early Islamic Mysticism* (New York: Paulist Press, 1996; Classics of Western Spirituality series).

P. J. Stewart, *Unfolding Islam* (Reading, England: Garnet Books, 1994).

THEATER OF CONFLICT

Hatem Abu-Lebdeh, *Conflict in the Middle East* (Lanham, MD: University Press of America, 1997).

Deborah Amos, *Lines in the Sand: Desert Storm and the Remaking of the Arab World* (New York: Simon & Schuster, 1992).

John Bulloch and Harvey Morris, *The Gulf War* (London: Methuen, 1989). Deals with the Iran-Iraq War.

Tom Clancy and Fred Franks J., *Into the Storm: A Study in Command* (New York: Putnam Publishers, 1996).

Anthony H. Cordesman, *Kuwait: Recovery and Security After the Gulf War* (Boulder, CO: Westview Press, 1997).

Frederick Denny, *Introduction to the Middle East,* 2nd ed. (New York: Macmillan, 1994).

Robert W. Fernea and Elizabeth Fernea, *The Arab World: 40 Years of Change* (New York: Doubleday/Anchor Books, 1997). Updated and expanded version of the authors' *The Arab World: Personal Encounters* (New York: Doubleday, 1985).

Robert O. Freedman, ed., *The Middle East from the Iran-Contra Affair to the Intifada* (Syracuse, NY: Syracuse University Press, 1991).

Thomas L. Friedman, *From Beirut to Jerusalem* (New York: Farrar, Straus & Giroux, 1989).

Michael Gordon and Bernard E. Trainor, *The Generals' War* (Boston: Little, Brown, 1995).

T. M. Hawley, *Against the Fires of Hell: The Environmental Disaster of the Gulf War* (New York: Harcourt Brace Jovanovich, 1992).

Michael Hickey, *Gallipoli* (North Pomfret, VT: Trafalgar Square, 1998).

James Jankowski and Israel Gershoni, eds., *Rethinking Nationalism in the Middle East* (New York: Cambridge University Press, 1997).

Leo Kamil, *Fueling the Fire: U.S. Policy and the Western Sahara Conflict* (Lawrenceville, NJ: Red Sea Press, 1996).

Robert D. Kaplan, *The Arabists: The Romance of an American Elite* (New York: Free Press; Simon & Schuster, 1995).

Sandra Mackey, *Passion and Politics: The Turbulent World of the Arabs* (New York: Dutton, 1992).

Musallam A. Musallam, *The Iraqi Invasion of Kuwait: Saddam Hussein, His State and International Power Politics* (New York: St. Martin's Press, 1996).

Schiff, Ze'ev, *Israel–Syria Negotiations: Lessons Learned, 1993–1996* (Washington, D.C.: Washington Institute for Near East Policy, Policy Papers Series, 1997).

ALGERIA

Kay Adamson, *Algeria: A Study in Competing Ideologies* (New York: Sterling Publishing, 1997).

James Ciment, *Algeria: The Fundamentalist Challenge* (New York: Facts on File, 1997).

Abder-Rahmane Derradji, *The Algerian Guerrilla Campaign: Strategy and Tactics* (Lewiston, NY: Edwin Mellen Press, 1997).

Graham Fuller, *Algeria: The Next Fundamentalist State?* (Santa Monica, CA: Rand Corporation, 1996).

Robert Malley, *The Call from Algeria: Third Worldism, Revolution and the Turn to Islam* (Berkeley, CA: University of California Press, 1996).

John Ruedy, *Modern Algeria: The Origins and Development of a Nation* (Bloomington, IN: Indiana University Press, 1992).

Martin Stone, *The Agony of Algeria* (New York: Columbia University Press, 1997).

Michael Willis, *The Islamist Challenge in Algeria* (New York: New York University Press, 1997).

BAHRAIN

Michael Jenner, *Bahrain: Gulf Heritage in Transition* (London: Longman, 1984).

Fred H. Lawson, *Bahrain: The Modernization of Autocracy* (Boulder, CO: Westview Press, 1989).

Mahdi A. al-Tajir, *Bahrain, 1920–1945: Britain, The Shaykh and the Administration* (London: Croom Helm, 1987).

EGYPT

Joel Gordon, *Nasser's Blessed Movement* (New York: Oxford University Press, 1992).

Thomas W. Lippman, *Egypt after Nasser* (New York: Paragon Books, 1992).

Peter Woodward, *Nasser* (London: Longman, 1992).

IRAN

Janet Afary, *The Iranian Constitutional Revolution, 1906–1911* (New York: Columbia University Press, 1996).

Huseyin Agha, *Syria and Iran: Rivalry and Cooperation* (London: Pintner/Royal Institute of International Affairs, 1995).

James A. Bill, *The Eagle and the Lion: The Tragedy of American-Iranian Relations* (New Haven, CT: Yale University Press, 1988).

Patrick Clawson, *Business as Usual: Foreign Policy Options toward Iran* (New York: American Jewish Congress, 1997).

Anoushirvan Ehteshami, *After Khomeini: The Iranian Second Republic* (London: Routledge, 1995).

Graham Fuller, *The "Center of the Universe," The Geopolitics of Iran* (Boulder, CO: Westview Press, 1991).

James F. Goode, *The U.S. and Iran: In the Shadow of Musaddiq* (New York: St. Martin's Press, 1997).

Shireen Hunter, *Iran after Khomeini* (New York: Praeger, 1992).

Mehran Kamrava, *The Political History of Iran: From Tribalism to Theocracy* (New York: Praeger, 1992).

R. K. Ramazani, ed., *Iran's Revolution: The Search for Consensus* (Bloomington, IN: Indiana University Press, 1990). Published in conjunction with the Middle East Institute).

John Simpson and Tira Shubart, *Lifting the Veil: Life in Revolutionary Iran* (London: Hodder & Stoughton, 1995).

Robert Tinberg, *The Nightingale's Song* (New York: Simon and Schuster, 1995).

W. T. Workman, *The Social Origins of the Iran–Iraq War* (Boulder, CO: Lynne Rienner Publishers, 1994).

IRAQ

John Bulloch and Harvey Morris, *Saddam's War* (London: Faber and Faber, 1991).

John Kelsay, *Islam and War: A Study in Comparative Ethics* (Louisville, KY: Westminster/John Knox Press, 1993).

S. T. Laizer, *Martyrs, Traitors and Patriots: Kurdistan after the Gulf War* (London: Zed Books, 1996).

Pebe Marr, *Iraq, Troubles and Tensions* (Washington, D.C.: National Defense University, INSS, 1997).

Yitzhak Nakash, *The Shi'is of Iraq* (Princeton, NJ: Princeton University Press, 1994).

Daniel Silverfarb, *Twilight of British Ascendancy in the Middle East: A Case Study of Iraq, 1941–1950* (New York: St. Martin's Press, 1994).

Peter Sullivan, *Iraq's Enduring Political Threat* (Washington, D.C.: National Defense University/Institute of National Strategic Studies, 1996).

Eliezer Ta'uber, *Formation of Modern Syria and Iraq* (London: Frank Cass, 1995).

ISRAEL

Gad Barzilai, *Wars, Internal Conflicts and Political Order: Jewish Democracy in the Middle East* (Albany, NY: State University of New York Press, 1996).

Meron Benvenisti, *Intimate Enemies: Jews and Arabs in a Shared Land* (Berkeley, CA: University of California Press, 1995).

Boas Evron, *Jewish State or Israeli Nation?* (Bloomington, IN: Indiana University Press, 1995).

Norman Finklestein, *Image and Reality in the Palestine Conflict* (London: Verso, 1995).

—, *The Rise and Fall of Palestine: A Personal Account of the Intifada Years* (Minneapolis, MN: University of Minnesota Press, 1996).

Adam Garfinkle, *Politics and Society in Modern Israel: Myths and Realities* (Armonk, NY: M. E. Sharpe, 1997).

Calvin Goldscheider, *Israel's Changing Society: Population, Ethnicity and Development* (Boulder, CO: Westview Press, 1996).

Aziz Hardan, *On the Margins: The Arab Population in the Israeli Economy* (New York: St. Martin's Press, 1995).

Clive Jones, *Soviet Jewish Aliyah, 1989–1992* (London: Frank Cass, 1996).

Ahron Kellerman, *Society and Settlement: The Land of Israel in the 20th Century* (Albany, NY: State University of New York Press, 1993).

Yehuda Lukacs, *Israel, Jordan and the Peace Process* (Syracuse: Syracuse University Press, 1996).

Yitzhak Rabin, *The Rabin Memoirs,* 2nd ed. (Berkeley, CA: University of California Press, 1996).

Eliezer Ben Rafael, *Language, Identity and Social Divisions: The Case of Israel* (New York: Oxford University Press, 1994).

Glenn Robinson, *Building A Palestinian State: The Incomplete Revolution* (Bloomington, IN: Indiana University Press, 1997).

Nadim Rouhana, *Palestinian Citizens in an Ethnic Jewish State: Identities in Conflict* (New Haven, CT: Yale University Press, 1997).

Sara Roy, *The Gaza Strip: The Political Economy of De-Development* (Washington, D.C.: Institute for Palestine Studies, 1996).

Kirsten Schulze, *Intervention, Israeli Covert Diplomacy and the Maronites* (New York: St. Martin's Press, 1997).

Gabriel Shaffer, *Moshe Sharett: Biography of a Political Moderate* (New York: Oxford University Press, 1995).

Ira Sharansky, *Policy Making in Israel* (Pittsburgh, PA: University of Pittsburgh Press, 1997).

JORDAN

Randy Deshazo and John Sutherlin, *Building Bridges: Diplomacy and Regime Formation in the Jordan River* (Lanham, MD: University Presses of America, 1996).

Andrew Shryock, *Nationalism and the Genealogical Imagination: Oral History and Textual Authority in Tribal Jordan* (Berkeley, CA: University of California Press, 1997). Comparative Studies on Muslim Societies, Vol. 23.

KUWAIT

Abdul-Reda Assiri, *Kuwait's Foreign Policy* (Boulder, CO: Westview Press, 1990).

Jill Crystal, *Kuwait: The Transformation of an Old State* (Boulder, CO: Westview Press, 1992).

Jill Crystal, *Oil and Politics in the Gulf: Rulers and Merchants in Kuwait and Qatar* (New York: Cambridge University Press, 1995).

LEBANON

Youssef Choueiri, ed., *State and Society in Syria and Lebanon, 1919–1991* (New York: St. Martin's Press, 1994).

Deirdre Collings, ed., *Peace for Lebanon? From War to Reconstruction* (Boulder, CO: Lynne Rienner Publishers, 1994).

Carolyn Gates, *The Making of the Lebanese Merchant Republic* (New York: St. Martin's Press, 1997).

Michael Gilsenan, *Lords of the Lebanese Marches: Violence and Narrative in Arab Society* (Berkeley, CA:) University of California Press, 1996).

William Harris, *Faces of Lebanon: Sects, Wars, and Global Expansion* (Princeton, NJ: Markus Wiener Publishers, 1997).

Magnus Ranstorp, *Hizb'Allah in Lebanon* (New York: St. Martin's Press, 1997).

Nazih Richani, *Dilemmas of Democracy and Political Parties in Multiethnic Societies: The Case of the PSP in Lebanon* (New York: St. Martin's Press, 1997).

Elie Salem, *Violence and Diplomacy in Lebanon: The Troubled Years, 1982–1988,* Vol. 1 (New York: St. Martin's Press, 1995).

Raghid El-Solh, *Lebanon and Arabism* (New York: St. Martin's Press, 1996).

LIBYA

Guy Arnold, *The Maverick State: Libya and the New World Order* (London: Cassell Academic Press, 1997).

Scott L. Bills, *The Libyan Arena: The U.S., Britain and the Council of Foreign Ministers, 1945–1948* (Kent, OH: Kent State University Press, 1995; American Diplomatic History Series #8).

Mary-Jane Deeb, *Libya's Foreign Policy in North Africa* (Boulder, CO: Westview Press, 1991).

Judith Gurney, *Libya: The Political Economy of Oil* (New York: Oxford University Press, 1996).

Mansour El-Kikhia, *Libya's Qaddafi: The Politics of Contradiction* (Gainesville, FL: University Presses of Florida, 1997).

Salah Saadany and Mohamed M. El-Behairy, *Egypt and Libya from Inside, 1969–1976* (Jefferson, NC: McFarland Publishers, 1994).

Dirk Vandewalle, *Qadhafi's Libya, 1969–1994* (New York: St. Martin's Press, 1995).

MOROCCO

John P. Entelis, *Culture and Counterculture in Moroccan Politics,* rev. ed. (Lanham, MD: University Presses of America, 1996)

James Miller and Jerome Bookin-Weiner, *Morocco: The Arab West* (Boulder, CO: Westview Press, 1998).

Stefania Pandolfo, *The Impasse of the Angels: Scenes from a Moroccan Space of Memory* (Chicago, IL: University of Chicago Press, 1997).

Christine Ronan, *North Africa: Morocco* (New York: HarperCollins, 1997).

OMAN

Calvin H. Allen, Jr., *Oman: The Modernization of the Sultanate* (Boulder, CO: Westview Press, 1987).

Miriam Joyce, *The Sultanate of Oman: A Twentieth Century History* (Westport, CT: Greenwood Publishing Group, 1995).

Joseph A. Kechichian, *Oman and the World: The Emergence of an Independent Foreign Policy* (Santa Monica, CA: Rand Corporation, 1995).

QATAR

Jill Crystal, *Oil and Politics in the Gulf: Rulers and Merchants in Kuwait and Qatar, 2nd ed.* (Cambridge, England: Cambridge University Press, 1995).

Steven Dorr and Bernard Reich, *Qatar* (Boulder, CO: Westview Press, 1996).

SAUDI ARABIA

Said Aburish, *The Rise, Corruption and Coming Fall of the House of Saud* (New York: St. Martin's, Press, 1996).

Shahram Chubin and Charles R. Tripp, *Iran–Saudi Arabia Relations and Regional Order* (New York: Oxford University Press, 1997). Adelphi Papers, International Institute for Strategic Studies, No. 304.

Anthony Cordesman, *Saudi Arabia: Guarding the Desert Kingdom* (Boulder, CO: Westview Press, 1997).

Sandra Mackey, *The Saudis* (Boston: Houghton Mifflin, 1987).

Rashid Nasser and Esber Shaheen, *Saudi Arabia and the Gulf War* (Joplin, MO: International Institute of Technology, 1992).

Andrea Pampanini, *Cities from the Arabian Desert: The Building of Jubail and Yanbu in Saudi Arabia* (Westport, CT: Greenwood Press, 1997).

SUDAN

Sharon E. Hutchinson, *Nuer Dilemmas: Coping with Money, War and the State* (Berkeley, CA: University of California Press, 1996).

Osman El Nazir and Govind Desia, *Kenana—Green Gold of Sudan, Multinational Venture in the Desert* (New York: Columbia University Press, 1997).

Abdel Sidahmed, *Politics and Islam in Contemporary Sudan* (Concord, MA: Paul & Company, 1996).

Peter Strachan and Chris Peters, *Empowering Communities: Lessons from West Sudan* (Atlantic Highlands, NJ: Humanities Press International, 1997).

John O. Voll and Sarah Potts Voll, *The Sudan: Unity and Diversity in a Multicultural State* (Boulder, CO: Westview Press, 1985).

SYRIA

Raymond A. Hinnebusch, *Peasant and Bureaucracy in Ba'thist Syria* (Boulder, CO: Westview Press, 1989).

Martha N. Kessler, *Syria: Fragile Mosaic of Power* (Upland, PA: Diane Publishing, 1995).

Volker Perthes, *The Political Economy of Syria under Asad* (New York: St. Martin's Press, 1997)

Daniel Pipes, *Syria beyond the Peace Process* (Washington, D.C.: Institute for Near East Policy, 1996, Vol. 40).

Patrick Seale, *Asad of Syria: The Struggle for the Middle East* (Berkeley, CA: University of California Press, 1989).

Eliezer Ta'uber, *The Formation of Modern Syria and Lebanon* (Portland, OR: Frank Cass, 1995).

TUNISIA

Derek Hopwood, *Habib Bourguiba of Tunisia: The Tragedy of Longevity* (New York: St. Martin's Press, 1992).

Kenneth J. Perkins, *Tunisia: Crossroads of the Islamic and Mediterranean Worlds* (Boulder, CO: Westview Press, 1986).

—, *The Historical Dictionary of Tunisia,* 2nd ed. (Metuchen, NJ: Scarecrow Press, 1997).

TURKEY

Henry Barkey and Graham Fuller, *Turkey's Kurdish Question* (Lanham, MD: Rowman & Littlefield, 1997).

Graham Fuller, *Turkey's New Geopolitics* (Boulder, CO: Westview Press, 1993).

Michael Gunter, *The Kurds and the Future of Turkey* (New York: St. Martin's Press, 1997).

M. Sukru Hanioglu, *The Young Turks in Opposition* (London: Oxford University Press, 1995).

Paul B. Henze, *Turkish Democracy and the American Alliance* (Santa Monica, CA: Rand, 1993).

Halil Inalcik, *The Middle East and the Balkans under the Ottoman Empire: Essays on Economy and Society* (Bloomington, IN: Indiana University Press, 1993). Turkish Studies, Vol. 9.

Resat Kasaba and Sibel Bozdogan, eds., *Rethinking Modernity and National Identity in Turkey* (Seattle, WA: University of Washington Press, 1997).

Hasan Kayali, *Arabs and Young Turks: Ottomanism, Arabism and Islamism in the Ottoman Empire, 1908–1918* (Berkeley, CA: University of California Press, 1996).

Bruce Kuniholm, *The United States and Turkey* (New York: Scribner's, 1998).

Andrew Mango, *Turkey: The Challenge of a New Role* (Westport, CT: Praeger, 1994).

Justin McCarthy, *The Ottoman Turks: An Introductory History to 1923* (White Plains, NY: Longman, 1996).

Hugh Poulton, *The Top Hat, the Grey Wolf, and the Crescent: Turkish Nationalism and the Republic* (New York: New York University Press, 1997).

Libby Rittenberg, ed., *The Political Economy of Turkey in the Post-Soviet Era* (Westport, CT: Greenwood Publishing Group, 1997).

William Spencer, *The Land and People of Turkey* (New York: HarperCollins, 1990).

Bahri Yilmaz, *The Challenges to Turkey: New Role in International Relations* (New York: St. Martin's Press, 1996).

UNITED ARAB EMIRATES

Hassan Hamdan Al-Alkin, *The Foreign Policy of the U.A.E.* (London: Saqi Books, 1989).

Farhang Mehr, *A Colonial Legacy: The Dispute over the Islands of Abu Musa and the Greater and Lesser Tunbs* (Lanham, MD: University Presses of America, 1997).

Malcolm C. Peck, *The UAE: A Venture in Unity* (Boulder, CO: Westview Press, 1986).

Peter Vine, *The United Arab Emirates, Heritage and Modern Development* (New York: State Mutual Book and Periodical Service, 1995).

YEMEN

Robert Burrowes, *Historical Dictionary of Yemen* (Metuchen, NJ: Scarecrow Press, 1995).

Paul Dresch, *Tribes, Government and History in Yemen* (New York: Oxford University Press, 1989, 1994).

Ulrike Freitag and William Clarence-Smith, *Hadhrami Traders, Scholars and Statesmen in the Indian Ocean, 1750s to 1960s* (Leiden, the Netherlands: E. J. Brill, 1997).

F. Gregory Gause, *Saudi-Yemeni Relations* (New York: Columbia University Press, 1990). Middle East Institute books.

Fred Halliday, *Revolution and Foreign Policy: The Case of South Yemen, 1967–1987* (Cambridge, England: Cambridge University Press, 1990).

REGIONAL STUDIES

Frederick F. Anscombe, *The Ottoman Gulf: The Creation of Kuwait, Saudi Arabia and Qatar, 1870—1914* (New York: Columbia University Press, 1997).

Robert Bowker, *Beyond Peace: Search for Security in the Middle East* (Boulder, CO: Lynne Rienner Publishers, 1996).

Norman Daniel, *Islam and the West: The Making of an Image* (Rockport, MA: Oneworld Publications, 1997).

John P. Entelis, *Islam, Democracy and the State in North Africa* (Bloomington, IN: Indiana University Press, 1997).

Ziva Flamhaft, *Israel on the Road to Peace: Accepting the Unacceptable* (Boulder, CO: Westview Press, 1996).

Aaron Klieman, *Approaching the Finish Line: The U.S. in Post-Oslo Peacemaking* (Ramat Gan, Israel: Besa Center for Strategic Studies, Bar-Ilan University, 1995).

Michael Laskier, *North African Jewry in the Twentieth Century: The Jews of Morocco, Tunisia and Algeria* (New York: New York University Press, 1997).

Susan Waltz, *Human Rights and Reform: Changing the Face of North African Politics* (Berkeley, CA: University of California Press, 1995).

WOMEN'S STUDIES

Evelyne Accad, *Wounding Words: A Woman's Journal in Tunisia.* Trans. Cynthia Hahn (Portsmouth, NH: Heinemann, 1996).

Judith Caesar, *Crossing Borders: An American Woman in the Middle East* (Syracuse, NY: Syracuse University Press, 1997).

Ayala Emmitt, *Our Sisters' Promised Land: Women, Politics and Israeli-Palestinian Coexistence* (Ann Arbor, MI: University of Michigan Press, 1996).

Kathy Ferguson, *Kibbutz Journal: Reflections on Gender, Race and Militarism in Israel* (Pasadena, CA: Trilogy Books, 1995).

Lucy Garnett, *The Women of Turkey and Their Folk-Lore Set* (New York: AMS Press, 1977).

Nilufer Gole, *The Forbidden: Modern Civilization and Veiling* (Ann Arbor, MI: University of Michigan Press, 1996).

Sondra Hale, *Gender Politics in Sudan: Islamism, Socialism and the State* (Boulder, CO: Westview Press, 1996).

Deborah A. Kapchan, *Gender on the Market: Moroccan Women and the Revoicing of Tradition* (Philadelphia: University of Pennsylvania Press, 1996).

Mona Al-Munajjed, *Women in Saudi Arabia Today* (New York: St. Martin's Press, 1997).

Annemarie Schimmel, *My Soul Is a Woman: The Feminine in Islam* (New York: Continuum Publishing, 1997).

Judith E. Tucker, *In the House of the Law: Gender and Islamic Law in Ottoman Syria and Palestine* (Berkeley, CA: University of California Press, 1998).

Madeline C. Zilfi, *Women in the Ottoman Empire: Middle Eastern Women in the Early Modern Era* (Leiden, the Netherlands: Brill Academic Publishers, 1997).

LITERATURE IN TRANSLATION

Pedro Antonio de Alarcon, *Diary of a Witness* (Memphis, TN: White Rose Press, 1988). Translated by Bern Keating.

Samar Attar, *Lina, Portrait of a Damascene Girl* (Colorado Springs, CO: Three Continents Press, 1994).

Imam Khomeini's Last Will and Testament. Published in English by the Embassy of the Democratic and Popular Republic of Algeria, Iranian Interests Section, Washington, D.C.

The Intimate Life of an Ottoman Statesman: Melek Ahmed Pasha (1558–1662), as portrayed in Evliya Celebi's *Book of Travels (Seyahatname)* (Albany, NY: State University of New York Press, 1991). Translated by Robert Dankoff.

Herbert S. Joseph, ed., *Modern Israeli Drama, an Anthology* (Rutherford, NJ: Fairleigh Dickinson Press, 1983).

Yeshayahu Koren, *Funeral at Noon* (South Royalton, VT: Steerforth Press, 1996). English version of *Levayah ba-tsohorayin.*

Djanet Lachmet, *Lallia (Le Cowboy)* (New York: Carcanet Books, 1986). Translated by Judith Still.

Carol Magun, *Circling Eden: A Novel of Israel in Stories* (Chicago: Academy of Chicago Publishers, 1995).

Hanna Minah, *Fragments of Memory: A Story of a Syrian Family* (Austin, TX: University of Texas Press, 1993).

H. T. Norris, *The Berbers in Arabic Literature* (London: Longman, 1982).

Nicolas Saudray, *The House of the Prophets* (New York: Doubleday, 1985).

Dan V. Segre, *Memoirs of a Fortunate Jew* (Bethesda, MD: Adler & Adler, 1987).

Charles G. Tuety, *Classical Arabic Poetry* (London: Kegan Paul International, 1985).

Abdullah al-Udari, *Modern Poetry of the Arab World* (New York: Penguin Books, 1987).

CURRENT EVENTS

To keep up to date on rapidly changing events in the contemporary Middle East and North Africa, the following materials are especially useful:

Africa Report
Bimonthly, with an "African Update" chronology for all regions.

Africa Research Bulletin (Exeter, England)
Monthly summaries of political, economic, and social developments in all of Africa, with coverage of North–Northeast Africa.

Current History, A World Affairs Journal
One issue per year is usually devoted to the Middle Eastern region.

Middle East Economic Digest (London, England)
Weekly summary of economic and some political developments in the Middle East–North African region generally and in individual countries. Provides special issues from time to time.

PERIODICALS

The Christian Science Monitor
One Norway Street
Boston, MA 02115

The Economist
25 St. James's Street
London, England

Le Monde (Weekly edition, in English)
7 Rue des Italiens
Paris, France
A summary of the previous week's news, with separate sections on various geographical regions. The Middle East and North Africa are treated separately.

The Middle East and North Africa
Europa Publications
18 Bedford Square
London, England
A reference work, published annually and updated, with country surveys, regional articles, and documents.

The Middle East Journal
1761 N Street, NW
Washington, D.C. 20036
This quarterly periodical, established in 1947, is the oldest one specializing in Middle East affairs, with authoritative articles, book reviews, documents, and a quarterly chronology.

Middle Eastern Studies
Gainsborough House
Gainsborough Road
London, England
A quarterly historical magazine.

New Outlook
9 Gordon Street
Tel Aviv, Israel
A bimonthly news magazine, with articles, chronology and documents. Reflects generally Israeli leftist peace-with-the-Arabs views of the movement Peace Now with which it is affiliated.

Index